THINK
WORLD RELIGIONS

• ROY R. ROBSON •

University of the Sciences in Philadelphia

D1406634

Prentice Hall

Boston   Columbus   Indianapolis   New York   San Francisco   Upper Saddle River
Amsterdam   Cape Town   Dubai   London   Madrid   Milan   Munich   Paris   Montreal   Toronto
Delhi   Mexico City   Sao Paulo   Sydney   Hong Kong   Seoul   Singapore   Taipei   Tokyo

Editorial Director: Craig Campanella
Editor in Chief: Dickson Musslewhite
Publisher: Nancy Roberts
Development Editor: Maggie Barbieri
Editorial Assistant: Nart Varoqua
Director of Marketing: Brandy Dawson
Senior Marketing Manager: Laura Lee Manley
Marketing Assistant: Pat M. Walsh
Managing Editor: Maureen Richardson
Project Manager/Production: Cheryl Keenan
Operations Specialist: Amanda Smith
Manager of Design Development: John Christiana
Art Director, Text and Cover: Laura Gardner
Line Art and Illustrations: Words & Numbers
Manager, Visual Research: Beth Brenzel

Photo Researcher: Kathy Ringrose
Image Permission Coordinator: Annette Linder
Manager, Rights and Permissions: Zina Arabia
Manager, Cover Visual Research & Permissions: Karen Sanatar
Front Cover Art: Marie Docher/Getty Images
Back Cover Art: istock
Media Director: Brian Hyland
Media Editor: Rachel Comerford
Composition and Full-Service Project Management: Lauren Pecarich, Adam Noll, Matt Skalka, Russ Hall, Ally Brocious, and Matt Gardner/Words and Numbers, Inc.
Printer/Binder: Courier/Kendalville
Cover Printer: Lehigh-Phoenix Color
Text Font: Helvetica Neue Light

Credits and acknowledgments borrowed from other sources and reproduced, with permission, in this textbook appear on appropriate page within text or on page 304.

Library of Congress Cataloging-in-Publication Data

Robson, Roy R.
  Think world religions / Roy R. Robson.
     p. cm.
  Includes bibliographical references and index.
  ISBN-13: 978-0-205-77362-6 (student edition : alk. paper)
  ISBN-10: 0-205-77362-1 (student edition : alk. paper)
  ISBN-13: 978-0-205-77590-3 (examination edition : alk. paper)
  ISBN-10: 0-205-77590-X (examination edition : alk. paper)
  1. Religions--Textbooks. I. Title.
  BL80.3.R62 2011
  200--dc22   2010015825

10 9 8 7 6 5 4 3 2 1

Prentice Hall
is an imprint of

www.pearsonhighered.com

Student Edition
ISBN-10:   0-205-77362-1
ISBN-13: 978-0-205-77362-6
Examination Edition
ISBN-10:   0-205-77590-X
ISBN-13: 978-0-205-77590-3

This book is written in memory of my father,
Joe Brooks Robson, on the fifth anniversary
of his death.

He taught me to mix high seriousness with soaring
silliness. Years before Bart Simpson said it, my
father's favorite prayer went like this:

Rub a dub dub,
Thanks for the grub.
Yeah, God!

BRIEF CONTENTS

CONTENTS

01 THINKING ABOUT RELIGION 2

02 TALKING ABOUT RELIGION 10

03

HINDUISM:
THE ETERNAL LAW 22

04

HINDUISM:
LAW AND LIFE 38

05

BUDDHISM: BECOMING AWAKE 52

06

BUDDHISM: AWAKENING THE WORLD 68

07

EAST ASIAN SACRED WAYS:
THE ETERNAL DAO 82

08

EAST ASIAN SACRED WAYS:
HARMONY IN THE WORLD 102

CONTENTS

13

ISLAM: SUBMISSION AND FAITH 204

14

ISLAM: THE PILLARS AND THE UMMA 226

15

RELIGIONS OF PLACE:
A SACRED WORLD AROUND US 250

16

NEW RELIGIONS:
A QUEST FOR THE SACRED 272

A MESSAGE TO STUDENTS

In a rural Russian village called Sepych, an Orthodox Old Believer priest opens a book called *The Navigator*. It's huge—leather covers stretch over wooden boards, the pages are thick and heavy. Brass clasps usually keep the book shut, but the priest has clicked them open, letting small leather straps fall away. Hefting the tome, the priest looks out over the crowd of peasants, townspeople, scholars, and visitors. *The Navigator*, he explains, "tells us literally everything"—how to pray, how to live with one another, and how to get to heaven. Even though it was compiled centuries ago, the priest feels sure *The Navigator* will apply to any modern situation. If you have a question, he says, *The Navigator* has an answer (Rogers 1–3).

Please do not think of *THINK World Religions* like *The Navigator*. When you take a new class, it's easy to use the course textbook as an encyclopedic source. It's heavy, important, and hard to read. You only consult it when getting ready for an exam, or when the professor refers to it in class. In other words, it's like *The Navigator*—a big important book that should contain everything you need to know, but probably won't often consult.

How could any book contain the wisdom of sacred traditions that span the last 5,000 years? Since that's just not possible, don't rely on this book as the only place you look for information on world religions. Instead, use *THINK World Religions* as a way to begin the dialogue with your instructor, other students, and the greater community around you.

I hope that you'll use *THINK World Religions* like a travel guide. It may contain information about something familiar—maybe your own religious tradition—but it will also point the way toward new places, ideas, and people. Like any good guide, this book should bring up many more questions than it answers. You'll notice a few other things. The tone is less formal and more conversational than other textbooks. It contains stories and examples from my experiences that I hope will connect to your life. Each element of the chapter works with every other one: You'll learn by reading the text, studying pictures, and interpreting charts or graphs. Don't skip the block quotations or text boxes because you expect them to be filler; a good guidebook packs every page with important information for your journey.

THINK World Religions will emphasize conceptual knowledge and critical thinking over rote memorization of facts. The text will help you consider how each religion grapples with a series of important ideas. To guide you through your exploration of these ideas, *THINK World Religions* will introduce four questions that will recur throughout the text:

- "Is there a god?"
- "What does it mean to be human?"
- "How do humans interact with the sacred?"
- "How does the sacred become community?"

By asking the same questions of each religion, you will be able develop your own critical thinking skills through comparison, contrast, and analysis.

    THINK World Religions will integrate the social, cultural, and political aspects of each religion within the context of these four questions. By using them as an organizational theme, you will be able to consider both similarities and differences more easily among many faiths. While developing critical analysis skills, the organization of the textbook will also help you participate in classroom discussions and shape your individual projects.

    We'll study each religion in two chapters. The first will cover the questions of divinity and humanity, giving you an overview of the tradition. The second chapter in the paired set brings the human experience to bear in the context of the tradition, and explores how ordinary people practice it in the world today.

Common Features of Religions

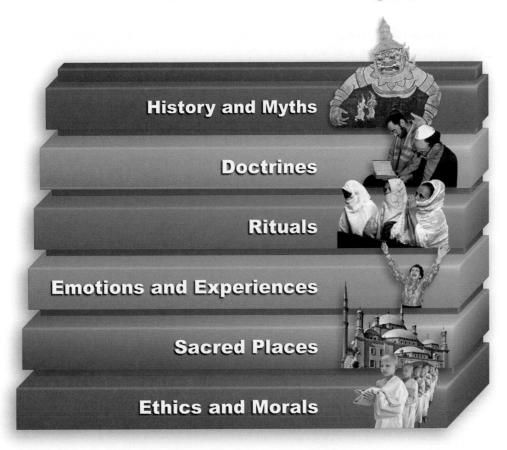

History and Myths

Doctrines

Rituals

Emotions and Experiences

Sacred Places

Ethics and Morals

THINK World Religions has many special features that will make your journey through the different faith traditions more meaningful:

A Sacred Place: This feature will describe a religious location. It may be a temple, cathedral, or a garden. The book has some great illustrations to let you peek inside buildings and imagine yourself walking through them. Because they're similar in style from one chapter to another, the drawings also lend themselves easily to comparisons.

A Hindu Temple	St. Stephen's of Walbrook
The Fogong Si Temple	Selimiye Mosque, Turkey
Chang Ling	The Tipi
The Central Synagogue	Stonehenge

A Sacred Action and a Place in the World: After learning a little bit about a place, you'll read about some activity that illustrates the religion we're studying. This may be a special event or an everyday occurrence, and we'll refer back to it often. In the second paired chapter of a particular tradition, we'll turn attention to some way in which experience and religion interact. Likewise, it will offer insight to help you in your own observations of the world around you.

Internal Conflicts and Contemporary Issues: You'll find text boxes integrated into each chapter that bring up topics distinct to each religion or related to today's society. These may include marriage, politics, or gender issues. These boxes will give you ideas for your own reading and research.

Religion + Box: If the Internal Conflict text box points you inside a religion, this one will send you to the outside world. Examples may include religion + science, religion + technology, or religion + nature.

THINK World Religions Box: Each chapter contains at least one THINK World Religions box. The information in this box will help you relate the religious traditions being discussed to some other pertinent topic.

Key Terms: Key terms are printed in bold throughout the chapter, and can also be found at the end of the chapter for easy reference.

Questions for Study and Review: Appearing in every chapter of the book, these questions will help you review what you've learned and assess your knowledge. Answering these questions will take some critical analysis of the chapter content.

For Further Study: You'll notice that this book will refer to a few main sources in each chapter. I've selected books that are easy to find in a bookstore or library. They range from general introductions to scholarly works. You can find a list of the bibliographical information about those books, other good printed sources, and important Internet sites at the end of each world religion.

The ThinkSpot.com and Other Internet Resources: At TheThinkSpot.com, you will have access to online material that has been arranged specifically for use with *THINK World Religions*. You will find links to other Web sites and videos that will enhance your understanding of the religion. Finally, you'll be able to download flashcards and summary sheets to help you study and review what you've learned.

ACKNOWLEDGMENTS

Many people have helped me in the adventure of writing *THINK World Religions*. Although there are too many to name every one, I would like to single out a few people who particularly aided me along this road. Faculty and students at the University of the Sciences have read chapters, made comments, and borne with me when I had my head in a book or was typing away madly. I'd like to thank four colleagues in particular: Professors Laurie Kirszner, Robert Boughner, Kevin Murphy, and Christine Flanagan. My students have read this book in draft form. They've offered student perspectives, great ideas, and incisive questions. Thank you to

Megan Burzynski	Bhaumik Jani
Laura Caccioppoli	Susannah Price
Vinay Daryani	Matthew Stratton
Juliet Franklin	Tiffany Weiss
Carl Gerdine	

Yuqian Liu and Zhimeng Jin came to my rescue when I needed immediate help with a source in Mandarin. Two new members of our family, Kurniawan Rusly and Devie Sari Dewi Pawlak, also translated and explained information in Mandarin and Bahasa. My thanks to them.

My editorial team at Pearson has provided the vision, guidance, and support to make this book possible. Always ready to help, they also let me control more of the writing, editing, and design process than I could have expected. Thank you especially to Nancy Roberts, Cheryl Keenan, and the hardworking design, editorial, and permissions folks in Upper Saddle River, NJ.

The editorial board for this book has taught me new ways to look at world religions and new paths to follow. They guided me back on the straight and narrow when I strayed too far from the needs of students. Thank you to

Charlene Burns	University of Wisconsin–Eau Claire
Ivory Lyons	Mount Union College
Andreas Reif	Southern New Hampshire University
Robert Steed	Hawkeye Community College
Steve Young	McHenry County College

Maggie Barbieri has guided me through every step of the process. An experienced editor and a writer of great talent and success, Maggie has allowed me to develop my own voice while still nudging me in the right direction. She might think of herself as an old-time Catholic schoolteacher, but really, Maggie's more like a great coach: She can do everything better than the players, but uses that knowledge to help them excel.

My highest praise and deepest thanks, though, go to my wife and colleague, Kim Robson. We share both a family and a career at the University of the Sciences, and she makes my research and writing possible with her good humor, her professional opinions, and her constant, consistent, loving support.

Happy reading!

Roy R. Robson is professor of history and director of the Honors Program at University of the Sciences in Philadelphia. He teaches courses on world religions, European and Russian history, and the concept of time in religion and science.

Robson writes extensively on history and world religions with an eye toward religious experience, focusing on how people interpret and experience religions across time. His last book, *Solovki*, won praise from *The New Yorker, The Times (London)*, *Condé Nast Traveler*, and the *Journal of Modern History*. He edits a series of books on Orthodox Christianity for Northern Illinois University Press.

Professor Robson has received fellowships, grants, and prizes from the National Endowment for the Humanities (NEH), Fulbright-Hayes, the American Council of Learned Societies, the Social Science Research Council, the Templeton Foundation, and other organizations. In 2009, the NEH awarded him a Teaching Development Fellowship to expand his course on the concept of time.

When asked why he wanted to write *THINK World Religions*, Robson responded:

"My teaching career has led me toward writing a book like this. I began teaching at Boston College, where I also received my doctorate. BC is a Roman Catholic school run by the Society of Jesus (the Jesuits). Around many corners of the beautiful campus, you're likely to run into a statue of the Virgin Mary or a priest in a Roman collar. Even so, BC has reached out to people of other traditions. Mary Daly, the radical feminist theologian and critic, taught nearly all of her career at Boston College, even while trying to undermine the church that had founded the university.

After Boston College, I taught for three years at Fayetteville State University in North Carolina. Fayetteville State challenged all of my assumptions about geography, education, and race. At FSU, I learned to speak directly about difficult issues like race relations or religious conviction. Rather than avoiding a conversation, I now realize that talking about differences can actually honor each person and view, rather than sweeping them all under the carpet.

Since 1997, I've taught at University of the Sciences in Philadelphia. Here, I interact with students from cultures around the world. My courses on history, world religion, time, and cosmology are filled with Christians, Muslims, Jews, Buddhists, Hindus, and atheists. They were the impetus to write *THINK World Religions*.

Working with my students and writing this textbook reminds me to be intellectually humble. How can any one person make sense of the world's religious traditions? My students and I try to ask pertinent questions, but we also try to remain open to ideas that we could never have imagined. That's how I have approached this book—not so much an encyclopedia as a guide toward deeper study."

Early mornings, look for Professor Robson rowing on the Schuylkill River in Philadelphia. Sunday afternoons in the autumn, he'll be wearing his lucky Pittsburgh Steelers T-shirt. On Monday nights, you'll find him rehearsing with the college choir as a bass/baritone.

Professor Robson lives in Lansdowne, Pennsylvania, with his wife Kim, three dogs, and two cats.

<<< On the right: Rev. Jeremiah Wright.
On the left: President Barack Obama.

How does religion influence
politics?

RELIGION AS A FIELD OF STUDY

THE FOUR QUESTIONS

CRITICAL THINKING WITH THINK WORLD RELIGIONS

During the

2008 presidential campaign, Democratic nominee Barack Obama found himself in the middle of a heated debate. For years, Obama had been attending Trinity United Church of Christ in Chicago. The church had a strong connection with black Chicagoans, owing in part to its focus on African-American issues and strident sermons by the church's head pastor, the Reverend Jeremiah Wright.

In urban Chicago, Rev. Wright had led the Trinity United parish for many years without receiving much media attention. When Barack Obama ran for the presidency of the United States, Wright's sermons and his alleged influence on Obama became newsworthy. Many suburban and rural Americans despaired to hear a black preacher blame the U.S. government and culture for problems ranging from poverty to AIDS. Although Wright seemed a fiery prophet to some, he came across as a hateful and offensive hypocrite to others (Cooper A21).

You may remember what happened—Obama sought political middle ground, but Wright amped up his remarks. He publicly wondered if America's own foreign policy had brought about the attacks of September 11th, 2001, and linked a lack of support for AIDS in Africa to American racism. As the election wore on, Obama realized he had to respond to his Republican opponents, who tried to link his views to that of Wright. In Philadelphia at the

National Constitution Center, Obama gave an extremely persuasive and well-reasoned speech on race and religion in contemporary America. Yet, in the end, he had to sever ties with his church to quell talk that he and Wright agreed on controversial issues (Zeleny A1).

So, how does this tale of Rev. Wright and President Obama relate to a world religions textbook? As you can see from this recent series of events, religion rarely stays inside a building or a book. For billions of people throughout history, religion has combined social, philosophical, cultural, and personal experiences that elude scholarly boundaries or governmental decrees. To understand world religions, you'll need to be willing to look far beyond the prayer rug, pew, or monastery.

Religion seems to wax and wane in the American consciousness. You might go for months without hearing a report about the Pope or the Dalai Lama, but then you'll be bombarded with news of Burmese monks, Pentecostal preachers, or children who see visions of the Virgin Mary in the skies above Medjugorje in Bosnia and Herzegovina. Lately, the best sellers lists groan with books both attacking religion and defending it. As I write this, a book called *God Is Not Great: How Religion Poisons Everything* is battling it out with *The Case for God*. Clearly, religion affects people in every possible positive and negative way.

THINKING ABOUT RELIGION

Why are you taking this class? If you're like most students, Introduction to World Religions might sound interesting, but it's also probably a general education requirement. A few decades ago, however, students like you could not take a "religious studies" class, because the discipline did not yet exist. In fact, most universities did not open religious studies departments until the 1960s. Because it is so young, religious studies continues to define how and why it studies religious traditions. You'll see that as we survey a little history.

For thousands of years, scholars tended to delve deeply into their own religious tradition rather than someone else's. For example, Thomas Aquinas wrote important things about Christianity from the point of view of a Christian. This approach can be very powerful, because someone like Aquinas spent much of his life thinking deeply about his faith. At the same time, however, Aquinas never questioned Christianity's basic tenets, which limited his analysis. For our purposes, this kind of scholar is an "apologist." This doesn't mean that Aquinas was apologizing for his faith. In this case, apologist refers to a person explaining or defending religion from the inside rather than the outside.

By the late 19th century, however, another kind of scholar began to appear on the academic scene. These men (almost never women) sought to analyze religion from the outside, not defending any one tradition but trying to understand them all. They were consciously not apologists and instead focused on two general questions: "What is religion?" and "How did it begin?" (In many respects, these issues continue to linger in the minds of religion scholars even today.) Two men in particular, F. Max Müller and Rudolf Otto, developed the system to answer these questions. Müller excelled in languages, and he argued that no one could understand a religion without first learning how to read its sacred texts. He translated the great Hindu text the Rig-veda into English for the first time. Müller became convinced that he could study religion scientifically, applying methodology he learned from textual analysis and linguistics. Like others of his time, Müller hoped that rational scholarship would ultimately clarify both the definition and origin of religion. In 1873, he published *Introduction to the Science of Religion*, which helped launch Religious Studies as a distinct discipline.

Rudolf Otto continued with Müller's approach. Otto argued that all religions interacted with "the holy," which he defined as something ultimately good that both interacts with and transcends everyday life. Unlike morals, ethics, ideas, or feelings, Otto claimed

that "the holy" somehow existed timelessly on its own: "[L]ike every absolutely primary and elementary datum, while it admits to being discussed, it cannot be strictly defined" (Otto 7). You might think of "the holy" as a religious atom—the building block of all religions (Capps 68–71; Forward 1–6, 15–19).

If you slog your way through Müller and Otto's writing (Otto is particularly hard going) you'll see that they often write about religion in comparison to Christianity. This made it impossible to have a truly impartial study.

Although Müller and Otto respected religion, other scholars scorned it as a remnant of the irrational past. Karl Marx famously declared, "Religion is the opiate of the masses"—a drug given by society's rich and powerful so that they could keep others oppressed by promising them a better afterlife. To Marx, religion functioned as a brake on the progress of humanity and should be eradicated from society (Capps 40–41). As a result, Marxist governments from Russia to China and South America have targeted religious institutions. In the early 20th century, for example, Marx's analysis of religion motivated leaders of the USSR to murder thousands of priests, monks, and nuns in order to break the power of the religion "drug" in Russia.

Other important European thinkers shared Marx's dim view of religion, although their students rarely took to murder as a result. Friedrich Nietzsche, for example, famously proclaimed that the development of rationality and science had killed God (Nietzsche 168). (A philosophy major's T-shirt reads "God is Dead—Nietzsche" on the front and "Nietzsche is Dead—God" on the back!) Although different in approach from Nietzsche, Sigmund Freud also called for the death of religion. In *The Future of an Illusion*, Freud argued that religion sprang up from unconscious wishes and neuroses, not from any external reality. As human beings become aware of these issues, Freud reasoned, religion will wane in importance (Capps 40–41).

Although Marx, Nietzsche, and Freud had an enormous effect on other scholars, many rejected their

<<< From top to bottom: Four Muslim women from Morocco are clad in traditional hijabs; an aboriginal man performs a ceremony, clutching a box that contains the skulls of his ancestors; Wiccan followers join hands in a sacred circle. **Which of these photos fit your idea of "religion"?**

atheistic view of religion. Three men—William James, Max Weber, and Emile Durkheim—developed the methodology and assumptions of modern religious studies. William James claimed that religion came from some deeply personal experience. Because of that, he believed it's impossible to condemn or to praise religion in general, since every one of us perceives it differently (Capps 41–45; Forward 10–11). In James' own words: "As there seems to be no one elementary emotion, but only a common storehouse of emotions upon which religious objects may draw, so there might conceivably be no one specific and essential kind of religious object, and no one specific and essential kind of religious act" (James 28). With this statement, James refuted any idea of a religious "atom" that underlies all traditions across the world.

Unlike James, who was interested in individuals, Emile Durkheim focused on religion's social role. In his monumental work *The Elementary Forms of Religious Life*, Durkheim showed how beliefs and practices helped create a cohesive community. Following Durkheim, the American anthropologist Clifford Geertz further refined this idea by focusing on rituals such as weddings, funerals, or even cockfights that bound people together in family, social, and community units (Capps 162–168; Martin 6–8; Winzeler 4–19, 261–270).

Max Weber's work complemented Durkheim in many ways, but it sharply contrasted with Marx's view of religion. Among these scholarly superstars, Weber has probably had the most enduring influence, as many scholars even call him the father of sociology. In *The Protestant Ethic and the Spirit of Capitalism*, Weber linked Protestant Christian views of money and work to the creation of the capitalist economic and social system. He agreed with Marx that religion influenced social relationships and actions, but he did not condemn religion in the way Marx had done (Capps 162–168; Martin 13–15).

Mircea Eliade, the great Romanian academic, came a generation after the "big three" and concentrated on the study of myths and rituals. Teaching at the University of Chicago for many years, he influenced generations of students and other scholars. According to Eliade's theory, religion differentiates between the "profane" everyday world and the "sacred" world of higher truth. Eliade emphasized the idea of hierophanies, events like rituals or sacred places that link our lives to something bigger than we are (Capps 139–45).

In the past 20 years, however, scholars have begun to question the theories of each of the people we've just encountered. Following a trend called "postmodernism," today's professors often look for ways in which one religious "voice" seeks to drown out all the others. The dominant voice has come to be called a "master narrative," and scholars try to uncover the competing voices that have been silenced by the power of gender, violence, wealth, or prestige of the dominant group. For the postmodern student of religious studies, there can be no single definition of religion, and even the term "religion" itself comes under scrutiny. Maybe there is no such thing as religion as something distinct from the rest of human culture. By this way of thinking, religion was not so much defined by its 19th-century observers as it was developed in their minds.

Postmodernism has brought exposure to many ideas, stories, and people that had never before received any scholarly attention. This movement has led us to understand that we can never assume that definitions have the same meaning to everyone, or that all people who call themselves "religious" mean the same thing. Postmodern emphasis on power relationships, however, can de-emphasize mysticism or other nonrational phenomena. The trick for postmodern religious scholars will be to not fall into the same trap as their predecessors, who claimed that theirs was *the only* way of understanding religion, instead of *one of many* ways.

Asking Questions about Religion

In this book, we will not try to discover the source of all religions. We will not look for attributes that all religions share, nor claim that one religion is better than all the others. Instead, we'll look at the most prominent religions in the world and ask them the same four questions:

1. Is there a god?
2. What does it mean to be human?
3. How do humans interact with the sacred?
4. How does the sacred become community?

Each religious tradition may develop its own answers to these questions or perhaps not answer them at all. I remember that my undergraduate advisor had a poster on her door, which I can still see in my mind's eye. It quoted Rainer Maria Rilke, reminding us students not to preoccupy ourselves with memorizing answers. Instead, it said, "Try to love the questions themselves" (Rilke 35). Dr. Jones' poster may have been more powerful than I ever imagined, because now I ask students to do the same thing: Concentrate on the questions, and the answers will arrive.

▶ THE FOUR QUESTIONS

Is There a God?

Imagine God. Can you? Can we really guess what God might look like? For example, does God look like the character on the next page—a really, really old guy with a long beard and white robes floating in the sky? Or maybe God looks more like a squat, round man sitting cross-legged with a big smile on his face.

Representations of gods are different over time and across cultures. Many religions conceive of one god who looks like a man. Some religions recognize multiple gods, both male and female. Some forbid the depiction of God in any shape or form. In *THINK World Religions*, we'll explore many different traditions, some of which may not even have a god.

DO YOU HAVE TO BELIEVE IN A GOD TO BE RELIGIOUS?

Must a person believe in a god to be religious? The answer depends on whom you ask. Some people warn of harsh punishment for those who renounce their god. However, others might say that you could follow their religion without acknowledging any god at all.

Another way to look at this issue would be to ask if a religion has no god, one god, or many? Traditionally, scholars group religions together by those who perceive just one divine being (monotheists) versus those who understand there to be many gods (polytheists). That sounds a lot simpler than it really is. For example, many Hindus would say that there are countless deities but only one divine essence. Christians, on the other hand, perceive their God as one nature fused from three distinct "persons."

In yet other religious systems, followers may differ on the question of a god existing at all. One can easily be a Buddhist but not accept any divine being, or follow Daoism with only a vague idea of one. If you are religious, does your tradition include a god? If so, can you imagine not having one? How would it be different from what you experience today?

What Does It Mean to Be Human?

You have to admit, it's hard to objectively define what it means to be human. After all, we can't completely divorce ourselves from our senses, ideas, and backgrounds. One way we might shed light on contemporary perceptions comes from popular culture, because movies or music must find an audience to make money. So, how are human beings shown in popular culture? Let's look at two well-known examples: *South Park* and Hello Kitty.

Picture in your mind an evil little eight-year-old named Eric Cartman. Do you know anyone who could get away with bigoted, anti-Semitic, mean-spirited talk and actions like his? Probably not. So, why is a character as nasty as Cartman so popular? What is it about our culture and our humanity that resonates with this character? Although its audience is mostly adults, *South Park* tries to show a view of the world from a child's perspective on adult themes, which is part of what makes Cartman so subversive and interesting. His character embodies the worst in us, saying things out loud that people might think, but would never utter in public. For the writers and fans of *South Park*, that picture of humanity rings true—we try to be good on the outside, but inside we're full of nasty and sometimes hateful feelings. We keep it bottled up, but just barely so. Can you identify with that?

Maybe Cartman's brand of humanity is too abrasive for you. Let's take a look at another cartoon perspective—Hello Kitty. She's an adorable little cat. She carries a purse or a teddy bear; she giggles. Preadolescent girls *love* Hello Kitty, and students around my university sometimes still carry backpacks adorned with her cute, mouth-less face. What does Hello Kitty show us about our own humanity? She's a cat, but she's human-like—she is anthropomorphized. Does she symbolize childhood and innocence, the opposite of Cartman? Does her popularity indicate something about our culture's fascination with the young and the childlike? Is that culturally permissible?

On Facebook, you can take "quizzes" to figure out which cartoon character, movie star, or ice cream flavor best describes you. Likewise, by considering either Hello Kitty or Eric Cartman, we can learn more

∧ ∧ **Do you envision an** elderly, white-haired man **when you think of God?** Does your answer reflect the pop culture of your society?

about how we perceive ourselves and how others see us. What makes us human? What is acceptable behavior? How might that change with age? How do animals resemble people, or people act like animals? What can we learn about ourselves when considering Cartman or Hello Kitty?

How Do Humans Interact with the Sacred?

If you are religious, what do you do? Maybe you attend weekly church services, hike through the woods, or find enlightenment in a sweat lodge. You may sip wine from a cup or smoke ganja from a pipe. You may sit quietly or twirl in circles. You may cry, sing, or stay silent. Human beings have developed nearly countless ways to interact with the sacred world around them. As we learned from Mircea Eliade earlier in this chapter, people can have strong experiences at sacred places or through sacred actions. We'll describe both of these in each chapter of *THINK World Religions*, but you might consider some other ways that human beings have sought interaction with the divine.

THOUGHTS AND WORDS

In the Western world, we tend to use the term "prayer" as a shorthand for all interaction with the sacred world. More specifically, prayer may be defined as a verbal communion using some sort of language. Individuals may pray directly or as a group, with set language, spontaneous words, or even "in tongues."

ACTION AND INACTION

What do whirling dervishes, snake handlers, fire walkers, and beggars have in common? They may all be communicating with the sacred world. Singers and dancers may also experience an otherworldly feeling, while two people climaxing in sexual ecstasy may see a divine revelation.

On the other hand, religions across the world also value absolute quiet—complete inaction—as a paradoxical way to interact with a world beyond ourselves. In the most extreme cases, people can move themselves into a meditative state that drops blood pressure and heart rate so low they can barely be measured. In these situations, lack of action seems to lead people close to physical death and back again.

WHAT ABOUT VIOLENCE?

Can bloodshed help human beings communicate with the divine? Throughout history, people of many religions have claimed a sacred purpose for violence directed at other people. In some cases, religious people have even turned violence toward themselves.

Given the high stakes of religion and violence, it's worthwhile to consider why people might believe that religion is a matter of life and death. On September 11, 2001, for example, a small band of radical Islamists (people who believe in a very conservative, politicized Islam) hijacked airplanes and crashed them into the Pentagon, the World Trade Center, and a rural Pennsylvania field. To most Americans, these acts were an incomprehensible horror. However, to members of al-Qaeda, it glorified God and sent the attackers directly to heaven. The al-Qaeda leader, Osama bin Laden, who orchestrated the attacks, justified them as a way to punish the United States for its meddling in the politics of Muslim nations. Bin Laden's opinions differ wildly from most Muslims, especially in his support of the murder of innocent people (Kean 55–62). His concept of *jihad*, or struggle, grew out of a form of Islamic fundamentalism,

∧
∧
∧ Cartoons help show our true ideas about humanity to ourselves. **How is Cartman an exaggeration of real people? How does Hello Kitty help us understand what we value as a culture?**

which claims that Western culture offends Islam. From this perspective, attacks against the United States become holy acts, supposedly preserving the basic virtues of Islam against foreign influence.

How Does the Sacred Become Community?

Finally, in *THINK World Religions* you will explore social aspects of religious traditions. As you can imagine, how people interact with the sacred can also affect their relations with each another. It's hard to overestimate the relationship between religion and community. In fact, some scholars argue that environment can predict your religion approximately 90 percent of the time. If you didn't grow up in India or among Indian émigrés, what is the likelihood of your being Hindu? If your great-grandparents hadn't come from England, would you likely be Episcopalian? This linkage between religion and society seems to fly in the face of American individualism, but it surely exists. When I lived in rural North Carolina, for example, we used to joke that there were two Jews and one Orthodox Christian in our whole county, and definitely no Buddhists. On the other hand, I could walk to three Baptist churches from my front door.

Do You Have Other Questions?

I hope so. If you think back to the questions on the study of religion, you'll quickly come up with many other possible questions. What role does gender play? Who has power and how do they wield it? What myths or rituals characterize each religion? Do people perceive a huge gulf between themselves and the sacred world? What role do animals play in religion? How do religions affect the environment?

I can imagine you or your instructor wanting to explore these or other questions about religion. The most important purpose in *THINK World Religions* may be developing the skills to inquire deeply and broadly of religion, culture, or society. You may decide that the four questions in this book may not be the best ones to ask. If that's the case, I will feel like I've accomplished my goal and perhaps the goal of my advisor from many years ago.

▶ CRITICAL THINKING WITH *THINK WORLD RELIGIONS*

The Visual Summary

Appearing at the end of the chapter, the Visual Summary may be the first tool you use to study the *THINK World Religions* text. This graphic will provide visual aids to help you remember major ideas from the chapter and will look the same each time you see it. You can rely on the Visual Summary to help you understand how various religions have similar or different attributes.

Doing Research on Religions

As you read about each religion in *THINK World Religions*, your instructor may ask you to do additional research. This may include presenting oral or written reports, creating or participating in a wiki, or looking at primary sources such as holy books or pictures. You may be asked to explore familiar or foreign religions.

To do this, consider using the techniques of ethnography, which offer a way to learn about people by observing and talking. Ethnographic research often includes watching repeated actions over time. For the study of religion, this may mean observing the way people move around in a cathedral, synagogue, mosque, or temple. Do the worshippers pause at certain times? Do they gesture or utter repeated phrases? Do they wear special clothing?

You may even be able to use ethnographic techniques to answer the four questions about a particular religion. Do members of a religious tradition keep to themselves or preach on a street corner? Do people interact with works of art in their sacred places? What could that tell us about the religion? By closely observing people, you may be able to tease out the relevance of their actions and see how their ideas relate to their gestures.

Creating a Question Matrix

THINK World Religions introduces each religion in the same way, so each pair of chapters will follow a predictable structure. Once you get used to it, you can begin to create a chart to help you understand each religious tradition that we cover. At the bottom of this page is an example of a Question Matrix.

You can fill in the matrix with information as you work through each chapter. Completing the matrix will help you "think vertically," or study how a single religion answers the four questions. It will also help you "think horizontally," or study how different religions answer one of the four questions.

Important Parts of the Book

As you can see, *THINK World Religions* has been designed to help you understand world religions from different perspectives. Let's take a closer look at the features you can expect to see throughout this book.

TWO CHAPTERS PER RELIGION

In this book, each religion will be covered in two chapters. The first one will explore these questions:

- Is there a god?
- What does it mean to be human?

This chapter will generally also focus on historical development rather than contemporary issues.

The second chapter devoted to each religion will take a different approach. This chapter will answer these questions:

- How do humans interact with the sacred?
- How does the sacred become community?

We'll spotlight contemporary issues in this chapter. You will explore the ways in which religious people communicate with each other and with their world. You will see what can happen when different religious groups must coexist side by side. Finally, you will learn how religion plays a role in societies all over the world.

Different religions have overlapping concepts, and it can be challenging to keep them straight. Create your own Question Matrix to organize information as you read through this book.

A Question Matrix

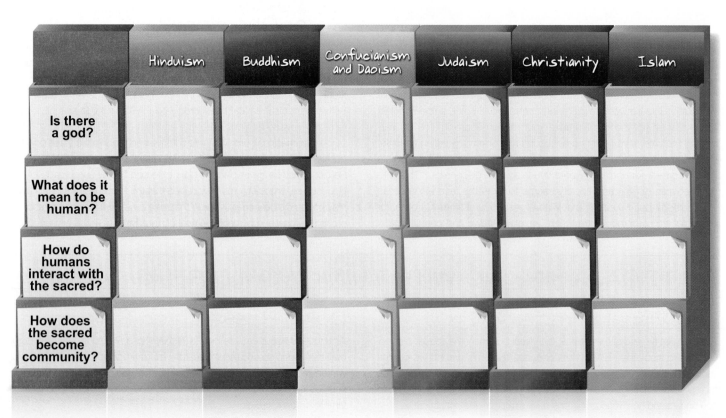

	Hinduism	Buddhism	Confucianism and Daoism	Judaism	Christianity	Islam
Is there a god?						
What does it mean to be human?						
How do humans interact with the sacred?						
How does the sacred become community?						

∧
∧ In what ways are the religious and the nonreligious in these images similar? In what ways are
∧ they different?

FEATURES OF THE BOOK

You can expect to see the following features in every chapter pair in *THINK World Religions*.

A Sacred Place

In the first chapter, the Sacred Place feature will describe a religious location. It may be a temple, cathedral, or a garden. The book has some great illustrations to let you peek inside buildings and imagine yourself walking through them. Because they're similar in style from one chapter to another, the drawings also lend themselves easily to comparisons.

A Sacred Action and a Place in the World

After learning a little bit about a place, you'll get to read about some activity that illustrates the religion we're studying. This may be a special event or an everyday occurrence, and we'll refer back to it often. In the second chapter of the group, we'll turn attention to some way in which geography, activity, and religion interact. Likewise, it will offer insight to help you in your own observations of the world around you.

Internal Conflicts and Contemporary Issues

You'll find text boxes scattered across each chapter that bring up topics distinct to each religion or related to today's society. These may include marriage, politics, or gender issues. Reading through these boxes, may give you ideas for your own reading and research.

Religion + Box

If the Internal Conflict text box points you inside a religion, this one will send you to the outside world. Examples may include religion + science, religion + technology, or religion + nature.

THINK World Religions Box

Each chapter contains at least one THINK World Religions box. The information in this box will help you relate the religious traditions being discussed to the outside world. Outside of the sacred, what place does the tradition have in the world around us? This box will answer that question.

Key Terms

Watch for key terms printed in bold throughout the chapter, and then check your understanding against the definitions in this section.

Questions for Study and Review

Appearing in both chapters, these questions will help you review what you've learned and assess your knowledge. Answering these questions will take some critical analysis of the chapter content.

For Further Study

You'll notice that this book will refer to a few main sources in each chapter. I've selected books that are easy to find in a bookstore or library. They range from general introductions to scholarly works. You can find a list of the bibliographical information about those books, and important Internet sites at the end of each world religion. Don't be fooled by some of the book titles—the *Idiot's Guide to Judaism* is a best-selling and clear introduction to that faith!

THE THINKSPOT.COM AND OTHER INTERNET RESOURCES

At TheThinkSpot.com, you will have access to online material that has been arranged specifically for use with *THINK World Religions*. You will find links to other Web sites and videos that will enhance your understanding of the religion as well as to download flashcards and summary sheets to help you review what you've learned.

OTHER MEDIA SOURCES

There has been a lot of debate surrounding the reliability of Web sites such as Wikipedia, which depends on user-generated content. As you're researching different world religions, you may find Wikipedia to be a useful jumping-off point because of its easy navigation and wide variety of topics. However, your best strategy may be to get an idea of the answer using Wikipedia and then confirm what you've read using your library or other Web sites. One of my favorites is *religionfacts.com* because it puts a lot of information in one place.

You may find it useful to visit sites such as YouTube to watch videos of religious activities. I check it regularly to see what people find intriguing or important enough to put on the Web. Just keep in mind that the videos uploaded to YouTube may be as unreliable as the content in Wikipedia. Always cross-reference your online sources.

You can use the information contained in *THINK World Religions* along with your Question Matrix to help you to root out unreliable information. In fact, finding biases in an online resource can be kind of fun. Is the writer mainstream or an apparent member of a fringe group? Does he or she try to change your mind or sell you something? If so, how persuasive is the argument or the sales pitch?

<<< Steeler Nation reveres
Super Bowl winners, **so long
as they play Steeler Football.**

Q CAN WE DESCRIBE STEELER NATION
AS A RELIGION?
WHY IS RELIGION SO DIFFICULT TO
TALK ABOUT?
THE BIG QUESTION: IS RELIGION TRUE
OR FALSE?

I am a fan,

of the Pittsburgh Steelers, and so a citizen of Steeler Nation. Each one of us has our own stories and memories, but we all believe that the Steelers symbolize the grit, hard work, and team spirit that Steeler Nation loves.

I grew up in western Pennsylvania, an area known for producing some high-quality football players. Hall-of-Famer Joe Namath came from Beaver Falls, south of our home, and my mother grew up with the father of Freddy Biletnikoff, the Oakland Raider's legendary wide receiver. Blue collar or white collar, likely your dad worked for some kind of industry. We loved the tough players on the region's teams, full of long Slavic names that sounded like the kid next to you in class. We called the great Steeler linebacker Jack Ham "Dobre Shunka," Polish for the "Good Ham." It was Steeler country in the 1960s and 70s, when the team won four Super Bowls. Where I grew up, people worked in steel mills and paper mills and ore docks. We prided ourselves in working-class teams. The trouble was that our city was also Browns country and Bills country. We wore down-to-earth colors: black and gold or, well, brown for the Browns. No one wanted to be a Miami fan and be seen in aqua and orange.

Don't think it's just geography that made me a fan. I like the Steelers' history and values, too. The team is owned by the Rooney family, who still lives in Pittsburgh, and the management really cares about the "home" aspect of "home team." The

Steelers don't buy high-priced players at the top of their game. Instead, they cultivate talent within their organization. The Steelers patiently train and develop players over time, illustrating the long-term vision and loyalty we cherish over in western PA. The Rooneys commit themselves to their players and their city, sometimes even seeing them through difficult times. For example, Rocky Bleier was kept on the Steelers roster in the 1970s after he returned from Vietnam, just so he could recover from major injuries. Rocky paid them back by helping win two Super Bowls, running with one foot shorter than the other from his war wounds. In the past few years, the Steelers have kept Fast Willie Parker even when he's been hurt more often than playing.

These traditions, coupled with some unexpected surprises, keep me coming back to watch football week after week, season after season. I value teamwork and look for it in my team. The players aren't all angels but they do good work and they don't tolerate divas. I like that. The Steelers give me a reason to root for them. They become "local" players, even if they weren't born or raised in Pittsburgh.

There's something else, too. Behind all the reasons I can tell you for being a Steelers fan—the history, the family connections, the values—there's also an intangible aspect: I just like them. When I see all the other Steelers fans waving their yellow "Terrible Towels," I feel like I'm really part of something special. I *am* part of something special.

11

TALKING ABOUT RELIGION

CHAPTER 02

Steeler Nation or Church of the Steelers?

But how much of my decision to support the Steelers is really a choice? How much of it is based on things over which I have no control?

I know that part of the reason I like the Steelers is the fact that they're a local team. But I didn't choose to be born near Pittsburgh. My parents could just as easily have bought a house in Cleveland or Buffalo, and, if they had, you'd be reading opening pages about the Browns or the Bills. My family could have moved to another town when I was young and still developing team loyalty. Would I have changed teams if every time "my" team lost, everyone around me cheered? Maybe I would have been turned off to football entirely. How much of my Steeler Nation citizenship can be attributed to chance? Probably more than I'd like to admit.

I'm sure my family also had a big impact on my choice of team to support. I come from a long line of Steelers fans. Cheering for the same team with my cousin Harry or Uncle Peter made me feel like I was a part of the adult world, if only for a few hours a week. But then there were my brothers-in-law, who actually prefer the Browns. I remember being young and clinging fiercely to "my" team while my sisters' husbands teased me when we lost a game. No doubt, the "anti-Steelers" family members made me more of a fan than my own immediate family.

All in all, I think my decision to be a Steelers fan is probably a mix of geography, family influence, and my own personal opinion. If I'd been born elsewhere, I'd probably not root for the Steelers. Having lived around the country and in Europe, I could have become a Patriots fan or even started to follow soccer. But it's hard to shake that Steeler loyalty. I might not have really chosen it, but I'll keep my membership in the Steeler Nation.

▶ CAN WE DESCRIBE STEELER NATION AS A RELIGION?

Characteristics of Religions

You'll remember from the last chapter that many scholars have tried to define "religion" over the past two centuries, but that each time there seems to be something to disprove the definition. Instead of falling into that trap, I'd like to consider a number of characteristics that many religions share. You may notice, though, that this list might also apply to other situations, like loyalty to a football team.

Which elements of the Steeler Nation seem religious, and which elements do not? To answer these questions, let's look carefully at six characteristics that religions tend to share.

HISTORY AND MYTHS

All religions have some sort of history, often told as a sacred story, or **myth**, that underlies the practices and beliefs of its people. In everyday speech, we tend to use that term to mean a story that is not true. In the study of religion, though, "myth" has no negative connotation—it simply means a story that explains the world. You may be familiar with creation myths from the Bible or Greek and Roman mythology, which explain how the world came to be. Religions tend to rely on myths to educate and to explain the world in a

narrative way—a story that shows us where we have been, so that we might guess where we're going.

You knew it was coming: do you want to hear a few Steeler myths? I can think of quite a few stories that may very well qualify as religious history and myth in the way I've just described. Many new Steelers fans are surprised to learn that in 1943, the team paired up with their cross-state competitors, the Eagles. At that time, men were

>>> How are the characteristics of religion similar to the characteristics of a sports team?

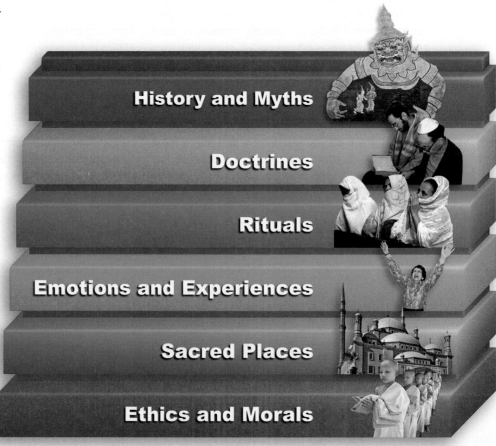

Common Features of Religions

History and Myths

Doctrines

Rituals

Emotions and Experiences

Sacred Places

Ethics and Morals

shipping off to war in Europe and North Africa. Back home, the National Football League (NFL) thought it would shut down because there simply weren't enough men left to play on the teams. Instead, the NFL decided to consolidate the number of teams. At a time of such fear and tragedy abroad, the newly created "Steagles" gave folks back home something to cheer about each week of the season. To me, that's a great historical story, reminding us to keep American traditions alive in the face of very difficult times.

And as for mythic tales, Steelers fans have those, too. For example, in December 1972 the Steelers won their first division title in 40 years. They nearly lost, but for one spectacular catch. During the final play, the Steelers receiver was hit hard by a defensive player from the opposing team (the Raiders). The ball flew out of the receiver's hands and was caught, seemingly miraculously, by Steelers running back Franco Harris, who ran the ball in for a touchdown. Considered one of the greatest moments in the history of football, to this day it's referred to as "the Immaculate Reception," in reference to the Roman Catholic dogma of the Immaculate Conception.

Then, 33 years later, the great Jerome Bettis uncharacteristically fumbled the football in a playoff game. An Indianapolis Colts player picked up the ball, and no Steeler seemed able to avert disaster. Out of nowhere, quarterback Ben Roethlisberger tackled the Colt by holding on to his shin, thus saving the game. What's that play called? Either "The Tackle" or (my favorite) "The Immaculate Redemption." It's a perfect example of a myth, because it shows failure (the abnormal fumble), salvation (the impossible tackle), and divine providence—the Steelers went on to win the Super Bowl.

DOCTRINES

Religions also tend to develop **doctrines**, a set of principles that often guide people's understanding or actions. In Islam, for example, there is one core doctrine that all Muslims must believe: "There is no other god but God, and Mohammed is the Prophet of God."

As you may have guessed, Steeler Nation has some doctrines of its own. Doctrine #1: *Steelers play physical football*. No namby-pamby pretty boys on our team. Steelers can hit. Doctrine #2: *Steelers hire head coaches from the ranks of defensive assistants*. They're not stars from other teams lured away by huge paychecks. The Steelers choose former defensive coaches to become their leaders because they understand the core philosophy of Steeler football—see Doctrine #1.

Just as the team lives and works by some simple doctrines, fans also play by certain rules. For example, members of Steeler Nation don't like the Cleveland Browns. Don't ask why; it's just a fact. All Steelers fans know this, and they don't require a logical reason to follow this simple, straightforward rule of fandom. We also don't like the Ravens, the team that the Browns became when they moved to Baltimore in 1996. Ravens are Browns in another ugly uniform.

It is not enough for us to simply dislike the Ravens and the Browns. We must also voice our displeasure openly. One of my favorite signs in a playoff game said "To us, you're still the Browns, and you still suck." I should note that this did

> **Myths** explain important ideas about the world through narrative stories.
>
> **Doctrines** explain how to understand the world and how to behave based on a specific religion.
>
> **Rituals** are repeated actions that have meaning.

not make the guy with the sign any friends in Baltimore. Such behavior would surely get you in trouble in religions situations too.

RITUALS

In my first job as a professor, I loved to come into the office, turn on the lights, make coffee, turn on the computer, check my e-mail, and pour my coffee. I always started my day in that order, which helped me to feel comfortable and able to focus. My actions might be considered **rituals**, because I repeated them and found solace in doing so. Religions also have rituals, which are often more important than doctrines to members of that tradition.

Religions tend to develop distinct rituals that help define life within that tradition. While Buddhists might regularly leave fruit in front of a statue of the Buddha, Daoists might burn incense in front of a shrine or practice tai chi to develop their own inner life. As we have seen in Chapter 1, scholars such as Clifford Geertz and Mircea Eliade have studied rituals extensively, showing how they bond people together in time and space while also linking them to their spiritual world.

What's the most important Steeler Nation ritual? No doubt, it's the Terrible Towel, started in 1975 by the famed Pittsburgh sportscaster Myron Cope. The ritual goes something like this: bring the towel with you to games, whether you are watching the Steelers in the stadium or on television. Whenever the team needs to be pumped up, swing the towel over your head and cheer wildly. Check it out some time on TV—there seem to be as many Steeler fans as home fans when the team is playing an away game.

<<< This guy is definitely following the fan doctrines of Steeler Nation.

∧
∧ **Rituals help members of a community bond together.** Why would fans create a ritual like the
∧ Terrible Towel?

Staying true to hometown values, all profits earned from the sale of Terrible Towels go to a charity to help a local school for children and adults with disabilities—one that Myron Cope's son attended. Like religious rituals that can move from one tradition to another, swinging towels at sporting events has gone beyond the borders of Steeler Nation. Other teams call them "rally towels," and their fans use them just as Steelers fans do.

EXPERIENCES AND EMOTIONS

Religions often develop shared experiences that produce emotional responses in people. This is not to say that all religious phenomena exist to make people feel good. The point here is that experiences help create feelings, which then help people better interact with their world.

Religions often also rely on shared experiences to support believers in good times and bad. They may include rituals to support life's major events—births, weddings, and deaths—but also everyday experiences like eating. In this way, emotion and experience intertwine with religious practice. You can imagine how this happens: having a parent or a child die can be an excruciating, debilitating experience. For millennia, religious traditions across the globe have helped people make sense of and cope with forces outside their control.

Being a sports fan gives me, on a much smaller level, some of the same intertwined emotions and experiences. I look forward to watching the game and talking about it with my friends and family. We celebrate wins together, and we mope about losses, too. We take pride in reliving great moments after the game. In fact, Steelers fans are so loyal to their team that a recent panel of sports writers ranked us the best in America.

SACRED PLACES

As we learned in Chapter 1, religions often set off some places from the rest of the world. In this way, they become sacred. They could be mountains, buildings, or caves. For example, followers of Hinduism may visit temples dedicated to one or more gods and goddesses. They may also visit rivers, which both embody a goddess and provide a place to wash away your sins. Likewise, a Native American may find strength in walking the land where his grandfather lived, while a Daoist may remove herself away to a sacred mountain. Spaces can be created or found, modest or grandiose. They share only their power as spots separate from the mundane world.

You can see where I'm going with this in regard to the Steelers, right? Three Rivers Stadium has given way to Heinz Field, both built at the confluence of the Ohio, Allegheny, and Monongahela rivers. How special is that little corner of land, surrounded by water and bathed in light from thousands of bulbs, shaking from fans' cheers? The team has sold out more than 300 consecutive home games. The Immaculate Reception happened at that spot, and Troy Polamalu miraculously hauled in a one-handed interception there in September 2009.

ETHICS AND MORALS

Surely, not all religions must provide ethical or moral codes. The ancient Roman civil religion, for example, did not give much guidance in these areas. Yet, most traditions do offer codes of conduct that apply to personal and social situations. Religions may also help people understand how to interact with the nonhuman world, including nature, animals, or unseen cosmic forces. Some traditions self-consciously adapt to the changing world, while others seek to slow down the rate of change and retain moral and ethical codes from generation to generation. In many cases, adherents perceive a code of conduct as coming directly from a sacred or divine source. Others, however, emphasize the human development of ethical codes.

I've already mentioned some of the ethical and moral behavior that we fans expect from our Steelers. Above all, there shall be no superstars. The team's long history of success grows from the efforts of the entire team, not a few hotshots. Here are a couple more:

- Thou shalt honor the Rooney family, for they have supported you.

- Thou shalt not question the coach in public.

- Thou shalt not dance in the end zone, but thou shalt hug the receiver or kicker who makes a play.

    You get the idea, right?

WHERE IS THE THOR OF PITTSBURGH FOOTBALL?

As you've read, the actions, beliefs, rituals, and moral code of the Steeler Nation stack up pretty well against religion as we've described it here. Yet we seem to be lacking one thing: a deity. Sure, Ben Roethlisberger's a great quarterback, but even he or Mean Joe Greene can't claim divine status. That lack of a god may not preclude us from calling Steeler Nation a form of religion, but it does make it look less like the religious traditions most prominent in American society. And those are the strength and weakness of describing religion rather than defining it—we may not ever come to a final conclusion.

∧
∧ Why might the Steelers decide to place their stadium at the confluence of the three rivers in Pittsburgh? Could that spot have symbolic meaning?

The Steeler Nation

You know the old saying—don't talk about religion or politics in polite company. Why does religion in particular ignite so many disagreements, arguments, and even war? Before we explore these questions, though, let's turn back again to our surrogate religion to see what we can learn by thinking about football rivalries. I've been planning to see the Baltimore Ravens play the Steelers this year, and I've got to decide whether I'll wear black and gold to the game in Baltimore. On the one hand, I don't want to offend the locals or endanger my niece, who will go with me. On the other hand, though, I want people to know that I support the Steelers against their rival Ravens. Where is the line between getting along and giving in? I don't really know.

∧
∧ **How can you be detached or objective**
∧ **when your team is going head-to-head**
with its rival?

Here's another example: I never had a Steelers sticker on my car when I lived near Pittsburgh. Now that I work in Philadelphia, Eagles territory, I show my Steeler pride on the back window of my Toyota. Living near so many Eagles fans, I could have chosen to convert to Eagles fandom, but I didn't. Loyalty "my" team ran too deep. I didn't want to change religions! Perhaps it could be possible for me to "believe" in both the Steelers and the Eagles. You would think I would be able to do it. I am an adult, right? Logically, I should be able to enjoy watching any game. And if I'm in a room full of Eagles fans, it would be a lot more fun to root for the group's team than to be the lone holdout. Why not just join in when it's convenient?

After all, when it comes to baseball, I have no such deeply held loyalties. I can have a great time rooting for either the Pirates or the Phillies. Maybe it's because the Pirates are so bad, and the Phillies have won the World Series. The teams are so out of step that they don't even seem to compete with each other. On the other hand, the Steelers and Eagles regularly make it to the playoffs, contending for the Super Bowl. They both command rabid loyalty, which forces me to choose between them. In a way, that's good because it makes for better football, and it reaffirms my faith in my team. An Eagles victory might mean lots of teasing from my students on Monday morning, but that only increases my devotion to Pittsburgh. My situation illustrates another issue: it seems easier to disagree with people similar to you (like Eagles fans) than with folks who hold vastly different beliefs (like rugby fans). In the second case, the gulf feels too wide for any real fight.

So, in the case of football, my loyalties persist, but I've become a little more broad-minded with baseball. I think we can use this situation to help us think about the depth of commitment millions of people feel toward their religion. No matter how difficult—whether persecuted, ridiculed, or attacked—these people still maintain their faith. Others, however, feel less intense loyalty to their tradition and may change religions based on geography, changing social conditions, or a new political atmosphere. They may introduce a new religion into their lives by marrying someone of a different faith. Perhaps they'll take on their mate's tradition, meld the two together, or leave both traditions for something new.

Strategies for Studying World Religions

Can you really like the Steelers but respect the Eagles? Can you believe in one religion and still take the time to learn about others? Some of the most dearly held beliefs of another religion might completely contradict a value that is important in your religion. Can you appreciate why others believe as they do, even if you disagree with that belief? You are the only one to answer these questions. Keeping all this in mind, here are some strategies for studying world religions.

YOU CAN DO IT

You can study religion whether or not you are personally religious. More important than verifying your opinions, try to realize how other people's belief systems, myths, morals, and deities powerfully affect the world—

even if you personally do not acknowledge their existence or worth. People may be willing to live and die for their religions. You can thus appreciate and respect the deep feelings others have, even if you do not share them.

YOU DON'T HAVE TO GIVE UP YOUR VALUES

Although you will be studying world religions, you will never be asked to change your own religious outlook. You may be asked to imagine what your life might be like as a Christian, Daoist, or Buddhist, but these thought exercises are meant only to help give you some deeper insights, not convince you to convert.

YOU CAN USE COMPARISONS AND METAPHORS

Try using comparisons or metaphors if you are having trouble comprehending a religious concept. Of course, that's the point of talking about the Steelers in this chapter. Often, comparisons or metaphors can remove passion from a discussion. For example, if you can compare a religious action or value to something a football fan might do, then you may be able to figure out why people act in ways that seem unusual to you.

Try using the "four questions" method to study how religions arrive at answers to similar questions. Remember, too, that you may find other questions more useful than the ones we use in this book. Consider, for example, questions about beauty and ugliness, strength and weakness. Explore those concepts, so very different from the four questions in this book, and who knows how you'll change your analysis.

As you compare the answers to the four questions for different religions, keep in mind that one answer is not necessarily better than another. The question matrix will help in this regard because it creates visual patterns from verbal ideas. Look for similarities and differences among the various religions. Doing so may help you take the "right" and "wrong" out of the discussion and lead you more toward "if this, then that."

For me, it's useful to fall back to things I know, as I've done in this chapter with the football metaphor. What if we asked specific questions about professional football but put aside our emotions? Even this can be difficult, but it's worth trying. For example, I might study the relationship each team has with its host city by looking at its colors. Red, white, and blue clearly refer to New England's role in the creation of the United States. The Mariners sport aquatic colors. The trick for me, though, would be not going off topic to explain why the coolest helmets are black and gold with a team logo on just one side instead of both. I would have to include Steeler black and gold in a box along with other teams in my question matrix. Then I'd see that the Steelers followed the colors of U.S. Steel, which is a century-old manufacturing company based in Pittsburgh. That fact may then help explain why Steeler Nation thinks of itself in blue-collar terms.

As another example, you could compare statistics from one player to another, or one religion to another. What can we learn by knowing Hines Ward's catching average compared to Terrell Owens? How does Islam's growth in Western China compare to the same numbers for Western Europe? From this perspective, we can learn about subjects by emphasizing dispassionate data.

Making comparisons like the ones I just described, however, doesn't keep me from having favorites of my own. It does give me a way to talk with less emotion, though, which may help to foster some forms of analysis. It's like that quote from the old detective TV show *Dragnet*: "Just the facts, ma'am."

Finally, don't forget that one's religion, like one's team loyalty, most often grows out of a mixture of geography and history. Personal choices may change people's religious predilection, but more often than not, they tend to return to the system in which they were raised. It's perfectly common for someone to live his or her whole life without making a conscious choice about religion, which tends to help maintain tradition for generations.

▶ THE BIG QUESTION: IS RELIGION TRUE OR FALSE?

What Is Truth?

The study of religion brings up an important question, and scholars have wrestled with it for many years. Is religion "truthful" or "true"? Although it may seem that these two words refer to the same thing, I'll press you to explore these ideas a little more deeply.

In 2005, comedian Stephen Colbert coined the term **truthiness**. "Truthy" ideas may seem true at first, but if you dig deeper into the issue and discover the facts, you are likely to find a truthy statement to be verifiability wrong. These falsehoods, however, are repeated over and over again until we accept them as real. Why? Because it helps us feel good or helps politicians get what they want without sounding like they're lying.

On the other hand, I would define **truthfulness** as seeking truth or living in a way that honors an uncomfortable truth over a comfortable lie.

A truthful life is a genuine and authentic one. When viewed from this perspective, the opposite of truthfulness is therefore not falsehood, but hypocrisy. Thus, when we study people through their own eyes, it's not so hard to accept the truthful way they are living, even if you don't share their perceptions.

OK, so we now have a handle on truthfulness versus truthiness. But what about truth itself? Can a religion be true? I tell students that true religion reveals something authentic about someone's life. That's easy enough to say. But what, then, is the opposite of truth? I think a lie is definitely the opposite of truth. But what about an opinion? Is that the opposite of truth? Or can we learn a greater truth about people in general by valuing their unverifiable opinions? Can two truths contradict one another? And can personal experiences color the way different people value one truth over another? These are some difficult questions to answer (Andrade).

THINK World Religions

Truthfulness vs. "Truthiness"

What does it mean to be truthful? In 2005, American TV satirist Stephen Colbert challenged his audience to consider the relative values of truthfulness and "truthiness." Whereas truthfulness relies on factual accounts to validate a person's beliefs, truthiness does just the opposite. It relies on a person's gut feelings to define truth, regardless of the facts. When asked about the segment in an interview, Colbert replied, "It used to be, everyone was entitled to their own opinion, but not their own facts. But that's not the case anymore. Facts matter not at all. Perception is everything. It's certainty" (Andrade).

^
^   **Stephen Colbert** is the satirist and
^   host of Comedy Central's *The Colbert
    Report*.

Can There Be More Than One Truth?
TRUTH THROUGH MONOLOGUE VS. TRUTH THROUGH DIALOGUE

This book does not ask you to believe that any religion is true for *you*. It does, however, ask you to accept that it is true for *someone*. Additionally,

I hope you will think about each religion with the same sense of respect you would want from others learning about your own.

In other words, *THINK World Religions* puts great store in the power of dialogue rather than monologue. If you have studied ancient Greek or Shakespearean plays, you have had some experience reading both of these. In each case, characters work through a dilemma and seek the right course of action. Truth through dialogue seeks to learn through input from more than one person, source, or place. It does not seek to impose one's views on another person. In fact, the truth may come from many rather than one voice. In a dialogue, speakers have no choice but to modulate their own ideas to consider those of others (Thomlinson).

Truth through a monologue, on the other hand, seeks to find a single truth that can be applied to a situation. Monologues can deeply nurture a person's spirit and intellect, but they can also embody self-serving behavior. In a play, monologues express inwardly directed thoughts for the outside world to hear. They allow the speaker to concentrate privately, away from interactions with other characters. Monologues by their nature reveal much about a person, but less about a relationship.

THINK World Religions

Pontius Pilate: "What Is Truth?"

In the Christian New Testament, the Roman prefect Pontius Pilate must decide if Jesus is guilty of plotting against Rome and should be crucified. In the Gospel of John, Pontius Pilate and Jesus engage in the following dialogue:

"Pilate asked him, 'So you are a king?' Jesus answered, 'You say that I am a king. For this I was born, and for this I came into the world, to testify to the truth. Everyone who belongs to the truth listens to my voice.' Pilate asked him, 'What is truth?' After he had said this, he went out to the Jews again and told them, 'I find no case against him." (John 18: 37–38)

Let's go back again to Chapter 1. I believe that the search for a solitary truth relates closely to apologetic writers such as Thomas Aquinas or Ayatollah Khomeini, who led the Islamist revolution in Iran. Their thoughts and words illustrate their worlds for us, but they represent a single voice from a single perspective. Finding truth through dialogue more closely resembles our task in *THINK World Religions*. Imagine all the voices in this book—mine, yours, adherents from the past, seekers in the present, and those who doubt everything. It's as if we're in a conversation with people from all over the world. In this way, learning about others' traditions, ideas, and perceptions of the world while voicing your own helps create a dialogue of many voices, out of which, I hope, will come truth.

Back to Steeler Nation

As I prepared to write this conclusion, I scanned the sports page for news of Steelers. But here in Philadelphia, everything was about the Eagles—which player was healthy, which one had contract problems, who would be starting in the next game. It made me want to turn to the comics section. Using my strategies for understanding and comparing other religions, however, I read stories about the Philadelphia team and looked at the pictures of the fans. But though I am working to understand the workings of this "other" team, I've got to admit it—there's still a Steelers sticker firmly affixed to my car.

<<<

Members of the Steeler Nation are proud to display their loyalty **with logos such as this one.**

CAN WE DESCRIBE STEELER NATION AS A RELIGION?

Steeler Nation shares many of the characteristics of a religion. Members of Steeler Nation are well versed in the team's history and myths. They also follow the team's doctrines and rituals, such as the use of the Terrible Towel. Additionally, there are many emotions and shared experiences that bring Steeler fans together, no matter what their background. The team's stadium can be compared to the sacred places of religions. Finally, the team upholds certain morals and ethics, just like a religion.

?

THE BIG QUESTION: IS RELIGION TRUE OR FALSE?

It is difficult to define religion as true or false or to prove that all the ideas and theories that make up the foundation of a particular religion are correct. From the point of view of a World Religions class, it makes more sense to ask if a religion gives meaning to people's lives than if it is true or false.

WHY IS RELIGION SO DIFFICULT TO TALK ABOUT?

Many people prefer to keep their religious lives to themselves, for fear that their beliefs will not be accepted by those around them. Additionally, many people often find it hard to find a common ground with people who follow a different tradition. Failure to do so can lead to heated debates, arguments, and even fights.

<<<

Is religion true or false?

>>>

Religion **has often been at the** root of many fights and arguments.

REVIEW

Summary

CAN WE DESCRIBE STEELER NATION AS A RELIGION?   p. 12

- While Steeler Nation may not be currently acknowledged as such, it contains many characteristics of religion—history and myths, doctrines, rituals, experiences and emotions, sacred places, and an ethical and moral code.

WHY IS RELIGION SO DIFFICULT TO TALK ABOUT?   p. 16

- Spiritual beliefs can run extremely deep, and many people view religion as a personal matter. Often, it's challenging to find a common ground among belief systems, and religious discussions can lead to arguments and even violence.

THE BIG QUESTION: IS RELIGION TRUE OR FALSE?   p. 17

- It's hard to define what is "true" and what is "truthy." Should people's opinions be considered when studying religion? Is there one objective "truth?" There is no easy answer, but for the purposes of this book, you'll find it helpful to focus more on the meaning and value associated with each religion, not the facts.

Key Terms

Myths explain important ideas about the world through narrative stories. *12*

Doctrines explain how to understand the world and how to behave based on a specific religion. *13*

Rituals are repeated actions that have meaning. *13*

Truthiness refers to a satirical idea describing verifiable falsehoods repeated so often that they seem to be true. *17*

Truthfulness seeks the truth or tries to find a way to live authentically or genuinely. *17*

Find it on

www.whirlingdervishes.org

You are probably familiar with many of the religious traditions and their practices found in the United States. For instance, you probably can conjure up a mental image of a boy or girl at their bar or bat mitzvah or a young child receiving the Holy Eucharist for the first time. You have probably even seen images of people making a pilgrimage to Mecca. You may not be familiar with a more mystical tradition—Sufism—a tradition that derives from Islam and in which you can find whirling dervishes. Visit the ThinkSpot for more information on Sufism and to see video of the mystical whirling dervishes.

- http://www.youtube.com/watch?v=vsLP9syh0EU&feature= related

What constitutes a religious tradition? You'll have a fuller understanding once you read this textbook. Some people have very strict ideas about what makes a religion, while others … well, not so much. Go to the ThinkSpot and watch this video about Deadheads, those people who follow the band The Grateful Dead

with an unfailing devotion. Religion or not? You decide.

- http://www.youtube.com/ watch?v=7xMDlcsUMmA

- http://www.post-gazette .com/sports/columnists/ 20001214thebig1.asp

- http://www.youtube.com/ watch?v=RwYkqErKJ08& feature=youtube_gdatahttp://www.youtube.com/watch?v=R wYkqErKJ08&feature=youtube_gdata

Many people have their favorite sports teams and their favorite sports moments. The Pittsburgh Steelers, however, are my team and one to which I'm extremely devoted. They hold a special place in my heart. Does that make my love for the Steelers approach the divine? Hard to say. But if you're interested in learning more about the Steelers and what they mean to other people, go to the ThinkSpot. (And if you can watch the video of the end zone catch and not believe that some kind of higher power was involved, we need to talk.)

Questions for Study and Review

1. **What are the main characteristics of religion?**

   Religions tend to share six characteristics, although not every tradition has each one.

   1. *History* forms the foundation for beliefs and practices. Similarly, myths explain the existence of the world, or how things came to be the way they are today.
   2. *Doctrines* help to define the moral code or appropriate behavior for the members of a group.
   3. *Rituals* may include actions such as religious services or public celebrations.
   4. Religious *emotions* and *experiences* generate feelings which tie people closer to their beliefs and help them relate to one another and the world around them.
   5. Religions often have *sacred places*: a home or church, a spot for prayer or ceremony, or a hallowed ground with great historical significance.
   6. *Ethics and morals* offer codes for living in the world.

2. **Discuss some of the ways in which Steeler Nation is similar to a religion.**

   Steeler Nation shares each of the six characteristics of religion. The team's history and myths have nourished generations of loyal fans, who pass their experiences down to the next generation. As with religion, geography has played a strong role in the cultivation of new fans. Both the players and the fans have a set of rituals they follow before, during, and after each game. The game day emotions and experiences also bond fans together. The one main characteristic the Steeler Nation does not have is a god or deity to worship.

3. **What methods or practices can you use to study different religions?**

   You can adopt a few different methods to help you objectively study different religions. Using comparisons or metaphors is one way. Putting together charts using the four questions or statistics can also help neutralize feelings and emotions. Finally, trying to put yourself in another's shoes while studying a particular religion is a method that many find successful. Doing so allows you to experience, if only for a brief time, the different components of that particular religion.

For Further Study

BOOKS:

Baker, William J. *Playing with God: Religion and Modern Sport*. Cambridge, MA: Harvard University Press, 2007.

Capps, Walter H. *Religious Studies: The Making of a Discipline*. Minneapolis, MN: Fortress Press, 1995.

Forney, Craig A. *The Holy Trinity of American Sports: Civil Religion in Football, Baseball, and Basketball*. Macon, GA: Mercer University Press, 2007.

Forward, Martin. *Religion: A Beginner's Guide*. Oxford, UK: Oneworld Publications, 2001.

Price, Joseph L., Ed. *From Season to Season: Sports as American Religion*. Macon, GA: Mercer University Press, 2001.

Winzeler, Robert L. *Anthropology and Religion*. New York: AltaMira Press, 2008.

WEB SITES:

Academic Info: Religion Gateway.
http://www.academicinfo.net/Religion.html

Belief-o-Matic.
http://www.beliefnet.com/Entertainment/Quizzes/BeliefOMatic.aspx

Religion Facts. http://www.religionfacts.com

Religious Worlds: an information source for religion, religions, religious studies. http://www.religiousworlds.com

Sacred Texts. http://www.sacred-texts.com

Writing Papers about Religion. www.unc.edu/depts/wcweb/handouts/religious_studies.html

Q

IS THERE A GOD?
WHAT DOES IT MEAN TO BE HUMAN?

For nearly

4,500 years, people around the globe have followed rituals, memorized texts, and revered the many gods of Hinduism. It continues to be based in the southern section of Asia, including India and Sri Lanka. Although the divine infuses all things, Hindus may choose to worship one, two, or many gods. Some may put their trust in a particular god and make sacrifices to it. Others may seek enlightenment—the experience of absolute knowledge and understanding.

Here's a tip at the beginning of our study of Hinduism: As you learn about its many traditions, you're likely to use the word "and." A simple enough term it will help you understand the complexities of Hinduism, where different ideas layer and complement each other. Avoid using "not" and "or," remember to say "and," and you'll be well on your way. For example, Hindus revere both one god *and* millions of gods.

To help you begin to understand the deceptively simple idea of "and," envision the process of creating sand art. (Although many cultures use sand in their artistic and religious artwork, here the analogy refers only to craft class.) You may have done this as a child, pouring different colors of sand into a clear glass jar, and then moved them around to form patterns, layers, and designs. Do it enough times with some help, and you can create really complex patterns and images.

If you look closely, you can see each individual piece of sand. The picture comes from the layers as they've been moved by the knife: red *and* green, yellow *and* blue. Each bit, each layer is an essential part of the art. But no single grain or layer alone can make the design. If you add a layer or shake the jar a little, the art takes on a new shape, transformed by outside forces in much the same way that Hinduism has reshaped itself in response to outside influences. With each successive level, the sand art—like Hinduism—becomes more complex without losing the layers below it.

Like the sand in your glass, different groups of people have molded and changed what it means to be a Hindu over thousands of years. Just as the sand art has many distinct layers, so too does Hinduism. As you turn the jar, the layers mingle together and yet remain distinct. So it is with Hinduism: Many ideas, practices, philosophies, and relationships lay atop one another. Because there is no single source of authority—no "church"—in Hinduism, diametrically opposed ideas often exist simultaneously. Like sand in a jar, you may sometimes see one layer, sometimes another. Just remember that each layer interacts with the others to create the whole picture, which is a way of life called *Hinduism*.

HINDUISM:
The Eternal Law

A Hindu Temple

WALK INTO THE BRIHADEESHWARA TEMPLE IN THANJAVUR, INDIA AND PREPARE TO BE AMAZED. A path of columns welcomes you, a man-made mountain towers beyond it. Though undeniably ancient, this building is also feels alive. Statues peer out from niches, surrounded by wall paintings vivid with blue, gold, and red. There are people and smells, chanting and laughter, darkness and bright light. A few folks drape a sculpture (half elephant, half man) with flowers. Making your way inside, pass a huge figure of a bull, watching intently.

At the front of the temple, directly under the peaked tower, is a huge Lingam and Yoni. This is a temple dedicated to Shiva, the god of destruction, and transformation. People may be leaving offerings, bowing down, or walking around the Lingam and Yoni.

Visit a Hindu temple in your community and it's unlikely to be nearly so impressive as the Brihadeeshwara. Yet it should feel similar—there may be a tower, a water source for ritual bathing, an outer room and an inner chamber that holds the deities to whom the temple is dedicated. And you'll feel the same rush of your senses as you take in the color, fragrance, and sounds that characterize Hindu worship.

Cross section of the
Brihadeeshwara Temple

Shiva as Lingam and Yoni—Penis and Vagina.
This teaches us that Shiva is responsible for both destruction and rebirth. The Lingam has the Om painted on it, and Nandi—Shiva's protector bull—looks on. Nandi reminds us of cattle's sacred place in Hindu society.

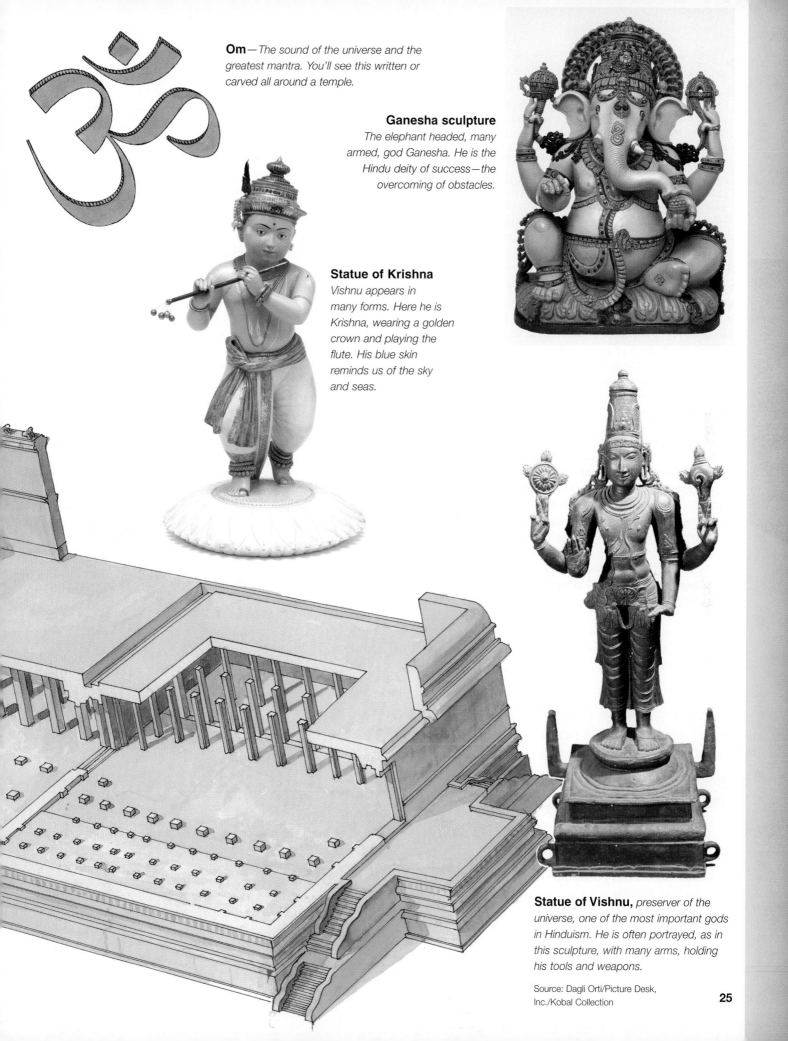

Om—*The sound of the universe and the greatest mantra. You'll see this written or carved all around a temple.*

Ganesha sculpture
The elephant headed, many armed, god Ganesha. He is the Hindu deity of success—the overcoming of obstacles.

Statue of Krishna
Vishnu appears in many forms. Here he is Krishna, wearing a golden crown and playing the flute. His blue skin reminds us of the sky and seas.

Statue of Vishnu, *preserver of the universe, one of the most important gods in Hinduism. He is often portrayed, as in this sculpture, with many arms, holding his tools and weapons.*

Source: Dagli Orti/Picture Desk, Inc./Kobal Collection

▶ IS THERE A GOD IN HINDUISM?

Puja is the ritual by which Hindus connect with their gods and goddesses; the puja can be held by a priest in a temple or by Hindu followers themselves in the home.

Sanatana dharma is the term Hindus use to refer to their religion and life; it translates roughly as "eternal law" or "eternal virtue."

Dharma can mean religion, universal law, application of universal law to Indian society, regulation of life through universal law, social responsibilities and duties, and the virtuous path of life.

Caste system divides people into separate social groups that have varying rights, responsibilities, professions, and status.

Do Hindus worship one god or many? Although it may seem strange, the answer to this question is "yes." As you have read, Hindu families venerate different gods or goddesses. Even members of the same family may focus on different deities of their choosing. When a Hindu family performs a **puja**, members may direct the ceremony to one of many different gods. That being said, some strains of Hinduism also emphasize a single force in the universe that has created everything—even itself—and thus links all things in the cosmos. In that case, a Hindu might answer that there is both one god and many gods all at the same time.

Dharma

Although we've been using the word "Hinduism," its adherents often prefer another term: **Sanatana dharma**, a Sanskrit term approximately translated as "eternal virtue" or "eternal law" (Klostermaier *Beginner's Guide*, 7). If we spend a little time exploring the many shades of meaning in "dharma," we'll also better understand the complex relationships and layers that characterize Hindu perceptions of the world and the divine. In fact, learning a little about the word dharma will also teach us about the paradoxical unity and diversity of the divine in Hinduism.

Dharma means "religion." In fact, it goes beyond that idea in the sense that other belief systems use the term. In Sanskrit, it means "to hold together," as in holding the whole universe together. In this way, dharma acts as a universal glue.

It makes sense, then, that dharma also means "universal, timeless law." As the guiding force of the universe, dharma affects everything—not just rocks, plants, or people, but also ideas, time, and space. Dharma organizes all of this as a universal law that exists outside of time.

Dharma also means "regulation of life through universal law." In a typical Hindu household, you will find a shrine devoted to the gods primarily worshipped there. Dharma regulates when to perform puja to those gods, when to marry, and when to set out or return on pilgrimage.

The law of all the cosmos, dharma may also be defined as the "application of divine law to Indian society." Dharma encompasses the spiritual and practical aspects of Indian life and includes abiding and enforcing laws. Laws are dharma. Following the law is dharma.

Thus, dharma also means "social responsibilities and duties." If everything is cosmically connected, then your place in society fits into some kind of universal harmony. We can see this most clearly through the Indian castes and subcastes that have developed over thousands of years. The **caste system** structures society by applying different prerogatives and responsibilities to various groups. Some castes have more power, prestige, and prominence than others. Professions, status, and even names fall under caste traditions. Unlike social classes in the United States, the caste system does not derive from wealth. A high-caste priest, for example, may have much less money than a lower-caste banker. (We'll learn much more about castes throughout this chapter and the next.)

It makes good sense, then, to imagine dharma as also meaning "the virtuous path of life." And so sanatana dharma refers both to eternal law and eternal virtue. To fit into the cosmic harmony, to follow universal law, to live appropriately to your place in life: These all represent virtuous actions that can lead a person to ever-higher states of enlightenment.

Sacred Texts and Traditions

How do Hindu families choose which deities to worship? Where do they learn the steps of the puja and the actions they must take to live in concert with dharma? As in other traditions, they

>>> **What acts of reverence to a spirit or deity are you familiar with?** What functions do they serve?

A SACRED ACTION ▶▶▶

The Puja

When Hindus want to show reverence to their gods, they may conduct a ceremony called a puja in a temple like the one we just read about. They may also offer puja in public spaces or even at home. Ranging from simple to highly elaborate, all pujas follow traditional structure and link human beings to particular gods. People will often visit different temples when they want to connect with different gods or goddesses. A woman hoping to become pregnant, for example, might visit the temple of Sarasvati, a Hindu goddess of fertility.

You'll be most likely to attend an elaborate puja in a temple, conducted by a Hindu priest who may even live there. You will arrive in the temple after bathing in a ritual bath outside and might watch the priests wake up deities that reside there, dress them, feed them, and put them to bed every day. An oil lamp flickers in front of the deities, a small sacrifice to the god in the temple. By attending and watching, you avail yourself to the temple gods, who may then aid you (Kanitkar and Cole 65). It can be an elaborate set of steps, as we see in the chart on the opposite page. Take a few minutes to imagine yourself watching—or doing—these sacred actions, for we'll refer back to them throughout the next two chapters.

The 16 Steps of a Temple Puja

Step 1 The priest and followers sit or stand before the statue and focus on its characteristics. Participants invoke mental images of the deity and combine them with their own thoughts, so the deity and the statue commingle in their minds.

Step 2 The priest touches the statue and offers the deity a seat.

Step 3 The priest washes the statue's feet with water.

Step 4 The priest offers water to the deity so that he may wash his hands.

Step 5 The priest offers water to the deity so that he may wash his mouth and face. The priest then offers a mixture of milk and honey to the deity.

Step 6 The statue is bathed again.

Step 7 The priest offers the deity a garment. The priest may drape cloth over the statue, or may use flowers in place of cloth.

Step 8 The priest offers colored powders to the deity.

Step 9 The priest offers adornments to the deity. These can be gold or silver, or they can be precious stones.

Step 10 The priest offers flowers to the deity.

Step 11 The priest chants holy names as he places the flowers on the statue.

Step 12 The priest offers a stick of incense to the deity. The priest then lights it and draws circles in the air with the lit incense.

Step 13 The priest lights an oil lamp and offers it to the deity.

Step 14 The priest offers the deity food, such as fruits, rice, or sweets.

Step 15 The priest then recites prayers for the statue while circling a flame in front of the statue.

Step 16 The priest offers flowers at the feet of the statue, symbolizing surrender to the deity. Participants bow in front of the deity and offer songs and prayers. Sometimes, the food offering, which has now been blessed, is retrieved and eaten by the participants.

Source: Kanitkar, Hemant, and Owen Cole. *Teach Yourself Hinduism* (Chicago: McGraw-Hill, 2003), 65–69.

∧
∧ Although the priest conducts the ritual actions of the puja, the other participants still reap
∧ the rewards of being in the presence of the deity. When a god enters the statue, he can see the participants, and they can also see the god. How might this establish and strengthen a bond between Hindus and their deities?

Sruti means "scripture" in Sanskrit and refers to the Vedas as well as the other sacred texts of Hinduism.

Smrti refers in Sanskrit to sacred Hindu traditions, both orally transmitted and written down.

Puranas often teach morality lessons or offer parables of right living in Hinduism.

Vedas are the ancient texts brought to India by the Aryans around 2500 BCE; these are the sacred texts of Hinduism.

Upanishads are Vedic texts that focus on the relationship between the human and the divine.

Brahman is the original source of all things and the composition of the cosmos in Hinduism.

Brahma is often considered to be the creator of the world in Hinduism.

Vishnu is the Hindu protector of the world.

Shiva is the Hindu god of transformation and destruction that ultimately leads to new creation.

rely on sacred texts and traditions. Given its long age and layers, it's no surprise that Hinduism can look to many different texts as the basis for understanding cosmic reality. To get a handle on the great diversity, we'll talk about three important forms of knowledge: **sruti** (scripture), **smrti** (tradition), and **Puranas** (stories).

SRUTI AND SMRTI: THE VEDAS

The oldest and most basic texts of Hinduism began as stories handed down orally. Although we refer to them as the **Vedas**, you might also hear them simply called "scripture," or sruti. Not so much narratives of ancient times or people as teaching about the divine essence of all things, the Vedas link cosmic structures to social organization and personal virtue. Here are a few things you should remember:

- The Rig-veda (or Rgveda) is the oldest and most important of the four Vedic texts, bringing together about 1,000 hymns. For centuries, only a few people learned the Rig-veda, passing it down secretly from generation to generation with incredible precision.

- So central to Hindu life are the Vedas that they have attained status of both sruti and smrti—scripture and tradition.

- As keys to the physical and metaphysical universe, the Vedas also contain significant coded astronomical data.

- The newest Vedic texts (written from the 8th to the 3rd centuries BCE) are called the **Upanishads**. They weave together stories, discussions, and instructions designed to help human beings understand and interact with the cosmos. Much of the material that we'll study in this chapter derives originally from the Upanishads.

PURANAS: THE "BIBLICAL STORIES" OF HINDUISM

Unlike the Vedas, which describe the universe through sacred words, the Puranas are a collection of myths, legends, lessons, and stories originally meant to simplify and teach the Vedic texts to all Hindu followers. Even today, people across India know stories from the Puranas, and you might see them dramatized in a Bollywood film. The intellectual teachings and hymns of the Vedas, combined with the stories in the Puranas, provide us with a rich description of the complex web of Hindu gods and goddesses.

In addition to the Vedas and the Puranas, Hindus treasure a number of great epic stories (like the Ramayana—the story of Rama) that might be considered the "history of dharma." Although we will consider some very esoteric ideas in other parts of this chapter, it's useful to remember that most Hindus know their tradition through these narratives, poems, and teachings. For them, the subtleties of philosophy play a minor role in comparison to the local customs and stories that they've learned since childhood.

Nevertheless, the combination of these traditions—both written and oral—comprises the underlying structure of sanatana dharma. A famous way to remember this is the saying that "Sruti and smrti are the eyes of dharma, but the Purana is its heart. On no other foundation does it rest than on these three" (Klostermaier 55).

Brahman: Source of All Divinity

One important strain of Hinduism, based especially on the Upanishads, brings together all the Hindu deities into a single source called Brahman. The philosopher Adi Shankara developed an important interpretation of Brahman in the 8th and 9th centuries CE, and

Main Concepts of Hinduism

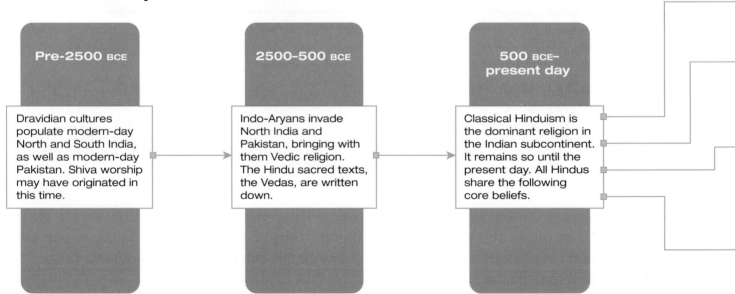

Pre-2500 BCE

Dravidian cultures populate modern-day North and South India, as well as modern-day Pakistan. Shiva worship may have originated in this time.

2500–500 BCE

Indo-Aryans invade North India and Pakistan, bringing with them Vedic religion. The Hindu sacred texts, the Vedas, are written down.

500 BCE– present day

Classical Hinduism is the dominant religion in the Indian subcontinent. It remains so until the present day. All Hindus share the following core beliefs.

much of our understanding comes from his work. Other Hindu traditions differ, but Shankara's teaching can help explain the paradox of both one and many gods in Hinduism.

Brahman includes both matter and creative force. Brahman has existed for all time and space and, in fact, *is* all time and space. You may know of other religions in which one creator made all things. At the moment of creation, however, Brahman did not stand outside the world and create it. Instead, Brahman *became* the world, infusing and multiplying itself into all things. Brahman emanated outward, creating everything: rocks, animals, rivers, and air. Brahman is the divine. Brahman is creation. Brahman is dharma.

ALL GODS ARE BRAHMAN

As all of everything comes from and is Brahman, so must Brahman include all the gods of Hinduism. From this point of view, Hindus may simultaneously worship one source for all divinity and also a multiplicity of deities. When a Hindu family goes to a temple to connect more closely with the god Vishnu, they may recognize him as a powerful aspect of Brahman. And remember: Vishnu, his followers, the temple, the earth it's built on, and the air surrounding it all connect with one another, since they are all Brahman. It's worth repeating that even Brahman itself is composed of Brahman, making Brahman both the creator *and* creation.

So, why have all those different gods if they all are One? Some people don't much think about Brahman, but concentrate instead on the gods of their neighborhood or family. Yet each god and goddess can also represent an aspect of Brahman. Some embody a powerful force like life or death. Others personify things like home and hearth or safe travel. So, let's ask our question again: How many gods are there in Hinduism? There is one: Brahman. Yet, as we'll soon learn, there are also three: **Brahma**, **Vishnu**, and **Shiva**. And, finally, there are perhaps 330 million gods and counting.

Three Main Gods of Hinduism

Hindus often worship at least one of the three primary aspects of creation that represent elemental aspects of human existence—life, death, and the external world.

- Brahma created the world.
- Vishnu protects and preserves the universe. He embodies goodness and appears on earth in many ways.
- Shiva transforms the universe, destroying the old and ushering in new creation.

Although they are often called the primary gods of Hinduism, Brahma, Vishnu, and Shiva do not all receive the same favor from Hindus. For example, they often pay less attention to Brahma than Vishnu or Shiva, since Brahma's work has already been finished—the world has been created. Therefore, he interacts with us to a much lesser degree than Vishnu or Shiva, who constantly affect our lives. For that reason, millions of Hindus worship and commune with these two gods in their many forms.

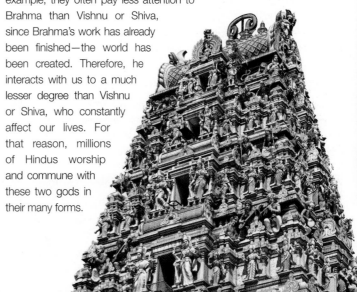

>>> **Hindu art and architecture depict many gods and goddesses.** What do you think is the value of painted or sculpted images of gods?

Everything in the world originates from Brahman. Brahman is the one source for all divinity.

Humans are imperfect and distracted by the illusory world, which is known as maya.

The Hindu Pantheon is comprised of three primary gods and up to 330 million lesser gods. All gods are simply aspects of the one divinity, Brahman. Hindus connect directly with the gods through a ceremony called a puja.

The Vedic sacred texts, the *Upanishads* offer these four Great Sayings that when meditated upon will lead the Hindu to a greater understanding of Atman, which is Brahman.

Humans are disconnected from Brahman. Because of this, they are stuck in a cycle of rebirth and death called samsara. They must work hard to break the cycle and avoid reincarnation.

To transcend maya, humans must focus on Brahman through true self-knowledge. Knowledge of the self is known as Atman. Humans also connect with Brahman through the many gods and goddesses.

The three primary gods are Brahma, the creator, Vishnu, the preserver and protector, and Shiva, the destroyer.

Part of breaking the cycle involves removing the karma that a person collects throughout his or her many lives. Good works create good karma. Evil deeds or neglecting Brahman result in bad karma.

Brahman is wisdom.

The Self is the Ultimate.

That you are.

I am Brahman.

Beliefs and Science

How can an ancient belief system like Hinduism relate to cutting-edge science? Surprisingly, Hindu perceptions of Brahman correlate in some ways to the big bang theory. Now widely accepted as the best scientific model of creation, the big bang theory states that all the matter in the universe is expanding because it originated from a single point. At the beginning of the known universe, this singularity spewed out all the matter we now see and experience. How do you think a Hindu might interpret the big bang in terms of Brahman?

the THINK SPOT
www.thethinkspot.com

Primary Gods: A Closer Look

Each of the main gods is generally male, but can also be experienced as female. Very often, you'll see a male god linked somehow to his female consort (Kanitkar and Cole 25–34). Here are descriptions of a few of them.

VISHNU AND LAKSHMI

Hindus widely revere Vishnu through the many forms in which he has appeared on earth. Vishnu manifests himself whenever human beings most need salvation from natural disasters or ruthless rulers. Although Brahma gets credit for creating the world, Vishnu often plays a part as well; he is often portrayed sleeping, with Brahma growing from his navel as a lotus flower. When Vishnu wakes up, the world will end, so Vishnu's consort Lakshmi massages his feet to keep him comfortable. At other times, Hindus depict the god reclining on a lotus blossom floating in the water. He wears a necklace of precious jewels and holds a lotus, mace, conch shell, and a discus in his four hands. You'll see these same objects as part of a puja to Vishnu.

Vishnu's consort, Lakshmi, appears as his wife when he comes to earth as an avatar. In Hindu art, you'll often see her as a beautiful woman holding two lotus blossoms and gold coins. During Diwali, the celebration of light, Hindus often make a special veneration to Lakshmi.

By tradition, Vishnu has come to earth 10 times, appearing in as many forms called avatars (yes, just like the movie). You'll most likely hear of Krishna (also spelled Krshna) and Rama. Often given the title "Lord," these two avatars appear regularly in temples, songs, stories, and even movies. Yet Krishna came eight other times, too, turning himself into animals and even the Buddha. Listed are the incarnations of Vishnu:

- Matsya—The Fish: Vishnu saved the ancient Hindus from a giant flood by transforming into a giant fish.
- Kurma—The Tortoise: When the ocean churned and became treacherous, Vishnu saved the people by coming to them as a giant turtle.
- Varaha—The Boar, who slew the demon Hiranyaksha.
- Narasimha—Half-Man, Half-Lion: In this form, Vishnu slew the demon Hiranyakashipu.
- Vamana—The Dwarf, who tricked the ruthless demon king Bali. After this event, Bali became ruler of the underworld.

∧∧∧ This painting depicts Vishnu with his consort Lakshmi. **Brahma grows from Vishnu's navel, and sits on a lotus blossom. What does the depiction of the female add to the concept of the god?**

Hindu Gods and Goddesses

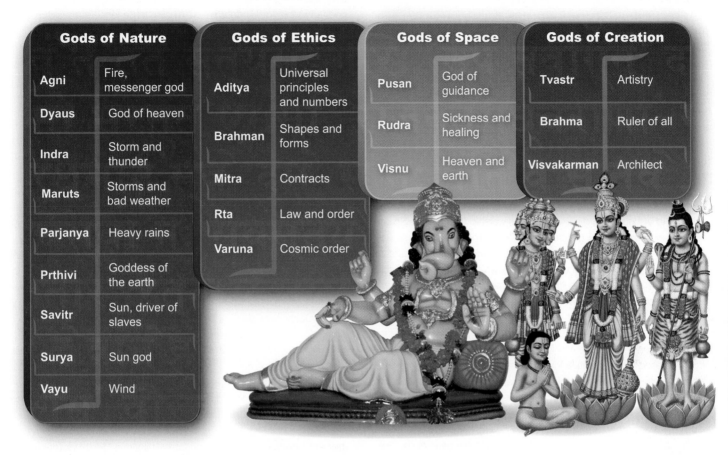

Gods of Nature	
Agni	Fire, messenger god
Dyaus	God of heaven
Indra	Storm and thunder
Maruts	Storms and bad weather
Parjanya	Heavy rains
Prthivi	Goddess of the earth
Savitr	Sun, driver of slaves
Surya	Sun god
Vayu	Wind

Gods of Ethics	
Aditya	Universal principles and numbers
Brahman	Shapes and forms
Mitra	Contracts
Rta	Law and order
Varuna	Cosmic order

Gods of Space	
Pusan	God of guidance
Rudra	Sickness and healing
Visnu	Heaven and earth

Gods of Creation	
Tvastr	Artistry
Brahma	Ruler of all
Visvakarman	Architect

Source: Michaels, Axel (Barbara Harshew, tr.) *Hinduism; Past and Present* (Princeton: Princeton University Press, 2004), 16.

∧
∧ These are some of the principal gods and goddesses of Hinduism. To what extent do some
∧ gods have human qualities or do people have godlike qualities?

- Parashurama—Rama with the Ax: The people of the Kerala region especially revere him as their protector, though Parashurama also came to conquer the entire earth.

- Rama—Present in Everything: Embodying the right way to live, you can read of Rama's heroic deeds in the Ramayana.

- Krishna—Source of Dharma: Krishna vanquished the wicked and restored eternal law to the world when it had been broken.

- Buddha—the Enlightened One: Although Buddhists revere him as the "awakened one," Hindus see him as an avatar of Vishnu, who came to bring enlightenment to the world.

- Kalki—The Avatar Yet to Come: Hindus await the coming of Kalki, the next avatar, who will arrive on a white horse and end our current Age of Darkness.

SHIVA AND PARVATI

Shiva may be the oldest god in the Indian tradition, perhaps even predating the Vedas. Shiva worshippers (like those at the Brihadeeshwara Temple we described in the beginning of this chapter) concentrate on the changing elements of the human condition—death and regeneration, uncertainty and fear, and the transformation of the human body and psyche during the course of human life. You'll often see Shiva portrayed as a stylized penis and vagina, a warrior, or a dancer. Each of these encapsulates one element of Shiva's vast power.

Shiva's most well-known wife is Parvati (also known as Shakti), although he is known to have many other wives as well. They had two sons, Ganesha and Kartikeya (also known as Murugan). Even if you've seen very little Hindu art, you may still recognize Ganesha with his elephant head and human body. At the

<<< Vishnu has traveled to Earth numerous times. As the avatar Narasimha, Vishnu came to Earth as a half man, half lion. How might the direct influence of the gods affect the lives of people?

Brahmins are the priestly caste.

Ksatriyas are the warrior or governmental caste.

Vaisyas are the caste of farmers, merchants, businesspeople, and professionals.

Sudras are laborers and servants.

Untouchables, also called "outcastes," "dalits," or the "scheduled castes," and represent a group below the four traditional castes.

Brihadeeshwara Temple, some worshipers may go directly to worship Ganesha, bypassing Shiva and Parvati altogether.

THE GODDESSES SHAKTI, DURGA, AND KALI

In addition to Vishnu and Shiva, many Hindus worship the goddess Shakti (who may also receive the general name Devi, "The Goddess," and is sometimes linked to Shiva). As you might now expect, Shakti appears in many forms: sometimes helpful but maybe malevolent, often pleasant but also ferocious. Shakti translates literally as "power" and may characterize the female aspect of male gods. For example, the god Brahma is usually represented as fire. The heat from the fire, however, is its *power*—Brahma's Shakti. We can see this duality in many gods. Parvati, for example, is the power of sensuality, sexuality, and love. Umma is the power of childbirth and motherhood (not to mention the name of Uma Thurman, actress and daughter of a well-known scholar of India, Robert Thurman). Shakti embodies positive power, while Durga manifests the strength of violence. Parvati takes the form of a warrior when she is Durga, carrying the weapons of many other gods so that she might slay demons.

Durga controls her violence and consorts with the male gods. The goddess Kali, though, is fierce and powerful. No second fiddle to male gods, Kali steps on them while wearing jewelry made of bones with her blood-red tongue sticking out.

Rocks, Rivers, and Animals

Even this listing of Vishnu's avatars cannot come close to the richness of gods available for Hindu worship. They can be local, even village gods. They can have multiple faces, appearances, avatars, and consorts. They can be rocks (Shiva is often depicted this way), animals, or even rivers. The Ganges River, often called the Mother Ganga, flows from the high Himalayas through the heart of India, bringing spiritual and physical blessings to those who come to her. The beautiful opening photograph in Chapter 4 illustrates the many layers of meaning that the Ganges can offer to humanity. The woman in the photo can bathe herself in the water to be cleaned physically or spiritually; she can ask Mother Ganga for help by performing a ritual in the water. Finally, the woman will receive particular blessings if she dies near the river and has her ashes strewn upon it.

Go to any Hindu temple dedicated to Vishnu, and you'll likely see a murti of Hanuman, the most famous animal god. As a monkey, Hanuman helped Rama (an avatar of Vishnu) defeat Rama's enemies and save his consort, Sita. Follow pilgrims along the road outside of Jaipur and you'll come to the Galta Temple, built into the rocks and home to monkeys who roam around the complex. They'll gaze at you calmly, accept a food offering from your hand, and watch from above as people come and go.

In Deshnok, Rajastan, however, you'll be surrounded by the rats of Karni Mata. According to legend, goddess/woman Karni Mata was so distraught by the death of one of her clan that she struck a deal with Yama, the god of death. From that day forward, all of Karni Mata's clanspeople would be reincarnated as rats until they could be reborn into the clan. Today the famous temple devoted to her houses more than 20,000 rats at any given time. They run around the temple grounds, clean and happy as they consume sweets, large bowls of milk, and portions of grain brought by pilgrims. Believers touch, bow down, and watch the rats. Pilgrims may share a bowl of food with them and try to touch one of the rare white ones, which represent the sons of Karni Mata herself.

▶ WHAT DOES IT MEAN TO BE HUMAN?

The Caste System

It's nearly impossible to think about the human condition in Hinduism without also considering the caste system. One of the oldest social structures in India, it divides people into separate social groups (called "castes") based on family background and occupation. Although many societies have class-based social structures, the caste system refers specifically to India and is particularly important to Hindus.

THE MAIN SOCIAL CASTES

According to the *Purusha Sukta*, a story in the Rig-veda, human beings originated from the sacrifice of a primeval being called Purusha. From his death came four types of humans: *brahmins*, *ksatriyas*, *vaisyas*, and *sudras*. The part of Purusha's body from which the group comes thus corresponded to that group's place in society. Even today, the broad outlines of these groups—the castes—can be seen in Indian society.

Brahmins came from Purusha's head and are the highest stratum of society, the priestly caste. Brahmins study the Vedas, perform rituals, and act as teachers and advisors in society. From Purusha's arms came the **ksatriyas**, also known as the *rajanya*, traditionally the protectors, warriors, and royalty of India. In modern times the ksatriyas often still serve as government administrators. The **vaisyas** emerged from Purusha's thighs, and thus carry much of the weight of society. This group includes businesspeople, farmers, and merchants. In my university, for example, many students from a subcaste of this group come to study pharmacy and medicine. Finally, the **sudras** came from Purusha's legs and make up the lowest social group in the myth. They are laborers and servants (Klostermaier *Beginners Guide*, 38–39 and Klostermeier *Survey*, 334).

You may remember reading about the **untouchables** of Indian society,

>>> **Two untouchable children beg on the streets of Jaipur, India.**
According to the Rig-veda, untouchables weren't born of Purusha. Indian culture and politics have long struggled with their role and rights.

The Story of Purusha from the Rig-veda

A thousand heads hath Purusha, a thousand eyes, a thousand feet.

On every side pervading earth he fills a space ten fingers wide.

This Purusha is all that yet hath been and all that is to be;

The Lord of Immortality which waxes greater still by food.

So mighty is his greatness; yea, greater than this is Purusha.

All creatures are one-fourth of him, three-fourths eternal life in heaven.

....

When Gods prepared the sacrifice with Purusha as their offering,

Its oil was spring, the holy gift was autumn; summer was the wood.

....

When they divided Purusha how many portions did they make?

What do they call his mouth, his arms? What do they call his thighs and feet?

The Brahmin was his mouth, of both his arms was the Rājanya made.

His thighs became the Vaiśya, from his feet the Śudra was produced.

The Moon was gendered from his mind, and from his eye the Sun had birth;

Indra and Agni from his mouth were born, and Vayu from his breath.

(Rig-veda Book 10, Hymn 90, http://www .sacred-texts.com/hin/rigveda/rv10090.htm)

the **THINK**SPOT
www.thethinkspot.com

Jati is a subclass of the Hindu caste system.

Atman is the true self; Hindus work to achieve understanding of atman.

Moksha is the experience of oneness with the entirety of creation.

Maya is the illusory, transient world that distracts Hindus from the universal truth that Brahman is in all things.

of Brahman, then all people must be Brahman, too, right? Right! All people are Brahman, just as all things are Brahman. But the problem with humanity, as many Hindus see it, is that we are not "in tune" with Brahman. We experience the world through our short, imperfect lives that seem to be reality, but really only create an illusion. Thus, we humans have some work to do, if we are really to see ourselves as part of Brahman.

BECOMING ENLIGHTENED

This process of tuning into Brahman may better be termed "enlightenment," for it includes both personal knowledge and experience. The spiritual path of Hinduism leads toward knowledge of the enlightened self, called **atman**. Like everything else in the universe, atman is composed entirely of Brahman. To live in concert with Brahman, human beings must connect with and develop atman. It's not an easy task and may take many lifetimes to achieve. Truly knowing the atman requires you to transcend all explanations, definitions, and descriptions of the cosmos. Brahman cannot be defined in any terms other than itself, so all attempts to quantify or to explain it come up short. In knowing atman, you will also perceive Brahman in its ineffable nature (Klostermaier *Beginners Guide*, 106).

Once you truly know yourself, you will also know Brahman, and you attune yourself to the divine nature of everything. Ultimately, the source, the process, the power, and the physical reality have no differences, only separate forms. Once you achieve this all-knowing state, you will be deified—your existence as Brahman will connect with your understanding of the Brahman. Like the gods, you will know yourself as Brahman. You will have achieved **moksha**—the experience of oneness with the entirety of creation. For some Hindus, this is the ultimate goal of life.

Most people, though, go through their day doing their jobs, providing for their families, and caring for their parents or children. Like believers of many religions, they see little need to delve constantly into philosophical and religious questions. Rather, these everyday Hindus will continue to worship gods beloved in their village or city and to celebrate births and mourn the deaths of their loved ones. Yet the philosophical system that we just read about is an important part of the intellectual life of Hinduism, even if it doesn't always seem connected to everyday life. These ideas, after all, help define what it means to be a human being in Hinduism.

MAYA: THE ILLUSION

If we, and our thoughts and laws and energy and desires, come from Brahman, why should it be so difficult to achieve moksha? Unfortunately for us, our everyday cares and worries cause us to focus too narrowly on changeable phenomena and to forget the larger reality of an unchanging Brahman. Our world of bills and grades is actually an illusion, called **maya**. Maya includes the world around you, the commercials on television, the soft pillow for your head at night—anything that causes you to lose sight of atman. Paradoxically, though, even maya is part of Brahman, since *everything* is Brahman. Think of it this way: If the glass jar holding our sand art were clouded and dirty, it would make the layers inside darker and harder to see. That cloudiness is maya, which keeps us from seeing the truth of Brahman.

Here is a story from the Upanishads to illustrate these ideas: A young man named Svetaketu returns home after 12 years at school. He proudly

---

sometimes called "outcastes," "dalits," or the "scheduled castes." These are the people who officially did not fit into the system described here. These lowest rungs of society have traditionally lived in exceedingly poor conditions and have been forced into the worst jobs, especially those related to death, garbage, and excrement. The British government began trying to break down the caste system's greatest iniquities in the 19th century, but significant change only began in the later 20th century, when economic modernization, urbanization, and education started to offer a better life to the lower class. In fact, K. R. Narayanan, originally a dalit, was elected president of India in 1997 (Klostermaier *Beginners Guide*, 39–40).

Because this system originated in a Hindu creation story, many Hindus see a divine will and structure in the castes, which date back thousands of years. Castes reform themselves continually through countless interpersonal negotiations, economic changes, outside forces, marriages, and generational turnover. People from different areas disagree on caste duties or prerogatives, so even the same word may have more than one meaning. In fact, if you were to look at every subclass, or **jati**, you would have over 3,000 groups to cover, each with its own rules regarding social activities. And so, like many structures in a traditional society, people in the caste system might describe it as unchanging, but in fact it evolves constantly across time and geography.

Human Beings: Out of Touch with Brahman

The Rig-veda closely links Purusha and Brahman, the divine force that both created and makes up the universe. So, if everything in the world is made

relates his academic accomplishments to his father, who gently asks if Svetaketu has come to understand that which cannot be understood. Confused, Svetaketu admits he learned nothing like that lesson. His father then tells Svetaketu to bring him a fig and instructs his son to split it open. "What do you see in the fig?" the father asks. "I see seeds," replies Svetaketu. The father then instructs Svetaketu to cut one of the seeds in half. "What do you see now?" asks the father. "I see nothing," is Svetaketu's honest response. "That which you cannot perceive," the father explains, "is the substance that will one day become a mighty fig tree. That is atman. It is the true self" (Klostermaier *Beginners Guide*, 107).

For another illustration, let's go back to our jar of sand art. What keeps the sand in its pretty layers, sheltering it from wind? Of course, it's the glass jar. But what is glass made of? Sand! We humans perceive the glass and the colors and the grains as separate and discrete bits of reality. Although that's true on one level, such distinctions mask a deeper reality in which all things share the same essence. Maya shows us color and art and glass and sand. Yet, ultimately, everything is sand. It is all one, just as everything in the world is all Brahman.

REINCARNATION

As long as we are distracted by maya, the illusory world, we cannot achieve true understanding of ourselves—we cannot perceive atman. And as long as we are unable to do that, we will not be able to unite with Brahman. The problem for Hindus is that maya is a world of change, whereas Brahman is the essence of permanence. Brahman is and always has been. How can anyone hope to experience permanence in a world of change?

Hindus generally believe that as they cycle through many lives, a process called **reincarnation**, their souls may exist as people, animals, and even plants. To break the cycle of rebirth, Hindus must follow dharma, living their lives according to the cosmic harmony of laws and virtues set out through sanatana dharma. The more closely you follow dharma, the more likely you'll be reincarnated upward toward moksha. If you disregard dharma, however, you're sure to be come back to earth in a lower form of being, forced to take longer on the dharma path.

Another way to think about reincarnation, though, relates to the problem of permanence and change. To the extent that we live with an eye toward the future, thinking about pleasure, sorrow, love, or death, we stay trapped inside **samsara**, the wheel of time, and continue to be reincarnated. When we see people aging, trees growing tall, or mountaintops crumbling, we perceive change—ultimately illusory—that keeps us locked on the wheel of time.

Yet we know that Brahman must be constant and unchanging, since it incorporates all matter and energy. The ultimate challenge for us, therefore, is to recognize this unchanging and ever-present quality of Brahman; to live without change inside a world that *appears* to change. As we experience permanence instead of change, we become closer to the true self, atman. And, of course, the closer we come to that, the nearer we move toward living in concert with Brahman.

This is tough stuff to understand, because it opposes much contemporary Western thinking. We're taught to look toward the future, to study now so we can get a better job later, or at least to put off a pub crawl until final exams are finished. In fact, we constantly worry about the future, don't we? Have you ever fretted about an ill relative? Have you ever considered

earning a promotion at work? Maybe you've looked forward to a date with someone new. These seem completely normal, but Hinduism teaches us that you lose sight of your unchangeable atman whenever you worry about change. Imagine the difficulty of continually focusing on the unchanging Brahman just as everything around you seems to change. It is one thing to be aware of Brahman; it is entirely another matter to live one's life with the sure knowledge of Brahman's permanence. Thus, it takes many lifetimes to see past the illusion of change and perceive the oneness underneath it.

Here's a paradox: To stop being reborn and experiencing redeath, we must somehow live without alteration in a world of change (Michaels 264). To do that, we must circle back to the concept of dharma that we discussed in the beginning of this chapter. As you may remember, dharma has many meanings. They include:

- Religion
- Cosmic and timeless law
- Application of cosmic law
- Social responsibility
- Virtuous life

If we look at all of these aspects together, we can begin to see a pattern for our lives. We should understand our appropriate place in our community, society, and universe through the application of dharma to our own existence. Our little spot in history exists specifically because we fit into a larger synchronized whole. If we live according to the laws applying to us, we will then begin to experience the unchanging harmony of Brahman. When we die and are born again, we will move a little higher on the path toward moksha. If, however, we choose to disregard our place in society and the universe, if we live outside the expectations of our caste and subcaste, we doom ourselves to rebirth at a spot further away from moksha, and we'll take that much longer to attain our final goal.

Dharma and Karma

You can imagine many different ways to interpret the ideas we have just encountered. Critics of religion might say that the system exists only to keep elites in their place by offering people below them the chance to progress, but only in the next life. Other observers might perceive it as a way to give the downtrodden masses some hope that their lives are not futile, but rather part of an important cosmic plan. Still others might imagine an economic motive, so that most people would not leave the jobs and land traditionally fulfilled by their caste or jati.

Although all of these interpretations make sense, Hindus offer yet a different explanation, focusing on the idea of **karma**: Your own actions in a prior life have determined the body into which you've been born in this life (Kanitkar and Cole 103–104). To the extent you now follow dharma, live virtuously, and seek to understand atman, you will gain good karma that ultimately determines how you will be reborn. If, however, you reject dharma and focus on the changing world around you, in the next life you'll find yourself in a worse situation than you have today. The only way to break away from samsara, the wheel of time, is to guide yourself slowly through your many lives by following the dharma of each life. In doing so, you will ultimately come to perceive that all things are not different, but rather connected through Brahman.

THE EFFECTS OF LIVING

Let's apply the dharma/karma theory to everyday life. For each of our actions there is a visible effect. But there is also an invisible, karmic effect. If you give a hungry person food, your actions have a positive effect on someone else. If you steal food from a hungry person, your actions have a negative effect.

Cows and Hinduism

Driving through New Delhi, you'll have to contend with cars, bicycles, scooters, and cows. Yes, they roam the highways and backstreets of this huge city, competing for space on the road and sidewalks with millions of other people and animals.

Hindus generally consider cows to be holy animals, perhaps because Krishna appeared as Govinda the cowherd in one of his many manifestations. Cows, like the river Ganges, also represent birth, growth, and nourishment. Although the prohibition on eating beef varies by caste and geography, you won't find hamburgers in McDonald's. By long tradition, cows can be fed and milked but much more rarely slaughtered for food. Instead, poor Hindus in central India let their cows loose after they've stopped giving milk. This way, the farmer does not have to feed her, but does not take on the bad karma of killing her either.

It's not a good situation. According to one activist, a recent post-mortem on an urban cow "revealed 14 kilos (31 lbs) of plastic" in her stomach (*Agence France Presse*, 2008). As a result, city officials claim to have recently taken some 20,000 cows off the streets. To do this, they employ "cow catchers" like Brajveer Singh, who usually uses old-fashioned methods like lassos and tough-as-steel arms to hold on to the cows: "The key is, once you have the horn in your hand, try hard not to let go" (*New York Times*, 2008).

Yet the problem persists, and it illustrates issues related to the many layers of belief, tradition, and opinion in Hinduism. On the one hand, taking care of cows seems inconsistent with the practice of letting them rummage through garbage and risk getting killed by passing cars. On the other hand, the sight of cows among human beings in New Delhi also reminds us of our shared existence with all other forms of life.

In fact, the Indian Constitution clearly states that "It shall be the duty of every citizen of India to have compassion for living creatures." And so, Hindu and animal rights advocate Raj Panjwani has legal basis when he fights for compassionate care for the original "sacred cows." Panjwani notes that "India also has possibly the largest vegetarian population. Despite this, animals in India continue to suffer enormously and in staggering numbers even though the constitution mandates that every citizen have compassion toward all living creatures" (*The Dominion Post*, 2008).

As Hinduism expands across the world, other tensions arise. In December 2007, Veterinarians from the Royal Society for the Prevention of Cruelty to Animals (RSPCA) put down a cow owned by a British Hindu temple, claiming that it was suffering from quickly declining health. This created an international tussle, with Hindus staging a mock-slaughter in front of the English House of Parliament and sending the ashes of the beloved cow for burial in the Ganges River. The Anglican Church stepped in to try and soothe the pain created by the situation, and the Hindu community accepted a gift of a new cow for its cattle sanctuary. A spokesman for the group, Kapil Dudaki, said that "It is a wonderful gesture and we gladly accept it. . . . To see a cow killed on the temple's grounds was utterly devastating" (*The Independent*, 2008).

The controversy has apparently resolved itself as worshippers celebrated the birth of a calf to the new cow in its herd. Named "Gangotri" after the cow who had been killed by veterinarians, the cow has become a symbol for British Hindus: "In the Hindu tradition, cows symbolise mother earth. We believe there is a connection between man, the cow and the environment" (*The Guardian* London, 2009).

You can see the visible effect of helping another or refusing someone's help, but you will not perceive the karmic implications of your actions. The Hindu soul achieves karmic credits by doing good works, through meditation, or through rebirth. The soul generates negative karma by becoming distracted by maya or by actions that cause injury to others.

GOOD KARMA, BAD KARMA

As you can see, appropriate actions (including even breathing and thought) build up good karma, while inappropriate ones create bad karma. When you die, the total good and bad karma you have produced over your lifetime affects your next life. You can be reborn into a higher state or a lower one. You could even be reborn as a bug! The important concept to remember is that no one exists by chance; we all live our lives based on the actions we took in our previous life. (Interestingly, you can also think about karma as being all negative. You don't want to create bad karma by your actions. Rather, you want to "use up" bad karma by being reincarnated. The result, however, is the same—each deed has a karmic consequence on your future.)

Moksha: Breaking the Cycle

Karma also describes the trajectory each of us takes toward the enlightenment of being free from samsara, the wheel of time. Once you have used up all your karma, you achieve moksha, full identification with Brahman. After moksha, there is no change—no rebirth and no more death. When a Hindu achieves moksha, he or she no longer creates karma, but rather experiencing the perfect unchanging unity of atman and Brahman, of which we have always been made but have not always understood.

The Upanishads express much of the underlying philosophy behind karma and moksha. Specifically, the Upanishads identify four Great Sayings that, when meditated upon and internalized completely, will lead atman to complete unity with Brahman. And so, many Hindus concentrate on the four Great Sayings:

- That you are.
- I am Brahman.
- The Self is the Ultimate.
- Brahman is wisdom.

Although they seem to be simple utterances, these phrases encapsulate the relationship of Brahman with human beings. When watching a temple puja or giving fruit to feed a divine sculpture of Rama or Hanuman, a Hindu treads the path toward the realization that everything—the gods, the fruit, and the self—are embodied in the words "I am Brahman" (Klostermaier *Beginners Guide*, 109–113).

Summary

IS THERE A GOD IN HINDUISM?
p. 26

- Everything comes from and is made of Brahman.
- Hindus often worship at least one of the three main gods: Brahma, Vishnu, and Shiva. There are up to 330 million other deities that may receive devotions as well.

WHAT DOES IT MEAN TO BE HUMAN?   p. 32

- According to a story in the Rig-veda, human beings originated from the sacrifice of Purusha. From his death came four types of humans: brahmins, ksatriyas, vaisyas, and sudras.
- Hindus believe that we cycle through many lives in the process of reincarnation. Our souls may exist as people, animals, or plants.
- Reincarnation is governed by the idea of karma: Our actions in a prior life have determined the bodies into which we've been born in this life.

Key Terms

Puja is the ritual by which Hindus connect with their gods and goddesses; the puja can be held by a priest in a temple or by Hindu followers themselves in their homes.   26

Sanatana dharma refers to Hindu religion and life; it translates roughly as "eternal law" or "eternal virtue."   26

Dharma can mean religion, universal law, application of universal law to Indian society, regulation of life through universal law, social responsibilities and duties, and the virtuous path of life.   26

Caste system divides people into separate social groups that have varying rights, responsibilities, professions, and status.   26

Vedas are the most sacred texts in Hinduism.   28

Sruti means "scripture" in Sanskrit and refers to the Vedas as well as the other sacred texts of Hinduism.   28

Smrti refers in Sanskrit to sacred Hindu traditions, both orally transmitted and written down.   28

Puranas often teach morality lessons or offer parables relating to correct living in Hinduism.   28

Upanishads are Vedic texts that focus on the relationship between the human and the divine.   28

Brahman is the original source of all things and the composition of the cosmos in Hinduism.   29

Brahma is often considered to be the creator of the world in Hinduism.   29

Vishnu is the Hindu protector of the world.   29

Shiva is the Hindu god of transformation and destruction that ultimately leads to new creation.   29

Brahmins are the priestly caste in the Hindu caste system.   32

Ksatriyas are the warrior or governmental caste in the Hindu caste system.   32

Vaisyas are the caste of farmers, merchants, businesspeople, and professionals in the Hindu caste system.   32

Sudras are laborers and servants in the Hindu caste system.   32

Untouchables, also called outcastes, dalits, or the scheduled castes, represent a group below the four traditional castes in Hinduism.   32

Jati refers to a subcaste of the Hindu caste system.   33

Atman is the true self; Hindus work to achieve understanding of atman.   33

Moksha is the experience of oneness with the entirety of creation in Hinduism.   33

Maya is the illusory, transient world that distracts Hindus from the universal truth that Brahman is in all things.   33

Reincarnation is the concept in which a soul moves from one being to another after death.   34

Samsara is the wheel of time, or cycle of rebirth and re-death.   34

Karma is the effect of a person's actions; good actions result in good karma, and bad actions result in bad karma.   34

Find it on THINKSPOT
www.thethinkspot.com

○ www.templepujari.com

You've read the chapter and now you're interested in finding out how to offer puja in your home. Where do you begin? Go to the ThinkSpot, where you'll find illustrations of pujas located in different parts of the world, as well as different deities and their histories. The virtual puja introduces you to the temple gods and the blessings they have to offer.

○ http://www.pbs.org/wnet/nature/holycow/video.html

Cows are "Hinduism's Sacred Animal." To watch streaming video that illustrates how the cow is revered in India, go to the ThinkSpot to watch "Holy Cow," a Nature video that is part of PBS's video library.

Questions for Study and Review

1. How do dharma and karma relate to one another in Hinduism?

Dharma is the moral law that is encoded in the Vedas and through smrti, sruti, and the Puranas. When a Hindu lives in accordance with dharma, he or she earns good karma. If the Hindu is reincarnated, the next life will be positively affected by the good karma and will be closer to achieving moksha, or freedom from samsara.

2. Do Hindus believe that they can affect their future? Support your answer with an explanation.

Yes. Hindus believe that they can affect future lives with behaviors in the current life. This is the idea behind karma. When a person acts in accordance with dharma, achieves a greater understanding of atman, or offers the ultimate sacrifice of death, he or she earns good karma. This karma follows the person into the next body and life. On the other hand, if a person neglects atman or does not participate in good works, he or she can develop bad karma, which also follows the Hindu into the next life. Bad karma can even cause a person to be reborn as an animal or plant, beings that are much further removed from knowing Brahman than any human being.

3. Why do Hindus participate in the puja? Where can you expect to find one being held?

Hindus participate in the puja to become spiritually closer to the gods and goddesses that are most important to them. Because all gods and goddesses are aspects of Brahman, having the connection with a deity during puja brings the Hindu in connection with Brahman itself. Puja can be held in a temple, in a public space, or even in the home of a Hindu family. Many devout Hindus practice in their own homes.

4. Hindus refer to their religion as sanatana dharma, or eternal law. How does this eternal law relate to Brahman?

Hindus believe that everything originates with Brahman. Everything that can be seen, such as people, animals, rocks, and water, are all Brahman. Laws and moral codes are also Brahman. Because laws and moral codes are Brahman, they are all interconnected with people and with the world. To live in accordance with these eternal, timeless laws is to live in concert with Brahman. Hindus are always working to achieve unity with Brahman. Living in accordance with sanatana dharma is one way they are able to strengthen their connection to Brahman.

HOW DO HUMANS INTERACT WITH THE SACRED? HOW DOES THE SACRED BECOME COMMUNITY?

A woman

bathes in the Ganges River. What could be simpler? After all, Hindus repeat this simple act millions of times every year. But, like many aspects of sanatana dharma, her bathing layers meaning upon meaning. Her actions symbolize the richness and complexity of Hindu traditions and symbols.

First, consider the Ganges, a river in northern India that flows more than 1,500 miles from its source in the Himalayas to the Bay of Bengal. Mother Ganga, as Hindus call it, contains all the promise and problems of India between its shores. More human waste, industrial runoff, burnt remains, and urban sewage are dumped into the Ganges than any other river in the world. And yet it provides drinking water and irrigation to feed a hungry land. It teems with every kind of pollutant, yet cleanses the souls of those who wash in her. The Ganges embodies the goddess Ganga while struggling to provide its traditional sweet water to the millions of pilgrims who seek her during life and find solace in her waves after death.

Bathing in the Ganges reminds us of the importance of purity and ritual in Hindu belief. An annual ritual bathing festival takes place here in February. The waters of the river cleanse the believer of the pollution and impurities contracted through improper actions or through interactions with other people or certain foods (Michaels 184–186). Beyond the bathing rituals, every day at dawn, pilgrims come to the river to pray, to set votive lights, flower garlands, and other offerings afloat on its surface, to drink from the river and to take away vials of the water. The river is also the place where the cremated remains of the dead come to rest after being consumed in funeral pyres on the river's banks, to be returned to heaven by Mother Ganga.

And so the woman comes, stepping gingerly from the steps into the water as it slowly flows past. Sari afloat, she immerses herself both in the water of Mother Ganga and in her devotions. With the Ganges, there is a sense of paradox and unity. The water is full of both pollution and the divine. It nourishes Indian soil and accepts the bodies of countless Hindus who desire a watery burial in it. Then it flows to the sea, mixing with the ocean.

HINDUISM: Law and Life

CHAPTER 04

The Bharatiya Temple

As we saw on the previous page, the Ganges River, or Mother Ganga as some call it, holds a sacred place in Hindu society. Yet Hinduism has another mother—the Earth. In the United States, Hindu priests bring earth from India to Pennsylvania as they prepare to consecrate statues, welcoming deities into their stone likenesses. The priests mix dirt and water that has been carried thousands of miles from the seven sacred rivers of India to an old farm in Pennsylvania. It's an appropriate ritual, for Hinduism—like the earth and water—has now left its Asian shores to become part of America's religious landscape.

Usually the steps to the Bharatiya Temple are white, but for one weekend they are ablaze in orange and red for the Prana Pratishtha Mahotsava. Hindus from all over the United States descend on the tiny Pennsylvania town of Chalfont, near Philadelphia, for five days of cere-monies and celebrations. They take part in events that transform mere statues of the gods into **murtis**—places where the deities actually reside.

The Indian population in the Philadelphia region has grown in the past 20 years, and by 1999 the local Hindus and Jains had formed an organization, bought land, and begun transforming an old farmhouse into a place of worship (O'Reilly B1).

As word of this gathering place spread through the region, atten-dance at puja and other activities increased. Within a year, the farm-house was bursting at the seams, and the community began construc-tion of its temple, which opened in 2004. It took five more years to finish all the work. Now, at the dawn of a new decade, sculptures replace pictures that had previously hung on the walls.

Growing out of the Pennsylvania farmland, the temple represents the expansion of sanatana dharma from India to the United States. But more than a symbol, the building is now a true Hindu temple,

---

>>> **A temple entrance** is specially decorated for the Prana Pratishtha Mahotsava. **How does this ceremony compare to your own rituals of celebration?**

the physical house of the deities. At home in Chalfont, Hindus can worship according to ancient sruti and smrti in a new land. A saying reminds everyone who attends, "Building a temple gains good karma, but performing the Prana Pratishtha is much beyond" (*http://pranpratishtha.ettitudemedia.com*, Retrieved October 2, 2009).

▶ HOW DO HUMANS INTERACT WITH THE SACRED?

Hindus interact with the divine at nearly every level of human existence: mental, physical, emotional, historical, mystical, and social. Such rela-tions in turn give rise to a huge variety of practices and rituals. These overlie one another, as if in layers like the sand art we discussed in Chapter 3. If this concept seems a little difficult to grasp, recall that Hinduism is a religion of "and," rather than "or."

Also think back to the many meanings of the term dharma, which embodies religion, law, way of life, and virtuous action. We will investigate human–divine interaction through three different dharma paths, any of which might be taken by a Hindu believer (Klostermaier *Survey*, 155–239):

- The Path of Works—emphasizing Vedic sacrifices and rituals. This oldest form of Hinduism has been growing in popularity again in India.

- The Path of Devotion—focusing on devotion and love. Many mil-lions of followers take this route.
- The Path of Knowledge— stressing education and contempla-tion. The most intense course, the Path of Knowledge can lead a Hindu toward renunciation of the world in the quest for spiri-tual knowledge and unity with the divine.

The Path of Works: Sacrifice, Purity, and Ritual

You have already read about puja in Chapter 3, which can take place in the temple or in the home. In the new temple in Pennsylvania or any of thousands of places every day, Hindu priests perform pujas to wake up deities, dress them, feed them, or put them to bed. These are a form of sacrifice to the gods, a gift of time and attention.

VEDIC SACRIFICE

Another way to connect with the gods, however, can be seen in an extremely ancient practice of sacrifice, or **yajna**. It is the original basis of Hinduism, developed thousands of years ago during the Vedic period.

Vedic scriptures point out that sacrifice has been essential since the beginning of time, forming the essence of Vedic Hinduism. The Vedas teach that the gods found pleasure by receiving offerings from their devotees. The gods then produced harmony and order in the cosmos. Good weather, bountiful crops, good health and long life, and success and prosperity of all sorts—including offspring—could result from proper sacrifice.

It is crucial to understand that, in the ancient Vedic world, all beings existed for sacrifice to the gods. However, only a precisely trained priest could make a powerful sacrifice. If he did not recite words correctly, for example, the sacrifice might not have been acceptable to the deities. This placed both tremendous power and responsibility with the priests. On the one hand, they controlled the world around them through sacrifice. On the other hand, a priest could easily make a fatal error in a ritual that included the recitation of long, intricate texts by heart. The high stakes for these rituals helped ensure the Brahmins' leading place in Indian caste society.

But back to the sacrifice: As you move up the karmic ladder from plants through animals and human beings, sacrifices become ever more powerful. In early Hinduism, birds and other animals, especially goats, made up the most common sacrifices. Priests often also used clarified butter (called *ghee*), cakes of grain, and an intoxicating drink called *soma* as offerings. In fact, *soma* has been lost to history, although scientists continue to guess from what plant it might have been derived.

Goats and horses carried even more power than ghee and soma, but there was a final sacrifice, even more powerful than animals. Until the 19th century, Hindus occasionally sacrificed human beings. Most famous of these were supposed to be a form of suicide, when a widow would sacrifice herself on her husband's funeral pyre. (We'll discuss this in more detail later in this chapter.) The goddess Kali, that wild torrent of power, also demanded human sacrifices. Even in present-day India and abroad, newspapers occasionally report a ritual murder allegedly performed to appease the goddess (*Hindustan Times*). Although no Hindu leaders condone human sacrifice, the pace of other Vedic sacrifices has grown in the past few decades. Ironically, the revival of Hinduism's most ancient form of worship has been underwritten by newly wealthy Indian businessmen, who can afford to pay for the elaborate sacrificial rituals.

The Vedic tradition of sacrifice offers a fascinating paradox with the Hindu tradition of ahimsa, which promotes nonviolence and avoids killing. You saw a glimpse of this in Chapter 3, when you read about the place of cows in Indian society. Ahimsa, however, developed in Hinduism as it incorporated elements from Buddhism and Jainism, where the concept plays a central role. Thus, one Hindu might save money to pay for a sacrifice, but another one—more attuned to ahimsa—would ask, "How can a human being kill another living thing when we too might have been— or might yet be—reincarnated in nonhuman form?"

RITUAL PURITY

For ritual sacrifice to work, all participants—including the object to be sacrificed—must have ritual purity. You may remember that Hindu temples often include outside bathing areas, so people can walk into the sacred place cleansed of both dirt and impurity. When you visit a temple, you'll undoubtedly be asked to take off your shoes before entering. As you can imagine, this small gesture keeps the temple clean from outside dirt and retains its ritual purity, too.

INTERNAL CONFLICT

Ahimsa and Social Movements

The practice of ahimsa has strongly influenced political and social movements across the world for the past century. In leading a struggle for Indian independence from Great Britain, Mohandas Gandhi developed his theory of *satyagraha*—nonviolent resistance—in part from ahimsa. He insisted that his followers respond to British violence with nonviolent actions, sparing lives and preventing bloodshed. Gandhi successfully led a peaceful campaign that resulted in India gaining its independence in 1947. In the process, however, he enraged other Hindus who saw him as overly welcoming of Muslims in India and too friendly with non-Hindu religions. In 1948, just months after Indian independence, a militant nationalist assassinated Gandhi.

Gandhi's success has inspired social leaders around the world to adopt his views of ahimsa and satyagraha in their struggles against injustice. In the 1950s and 1960s, Martin Luther King, Jr. led nonviolent protests—such as bus boycotts, restaurant sit-ins, and marches—against racial segregation in the United States. In the 1990s, Nelson Mandela led a similar nonviolent protest against racial segregation and apartheid in South Africa, where Gandhi once lived.

Imagine yourself in the shoes of both a nonviolent protestor and the soldier standing across from her. Why do you think that nonviolent protests sometimes initiate radical social change, but other times fail?

>>> Mahatma Gandhi, Martin Luther King, Jr., and Nelson Mandela all found inspiration in the Hindu practice of ahimsa. How did their nonviolent approaches promote social change?

The idea of ritual "cleanness" (sometimes opposed to healthy "cleanliness") appears in many traditional religions, offering a way to communicate with the sacred world, which by nature is pure. Although it might have some ties to hygiene (as in the temple baths), ritual cleanness may not relate at all to personal hygiene or tidy housekeeping. Instead, rules of ritual purity teach believers to avoid contact with particular human beings, animals, places, or actions that might threaten to make them unclean. Origins of such practices vary widely by religion, tradition, time, and scripture.

Hinduism has developed rules for keeping adherents ritually pure and restoring ritual purity to objects or people who have been polluted. These processes help harmonize people with their cosmic world, in turn creating good karma. As in any area of Hinduism, perceptions and practices of ritual purity vary widely, and they're often exceedingly complex. However, a very general rule to remember is that all impurity stems from the experience of change in one form or another. If Brahman is permanence, change should be avoided (Michaels 184–186).

Today, Hindus who live in rural villages tend to emphasize ritual purity far more than their co-religionists residing in cities or outside traditionally Hindu countries. One might argue that urban Hindus find issues of purity and pollution to be less important since they have to interact with people of many backgrounds and traditions. After all, cities change rapidly, but villages resist altering their traditional course.

In addition to its religious power to link people with gods, ritual purity can serve a number of other functions. Caste differentiation in India illustrates the social power of ritual cleanness, because all upper castes have traditionally viewed outcastes as completely unclean. As you contemplate different questions about religions, consider this one, which will reappear in different chapters: To what degree do sacred activities also affect other parts of human life, like politics or economics?

RITUALS AND FESTIVALS

As repeated actions with sacred meanings, rituals occur across the spectrum of Hindu interaction with the gods. As we discussed in Chapter 3, puja is ubiquitous, and it can contain elements of ritual purification. In reading the many steps of sacred action in a temple puja, check back to see where ritual purity might have a place.

Although they often do—remember the ritual bath in the Ganges from the beginning of this chapter—ritual actions may not relate directly to issues of purity. Later in this chapter, we'll examine rituals that relate to important points in a person's life. But, for now, let's turn our attention to some of the great festivals that represent ritual communication between

∧
∧ During the joyous and colorful
∧ celebration of Holi, Hindus may find themselves covered in brightly hued powders. How might this relate to the celebration of the end of winter and the start of spring?

Hindus and their deities. Unlike the puja, which can be performed privately, festivals include whole communities. Given the great diversity of Hinduism, you can find a holiday being celebrated nearly all the time in some corner of a city or village in India.

A festival brings together many elements—food, sacrifice, time, place, people, history, and myth. No doubt, some Hindus celebrate without knowing the "real" meaning behind an important day. Yet the participation of many folks in one place at one time creates a feeling—an experience—crucial to the religious life of Hinduism. It reminds Hindu believers that sanatana dharma encompasses all of life, rather than being constrained to a few minutes of puja in the morning or evening.

Let's use the Holi festival as an example. Occurring in February or March, it celebrates Vishnu, Krishna (his avatar), and the arrival of spring. Hindus may abandon their usual activities at school or work, dress up in bright clothing, and throw colored powders at one another. They light a huge bonfire to symbolize the destruction of the demon Holika, dance in the street, and revel in colorful, crazy exuberance. Then, at the end of the festival, people bathe, change into clean clothes, and resume proper social conduct. In Holi, Hindus simultaneously take part in rituals that celebrate a new season, disgrace a demon, and solidify relationships between friends and family. These actions—from throwing colored powder to eating special food or building the fire—help them communicate with the divine world (Michaels 310–313).

Festivals can align with personal pilgrimages—journeys taken for spiritual or religious reasons. Hindus from across the United States, for example, set off on a pilgrimage in May 2009 to the watch the consecration of the new temple in Pennsylvania. In a traditionally Hindu land like India, though, thousands of pilgrims crisscross the land every day, traveling by crowded railways, automobile, or on foot to destinations related to gods, events, or natural sacred places. In Chapter 3, we mentioned the animal-god temples that attract thousands of believers every month. Perhaps the most famous pilgrimage destination, however, is the ancient city of Varanasi, called the "City of Temples" because of its spiritual significance (Kantikar and Cole, Chapter 9).

Sometimes called the largest gathering of people in the world, Hindus travel to the Ganges for the Maha Maha Kumbh Mela, arguably the most important pilgrimage date in all of Hinduism. During a recent celebration, more than 70 million Hindus participated in the 15-day pilgrimage—that's the equivalent of 25 percent of the U.S. population all traveling at one time over 44 days of communion with the divine!

The Path of Devotion: *Bhakti*

Unlike the killing of animals or leaving fruit before a murti, the **bhakti** path of devotion focuses on a person or group's devotion to a specific god, relying on the deity's grace for help and strength. Bhakti (from the Sanskrit *bhaj*, meaning "to share" or "to love") developed in South India in two periods around 600 and 900 CE. Bhakti hearkens back to the older Vedic sacrificial rituals. Yet bhakti doesn't grow out of fear of cosmic disharmony, which often then promotes ritual sacrifices or purifying baths. Instead, followers of the bhakti path seek to find a consensual relationship between themselves and their gods. In bhakti, a person often perceives one deity as supreme and trusts in the grace of that god for aid and comfort. Bhakti does not involve sacrifice in the Vedic sense, but instead cultivates emotional connections (Michaels 253–254). In this way, believers often anthropomorphize the gods, attributing human characteristics and purposes to them. People tend to devote themselves to gods who represent traits that the practitioner would like to develop, too. Imagine how young couple might look to Vishnu and Lakshmi for guidance in their marriage, or how an injured son would seek solace from Ganesha, whose head had been cut off by his father Shiva in a rage.

Daily activities at a temple—such as the one just dedicated near Philadelphia—may mix sacrificial, ritual, and bhakti elements. For example, while a priest cleans and awakens a murti of Rama as the sun rises, another person may stand at the back of the temple, singing a song of praise, wearing a special piece of clothing, or perhaps a bit of jewelry related to Rama. In fact, followers of the bhakti path desire to see a deity and to be seen in return. In the presence of a murti, a person may sit quietly, gazing at the statue and gaining strength from its presence. Yet she may also offer a verbal prayer, read the story of Rama's life aloud, or repeat a *mantra*—a word that may have no literal meaning, but hold important mystical connotations. (The most important mantra is "**om**," the sound emanating from all the cosmos.) Each of these actions shows her devotion for Rama and implicitly asks for Rama's affection in return (Michaels 257).

$\land\atop\land\atop\land$ The control of one's breathing (pranayama) is one of the focal efforts in yoga, so that one can reach kaivalya. How long do you think one waits to achieve kaivalya? How do you think that ultimate freedom varies from person to person?

The Yogic Paths of Knowledge

This path toward moksha can be taken by any person through education of mind and body. No matter your caste or personal situation, you can dedicate yourself wholly to this course, even excluding all other responsibilities. It is the ultimate **path of knowledge**, seeking a cosmic understanding of all things. Like other Hindu forms of communication with the divine, the path of knowledge regularly overlaps with traditions of sacrifice, ritual, and devotion. Even more confusing for an outsider, the many yogic pathways of knowledge also intersect with one another, creating a rich map of philosophy, mysticism, and experience on the road to enlightenment.

In the West, we tend to equate the term "**yoga**" with postures that help us stretch, concentrate, and grow more physically limber. In

Bhakti is a form of devotion by Hindu individuals and groups toward a specific god.

Om is the sound of the universe and the sound emanating from all Brahman.

Path of Knowledge is a means by which one can arrive at an understanding of all things in Hindu belief.

Yoga generally refers to any religious practice, but it is often used in connection with the development of physical and spiritual discipline toward the goal of kaivalya.

Kaivalya is the experience of ultimate timelessness or detachment in Hinduism.

Hinduism, however, yoga refers to any kind of religious practice, not specifically physical postures like "downward facing dog." Think of it as spiritual and physical stretching on the long road toward ultimate consciousness. The goal of yoga is to achieve **kaivalya**, the experience of ultimate timelessness. Travel on this path requires a guide: a *guru*. More than just a teacher, a guru can have an immense influence on a person's spiritual development. He (less often she) can guide you through vast amounts of arcane study, including philosophy, theology, psychology, physics, textual study, languages, physical activity (including physical yoga and martial arts), and meditation. No matter what you're learning, though, your goal must be to push past maya and to experience unifying consciousness, your atman.

Traditionally, the yogic path describes four potential states of human consciousness, as described in a story from the Upanishads:

1. Wakefulness, in which we perceive the "gross" material world.
2. Dreaming, when we begin to understand a more "subtle" reality than when awake.
3. Dreamlessness, in which we blissfully open ourselves to the universal soul.
4. Pure Consciousness, where we traveled past cognition, dream, knowledge, and bliss. It is the unity of all, the atman (Klostermaier *Beginners Guide*, 104–105).

To achieve the state of pure consciousness, a person needs both physical and mental power, which you derive from the kinds of yoga described above.

As you gain power, you also find spiritual release as your self (*purusha*) breaks free from the repression of matter (*prakriti*) (Klostermaier *Beginners Guide*, 116–122). This is tough philosophical work, so don't be surprised if you need some time to understand even a little bit about purusha and prakriti. They denote two aspects of Brahman, and together they create the universe. In the most general sense, purusha usually relates to forces of spirit, oneness, and consciousness. Prakriti, on the other hand, often refers to creation, including everything variable and changeable in life. Connected to our old friend maya (illusion), prakriti seems more real to us here on Earth, since we're generally taught to concentrate on things that have been created: buildings, wealth, even families.

If you choose the path of knowledge, your goal will be to stop caring about the ever-changing life of this world and to transcend through lightness to a final experience of pure consciousness. This takes years of training both your mind and body. In the West, you mostly learn asana—postures—that help you to control your breathing, the first step toward awakening your atman. At that point, you can begin to prepare for the intense concentration and trance states that open the doors to true knowledge and experience.

We can roughly equate purusha to the human soul, whereas prakriti aligns with the mind and body. Given that human beings have both purusha and prakriti, a traveler on the yogic path hopes to move past the maya—illusion—created by prakriti. When you fully realize that prakriti exists, but you don't let it impede your understanding of purusha, your job will be done. You will have unmasked the illusion of change and experienced the unchanging unity of the universe. You will have achieved moksha.

The Yoga Ladder to Enlightenment

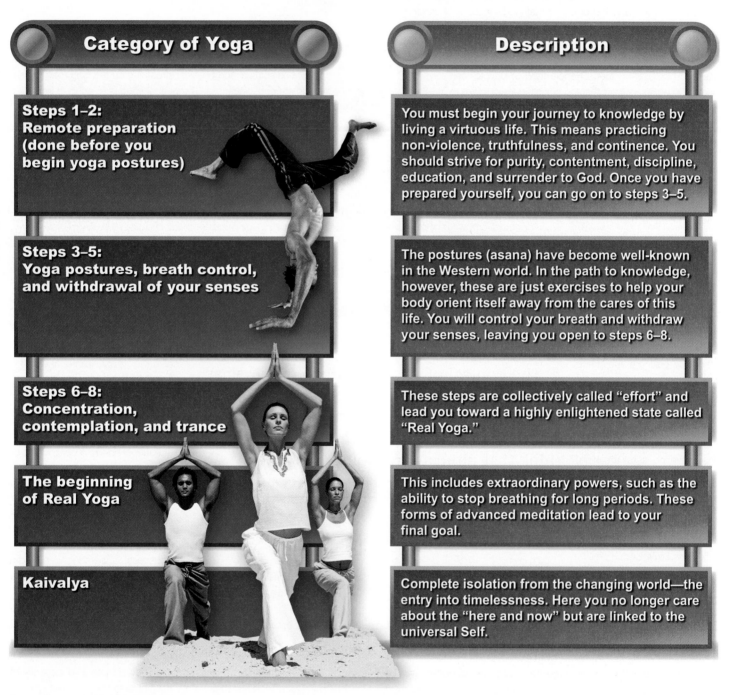

Category of Yoga	Description
Steps 1–2: Remote preparation (done before you begin yoga postures)	You must begin your journey to knowledge by living a virtuous life. This means practicing non-violence, truthfulness, and continence. You should strive for purity, contentment, discipline, education, and surrender to God. Once you have prepared yourself, you can go on to steps 3–5.
Steps 3–5: Yoga postures, breath control, and withdrawal of your senses	The postures (asana) have become well-known in the Western world. In the path to knowledge, however, these are just exercises to help your body orient itself away from the cares of this life. You will control your breath and withdraw your senses, leaving you open to steps 6–8.
Steps 6–8: Concentration, contemplation, and trance	These steps are collectively called "effort" and lead you toward a highly enlightened state called "Real Yoga."
The beginning of Real Yoga	This includes extraordinary powers, such as the ability to stop breathing for long periods. These forms of advanced meditation lead to your final goal.
Kaivalya	Complete isolation from the changing world—the entry into timelessness. Here you no longer care about the "here and now" but are linked to the universal Self.

Source: Klostermaier *Hinduism Beginner's Guide* 116–122.

∧ The eight steps begin with leading a virtuous life. Why do you think this is necessary to
∧ proceed through the subsequent steps?
∧

► HOW DOES THE SACRED BECOME COMMUNITY?

Let's go back to our sand art idea from Chapter 3. We discussed how the individual grains of sand interact with one another to create layers and pictures. In the same way, Hinduism relies on the communication between ourselves (the grains) and our communities (the bands of sand) to create cosmic harmony (the whole jar). Similarly, Hinduism relies on the family and the caste to integrate sanatana dharma into society.

> **Life cycle rituals** are performed at the important stages of a person's life, such as birth, marriage, and death.
>
> **Thread ceremony**, also called the second birth, is a coming-of-age ceremony in which a boy's hair is shaved except for a topknot and he is initiated into Hindu education.
>
> **Pandit** studies and teaches Hindu law.

Religion and the Family

Hindu families mark different stages of life by performing **life cycle rituals** at important events such as birth, marriage, and death. Although one might celebrate as many as 16 of these practices, very few people actually experience each one. Instead, most Hindus take part in a select few. We'll look at birth, second birth, marriage, renunciation, and death.

BIRTH AND SECOND BIRTH

Shortly after birth, Hindu children receive their names and horoscopes. Far removed from popular magazines or the back of the newspaper, these horoscopes orient the child in the universe, noting auspicious days. The family remembers these days as they take care of the children, often doting on youngsters until they come of age. Traditional families still tend to concentrate their energy and wealth on boys, since they will someday take responsibility for family rituals and sacrifice. Other families coddle all their children, knowing that modern girls often assume religious responsibilities if no men are present. In either case, custom dictates that young children have few responsibilities, even getting spoiled by their older siblings, parents, and extended family.

All of that easy life stops for a young boy when he reaches about eight years old. At that point, Hindu families will begin preparing for his **thread ceremony**, a coming-of-age ritual also known as second birth. The passageway from childhood to responsibility begins with a ceremonial head-shaving, leaving the youth with only a topknot of hair, obvious to anyone who sees him. From this point onward, he must begin his education. He may study the Vedas, memorize passages for repetition, and learn about appropriate rituals and sacrifices for local gods. Given Hinduism's great complexity, boys used to take a 12-year sojourn away from home for their education. Today, however, he may attend a school and study with a **pandit**, or scholar of Hindu law.

As you can imagine, the thread ceremony traditionally applied only to upper-caste boys. Modern Hinduism, however, has expanded the ritual to youths in any of the top three castes and has broadened the range from eight through twelve years old. Even some girls now celebrate a second birth ceremony. Members of the sudra caste and untouchables still cannot receive the sacred thread, an illustration of the power of caste even today.

^^^ A wedding couple performs the fire-lighting ceremony. In this context, how might fire suggest the virtues of humility and selflessness?

MARRIAGE

If you have Hindu friends or have watched a Bollywood movie, you'll already know stories about Hindu marriage: you must marry only in your caste; parents pick your mate, whom you might not see until the wedding; arranged marriages last longer than "love marriages." To be sure, there are kernels of truth in each of those statements, but real life complicates Hindu marriage far more than you might see on screen or in a novel.

For example, child marriage has largely died out in India. For centuries, parents sometimes arranged marriages for their young children. By law in 1860, girls could be married at the age of 10. This later increased to 12 in 1891 and 14 in 1929. Today, a bride must be at least 18, and her groom must be 21 (Michaels 113–120). In the most traditional parts of Indian society, the parents of a couple may still arrange the marriage when both the bride and the groom are young, with the understanding that the two will wed when they are older. In this case, love plays no role in the decision, although all parties hope the couple will grow to care for one another over time. Instead, marriage joins two clans, forming an alliance to strengthen finances and to bolster both families' genealogies. Brides become part of the groom's clan, which can be defined either genetically or ritually. (Through this malleable system, families can even slowly migrate between jatis and castes.)

Weddings include several different ceremonies that take place over an extended period and include families and friends, dancing and eating. One of the most serious moments, however, comes as the new couple lights a sacred "domestic fire" in their home. Dating back to Vedic times, this ancient ritual invokes one of the few gods left from the Vedic tradition, Agni, a word denoting both fire and the god of fire. By tradition, the ritual especially honors the bride, the new head of a household. Once lit, the sacred fire will help produce "happiness, fidelity, and progeny" (Klostermaier 45).

Given the potential for economic and karmic gain, Hinduism celebrates marriage above most other rituals. Yet today, village and urban Hindus often differ. Rural Hindus still tend to associate marriage with strengthening the system of kinship that permeates local society. In urban areas, however, more and more couples find each other and get married, sometimes to the chagrin of their elders.

That being said, most marriages still do follow many aspects of tradition. They usually occur within the same caste, and the couple seeks parental approval. Couples who hope to marry someone outside their caste may encounter opposition or anger. I will never forget two very good students of mine, both Hindus from the same region of India. They shared a heritage, language, and interest in science. They met and fell in love during college, only to break off their engagement when one parent would not agree to a mixed-caste marriage. Not a Hindu myself, I had never previously witnessed this collision of U.S. collegiate life and traditional Hindu culture. Describing the situation, one of the students sighed and hoped that they would marry in their next life.

Although civil divorce exists in Indian law (not to mention in other countries where Hindus live), Hindu tradition strongly discourages couples from breaking apart for any reason. Given that, it's very hard to claim that arranged marriages are more successful than ones made for love. They do, however, tend to last longer and contribute to a highly developed sense of Hindu identity that includes family, clan, jati, and caste.

Outside marriage, or after your spouse has died, some Hindus will assume a whole new place in their community. They will leave family and friends, home and job. They will wander the land without following the guidelines of their jati or caste. They have renounced the world. Sometimes called "forest dwellers," or, more generally, renunciants, these people renounce their communal roles to follow the path toward moksha. If you travel to India, you're bound to see a holy wanderer—a **sadhu**—when you come near a sacred place, a temple, or even standing alone in the wilderness. By giving up his traditional place in society, the sadhu frees himself from prescribed duties but also from the shelter of caste identity and familial relations. He (or sometimes she) may follow a charismatic guru, develop extraordinary physical abilities, or practice meditative exercises to overcome maya. These people play a part in Hindu society that most of us can barely imagine, for they have left everything behind for an intensive search for the divine.

Hindu Views of Death

The final ritual occurs at death. Over thousands of years, Hinduism has developed many different funeral rites. Most people will follow these steps: After a loved one's death, mourners place the corpse on the floor with the head pointing south, the ritual direction of the dead. Family members then prepare the body by bathing it, trimming hair and nails, and wrapping a shroud around the corpse. Soon after death, mourners light an oil lamp and keep it burning for three days. As they do this, the family members acknowledge that they have become ritually impure through contact with the body. They will have to ceremonially purify themselves at the end of the funeral process.

Only very few Hindus receive a burial in the Western sense. Instead, they are usually cremated, and family members scatter the ashes, often in a sacred river. A death priest, assisted by the eldest son of the deceased, performs the funeral rites, and the son often lights the funeral pyre. (Today, the eldest daughter may take on these responsibilities if the deceased has no son.)

The priest and family may ask the god of fire, Agni, to take the body to the place of the fathers. The family then gathers the ashes left after the cremation, saving them to be scattered at a sacred place on a propitious day.

The cremation signals the beginning of the mourning period and the family ritually bathes as a step toward ritual cleanness. Survivors often won't eat salt or wear leather to help rid their spirits of the impurity arising from death. On the 11th day, after one more ritual, the family rejoins society. At this point, the family members hope that their loved one has found a new place in a better body, born again a bit further along the path toward enlightenment.

Unlike the family of the deceased, people who work around death never lose the taint of ritual impurity. This leads to one of the paradoxes of the caste system: Cremators, although impure, can eventually become low-status Brahmins. "Death priests," however, so regularly interact with death that they are regarded as untouchables.

THE AFTERLIFE

In the ancient Vedic tradition, life after death depended on a person's gender, caste, and funeral ritual. A high-caste man would join his ancestors, but only if proper last rites had been performed. His afterlife would then be spent (poetically) on the cool moon (Klostermaier *Beginner's Guide*, 46–47). The Rig-veda explains that those who have entered the afterlife can influence what happens on Earth, so the living ought to continue performing rituals to keep the deceased appeased.

Starting around 500 BCE, however, reincarnation began to take the place of Vedic teachings regarding life after death. As we've learned, the concept of reincarnation explains that a person's soul continually goes through the process of being born, dying, and being reborn. The reincarnation of a living thing depends both on the soul's karma and its desire to be born again to enjoy the pleasures of Earth. Good karma will lead to a higher level of rebirth but also a diminishing desire for worldly delight. Put another way, the soul will only cease the cycle of rebirth and attain unity with the divine when it becomes bored with worldly gratification and seeks further spiritual experiences.

Hindu's Life-Cycle Sacraments

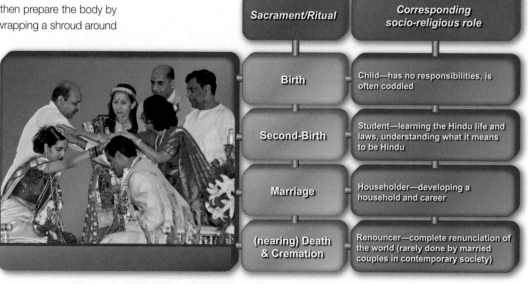

Sacrament/Ritual	Corresponding socio-religious role
Birth	Child—has no responsibilities, is often coddled
Second-Birth	Student—learning the Hindu life and laws, understanding what it means to be Hindu
Marriage	Householder—developing a household and career
(nearing) Death & Cremation	Renouncer—complete renunciation of the world (rarely done by married couples in contemporary society)

∧
∧ Might these rituals have parallels in other religions or in secular
∧ ritual ceremonies? Which, if any, seem particular to Hinduism? Why?

Sati: Ritual Widow Burning

It's against the Indian law and nearly never followed today, but ritual wife burning—known as **sati**—casts a long shadow over Hindu culture. Either voluntarily or by force, a widow would be burned along with her dead husband. Sati emphasized the lasting marriage between the couple, with the widow dressed in wedding clothes before being burned on the funeral pyre. As a result of her ritual suicide, the woman gained tremendous respect from the living. Family members might mark the spot of her death with stones, and even build shrines to her as a local deity. Yet Hindu traditions sometimes also describe the need to play loud music during a funeral. Did this encourage the wife toward suicide or cover her screams if she were pushed by members of her family? Traditionalists, scholars, feminists, and modernists may all have different answers to that question.

the **THINK**SPOT
www.thethinkspot.com

Sati was a funeral practice in which a widowed woman would, voluntarily or by force, be burned on a pyre with the body of her husband.

Varna means "color" and refers to caste in Indian society.

Sanatana Dharma and the Caste System

Think back to Chapter 3 and our comparison of Hinduism to sand art. Every layer and every grain in the jar helps create the final picture. Each layer depends on the others to help make the image and avoid falling into the wrong place. The principles of the sanatana dharma are like layers of sand in the jar: Take away even one, and the picture won't be finished. Many Hindus see caste in a similar way—each person fits into the picture at a particular place.

As you know, you can follow dharma by living appropriate to your caste (also called a **varna**) and jati. It's a lot easier to describe caste and jati in theory, however, than to define them in real life. Especially if you have grown up in a rural Hindu village, the caste system includes nearly endless overlapping beliefs, traditions, teachings, and customs that make it impossible to discern differences among family, clan, jati, and caste. In fact, Hindus often use the terms "varna" and "jati" interchangeably.

For the most part, Hindus are born into a specific varna and jati. As they grow up, Hindu children learn how their varna and jati determine appropriate behavior. How you greet others, speak, eat, give gifts, or pay for services all relate to your jati. Your place in the family and your age will further affect how you interact with the world around you.

As you might suspect, higher caste generally confers higher ritual purity, more prescribed rituals to be performed, higher social prestige, and proximity to moksha. Members of lower castes may not have to follow so many explicit rules regarding ritual cleanness or food preparation, but they also receive far lower prestige from society and can expect to have longer paths toward enlightenment.

Caste constantly reminds every person that his place in society results from actions taken during previous lives. Therefore, it makes good sense to follow sruti (scripture) and smrti (tradition) to create good karma. Violating sruti and smrti has the opposite effect, developing bad karma that you'll have to wash away through religious rituals, pilgrimage, or perhaps gifts to the temple.

As you learned in Chapter 3, good karma speeds your way toward moksha, while bad karma keeps you unenlightened. Although it may sound silly, I often think about this as a cosmic game of Chutes and Ladders. You spend life living according to sanatana dharma, accumulating good karma as you move along the path toward moksha. Break the dharma rules, though and you may slide down the chute to a lower social caste. On the other hand, if you leave the troubles of the world behind and become a sadhu, perhaps you'll find a ladder that leads you quickly toward enlightenment.

Religion + GENDER

Women in Hinduism

Male gods. Widow burning. These things make you wonder: What role do women play in Hinduism? Some scholars argue that, during the ancient Vedic times, women actually had a prominent role in the religion. Women were allowed to study the Vedas, some participated in sacrifice, and others traveled to war with male caste members. Many Vedic hymns sing the praises of women and goddesses.

As the Vedic tradition spread and began to develop its many ritual levels, men began to take control of society. Women moved into the domestic sphere, where they tended the sacred domestic fire and looked after children. Women's duties in the home were often so great that they were taught that they ought not go out in public. Yet other Hindu traditions and texts, including the Puranas, offer pictures of free, powerful women who live outside traditional restrictions. Not just a consort to a male god or his feminine aspect, the goddess became a powerful force in her own right. Don't forget Kali's terrible influence or Shakti's erotic power. Closer to earth, some women have become important gurus and spiritual advisers called Mas (or "Mothers"). They are renowned among devotees for their spiritual power and insight.

In the 20th century, as India has developed modern forms of education, economy, and politics, women have taken increasingly larger roles in society. Indira Gandhi remains an icon of female political power, and the exploding technology sector looks for women to fill its huge employment needs. Still, women in the countryside tend to be undereducated and economically disadvantaged. Traditionalist Hindus have been slow to accept changes that would give women more modern political or social rights, preferring instead to uphold older traditions. Coupled with issues of the economy, caste, and education, the particularly Hindu role of women in India continues to evolve (Klostermaier *Survey*, 361–376).

Gandhi, Hinduism, and Politics

Mohandas Gandhi (later called "Mahatma," the Great Soul) originally wanted to become a medical doctor. His place in Hindu society, however, did not allow this profession, so he became a lawyer and moved to South Africa. When the government there forced all Indians to be registered and fingerprinted, Gandhi began his life of social activism and passive resistance. He believed that it was better to go to prison than to follow an unjust law.

When Gandhi returned to India in 1915, Great Britain ruled the subcontinent as a colony. In 1919, in reaction to harsh British measures, Gandhi began to support Indian nationalism and to train others in passive resistance. He encouraged nonviolent protests based on the commandments of the *Bhagavad Gita*. He inspired a powerful sense of nationalism long dormant in India.

Gandhi also hoped to reform some aspects of Hinduism, which made him countless enemies among Hindu traditionalists. He identified and spoke out about areas of Hindu belief that he thought could be improved, including women's rights. Gandhi encouraged women to fight for independence alongside their husbands. He even nominated a woman for president of the Indian Congress. Likewise, Gandhi fought for the rights of the outcastes—the untouchables—whom he renamed **Harijan**, or "people of God." In this way, Gandhi sought to preserve Hinduism while bringing a modern sense of fairness to Indian society.

Gandhi's belief in nonviolence extended to the active care and love of all beings. Although he was devoutly Hindu, Gandhi tolerated and accepted people of all religions, looking even to the Russian Christian writer Leo Tolstoy for inspiration. He reached out to all levels of society, not just the upper middle class of his jati. This helped to foster a single national identity for India, rather than multiple ones based on caste, jati, language, religion, or region.

Today, Hindu nationalists have separated themselves from secular nationalists, and they battle for political power. Traditional Hindus have, for example, prohibited the slaughter of cattle in areas they control, even though Indian Muslims and Christians regularly eat beef. Far worse, Muslims' and Hindus' disagreements regularly flare into violence, especially when sites sacred to both traditions seem to be threatened. At the geographical edges of India, Hindu and Muslim groups also fight with Sikh and Kashmiri separatists. All of these movements undermine the carefully crafted "Indian" identity that Gandhi hoped all would share. In the contemporary political world, Hindu nationalists have transformed his ideas into ideas have transformed into "Hindutva," political Hinduism, which Muslims sometimes counter with "Islamism," a politicization of Islam. Yet, the competition for political, economic, and social power in modern India—the world's largest democracy—continues to illustrate the power of Hinduism and other religious traditions in the region. Thus, while Gandhi hoped to use Hinduism as a springboard for harmony in India and the world, his successors sometimes focus on the distinctions between Hinduism and other traditions in their quest for political influence (Ashutosh).

Harijan means people of God, a term used by Gandhi for the outcastes of the Hindu caste system.

Creating good karma isn't as simple as it sounds. You should act appropriately because sanatana dharma tells you its right, not because you want to act a certain way. Called "desireless action," a good life helps to create harmony in the world by keeping the element of unpredictable desire out of the system. For example, a businessman should develop his firm because that's appropriate to his place in society. Act with greed or personal ambition, though, and he will accumulate bad karma.

Desireless actions have three important effects. First, they help drain bad karma from your person's soul, ultimately helping you along the path to enlightenment. You will also focus on permanence instead of change, piercing through maya to see the atman just behind it. Finally, you will help to preserve social and dharma harmony. In other words, they're not rocking the dharma boat.

Think back to the sand art example. If you imagine yourself as a grain of sand in the jar, what would happen if you decided to change positions or move to another location? You might not alter anything significantly, but you might upset the balance of the total structure. Similarly, many Hindus see greater good in sustaining their position, rather than introducing confusion and change by acting according to personal whim, ambition, or expediency.

Conclusion

Our jar of sand reminds us that Hinduism's ideas and philosophies, practices and rituals, relationships and structures lay like bands of colored sand on top of each other; move the sand with a spoon and you'll change the patterns. Even so, you'll never change the basic unity of sand and glass.

Like the sand art, Hinduism embraces the paradoxes of one and many, of change and permanence. It accepts one, three or countless gods. Humans also live a paradoxical existence, striving for moksha in the midst of maya. By way of rituals, sacrifices, devotions, and study, a Hindu may attain higher levels of consciousness. Yet enlightenment often comes through long karmic struggle, rooted in family rituals, and communal responsibilities. When Hindus help build a new temple or attend a puja, they simultaneously cement spiritual and social bonds.

Like the Hindu deities Brahma and Shiva, Vishnu is a manifestation of Brahman. How do the different forms of their gods allow Hindus to relate to them in a personal way?

V
V
V

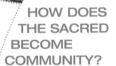

The funeral rites in Hinduism involve the cremation of the deceased on a pyre, often by a river where the ashes will be scattered. What does the scattering of ashes on a sacred river say about the Hindu view of humanity?

V
V
V

IS THERE A GOD?

Hindus can worship either one or numerous gods. Many believe that all divinity originally comes from one source: Brahman. This source can manifest itself in many forms, thus the Hindu worship of multiple gods. People often show devotion or make sacrifices to the god that they relate to the most. Hindus call upon certain incarnations of Brahman during specific events such as weddings or funerals. The three primary deities—Brahma, Vishnu, and Shiva—represent the most elemental aspects of human existence.

HOW DOES THE SACRED BECOME COMMUNITY?

Just as individuals interact with the gods, so does society as a whole. For Hindus, this begins with the family and at the beginning of life. Hindus normally focus on major events such as birth, second birth (or coming of age), marriage, renunciation of the world, and death. Finally, when Hindus follow the teachings of sanatana dharma, they are acting according to religious, social, ethical, and moral precepts. In this case, there is no difference between religious dharma and social dharma.

WHAT DOES IT MEAN TO BE HUMAN?

Humans, gods, animals, and the planets all come from Brahman. Our day-to-day experiences, though, cause us to lose sight of this ultimate reality. However, as human beings, we can work toward enlightenment. Hindus believe a person's soul will be reincarnated until that person achieves enlightenment, called moksha.

HOW DO HUMANS INTERACT WITH THE SACRED?

Hindus interact with the sacred world through puja ceremonies, rituals, sacrifices, and personal or communal devotion. These practices allow individuals to interact with the divine on spiritual, mental, physical, and emotional levels. More generally, Hindus interact with the divine whenever they follow dharma. Hindus may also choose the path of knowledge, seeking oneness with Brahman through the yoga tradition.

<<<
A Hindu bride and groom at their wedding. How would rituals of marriage and birth help to support Hinduism?

>>>
A brahmin priest dispenses blessings in a temple. How might public worship affect both individuals and the community?

REVIEW

Summary

HOW DO HUMANS INTERACT WITH THE SACRED?   p. 40

- The Vedas teach that the gods produced harmony and order in the cosmos after receiving offerings from their devotees. Animals—and in the past, sometimes even humans—are offered as sacrifices to the Hindu gods.
- While the puja can be performed in private, festivals often include entire communities. The festival of Holi celebrates Vishnu, Krishna, and the arrival of spring. Hindus dress in bright clothing, throw colored powders at one another, and light a bonfire to symbolize the destruction of the demon Holika.

HOW DOES THE SACRED BECOME COMMUNITY?   p. 45

- The ritual of second birth begins with a ceremonial head-shaving and marks the passage from childhood to responsibility. From this point onward, a Hindu child must begin his education.
- During a Hindu wedding, a sacred "domestic fire" is lit in the couple's new home. Once lit, the sacred fire—associated with the ancient god Agni—will help produce happiness, fidelity, and progeny.
- Hindus often follow strict rituals following death, including cleansing, cremation, and a scattering of the ashes. Survivors may adhere to strict rules, such as not eating salt or wearing leather, to rid their spirits of the impurity of death.

Key Terms

Murtis are statues of Hindu deities in which the god is present.   40

Yajna is the sacrifice that Hindus use to connect to deities.   41

Bhakti is a form of devotion by Hindu individuals and groups toward a specific god.   43

Om is the sound of the universe and the sound emanating from all Brahman.   43

Path of knowledge is a means by which one can arrive at an understanding of all things in Hindu belief.   43

Yoga generally refers to any religious practice, but it is often used in connection with the development of physical and spiritual discipline toward the goal of kaivalya.   43

Kaivalya is the experience of ultimate timelessness or detachment in Hinduism.   43

Life cycle rituals are performed at the important stages of a person's life, such as birth, marriage, and death.   45

Thread ceremony, also called the second birth, is a coming-of-age ceremony in which a boy's

hair is shaved except for a topknot and he is initiated into Hindu education.   45

Pandit studies and teaches Hindu law.   45

Sati was a funeral practice in which a widowed woman would, voluntarily or by force, be burned on a pyre with the body of her husband.   47

Varna means "color" and refers to caste in Indian society.   47

Harijan means people of God, a term used by Gandhi for the outcastes of the Hindu caste system.   48

Find it on

- As you read in this chapter, ahimsa has had a strong impact on political and social movements around the globe. Want to learn more? Go to the ThinkSpot to view a video of Sri NV Raghuram, who is interviewed about his views on ahimsa and what it means to the world. (http://www.youtube.com/watch?v=wng1H0PB9RI&feature= youtube_gdata)
- You can view a video from Planet Earth entitled "Our Loving Home," which explores the idea of ahimsa and how it relates to agriculture. (http://video.search. yahoo.com/video/play?p= Ahimsa&ei=UTF8&vs=video. yahoo.com&vid=0001305132293)

- Dance plays an important role in Hindu worship. Go to the ThinkSpot to learn more about how dance is integrated into religious pratice and why it is symbolic. Find out which deities are worshipped through dance and why by watching this informative video.

http://www.youtube.com/watch?v=YKr4yUB6RP4&feature= youtube_gdata

Questions for Study and Review

1. **Describe two ways in which a Hindu can achieve purity.**

   A Hindu can achieve purity by cleansing him- or herself after going through the unavoidable changes that they experience every day, such as waking, moving from place to place, and eating. A Hindu can also achieve purity by avoiding impure things, such as the killing of animals or interacting with members of different age groups or social castes.

2. **How is the movement of devotion, or bhakti, related to both sacrifice and ritual? Give two examples.**

   Bhakti relates to both sacrifice and ritual. Bhakti includes many ritualistic activities, such as saying the name of the god or goddess, singing songs in honor of the deity, and dressing in or bearing Hindu symbols. Additionally, the follower may take pilgrimages to holy places connected to a particular god. Daily sacrifices in the home or temple are also practices of bhakti.

3. **What is the practice of yoga?**

   The term "yoga" can be used for many religious practices. Specifically, though, yoga connotes a form of education. People begin by living a virtuous life, then learn to discipline their bodies and breathing through yoga postures leading to greater insight and, finally, kaivalya—timeless existence.

4. **For Hindus, what is the relationship between karma and reincarnation?**

   Karma affects reincarnation. Your actions in one life can influence your social and religious position in the next.

For Further Study

BOOKS:

Fowler, Jeaneane. *Hinduism: Beliefs and Practices.* Eastbourne, UK: Sussex Academic Press, 1997.

Kanitkar, V. P. *Teach Yourself Hinduism.* London: Teach Yourself, 2003.

Klostermaier, Klaus K. *A Survey of Hinduism*. Albany: State University of New York Press, 2008.

Klostermaier, Klaus K. *Hinduism: A Beginner's Guide*. Oxford, UK: Oneworld, 2008.

Knott, Kim. *Hinduism: A Very Short Introduction*. New York: Oxford University Press, 2000.

Michaels, Axel, and Barbara Harshav, trans. *Hinduism: Past and Present*. Princeton, NJ: Princeton University Press, 2004.

WEB SITES:

Sacred Texts: Hinduism. http://www.sacred-texts.com/hin/index.htm

ReligionFacts: Hinduism. http://www.religionfacts.com/hinduism/index.htm

Srirangam Temple. http://www.srirangam.org/index.html

Hinduism Today. http://www.hinduismtoday.com

<<< The Potala Palace in Lhasa, Tibet, is the largest structure in that country. Begun in the seventh century CE, the building has served as both the monastery-residence of the Dalai Lama and the center of the Tibetan government.

In Chapters

3 and 4, we discussed how the word "and" could help to explain the layers of history, tradition, and meanings in Hinduism. Each new generation places new levels on top of old ones, or perhaps digs down to see the ancient layers that have been hidden in the past. You might think of Buddhism as more layers set on top of Hinduism, and indeed many Hindus perceive it in just that way. Vishnu came to Earth, remember, in the avatar of the Buddha, bringing comfort and enlightenment to a people in need. Buddhists, however, tend to discount the Hindu version of their tradition. Instead, Buddhists point out that their religion and Hinduism sprang from the same sources but experience the world differently. For Buddhists, the world suffered an uneasy sleep until a man named Siddhartha found ultimate knowledge while meditating under a tree more than 1,000 years ago. Only then could we humans awaken to the reality of the world around us. As time has passed and Siddhartha's message traveled around the world, Buddhism has journeyed along different paths, each with unique characteristics but all leading back to the general principles set forth by the Buddha.

In Chapters 5 and 6, you will encounter many of the terms and concepts found in Hinduism, but with new meanings. For example, the Hindu idea of dharma transforms in Buddhism to mean "the teachings of the Buddha." The concepts of karma and samsara also reappear with their own Buddhist meaning. Yet dharma, karma, and samsara still retain shades of meaning from Hinduism, making it important to keep the religious context of Indian Hinduism in mind as you study Buddhism in the chapters that follow.

In Chapters 5 and 6, we will focus on the South and Southeast Asian regions, moving on to the United States. In Chapters 7 and 8, we'll turn our attention to Buddhist traditions in East Asia. This makes talking about a single "Buddhism" pretty tricky, because the term means different things to various people across place and time. For instance, I have Buddhist friends, family, students, and colleagues coming from places as far apart as Indonesia and New Jersey, each of their traditions teaches different things about the divine beings. They're all Buddhist, but they don't agree on Buddhism.

BUDDHISM: Becoming Awake

A Sacred Place

The Fogong Si Temple

THE FOGONG SI TEMPLE SEEMS TO GROW FROM ITS NATURAL SURROUNDINGS. NICKNAMED THE TIMBER PAGODA, IT'S MORE THAN 950 YEARS OLD, THE TALLEST ALL-WOOD STRUCTURE IN THE WORLD. Like a tree, it has no nails or screws holding it together. You'll strain your neck looking up to the top, rising five stories and 221 feet into the blue sky. Each octagonal floor grows upward from the last one, a little bit smaller and circled round with a wooden roof. Five stories represent both the Buddhist elements of existence and the steps toward enlightenment.

Standing witness to Buddhism, the pagoda has weathered invasion, disrepair, and hatred from an atheist communist government. As Buddhism slowly opens its mysteries to you, so does the Timber Pagoda: there are hidden floors, concealed from the outside but evident as you climb the interior stairs.

Stop at the vendor to try a local delicacy, Liang Fen (cold potato noodles with vegetables), then climb a few steps and walk through the massive red doors, quietly into the main hall. Above you, thick wooden supports nestle into one another like Lincoln Logs. But your eye is drawn first to the huge Buddha looking serenely toward you. He is seated in the lotus position, one hand in his lap, the other raised in blessing and welcome. The Buddha is huge—his head rises 30 feet. He is Shakyamuni—Sage of the Shakyas, the Buddha's clan.

The word "pagoda" describes East Asian Buddhist buildings like the one you see here. It is equivalent to the Indian "stupa," the earthen mound built over Buddha's burial place. It can still refer to a burial mound, but over the centuries the term also came to describe a sacred building representing the Buddha's physical presence. As Buddhism moved north into China, Japan, and Korea, stupas took on local characteristics and became known as pagodas.

Inside the pagoda, red and green painted figures surround the Buddha. They portray the journey from ignorance and suffering to knowledge and enlightenment. Climb the stairs and encounter the Buddha and his companions again and again, each time in a higher spiritual level—from belief to understanding to wisdom, experience, and dharma. Some statues wear a saffron cape around their carved shoulders, reminder of Buddha's asceticism.

By the time you reach the eighth floor, turn to look outside. You can see for miles from this height, just as an enlightened one distinguishes the truth through clouds of desire and suffering. And here, at the top, sits the Buddha with a retinue of enlightened ones, each with a crimson cape. Together, they embody the highest level of spiritual enlightenment.

Finally, look up one more time and you'll see a **mandala** painted on the coffered ceiling. It is a spiritual map, to lead you from the world of suffering to one that knows no anguish.

SOURCE: Based on http://www.yingxian.gov.cn/950/

Interior of
The Fogong Si Temple

When you travel to Buddhist temples you may find him in many positions—here he reclines as he peacefully prepares for death.

Shakyamuni—Here is the Buddha in the classic pose, welcoming you to the Timber Temple and offering his help in the climb toward enlightenment.

The original stupa was a mound of dirt pled over the Buddha's dead body. **Stupas** can take on many different styles, shown here from Laos.

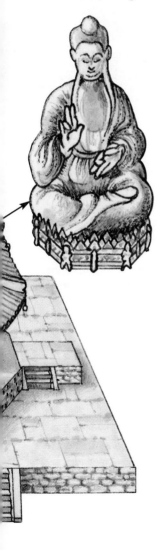

Buddhists sometimes depict the **"Five Buddhas" of meditation and enlightenment** in tapestry or painting instead of sculpture, as in the Timber Pagoda.

"The Five Buddhas." Votive painting on silk from Gansu province, China. The Granger Collection.

IS THERE A GOD?

God or Gods in Buddhism: No, Yes, and Maybe

Unlike other religious traditions, Buddhism can exist without a supreme creator. While Hinduism, for example, emphasizes the need for atman (the self) to join with Brahman in a union of creation and creator, Buddhism takes the opposite path, claiming no Brahman and therefore no atman. To explain this concept, Buddhists use the term **anatman**, which means "the absence of atman." We will learn more about this idea later in the chapter.

LESSER GODS CAN EXIST

So, what kind of gods might there be in Buddhism? Since its inception, Buddhism has been in contact with other spiritual traditions.

Buddhists do generally agree that our earthly life does not reflect all existence. In many cultures, therefore, Buddhists imagine a realm inhabited by deities with whom we can communicate. However, Buddhists believe that because there is no all-powerful creator, these deities can die and be reincarnated, just like human beings, animals, and insects. They're just on a higher level than us on Earth.

So, as Buddhism expanded from India to the rest of Asia, local Buddhists retained their own deities. In Sri Lanka and Thailand, for example, it is possible to ask a local deity for assistance with the weather or your health, but this does not preclude a Buddhist from looking directly to the Buddha for the ultimate help of breaking out of the cycle of reincarnation. This adaptability has allowed Buddhism to be easily integrated into the existing cultures.

IS THE BUDDHA A GOD?

Another simple question, yet another difficult answer. As you'll see reading his biography, Siddhartha (who became the Buddha) never claimed divine status. When asked who he was, Siddhartha answered, "I am awake." Some later Buddhists, however, have understood the Buddha as a deity.

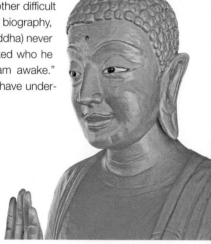

>>> This is a Thai statue of the Buddha. Although the Buddha is the central figure of Buddhism, he is not a god like Brahman in Hinduism. Some Buddhist traditions believe that the Buddha may be a deity. How might the view of Buddha as a god have developed?

A SACRED ACTION >>>

Alms-Giving

Most likely, the monks have arisen before you have, joining together for a period of intense meditation as the sun rises. Then they leave the monastery in a line, following each other through the neighborhood clad in brightly colored robes of orange, yellow, or red. Each monk carries an iron alms bowl as he walks through the town. Sometimes, drummers lead the procession, announcing that it is time to give food to the monks. You can join neighbors who wish to give to the monks—sit or kneel on the side of the road and place a donation in the bowl. If you've been staying with a family, the mother of the house may have made something special for the monks, but you can also just give rice.

When they get back to the monastery, the monks will divide the food they've been given and use it for a morning meal. In many places, because the monks generally do not handle money or cook, they rely on daily alms-begging to obtain all their food. In fact, in some monasteries the monks will not eat again until tomorrow morning, when the ritual begins again. Monastic life, including the alms-giving tradition, has adapted to new places and regions. Monks who reside in colder climates may not participate in daily alms-begging, or they may be permitted to wear additional clothing in order to keep warm. In urban areas, heavy traffic may inhibit this sacred activity. When Thai monks first arrived in Southern California, for example, they had to purchase their own food from local grocery stores rather than collecting alms.

Whether in Laos or Los Angeles, though, begging rounds and alms-giving are sacred actions for both the givers *and* the receivers. For the monks, collecting food or other donations reinforces their commitment to living a simple life in honor of Buddhist traditions. For the lay public, the act of donating builds good karma through philanthropy.

<<< Buddhist monks collect alms in Thailand. How do you think this act transfers spirituality to the giver of alms?

The Life of the Buddha

The Buddha's life story, like that of many religious figures, contains elements of the magical and the supernatural. Stories about the Buddha's birth, life, and death not only recount the events of the leader's life but also act as a parable for his followers (Keown 16–30; Maguire 3–18; Olson 3–18).

The man who would become the Buddha was born Siddhartha Gautama in the mid-sixth century BCE near Lumbini, in the foothills of the Himalayan mountains in what is now southern Nepal. Due to centuries of retelling and legend, stories of the Buddha's life contain both facts and fables. His people were called the Shakyas, probably among the local elites of the Kshatriya caste of warriors and rulers. Most accounts refer to his parents, Suddhodana and Maya, as a king and queen. Maya, however, had taken a vow of celibacy so the couple had no children. One night, during a full moon, legend tells that Maya dreamed of a white elephant, a good omen in Indian culture. Accounts of the creation story vary. Some claim that the elephant circled Maya's bed three times, while others say that the elephant had six tusks. Most agree that the Buddha was conceived when, in Maya's dream, the elephant entered her womb through her side. Maya and Suddhodana's counselors advised them that the dream meant that she would give birth to a son who would be either a great ruler or religious leader.

Maya traveled to her parents' home, as was customary, to give birth. When she and her escort reached a garden in Lumbini, she went into labor. Holding onto the branch of a sala tree, she gave birth to her child. Some stories describe the earth quaking and angels or deities surrounding the babe and bathing him. Others relate that Siddhartha immediately took seven steps and then proclaimed that he would become enlightened in this lifetime. (The number seven recurs in many Buddhist stories.) Though he would later become known as the Buddha, his parents named the baby Siddhartha, meaning "every wish fulfilled."

Seven days after she gave birth, Maya died. Her sister Prajapati raised Siddhartha and married Suddhodana. Fearing that his son would leave royal life to pursue his religious destiny, Suddhodana provided his child with every comfort. At the age of 16, Siddhartha married a woman named Yasodhara, and soon she bore a son named Rahula. Yet, as a young adult, Siddhartha tired of palace life and began to yearn for a more meaningful existence. Whenever he wandered away from the palace, his father arranged for any unpleasant sights to be removed, so that Siddhartha wouldn't be tempted to think about them. However,

Mandalas are geometric designs symbolic of the universe. They act as spiritual maps, leading one to a world beyond suffering.

Anatman literally means "not self." In contrast to the Hindu concept of atman, Buddhists do not believe that there is an essential self that moves from one body to another as we are reincarnated.

Samana is a wandering religious beggar.

∧∧∧ This Tibetan *tangka*, or public artwork, depicts the life of the Buddha. **How might this picture relate to a written narrative?**

Siddhartha's destiny was too strong, and the gods stepped in and presented him with four signs: an old man, a sick man, a corpse, and a monk. The first three showed Siddhartha that existence was impermanent, and the fourth sign encouraged him to look for a spiritual answer to humanity's problems.

SEARCH FOR ENLIGHTENMENT

Shortly after encountering the four signs, Siddhartha left his family and comfortable palace life to seek enlightenment. At the beginning of this quest, Siddhartha became a **samana**, a wandering religious beggar.

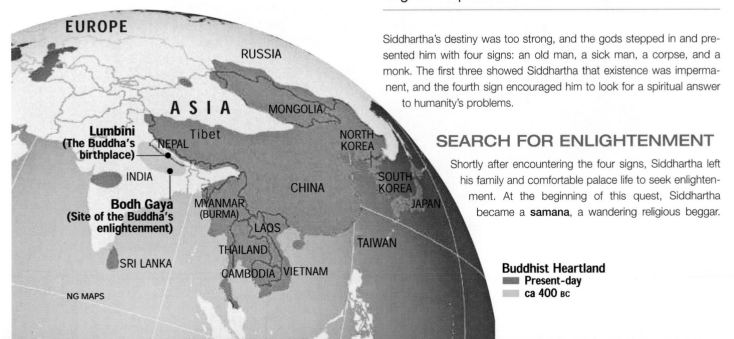

EUROPE

RUSSIA

ASIA

MONGOLIA

Lumbini
(The Buddha's
birthplace)   Tibet

NEPAL   NORTH
KOREA

INDIA   CHINA   SOUTH
KOREA

JAPAN

Bodh Gaya
(Site of the Buddha's
enlightenment)   MYANMAR
(BURMA)

LAOS

TAIWAN

THAILAND

SRI LANKA   CAMBODIA   VIETNAM

NG MAPS

Buddhist Heartland
Present-day
ca 400 BC

The Samana movement was well established in India at this time, and many other religious seekers followed this same path. Siddhartha learned how to enter deep states of meditation, but he felt troubled that, even in his heightened sense of reality, he could not answer ultimate questions about suffering and change.

For the next six years, Siddhartha experimented with extreme asceticism as a path to enlightenment. Various narratives describe how he attempted to hold his breath for long periods, slept in cemeteries, consumed cow manure, and stopped eating almost completely. Contrasted to his early life of ease, this experiment convinced Siddhartha that neither extreme self-indulgence nor asceticism lead to enlightenment. From this came Siddhartha's concept of the Middle Path that counsels moderation in all things. He chose to resume eating and to return to meditating.

SIDDHARTHA'S ENLIGHTENMENT

Once he resumed meditation, Siddhartha quickly progressed, and he found complete enlightenment in a single night. Sitting beneath a tree that came to be known as the Bodhi (enlightenment) Tree, he had sunk into a profound stillness when he encountered Mara, the essence of evil, who desperately wanted to prevent Siddhartha from gaining enlightenment. Mara tormented him, first by trying to have his three daughters seduce Siddhartha. Failing in this, Mara deployed armies of demons and even elements of nature against Siddhartha, who remained unmoved. Finally, in an effort to take the symbolic throne of power for himself, Mara demanded that Siddhartha give up his seat for him, gesturing to the myriad demons attending him and sneering at Siddhartha's lack of witnesses. Utterly composed, Siddhartha simply touched the earth

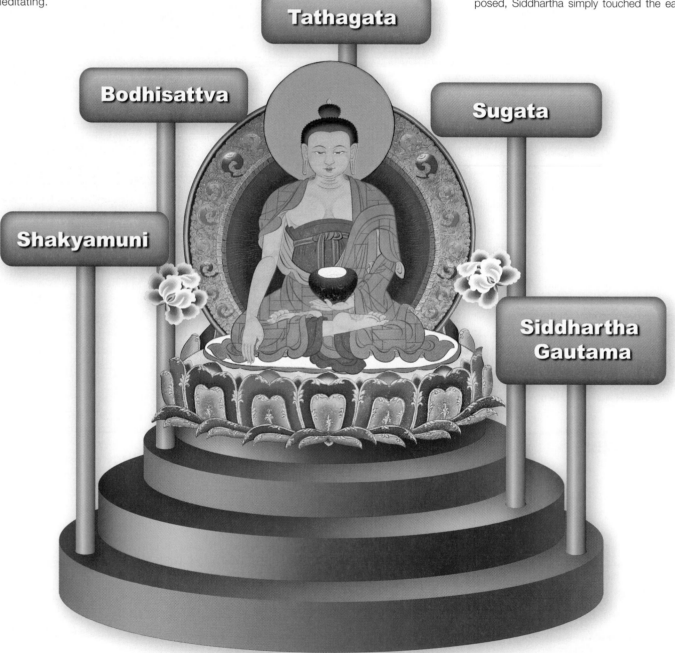

Tathagata

Bodhisattva

Sugata

Shakyamuni

Siddhartha Gautama

Why would a religious leader such as the Buddha acquire different names?

with his finger, and the earth roared, "I am his witness." Mara and his forces withered away in defeat (Maguire 37–38).

After this cosmic battle, Siddhartha's meditation went through three periods, or watches. During the first watch, he remembered his previous births and deaths in detail. During the second, he realized that our deeds in one life will determine our next life. Finally, in the third watch Siddhartha perceived his own enlightenment:

> Many houses of life have held me. Long have I sought to find him who made these prisons of the senses. But now, you builder, I have seen you at last. Never again will you construct such houses of pain! The walls are broken and the ridgepole shattered! Now that the bond of ignorance and craving are sundered, deliverance is obtained for all! Wonder of wonders! Intrinsically all living beings are buddhas, endowed with wisdom and virtue! (Maguire 12)

From that day onward, Siddhartha would teach these simple ideas to the world. Not Brahma, Vishnu, or Shiva: He was the Buddha—the awakened one.

As you wandered through the Fogong Si Temple at the beginning of this chapter, you saw that the Buddha had a specific name—Shakyamuni. Over the centuries, people have thought up many names for him, referring to different aspects of his life. Here are some of them (Maguire 16):

- **Bodhisattva:** "a being of enlightenment." This term can refer to the Buddha specifically or more generally to those who attain nirvana but choose to stay on Earth to help others find enlightenment.
- **The Buddha:** "the awakened one."
- **Shakyamuni:** "sage of the Shakya clan." At the time of his birth, the Buddha's people were known as the Shakyas.
- **Siddhartha Gautama:** the Buddha's name at birth. Siddhartha means "every wish fulfilled."
- **Sugata:** "the happy one."
- **Tathagata:** "the thus-perfected one."

THINK World Religions

Some Sanskrit and Pali Equivalent Terms in Buddhism

Scholars of Buddhism often interchange Pali and Sanskrit versions of the same term. We will use only the Sanskrit terms in this chapter for ease, but you may come across the Pali versions in other places. With a bit of practice, you'll get comfortable with both Sanskrit and Pali words.

the THINK SPOT
www.thethinkspot.com

Sanskrit Word	Pali Word
Anatman	Anatta
Atman	Atta
Bodhisattva	Bodhisatta
Dharma	Dhamma
Mantra	Manta
Nirvana	Nibbana
Skandha	Khanda

THE BUDDHA'S TEACHING AND THE SANGHA

After his enlightenment, Buddha chose to share what he had learned. This began a religious teaching career that spanned almost 40 years. The Buddha's early teachings have a special place in Buddhist tradition, and his very first sermon is called "the turning of the wheel of the dharma." A group of ascetics banded around the Buddha shortly after his enlightenment, and they received this wisdom. The sermon laid out the principles of the Middle Path, the Four Noble Truths, and the Noble Eightfold Path. You will learn more about these ideas later in this chapter.

Many of the Buddha's listeners became enlightened themselves and began to teach, too. From these men, the Buddha created an order of monks, or **sangha**. He founded a similar institution for nuns, although it never thrived to the same extent as the order of monks, perhaps because the Buddha himself did not live with the women. Gaining followers, the Buddha traveled across India for the last half of his life, teaching about the path to enlightenment.

Much like the story of his birth, narratives of the Buddha's death describe many miraculous elements. At 80, his health failing, the Buddha continued to teach. Eventually, he came to the town of Kusinara and lay down between two sala trees—the same species that his mother had grasped while giving birth. Some stories claim that the Buddha succumbed from food poisoning, but others state that he recovered from that incident, dying instead of natural causes. As his body gave up its life, the sala trees then bloomed out of season, the earth quaked, and a funeral pyre lit of its own accord.

Principles of Buddhism

What can we learn from this man who claimed no godly mantle but who has inspired millions of people? Paradoxically, the Buddha taught very simple ideas that grew into highly complex systems. He used words familiar to his audience—dharma, karma, samsara—but explained them in new ways to offer a different form of enlightenment than that of Hinduism. We'll try to take the same path as the people who first listened to the Buddha, applying our knowledge of Hindu tradition to figure out how Buddhism offers its own path to enlightenment. Here are a couple of questions to consider:

- Why do you think the Buddha opted to use these terms instead of coining new ones?
- Does this choice show Buddhism as an evolutionary or a revolutionary change in Indian religion? Could it be both?

DHARMA, KARMA, AND SAMSARA

You remember that in Hinduism, humans strive through many lives to experience unity with Brahman, and thus oneness with all creation. When Siddhartha Gautama began his quest for enlightenment, he too sought Brahman, "he who made these prisons of the senses." On the night of his enlightenment, though, the Buddha saw that there was no "prison builder," no creator of the universe—no Brahman. Rather he realized that "all living beings are buddhas, endowed with wisdom and virtue." In a sense, then, the Buddha subtracted Brahman from Hinduism and replaced it with the **Four Noble Truths** as the essence of **dharma**. For Buddhists, dharma equals the Buddha's teaching, especially in relation to the structure of the universe. (Some of Buddhism's appeal may have come originally from its simplicity in contrast to the Vedic tradition. Why do you think that might be the case?)

You'll notice that Buddhist dharma provides a concise explanation for life. Although we will identify many different trends in Buddhism, they all spring from this set of first principles:

1. Life is suffering, or **duhkha**.
2. Suffering is caused by desire.
3. It is possible to end suffering.
4. There is a path to follow to end suffering.

Levels of Existence

Level	Realm	Description	Reason for Rebirth Here
6–31	Heaven/Gods/Devas	Blissful; Followers have achieved higher levels of meditation and gods have overcome desire. The potential downfall is that beings in this realm may become complacent, neglect their spiritual duties, and ultimately be reborn in a lower realm.	Life of good deeds without achieving enlightenment due to maintaining a sense of self.
5	Human	Considered the Middle Path of Samsara. Characterized by constant change and opportunity. Humans can choose a life of devotion and spirituality, and thus have the potential to break the cycle of reincarnation.	Life of good and bad deeds, moderation.
4	Titan/Asura	Warrior realm of violent, competitive beings who desire superiority. Inhabitants are jealous of gods and battle with them constantly.	Life of devotion on the outside, while secretly harboring feelings of jealousy, hate, and dissatisfaction.
3	Ghost	Populated by former humans consumed by greed and still bound to the earth. Constantly hungry and thirsty with huge stomachs and small mouths. Sometimes called the "hungry ghost realm."	Life of greed, lack of charity to the less fortunate.
2	Animal	Overlaps with human realm. Undesirable since animals are motivated by their physical needs and are unable to make conscious decisions.	Life of ignorance of the moral laws of karma.
1	Hell	Comprised of 18 different hells, both hot and cold. Extreme suffering, but there is a chance to be reborn somewhere else once karma runs its course.	Life of conscious evil. Individuals were overcome by hatred, anger, or aggression.

Source: Keown, Damien. *Buddhism: A Very Short Introduction*. (Oxford: Oxford University Press, 1996), 38.

∧
∧ **This chart depicts samsara, the six levels of existence.** If this were portrayed as a
∧ circle, as it often is in Buddhist art, how would it add to an understanding of the six levels?

From a glance, you'll see the simplicity of this system—the first two truths focus on the problem of existence, while the latter two propose a solution. Let's delve deeper into the meaning behind each of them.

Think back to the four signs that the Buddha encountered before his enlightenment: an old man, a sick person, a corpse, and a religious man. Like them, everything in the world ultimately changes: we experience sickness, pain, and, eventually, death. Friends, loved ones, and strangers alike face physical hardship, and ultimately we possess no power against changes brought on by time. We also suffer from emotional hardships such as disappointment, dissatisfaction, and depression. In fact, even when life is fine, we can't get rid of that feeling that good times will soon flee. Though this worldview may sound despairingly pessimistic, Buddhists see it as realistic (Keown 46–58; Maguire 86–90).

The second truth explains that suffering comes from desire. English translations of Buddhist texts often use the word "craving" instead of "desire," which may be more helpful in understanding this concept. Craving implies that we want something but do not need it. Buddhism describes three forms of desire or craving:

1. sensual pleasure (desire for tastes, touches, sights)
2. existence (desire for life as we know it, fear of death)
3. destruction (desire to end suffering, desire to avoid anything unpleasant)

For example, I sometimes crave ice cream, going back for seconds or even third helpings. Ultimately, though, I know that it puts on the pounds and clogs my arteries. My craving doesn't give me what I want—it just creates more craving. And so we cannot achieve enlightenment by craving or desiring it. We must learn to overcome desire, even the desire *not* to desire.

The Buddha's use of the term **karma** should sound similar to you, because it relates closely to Hinduism. Karma dictates that every action and every thought affects a person in two ways:

1. immediately, with visible effects
2. later, with consequences that you cannot see but that will change your future

When you die, the sum of your actions during your lifetime helps determine your situation in the next life. Back at the beginning of the chapter, we read about the morning tradition of begging. The monks developed good karma both by shaking off their desire for food and by offering other people the opportunity to give alms. Everyone who offered food to the monks also gained karma, as they gave charity to holy men.

In Chapter 3, you learned that **samsara** is "the wheel of time" in the Hindu tradition. Buddhism develops this concept even further, using it to illustrate our human bondage to time. Samsara reminds us that nothing—nothing—escapes change. All is impermanent. To illustrate this, Buddhism traditionally divides samsara into six realms of existence, moving from a form of hell at the bottom to a kind of heaven at the top.

The gods, called **devas**, live in the highest few levels. In those realms Buddhists distinguish some 31 subdivisions, and the eight highest correspond to Buddhist levels of meditation. This is a crucial idea: By equating the upper levels of samsara to stages in meditation,

> **Four Noble Truths** are the essence of Buddhist dharma; they state that life is suffering, suffering is caused by desire, it is possible to end suffering, and there is a path to follow to end suffering.
>
> **Dharma** refers generally to the teachings of the Buddha, and is also the law that the universe follows.
>
> **Duhkha** is the Sanskrit word for suffering, which Buddhism states is the primary condition of life.
>
> **Karma** as used in Buddhism is very similar to the Hindu term. Every action has both an immediate and a later effect. Karma determines one's status in the next life.
>
> **Samsara** is the wheel of time, the cyclic life of all beings. In Buddhism, it represents our bondage to time and our inability to escape change.
>
> **Devas** are gods who live in the highest realms of existence in Buddhism.
>
> **Nirvana** is enlightenment, the ultimate goal of Buddhism. After a Buddhist becomes enlightened, he or she reaches a state of existence in which suffering ends and the cycle of rebirth and reincarnation is broken.

Buddhism links the external world to the internal one. In other words, there is no wall between "inside" yourself and the world "outside." As you advance through the levels of meditation, you will become aware of higher levels of existence that had been inaccessible to you at lower mental states.

NIRVANA

Consider the consequences of samsara and dharma. Every being in the cosmos, even deities, exists in a world of craving and suffering. Yet the Four Noble Truths teach us that we can eliminate suffering if we get rid of desire. We can lead lives of wisdom and virtue rather than lives consumed by cravings. When we attain a state of perfect wisdom and perfect virtue, we have reached **nirvana**, the ultimate goal of Buddhism (Keown 47).

If we reach enlightenment, we'll live out the rest of our days in that state, just as the Buddha did. When we die, we will no longer be reincarnated but will continue to exist in nirvana, a term that means "quenching," or "blowing out," as in the flame of the candle as it goes dark. Think of desire and suffering as fuel for the flame. When we take them away, the flame goes out. That sweet darkness afterward is nirvana, a new state of existence that we cannot fully imagine (Keown 56).

As you might imagine, Buddhists can speculate nearly endlessly about nirvana. For example, consider the following questions:

- What is the difference between this world (samsara) and nirvana?

- If you can achieve nirvana here on Earth, then is Earth part of nirvana?

- If nirvana is the absence of suffering, and all life is suffering, does that mean nirvana is no-place and no-thing, just as people are not-self?

- If nirvana is a kind of emptiness—blowing out of the candle—does it mean there is nothing there? Or does it mean there are simply no desires and so no suffering in nirvana?

▶ WHAT DOES IT MEAN TO BE HUMAN?

To begin our path toward nirvana, we must first define who we are—or who we are not. Unlike Hinduism, Buddhism teaches that there is no ultimate self—atman—who can experience unity with Brahman. Instead, Buddhists describe human beings as anatman, no-self. The Buddha taught that nothing in the cosmos remains constant; everything is subject to change. Therefore, we too have no permanent existence, no unchangeable or essential soul. Buddhists believe that we crave the idea of ourselves as something distinct and special. The first step toward enlightenment occurs when we realize that, rather having a static "self," we constantly change and develop in new ways. To do so, we must let go of our attachments to material things such as our bodies, and even our spouses and families. Because *everything* is impermanent, craving *anything* leads to suffering.

Let's think a little more about anatman—not-self. What is not me? That chair is not me (that's easy), but this thought is also not me, and that emotion is also not me. Think back at your life—the person you are today is not the one you were 10 years ago, or who you will be 10 years from now. Once you were physically smaller, mentally less developed, and psychologically unsophisticated. As you age, your body changes, but so too does your mind. So, who are you, if you keep changing?

Instead of a single self—me—Buddhism explains that we are each made up of five elements, called **skandhas** or **kandhas**, which mean "aggregates" or even "piles of stuff." They include

- forms—the material world

- feelings—our sensual interaction with the material world, including our emotional attachments to it

- perceptions—the desires, ideas, and sights and sounds of the world around us

- will—the part of us that intends to do something, that chooses our karmic path

- consciousness(es)—our state(s) of mind.

These skandhas interact with one another by constantly combining, breaking apart, and recombining. Just as the chair is "not me," each of these elements is also "not me." Piled up, though, the five elements do cook up a personal stew of characteristics that we call "me." Ultimately, though, there is nothing about us that cannot be changed—no soul that can be identified as "me." Consequently, we have no atman, no cosmic self that moves from one body to another. (If this is difficult to grasp, don't worry—we'll talk more about the relationship of anatman and reincarnation later on.)

Still, Buddhism won't go so far to say that we are nothing, because that too flies in the face of the evidence. (If we were nothing, how could I write this chapter? How could you read it?) Instead, the Buddha counseled us to stay on the Middle Path:

- We are *not* nothing.

- We are *not* eternal.

- We are *between* nothing and eternal.

In other words, we are what we are—a changing bundle of physical, sensual, emotional, and rational attributes. When we realize we are selfless, it also becomes easier to become selfless—why worry about a self that doesn't exist?

Let's go back to the Fogong Si Temple from the beginning of this chapter. As you climbed the stairs, each floor revealed another version of the Buddha. Though you might change—losing breath or feeling the noodles in your stomach—the Buddha stayed the same. He appeared again and again, yet each time he sat in the center of the room, completely at peace. Ultimately, we too want to stop circling around the Buddha. Instead, we hope to join him in the middle of the room, rather than frantically walking in circles.

Now let's go back to the monks who beg for food. What might happen if no one gave them rice? If they do not eat, won't the monks die? Eventually, yes, but death simply dissolves our present pile of stuff until it gets piled up in some other way. So, the monks strive neither to crave food nor to give it up completely.

This brings up two big problems: First, how can we get to nirvana without craving it? Second, if we have no soul, how does our karma move from one life to another? To find some answers, let's go back to the idea of the flaming candle. The wick, oxygen, and heat combine to create the flame. What if you set a matchstick next to the flame? Both would burn, flames mingling with one another even as they burn different fuel. So it is with our lives: When we die, our flames simply take on new fuel. We stop existing as one candle as we become another one. Our karma affects the size of the new candle and how it burns. But here is the important part—the more we desire to burn brightly, the bigger candle we create for our next life. If we could just let go of that craving for heat and light, we would let the candle burn down naturally, finally using up all the wax, wick, heat, and air. And then, like the candle, we could simply go out.

The Eightfold Path

Just like all sentient beings—from animals to deities—we hope to attain nirvana. That being said, we're stuck right now as human beings, somewhere on the path between bugs and gods. To help us along, the Buddha has offered the Eightfold Path, a roadmap to move us toward wisdom, virtue, and meditation (Keown 58). The Eightfold Path treads the Middle Way

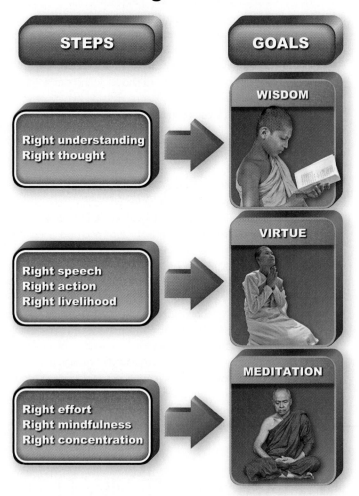

The Eightfold Path

STEPS	GOALS
	WISDOM
Right understanding **Right thought**	
	VIRTUE
Right speech **Right action** **Right livelihood**	
	MEDITATION
Right effort **Right mindfulness** **Right concentration**	

 How do the steps and goals of the Eightfold Path complement one another?

A U.S. Army Chaplain Who Is a Buddhist

In late 2009, the U.S. Army prepared to send its first Buddhist chaplain to the Middle East. Thomas Dyer, formerly a Marine reservist and then a Southern Baptist minister, converted to Buddhism as a result of practicing meditation. He prefers to see himself as a chaplain who happens to be a Buddhist, instead of a chaplain only for Buddhists. Dyer's wife and children have remained Christian, a choice he supports.

When he joined the National Guard, Dyer found that he had something to offer to soldiers whose experiences in Iraq left them very troubled. Dyer said that meditating with one combat veteran in particular brought solace to that soldier. Army recruiters invited Dyer to sign up as a chaplain, and after consulting with his teacher, a Tibetan monk, he agreed. Yet Dyer also feels the paradox of being a Buddhist soldier: "Is military service what we call right livelihood? Most Buddhist teachers are moving to say 'yes' because the potential to do good and to protect is there. And it is not beneficial to *not* participate in civil action when peoples and nations around the world are suffering. It is something that has become necessary, we might say" (Martin).

the THINKSPOT
www.thethinkspot.com

Skandhas (or **Kandhas**) are five elements that combine to form an individual

Theravada means "teaching of the elders" and refers to the most ancient Buddhist tradition.

Tripitaka are the sacred texts of the Theraveda.

Mahayana means "the great vehicle," and is a branch of Buddhism developed after Theravada.

Arhat is a person who has achieved enlightenment, a "worthy one." In the Theravada Buddhist tradition, to become an arhat is the goal of humanity.

Bodhisattva is a person who has achieved enlightenment but chooses to stay on Earth to help others reach enlightenment rather than entering nirvana. Becoming a bodhisattva is the goal of Mahayana Buddhists.

between the extremes of asceticism and self-indulgence, both of which the Buddha experienced and rejected. In its three goals, the path shows us how to live as Buddha did. Because we do not have an unchanging "self," we can use our actions, ideas, perceptions, attitudes, and other traits to create a new self. If we act the right way, we'll continue the path toward enlightenment. On the left is the Eightfold Path in graphic form.

The first two "rights" help us achieve wisdom. We develop the "right understanding" when we accept the Four Noble Truths. Our "right thought" focuses our minds on moral ideas and avoiding malicious thought.

Virtue comes next. It includes "right speech," which means that we do not speak ill of others, lie, or gossip, and that we refrain from using crude or abusive language. "Right action" means that we behave morally—not killing, stealing, lying, or becoming unchaste or intoxicated. "Right livelihood" teaches us to avoid any profession that harms other beings. For example, we should never work in a slaughterhouse but instead choose a profession that helps others, such as nursing (Keown 57–58; Maguire 90–95; Olson 54–58).

Finally, "right effort," "mindfulness," and "concentration" move us from the world of craving to the mental pace where suffering can end.

The Human Condition in Theravada and Mahayana Traditions

As it spread across Asia, Buddhism developed into two main branches: Theravada ("teaching of the elders") and Mahayana ("great vehicle"). The older and more traditional group, **Theravada**, dates to around 300 BCE. It focuses on a relatively small number of the Buddha's teachings and tends to emphasize monasticism. The sacred texts of the Theravada are called the **Tripitaka**, or "Three Baskets." Theravada once prospered in India, but is now most popular in Sri Lanka, Myanmar, Cambodia, and Thailand. Like other forms of Buddhism, Theravada adapted to fit existing local traditions, which contributed to the religion's establishment in many different countries (Maguire 37–38). We'll look closely at Theravada's different forms of sacred activities in Chapter 6.

As Theravada's younger sibling, **Mahayana** Buddhism developed around the first century CE. Meaning "great vehicle," Mahayana spread outward across Asia, growing new branches as it moved across the Himalayan Mountains and the Pacific into Japan. (Mahayana Buddhists often describe the Theravada as Hinayana, or "lesser vehicle," a rather pejorative nickname.) Mahayana tends to emphasize both lay and monastic life to a greater extent than Theravada. Mahayana also follows a different set of sacred texts, called sutras, shastras, and tantras (Keown 60–61; Maguire 35–38). We'll discuss Mahayana in Chapters 5–8, because it exists across Asia in different forms.

TO BECOME AN ARHAT OR A BODHISATTVA?

Theravada teaches that humans ultimately seek to become an **arhat**, or "worthy one." Arhats have become enlightened and will achieve nirvana, having overcome the "the five fetters:" craving for life in a physical realm, craving for life in a nonphysical realm, pride, restlessness, and ignorance. Mahayana, on the other hand, seeks the enlightenment of both the self and others by becoming a **bodhisattva**, or "one with an enlightened essence." Both traditions seek enlightenment, but they perceive the relationship between enlightened and unenlightened humanity in very different ways. An arhat dies and experiences nirvana, never to be born again. A bodhisattva, on the other hand, voluntarily chooses to be born again in order to help others achieve enlightenment and, ultimately, Buddhahood. Theravada Buddhists would say that it is presumptuous to believe that a person could become a Buddha and then come back to the world; Mahayana Buddhists argue that only the selfish person would achieve arhat but then move directly into nirvana, leaving so many suffering beings behind (Keown 59–61; Maguire 35; Olson 102–103).

THE BUDDHA IN MAHAYANA: THREE BODIES

Mahayana also has a unique view of the Buddha and his body, which complicates Mahayana's perception of the human condition. In Mahayana cosmology, the Buddha exists in three dimensions, or bodies:

- The earthly body (also called the body of transformation)—this was the Buddha's human body when he lived on Earth.

Buddhist Texts

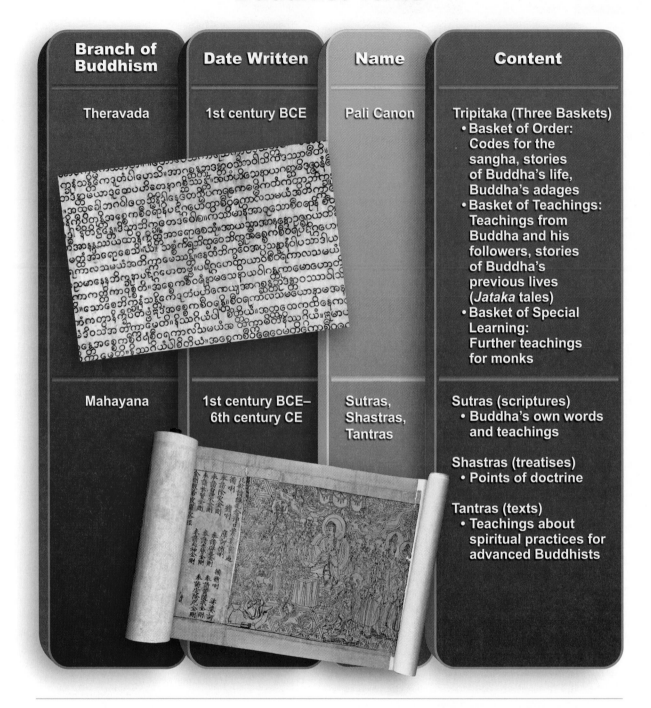

Branch of Buddhism	Date Written	Name	Content
Theravada	1st century BCE	Pali Canon	Tripitaka (Three Baskets) • Basket of Order: Codes for the sangha, stories of Buddha's life, Buddha's adages • Basket of Teachings: Teachings from Buddha and his followers, stories of Buddha's previous lives (*Jataka* tales) • Basket of Special Learning: Further teachings for monks
Mahayana	1st century BCE–6th century CE	Sutras, Shastras, Tantras	Sutras (scriptures) • Buddha's own words and teachings Shastras (treatises) • Points of doctrine Tantras (texts) • Teachings about spiritual practices for advanced Buddhists

∧∧∧ The Pali Canon (top) is the main body of Theravada scriptures, while the sutras (bottom), shastras, and tantras make up the Mahayana scriptures. How do you think two traditions can arise out of a single religion?

- The heavenly body (also called body of bliss)—this was Buddha's body in a heaven-like realm; bodhisattvas can see this Buddha, but human beings cannot.

- The transcendent body (also known as the body of essence)—this embodies Buddha as the ultimate truth, a cosmic entity.

As you might imagine, scholars often compare this Three Body concept to the Christian idea of the Holy Trinity (which we will discuss in Chapter 11). That's a useful idea, because it illustrates for Christians the ways in which the Buddha can simultaneously exist as a human being, a universal (divine) being, and a link between the absolute and the human. In fact, the Three Body concept also helps to explain the "maybe" answer to our first question: "Is there a god?" By Mahayana reckoning, the Buddha *may be* understood as being both human and divine (Keown 61–64; Olson 180–181). We will explore this concept in more detail in Chapter 6.

King Ashoka and the Spread of Buddhism

The story of the Indian king Ashoka illustrates how Buddhist ideas grow and spread across large geographic areas. Ashoka ruled the Indian Mauryan dynasty from about 270 to 230 BCE. He concentrated on military adventures and brutality through much of his early reign, and Ashoka himself witnessed bloodshed in battle. Thousands of men were murdered at his orders, leaving children without parents and women without husbands.

Eventually, Ashoka realized the futility of his military gains. Seeking peace and enlightenment, he converted to Buddhism and promoted it across his realm. Ashoka encouraged vegetarianism and prohibited the unnecessary killing of animals. He sought peace with neighboring kingdoms and devoted himself both to his subjects and to the principles of Buddhist dharma. Most significantly, he erected a series of "rock edicts" that proclaimed his moral code and societal reforms. These edicts were inscribed on stone pillars and displayed in India, Nepal, Pakistan, and Afghanistan. King Ashoka's devotion and contribution to Buddhist art in the form of the rock edicts contributed to the spread of Buddhism in Asia, and his story continues to serve as a parable in Buddhist philosophy.

>>> India uses this Pillar of Ashoka with four lions as a national emblem. Why do you think that the modern-day government would choose to use a symbol of Ashoka's reign, over 2,000 years earlier?

INTERNAL CONFLICT

Buddhism and Gender

Over the centuries, men and women have had a complex relationship in Buddhism. Given its deep focus on monasticism, there's little wonder that gender relations have not always been easy. In addition, early Buddhism developed in an Indian society that sometimes revered women while also fearing female goddesses such as Kali. That being said, men held most day-to-day political and religious power in ancient India. Women tended to have more control over domestic and child-rearing activities.

Buddhist teachings, especially as they relate to monasticism, have often viewed women as a threat to male enlightenment. For that reason, monks developed elaborate rituals to keep them away from the other sex, for even celibate men could not always resist an attractive woman. In practical terms, though, this system tended to subordinate nuns to monks.

The Buddha also taught, however, that all human beings could achieve enlightenment, regardless of gender. In fact, a woman traumatized by the loss of a husband or child could find a safe haven with Buddhist nuns. Once on the dharma path, women could then achieve the status of arhat, living out their earthly years by teaching or writing poetry about enlightenment. They had much to offer, since they suffered in five ways that men never experienced: the menstrual cycle, pregnancy, childbirth, inferiority to men, and submission to family.

Today, Theravada Buddhism still tends to emphasizes male monasticism and leadership. Theravada Buddhist countries do not recognize an official order of nuns, but women have created informal organizations in Sri Lanka, Thailand, and Myanmar. Nuns also teach privately and occasionally officiate at family ceremonies. Since they may handle money, some nuns assist monasteries with financial matters. Mahayana lands, on the other hand, have long cultivated female monasticism. In modern perceptions, Buddhist women may thus seem both oppressed and liberated; they rarely hold positions of real power but are also quite autonomous from male monastic authority (Maguire 221–225; Olson 110–122).

REVIEW

Summary

IS THERE A GOD?   p. 56

- Some Buddhists believe the world is inhabited by deities with whom we can communicate. However, Buddhists generally believe that there is no all-powerful creator.
- The Buddha was an enlightened teacher, but he never claimed to be divine. Some traditions, however, define Buddha in terms that come close to a god.

WHAT DOES IT MEAN TO BE HUMAN?   p. 61

- Buddhism explains that we are each made up of five elements, called skandhas or kandhas. They are *forms*, *feelings*, *perceptions*, *will*, and *consciousness*.
- The Eightfold Path acts as a roadmap to move humans toward wisdom, virtue, and meditation.
- In Mahayana cosmology, the Buddha exists in three dimensions: The earthly body, the heavenly body, and the transcendent body.

Key Terms

Mandalas are geometric designs symbolic of the universe. They act as spiritual maps, leading one to a world beyond suffering.   *54*

Anatman literally means "not self." In contrast to the Hindu concept of atman, Buddhists do not believe that there is an essential self that moves from one body to another as we are reincarnated.   *56*

Samana is a wandering religious beggar.   *57*

Sangha is the name for the monastic order created by the Buddha. Although the Buddha created the order for men only, he later created a separate order of nuns.   *59*

Four Noble Truths are the essence of Buddhist dharma; they state that life is suffering; suffering is caused by desire; it is possible to end suffering; and there is a path to follow to end suffering.   *60*

Dharma refers generally to the teachings of the Buddha, and is also the natural law that the universe follows.   *60*

Duhkha is the Sanskrit word for suffering, which Buddhism states is the primary condition of life.   *60*

Karma as used in Buddhism is very similar to the Hindu term. Every action has both an immediate and a later effect. Karma determines one's status in the next life.   *61*

Samsara is the wheel of time, the cyclic life of all beings. In Buddhism, it represents our bondage to time and our inability to escape change.   *61*

Devas are gods who live in the highest realms of existence in Buddhism.   *61*

Nirvana is enlightenment, the ultimate goal of Buddhism. After a Buddhist becomes enlightened, he or she reaches a state of existence in which suffering ends and the cycle of rebirth and reincarnation is broken.   *61*

Skandhas (or **Kandhas**) are five elements that combine to form an individual.   *62*

Theravada means "teaching of the elders" and refers to the oldest Buddhist tradition.   *63*

Tripitaka are the sacred texts of the Theraveda.   *63*

Mahayana means "the great vehicle," and is a branch of Buddhism that developed after Theravada.   *63*

Arhat is a person who has achieved enlightenment, a "worthy one." In the Theravada Buddhist tradition, to become an arhat is the goal of humanity.   *63*

Bodhisattva is a person who has achieved enlightenment but chooses to stay on Earth to help others reach enlightenment rather than entering nirvana. Becoming a bodhisattva is the goal of Mahayana Buddhists.   *63*

Find it on

- Many people are fascinated by Buddhist monks and their way of life. Are you one of those people? If so, visit the ThinkSpot to learn more about the Buddhist monk lifestyle and how you, as a lay person, can relate to someone practicing the oldest living tradition. http://www.buddhanet.net/e-learning/buddhistworld/layguide.htm

- The Dalai Lama –the 14th such designated person—is a well-known figure in the Buddhist tradition and someone you may have seen before. The current Dalai Lama has been very vocal about certain political issues and has been interviewed on many occasions. Listen to what the Dalai Lama has to say about his legacy and the prospect that he may be the last Dalai Lama to hold that title. http://www.cnn.com/video/?/video/world/2010/02/26/nr.nguyen.dalai.lama.cnn

- Would you like to try your own meditation? Listen to this clip of Buddhists chanting while focusing on the beautiful waterfall. Om Mani Padme Hum is a Tibetan incantation that promises absolution from sin. http://www.dailymotion.com/video/x3ourh_om-mani-padme-hum_music

Questions for Study and Review

1. What are the Four Noble Truths of Buddhism?

The Four Noble Truths state that: 1) life is suffering, 2) suffering is caused by craving, 3) suffering can end, and 4) the way to the end of suffering is to follow the Eightfold Path. These truths were revealed to the Buddha on the night of his enlightenment and serve as one of the main principles of Buddhist thought.

2. Discuss the significance of daily alms-begging.

Begging for food represents a monk's quest to rid himself of desire. If he receives food, he will eat, but if he receives nothing, then he eats nothing. More practically, monks rely on donations for their food supply because they are prohibited from handling money or cooking food. For those who donate, the monks have provided an opportunity to build good karma by performing an act of charity.

3. How does the Eightfold Path relate to anatman?

The Eightfold Path offers a series of steps to help Buddhists change their lives. Because Buddhists do not believe in an unchangeable soul, they say that the Eightfold Path will help them to develop a better anatman, or aggregation of characteristics of self.

4. List three differences between the Theravada and Mahayana forms of Buddhism.

Theravada Buddhism is more conservative and traditional than the Mahayana branch. In Theravada Buddhism, the goal is to become arhats, "worthy ones" who are enlightened. In Mahayana Buddhism, human beings strive to become bodhisattvas. A bodhisattva is also one who has reached enlightenment, but who chooses to help human beings reach enlightenment rather than making the final step away from samsara. A third difference between the two groups is their sacred texts. For the Theravadas, the Tripitaka is the sacred text. For the Mahayana Buddhists, the sacred texts are the sutras, shastras, and tantras.

HOW DO HUMANS INTERACT WITH THE SACRED?

HOW DOES THE SACRED BECOME COMMUNITY?

Like a

perfect piece of jewelry adorning the Burmese landscape, the Shwedagon Pagoda sits in golden splendor at the top of a hill overlooking Yangon, Myanmar's largest city. (The historic name of Yangon is Rangoon; Myanmar was known for centuries as Burma. Many people prefer the old names, associating the new ones with today's brutal military government that took power in 1988.) The Burmese have long treasured their gold and jewels, so they built a temple to reflect the sacred beauty of Buddhist teaching. The main stupa recalls the Buddha's burial mound, built as a shrine to hold hairs from his head.

It's no surprise that Shwedagon is called the "Golden Hill," as stupas from dozens of temples, each covered in gold, reflect early morning light. Thousands of bells peal as worshipers and visitors climb the stairs toward the temple. In the center of the Shwedagon Temple, a huge emerald catches the light and refracts it toward the thousands of other rubies, diamonds, and other gems. Light filters through the smoke rising from incense burners that run for hundreds of feet along the temple walls. People bring flowers to the temple, their fragrance mixing with the incense and their colors mingling with the saffron robes of Buddhist monks.

The Shwedagon Temple embodies one of the great Buddhist paradoxes. On the one hand, Buddhism reminds us that the cares of this world—wealth, beauty, and status—will die away like the incense snaking its way into the morning air. Yet inside this world of suffering, Buddhists have also built temples of great wealth, adorning them with the most beautiful things on earth—gold and silver, tinkling bells and monastic chants, rubies, and freshly picked flowers.

BUDDHISM: Awakening the World

CHAPTER 06

Protests in Myanmar

In the capital city of Yangon, hundreds of Buddhist monks cloaked in saffron-hued robes protested on Wednesday, September 19, 2007. They objected to an increase in fuel prices announced by the State Peace and Development Council, the region's ruling military junta. For poor people, higher costs of fuel robbed them of money to take the bus into work or even to buy food for their families. The rich members of the junta, of course, felt no pain as they continued to pillage from the country's meager economy, but the monks were standing up for the very poorest people.

Thousands of monks (roughly equivalent in number to their brothers in the army) took to the streets. They turned their begging bowls upside down, refusing to accept alms from members of the government. "In a staunchly Buddhist country," explained one Buddhist abbot, "such a boycott is the most severe form of punishment for a Buddhist. The boycott brings extreme shame to the ruling junta" (Chopra).

Protests began after authorities in the town of Pakokku assaulted monks during a peaceful demonstration against the increased fuel prices. "Reverend clergy, may you listen to my words," said one Buddhist leader, "the violent, mean, cruel, ruthless, pitiless kings—the great thieves who live by stealing from the national treasury—have killed a monk at Pakokku and also arrested reverend clergymen by trussing them up with rope. They beat and tortured, verbally abused and threatened them. The clergy . . . must boycott the violent, mean, cruel, ruthless, pitiless soldier kings" (Buncombe).

One of the most important and virtuous actions a Buddhist can do is to give alms to monks. By refusing these alms, the monks denied the giver, in this case the military, the opportunity to garner merit to enjoy a better life, both in this one and in the next.

Because the governing military junta funds the refurbishment of many of Yangon's temples, the government was able to close the sacred buildings. Hundreds of monks found themselves barred from entry to the city's temples. This ban included the most revered of the city's temples, the Shwedagon Pagoda. Monks marched for hours through the city. As the protests raged on, soldiers raided monasteries, beating the monks and taking them into custody. The Shwedagon Pagoda continued to be the center of many of the protests, as monks attempting to enter the temple clashed with police officers, resulting in several arrests. At the Sule Pagoda, the site of one of the largest protests, a similar confrontation took place.

Initially, sympathizers didn't take part in the protests, for fear of retaliation from the junta. However, as public sympathy toward the monks grew, more marches and rallies occurred in neighboring towns, with protesters facing tear gas, gunshots, and arrest. The number of monks protesting the junta grew to hundreds of thousands, followed by increasing numbers of public supporters, who aided the marching barefoot Buddhists by giving them water, food, flowers, and healing ointments. As public outrage continued, many world leaders expressed their anger and concern. The Asian Human Rights Commission said that "Only under the most compelling moral circumstances will a monk refuse the alms that have been offered, as to do so is to refuse to acknowledge the alms-giver as a part of the religious community. It amounts to an act of excommunication. However, the view of monks in Burma today is that such an extraordinary moment has arrived" (Buncombe).

The simple act of turning their bowls upside down brought Myanmar's catastrophe to the headlines. It also led to an interesting question—what is the correct role for Buddhists in society? Should they work to alleviate suffering only through the Eightfold Path, or does Buddhism also make room for political and social action? Were the monks' protests inappropriate for men devoted to the cause of peace, or did their actions help give spiritual strength to a downtrodden Buddhist community?

∧ **Buddhist monks pray with**
∧ **overturned alms bowls.**
Such a simple action is nonetheless a powerful sign of protest.

▶HOW DO HUMANS INTERACT WITH THE SACRED?

Buddhists often describe dharma, Buddha, and sangha as the **Three Jewels**. To understand how Buddhists interact with their sacred world, we'll follow the example of Buddhist monks, who invoke the Three Jewels when they enter monastic life:

1. "I take refuge in the Buddha."
2. "I take refuge in the dharma."
3. "I take refuge in the sangha."

Lay Buddhists also rely on the Three Jewels, and they offer us a good introduction to Buddhists' interaction with the sacred.

The First Jewel:
Taking Refuge in the Buddha

As you climbed up the stairs of the Timber Temple in the Sacred Place we studied in Chapter 5, you saw multiple statues of the Buddha at every turn. Go into nearly any Buddhist temple and you'll find the same thing— statues of Buddha smiling, sitting in the lotus position, or even lying down. Sometimes he will be fat, other times slim. His face will look Thai, Indonesian, Japanese, or Chinese. By sculpting him in many positions and making him look like people who live in that region, Buddhists remind themselves that the Buddha offered a way that rose above race, ethnicity, or language.

Following the Buddha means living like him, according to the Eightfold Path. If you choose a monastic life, you'll closely tread in the footprints left by the Buddha. You'll wear similar clothing, shave your hair, and foreswear sex and meat. You'll live with other monks and perfect your meditational techniques. By living like him, you too may achieve enlightenment. Yet any lay Buddhist can also take refuge in the Buddha. By living and thinking rightly, you'll build a more enlightened version of yourself. By offering incense, you'll remind yourself of the sweetness of the Buddha's teaching and the impermanence of the world. By gazing at the Buddha, you'll realize how he resembles you, and learn that you can be like him.

Λ
Λ How would you imagine a Buddha who fits
Λ into your ethnic or national tradition?

> **Three Jewels** of Buddhism are Buddha, dharma, and sangha.
>
> **Tantra** is a set of instructions said to be given by the Buddha to a group of his students. These teachings are widely used in Tibetan Buddhism.

Buddhist art, especially in mandalas, the sacred, circular diagrams used for meditation. The mandala's shape reflects the celestial home of the Buddha. The outermost ring represents the cosmos and the middle circle often symbolizes the Buddha himself. He might make hand gestures, indicating forms of preaching and mediation. All of this may surround a swastika or four dots, graphic reminders of motion and eternity (Olson 215–216).

A bodhisattva embodies virtues known as the "Six Perfections," each of which can help us toward enlightenment. Starting with generosity—a virtue that Buddhists develop through giving to the poor, the monks, and the temple—the bodhisattva then moves upward through the phases of existence that ends with wisdom. Once he or she has attained that level of existence, the bodhisattva's compassion for us leads the enlightened one back to this world, even though nirvana exists just a moment away.

SPECIAL ASPECTS OF MAHAYANA BUDDHISM

In Chapter 5, we briefly discussed the differences between the Theravada concept of arhat and the Mahayana idea of bodhisattva. Let's see how those distinctions affect the way in which Buddhists interact with their sacred world.

For the Mahayana Buddhist, the path toward enlightenment comes with a guide who has already been there and wants to show you the way. That's the essential power of a bodhisattva—the ability to help the unenlightened toward their goal. In fact, the Mahayana tradition takes the bodhisattva idea to another level, saying that enlightened beings can actually become Buddhas too. In the latter stages of enlightenment, the bodhisattva is ensured entry into nirvana, and often becomes so powerful that he or she is worshipped with almost as much fervor as the Buddha. (We'll discuss this in Chapters 7 and 8 as it relates to East Asia.)

You can visualize the relationship between bodhisattvas and the Buddha by recalling the sculptures of the Five Buddhas on the second floor of the Timber Temple. This group of statues represents the historical Buddha plus four bodhisattvas who became Buddhas. You'll also find the Five Buddhas in other forms of

>>> The Six Perfections are integral to the Bodhisattva tradition. How might they help a Buddhist live his or her everyday life?

The Six Perfections of the Bodhisattva

6 **Wisdom**

5 **Meditation**

4 **Courage**

3 **Patience**

2 **Morality**

1 **Generosity**

THE TIBETAN BUDDHIST TRADITION: A UNIQUE FORM OF MAHAYANA

Buddhism began to move northward into the Himalayan Mountains around the 3rd century CE. For about seven hundred years, Buddhism cycled between favor and disfavor in the mountain kingdom, developing alongside indigenous traditions (especially one called "Bon") that helped to give Tibetan Buddhism its distinctive characteristics. By the 10th century CE, Buddhism had finally secured its central place in Tibetan culture, as it remains today.

Tibetan Buddhism relies on teachings called **tantras**, which are attributed to the Buddha himself. It also integrates the work of shamans, indigenous holy men who complement Buddhist teaching with magical insights based on local traditions. In fact, the Mahayana path in Tibet grew so distinct that it has received its own name—Vajrayana, meaning the Thunderbolt Way or the Diamond Way. The "Diamond" Way indicates a clear, perfect, and strong path. "Thunderbolt" conveys the idea that enlightenment can come in a moment, not necessarily over many lifetimes (Olson 206–217).

Over the past few centuries, Tibet's political and religious structure merged into a single entity. Monasticism developed to a high degree and monasteries provided both religious and political leadership. There are two major divisions of Tibetan monasticism: Red Hats and Yellow Hats, based on the color robes worn by each group. The Red Hats are the older school, often called the "unreformed" branch. Much of the Red Hat tradition comes from oral transmission of sacred ideas, added to the new

Secret Tantric Practice

As Vajrayana Buddhists move upward through each level of meditative practice, their teachers introduce them to ever-more esoteric practices, which had earlier been kept secret. As a result, scholars often refer to Tibetan Buddhism as Esoteric Tantrism, since it offers important knowledge only to those who have been appropriately educated and initiated.

You can even interact with the sacred through sex. On the one hand, it seems strange that Buddhists might embrace sexual desire as a tool for enlightenment, since the tradition usually advocates celibacy. On the other hand, Tantric Buddhists believe that sex can actually help break the cycle of Samsara through a mystical union of two people that dissolves the self.

The tantric sexual process tends to be oriented toward male enlightenment, though not absolutely. Here's how it works: Each person must recognize sacred power embodied in his or her mate, demonstrated by making offerings to each other as if communing with the Buddha. Then the man draws a mandala on the floor and the woman sits on top of it, further linking the universe to her body. He continues to worship her using flowers, incense or ghee lamps, perhaps also giving her jewelry, clothing, or perfume. The woman embodies enlightenment and selflessness, which the man worships. However, he hopes to consummate their union without giving himself into pure sexual desire. Instead, both people move with an intimate and ritualized choreography that both intensifies their sexual interaction and also casts off their personal desires. In the end, the man hopes to share in the changelessness that he perceives in his female partner, just as he would interact with the Buddha (Olson 217–224).

discovery of secrets left behind by specific Buddhas. There are four distinct groups of Red Hats, each of which follows its own revered monks and teachers.

The Yellow Hats reformed some Red Hat traditions, and are best known for their leader, the Dalai Lama. In general terms, the term **lama** refers to a teacher of the dharma who has attained high levels of spiritual development and authority. The highest of all is the Dalai Lama, the "ocean of wisdom" sometimes known as the "god king" of Tibet, as he has traditionally directed both religious and political policy toward the attainment of enlightenment.

As a bodhisattva, the Dalai Lama chooses to return to the Earth each time he dies, to continue helping Buddhists along the way to nirvana. Shortly after a Dalai Lama dies, members of the Yellow Hat monks begin to search for his new incarnation. They look for signs from the deceased lama, in addition to information offered by Buddhist sages and oracles. The test for a new lama comes when a certain youth meets the monks—if the child can pick out the dead Dalai Lama's effects from among many objects, it's clear that he has come to take back his own possessions. The child then leaves his family, becomes the object of intensive training in Buddhism, and finally assumes the role of supreme Tibetan Buddhist leader.

Tibetan tradition distinguishes itself from other forms of Buddhism through its use of Tantric practices inherited from India and further developed in Tibet.

They take many forms, including hand gestures, visualizations, **prostrations**, and sacred **mantras**. By making particular sequences of hand gestures and movements, these Buddhists exhibit both their humility and their wish for enlightenment. Mantras aid in meditation, and visualization offers a way to control bodily activities such as temperature and respiration.

The Second Jewel: Taking Refuge in the Dharma

The Buddha did not create an intricate set of doctrines. Instead, he developed principles to illustrate the Four Noble Truths, helping his followers to move along the path toward enlightenment. As a result, Buddhism relies on lists of precepts that grow longer and more complex as you rise through the levels of enlightenment. You've already seen hints of this in Chapter 5, when we described the Four Noble Truths and the Eightfold Way with its three divisions. In this chapter, we'll concentrate on the Three Jewels of Buddhism: Buddha, dharma, and sangha.

Lists of precepts tend to define the dharma in ever-more exacting ways, which means that the number of precepts tends to get bigger and bigger. In general, though, they all derive from five basic concepts:

- Abstain from taking life
- Abstain from taking what has not been given
- Abstain from inappropriate sexual conduct
- Abstain from false speech
- Abstain from alcohol [or drugs] that cause carelessness (Maguire 137–142.)

The first principle teaches us that all beings have the right to live. This leads many Buddhists toward vegetarianism, though even monks sometimes eat

<<< **His Holiness Tenzin Gyatso** is the 14th Dalai Lama in the Yellow Hats tradition.

meat if it has been given to them. The second reminds us to respect the rights and welfare of others, while the third shields Buddhists from reckless masturbation, promiscuous sex, adultery, and rape. (Tantric sex, of course, appropriately focuses on enlightenment.) The fourth guideline requires Buddhists to refrain from lies, for they create bad karma. The fifth, prohibiting the use of alcohol or drugs, helps Buddhists to remain mindful and to concentrate on enlightenment rather than on physical pleasure.

Lists of precepts, like many Buddhist traditions, vary by time and place. Monks typically follow—and memorize—many more than lay believers. These may include observing the correct mealtime (once a day after sunrise but before noon); avoiding music, dance, and entertainment; relinquishing vain objects such as jewelry, perfume, and makeup;

Lama is someone who has achieved a certain level of spirituality and has the authority to teach others.

Prostration is an act of bowing down to the ground.

Mantra is a sacred verbal formula repeated in meditation.

and abstaining from sleeping in luxurious beds or sitting in lush seats (Maguire 137–142). A good Buddhist remembers that these should be guides rather than laws—following a precept ought never to become an end in and of itself. Rather, each one is a signpost on the road toward breaking the power of Samsara.

The Five, Eight, Ten, and Sixteen Buddhist Precepts

FIVE PRECEPTS

Abstain from:
- Harming living beings
- Taking things not freely given
- Sexual misconduct
- False speech
- Using intoxicating drinks and drugs that cause heedlessness

EIGHT PRECEPTS

Abstain from:
- Harming living beings
- Taking things not freely given
- Sexual misconduct
- False speech
- Using intoxicating drinks and drugs that cause heedlessness
- Taking untimely meals
- Singing, dancing, playing music, and watching grotesque mime
- Using garlands, perfumes, and personal adornments, or sitting and sleeping in luxury

TEN PRECEPTS

Abstain from:
- Harming living beings
- Taking things not freely given
- Sexual misconduct
- False speech
- Using intoxicating drinks and drugs that cause heedlessness
- Taking untimely meals
- Singing, dancing, playing music, and watching grotesque mime
- Using garlands, perfumes, and personal adornments
- Sitting or sleeping in luxury
- Receiving money

SIXTEEN PRECEPTS

THREE JEWELS:
- Taking refuge in the Buddha
- Taking refuge in the dharma
- Taking refuge in the sangha

THREE PURE PRECEPTS:
- Not creating evil
- Practicing good
- Actualizing good for others

TEN GRAVE PRECEPTS:

Abstain from:
- Harming living beings
- Taking things not freely given
- Sexual misconduct
- False speech
- Using intoxicating drinks and drugs that cause heedlessness
- Taking untimely meals
- Singing, dancing, playing music, and watching grotesque mime
- Using garlands, perfumes, and personal adornments
- Sitting or sleeping in luxury
- Receiving money

Further divisions into hundreds of possible precepts to be memorized and followed by monks and nuns

The Precepts provide Buddhists guidelines for daily life. Why do you think the list grows and grows?

MERIT AND GIVING IN THERAVADA BUDDHISM

From studying the lists of precepts, you can see how a Buddhist interacts with the sacred world through a mixture of virtuous actions, morality, and purity. The Theravada tradition places a lot of importance on monastic begging, which offers lay people the opportunity to give alms. When you read the first pages of Chapter 5, this may have seemed a little odd—why didn't the monks just make their own breakfast? Yet, as the description of monks in Myanmar has shown the world, there is great spiritual power and benefit to the process of giving and receiving. Lay people also earn merit by giving robes for the monks to wear or donating money to Buddhist monasteries and temples. Even one's presence at Buddhist sermons and the celebration of others' gift-giving can earn merit (Keown 42–43).

A legend about King Ashoka illustrates this idea. Two young boys named Jaya and Vijaya were playing in the dirt one morning when the Buddha came to seek alms. Jaya, lost in his imaginary world, was pretending that his dirt was grain. Seeing the Buddha, the young boy threw a handful of dirt into the Buddha's bowl. Vijaya approved of this donation by making a gesture of greeting called the **anjali**, his hands pressed together in front of his chest. Although Jaya's contribution to the bowl was only dirt, the Buddha perceived the boys' pure sincerity. Jaya was reborn as the great king Ashoka, and Vijaya as his first minister (Olson 104–105; Keown 42–43).

MEDITATION

The statues of Buddha in the Timber Temple or the Shwedagon Pagoda often portray the Buddha sitting in a lotus position, eyes

<<< In an advanced state of meditation, Buddhist monks can dramatically alter their blood flow, breathing, and even body temperature.

Religion + HEALTH

MIND OVER BODY

Years of practice and the ability to completely focus on mediation give monks incredible control over their bodies. Herbert Benson, a Harvard University medical professor, has conducted experiments with Tibetan monks. In a room set to 40°F, monks wearing thin robes were covered in sheets that had been soaked in 49° water. The average person would begin to shiver uncontrollably and fall into hypothermia. The monks, however, raised their body temperature through meditation until the cloth began to steam. Within an hour, the monks had dried the sheets and stayed completely comfortable. They could do this at will.

Benson found that monks could do the opposite too, using their meditative state to slow their metabolism. When we sleep, we typically use about 10–15 percent less oxygen than when we are awake. The most adept Buddhist monks, however, can slow their oxygen rate by 64 percent, before returning to regular breathing patterns. "It was an astounding, breathtaking [no pun intended] result," said Benson.

Modern brain imaging also confirms what Buddhists have always said—meditation decreases blood flow to the brain while at the same time making some areas more active.

As a medical doctor, Benson's mind turns to the practical application of these techniques. "More than 60 percent of visits to physicians in the United States are due to stress-related problems, most of which are poorly treated by drugs, surgery, or other medical procedures," he says, explaining that meditation could take the place of these highly intrusive and expensive procedures (Cromie).

>>> Modern science has begun to study the effects of meditation on the brain. Note how the left scan has less color than the right one. That's because the left brain scan shows a person not meditation, while the right image was taken after the person began to meditate. Physicians and scientists learn more about both meditation and health in such studies.

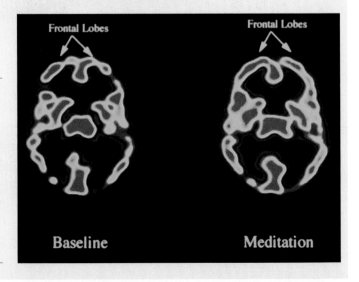

Frontal Lobes   Frontal Lobes

Baseline   Meditation

slightly downward but open—the classic meditative pose. Related to yoga in Hinduism, Buddhist meditation offers a powerful way to interact with the sacred world. Anyone can learn contemplative practices, but in Asian societies monks are more likely to meditate than lay Buddhists, who typically rely on giving and merit (Keown 88–89). Not a sleeping state, meditation produces a high degree of consciousness that includes thoughts, feelings, and perceptions of external circumstances. Rather than dulling consciousness (in the way alcohol can do), meditation raises a Buddhist's perception of the world and his or her control over it. In the most extreme examples, monks in meditation can produce phenomenal mental and physical results.

Anjali is a gesture of greeting one makes by putting the palms together at the chest.

To begin developing a meditative state, Buddhism teaches that we must clear our minds of four "cankers": sexual desire, the desire to live, false views, and ignorance. These overlap with seven more unconscious desires—sexual drive, anger, arrogance, wrong opinions, doubt, craving for life, and ignorance (Olson 95–100). Monks must also conquer greed, hatred, and delusion by replacing them with the product of meditation: charity, love, and knowledge.

▶ HOW DOES THE SACRED BECOME COMMUNITY?

So far we have studied two of the Three Jewels: Buddha and dharma. The final one is sangha, the Buddhist monastic community. While monks directly take refuge in the sangha, lay Buddhists can also find safe haven in the traditions of these Buddhist communities. To the extent that a Buddhist lives in the sangha, he or she replicates the Buddha's own teaching and life.

In ancient times, Buddhist monks often lived a nomadic life, begging for food, meditating, and teaching. The rainy monsoon season in South Asia forced monks to seek shelter for several months each year. As a result, early Buddhist groups established retreats (also called sanghas), for the monks. Over time, people began returning to the same place each season and the sanghas developed into monasteries, sometimes even growing into universities for Buddhist education (Olson 88–95).

Though closed to the public in order to ensure the monastic refuge, Buddhist sanghas play active roles in the community, often providing a central meeting place or focus for religious activities. This also allows lay people to take refuge in the sangha. Of course, the reciprocal arrangement of begging and alms-giving (especially in the Theravada tradition) helps spread good karma to everyone involved.

Monastic Life

To join a sangha, your first step will be to renounce the world and adopt a state of homelessness. One must also exchange worldly riches for a life of poverty, but only if parents or spouses accede to your wish. You cannot use the sangha to escape from debt or to find health care. Upon arrival, you may be instructed to recite the Three Refuges, have your head shaved, and don a robe instead of your worldly wardrobe. You'll receive a begging bowl, two more robes, a sewing needle, razor, and a water strainer to strain insects from your drinking water (so not to kill any living thing) (Olson 90–95).

Beginning as a novice, you will gradually work your way into higher positions in the sangha as you deepen your commitment and tread farther along the dharma path. You'll offer respect to the elder monks who lead the sangha and often act as a spiritual mentor for novices.

More than 200 rules guide and govern monastic life. They grow out of four cardinal precepts: no sex, no killing, no stealing, and no false proclamation of spiritual powers. You will learn these

rules by heart, joining the other monks or nuns in chanting them out loud. As you realize which rules you have disregarded, you'll have regular opportunities to confess your shortcomings to the group.

OUTSIDE THE SANGHA: THE RELATIONSHIP BETWEEN LAY AND MONASTIC LIFE

The relationship between monastic and lay life in Buddhism varies widely across traditions and regions. In Thailand, monasteries meet many of the community's needs by providing teachers for adults and children, creating a space for religious ceremonies, and acting as a center of village administration. Lay Buddhists often honor their monastic brothers, ceremonially thanking them for their service and piety. These customs combine to allow the laity to take an active role in the monastery and take refuge in the sangha (Olson 134–138).

At one time, monasteries monopolized the rural Thai educational system. Now, however, fewer young boys seek out the monasteries to receive their education and become novices. Instead, adolescents and young men may be ordained to complete a sort of novice training for a few weeks or months, perhaps to earn merit on behalf of a deceased loved one. After the boy experiences this brief monkhood, he usually returns to his family. This tradition helps build a strong relationship between the Thai village and the monastery. Even though they have returned to lay life, many men retain bonds with the members of the monastery and among the other villagers who have lived there (Olson 134–140).

In Myanmar, monks lead more separate lives from the community than you'd typically see in Thailand. The monasteries are established outside the villages instead of as part of them, and monks interact with lay Buddhists with far more formality than in other cultures. Here, boys living in the monastery tend to be more "sons of Buddha" rather than "sons of the village," as in Thailand.

Local tradition dictates that deceased lay people are buried while monks and their families receive cremation. Either way, the border between life and death is a fluid one. Living relatives, for example, place pieces of string in the coffin to symbolize themselves and their relationship to the dead person. Monks help families to grieve by chanting mantras that drive the dead person's ghost away from the household and toward its reincarnated body (Olson 136–140).

Sri Lankan culture offers yet another way for monks and laity to interact. There, the lay people take a more active role than in other Buddhist societies by preaching, teaching, and sometimes even questioning monks' holiness (Olson 136).

Monastery and Laity: Tibetan Buddhism

Tibetan Buddhists have sought to recreate the "three refuges" in their national life by aligning their religious and political systems along Buddhist precepts. The Dalai Lama embodies this linkage as the spiritual and political leader of the nation. A few pages ago, we read how Jaya's dirt offering to the Buddha allowed him to be reborn as the great king Ashoka. In Tibet, the Dalai Lamas have sought to play a role similar to that of Ashoka, using the economic and political system to further development of Buddhism. As an incarnate bodhisattva, the Dalai Lama is a living embodiment of enlightenment. His followers can therefore take refuge in the Buddha through him. Likewise, as a political leader, the Dalai Lama can pass laws that reflected the dharma. Before the Chinese invasion of 1950, Tibet had more Buddhist monks per capita than anywhere else in the world, and spent a large percentage of its wealth maintaining monasteries across the country. In this way, the Tibetan system blurred the lines between government, monastery, and community in order to create a kind of national sangha, a society where all Buddhists could take refuge.

Buddhism Without a Monastic Sangha: Buddhism Comes to the West

Though it had spread across Asia, Buddhism had nearly no presence in United States until the 1860s, when a large influx of Asian immigrants arrived in America. During the Gold Rush of 1849, many Chinese men traveled to California to work on railroads and in the gold mines. By 1870, tens of thousands of Chinese immigrants were living in the United States, establishing temples and shrines as they settled permanently. Yet they stayed more or less isolated from the largely Judeo-Christian society. Failure to adopt mainstream American cultural beliefs eventually led to discrimination and the passing of the Chinese Exclusion Act of 1882, which prohibited Chinese immigration to the United States. This effectively stunted the spread of Buddhism in America (Maguire 165–196).

One turning point in the rise of popularity of Buddhism occurred at the Chicago World's Fair of 1893, during The World's Parliament of Religions. The Old World and the New World were, for a moment brought together, marking a step toward cultural and religious tolerance in the United States. Many religious leaders spoke publicly, including a Sri Lankan Theravada Buddhist and a Zen Buddhist from Japan (Maguire 167–168).

∧
∧ **When East meets West**—a Buddhist monk wearing Converse "Chuck
∧ Taylor" Allstars sneakers.

Tibet and China

Relations between the Himalayan country of Tibet and neighboring China have been strained for centuries. Although China claimed this territory in 1720, Tibet has primarily functioned as a separate country, and in 1913 the 13th Dalai Lama proclaimed its complete independence with himself as the spiritual and political leader.

After a takeover of China by communists in 1949, the new Chinese government reinstated its influence over Tibet and enforced its claim to the "hermit kingdom." In 1959, Tibetans rose up against communist rule and the 14th Dalai Lama fled to India and exile. In 2009, 50 years later, the Dalai Lama still cannot return to Tibet. China regularly attacks the Dalai Lama and promotes a version of history in which the Tibetan people asked the Chinese government to integrate Tibet into the communist system.

Tibetans want to be able to practice Buddhism, preserve their culture, and limit the number of ethnically Han Chinese in Tibet (NBC). While Tibetans stage protests and voice their unhappiness over this rule, the Chinese government maintains that it acts as a positive influence in Tibet by building roads, hospitals, schools, and factories to stimulate the economy (Stewart).

In an effort to find a resolution, the Dalai Lama has adopted a nonviolent approach following the Buddhist "middle way." His plan would allow greater autonomy for Tibet, assure freedom of religion and culture, but accept China's political rule. The Dalai Lama's exile, nonviolent protests, and efforts to achieve peace with China have gained worldwide attention over the years. In 1989, he was awarded the Nobel Peace Prize for his efforts. However, in a 2009 interview with NBC News, the Dalai Lama lamented that his tactics over 50 years have not borne fruit, saying "I publicly accept failure of our approach" (NBC).

Now more than 70 years old, the Dalai Lama's health has begun to falter. If he dies before signing an agreement with China, many observers fear that there will be no way to find peace in the region. The next Dalai Lama will take time to be found and may be a young child who would be unable to rule immediately. China will likely try to influence the identity of the next Dalai Lama, following a pattern they've established with other Tibetan lamas. But until then, the Dalai Lama continues to take the long view. Though reviled by the Chinese government as a "jackal clad in Buddhist monk's robes," he muses that "not getting what you want is often a wonderful stroke of luck" (MacKinnon).

∧∧∧ Buddhists show their love and loyalty to the Dalai Lama and a free Tibet. How might both of these photos illustrate that love? Do the images fit your conception of Buddhism?

∧
∧
∧ **Buddhist traditions can change according to circumstances.** Why do you think that these Los Angeles monks stay inside to receive alms, rather than begging on the street?

Many Westerners have tended to gravitate to Mahayana traditions with their emphasis on lay Buddhism. However, Theravada Buddhists have also flourished in the United States. In 1966, the first Theravada monastery in the United States was built in Washington, DC, followed closely by the Wat Thai Center in Los Angeles. Today, there are more than 150 Theravada monasteries throughout the United States (Maguire 170–175).

Zen Buddhism (a form of Mahayana that we will discuss in more detail in Chapters 7 and 8), was the first branch of Buddhism to appeal to a large group of Americans. Interest in Zen soared after World War II due to the large number of American soldiers stationed in Japan (Maguire 178–88). The 1960s counterculture embraced Zen, as author Jack Kerouac published *Dharma Bums* and *Wake Up: A Life of The Buddha*. In fact, Zen has become so much a part of the American cultural landscape that it's even used as shorthand, as in "I tried to be Zen about failing the physics exam." The first book I read as a freshman in college was Robert Pirsig's *Zen and the Art of Motorcycle Maintenance*. Years later, that classic hybrid of American and Zen philosophy has spawned another bestseller, Matthew P. Crawford's *Shop Class as Soulcraft*.

Conclusion

Think back to the beginnings of Chapters 5 and 6. You can almost imagine a movie in your mind: a peaceful temple with a large Buddha image at the center; monks quietly leaving in the early morning hours to beg for food from their community. But that peaceful scene is shattered by a shot of Myanmar monks defying police, leading protests against the government, and enduring beatings and killings. Both of these scenes illustrate important aspects of modern-day Buddhism.

By protesting with their begging bowls overturned, the Buddhist monks acted with both religious and political resolve. This portrayed the rulers of Myanmar as outside the sangha, shunned from the sacred community. By rejecting alms from the military government, the monks also refused to let the leaders develop good karma through giving. Instead, the monks' actions spotlighted leaders' desire for power and wealth, which ultimately hurt both themselves and the people of Myanmar. In turning over their bowls, the monks showed the world that the citizens of Myanmar had been forced to suffer for the actions of their leaders, whose cravings had bankrupted the nation.

The Buddha provided a path away from suffering and toward enlightenment. **Does this make him a god? That depends.**

∨∨∨

Buddhists believe humans are made up of four different parts that constantly interact and change: **body, senses, mind, and consciousness.**

∨∨∨

IS THERE A GOD?

Is there a god? Maybe. Calling himself simply "one who is awake," the Buddha never claimed to be a god. Yet some Buddhists do describe him in terms that resemble the divine, with an earthly, heavenly, and transcendent body. Additionally, many Buddhists acknowledge a realm inhabited by deities who can die and be reincarnated, just like humans, animals, or insects. These deities exist on a higher level than those on earth. Assistance from local gods does not preclude a Buddhist from looking to Buddha for help with the ultimate goal of breaking out of the cycle of reincarnation.

HOW DOES THE SACRED BECOME COMMUNITY?

The sacred can become community through the sangha. Often, the monastery is a vital part of the community where it is located. Additionally, monks provide lay people the opportunity to give freely, which in turn provides the lay people a chance to take refuge in the sangha. Finally, the sangha can grow to become an entire nation (like Tibet) or a community of Buddhists without a centralized monastic structure (as in the USA).

WHAT DOES IT MEAN TO BE HUMAN?

In Buddhism, human nature has no independent soul, but rather a constantly changing mixture of different characteristics. Humans can work toward enlightenment and nirvana by following the Eightfold Path. While they work toward this goal, people must realize that nothing is permanent and they themselves, as well as the world around them, is constantly changing.

HOW DO HUMANS INTERACT WITH THE SACRED?

Buddhists interact with the sacred in many ways, but especially by taking refuge in the Three Jewels of Buddhism. Followers can interact with the sacred by striving to live like Buddha, by obeying his teachings, and by contributing to the sangha. Interactions with the sacred have been codified in many lists of precepts, including the Six Perfections, and The Five, Eight, Ten, and Sixteen Precepts.

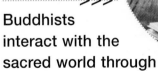

<<< **Thai Buddhist** renunciants collect alms.

>>> **Buddhists interact with the sacred world through** virtuous actions, morality, and purity.

REVIEW

06

Summary

HOW DO HUMANS INTERACT WITH THE SACRED?   p. 70

- To follow the Buddha means to live like him according to the Eightfold Path. By living and thinking rightly, you'll build a more enlightened version of yourself.

- Tibetan Buddhists have developed their own tradition. They emphasize tantric rituals, which include hand gestures, visualizations, prostrations, and sacred mantras. Mantras aid in meditation, and visualization offers a way to control bodily activities such as temperature and respiration.

HOW DOES THE SACRED BECOME COMMUNITY?   p. 75

- Though closed to the public in order to ensure monastic refuge, Buddhist sanghas play active roles in the community, often providing a central meeting place or focus for religious activities.

- The Dalai Lama is a living embodiment of enlightenment. His followers can therefore take refuge in the Buddha through him. Likewise, as a political leader, the Dalai Lama can pass laws that reflect dharma.

Key Terms

Three Jewels of Buddhism are Buddha, dharma, and sangha.   *70*

Tantra is a set of instructions said to be given by the Buddha to a group of his students. These teachings are widely used in Tibetan Buddhism.   *71*

Lama is someone who has achieved a certain level of spirituality and has the authority to teach others.   *72*

Prostration is an act of bowing down to the ground.   *72*

Mantra is a sacred verbal formula repeated in prayer and meditation.   *72*

Anjali is a gesture of greeting one makes by putting the palms together at the chest.   *74*

Find it on

- http://www.youtube.com/watch?v=Sv4oNQySSzY
  Visit the ThinkSpot to watch a fascinating video from England's SkyNews. It shows Buddhist monks protesting the oppressive regime in Burma. Videos of monks in prayer and in nonviolent protest abound in this clip which also provides a clear and concise explanation of the problem in Rangoon and the role of the monk in the Burmese family and society.

- http://www.ehow.com/how_2073363
  _become-buddhist-monk.html

It has been said that you can find just about anything on the Internet. In the case of becoming a Buddhist monk, this certainly is true! Searching for information as to how to become a Buddhist monk returned countless sites devoted to this endeavor. We picked the most straightforward and accessible information available and have included it on the ThinkSpot for you.

Questions for Study and Review

1. All Buddhists take refuge in the Buddha, dharma, and sangha. Explain what each of these means as well as the meaning of "taking refuge."

"Taking refuge" means participating and practicing; taking refuge in the Buddha means modeling your life after the Buddha's. When you take refuge in the dharma, you use the Buddha's doctrine as a guide by which to live. For monks, this means taking the vow of poverty and becoming an ordained monk. For lay Buddhists, it can mean giving to the monastery.

2. Describe the Bodhisattva tradition of Mahayana Buddhism.

The Bodhisattva is a tradition in which an enlightened person purposefully chooses to be reincarnated, coming back to this world to help others achieve enlightenment, as illustrated in representations of the Five Buddhas, the historical Buddha and four bodhasittvas who became buddhas.

3. In Buddhism, what is the goal of meditation?

Buddhist meditation leads to greater enlightenment. It can be learned by anyone, but is more likely to be done by a monk because the mind must be trained. It also must be totally clear and pure, so that the so-called "cankers" (sexual desire, the desire to live, false views, and ignorance) can be eliminated. These cankers often reside in us unconsciously and can consume our minds if they are not counteracted. Masters of meditation can gain control over their entire bodies to achieve this. They can even control their breathing and body heat.

4. How did Buddhism become recognized in the Western world? Provide two examples.

1. Initial Chinese immigrants, most of whom were Buddhist, came to the western United States during the Gold Rush of 1849. Eventually settling down, they established monasteries and shrines.

2. The influence of the Dalai Lama has provoked a greater understanding and familiarization of Buddhism as well as the history of Tibet.

For Further Study

BOOKS:

Armstrong, Karen. *Buddha*. New York: Viking Adult, 2001.

Dalai Lama. *The World of Tibetan Buddhism: An Overview of Its Philosophy and Practice*. Somerville, MA: Wisdom Publications, 1995.

Keown, Damien. *Buddhism: A Very Short Introduction*. Oxford, UK: Oxford University Press, 1996.

Maguire, Jack. *Essential Buddhism: A Complete Guide to Beliefs and Practices*. New York: Pocket Books, 2001.

Olson, Carl. *The Different Paths of Buddhism: A Narrative-Historical Introduction.* New Brunswick: Rutgers University Press.

Rahula, Rapola. *What the Buddha Taught: Revised and Expanded Edition with Texts from Suttas and Dhammapada*. New York: Grove Press, 1974.

WEB SITES:

Buddhist Temples: Paths to Salvation.
http://www.buddhist-temples.com

Buddhanet: Buddhist Education and Information Network.
http://www.buddhanet.net

Sacred Texts: Buddhism.
http://www.sacred-texts.com/bud/index.htm

<<< The calm of an early spring morning. Might this photo, like the symbol below, represent the Supreme Ultimate? How?

Q

IS THERE A GOD?
WHAT DOES IT MEAN TO BE HUMAN?

You've likely seen the symbol on this page, maybe even as a friend's tattoo. In the west, we often call it the "yin/yang." In Chinese, it is called the taiji or the tai chi, meaning the "Supreme Ultimate." What do you think it means? The symbol is a circle, half white and half black. It's divided in a curvy way, as if the circle is rolling, not standing still. Neither of the halves of the circles is completely black or white. Each half contains a bit of the other color.

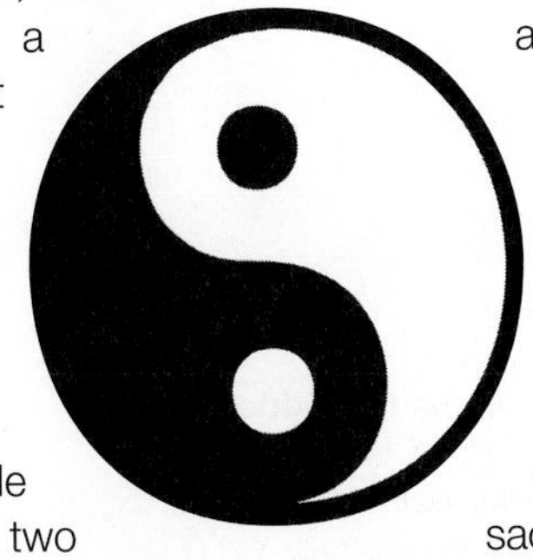

Each part of the image has significance. The circle itself stands for wholeness—the whole world, the whole cosmos, time, people, everything. The two colors swirling through the circle remind us that the universe constantly changes. The colors are deferent but equal—there is the same amount of black and white in the circle. They teach us that there are opposites in the world—up and down, male and female, good and bad, strong and weak, hot and cold, working in tandem with each other. For example, how can you understand hot unless you have experienced cold?

We also see that each half of the circle contains some of the other color in it. The black half holds a bit of white; the white half has a spot of black, showing us that there is a little of the opposite in everything and everyone—a little bad in everything good, and vice versa. Importantly, though, the opposites remain in equilibrium, reminding us that there must be harmony in the world. Finally, that rolling movement demonstrates that all things in life turn from good to bad and back to good.

By studying the Supreme Ultimate, we can glimpse the basis for East Asian sacred ideas. As you read this chapter, refer back to the Supreme Ultimate, because it will help you to organize the many shades of sacred traditions that date back thousands of years in China and other parts of Asia, especially Japan, Korea, and Vietnam. Both Confucianism and Daoism, our main topics for this chapter, have developed from ideas embodied in the Supreme Ultimate. Buddhism, which arrived from India about 2300 years ago, has also integrated the Supreme Ultimate into its perception of the world.

EAST ASIAN SACRED WAYS: The Eternal Dao

CHAPTER 07

Chang Ling

YOU'VE DECIDED TO SEE CHANG LING, THE GARDEN AND TOMBS OF THIRTEEN MING DYNASTY EMPERORS. Put on a good pair of sneakers and begin to stroll on the Sacred Way, more than four miles of dead-straight path toward your destination. As you walk, you'll pass 18 pairs of statues: stone guards stare down at you, bureaucratic officials note your appearance, and elephants (realistic and in bad humor) watch your progress. Getting closer to the Great Red Gate, a hulking ominous building, you must first pass mythical Qilin—the horned, hooved, mythical giraffe-like beasts that appear when a true sage has arrived on Earth.

Finally, step past the columns topped with dragons. Go through the gate. Down the stairs, sitting in a formal garden, is the huge Hall of Eminent Favors. Inside, you'll find the bronze statue of the Ming Dynasty emperor named Yongle. He sits on a throne looking a little like Confucius, a little like the Buddha. Gazing out of the hall, Yongle views a world both natural and contrived—each rock in its place, each tree perfectly coiffed, the world ordered according to the mandate of Heaven.

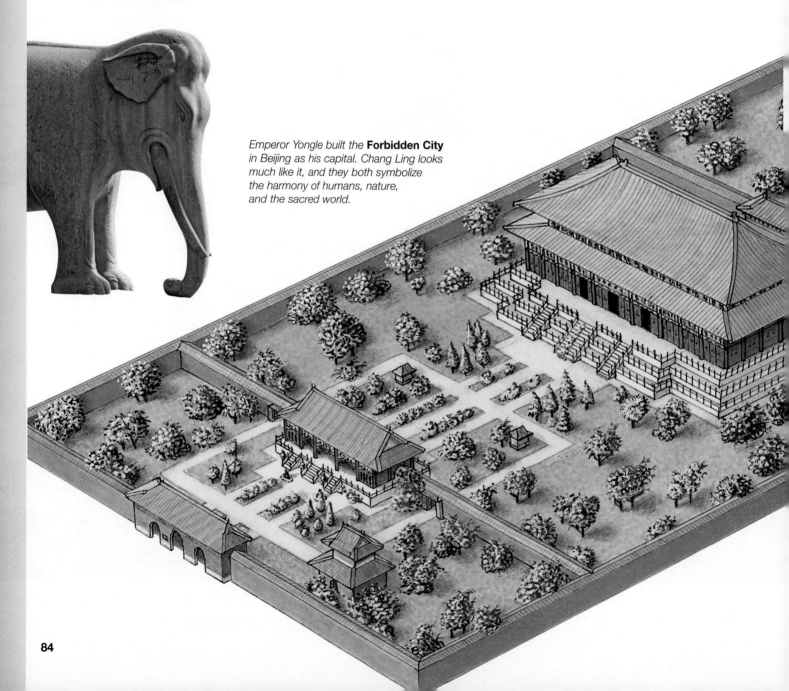

Emperor Yongle built the **Forbidden City** *in Beijing as his capital. Chang Ling looks much like it, and they both symbolize the harmony of humans, nature, and the sacred world.*

Why might the Great Red Gate look like the Buddhist pagoda in Chapter 5?

The Emperor Yongle (Yung-Lo) lived from May 2, 1360 to August 12, 1424. Note how solid he looks on his throne—what does that tell you about his reputation?

path as an illustration
sm—the way toward a
straight and narrow,
hing in its place.

The natural way of Daoism surrounds the organized way of Confucianism. So too does the garden surround the path.

By ancient tradition, the Chinese Emperor ruled by the Mandate of Heaven. All dragons and humans defended and served.

The Qilin

▶ IS THERE A GOD?

When we discussed Buddhism in Chapter 5, we learned that a god might exist or might not. The question becomes even more complicated to answer as we consider Buddhism alongside other East Asian traditions. Depending on whom you ask, which sources you read, or how you define god, you're bound to get different answers. In this vast area that includes China, Japan, Korea, Vietnam, and other countries, you may receive any (or all) of the following answers: "There is a god," "There are many gods," "There are no gods," or even, "It depends."

East Asia is huge, but China has dominated the region's politics and culture for many centuries. Many East Asian philosophical and religious ideas developed there, spreading and changing northward toward Korea, southward toward Vietnam, Laos, and Cambodia, and across the sea to Japan. One feature—the Dao—dominates this tradition. The Dao created everything, yet it's elusive. It lacks personality and a name like a Hindu god, but has creative power unlike the Buddha. We might think of it as a universal "power" rather than a "god." People from outside this tradition often find it difficult to grasp the concept.

That being said, people in this vast region sometimes also acknowledge one, several, or countless other deities. Your dead ancestors may be deified, and you too might become a god. So, yes, the best answer to the question "Is there a god?" in traditional East Asian religions may be

"It's complicated." In that case, we may have better luck studying what is *sacred* instead of looking only for *gods* in East Asia.

Dao, Qi, and Yin/Yang

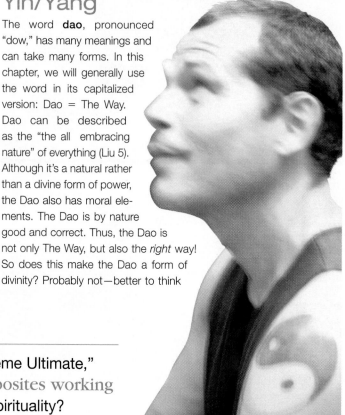

The word **dao**, pronounced "dow," has many meanings and can take many forms. In this chapter, we will generally use the word in its capitalized version: Dao = The Way. Dao can be described as the "the all embracing nature" of everything (Liu 5). Although it's a natural rather than a divine form of power, the Dao also has moral elements. The Dao is by nature good and correct. Thus, the Dao is not only The Way, but also the *right* way! So does this make the Dao a form of divinity? Probably not—better to think

>>> The yin yang, or Taiji symbol, means the "Supreme Ultimate," representing wholeness and the relationship of opposites working in tandem. How might this apply to the concept of spirituality?

A SACRED ACTION ▶▶▶

Tai Chi

Perhaps you have strolled through a park and come across a lone individual moving seamlessly from pose to pose in perpetual motion. Maybe you have happened upon a group in a public garden, moving wordlessly in unison. Without instruction, only by means of the connectedness of the group, all members seem to reach skyward and then retreat, or push at an invisible boulder and then roll it back again, going from one movement to another in harmony. They are practicing taijiquan, better known in the west as tai chi, an ancient form of martial arts. It is no accident that people practice tai chi outdoors, since the movements and poses seem to come from the very surroundings of nature, mimicking the breeze,

growing from the earth, floating like a cloud. You might describe their movements as a kind of dance, or perhaps meditation, or maybe exercise. It doesn't look so hard, but try to follow their patterns and you'll learn otherwise. So what's the point? Elegant and composed, in doing tai chi these people explore the world around them, learning too about the world inside themselves (Renard 206–207).

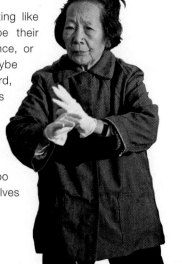

of it halfway between a neutral natural law (like gravity) and a divine being who controls nature (like Vishnu).

Qi (chi), pronounced "chee," emanates from Dao. Both matter and energy, qi constantly moves and alters according to no will of its own, but permeates everything in the cosmos; as a result, everything is interconnected in this organic whole (Liu 6–7). To explain the relationship of the Dao to qi, imagine the ocean from the point of view of a fish. The ocean (Dao) is made up of water (qi). It is everywhere, but it is not a static form of matter. Rather, you live in water, breathe it, push off it to swim, and swim through it. Water regulates your temperature and provides your food. All around you, water is a *thing*, but it is also *animated*—it does not just sit there but is constantly moving and changing. Like water, qi can be cleaner or dirtier, more pure or less so. The higher the being, the more pure its qi.

Dao can mean the path or the way; it encompasses the nature of everything.

Qi is matter or energy that comes from the Dao. Qi is the totality of things and is in perpetual motion.

Yet water does not equal the ocean. From a fish's point of view, the ocean churns water into waves, creating the currents and the tide. The ocean and its power constantly influence your fish-life, even though you cannot always perceive what is going on. As a fish, you can never hope to control the ocean or to see its edges. It is the life-giving reality, the absolute and everything. It is the "ultimate absolute." It is the Dao.

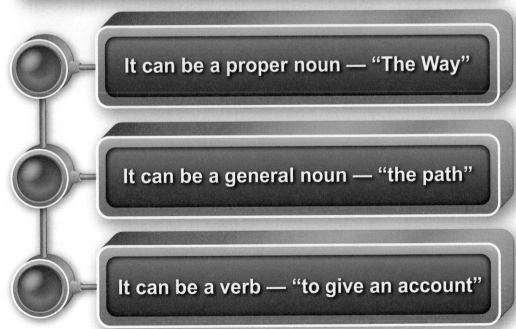

>>> Chinese is a character-based, rather than alphabet-based language. For this reason, Chinese characters can be written in many forms and also translated into English in many ways. How does its use as a noun, proper noun, or verb tie into the concept of the Dao?

Yin is passive energy and makes up a part of qi. Yin cannot exist without yang.

Yang, together with yin, makes up qi. Yang is active energy and cannot exist without yin.

Trigrams are symbols of three lines each that show how yin and yang interact in the world.

Divination tells the future by showing people their place in the cosmos.

YIN AND YANG

In the next step of our study on Dao and qi, however, the water metaphor breaks down. Like water and its two elements (hydrogen and oxygen), qi also has two parts—**yin** and **yang**. Unlike water and its elements, though, qi cannot be broken into component parts. What's more, the relationship of yin to yang changes constantly. The sum of yin and yang is qi, but you'll never know precisely how much of each one exists at any given moment. This might be understood as the "competitive cooperation" of yin and yang; one exists only because the other does, too. Together they make up something bigger: qi.

Now that we have looked at the ideas of Dao, qi, and yin/yang, think back to the symbol of the Supreme Ultimate. It represents the whole universe—the Dao. You can see matter (the black and white colors) and movement (the curvy line). Two dots—black inside of white, white inside of black—remind us that nothing exists without its opposite. The colors compete against one another, but they also rely on each other. Mix the black and white and you'll have a dreary field of gray rather than a vibrant image. (No one would get a tattoo of that.) Finally, we see that the Dao embodies the entire universe: Yin and yang constantly dance and compete with each other,

organizing qi, which in turn constitutes the Dao. Such wisdom in one little picture—no wonder people want it inked onto their bodies.

The *Yijing (I Ching)*

Much of our knowledge about these issues comes from a book called *Yijing (I Ching)*, "The Book of Changes." Written in bits and pieces, aphorisms and descriptions, the book took 1,500 years (2000 BCE to 500 BCE) to grow into its present form. Imagine it as a graphic version of the Dao in which we see yin and yang as lines rather than pictures. The Yijing represents yin as a broken line and yang as a solid one.

- broken line = yin (— —)
- solid line = yang (——)

Yin and yang have many metaphorical meanings. Generally, yin (black) passively accepts energy, while yang (white) actively creates it. Yin, as you might guess, represents the female, while yang is male.

You can always break the solid yang line into two yin lines or put together the two yin lines to create a yang. Groups of three called **trigrams**, produce a total of eight possible graphic images to illustrate how yin and yang create everything around us. Actually, trigrams represent not so much a word, existential state, or thought; rather, they characterize the movement of energy from below to above. In other words, trigrams illustrate changing nature, not a static existence. Trigrams appear static but they illustrate change, like snapshots of a runner in mid stride.

From eight trigrams we can create 64 hexagrams, each of which represents a changing force of nature—the shifting states of qi. Hexagrams also have metaphorical and moral meanings. These little combinations of lines bond natural phenomena, the flow of our lives, and morality. The lines, trigrams, and hexagrams remind us that

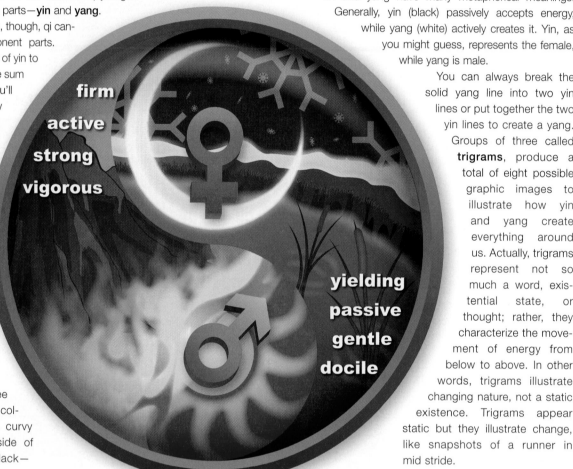

firm
active
strong
vigorous

yielding
passive
gentle
docile

Source: Liu, J., *An Introduction to Chinese Philosophy: From Ancient Philosophy to Chinese Buddhism*, (Malden, MA: Blackwell Publishing, 2005).

∧
∧ Yin and yang oppose each other but also work
∧ together. Yin represents femininity, the moon, the lake, water, and cold. Yang stands for masculinity, the sun, the mountain, fire, and heat. What other traits do you think yin and yang might symbolize? Do you think these are universal ideas or ones related just to one's culture?

The Eight Trigrams

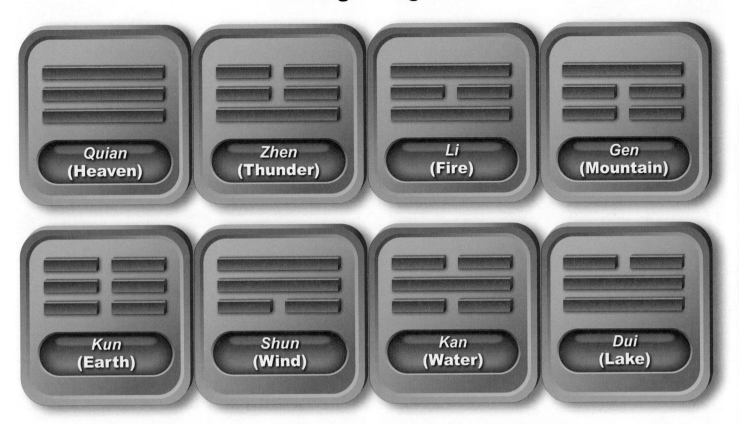

Source: Liu, J., *An Introduction to Chinese Philosophy: From Ancient Philosophy to Chinese Buddhism*, (Malden, MA: Blackwell Publishing, 2005), 27.

∧
∧ The eight trigrams depict different natural elements by combining "yin" lines with "yang"
∧ lines. **How do they relate to the Dao?**

we live as changing elements in a huge physical, cosmic, and moral force that embodies goodness. Using different techniques, a diviner can read the trigrams and hexagrams to help a person understand his or her place in a changing universe. Less fortune-telling than cosmic analysis, **divination** seeks to understand a person's place in a dynamic, interconnected universe unified through the Dao. I often think of divination as a cosmic GPS system, linking me to the cosmos and giving me direction, just as my GPS connects me to multiple moving satellites and tells me how to find my ultimate destination.

Confucianism, Daoism, and Buddhism: Syncretic Traditions in East Asia

The two great Chinese philosophical systems, Confucianism and Daoism, grow from the Dao, qi, yin/yang, and the Yijing.

This intermingling of Confucianism, Daoism, and Buddhism led to changes in all three. In some cases, one tradition took on characteristics

<<< **Does this look familiar?** The flag of South Korea includes both the Supreme Ultimate and four important trigrams. **Clockwise from top left, the trigrams represent heaven, water, earth, and fire.**

∧
∧ Merchants carried spices, silk, and other luxuries on the Silk Route. Philosophies and religions
∧ tagged along inside the hearts and minds of the traders as they trekked. How might beliefs
become transformed and adapted when introduced into a different cultural system?

of another. In other cases, however, one solidified its ideas in opposition to outside beliefs. In both situations, however, the presence of more than one tradition affected how each one developed and changed over time. Scholars call this phenomenon *syncretism*, and you've already studied it in regard to Hinduism and Buddhism. As you can imagine, though, it is sometimes impossible to figure out exactly what is Confucian, Daoist, and Buddhist. That's fine—we don't need to apply forced distinctions because we're studying the entire fabric of sacred life in East Asia.

THE DIVINE IN CONFUCIANISM

Before we can answer the question "Is there a god in Confucianism?" we should learn a little more about Confucius, his life in China, and his teachings. Like many words that have been brought into English, "Confucius" and "Confucianism" only approximate the real words as used in Chinese. In this case, scholars transliterated the name K'ung-fu-tzu (Wade-Giles) or Kongzi (Pinyin) into Confucius. They even added the "us" to make it sound more academically Latin! The Chinese usually call this tradition "Rujia." In the Western world, however, most

scholars and students (even those who speak Chinese) use the terms Confucius and Confucianism, so we will, too.

The man known as Confucius was born in 551 BCE, in Lu, a feudal state in today's Shandong Province of China. Although of aristocratic lineage, his family had been reduced to paupers by the time of his birth. Even at a young age, he demonstrated a predilection for learning and spent his life in pursuit of knowledge and self-improvement, seeking out masters to instruct him. Confucius learned the classical Chinese traditions of poetry and history and mastered the "six arts" of ritual, music, archery, charioteering, calligraphy, and arithmetic. He began teaching in his 30s.

Confucius initially aspired to a political career. Early on, he served in minor government posts (such as bookkeeping for granaries) and later worked as a magistrate and assistant minister of public works in his 40s and 50s. He hoped to expand education in China. Above all, Confucius became convinced that advancement of society grew from individual self-improvement. Learn to live in harmony with each other, he reasoned, and all of society would benefit. It is "virtuous manners," he taught, "which constitute the excellence of a neighborhood" (Confucius *Analects*, IV: 1). Not just pragmatism, Confucius reasoned that virtue would ultimately help people follow the Dao.

Confucius, like other Chinese, viewed the community as reaching backward to our ancestors and forward to our children. To maintain the flow of time as freely as possible, Confucius taught the importance of etiquette and tradition as the conduit for values, social norms, and harmonious existence. He called himself "A transmitter and not a maker, believing in and loving the ancients" (Confucius *Analects*, VII: 1).

Because of the troubled world in which he lived, Confucius thought it was more important to study society than the sacred realm, focusing on human issues instead of discussing "extraordinary things, feats of strength, disorder, and spiritual beings" (Confucius *Analects*, VII: 20). Even so, Confucius lived in a world inhabited by spirits of ancestors, of grain, of the land, and of many natural forces, called **shen**. Confucius actively sacrificed to the spirits of ancestors, but he focused on matters pertaining to this world, saying that a good life on Earth would bring

Shen are spirits of ancestors in traditional China.

harmony with the cosmos: "I do not murmur against Heaven. I do not grumble against men" (Confucius *Analects*, XXXVII: 2). Confucius didn't disown the shen, but instead linked life on Earth to that in the afterlife: "If you are not able to serve men, how can you serve their spirits?" (Confucius *Analects*, XI: 11). By showing obedience to the social order, he reasoned, a person simultaneously followed the "will of heaven," honoring the shen and following the Dao.

THE DIVINE IN DAOISM (TAOISM)

Let's return once again to the symbol of the Supreme Ultimate. Think about Confucianism as yang—active. In order for this to exist, there must also be a passive yin—Daoism. Based on the same underlying principles of Dao and qi, Daoists hope to *accept* the Dao passively rather than actively *pursuing* it through Confucian precepts. It's generally easier to understand Confucian ideas than Daoist ones, so don't be troubled if it doesn't come to you immediately.

Daoism grows from the writings of Laozi (Lao Tzu), the "Old Master," who may have never even existed. It is possible that he is an assemblage of many scholars of the fourth and third centuries BCE; however, because we do not know for certain, it is customary to study Laozi as if he were a real person. Tradition says that Laozi wrote out his ideas in a book called *Daodejing* (*Tao-Te Ching*) sometime in the sixth century BCE, which would have made Laozi a rough contemporary of Confucius. More likely, however, scholars compiled the *Daodejing* over the centuries, solidifying into its known form sometime in the first century CE.

The *Daodejing* explains that human can neither explain nor control the universe. This makes for some difficult reading. Its famous first lines go like this:

> As for the Way, the Way that can be spoken of is not the constant Way;
>
> As for names, the name that can be named is not the constant name.
>
> The nameless is the beginning of the ten thousand things;
>
> The named is the mother of the ten thousand things.
>
> Therefore, those constantly without desires, by this means will perceive its subtlety.
>
> Those constantly with desires, by this means will see only that which they yearn for and seek.
>
> These two together emerge;
>
> They have different names yet they're called the same;
>
> That which is even more profound than the profound—
>
> The gateway of all subtleties (Lao-Tzu 53).

In other words—you can never really understand ("name") something and hope to explain its essence. You can never achieve perfection by your own will and actions. In fact, the harder you try to understand The Way and follow The Way, the more it will elude you. Another way to think about this is to return to the scenario of the fish and the ocean. As a fish, you cannot understand the ocean (Dao) or control the water (qi). You would be foolish to think you could! Rather, you learn to swim by using the water around you, traveling long distances by surfing the tides and streams of the water. This is what it means to "realize the mystery" of the Dao.

THINK World Religions

The Analects

After his death, in 497 BCE, Confucius's followers compiled his teachings into a single volume, which is still our main source for understanding his ideas. It takes a while to get accustomed to Confucius's teaching and philosophical style. The little sentences, called analects, seem to hang in the air after you've read them. Here is a sample:

Confucius said, "There are three friendships which are advantageous, and three which are injurious. Friendship with the upright; friendship with the sincere; and friendship with the man of much observation—these are advantageous. Friendship with the man of specious airs; friendship with the insinuatingly soft; and friendship with the glib-tongued—these are injurious."

Confucius said, "There are three things men find enjoyment in which are advantageous, and three things they find enjoyment in which are injurious. To find enjoyment in the discriminating study of ceremonies and music; to find enjoyment in speaking of the goodness of others; to find enjoyment in having many worthy friends—these are advantageous. To find enjoyment in extravagant pleasures; to find enjoyment in idleness and sauntering; to find enjoyment in the pleasures of feasting—these are injurious."

Confucius said, "There are three errors to which they who stand in the presence of a man of virtue and station are liable. They may speak when it does not come to them to speak—this is called rashness. They may not speak when it comes to them to speak—this is called concealment. They may speak without looking at the countenance of their superior—this is called blindness."

Confucius said, "There are three things which the superior man guards against. In youth, when the physical powers are not yet settled, he guards against lust. When he is strong and the physical powers are full of vigor, he guards against quarrelsomeness. When he is old, and the animal powers are decayed, he guards against covetousness."

Confucius said, "There are three things of which the superior man stands in awe. He stands in awe of the ordinances of Heaven. He stands in awe of great men. He stands in awe of the words of sages" (Confucius *Analects*, XVI: 4–7).

www.thethinkspot.com

<<< On the left: the Jade Emperor; on the right: the Three Pure Ones. How do you think these gods relate to the concepts of harmony and The Way?

deity. Although known for centuries, Daoists began turning to the Jade Emperor in the first century CE to ask for favors. Early stories of the Queen Mother of the West emphasized her ferocity, a goddess with sharp teeth. Daoists slowly changed that perception, looking to her as the embodiment of a long life.

- *The Three Pure Ones* directly emanate from the Dao. The Celestial Worthy of the Way and Its Power, the Celestial Worthy of Primordial Beginning, and the Celestial Worthy of Numinous Treasure each embodies an aspect of the Dao. One of these three, the Celestial Worthy of the Way and Its Power is the deified version of Laozi himself.

- *Numens* live around us at all times. These spirit-beings associate themselves with specific places and people. Although we don't generally notice them, adept Daoists—those in tune with The Way—can communicate with these spirits. If you travel around China, you're likely to see dozens of small shrines to Tudi Gong, often just called "Grandpa." Chinese look to him as a sort of cosmic bureaucrat who can help them achieve wealth, help with

There is a moral element to this, too; as you act in harmony with the Dao, you also attain **De**, which might be translated as "virtue," though it also has shades of "excellence" and "charismatic force." Living on The Way produces virtue, making it a moral force in addition to its natural power. When you develop virtue in Daoism, you may also cultivate various other attributes and powers (Littlejohn 16–17; Liu 143). Here is Laozi's introduction to De. As you read it, consider how he might agree or disagree with Confucius.

> The highest virtue is not virtuous; therefore it truly has virtue.
> The lowest virtue never loses sight of its virtue; therefore it has no true virtue.
> The highest virtue takes no action, yet it has no reason for acting this way;
> The highest humanity takes action, yet it has no reason for acting this way;
> The highest righteousness takes action, and it has its reasons for acting this way;
> The highest propriety takes action, and when no one responds to it, then it angrily rolls up its sleeves and forces people to comply (Lao-Tzu 7).

As you read these lines, you may notice no references to deities or spirits. In fact, scholars often say that you can be a philosophical Daoist without paying attention to any supernatural beings or spiritual concerns. Yet Daoism, like Confucianism, developed in a culture that had long perceived spirits living around people. Religious Daoism has embraced the shen, explaining that human beings, deities, spirits, and demons all live in different relationships with the Dao. Though there are nearly limitless possible gods in the Daoist pantheon, you're most likely to hear about a few important ones:

- *The Jade Emperor and the Queen Mother of the West.* A mythic emperor of China, the Jade Emperor is the most famous Daoist

>>> How might you live differently if you perceived spirits and deities living around you all the time?

farming, and even aid in burying their dead. American readers learned about another numen, the Kitchen God, who watches over domestic activities, through Amy Tan's 1991 novel *The Kitchen God's Wife*, about the life of Chinese-American women.

Buddhism in East Asia

Constantly in contact with Confucianism and Daoism, East Asian Buddhists developed their own paths that incorporated words and ideas from these other traditions. We'll concentrate on three distinctive strains of Mahayana Buddhism developed in China and Japan: Pure Land, Chan (Zen), and Nichiren.

PURE LAND AND NICHIREN BUDDHISM

Pure Land Buddhism began in China in the second century CE. It expanded into Japan, where it became even stronger in the 1200s.

As a form of Mahayana Buddhism, Pure Land emphasizes the role of the Bodhisattva, the enlightened person who returns to Earth to help others on the path to enlightenment. Pure Land accentuates that tradition by claiming that people can move past the Bodhisattva level to actual Buddhahood. (In contrast, Theravada Buddhists tend to think that no one can attain Buddhahood other than the Buddha himself.)

Imagine a Buddha living among us. He would create a vast amount of merit from his good works, but none of that would be useful to him, because he'd already left the cycle of samsara. What would a Buddha do with such a huge amount of merit, of good karma? The Pure Land movement answers just that question. A certain Buddha named Amitabha (Amida in Japanese) decided to use his excess of merit to create a "buddha-field" called the Pure Land, a place of absolute beauty and calm, outside of time and space. Amitabha determined that this would be the last stop before nirvana. You don't have to be a monk or a scholar to find the Pure Land. Instead, you need only to rely on Amitabha, who will lead everyone there. In fact, Pure Land Buddhists have developed deep skepticism of traditional Buddhist paths to nirvana; they see monastic discipline, good deeds, and even meditation as forms of self-important craving that tends to produce suffering rather than enlightenment. Instead, the Pure Land Buddhists take refuge in the Buddha Amitabha. In some cases, this includes the frequent chanting of Amitabha's name, either as a form of devotion or in thanks for Amitabha's beneficence.

Like the Pure Land tradition, Nichiren simplifies Buddhism and hinges on the actions of a single person. Unlike other forms of Buddhism, though, Nichiren more clearly perceives the Buddha in terms that we might call god-like: The "primeval" Buddha has existed at all time and all places, coming to Earth as Sakyamuni in India to teach us. He still exists near us, but we simply cannot see the Buddha in his present form.

Nichiren ideas can best be understood through the contemplation of the Lotus Sutra, a 28-chapter text that explains how each one of us holds the seed of Buddhahood inside us. A monk named Nichiren

^^^ What kinds of people might be attracted to Pure Land Buddhism instead of other forms?

De is virtue attained by acting in harmony with the Dao.

Shonin began to teach the importance of the Lotus Sutra in the early 13th century, calling it the ultimate expression of the Buddha's true teaching. As a result, Nichiren Buddhists sometimes focus completely on this text, gazing on it rather than a statue of the Buddha. By repeating the words "namu Myoho renge kyo" ("salutation to the Lotus Sutra"), Nichiren Buddhists try to internalize and to live according to their beloved Sutra as the most pure path toward enlightenment.

CHAN (ZEN) BUDDHISM

Unlike Nichiren, Chan ("Zen" in Japanese) Buddhism completely rejects the idea of the Buddha as a god. Developing first in China and then in Japan, Chan shares many ideas with Daoism, as you'll soon see.

Like Pure Land and Nichiren, Chan Buddhism traces its history to the Mahayana tradition. Unlike those forms, though, Chan questions anything that it sees as contrary to early Buddhism, discarding elements that that might seem magical or deistic. Instead, Chan Buddhism argues that a disciple can receive enlightenment directly from a master, rather than slowly accreting knowledge over many lifetimes. They point to a famous story in which the Buddha chose to teach by silently holding up a flower. Only one of his students understood

^^^ Some Buddhists believe that Nichiren so understood the nature of reality that he could calm the seas.

> **Koan** is a seemingly meaningless statement meant to compel Chan followers to contemplate enlightenment.
>
> **Zhong** is loyalty, an important part of self-development according to Confucius.
>
> **Li** denotes rituals and rites in Confucianism.
>
> **Shu** complements zhou, and represents the Confucian concept of empathy or reciprocity.

this form of teaching and broke into a smile. He experienced enlightenment directly from the Buddha via the flower, rather than through years of study (Olson 225–229).

Therefore, Chan Buddhists claim that it is possible to gain enlightenment directly and instantaneously—not by doing something, but by doing *nothing*. You may hear echoes of Daoism in this statement. Chan emphasizes a simple form of meditation to help find enlightenment. Chan also looks to everyday life—a flower, a clod of dirt, a piece of trash—for sources of enlightenment. The point here is not to try too hard; enlightenment occurs to those who act naturally and spontaneously, much as if you were following the Dao. In fact, enlightenment can come in an instant—perhaps without a person's even knowing it will happen.

In fact, Chan even seeks enlightenment in the absurd or impossible. Often, Chan teachers give students a seemingly meaningless sentence—called a **koan** in Japanese—to contemplate. It might relate to nature or human life. The sentence has no rational meaning, but may help the student toward the perception that nothing in this life truly makes sense—only the Buddha brings enlightenment.

WHAT DOES IT MEAN TO BE HUMAN?

As you might guess, Confucianism and Daoism both concentrate on helping people to find and harmonize with qi and Dao. Yet the two focus their energy very differently. For Confucians, human beings exist primarily as social beings. Our life takes on meaning as we interact with other people appropriately to develop harmony in society. Daoists, however, concentrate on individual interaction with the Dao. If each of us could live harmoniously with the Dao, they reason, social problems would fix themselves. Let's look at each of these more closely. We'll leave Buddhism out of the picture for now but come back to it in Chapter 8.

The Confucian View of Humanity

Confucianism has developed a highly sophisticated view of human beings that emphasizes our connections to one another—family, ancestors, co-workers, and friends. Social harmony grows from our following the Dao, which is both moral and good. As we cultivate human nature, we'll naturally develop our moral character. Yet as human beings we also have the power to follow an immoral path that leads us ever further from the Dao and sows disharmony in society.

How do we achieve harmony? First, Confucianism teaches us that we must cultivate ourselves; we cannot hope to make the world better until we have improved ourselves. Confucian harmony can be achieved by loyalty and reciprocity, working together as yin and yang.

ZHONG—LOYALTY

According to the Confucian concept of **Zhong**, or loyalty, we all have a family of some sort. We are not just individuals but rather exist in a group from the time of our birth. For Confucius, developing loyalty to your family provides the structure for society to exist in harmony. When her kids were young, my sister used to have a sign that said "I'm the mommy: That's why." Confucius would have agreed, because he saw families as hierarchal systems, not a group of equals. Going further, he explained that the family was a microcosm for all society. Following this logic, we can create harmony in society if we each understand and fulfill our assigned roles in the hierarchal structure. Each of us needs to recognize when we are at the top, when we are at the bottom, and when we are equal (Liu 48–53).

In any social situation, we may simultaneously have three different roles—parent (leader), child (follower), and friend (equal). Your sense of loyalty and your actions all relate to that situation and the responsibilities dictated by it. A parent fulfills a different role than a child, though at some point the child too may grow up and have children. And so as roles change, duties also vary. The idea of loyalty, however, remains the same.

We express loyalty through our actions. Confucius has taught us that rituals and rites (called **li**) offer guidance as to how to act. In this case, rituals may not have any religious connotation. Rather, li encompasses the correct way to act with everyone, in every situation. Here is an illustration. What do you call your professor in this class? Doctor? Professor? Or Sue? You probably do not address her by first name. Why? Because you offer respect to the professor based on her knowledge, education, and position as leader of the class. What happens if you dislike the professor or disagree with her? Do you start calling her "Hey, you," or even worse? Of course not. But why? Because you like her? No, you use her title because of the hierarchal relationship. Like it or not, the professor has the power to pass or fail you in this class. For that reason, if no other, it will be better for you and the harmony of the class if you keep calling her "Professor."

Now let's imagine that you have finished school and continue on to graduate school. You come back to be a guest lecturer in this very class. The professor, whom you now respect and like, will probably tell you to call her "Sue." Why? Because your role is now different, so you are in a new relationship with the professor. You may call her by a first name but will feel awkward, because you remember that she is still the professor who taught you in class. Then, once you get your Ph.D. in religious studies and see your professor at a professional conference, you may feel more comfortable calling her Sue, because your roles are now as equals. In this situation, you have created harmony because you have understood your role as it has changed over time. You have been loyal to your role as student, graduate student, and peer. Accordingly, you act with the correct ritual with your professor, and thus you have made yourself better and created harmony in your world. You have followed the Dao.

SHU—RECIPROCITY AND EMPATHY

The other side of loyalty is **shu**, translated as "reciprocity" or "empathy." Shu embodies the Confucian Golden Rule. The Master said, "What you do not want done to yourself, do not do to others" (Confucius *Analects*, XV: 23). By remembering both li and shu, we can act appropriately to those below us and also refrain from getting angry if people do not act according to their

The Confucian System of Social Relationships

The ruler

The ministers

The subjects

Father Husband Teacher Friend Friend

Son Wife Student

Younger son

Source: Based on Liu, J., *An Introduction to Chinese Philosophy: From Ancient Philosophy to Chinese Buddhism,* (Malden, MA: Blackwell Publishing, 2005),

∧
∧ The hierarchy of a family is a guide for all relationships. How does your role in the family hierarchy affect how you interact with family members?

Confucian Moral Path

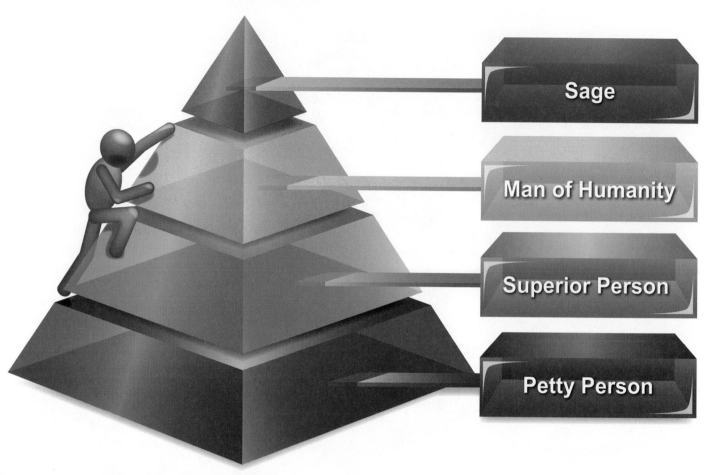

Source: Based on Liu, J., *An Introduction to Chinese Philosophy: From Ancient Philosophy to Chinese Buddhism,* (Malden, MA: Blackwell Publishing, 2005).

> Over time, people cultivate loyalty and empathy and move up in the hierarchy of morality. **What actions must individuals take to move up in the hierarchy of morality?**

proper roles. Shu teaches us to look past the mistakes of others, for you too may act inappropriately some day. The passive shu complements the active zhou (Liu 53–56).

Let's return to the classroom example. What if the professor overhears you referring to her as "Sue" to your friends, or what if someone in the classroom calls her "Sue"? She has two choices. First, she could scold you or the other student and remind you that it is inappropriate to call her by her first name. This would be completely acceptable by Confucian standards. However, it may make you feel uncomfortable or unwilling to take part in class because you have been reprimanded. Therefore, the principle of shu counsels the professor to acknowledge your inappropriate action another way. Perhaps she'll tell a story about a time when she embarrassed herself as a student by doing something similar to what you've done. Perhaps she'll refer to herself playfully as "Sue" for a class as a subtle reminder that only she should use her first name. You'll feel better because you have not been chastised and you'll remember to call her "Professor." You may even respect her more than before because she did not reprimand you but instead relied on shu to create harmony in the classroom.

What is the result of cultivating loyalty and empathy? Over time, you become a better person and move up the hierarchy of morality. The **petty person** occupies the lowest position, acting only according to his or her own wishes at the moment. With constant self-cultivation, however, an individual can develop into a **superior person** (sometimes also called a "gentleman"). The superior person constantly seeks The Way, acting according to zhou and li rather than self-interest or profit. A petty person will always try to find personal profit from a situation, even if it means acting with shady morality. A superior person, however, will constantly try to act correctly even when it offers less initial reward.

This is not an easy path to tread: Most of us will spend our lives trying to be a superior person. If we can then help nurture moral actions in the people around us, we may rise to the level of **man of humanity** as we use our own self-cultivation to help others become superior people. For this reason, to be called "humane" is a high compliment in Confucianism.

Finally, if you can lead many people—not just a few—toward moral actions, you may attain the position of **sage**. You have helped spread harmony outside the boundaries of your own life by aiding multitudes on

The Way. To be called a sage is the highest tribute in Confucianism because you have spread harmony far and wide. You can imagine how Buddhists might interpret this as a type of Bodhisattva: one who helps others toward enlightenment (Liu 56–60).

The Daoist View of Humanity

Although Daoism agrees with Confucianism on the importance of the Dao, the two philosophies depart very quickly. Instead of focusing on the family as a symbol of society, Daoism says that each person is a microcosm of the world. As qi flows through the world, so it courses through us, too. The more freely that qi can move through and around our body, the more closely we follow the Dao, resulting in good health and a long life.

Remember that Dao counsels inaction rather than Confucian deeds. Let's go back Laozi's text, which explains the Way through a series of losses and gains:

> Therefore, when the Way is lost, only then do we have virtue;
> When virtue is lost, only then do we have humanity;
> When humanity is lost, only then do we have righteousness;
> And when righteousness is lost, only then do we have propriety.
> As for propriety, it's but the thin edge of loyalty and sincerity,
>   and the beginning of disorder.
> And foreknowledge is but the flower of the Way, and the
>   beginning of stupidity (Lao-Tzu 7).

This cryptic passage challenges all the rituals and self-cultivation so prized by Confucians. Propriety only helps us fend off anarchy and disorder. No great goal in itself, proper behavior (like that described by Confucius) exists only after we have already lost righteousness, humanity, and virtue. According to this, we should not concentrate on propriety but rather on more lofty things like our relationship to the Dao.

And yet, if you spend your life trying to find The Way through your actions, you'll never experience the True Way, the True Reality. You cannot know everything; you cannot learn all the proper relationships, all the proper rituals, all the proper forms of address, in all situations at all times. If you think you can do this, you are mistaken! So, instead of working so hard to find The Way, you should relax. Once you stop, you may realize that you are already on The Way, and that you have naturally become one with the cosmos. When you *desire* The Way, as do the Confucians, you "see only the manifestations" of The Way, not The Way itself. The Daodejing explains that

> The softest, most pliable thing in the world runs roughshod over the firmest thing the world.

> That which has no substance gets into that which has no spaces or cracks.

> I therefore know that there is benefit in taking no action.

> The wordless teaching, the benefit of taking no action—
> Few in the world can realize these! (Lao-Tzu 12).

Your response to these lines may be something like "Huh?" That's probably because you are trying to understand them. Yet Daoism explains that, to the extent that we try to find The Way, we will ultimately fail. Our own efforts, no matter how noble, will never reveal The Way. If, however, we relax and act naturally, we will experience The Way. (Go ahead, but don't use this as an excuse not to study for your next exam.)

Here are two illustrations that may help explain the Daoist perception of human beings and The Way. First, recall the fish story from the beginning of this chapter. Water surrounds us, and we naturally swim with the currents and the tides. We do not need to be told to go with the flow or decide to follow the tide because it all happens naturally. Water surrounds us, the ocean is all around us, and we live naturally. Now, imagine that we decide to swim against the tide and end up on a beach. As fish, we suddenly cannot breathe. Being good fish, we try to help each other by spitting drops of water onto one another. This cools us a little and provides a bit of oxygen for our bodies. We are working hard, but ultimately we will fail and die.

Wouldn't it have made more sense just to move with the tides, surrounded by qi and Dao, living a long and healthy life? The harder we work, the more we swim against the tide and tire ourselves. Perhaps we'll even end up on dry land, sputtering out before we expire. The more we don't try to swim against the tide, though, the more effortlessly we will live in the water (qi) that makes up the ocean (Dao).

For another example, think back to the scene in the classroom. What if a new student arrived and did not know how to address the professor? What if he disrupted the class and called the professor "buddy" or "pal?" What if the professor's empathetic use of the Golden Rule didn't calm the situation? When you've got a

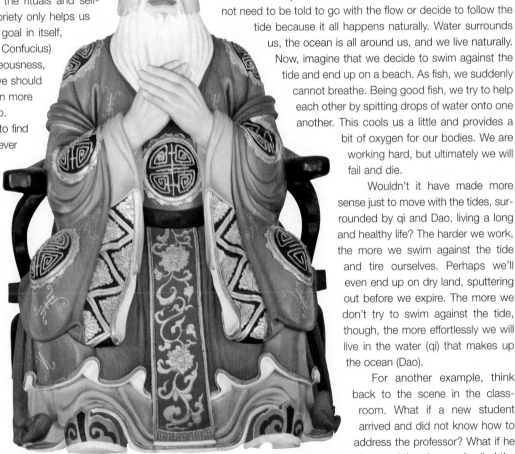

^ ^ ^ Why might you buy a statue of Confucius such as this in a Singapore shopping mall?

Wu wei is a Daoist concept that describes "action without effort" in Chinese. By practicing wu wei, we reflect nature rather than act against it.

Legalism assumes that all human beings act selfishly and need government and its laws to create a working society—in direct contradiction to both Confucianism and Daoism.

problem person like the one described above, all the rituals in the world will not restore harmony to the class. Daoism explains that we cannot continue trying—and ultimately failing—to produce harmony by our own actions. Instead, we should realize that any attempt to cultivate harmony is bound to fail, sooner or later. Rather than caring about titles or names, therefore, we should remember that "The Way that can be described" is not the True Way. Names, rituals, titles—all of this takes away from the real point of the class, which is learning. When we stop trying so hard to get it right, we'll be much more likely to learn.

Instead of acting according to some prescribed ("named") ritual, we should instead rely on **wu wei**, which means "action without effort" or "action without doing." In that case, we will never swim against the tide. We will not rely on titles or formality but instead interact naturally with each other. In doing so, we will experience The Way. By using wu wei, the professor in class might choose to sit quietly under a tree on campus and not lecture or pass out exams. Instead, she will wait until students converse with her and ask questions. In this manner, she does not care about the rituals of class (titles, lectures, and tests). By acting naturally, she is experiencing The Way and helping her students experience it, too.

The practice of tai chi that we read at the beginning of this chapter illustrates the essence of wu wei. In tai chi, you move through a series of poses that relate to the movements of animals in nature. Staying constantly in motion helps you experience the ever-changing flow of qi. Yet tai chi asks you to "do" nothing at all—rather, you are reflecting nature, acting without effort. What results from this wu wei? What happens if we can experience the Dao? Why practice tai chi? Daoists explain that health comes from living in harmony with the Dao, not necessarily harmony with society. Sickness

Λ
Λ Tantric Daoists believe that the power of
Λ the Dao can help you fly through the air. Here is Keanu Reeves doing just that in *The Matrix: Reloaded.* **Why do you think these ideas have become so attractive to Western audiences?**

and death derive from a poor relationship with the Dao, but health and longevity come from harmonious living with it. As you become one with the Dao, your senses become stronger, and your body becomes nearly magical because it constantly works with the energy around it. One tradition, sometimes called Tantric Daoism, teaches that you may find supernatural powers when you're aligned with the Dao. Far from philosophical Daoism, Tantric Daoism says that you may be able to fly through the air, jump over buildings, and run along the treetops, if only you could use the power of the Dao.

INTERNAL CONFLICT

Legalism

The Chinese philosophy called **legalism** suggests that both Confucianism and Daoism are naive in their desire to live according to the Dao. How many people in society will really develop morality? How many can live according to wu wei? Most people, said the legalist Hanfeizi, act according to their own self-interest. For example, a funeral director does not want people to die, but he profits from their deaths nevertheless. This doesn't make him bad. To the contrary, the mortician provides a service to society.

If we're selfish, according to Hanfeizi, we are also lazy. Why work if you don't have to? Why sweat out a hard class if an easy one will boost your GPA? This, Hanfeizi counsels, really can be a problem, because sloth can create many social problems—from removing sewage to planting rice, imagine what happens if no one does the difficult jobs.

The key to the legalist philosophy can be found in the law (no surprise). Given the right laws and their correct execution, society can become a well-oiled machine, with each person doing his or her job to develop resources and provide everyone with necessities—food, shelter, clothing, security. That's where the government steps into the picture. For legalists, neither the desire to be a Superior Man

nor accepting the Dao will change more than a handful of people. But bring out the troops, and people will do what's right:

> Here is a young man of bad character. His parents rail at him but he does not reform; the neighbors scold him but he is unmoved; his teachers instruct him but he refuses to change his ways. . . . But let the local magistrate send out the government soldiers to enforce the law and search for evil-doers, and then he is filled with terror, reforms his conduct, and changes his ways . . . for people by nature grow proud on love, but they listen to authority (Liu 185–186).

As a result of this observation, Hanfeizi wrote vast amount of criticism of Confucianism, offering his own recommendations to make sure governments run correctly and maintain stability in society.

Here's a joke: If a legalist, a Confucian, and a Daoist went into a bar, where would they sit? A legalist would sit where he's told, a Confucian would sit where he should, and a Daoist would sit wherever he sat, making no decision at all. OK, so it's not that funny, but it makes you think: Considering how different legalism is from Confucianism or Daoism, can you see any similarities?

THINK World Religions

The Immortals

In rare cases, Daoists argue that a person in perfect Dao harmony does not have to die at all; he or she can become immortal. The quests for long life, health, and immortality have therefore become hallmarks of Daoism. How many people have become immortal through the Dao? No one knows. However, "The Immortals," as they are symbolized through eight archetypal figures called The Eight Immortals, are the subject of many folktales. They fight evil and do good, much like modern-day super-heroes. The Eight Immortals represent various aspects of the human experience, such as male, female, rich, poor, noble, humble, old, and young. Each is often portrayed carrying an object that has a special function or meaning (Littlejohn 157–158).

To become immortal, according to the Daoists, is not to exist on just one side of the Supreme Ultimate—neither yin nor yang. Instead, an immortal is part of the whole circle, attuned to both yin and yang and therefore energized by the whole universe. As a person, how do you use both sides of the Supreme Ultimate—Confucianism and Daoism? Chinese traditional wisdom teaches us "to be a Confucian in interactions with the mundane world; be a Daoist when retreating back to one's inner world" (Liu 25).

>>> **Here are the Eight Immortals** as imagined in the book "Myths and Legends of China," 1922.

∧ Note the simplicity of the trees and the mountains in this ancient painting. What Daoist ideas are
∧ reflected in the artwork?

REVIEW

Summary

IS THERE A GOD?   p. 86

- Answers vary. Dao, or "The Way," is a common concept in East Asian spirituality. Dao emanates qi, which is made up of yin and yang.
- Confucianism seeks to pursue the Dao, while Daoism strives to accept it.
- Pure Land Buddhists focus on the role of Amitabha, Nichiren Buddhists center their worship on the Buddha, and Chan Buddhists seek enlightenment in the everyday.

WHAT DOES IT MEAN TO BE HUMAN?   p. 94

- Confucianism emphasizes connections between humans; we achieve harmony through loyalty to the social structure.
- Daoism views people as microcosms of the world, and stresses the importance of interacting naturally with one another.

Key Terms

Dao can mean the path, or The Way; it encompasses the nature of everything.   *86*

Qi is matter or energy that comes from the Dao. Qi is the totality of things and is in perpetual motion.   *87*

Yin is passive energy and makes up a part of qi. Yin cannot exist without yang.   *88*

Yang, together with yin, makes up qi. Yang is active energy and cannot exist without yin.   *88*

Trigrams are symbols of three lines each that show how yin and yang interact in the world.   *88*

Divination tells the future by showing people their place in the cosmos.   *89*

Shen are spirits of ancestors in traditional China..   *91*

De is virtue attained by acting in harmony with the Dao.   *92*

Koan is a seemingly meaningless statement meant to compel Chan followers to contemplate enlightenment.   *94*

Zhong is loyalty, an important part of self-development according to Confucius.   *94*

Li denotes rituals and rites in Confucianism.   *94*

Shu complements zhou, and represents the Confucian concept of empathy or reciprocity.   *94*

Petty person is the lowest position on the moral hierarchy of Confucianism. A petty person often seeks to make profit.   *96*

Superior person rises above a petty person and seeks, through self-cultivation, The Way, rather than personal profit; this term is used in Confucianism.   *96*

Man of humanity nurtures others to help them become superior persons in Confucianism.   *96*

Sage leads many people to self-cultivation and higher moral positions, and spreads harmony among multitudes of people. It is the highest level that a human being can attain in the Confucian moral hierarchy.   *96*

Wu wei is a Daoist concept that describes "action without effort" in Chinese. By practicing wu wei, we reflect nature rather than act against it.   *98*

Legalism assumes that all human beings act selfishly and need government and its laws to create a working society—in direct contradiction to both Confucianism and Daoism.   *98*

Find it on

http://www.metacafe.com/watch/3733444/chen_style_tai_chi_chuan/

Looking for a new and interesting way to exercise? To relax? Then Tai Chi may be for you. Go to the ThinkSpot to watch a video of someone practicing this ancient art which combines movement and meditation with martial arts. Learn about the "world inside yourself."

http://www.quotationspage.com/quotes/Confucius

"Forget injuries, never forget kindness." Sounds wise, right? This is just one of the sayings attributed to Confucius, and one that still resonates all these years after he is thought to have

said it. Go to the ThinkSpot to access more sayings of the father of Confucianism.

http://www.facebook.com/group.php?gid=2208321081&_fb_noscript=1

Do you participate in social networking sites? If you do, you might be interested to learn that Zen Buddhism has its own Facebook page. Go to the ThinkSpot to view the different discussions that take place, or maybe to write on Zen Buddhism's wall, as so many Facebook members have. This is faith in the 21st century.

Questions for Study and Review

1. **In East Asian religions, what is the meaning of yin and yang?**

   Yin and yang are parts of a whole. They are represented as a circle that is half white and half black. The halves of the circle are curved, and each half contains a bit of the other color. The yin and the yang represent the Supreme Ultimate in East Asian religions; they teach us that opposites in the world are equal and do not exist without each other. Each half of the circle defines the other half. The rolling shape of the halves demonstrates that things can turn from good to bad and back to good again. Each half of the circle contains a bit of the other color to remind us that there is a little bit of the opposite in everything and everyone.

2. **What is the Dao and how does it figure into East Asian spirituality?**

   The Dao is a central concept in East Asian spirituality. Sometimes called The Way or the Supreme Ultimate, it is the nature of all things. Dao is made up of qi, the energy of the universe.

3. **Briefly explain how Confucianism and Daoism differ with respect to the Dao.**

   While Confucianism teaches an active pursuit of harmony among people and with the Dao, Daoism teaches a passive approach to "finding" the Dao. Confucianism focuses on attaining harmony through transformation, whereas Daoism focuses on passive acceptance of The Way as a path to understanding it.

4. **Describe how wu wei, or "actions without effort" help people achieve harmony with the Dao, according to the Daoist perspective.**

   Wu wei is a way of acting naturally with others, rather than acting according to rituals or formality. By passively accepting the nature and flow of things and people rather than actively trying to understand and behave according to proper rituals and rules, one can experience The Way. In other words, we experience The Way when we stop seeking it. Once we experience The Way, we can live in harmony with the Dao.

<<< A woman practices tai chi in the early hours of the morning. How does this image reflect themes of East Asian spirituality?

Q

HOW DO HUMANS INTERACT WITH THE SACRED?
HOW DOES THE SACRED BECOME COMMUNITY?

The scene

has the simple beauty of a haiku poem: a woman, silhouetted against the morning sky, moves gracefully on rocks that resemble waves in their soft curves. She's in the Joshua Tree National Park in the USA. This image captures many questions that we're studying in relation to East Asian spirituality. How do people interact with nature? How does movement take on a sacred meaning? How can we find meaning in natural forms like gardens or stones? Can simplicity be more meaningful than sophistication? Can East Asian ideas retain their power as they move into new parts of the world?

In this chapter, we continue our discussion of East Asian sacred traditions, adding Buddhism to our investigation of Confucianism and Daoism. Here, the focus turns to humanity and society, finding relationships among Confucianism, Daoism, and Buddhism. Distinct yet interconnected, the East Asian sacred world searches for human enlightenment.

By this point in *THINK: World Religions*, you've gotten used to complex answers to easy questions. That will continue in this chapter, since Confucianism, Daoism, and Buddhism all perceive the world a little differently from each another. As you read, consider how these three traditions might interact with one another. Where does Buddhism seem to agree with one or the other traditions we studied in Chapter 7? Could you imagine following all three? Why or why not? To begin answering these questions, we will study ways that all three of these traditions interact with their sacred world and how their sacred becomes community. As you read, consider situations where Confucianism, Daoism, or Buddhism seems to be the most prominent, and also look for areas where they all work together.

EAST ASIAN SACRED WAYS:
Harmony in the World

Lion Dance in New York's Chinatown

"On the first and seventh days of the Lunar New Year, the narrow streets of New York City's Chinatown are transformed by nearly a dozen concurrent Lion Dance processionals. Individual groups animating colorful giant papier-mâché and silk lions weave their way from door to door to exorcize the evil spirits and to bring the blessings of good luck to businesses and social organizations. The dancers are students from the local [kung fu] schools of martial arts; in the ritual act they boldly demonstrate their strength, vitality, and skill. At this time Chinatown resembles a war zone—ignited firecrackers fill the air with deafening explosions and dense smoke, leaving the streets blanketed with lucky red paper debris. The sounds of drums, gongs, and cymbals herald the lions' approach—a signal for people to leave their jobs or private family celebrations to witness the festivities in the streets. A crowd forms around the Lion Dancers as they approach the entrance of a business. The space directly in front of the door is for the host, who pays for the ritual exorcism and concomitant blessing with a traditional red envelope containing lucky money. The crowds in the street move in close, surrounding the entrance and the performers. . . . Two performers animate the lion—one under the head and another under the tail. . . . At first, the lion emphatically twists and turns its head as it looks around. When the drumming changes its beat, the lion immediately shifts

into a series of three bows that gush forth with the power of an ocean wave, receding only enough to swell and crest forward again. The lion swings back its 40-pound head and then rushes forward, bowing to the door. The colorful papier-mâché head and silk body move as one luscious mass, the head kept low in deference to the host. At the end of the third bow, the dancers drop straight down in a low 'single-split' stance while the lion sniffs the ground. The kowtow complete, the lion thrusts up its head and stands tall. The drummer changes the beat again, and the group is ready to move to the next location. Before they depart, the host offers a sign of good luck with a hand gesture. Simulating the lion's kowtow, one hand is cupped over a loosely formed fist and gently shaken three times. Saying 'gung hei fat choi,' meaning 'best wishes for your prosperity,' the host acknowledges the ritual's conclusion. The whole sequence only lasts an average of three minutes, and the three-part kowtow approximately forty-five seconds" (Slovenz 74–75).

In Chapter 1, we read about ethnographic description as a way to study world religions. This is one of my favorites. Professor Madeline Slovenz helps us visualize the lion dance and hints at its importance to East Asian traditions. As we read through Chapter 8, think back to this scene, since it can tell us a lot about East Asians' interactions with the sacred world and their communities. For example, the dancing lion represents the story of a beast that made trouble in Heaven, only to have his head cut off by the Daoist god the Jade Emperor. The lion might also symbolize the taming of the New Year. Still other stories say that a lion ate the "vegetable of longevity" while the Buddha slept. Now, a smiling Buddha character often accompanies the lions when they dance, watching while they "eat" and spew out bok choi that has been elaborately hung from poles near businesses on the parade route (Slovenz 79, 83).

▶ HOW DO HUMANS INTERACT WITH THE SACRED?

Confucianism focuses on personal relationships and social order, but we can't forget that the Master lived in a world full of shen—spirits of ancestors and other supernatural beings. Once, when Confucius fell ill, his students asked if would be right to request help of the spirits. The Master agreed, quoting an ancient text: "Prayer has been made for thee to the spirits of the upper and lower worlds" (Confucius *Analects*, VII: 34). As it progressed after the Master's death, Confucianism continued to develop ways to create harmony in society and reach out to the spirits living around them.

East Asian people have continued this practice. Up until the beginning of the 20th century, everyone from the emperor (who took part in lengthy rituals linking him to the traditional gods) to the poorest farmer took part in regular ceremonies to honor various places and events. Some involved rituals of sacrifice; others celebrated the good fortune of

>>> What do you think this 14th-century artist was trying to tell us when he painted Lao-tze and Confucius gently holding the baby Buddha?

>>> How might keeping a tablet like this one from China, with your ancestors' names and dates, help you venerate their memory?

a new year. The lion dances occurring during the lunar new year celebration across the world continue that tradition, and often involve people from many backgrounds and religions. Before they use a new lion head, some groups offer a sacrifice to Guan Gong, the god of both war and virtue (Slovenz 82).

Confucius also explained that every social interaction had a ritual element that helped people understand how to interact with one another. In essence, he merged the sacred with the everyday by insisting on the correct way to do everything. After all, the Master said, "If his mat is not straight, he will not sit on it" (Confucius *Analects*, X: 9). He believed that all human relationships grew out of the family, which he said was the most important unit in society. This did not stop when a person died, so Confucius supported the veneration of deceased ancestors that had already developed in China. Today, when a member of an East Asian family dies, the family often holds funeral rites in the home, using an altar set up for just this purpose. It may be small and discreet, or it may take up an entire room of a house. In either case, the altar provides a place for family members to honor and venerate their ancestors. Funeral rituals vary, but they often include pouring wine for the departed, burning candles and incense (sometimes even paper money), and offering flowers or food.

Because a person has moved on to another world that might be similar to our own, a family takes care of its dead by giving these gifts. In Taiwan, for example, people commemorate *Qingming jie*, "Grave Sweeping Day," devoted to remembering the family ancestors (Smithsonian Institution). These traditions make particular sense in a culture imbued with family and community. Just because he is gone, Grandfather should not be forgotten: Without him your family name

^^^ Here is funny money to be burned in ancestor veneration. The cash is from the "Bank of Hell."

would not have survived, your reputation would have disappeared, and you would not exist. He may have left you an inheritance, perhaps money or family lore. Just because you can no longer see him does not mean he does not exist. In that case, why not respect him after death, just as you respected him when he was alive?

Veneration of Confucius

As we learned in Chapter 7, Confucius' followers began to venerate him after he died. In Qufu, where Confucius lived, a temple to his memory has stood for more than 2,000 years. As Confucianism spread and Chinese emperors embraced it as the state philosophy/religion, they built temples all over the country. In essence, people began to consider Confucius both a highly honored member of their families and a man who surpassed the sage, offering wisdom to last for millennia. Who more than Confucius blazed a path toward societal harmony? Who was a better teacher than the Master? In fact, the Taiwanese have even expanded the Confucius birthday commemoration into a celebration of all teachers on September 28, near the start of the school year.

Interacting with the Dao through Qi

In addition to venerating their deceased family, people from Daoist, Confucian, and Buddhist traditions also interact with their sacred world in

<<< Here is the inner gate to the Jianshui Confucius Temple, in China. In the *Analects*, the Master said, "When he entered the palace gate, he seemed to bend his body, as if it were not sufficient to admit him. When he was standing, he did not occupy the middle of the gateway; when he passed in or out, he did not tread upon the threshold" (*Analects*, X:4). What do these lines teach us about Confucian views of sacred places?

Alchemy is the ancient practice of transforming one matter into another. In Eastern Asia, practitioners focused on the transformation of the human body.

Falun Gong combines a system of exercise and movement with a spiritual emphasis on self-improvement.

other ways, including direct contact with spirits (shen). Just as often, however, people seek to harmonize with the Dao through their actions. As you cultivate a sense of harmony with qi, your physical and emotional life will develop too. In this way, East Asian traditions tend to combine elements that Westerners might call contemplation, exercise, psychology, and medicine. An East Asian person, on the other hand, might wonder why anyone would try to differentiate among physical vigor, emotional wellbeing, and spiritual health.

Given the interconnections among all forms of creation, some Daoists have hoped to learn how to transform one kind of matter into another. In medieval Europe, this practice—called **alchemy**—began as a search to turn lead into gold and helped to produce modern-day chemistry. In China, however, alchemy took a different turn, toward the transformation of the human body. Daoists might consume gold and mercury in tiny amounts by refining it from cinnabar. They chose these metals because they were changeable—gold could be molded but never tarnish; mercury was at once a liquid and a metal. In fact, the cinnabar's red color and the

luster of gold have become ubiquitous colors of good luck and good fortune in East Asia, tracing its way directly back to alchemy.

The idea of "good luck" also relates to East Asian divination as a way to interact with the world of qi. Although ancient, the Yijing still provides the template for learning about your place in the world. When performed by an adept practitioner, divination offers a way to interpret your relationship to the qi that surrounds you. Shared by Daoists and Buddhists alike, divination identifies auspicious times to engage in important events, such as marriage or changing jobs.

MARTIAL ARTS AND QI EXERCISES

Harmonizing with qi can include exercise and even ritual fighting. As with so many aspects of East Asian spiritual life, martial arts come in two distinct yet complementary forms. The "yin" types of martial arts are explosive and active. The "yang" types are receptive and passive, like the refined and controlled movements we read about at the beginning of Chapter 7.

The martial arts tradition in East Asia spans dozens of forms. In one way or another, they all teach you to develop your own qi while simultaneously exploiting the qi of the other person. To me, it's not so difficult to imagine developing qi (yin) power—we've all seen the amazing videos of a man breaking boards or bricks with only his hands.

It's harder to figure out how you might employ the "yang" philosophy of martial arts to control another through your own passivity. This may

∧
∧ These good luck plaques hang on the fence of the Four Gates Buddhist Temple in Jinan,
∧ Shandong Province, China. What might the plaques' owners hope to gain by hanging them on a
temple fence?

also remind you of the term "wu wei." Successful martial arts exploit the concept of effortless action—doing without doing. So let's think of another situation. Imagine that you are running toward someone, and just at the last moment, she catches your ankle or elbow, sending you spinning head over heels. That person has used your active, explosive qi against you. She remained passive, but her qi allowed her to stand firm against your movement. In this case, you might even say that she robbed you of your qi, because you expended energy but to no effect. Knowing how qi works, your opponent recognized your vulnerabilities and exploited them for her own gain. In other words, she understood the relationship of yin and yang better than you did. Her victory was more spiritual than physical, qi-based rather than muscular.

Each East Asian region has developed one or more martial arts. Many descend from the Buddhist Shaolin Monastery, whose monks developed Shaolin boxing and kung fu. The present-day abbot of the Shaolin Monastery explains that the monastery teaches fighting as a way to develop control, rather than to defeat an enemy (Shahar 20–22).

At this point, you may be scratching your head. How are ancestor veneration, Shaolin boxing, alchemy, divination, and acupuncture all forms of interaction with the sacred world? To be truthful, this

CONTEMPORARY RELIGIOUS ISSUES

Falun Gong

Falun Gong, a new version of the ancient qi gong tradition, appears in the news with sad regularity. The government of China calls it an "evil cult" and suppresses its followers. Traces of Falun Gong material get wiped off Chinese Internet sites, yet the movement continues to grow both inside China and across the world. Why?

For centuries, reform movements have grown from the fertile ground of Confucianism, Daoism, and Buddhism. Sometimes, these developed into sects of their own, such as Pure Land Buddhism. In other cases, they blossomed and then faded. Falun Gong is less than 20 years old, but it has spread rapidly across China and beyond its borders. To an outside observer, Falun Gong may look just like tai chi, with its system of exercise movements. Yet that's just the outward face of a system that borrows heavily from Daoism and Buddhism. Here, for example, is a passage from the Falun Gong's most influential book, the *Zhuan Falun*:

If you want to quit [smoking], it is guaranteed that you can do it. When you smoke a cigarette again, it will not taste right. If you read this lecture in the book, it will also have this effect. Of course, if you do not want to practice cultivation, we will not take care of it. I think that as a practitioner, you should quit it. I once used this example: Have you ever seen a Buddha or a Tao sitting there with a cigarette in his mouth? How can that be possible? As a practitioner, what's your goal? Shouldn't you quit it? Therefore, I have said that if you want to practice cultivation, you should quit smoking. It harms your body and is a desire as well (*Zhuan Falun* Lecture 7).

For years, the Chinese government has persecuted practitioners of Falun Gong, under the claim that the movement wants to undermine the government. The trouble began in the 1990s, when members of Falun Gong began to petition the government to formally recognize their religion. On April 25, 1999, some 10,000 people staged a silent, nonviolent protest outside government buildings in Beijing. Although Falun Gong's practitioners claim they were only seeking formal recognition for their movement, their organized action caused the Chinese government to fear its potentially widespread influence and ban it. In 2008 and 2009, the Chinese government detained more than 8,000 members of the Falun Gong movement; nearly 100 died while in custody. Falun Gong members claim that Chinese police have killed thousands of its members. Government officials counter that the movement creates cultish mind control, including its teaching of a "third eye" through which one can peer beyond the physical world (Ownby 121).

Today, followers of Falun Gong in China practice in secret to avoid arrest or persecution. The Chinese government, for its part, stands by its assertion that Falun Gong is a threat to the larger Chinese populace.

Here on a lawn in Connecticut, Falun Gong members don't look like revolutionaries. Why might the Chinese government think otherwise?

>>> Designed by the Chinese-American architect I. M. Pei, the Bank of China Tower in Hong Kong has long attracted criticism for its sharp corners, which negatively affect the neighborhood's feng shui.

question has vexed people from outside East Asia for centuries. The ideas about religion that we've discussed so far in *THINK World Religions* only partially apply to the East Asian experience. My advice to students is to try and remain open to the concept that qi exists inside everything and links everything. If that's the case, then we can pursue many paths to interact with this essential force. It may take a while to figure out how all these elements work together. As an old proverb says: When the student is ready, the master will appear.

My assurances, I know, don't help you much on a final exam. So, let's look at this a slightly different way: What do people want to achieve when they interact with qi? As you study each tradition, consider how a Daoist might describe Nirvana, or a Buddhist use the term wu wei. Some traditional Daoists, for example, argue that disharmony with the Dao shortens human life, so that living within the Dao could extend life and vanquish death. Others, however, define immortality in frankly Buddhist terms, emphasizing a spiritual transformation rather than a physical one (Littlejohn 156–160).

EAST ASIAN IDEAS COME TO THE WEST

The next few pages will introduce you to acupuncture and feng shui, two East Asian spiritual-physical phenomena that you've probably heard about. I remember that when I was young, my physician was deeply interested in acupuncture but could not actively prescribe it for his patients—it was just too far outside the American mainstream. Now, however, my health plan is considering paying for acupuncture, and I can go to a private clinic just a few blocks from my office, next to a bicycle shop and a brewpub! Likewise, I can stop into any Barnes & Noble and pick up books on acupuncture or feng shui—they're now part of the American culture.

∧
∧ How might tai chi help you live a longer life?
∧

You might recognize the term **feng shui** from TV shows about interior design or alternative health. Suddenly popular in America, feng shui traces its roots to East Asian ideas about qi. Similar to acupuncture, which studies qi in the body, feng shui searches for the effects of qi in a building or a place. For example, feng shui teaches that qi tends to get caught up in corners—because of the right angles in the room, it cannot flow effectively. To combat this natural tendency, a feng shui practitioner may recommend you soften the corners of a room with plants, a piece of furniture, or some other object. In this way, qi flows toward the object and gets redirected into the center of the room. Good Qi flow makes a space more comfortable and encourages health. You can see the effects of feng shui in the gardens described in the beginning of Chapter 7. Animal sculptures, walkways, and plants all fit together to provide a good conduit for qi, which in turn makes the place feel peaceful and look beautiful. Feng shui can also work with Confucianism. Had the Ming burial site been just a personal garden, the paths would have meandered through the space. But Confucian ritual calls for the path toward an emperor to be straight, which also may direct qi appropriately to and from the ruler.

INTERACTING WITH SACRED PLACES

For thousands of years, the Chinese have looked to their mountains as a place of refuge and beauty. Qi and Dao seem to be stronger there than at other places, and the mountains attract Confucians, Daoists, and Buddhists alike. For example, the great Confucian books of rituals—the *Rites of Zhou* and the *Book of Rites*—describe activities to be performed by the emperor at five holy mountains that represent the cardinal directions: Mount Tai (East), Mount Hua (West), Mount Heng (North), Mount Heng (with the same name, but symbolizing South), and Mount Song (Center). In fact, the *Book of Rites* says

Feng shui focuses on the flow of qi in a specific place (often a room or building).

that the emperor should travel to these mountains every five years to make sacrifices and to maintain the strength of the dynasty (Meyer 228; Shahar 12). The following passage, written by a Chinese

27 Steps toward Immortality

1. **Do not delight in excess. Joy is as harmful as anger.**
2. **Do not waste qi.**
3. **Do not harm the dominant qi.**
4. **Do not eat living things that contain blood.**
5. **Do not covet fame.**
6. **Do not try to teach the Dao to outsiders.**
7. **Do not forget the teachings of the Dao.**
8. **Do not try to cause action.**
9. **Do not kill; also do not speak of killing.**
10. **Do not study false texts.**
11. **Do not covet glory or strive for it.**
12. **Do not pursue fame.**
13. **Do not engage in activities that are pleasurable to the eyes, mouth, or ears.**
14. **Be humble and modest.**
15. **Do not partake in frivolous activities.**

16. **Be devout in religious services—be mindful and clear-headed.**
17. **Do not indulge in tasty food or fancy clothing.**
18. **Do not overextend yourself.**
19. **If you are poor and humble, do not pursue honor and wealth.**
20. **Do not do evil.**
21. **Do not set too many taboos; do not excessively avoid things.**
22. **Do not pray to or sacrifice for demons of the dead.**
23. **Do not oppose others strongly.**
24. **Do not assume yourself to be right always.**
25. **Do not argue with others over what is wrong or right. If you are engaged in debate, cede your side first.**
26. **Do not praise yourself for great wisdom.**
27. **Do not take pleasure in soldiering.**

Source: Littlejohn, Ronnie L. *Daoism: An Introduction*. (London: I.B. Tauris & Co. Ltd., 2009), 96–97.

∧
∧   One Daoist tradition offers a 27-step program toward immortality. Can you distinguish which
∧   of these steps we might consider to be spiritual, which ones physical, and which ones might be psychological? Does it matter?

Religion + MEDICINE

ACUPUNCTURE

East Asian physicians have practiced some form of **acupuncture** for more than 4,000 years. Daoist practitioners map out qi as it runs through the human body. You can imagine this flow as a river running through a valley. Like water puddling in a pool, qi in the body can get stuck, resulting in acute pain or discomfort that can turn chronic, if qi cannot find a way to travel freely. Acupuncturists redirect the flow of qi in the body by using tiny metal needles pushed into the person's skin at specific points on the body. The needles break up blockages of qi to relieve pain and restore general health.

In America and Europe, physicians have traditionally sought to distinguish among physical, mental, and emotional forms of sickness. They have often disregarded spirituality or sacred ideas when they relate to health. "Acupuncture may be an ancient treatment," says one prominent physician, "but in 4,000 years no one has managed to produce any proof that it actually works" (*The Pulse, 18*).

Instead, Western medical culture prefers evidence-based medicine, which tries to prove a direct relationship between an ailment and a treatment. When you begin to talk about qi, though, many physicians begin to feel uncomfortable. For that reason, some researchers have recently begun to translate acupuncture into language that Western physicians can understand. "In the past, it was easy for scientists to dismiss acupuncture as highly implausible when its workings were couched in these terms," says Adrian White, editor in chief of *Acupuncture in Medicine*. "But it becomes very plausible when explained in terms of neurophysiology" (*The Independent, 8*).

emperor in 645 CE, illustrates some ways that East Asian traditions combine nature, sacred places, and human spirituality:

> The sacred mounts contain fine soaring peaks and fields of wilderness with special markers where strange animals roar and dragons rise to heaven, and the spots where wind and rain are generated, rainbows stored, and crates beautifully dressed. These are the places where divine immortals keep moving in and out. The countess peaks overlap each other; thick vapor wraps green vegetation, layers of ranges move into each other, and thus sunlight is divided into numerous shining rays. The steep cliffs fall one thousand leagues into the bottom and the lone peaks soar to ten thousand leagues high. The moon with laurel flowers blooming in it sheds veiled light. The clouds hang over the pine trees with clinging vines. The deep gorges sound loud in the winter and the flying springs are cool in the summer. . . . Its rugged mass is forever solid, together with the Heaven and the Earth. Its great energy is eternally potent, in the span from the ancient to the future (Meyer 228–229, Shahar 12).

The Daoist tradition particularly reveres mountains as places where human beings can come close to the Dao and stand side by side with deities. While anyone can travel as a pilgrim to the mountains, adept Daoists learn to see hidden contours and caves hidden to regular eyes. Looking at it, your thoughts will fly to the real place beyond your geographic or physical limitations. You'll remember the Daoist hermits who have forsaken all social life to live in harmony with the Dao on a mountaintop. There, they say, the Daoist can distinguish the mountain's "real" shape—not just the craggy outline against the sky, but the qi outline, the essential nature of the place (Meyer 230). In fact, the great Zhongue Temple, among the oldest and most revered in Daoism, sits atop Mount Song.

∧∧∧ **Mount Hua,** China's sacred mountain of the west. Why do you think an emperor would write that mountains were places "where divine immortals keep moving in and out?"

∧∧ **A statue of Damo,** the legendary founder of Chinese Buddhism, looks over sacred Mount Song.

Acupuncture uses tiny needles to remove blockages of qi in the body.

Buddhists, too, perceive something sacred in the mountains. Legend says that an Indian Buddhist monk named Bodhidharma climbed Mount Song in the fifth century CE. Called "Damo" in Chinese, he meditated there for many years in a cave, arising to found the Shaolin Monastery on the mountain's western side. From its grottos, Damo taught the first Chinese Buddhist leader, Huike. The sacred mountain of the Confucians and Daoists had thus become a sacred place of Buddhism (Shahar 13).

Watching animals move naturally and beautifully on the mountaintop, the monks perfected movements that recreated their beauty and focused the mind into a meditation-like state. Over the centuries, those movements have grown into Shaolin's fighting tradition, the father of all East Asian martial arts. Even today, the Shaolin Monastery clings to the side of Mount Song. Here, thousands of pilgrims come every year to experience beauty, find communion with the Buddha, and learn Shaolin techniques of spiritual fighting.

Chan Buddhism also emphasizes nature, teaching its adherents to contemplate rocks, sand, and trees in a forest, on a mountain, or in a garden. In that peaceful place, you can let yourself be moved by the qi of the rock or sand. Daoists would say that you are being swept away by the Dao, but Chan Buddhists perceive it as a link with nirvana, the emptiness and beauty of nothingness.

<<< Here in Taiwan, Daoists and Confucians share a temple at this breathtaking spot.

▶ HOW DOES THE SACRED BECOME COMMUNITY?

As you can imagine from the information you have learned so far, traditional East Asian society has developed through a constant mixing of Confucianism, Daoism, and Buddhism (with a good dose of legalism and other philosophies). At any given point in the past 2,500 years, you'll be able to find influences of each of these systems. Halfway through the 20th century, however, a new philosophy—Marxist Communism—began to dominate Chinese society and influence others in the region. In a fascinating way, though, we can see elements of these earlier traditions even in Marxist thought.

Confucianism became the dominant belief system in China in the first few centuries after Confucius' death, in 479 BCE. With the succession of several ruling dynasties, though, Confucianism fell out of favor but was later reinstated numerous times. Near the beginning of the first century CE, Confucianism began to be overshadowed by the Buddhist influence, which had spread quickly throughout the region. For several hundred years, in fact, many people perceived Confucianism to be the sole purview of the learned classes, who had to memorize vast Confucian texts before passing a civil-service examination. Buddhism and Daoism, especially as they intertwined, appealed more to the lower classes, with their less-formal social and economic relationships. Daoism has generally been openly followed when members of the imperial family showed interest in it. When, however, the government perceived Daoism as a threat, Daoists had to beat a retreat (Renard 41–43).

Confucianism

Confucianism seeks to develop individuals within a community. Of all the ideas we've studied in Chapters 7 and 8, Confucius most clearly elaborated a sense of social order and its meaning. He based his philosophy on the development of humanity, which then spreads through a society and a government, creating a harmonious living organism. The Master taught that societies could be transformed by living according to the rules of humanity.

The more "human" you become, the more you will to become a sage, after which you can begin leading others toward the path of humanity. Followers of Confucianism, therefore, carry the burden of others' well-being on their shoulders. Here are three key Confucian concepts that illustrate this point:

- Everyone, including the poor, has to have adequate food, home, and work. How can one behave humanely when he or she is starving to death?
- War should only be undertaken when morally necessary, since it brings suffering to so many people.
- Everyone should learn and follow rituals. This preserves order in society.

Confucius believed that the process of individual and community growth came through free will rather than coercion. Because of this, he opposed the idea that a government should force people into submission:

The Master said, "If the people be led by laws, and uniformity sought to be given them by punishments, they will try to avoid the punishment, but have no sense of shame." (Confucius *Analects*, II: 3; see also Liu 62).

Punishing people, he reasoned, only scares them into acting humanely when others are keeping watch. Rather, Confucius argued for a society

What's in a Name?

You have read about the importance of strict Confucian social rituals. But how are you to know when someone else is in the cultural hierarchy relative to you? To solve this dilemma, Confucians developed the Rectification of Names. By clarifying all personal titles and connecting them to well-established rituals, people could incorporate new acquaintances into their lives. Once you understood the right name of each person in a society, they reasoned, you could treat him or her with the correct ritual and respect. You can imagine this happening in your classroom. If a person you don't know walks into the classroom and introduces himself or herself as "Professor," you immediately know how to behave in his or her presence. You'll also know what to expect (Liu 17–19).

As a professor, I think about the "rectification of names." I do not mind being called "Professor" or "Doctor," although I do not like to be called "Roy" or "Mr." in the classroom. I also want to be respectful of my students. At the beginning of every semester, I refer to my students as "Mr." or "Ms.," as a sign of respect that they are adults and have worked hard to be accepted to the university.

When should I change to using students' first names? Never? Or when we are more comfortable with each other in class? And should I make sure that students call each other by first names, or "Mr./Ms.," or something else? Is it OK for students just to refer to one another as "he" or "she" but not use a proper name? Finally, at what point should I expect my students to use my first name? As a student, what do you think?

I remember that my undergraduate mentor invited me to his house on my graduation day. We split a bottle of beer—a first!—and he told me to call him by his first name. Looking back on it, I realize that he was a Superior Man at work, making sure that he had rectified our names in a new, post-college atmosphere. I am still not sure what to call students, but I always remember how he made me more comfortable in our new roles, not equals, but no longer student and professor.

the THINK SPOT
www.thethinkspot.com

---

built upon virtue for virtue's sake. If every person would strive to think and act virtuously, then each person's intrinsic understanding of right and wrong would keep him or her on a path toward humanity. In this case, acting inappropriately makes you ashamed—a feeling that comes from inside, not outside, of yourself. Regardless of who is around to witness your behavior, your own sense of virtue will keep you on the right path. Confucius completes the argument this way:

> If they be led by virtue, and uniformity sought to be given them by the rules of propriety, they will have the sense of shame, and moreover will become good." (Confucius *Analects*, II: 3).

This self-directed virtuous thinking and behavior permeates East Asian culture. It's no wonder, since Confucianism provided the basis for Chinese civil service examinations for more than 1,000 years, ending only in the early 20th century. Although the system became corrupt toward the end of the imperial period, the exam's goal reminds us of Confucius' central role in Chinese society: To serve the empire, civil servants needed to understand how to act in all situations. Only when they had internalized the way to interact could they help run society (Liu 62).

Daoism

Confucian thinking—let's call it a philosophical "yang"—seeks to create a highly organized community based on virtuous individuals. In contrast—consider it "yin"—Daoism seems to care little about society. The great Daoist sages often lived alone in the wilderness or on a mountaintop. Its core practice, wu wei, doesn't seem useful for organizing or leading a society. Yet, as we have seen, Daoism became a state religion, too. Moreover, although it seems contradictory, Daoism has always believed that life in harmony with the Dao would lead to a more harmonious society. The *Daodejing* says:

> Cultivate The Way (Dao) in your village and the village's Virtue (De) will long endure.
>
> Cultivate The Way in your state, and the state's Virtue will be abundant.
>
> Cultivate The Way throughout the world, and the world's Virtue will be pervasive (*Daodejing* 54b, in Littlejohn 17).

Daoism's influence on East Asia has fluctuated over the centuries. During the Cultural Revolution in China, for example, practitioners of the Dao focused their attentions inward, largely in secret. In recent years, however, many East Asian people seem to be rediscovering Daoism, especially through the revival of qi gong. This upswing points to Daoism's power to organize people into peaceful groups, even if they are not communities in a formal sense. The people who gather in the morning to do qi gong in the park, for example, may not see each other during the rest of the day. Yet they do come together and share something, trying to focus qi in their lives. This intense concentration on qi, rather than on community organization, makes qi gong more acceptable to the government than Falun Gong, which the government distrusts.

The qi gong trend becomes stronger as people's lives change rapidly. The Chinese are transforming their country from an agricultural one to an industrial one at an alarming speed. To do this, millions of people have moved from the villages to the cities, where they experience the ups and downs of economic booms. In a world that seems out of control, where can you turn for peace and harmony? Perhaps you can find it through the Dao by developing your qi.

∧ **Japanese Buddhists** on a pilgrimage to the Nichiren temple in Minobu.

Community in East Asian Buddhist Traditions

When we studied Buddhism in Chapters 6 and 7, we spent a good deal of time learning about the relationship of monks to lay Buddhists. Communities grew in various ways based on how the monastic and laity interacted. In East Asia, this phenomena has continued but with a different emphasis. Consider the three forms of Buddhism that we've studied here: Pure Land, Nichiren, and Chan/Zen. All of them downplay the importance of monks in comparison to other forms of Buddhism. In this way, the Buddhist communities in this region may not cluster around monasteries, for enlightenment can be found in other forms of education.

Imagine yourself as a social outcast in contemporary Asian society. Perhaps a beggar or even a prostitute, you lack Confucian education. As a poor person, you may find it difficult to follow wu wei, since your belly is often empty. Now imagine you have been introduced to the Pure Land or the Lotus Sutra. Both of these offer solace to you even without a proper education or high social standing. You can live your life and hope for enlightenment by chanting the name of Amitabha Buddha or the Lotus Sutra. Likewise, you can find people like you in communities, sharing in these highly direct forms of Buddhism. Nichiren Buddhists congregate together, believing that theirs is the purest understanding of the Buddha. Pure Land followers, on the other hand, hope that *all* beings are eventually welcomed into the Pure Land because of Amitabha's huge store of

THINK World Religions

Chairman Mao and the People's Republic

In the early 20th century, a nationalist government ousted the last Chinese emperor and sought to create a quasi-democratic system in China while keeping most of its traditional culture. It did not last long—the Japanese invaded northern China in the 1930s, and China then became a theater of war during World War II. In the war's aftermath, the Chinese Communist Party, led by Mao Zedong (Mao Tse-Tung) successfully routed the nationalists, who fled to Taiwan. That's how it stands today—the Communist government controls the mainland, while tiny (but economically strong) Taiwan retains a more traditional Chinese culture.

Communism and traditional ways of life coexisted uneasily for about a generation, but then Chairman Mao called for a cultural revolution to root out traditional ideas. The Red Army and the Red Guards (volunteer units) burned family genealogy books, demolished temples, and destroyed ancient treasures. They rounded up intellectuals and sent them for "re-education" in the countryside, forcing professors and engineers to toil in rice paddies to become better communists. Survivors were lucky—thousands were murdered or died in labor camps.

The government called for the rooting out of the "Four Olds":

- Old Customs
- Old Culture
- Old Habits
- Old Ideas

By these, Mao meant the culture of ancient China, which embraced Confucianism, Daoism, and Buddhism. Even Mao, however, could not completely go against tradition. His famous *Little Red Book* reads as if Confucius or Laozi had suddenly become a communist. The content was different, but the aphoristic style was familiar to Chinese readers: "Anyone who sees only the bright side but not the difficulties cannot fight effectively for the accomplishment of the Party's tasks"; "The Three Main Rules of Discipline: Obey orders in all your actions. Do not take a single needle piece of thread from the masses. Turn in everything captured" (Mao).

From the 1970s through the 1990s, China struggled to regain the intellectual and scientific ground that it had lost during the Cultural Revolution. Resentment grew more strident, and in 1989, open protests broke out in Beijing. The government brutally put down the demonstrations and again jailed those who openly questioned its power. By the late 1990s, however, a new generation had risen to power, and they began to experiment with a fusion of communist politics, free-market economics, and traditional wisdom. Today in China, you'll easily find Mao's *Little Red Book* near a small statue of the Buddha or joss sticks for burning at a family altar. The present Communist leader calls for a "harmonious society," echoing Confucius far more than Mao!

⋀
⋀
⋀ Two views of the Cultural Revolution. On the left, marchers hold aloft a picture of Mao Zedong in Beijing. One the right, a crowd humiliates a man, perhaps an intellectual, by placing a huge dunce cap on his head.

the THINK SPOT
www.thethinkspot.com

^
^
^
^

A Chinese copy of the Lotus Sutra, c. 900 CE

merit. Only those who actively work against Buddha Amitabha will not gain entrance. This form of Buddhism, sometimes referred to as the "easy path to enlightenment," offers a different form of community than that to be found in Nichiren.

Different from Pure Land and Nichiren traditions, Chan (Zen) Buddhism teaches people to follow an uncomplicated yet well-reasoned and thoughtful path throughout life. Chan affects the Buddhist community in certain ways. For example, unlike other Buddhist monks (who only beg for food so not to become attached to this life), Chan monks believe in the importance of work. A day without work, says the Chan tradition, is a day without food. This approach to life can appeal to lay Buddhists, because it shows them the spiritual value in their jobs. Chan traditions, as we have seen, could also attract Daoists. The Chinese Chan master Lin-chi famously advised his disciples just to act ordinary, without trying to do anything particular. "Move your bowels, piss, get dressed, eat your rice, and if you get tired, then lie down. Fools may laugh at me, but wise men will know what I mean" (Olson 230).

Although a Chan master and not a Daoist, Lin-chi perceived the importance of wu wei, action through inaction.

Chan has had a huge impact across East Asia, and especially on Japanese culture. In some places, such as the highly ritualized Japanese tea ceremony, it seems that Chan, Confucianism, and Daoism all play a part. Even Japanese poetry developed as a form of Chan meditation. Haiku, the national form of poetry in Japan, is closely linked to the simplicity and natural beauty of Chan and the imponderable truth of a koan. To end this chapter, take a moment to contemplate this famous haiku by the master Basho (Olson 242):

On a withered branch
A crow has settled—
Autumn nightfall.

Conclusion

It may seem odd, but let's conclude this chapter by going back to the photograph at the beginning of Chapter 7. Look again, not just at the symbol of Taiji, but at the person himself.

First, take a good look at the man's head: If you focus your mind just right, doesn't he look like a living version of the Taiji? Imagine his hair to be the dark yang and his face to be the light yin. The hair even has a bit of light, and the face has bits of dark, just like the spots on the Taiji. So what is the point? We can use this picture to remember that the yin and yang of creation don't exist only as symbols. In the East Asian tradition, human beings are a part of the Supreme Ultimate; we include both yin and yang within us.

Similarly, the picture is of a guy—a real person—not just an idea. This can remind us that East Asian philosophy often focuses on the issues facing human beings and society, even to the apparent exclusion of gods or spirits. Daoism teaches that experiencing The Way can lead to immortality. East Asian Buddhism, while hoping for release from this life of suffering, also often concentrates on the human dimension. It links everyday life to enlightenment.

Why would the man get a tattoo of the Taiji? Perhaps he is a Daoist, Confucian, or Buddhist. Or maybe he wants something that won't lose its meaning, a better choice for permanent body art than his girlfriend's phone number or the name of his favorite football player. The yin and yang represent the harmony of the universe—constant but also constantly changing, like the ink on skin that moves, stretches, and ages. Finally, why is the guy smiling? Perhaps he feels, like Buddha's student, the joy of enlightenment through a simple flower, picture, or stone in a garden.

>>> **What does the tattoo of the taiji tell us about this man?**

The idea of the divine varies in East Asia depending on who you ask. Are there similar disagreements in other religions?

Through their actions, believers seek to harmonize with Dao. How is this similar to or different from Hindu beliefs?

IS THERE A GOD?

Not necessarily. Across East Asia, people will answer this differently. People may perceive Confucius as a man or a deity. The Dao has elements of divinity, but is a power, not a person. The Buddha might be divine in Nichiren Buddhism, but not Chan. And the Jade Emperor may be a Daoist god or just a folktale.

HOW DOES THE SACRED BECOME COMMUNITY?

The answer to this question depends on how the follower of the religion defines what it means to be human. Confucians interact with other people through a series of intricate rituals, which include formally recognizing one's place in society relative to everyone else. In contrast, Daoists reconcile their beliefs with the world by actively removing themselves from social obligations and constructs. East Asian Buddhists seek community through the laity more frequently than do other Buddhist traditions.

WHAT DOES IT MEAN TO BE HUMAN?

In all the East Asian religions, personhood is related to living a virtuous life. However, the different traditions describe different paths to virtue. Confucians put their faith in complex interpersonal rites and rituals. Daoists tend to value solitude and turning the mind inward. Chen Buddhists follow a path similar to Daoists, although they keep an eye toward the eventual break from Samsara.

HOW DO HUMANS INTERACT WITH THE SACRED?

In East Asian traditions, the sacred can be found nearly anywhere—from your ancestors' shen to a mountaintop to a garden. Humans can find many ways to interact with this sacred life, including rituals, martial arts, meditation, and divination. While Pure Land Buddhists look to Amitabha and Nichiren find enlightenment chanting the Lotus Sutra, Chan Buddhists hope for a flash of enlightenment from their contemplation of nature, work, or the absurd.

<<< The society of Eastern Asia has been influenced by the constant mix of Confucianism, Daoism, and Buddhism. How do you think this plays into modern-day politics?

>>> Because everything is part of the Dao, spirituality is carried over into all areas of life. How would this affect your daily actions?

Summary

HOW DO HUMANS INTERACT WITH THE SACRED?   p. 104

- Although Confucianism focuses on social relationships, it often includes a spiritual aspect as well. Confucius taught that every action has a ritual element, merging the sacred with the everyday. Since the family is seen as the most important unit of society, the veneration of ancestors—including Confucius—is common among believers.
- Daoists may practice divination as a way to interact with qi. Traditional martial arts, as well as alchemy and acupuncture, also provide a means of interacting with the sacred.

HOW DOES THE SACRED BECOME COMMUNITY?   p. 111

- Confucianism teaches a highly developed form of social order. Each human being should strive to move upward in the hierarchy of morality.
- Nichiren Buddhists come together to understand the Buddha, while Chan and Pure Land Buddhists focus on the everyday as a means of achieving enlightenment.
- Practitioners of Daoism seek to actively remove themselves from social bonds, and focus on qi rather than community organization.

Key Terms

Alchemy is the ancient practice of transforming one matter into another. In Eastern Asia, practitioners focused on the transformation of the human body.   *106*

Falun Gong combines a system of exercise and movement with a spiritual emphasis on self-improvement.   *107*
Feng shui focuses on the flow of qi in a specific place (often a room or building).   *108*

Acupuncture uses tiny needles to remove blockages of qi in the body.   *110*

Find it on

http://www.chinatownology.com/lion_dance.html
Want to see an authentic Lion Dance as performed at different locations around the world? Go to the ThinkSpot and take your pick from video postings from Paris, Singapore, or Cholon Chinatown. The dance is a spectacle of movement, light, and sound and an event you can now view from the comfort of your own room!

- http://www.falundafa.org/eng/home.html
Learn more about Falun Gong at the official Web site for this tradition. Read the information provided and decide for yourself: practitioners of an ancient faith system or revolutionaries?

Questions for Study and Review

1. **Explain how Confucianism and Daoism might be considered yin and yang to each other.**

   Confucius stressed the importance of recognizing social constructs. He considered following rituals to be the greatest of virtues. Confucians therefore tend to engage with others socially. Daoists, on the other hand, value inward thinking, so they may remove themselves from society and turn away from relationships with others. While Confucians tend toward action through ritual, Daoists prize wu wei—action without action.

2. **In what way Pure Land and Nichiren Buddhist traditions differ from the forms of Buddhism you read about in Chapters 5 and 6?**

   Pure Land Buddhists believe that Amitabha Buddha achieved enlightenment but stayed on Earth to help others. Because he continued to accumulate good karma that he no longer needed, he used it to create the Pure Land, where followers could be reborn on their way to enlightenment. The Pure Land does not shield the follower from samsara, but acts as a refuge for those not far along the path to enlightenment. Nichiren teaches that the ultimate message of Buddhism can be found in the Lotus Sutra, and contemplating it helps lead you toward enlightenment.

3. **In what way might a Chan rock garden help followers of Chan Buddhism?**

   As the Chan Buddhists create waves in the sand, they can contemplate the utter simplicity of everything. Chan rock gardens serve to focus the mind away from the complex, and inward toward enlightenment.

For Further Study

BOOKS:

Berthron, John H. and Evelyn Nagai. *Confucianism: A Short Introduction*. Oxford, UK: Oneworld Publications, 2000.

Confucius. Raymond Dawson, trans. *The Analects*. New York: Oxford University Press, 2001.

Lao-Tzu. Robert G. Henricks, trans. *Te-Tao Ching: A New Translation Based on the Recently Discovered Ma-wang-tui Texts*. New York: Ballantine Books, 1989.

Littlejohn, Ronnie L. *Daoism: An Introduction*. London: I.B. Taurus & Co. Ltd., 2009.

Liu, JeeLoo. *An Introduction to Chinese Philosophy: From Ancient Philosophy to Chinese Buddhism*. Malden, MA: Blackwell Publishing, 2006.

Renard, John. *101 Questions and Answers on Confucianism, Daoism, and Shinto*. New York: Paulist Press, 2002.

WEB SITES:

Chinese Ministry of Culture. http://www.chinaculture.org

I Ching: Book of Changes. http://www.pantherwebworks.com/I_Ching

"The Analects of Confucius" at *Sacred Texts: Confucianism*. http://www.sacred-texts.com/cfu/index.htm

Sacred Texts: Daoism. http://www.sacred-texts.com/tao/index.htm

Taiwan Culture Portal. http://www.culture.tw

ZenGuide. http://www.zenguide.com

<<< The magnificent interior
of the Dohany Synagogue
in Budapest, Hungary.

Q IS THERE A GOD?

WHAT DOES IT MEAN TO BE HUMAN?

You may

look at the magnificent structure at the left and be struck by its beauty. The synagogue, which bordered the Budapest Ghetto created during the Holocaust, is the largest synagogue in Europe and was consecrated in 1859. What you see in this photo represents a three-year restoration process that was necessitated after the original synagogue was nearly destroyed by the pro-Nazi Arrow Cross Party in 1939. The building was continually bombed in aerial raids during the Nazi Occupation and suffered severe damage. But like the Jewish people, who have a long and sometimes painful history, this building triumphed over its tragic past and continues to embody the faith, the trials, and the tribulations of the people of Israel, who, according to scripture, were "chosen" by God.

As you will learn in this chapter, Judaism is the oldest monotheistic religion and as such, holds a prominent place in our Western culture, having influenced other monotheistic religions with its doctrine. As we seek to answer the universal questions common to all religions, we will look at them through the lens of a religion that is anchored in both a place—Israel—and a culture, both of which inform the followers of this rich and historical faith.

JUDAISM:
A Chosen People Choosing God

CHAPTER 09

The Central Synagogue

EVERYONE SAYS NOT TO LOOK UP WHEN YOU'RE IN NEW YORK CITY BECAUSE YOU'LL LOOK TOO TOURISTY. But when you're walking on Lexington Avenue and get to 55th Street look up and to your right. There, in front of a tall pinkish skyscraper, you'll see the Central Synagogue. Its brown sandstone doesn't much stand out, but the two distinctive domes—green and gold with stars on the top of each tower—tip you off that this is a special place.

Climb the stairs, walk through the glass doors, and find yourself in another world from the hustle of midtown Manhattan. Stretching out before you is a long room, seven stories high and filled everywhere with a glow reflecting off warm, colored tile, gleaming walnut woodwork, and walls stenciled a riot of multihued designs. Yet somehow this majestic space seems warm and inviting, not overwhelming.

As your eyes adjust, you can start looking for themes. There are stars all around, the Star of David that you'd expect, but also five-pointed American ones and many others painted, applied, carved, and in stained glass. A towering cabinet in the front, called the ark, keep the Torah scrolls safe. Above it hangs a dome that looks like a Turkish turban. The whole effect is more Istanbul than New York. It's called the Moorish Revival style, recalling Judaism's history in the Middle East, Spain, and Europe.

Jewish immigrants built this striking synagogue in 1872, a congregation of "progressive" Jews who had found work as tailors or cigar makers on the lower East Side but began to be more successful and moved up town. They were German-speaking Czechs and children of the Haskalah, the Jewish Enlightenment. And so this would be a Reform synagogue, where men and women would pray together (rather than separated in a gallery), children would learn in English and Hebrew rather than Yiddish, and Christian neighbors would feel comfortable when they saw the pews, the *bema* (reading table) in the front rather than the middle of the room, and the pipe organ.

Look closely at the Torah scrolls when the rabbi slides open the wooden doors of the ark. There are eight of them, robed in blue and standing in front of a woven backdrop that seems to radiate light. On the far left in the back, one Torah has writing on the cover. It arrived in New York just recently. For decades, it lay buried in a metal box on the edge of a Jewish cemetery just outside the Auschwitz death camp. When found, it was missing a few panels of text. Jewish prisoners at the death camp secretly kept these sections, using them for prayer. They passed the Torah portions to others as they went to their horrible deaths. Somehow, a local Roman Catholic priest had kept them after World War II. He returned the panels, and the whole Torah found a new, safe home in New York's Central Synagogue.

If you're lucky to hear the organ played, listen for two unique sounds. The *shofar*, a ram's horn, calls Jews to prayer. The klezmer clarinet plays lead in klezmer, Eastern European Jews' folk music. Together on a pipe organ, they symbolize the many facets of Judaism in America.

Source: Based on Hardy, Hugh., *The Restoration of Central Synagogue*, New York: Central Synagogue 2002.

Interior of the
Central Synagogue, New York City
How is it similar to the Dohany Synagogue in Budapest?

A Torah Scroll, *hand-written on parchment. The Central Synagogue has more than one copy. They stay safe in the ark (as in "Ark of the Covenant") at the front of the synagogue.*

The shofar — *a ram's horn played like, well, a horn. The New Synagogue's organ has a pipe made to sound like a shofar.*

Men can borrow a **yarmulke** *(or* **kippah***) from a basket like this one near the doors. In some Jewish traditions, men wear these small hats continually, to remind them that God is always above them. The Central Synagogue offers them for special occasions or personal preference. Nowadays, sometimes women wear them too.*

The silver **yad** *has a tiny hand on it. "Yad" means hand in Hebrew. Torah readers use the yad to follow along the text as they recite, keeping the parchment clean and your real hands off it.*

121

Ethical monotheism is a foundational principle of Judaism that encapsulates three main ideas: 1) the need to recognize only one God; 2) the need to act appropriately toward God; and 3) the need to act appropriately toward other people.

Rabbi is a Jewish religious leader. The term literally means "teacher" or "scholar."

What Is Judaism?

For many people living in the western world, religion would not be imaginable without the influence of Judaism. Based on the idea of a covenant between God and his chosen people, Judaism is the oldest monotheistic religion. Although only a small minority of North Americans and Europeans are Jewish, the religion holds a central place in our culture. It was through Judaism that we first perceived the relationship of monotheism—the belief in a single god—linked to a universal standard of ethical behavior. This idea, often called **ethical monotheism**, has shaped the Western world in many ways. Judaism introduced ideas of "faith," "prayer," and "God" that have now become shorthand for "religion," "interaction," and "deity." Even scholars of religion—who pride themselves on finding neutral language—often slip back to using these words from the Jewish tradition as if they were universally appropriate to all religions. You may notice, for example, that the familiar word "God" suddenly has a capital "G" in *THINK World Religions*. That's because God in Judaism has no other proper name (like Brahma, for example), so we use the term "God" both as a description and a name. Yet, now that you think of it, don't we usually describe "God" this way, following the Jewish tradition?

A SACRED ACTION ▶▶▶

Bar and Bat Mitzvah

After practicing how to do it countless times, he has now wrapped a leather band around each arm, with a small portion of the Torah contained in a box attached to the bands. His *tefillin* now in place, he breathes a little nervously and hefts the scrolls into his arms from the ark at the front of the synagogue. Silver ornaments, hanging from the scroll, sway above him. All eyes focus on the boy who carries the words of God, his shoulders covered by a prayer shawl called the

tallith. Some people lean out into the aisle, touching the velvet cover with their hands or their prayer books. Making his way around the congregation and toward the front of the synagogue, the boy places the scrolls on a large reading table. In a few moments, he will begin to read the portion of the Torah appointed for that day. It's highly likely that he's nervous looking down at the parchment rolled out before him. It is the story of his roots and his tradition. It contains the commandments that, from this day forward, he should try to obey. For the first time, he has carried it on his arms in the leather *tefillin*.

The boy scans for the section he has recited over and over again in Hebrew school. Not to worry, because the **rabbi** gestures to it with a long silver wand ending in a tiny hand pointing the way, right to left, along the lines of text. His voice may shake and break—he's just 13 after all—as he begins to prove his literacy and his responsibility to the sacred covenant between God and Jews.

▶ IS THERE A GOD?

For the religions that we have studied in Chapters 3–8, the answer to this question has been "maybe," "sort of," "many," or "in some sense." To the contrary, Judaism exclaims, "Yes, there is a God—one and only one God." In fact, Judaism has defined itself through its relationship to a single creator God. To understand this connection, Judaism seeks to answer many questions. Here are a few important ones:

1. How do you prove that God exists?

2. How do you define God?

3. By what name or title do you call God?

4. How does God communicate with us?

Bar/bat mitzvah means "son/daughter of the commandment" and refers to a Jewish boy or girl reaching the age of a religious adult. A boy becomes a bar mitzvah at age 13, and a girl attains the status at age 12. Bar/bat mitzvah is also the name of the ceremony often held to celebrate this event.

Torah, meaning Law, refers to the first five books of the Hebrew Bible. However, the word can also be used to denote *all* Jewish religious texts and *all* Jewish law.

Proof of God

Can human beings prove the existence of a God who cannot be seen? For an answer, let's analyze the first words of the **Torah**, Judaism's sacred text. (By the way, the idea of finding meaning through text study is called "exegesis," and it plays a central role in Judaism.) Here is a

With the reading of the Torah in synagogue, a young boy (and, beginning in a few places as early as 1922, a young girl) publicly marks his place in the Jewish community. The ceremony isn't strictly necessary, but Jews throughout the world celebrate it, sometimes in their home synagogue or perhaps in Jerusalem. Before becoming a son or daughter of the commandments (the translation of **bar mitzvah** and **bat mitzvah**), Jewish kids do not have many responsibilities

to their families and communities. After that age, with or without the ceremony and its attendant party, the child takes on new roles. Even though this newly minted grown-up might not look it, standing there in a formal suit or party dress, the boy or girl has given an adult Torah blessing, received one in return from a parent, and can now say the words traditional to this day: "Today I am a man" or "Today I am a woman" (Robinson 157–59).

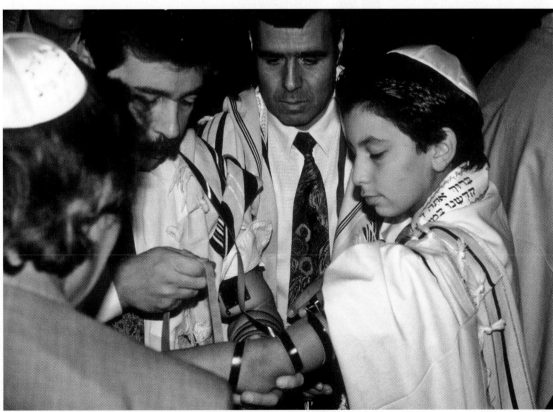

∧
∧   Here are photos from a Bat Mitzvah and Bar Mitzvah. Why do you think it took centuries
∧   before girls became eligible for this sacred ceremony?

Jewish Definition of God

God

- Created the universe
- Is always present
- Has no physical form
- Knows everything
- Needs no proof of existence
- Exists eternally
- Is the only God
- Judges fairly and mercifully
- Has no gender
- Is holy and perfect

∧
∧ **Which of these attributes seem common sense to you?**
∧ *What might that mean about your ideas about God?*

God separated the light from the darkness. God called the light Day, the darkness He called Night. And there was evening and there was morning, the first day" (Genesis 1:1–5). Ancient people of the Middle East would have understood the "unformed earth" and "deep waters" as explanations for a chaotic place where only God could create order. To do so, God would have to be incredibly powerful, not just "a" god but "the" God.

Definition of God

But doesn't this story also bring up some questions? What was that chaos that God turned into creation? Was God part of it or separate from it? In other words, can we define God? Well, yes and no. Remember the problem of describing the Dao in the East Asian tradition? We face a similar issue when trying to define God in Judaism. In Daoism, fish (people) could not define or understand the ocean (Dao) because they were inside it, unable to perceive its wholeness. Similarly, in the Jewish tradition, we cannot hope to understand God completely because we exist inside creation. There is simply no perspective from which we might see, feel, or define the totality of God. Nevertheless, like the Daoist fish, we can get a good sense of the ocean even if we cannot understand it completely.

Over thousands of years, Judaism has attributed a number of characteristics to God. You can see some of these in the diagram on the next page.

The Name of God

Try using the concept of "naming" as a way to understand the Jewish conception of God. Many parts of the Bible emphasize the importance of names as forms of identity. Later in Genesis, for example, Adam gets to pick out names for the rest of creation: "And the Lord God formed out of the earth all the wild beasts and the birds of the sky, and brought them to the man to see what he would call them; and whatever the man called each living creature, that would be its name. And the man gave names to all the cattle and to the birds of the sky and to all the wild beasts. . . ." (Genesis 2:19–20).

Names also create comparisons. Sometimes this is obvious, like "Junior." You could argue, though, that all names must be comparative in some sense because they differentiate one person from another. If you were alone on a desert island, your name would matter far less than it does when you're in your dorm. Confucius understood this when he counseled the Superior Person to "rectify names" to create order and harmony in society. In fact, the idea of "naming" arises in many cultures. The process illustrates the relationship between the "namer" and the "named." The girl's name "Tiffany," for example, tends to remind people of aspiration to wealth. "Sean" might recall a boy's Irish lineage.

How then, do we name a being—God—who has no comparisons? On the one hand, you might use descriptive terms, each of which reflects some facet of God's existence. On the other hand, giving God a name might also imply human characteristics, which Judaism avoids. So, it seems there are two possibilities: first, we can give God descriptive titles that aren't actual names. Alternatively, we can steer clear of any name all. Jewish tradition uses both of these strategies. In some cases, Jews refer to God as "The Name" or *Ha Shem*, to avoid giving a name to someone

---

quote that many of us know, even if we were not raised in the Jewish tradition: "In the beginning God created the heaven and the earth." (Genesis 1:1). A simple sentence, but take a closer look at what it implies. There is only one actor in this sentence: God. Not multiple gods or a general spirit, but a single entity. Likewise, we see only one action verb: "to create." And so, we can conclude that God—no one else—created heaven and earth, providing the backdrop for the rest of history.

Do we know anything about God in the passage? No—there is no description, just the fact of existence. Do we have knowledge about what happened *before* "in the beginning?" No—before this sentence there was nothing but God (Blech 4–7).

What did God do? God created everything. This statement has important implications. If God was the creator of everything, there is nothing outside of that "everything"—no time, place, or people that has *not* been created by God. In Jewish tradition, then, the very existence of the cosmos constitutes the proof of God. If there were no God, how could there be such a magnificent universe?

The act of creation meant that God took chaos—which already existed—and gave it order. The most recent Jewish translation of Genesis makes this clear in a poetic way: "When God began to create heaven and earth—the earth being unformed and void, with darkness over the surface of the deep and a wind from God sweeping over the water—God said, 'Let there be light'; and there was light. God saw that the light was good, and

who is above all names. Here are some other examples, in both Hebrew and English, of Jewish titles for God:

- *Adonai*/Lord
- *El Khai*/The Living God
- *El Olom*/God Everlasting
- *El Shaddai*/God Almighty
- *Eloheinu*/Our God
- *Tzur Yisroel*/Rock of Israel

You can see how certain names correspond to the characteristics of God outlined in the previous section. God is alive and always will be, God is all-powerful, God is ours, and God creates a foundation for Israel. One Jewish name for God illustrates the sacred importance of naming. Incorrectly translated as "Jehovah," it is the "Four-Letter Name", the Hebrew letters "Yud-Hay-Vav-Hay." You'll likely see it shortened as YHVH. The "Four-Letter Name" likely relates to the Hebrew word for "to be" and thus expresses the eternal nature of God.

Finally, you may see the word "God" written as "G-d" in Jewish discourse. In this tradition, writing down the word "God" carries the risk of later erasing or defiling God's name. Therefore, an observant Jew may choose to avoid writing "God" entirely by substituting "G-d" (Robinson 8–10; Seltzer 287–290).

How Does God Communicate with Us?

The final question from the beginning of this chapter asks how God communicates with followers of Judaism. The answer: through the Hebrew Bible, usually called the Torah. In the Hebrew Bible, the term Torah designates the first five books of the Bible—"the Law." After these come

The Talmud

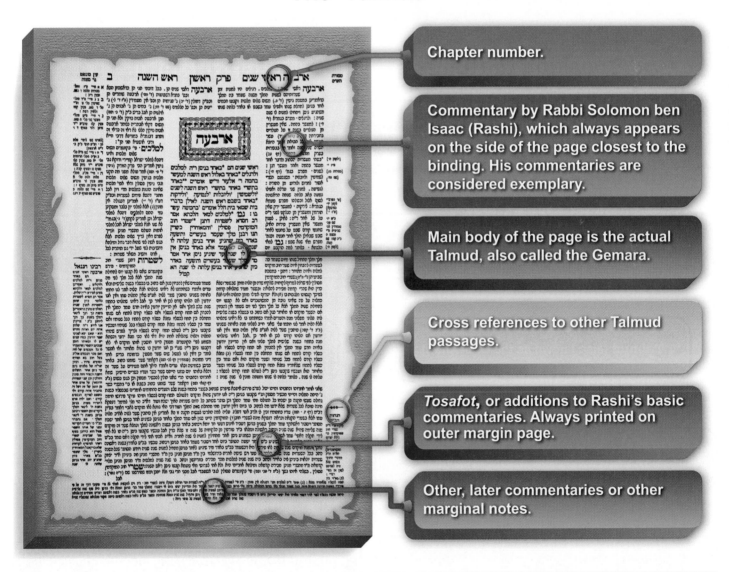

Chapter number.

Commentary by Rabbi Solomon ben Isaac (Rashi), which always appears on the side of the page closest to the binding. His commentaries are considered exemplary.

Main body of the page is the actual Talmud, also called the Gemara.

Cross references to other Talmud passages.

Tosafot, or additions to Rashi's basic commentaries. Always printed on outer margin page.

Other, later commentaries or other marginal notes.

The Talmud provides information on the writings in the Torah. What can you deduce about Jewish scholarship and tradition by studying the way Talmudic text is printed on the page?

Tanakh refers to three sets of religious texts—"the Law" (Torah), "the Prophets," and "the Writings" that constitute the Hebrew Bible.

Midrash interprets the Torah with an emphasis on everyday life.

Talmud, also called the "oral Torah," is a historical collection of rabbinical writings and commentaries on the Torah.

"the Prophets" and "the Writings." Together, the make up the **Tanakh** or, as we just mentioned, the "Hebrew Bible."

The first five books of the Torah describe the creation of the world, the development of human society, and God's relationship with humanity. They also contain laws that govern nearly all facets of life, from food to sex to travel. For millennia, however, scholars have studied and commented on these parts of the Torah, developing a huge number of opinions. The **Midrash** interprets the Hebrew Bible by expanding its stories to explain their meaning for everyday life. The **Talmud**, on the other hand, offers fewer Biblical interpretations than the Midrash. Instead, it concentrates on codifying and explaining Torah law. The Talmud existed orally for generations before it was written down, so it's often called the "oral Torah" to differentiate it from the "written Torah" of the Hebrew Bible. Just

THINK World Religions

Where Are the Pictures?

Take a look at this chapter and compare it to some of the others in this book. You'll likely notice that there are more text boxes but no pictures of God. That's on purpose. It illustrates the Jewish focus on texts and interpretation. Judaism (like Islam, which we'll study in Chapters 13 and 14) adamantly refuses to create pictures of God. To do so would anthropomorphize God—making a nonhuman being look like a human being. So, because it's impossible to interact with God using our senses, Jewish tradition relies instead on text. Jews believe that the Torah contains God's words. Others books, which we'll study in the next couple of pages, interpret God's words in different ways—through debate, textual analysis, and even humor. As a result, we will follow Jewish tradition and rely more on texts in Chapters 9 and 10 than in almost any other part of *THINK World Religions*.

God Speaking to Humans—The Structure of Jewish Laws

> **The Hebrew Bible (also known as the Tanakh)**

> **Torah ("Law"):** Five books—Genesis, Exodus, Leviticus, Numbers, Deuteronomy

> **Prophets:** 19 books

> **Writings:** 11 books

> **Talmud** (also known as the Oral Torah)

> **Midrash:** Interpretations of the Torah

> **Halakhah** ("The Way"): Law and ethics

> **Aggadah** ("The Telling"): Stories and explanations

> **Mishnah:** Study of the law

> **Mishneh Torah** (1178 CE): Digest of the Halakhah written by Maimonides and still used today

Source: Based on Robert M. Seltzer, *Jewish People, Jewish Thought: The Jewish Experience in History*, New York: Macmillan Publishing Co., Inc., 1989, 260–273.

to keep you on your toes: Because "Torah" means "Law," it's also possible to call the whole of the Tanakh (including the Torah) *and* the Talmud the "Torah."

The Talmud itself has two sections, the Halakhah (the Way) and the Aggadah (the Telling). The first of these—the Halakhah—guides Jews on their path toward ritual purity and holiness. The second—the Aggadah—emphasizes stories, explanations, and nonlegal elucidations of the Torah. Jewish scholars created two major versions of the Talmud, one in Jerusalem and the other in Babylon. Although they overlap, the Babylonian Talmud has become standard, often considered to be more complete than the Jerusalem Talmud (Seltzer 265–267).

Scholars continued to expand the Talmud by comparing many points of view. In the first two centuries of the Common Era, they compiled these into the **Mishnah**, a compendium of opinions regarding the Halakhah. Less Biblical interpretation than legal tract, the Mishnah delineates how and why Jewish laws need to be followed. It has six sections, each including up to a dozen "tractates." Together, they show us the areas deemed by the rabbis to be the most important in Jewish life:

1. *Zeraim* (Seeds) has one tractate on prayer and 10 more on agricultural concerns as they relate to the Talmud.
2. *Moed* (Set Feasts) describes how to celebrate holy days and other related issues in 12 tractates.
3. *Nashim* (Women) includes seven tractates covering legal issues of women, marriage, and family life.
4. *Nezrikim* (Damages) covers criminal and civil law in 10 separate tractates.

Mishnah is a compendium of opinions and teachings on the Talmud.

5. *Kodashim* (Holy Things) delineates how to serve in the Temple, emphasizing both forms of sacrifice and more general issues of holiness.
6. *Teharot* (Purifications) includes 12 tractates on ritual uncleanness and the ways to repair anything that has been defiled (Seltzer 260–267).

Even the Mishnah, however, is not complete. Each generation of Jews faces different problems and changing circumstances, necessitating new interpretations and applications of Talmudic law. From time to time, these too find their way into print. For example, Rabbi Moses ben Maimon (also known as Rambam and Maimonides), compiled and edited Talmudic law into a volume called the *Mishneh Torah*. Although writing centuries ago in medieval Spain, Maimonides's opinions still hold considerable sway in Judaism, especially his principles of Jewish faith (Seltzer 395; Neusner 137–138).

At this point, you may be wondering how all of this relates to the Jewish concept of God. It does seem confusing to figure out exactly which laws to follow and how to apply them to life. In the end, though, the Halakhah and the Aggadah boil down to just three important concepts. We might think of them as the core of ethical monotheism: All the commandments, laws, decisions, revisions, and interpretations of the Torah thus serve to bring Jews back to this core relationship between God and humanity.

▶ WHAT DOES IT MEAN TO BE HUMAN?

"In the Beginning"

The three elements of ethical monotheism mentioned in the last paragraph highlight the intimate link between God and humanity in Judaism. In the very first chapters of the Torah, we read that God created Adam and Eve (the original human beings) in God's image. Jewish teaching emphasizes not that we look like God (because God doesn't look like anything), but rather that we are naturally good like God. Like God, however, human beings also have our own will, meaning that we may choose *not* to act based on our natural goodness. On the following page is the text from Genesis, Chapter 3. The Hebrew is on the left to give you a feeling for how it might look on a Torah scroll.

As you will read, Adam and Eve had a choice: they could be creative and good, thus acting in God's image. Alternately, they could be destructive and evil—the opposite of God's image. As long as they happily lounged in Eden, naming animals and plants, they lived in harmony with God. When, however, Adam and Eve chose to eat the forbidden fruit, they exercised free will that brought on many consequences—banishment from Eden, a life of struggle, and eventual death (Blech 23–24).

The Human Condition: Abraham, Isaac, and Becoming a Chosen People

After describing the expulsion from the garden, the Torah turns to a discussion of the human relationship with God outside Eden. Abraham's sacrifice to God holds the most important clue to understanding Judaism's view of itself.

<<< This ancient mosaic comes from Beit Alpha, Israel and shows the Sacrifice of Abraham. It was probably made about 1,600 years ago.

א וְהַנָּחָשׁ, הָיָה עָרוּם, מִכֹּל חַיַּת הַשָּׂדֶה, אֲשֶׁר עָשָׂה יְהוָה אֱלֹהִים; וַיֹּאמֶר, אֶל-הָאִשָּׁה, אַף כִּי-אָמַר אֱלֹהִים, לֹא תֹאכְלוּ מִכֹּל עֵץ הַגָּן.	**1** Now the serpent was the shrewdest of all the wild beasts that the LORD God had made. He said to the woman, "Did God really say: You shall not eat of any tree of the garden?"
ב וַתֹּאמֶר הָאִשָּׁה, אֶל-הַנָּחָשׁ: מִפְּרִי עֵץ-הַגָּן, נֹאכֵל.	**2** The woman replied to the serpent, "We may eat of the fruit of the other trees of the garden."
ג וּמִפְּרִי הָעֵץ, אֲשֶׁר בְּתוֹךְ-הַגָּן—אָמַר אֱלֹהִים לֹא תֹאכְלוּ מִמֶּנּוּ, וְלֹא תִגְּעוּ בּוֹ: פֶּן-תְּמֻתוּן.	**3** It is only about the fruit of the tree in the middle of the garden that God said: 'You shall not eat of it or touch it, lest you die.'"
ד וַיֹּאמֶר הַנָּחָשׁ, אֶל-הָאִשָּׁה: לֹא-מוֹת, תְּמֻתוּן.	**4** And the serpent said to the woman, "You are not going to die,
ה כִּי, יֹדֵעַ אֱלֹהִים, כִּי בְּיוֹם אֲכָלְכֶם מִמֶּנּוּ, וְנִפְקְחוּ עֵינֵיכֶם; וִהְיִיתֶם, כֵּאלֹהִים, יֹדְעֵי, טוֹב וָרָע.	**5** but God knows that as soon as you eat of it your eyes will be opened and you will be like divine beings who know good and bad."
ו וַתֵּרֶא הָאִשָּׁה כִּי טוֹב הָעֵץ לְמַאֲכָל וְכִי תַאֲוָה-הוּא לָעֵינַיִם, וְנֶחְמָד הָעֵץ לְהַשְׂכִּיל, וַתִּקַּח מִפִּרְיוֹ, וַתֹּאכַל; וַתִּתֵּן גַּם-לְאִישָׁהּ עִמָּהּ, וַיֹּאכַל. ...	**6** When the woman saw that the tree was good for eating and a delight to the eyes, and that the tree was desirable as a source of wisdom, she took of its fruit and ate. She also gave some to her husband, and he ate. . . .
יג וַיֹּאמֶר יְהוָה אֱלֹהִים לָאִשָּׁה, מַה-זֹּאת עָשִׂית; וַתֹּאמֶר, הָאִשָּׁה, הַנָּחָשׁ הִשִּׁיאַנִי, וָאֹכֵל.	**13** And the LORD God said to the woman, "What is this you have done?" The woman replied, "The serpent duped me, and I ate."
יד וַיֹּאמֶר יְהוָה אֱלֹהִים אֶל-הַנָּחָשׁ, כִּי עָשִׂיתָ זֹּאת, אָרוּר אַתָּה מִכָּל-הַבְּהֵמָה, וּמִכֹּל חַיַּת הַשָּׂדֶה; עַל-גְּחֹנְךָ תֵלֵךְ, וְעָפָר תֹּאכַל כָּל-יְמֵי חַיֶּיךָ. ...	**14** Then the LORD God said to the serpent, "Because you did this, more cursed shall you be than all cattle and all the wild beasts: On your belly shall you crawl and dirt shall you eat all the days of your life. . . .
יט בְּזֵעַת אַפֶּיךָ, תֹּאכַל לֶחֶם, עַד שׁוּבְךָ אֶל-הָאֲדָמָה, כִּי מִמֶּנָּה לֻקָּחְתָּ: כִּי-עָפָר אַתָּה, וְאֶל-עָפָר תָּשׁוּב.	**19** By the sweat of your brow Shall you get bread to eat, until you return to the ground—for from it you were taken. For dust you are and to dust you shall return."
כ וַיִּקְרָא הָאָדָם שֵׁם אִשְׁתּוֹ, חַוָּה: כִּי הִוא הָיְתָה, אֵם כָּל-חָי.	**20** The man named his wife Eve, because she was the mother of all the living.
כא וַיַּעַשׂ יְהוָה אֱלֹהִים לְאָדָם וּלְאִשְׁתּוֹ, כָּתְנוֹת עוֹר—וַיַּלְבִּשֵׁם. {פ}	**21** And the LORD God made garments of skins for Adam and his wife, and clothed them.
כב וַיֹּאמֶר יְהוָה אֱלֹהִים, הֵן הָאָדָם הָיָה כְּאַחַד מִמֶּנּוּ, לָדַעַת, טוֹב וָרָע; וְעַתָּה פֶּן-יִשְׁלַח יָדוֹ, וְלָקַח גַּם מֵעֵץ הַחַיִּים, וְאָכַל, וָחַי לְעֹלָם.	**22** And the LORD God said, "Now that the man has become like one of us, knowing good and bad, what if he should stretch out his hand and take also from the tree of life and eat, and live forever!"
כג וַיְשַׁלְּחֵהוּ יְהוָה אֱלֹהִים, מִגַּן-עֵדֶן—לַעֲבֹד, אֶת-הָאֲדָמָה, אֲשֶׁר לֻקַּח, מִשָּׁם.	**23** So the LORD God banished him from the garden of Eden, to till the soil from which he was taken.
כד וַיְגָרֶשׁ, אֶת-הָאָדָם; וַיַּשְׁכֵּן מִקֶּדֶם לְגַן-עֵדֶן אֶת-הַכְּרֻבִים, וְאֵת לַהַט הַחֶרֶב הַמִּתְהַפֶּכֶת, לִשְׁמֹר, אֶת-דֶּרֶךְ עֵץ הַחַיִּים. {ס}	**24** He drove the man out, and stationed east of the garden of Eden the cherubim and the fiery ever-turning sword, to guard the way of the tree of life.

What do these two stories from the Torah **illustrate about** Jewish views on humanity?

אַ וַיְהִי, אַחַר הַדְּבָרִים הָאֵלֶּה, וְהָאֱלֹהִים, נִסָּה אֶת-אַבְרָהָם; וַיֹּאמֶר אֵלָיו, אַבְרָהָם וַיֹּאמֶר הִנֵּנִי.

1 Sometime afterward, God put Abraham to the test. He said to him, "Abraham," and he answered, "Here I am."

בַּ וַיֹּאמֶר קַח-נָא אֶת-בִּנְךָ אֶת-יְחִידְךָ אֲשֶׁר-אָהַבְתָּ, אֶת-יִצְחָק, וְלֶךְ-לְךָ, אֶל-אֶרֶץ הַמֹּרִיָּה; וְהַעֲלֵהוּ שָׁם, לְעֹלָה, עַל אַחַד הֶהָרִים, אֲשֶׁר אֹמַר אֵלֶיךָ.

2 And He said "Take your son, your favored one, Isaac, whom you love, and go to the land of Moriah, and offer him there as a burnt offering on one of the heights that I will point out to you."

גַּ וַיַּשְׁכֵּם אַבְרָהָם בַּבֹּקֶר, וַיַּחֲבֹשׁ אֶת-חֲמֹרוֹ, וַיִּקַּח אֶת-שְׁנֵי נְעָרָיו אִתּוֹ, וְאֵת יִצְחָק בְּנוֹ; וַיְבַקַּע, עֲצֵי עֹלָה, וַיָּקָם וַיֵּלֶךְ, אֶל-הַמָּקוֹם אֲשֶׁר-אָמַר-לוֹ הָאֱלֹהִים.

3 So early next morning, Abraham saddled his ass and took with him two of his servants and his son Isaac. He split the wood for the burnt offering, and he set out for the place of which God had told him.

זַ וַיֹּאמֶר יִצְחָק אֶל-אַבְרָהָם אָבִיו, וַיֹּאמֶר אָבִי, וַיֹּאמֶר, הִנֶּנִּי בְנִי; וַיֹּאמֶר, הִנֵּה הָאֵשׁ וְהָעֵצִים, וְאַיֵּה הַשֶּׂה, לְעֹלָה.

7 Then Isaac said to his father Abraham, "Father!" And he answered, "Yes, my son." And he said, "Here are the firestone and the wood; but where is the sheep for the burnt offering?"

חַ וַיֹּאמֶר, אַבְרָהָם, אֱלֹהִים יִרְאֶה-לּוֹ הַשֶּׂה לְעֹלָה, בְּנִי; וַיֵּלְכוּ שְׁנֵיהֶם, יַחְדָּו.

8 And Abraham said, "God will see to the sheep for His burnt offering, my son." And the two of them walked on together.

טַ וַיָּבֹאוּ, אֶל-הַמָּקוֹם אֲשֶׁר אָמַר-לוֹ הָאֱלֹהִים, וַיִּבֶן שָׁם אַבְרָהָם אֶת-הַמִּזְבֵּחַ, וַיַּעֲרֹךְ אֶת-הָעֵצִים; וַיַּעֲקֹד, אֶת-יִצְחָק בְּנוֹ, וַיָּשֶׂם אֹתוֹ עַל-הַמִּזְבֵּחַ, מִמַּעַל לָעֵצִים.

9 They arrived at the place of which God had told him. Abraham built an altar there; he laid out the wood; he bound his son Isaac; he laid him on the altar, on top of the wood.

יַ וַיִּשְׁלַח אַבְרָהָם אֶת-יָדוֹ, וַיִּקַּח אֶת-הַמַּאֲכֶלֶת, לִשְׁחֹט, אֶת-בְּנוֹ.

10 And Abraham picked up the knife to slay his son.

יאַ וַיִּקְרָא אֵלָיו מַלְאַךְ יְהוָה, מִן-הַשָּׁמַיִם, וַיֹּאמֶר, אַבְרָהָם אַבְרָהָם; וַיֹּאמֶר, הִנֵּנִי.

11 Then an angel of the Lord called to him from heaven: "Abraham! Abraham!" And he answered, "Here I am."

יבַ וַיֹּאמֶר, אַל-תִּשְׁלַח יָדְךָ אֶל-הַנַּעַר, וְאַל-תַּעַשׂ לוֹ, מְאוּמָה: כִּי עַתָּה יָדַעְתִּי, כִּי-יְרֵא אֱלֹהִים אַתָּה, וְלֹא חָשַׂכְתָּ אֶת-בִּנְךָ אֶת-יְחִידְךָ, מִמֶּנִּי.

12 And he said, "Do not raise your hand against the boy, or do anything to him. For now I know that you fear God, since you have not withheld your son, your favored one, from Me."

טוַ וַיִּקְרָא מַלְאַךְ יְהוָה, אֶל-אַבְרָהָם, שֵׁנִית, מִן-הַשָּׁמָיִם.

15 The angel of the LORD called to Abraham a second time out of heaven,

טזַ וַיֹּאמֶר, בִּי נִשְׁבַּעְתִּי נְאֻם-יְהוָה: כִּי, יַעַן אֲשֶׁר עָשִׂיתָ אֶת-הַדָּבָר הַזֶּה, וְלֹא חָשַׂכְתָּ, אֶת-בִּנְךָ אֶת-יְחִידֶךָ.

16 and said: "By Myself, I swear, the LORD declares, because you have done this and not withheld your son, your favored one,

יזַ כִּי-בָרֵךְ אֲבָרֶכְךָ, וְהַרְבָּה אַרְבֶּה אֶת-זַרְעֲךָ כְּכוֹכְבֵי הַשָּׁמַיִם, וְכַחוֹל, אֲשֶׁר עַל-שְׂפַת הַיָּם; וְיִרַשׁ זַרְעֲךָ, אֵת שַׁעַר אֹיְבָיו.

17 I will bestow my blessing upon you and make your descendants as numerous as the stars in heaven and the sands of the seashore; and your descendants shall seize the gates of their foes.

יחַ וְהִתְבָּרְכוּ בְזַרְעֲךָ, כֹּל גּוֹיֵי הָאָרֶץ, עֵקֶב, אֲשֶׁר שָׁמַעְתָּ בְּקֹלִי.

18 All the nations of the earth shall bless themselves by your descendants, because you have obeyed My command." (Genesis 22: 1–18)

Gentiles are non-Jews.

Incredibly, Abraham decided that he would sacrifice his son, if God so willed it. Yet many scholars and believers over the millennia have argued that God never actually intended for Abraham to murder Isaac, only to "put him to the test." So, what's the point? Why would God do such a thing, and why would Abraham respond in the way that he did? Judaism interprets the story as the interaction between two beings with free will—Abraham and God. Abraham (unlike Adam) chose to follow God; God therefore chose to bless Abraham and his offspring as a chosen people—"in thy seed shall all the nations of the earth be blessed."

Reading this passage, thousands of years after it was written, I still shudder. Sometimes I put myself into Abraham's position, or sometimes into Isaac's. What were they thinking? How complex a relationship must it have been for Abraham and God—receiving unbearable commands and wrestling with conscience and morality, with fear and love. Did Abraham struggle when he made the decision? How could he show his readiness to do God's bidding with those fateful words: "Here I am"? Did Isaac struggle as Abraham tied him and put him on the wood to be burned? Did he agree to be sacrificed? Did he later blame Abraham for putting him through this ordeal, or did he gain strength from hearing God's words?

Jews, too, have interpreted and debated this passage for millennia, because it creates the foundation of Jewish existence and identity. The Jewish Study Bible sums it up nicely by calling Abraham "the first Jew" (Berlin and Brettler 45). It's pretty clear that God sets apart Abraham for something special, blessing him and his progeny.

This idea of Jews being "chosen" can be interpreted in two ways. One approach comes directly from the words of the Torah: "For you are a people consecrated to the LORD your God: the LORD your God chose you from among all other peoples on earth to be His treasured people." (Deuteronomy 14:2). In this case, God chose the Jews as special

recipients of divine law, because Abraham had been willing to follow God's commands. Remember, though, that Abraham also chose God by using free will. We can therefore say both that God chose the Jews and that the Jews chose God. Here is another example of this idea from the Torah, as God speaks to Moses:

> "'Now then, if you will obey Me faithfully and keep My covenant, you shall be My treasured possession among all the peoples. Indeed, all the earth is Mine, but you shall be to Me a kingdom of priests and a holy nation.' These are the words that you shall speak to the children of Israel." Moses came and summoned the elders of the people and put before them all that the LORD had commanded him. And the people answered as one, saying "All that the LORD has spoken, we will do!" (Exodus 19:5–8)

Being "chosen" thus gave Israel, the Jews, a special relationship with God directly related to the concept of ethical monotheism; God acts ethically, and therefore Jews should respond the same way. As the chosen people, Jews therefore must follow more commandments than other groups. According to some traditions, Jews also consequently suffer more grievously than their neighbors *because* they are chosen, not *in spite* of being chosen.

Given the intense concern over being a "chosen people," you might wonder how Judaism views the rest of humanity. In a way, everybody else in the world has it easy—instead of the intensive commandments set out in the Torah for Jews, **gentiles** must only abide by the seven commandments given to Noah and his family, known as the Noahide Commandments. A righteous non-Jew is expected

1. To set up courts of justice (adjudication)
2. To refrain from blasphemy
3. To refrain from idolatry
4. To refrain from sexual immorality (e.g., incest, adultery)
5. To refrain from committing bloodshed
6. To refrain from robbery
7. To refrain from eating the flesh of a live animal (Seltzer 286)

THINK World Religions

Jews, Israel, or Children of Israel: Which Term Is Correct?

Those who practice Judaism generally refer to themselves as "Jews," although you may still hear terms such as "Children of Israel" or simply "Israel."

The word "Israel" can be understood in several ways. Abraham, the founder of Judaism, had two sons. By tradition, each fathered a separate "people" in the Middle East. One of Abraham's grandsons, Jacob, renewed Jews' covenant with God and thus received the name "Israel." He had 12 sons, each of whom in turn fathered one "tribe of Israel." In this usage, then, the word "Israel" means both the man (Jacob) and his progeny (the 12 tribes).

"Israel" also refers to the ethnic group of Jews living in the Middle East in biblical times, but can be expanded to include the religious community of all Jews. And, finally, Israel is the name of a modern nation, founded in 1948.

The word "Jew" refers to any genetic or spiritual heir to God's covenant with Abraham. This definition reminds us that being Jewish has a genetic component to it, often linked to the Semitic culture and language group in the Middle East. (This is where the term "anti-

Semitic" comes from). Historically, Semitic people shared social, religious, and economic ties and tended to be linked closely through marriage. Yet Judaism also offers the possibility that other people, even whole nations, could convert, becoming Jews by choice rather than inheritance. This undermines the argument that Jews are somehow completely separate (either for good or bad) from their neighbors, but it also complicates the definition of Judaism.

And so, the question of "Who is a Jew?" has no single answer. In contemporary Russian society, for example, you could have a "Jewish" ethnic description on your passport, though you may not be religiously Jewish or perceive of yourself as anything but Russian. In this case, your identity cannot be accepted or rejected, any more than being of Portuguese or Korean descent.

The issue is particularly difficult in present-day Israel, as the government constantly wrestles with the problem of Israeli citizenship, which is based in part on Jewish heritage but also on religious affiliation.

the THINKSPOT
www.thethinkspot.com

The Commandments: Words and Deeds

As we've seen, to be set apart—chosen—does not necessarily confer special power, but rather an intensified responsibility to God. Imagine a constant struggle by human beings to regain the purity lost with expulsion from Eden. In this way of thinking, the Torah's laws, customs, and traditions all nudge a Jew further along the path of righteousness. By following them, a Jew therefore turns away from death (the result of Adam's poorly used free will) and toward life (the result of God's free will).

This concept expresses itself through both words and deeds. In the story of Exodus, for example, God provided Israel with a blueprint for ethical speech and actions toward both God and other human beings. Here is a translation from the Torah of the Ten Statements (also often called the "Ten Commandments," especially by Christians). Note how each statement describes either the correct relationship between humans and God or of humans with each other (Blech 34–35). God asks for good words and good deeds.

> God spoke all these words, saying: [1:] "I the LORD your God who brought you out of the land of Egypt, the house of bondage: You shall have no other gods besides Me. [2:] You shall not make for yourself a sculptured image, or any likeness of what is in the heavens above, or on the earth below, or in the waters under the earth. You shall not bow down to them or serve them. For I the LORD your God am an impassioned God, visiting the guilt of the parents upon the children, upon the third and upon the fourth generations of those who reject Me, but showing kindness to the thousandth generation of those who love Me and keep My commandments. [3:] You shall not swear falsely by the name of the LORD your God; for the LORD will not clear one who swears falsely by His name. [4:] Remember the Sabbath day and keep it holy. Six days shall you labor and do all your work, but the seventh day is a Sabbath of the LORD your God: you shall not do any work—you, your son or daughter, your male or female slave, or your cattle, or the stranger who is within your settlements. For in six days the LORD made heaven and sea, and all that is in them, and He rested on the seventh day; therefore the LORD blessed the Sabbath day and hallowed it. [5:] Honor your father and your mother, that you may long endure on the land that the LORD your God is assigning to you. [6:] You shall not murder. [7:] You shall not commit adultery. [8:] You shall not steal. [9:] You shall not bear false witness against your neighbor. [10:] You shall not covet your neighbor's house: you shall not covet your neighbor's wife, or his male or female slave, or his ox or his ass, or anything that is your neighbor's." (Exodus 20:1–13).

Even if you're not Jewish or Christian, you may know the story: God gave these statements, written on stone tablets, directly to Moses. He took the tablets to the people of Israel, who had begun to worship a statue of a golden calf in his absence. When Moses saw the golden calf (which may have actually been a form of worship of God, not a calf itself), he smashed the tablets.

Repentant, the Jews finally took the tablets that Moses remade and placed them in a casket, placing "Ark of the Covenant" into the Holy of Holies at the center of the Temple. The story of the ark perfectly illustrates the Jewish perception of God's relationship to people: God gave Israel directives on how to live an ethical and holy life. After initially faltering in its faith, Israel came to value God's instructions. By creating the ark and placing it in the Temple, Israel then exalted the importance of God's words. The Jews' ancient first places of worship were not like the opulent

>>> Here are two pictures of Moses and the Ten Commandments by Jewish artists, Aron de Chavez (1674) and Marc Chagall (1966). How are they the same or different? Why?

Temple of Jerusalem, but rather tents in the desert because the Jews had not yet settled in their homeland.

In addition to the "Ten Statements," the Hebrew Bible further delineates Jewish commandments, called **mitzvot**. In fact, the Torah provides hundreds of specific commandments in the books of Leviticus and Numbers. These mitzvot have both symbolic and practical importance. They include:

- 248 positive commandments—things you should do, corresponding to a tradition that the human body has 248 parts.

- 365 negative commandments—things you should avoid, one for each day of the year.

The resulting 613 commandments (248 + 365) cover issues of morality, clothing, food, work, travel, prayer, and sex. They offer a web of interlocking ideas and actions that help Jews think about their relationship to God in every part of their lives (Robinson 195–223).

Many of the Torah commandments describe how to keep the Sabbath. One fascinating interpretation explains that the Sabbath recreates the relationship of God to humanity in Eden and offers a foretaste of a better world to come. On the Sabbath, as in Eden, people do not have to work or sweat, cook or clean. Instead, like Adam and Eve, they live in holy communion with God. Of course, human beings cannot keep the Sabbath perfectly because, well, we're not in Eden. If, however, we could keep the Sabbath perfectly *just one time*, we would recreate Paradise and end our estrangement from God (Neusner 89–91).

Cycle of the Relationship Between Israel and the Land

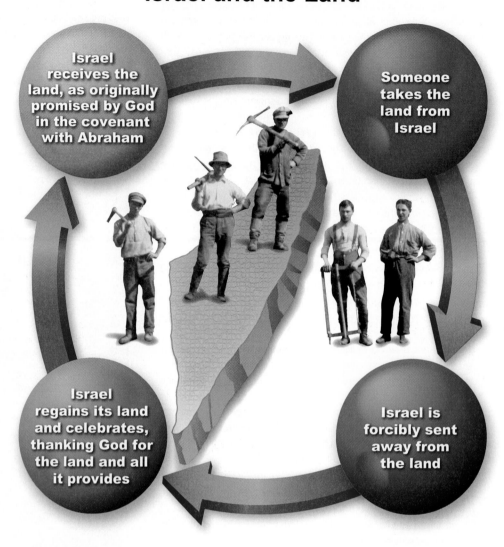

Israel receives the land, as originally promised by God in the covenant with Abraham

Someone takes the land from Israel

Israel regains its land and celebrates, thanking God for the land and all it provides

Israel is forcibly sent away from the land

∧∧∧ Many Jews see the relationship between Israel and the land as a cycle of gain and loss. What do you think motivated these early Israeli settlers?

History and Meaning: Cycles of Sin and Redemption

Israel's inability to keep a perfect Sabbath highlights the intrinsic tension built into ethical monotheism—imperfect humans can never replicate the faultless deeds of God. Knowing this, Jews often think of life as a continual cycle of success and failure in their struggle. In fact, some Jewish traditions interpret all history as a succession of losses and redemptions, each one played out on the land of Israel.

According to tradition, this cycle repeats itself, at least in some senses. The first sequence occurred when Jews fell into Egyptian bondage—an event dated around 1500 to 1200 BCE. The subsequent story of Moses, the plagues, Pharaoh's hardened heart, and Jews'

escape has even become standard fare for books and movies. (Cecil B. De Mille's *Ten Commandments*, made in 1956, has appeared on TV during the Passover-Easter season for more than 35 years. Only the *Wizard of Oz* has been shown more times on network TV.)

Along with Abraham's sacrifice of Isaac, the story of Exodus helps define the way Judaism developed its view of humanity. Through the power of God, Jews escaped Egyptian tyranny and slavery. God proved his love for the Jews by plaguing the Egyptians but "passing over" the Jews. This "Passover" would, of course, become one of Judaism's most important holidays, reminding people how they too can pass over from suffering to redemption.

In the Exodus story, Moses led his people out of bondage only to have them fall back into sin. Arriving in its own land after wandering the desert for 40 years, ancient Israel reached its pinnacle of influence and

Mitzvot are the commandments of God found in the Torah.

THINK World Religions

What Happens After We Die?

We cannot discuss how any religion views humanity without asking the ultimate question: What happens after we die? Judaism offers few specifics, believing that we can actually know very little about it during our earthly lives. Yet different ideas abound: Perhaps the afterlife is heaven, a place of bliss for those who live ethically and keep the laws. Maybe death is just a final end—afterward, just a lack of existence and nothingness. Or maybe death just moves us to another cycle of life—a form of reincarnation. Jewish thinkers have argued for all of these possibilities.

Judaism does believe, though, that eventually there will be a reckoning, a rebirth of the dead to life, when all people will account for their words and deeds. At that point—no one knows when God will judge—each person based on his or her earthly actions. This can console people who suffer hatred and injustice, because it promises eternal consequence for evil deeds (even if there doesn't seem to be any right now). In some, but not all traditions, this final reckoning coincides with the coming of a messiah, a Jewish leader who will reunite Israel and spread peace around the world.

the THINK SPOT
www.thethinkspot.com

Israel fell to Assyria, and Judah to Babylon. Starting in 597 BCE, Babylonian rulers forced some Israelites to leave Jerusalem, followed by tens of thousands more in 586 BCE. Although they had to live there for just 50 years (until 538), the "Babylonian Exile" strongly influenced Jewish identity, faith, and politics for generations to come.

Jews returned to Jerusalem in the fifth century BCE, a period traditionally called "Temple Judaism." Many events of this period influenced Judaism for centuries to come. In 516 BCE, Israel rebuilt the Temple that had been destroyed by Babylonians in 586 BCE. (It's called the "Second Temple," for obvious reasons.) Even with its religious focus rebuilt in Jerusalem, though, Israel endured Persian and Greek rule for much of the period. From 165 to 63 BCE, however, a rebellion first pushed out the foreign rulers and then recreated an independent Jewish monarchy. In 63 BCE, however, Israel fell to Rome, which installed both a Roman governor and a local Jewish king. In a crucially important event, Roman legions crushed an Israelite uprising in 70 CE, destroyed the Jewish Temple, and dispersed Jews throughout the Roman Empire. This began the period of Rabbinic Judaism that we know today.

Let's look a little more deeply at the years just before the Jewish insurrection, because it's a source for themes prominent in Jewish thought. During that period, we might consider three main groups. Most Jews were "regular" people—they worked the fields or in the villages, had children, prayed, and took animals to be killed sacrificially at the Temple if they lived near Jerusalem. (Temple offerings were then usually eaten.) Priests, however, lived separate lives, maintaining ritual purity so they could perform sacrifices in the Temple. In fact, many of the Torah's commandments focused on ways for priests to keep clean and holy. If the priests performed sacrifices, the scribes interpreted the Torah and acted as the historical conscience of Israel. They saw their position as historians, commentators, and keepers of the law, which offered eternal wisdom to Israel (Neusner 117–119).

In addition, we should also consider four groups within the Jewish elite called the Sadducees, Pharisees, Essenes, and Zealots. They tended to disagree with one another on religious and political issues. Although numerically small, these groups would have a major influence on Judaism for the next two millennia.

importance during the reigns of kings Saul, David, and Solomon. This period, from around 1050 to 920 BCE, endowed Judaism with many of its classic elements:

- The Temple—home to the Ark of the Covenant and altar for animal sacrifice
- Jerusalem—the holy city and capital of Israel
- The Psalms—poetry that explores humanity's relationship with God

Israel's decline began with its breakup into two kingdoms (Israel in the north, Judah in the south) and their subsequent fall to foreign powers.

THINK World Religions

A Psalm of Hope and Longing

For thousands of years, the words of Psalm 137 have comforted people exiled from their homes:

> By the rivers of Babylon,
>> There we sat,
>> Sat and wept,
>> As we thought of Zion.
> There on the poplars
>> We hung up our lyres,
>> For our captors asked us there for songs,
>> Our tormentors, for amusement,

>> "Sing us one of the songs of Zion."
> How can we sing a song of the LORD
>> On alien soil?
> If I forget you, O Jerusalem,
>> Let my right hand wither;
>> Let my tongue stick to my palate
> If I cease to think of you,
> If I do not keep Jerusalem in memory
>> Even at my happiest hour.
> (Psalm 137:1–6)

the THINK SPOT
www.thethinkspot.com

LA GRANDE HOSANNA, OU CÉRÉMONIES DU HUITIÈME JOUR DE LA FÊTE DES TABERNACLES.

1...Le Grand Prêtre va faire les libations sur le feu de l'Autel des Holocaustes. 2...Lévites qui portent l'eau et le vin pour les libations 3... Prêtres servant à offrir les sacrifices. 4...Troupes de Lévites portant des palmes à la main, et faisant sept fois le tour de l'Autel. 5...Chantres, et joüeurs d'instrumens qui chantent les Pseaumes et les Cantiques.

∧
∧ Here is an 18th-century attempt to illustrate how the Jewish Temple may have looked. Where
∧ might the artist have gotten his information?

- The Sadducees came from among the priestly Levites and emphasized the need for Temple sacrifice and following the written Torah. They rejected the oral Torah and questioned the concept of life after death.

- The Pharisees, on the other hand, were devoted to the idea that anyone—not just priests—could become holy. For that reason, Pharisees applied the laws of ritual cleanness to everyone, not just priests. They defended the oral Torah against the Sadducees as a relevant part of Jewish tradition and emphasized life after death.

- The Essenes created a quasi-monastic movement on the edges of Jewish society. They focused on ritual purity, small communities, and spiritual discipline.

- The Zealots hoped to drive the Romans from Israel and reinstate a Jewish state. They led uprisings against Rome and suffered a dramatic defeat at Masada in 73 CE. To prevent future uprisings, the Romans demolished the Second Temple, leaving only the Western Wall, which remains to this day (Seltzer 216–224).

The Roman army also forced Jews to leave their historic land of Israel and the city of Jerusalem. Within a few years, the priests and scribes lost their influence, just as the Temple and Israel had ceased to exist. The Jewish **diaspora** thus scattered Jews across many lands, exiled again from Jerusalem.

After the destruction of the Temple, priests could not perform sacrifices or other rituals. In their stead, Jewish teachers—rabbis—cultivated forms of worship that did not need the Temple. Over the next 10 centuries, this developed into the "Rabbinic" tradition of Judaism, which we will discuss in Chapter 10. The rabbinic system derived most closely from the Pharisaic tradition in its emphasis on holiness for all Jews. Without priests and scribes to lead them, Jews of all kinds slowly took on the responsibilities for studying and following the Torah. In place of the physical structure of the temple and its corresponding rituals, rabbis began to emphasize the Oral Torah, which could be orally passed down through the generations. (In Chapters 11 and 12, we will concentrate on another post-Temple phenomenon, the development of Christianity.)

In some important ways, the rabbinic tradition departed from Judaism as it had been practiced for centuries. Without a clear focus on the Temple and preparation of animal sacrifice, other parts of the Jewish tradition began to build up. Rabbis took on leadership of their communities as the roles of priest and scribe died away. This couldn't happen overnight. In fact, it took a couple of centuries for the new Rabbinical tradition to figure itself out: who would lead Israel and how it would relate to Jews' changing circumstances? Ultimately, the Rabbinic system did made sense for Jews spread around the world, because they did not have to rely on a single temple in Jerusalem for sacrifices. Instead, they looked toward prayer and good acts to link them to God, now that the Temple was destroyed.

As they dispersed across the Mediterranean and European world, Jewish people eventually assembled into two main traditions—Ashkenazi and Sephardic. The term "Ashkenazi" refers to Jews from France, Germany, and Eastern Europe. It is likely that Jews began to migrate to Europe after the Roman persecution and the spread of the

Diaspora refers to Jews being exiled from Israel to live around the world.

diaspora, but other evidence hints that they occupied these lands even earlier. Jews especially settled in areas they called the *Ashkenaz*, modern-day Germany. The term "Sephardic" refers to a smaller group of Jews from Spain, Portugal, North Africa, and the Middle East. Although they share a heritage and religion, the Ashkenazim and Sephardim often have different local traditions, languages, and religious opinions (Seltzer 345–348, 351–355).

Both Ashkenazi and Sephardic Jews interacted with the world around them based on their geographic, social, and political circumstances. Greek philosophy, Christian theology, and Muslim scholarship all affected Judaism. For example, Jewish thought in Muslim-dominated medieval Spain flourished, but the reconquest by Christian rulers in the 13th century introduced new tensions that ended with expulsion of Spanish Jews from their homes in 1492.

One of the great Rabbinic teachers of all time, Moses Maimonides (also known as Moses ben Maimon or Ramban), illustrates many of

∧
∧ You can see Roman soldiers carrying spoils from the Jewish Temple in this carving made in
∧ 81 CE, just a few years after the event happened. The Romans primarily saw this as a military victory, but how did it affect Jewish religious life?

Hasidim are members of a mystical and pietistic group in Judaism.
Haskalah is the Hebrew word for the Jewish Enlightenment.

these phenomena. He was born in the Jewish community of Cordova, Spain. During his lifetime, though, Maimonides' family had to wander through different parts of Spain and Northern Africa, settling finally in Egypt. There, he began a remarkable career that helped shape Judaism for ever after. Maimonides integrated Jewish thought with the Aristotelian philosophical system. In doing so, he sought to define exactly how Jews ought to perceive God and their faith. His 13 principles of faith still stand as a definitive description of Judaism. But that wasn't all; Maimonides wrote among the most important interpretations of the Torah (the *Mishneh Torah*) and the wonderfully titled interpretation of Jewish law called *Guide to the Perplexed*, which in fact expected the reader to have already mastered classical philosophy. Perhaps more than anyone else, Maimonides affected the way modern Jews understand their relationship to God, creation, and the rise and fall of sacrifice as a form of worship (Seltzer 393–408).

In large part through Maimonides and his followers, Rabbinic Judaism became normative in both Ashkenazi and Sephardic communities. Even so, complementary and competitive versions of Judaism have continued to develop. Jewry in 18th- and 19th-century Central Europe provides a good example. Most Jews of that period felt secure with Rabbinic leadership and an education system focused on learning, debate, and rational comprehension. Two important groups, however, offered new and potentially revolutionary ideas about Judaism. A minority group from Poland, the **Hasidim** turned toward mysticism in part as a reaction against rabbinic authority. The Hasidim sought a direct, nonrational communion with God, which could happen without decades of Torah study. They offered a charismatic alternative to the Rabbinic tradition and gained adherents quickly across central Europe. Communities with Hasidic Jews often stood out, as many Hasidim traditionally wore particular garments (including dark coats and hats). In fact, Hasidic and non-Hasidic communities in Eastern Europe often fought bitterly over the roles of leadership, learning, and tradition (Seltzer 487–496). We'll explore Hasidic ideas more in Chapter 10.

Within a few generations of the Hasidic movement, another trend challenged traditional European Judaism. In almost direct contradiction to

Hasidism, the **Haskalah** (Jewish Enlightenment) inspired Jews to turn their tradition of education toward non-Jewish subjects. In the late 18th and 19th century, European philosophers had begun to apply scientific concepts about Newtonian natural law to political, social, and even religious ideas. From this "Enlightened" point of view, rational Natural Laws governed all human activities. Perhaps equally importantly, Enlightenment thinkers also saw people as basically equal and argued that all people shared basic rights—kings happened to be royalty, but they had no "bluer blood" than everyone else. Likewise, religions might hold some sort of truth, according to the Enlightenment, but should not impose their views on other people.

Starting in late 18th-century Germany, followers of the Haskalah began to call for expanded integration of Jews into European society. To do this, they taught students Hebrew and local languages instead of Yiddish, which was the common language of Ashkenazi Jews. Even girls, who had been prohibited from Jewish education, found seats in Haskalah schools. No longer content with studying Torah and Talmud, followers of the Haskalah applied their energy toward the arts and sciences, medicine, and even agronomy. They looked to another Moses (like the original Moses and

>>> **Why do you think that medieval copyists would have made the pages of the Mishneh Torah so beautiful?**

∧
∧ Here are Hasidic men and boys in Czechoslovakia in the 1930s. What can you learn about them
∧ by studying how each one is dressed? Do some seem to want to be seen as more traditional
and others as modern? Are some in between?

Moses Maimonides) for guidance in this new kind of Judaism.

His name was Moses Mendelssohn (Seltzer 557–566). Mendelssohn sought to explain both Judaism to his Enlightenment counterparts, and also clarify the Enlightenment to Jews. In one of his most famous works, *Jerusalem*, Mendelssohn told his fellow Jews to leave their segregated villages and neighborhoods and to cautiously embrace the world around them:

> "Adopt the mores and constitution of the country in which you find yourself, but be steadfast in upholding the religion of your fathers, too. . . . stand fast in the place that Providence has assigned to you; and submit to

everything which may happen, as you were told to do by your Lawgiver long ago" (Seltzer 563–564).

The Haskalah also embraced European nationalism, which argued that distinctive ethnic and religious groups ought to have independent homelands. When applied to the people of Israel, nationalism became Zionism. Lacking a political home of their own, Zionists began to consider how Jews might return to Jerusalem and create a modern nation in their ancient patrimony. For Zionists, the ancient Passover saying "Next year in Jerusalem" had highly political meaning. If they could bring about the return of Jerusalem to Jewish rule, the diaspora that started in 70 CE could finally come to an end.

REVIEW

Summary

IS THERE A GOD?   p. 123

- There is one god—the capital "g" God—in Judaism. God is creator or the universe, and a being beyond human comprehension.
- God has no gender or physical form, but is always present and exists eternally.

WHAT DOES IT MEAN TO BE HUMAN?   p. 127

- Humans were created in the image of God, so they are all naturally good like God. However, we all have free will and can choose to act evilly (in opposition to God's image).
- God chose Jews as his chosen people, but they chose him as well through free will. As the chosen ones, Jews must follow stricter commandments (and sometimes suffer more) than gentiles do.

Key Terms

Ethical monotheism is a foundational principle of Judaism that encapsulates three main ideas: 1) the need to recognize only one God; 2) the need to act appropriately toward God; and 3) the need to act appropriately toward other people.   *122*

Rabbi is a Jewish religious leader. The term literally means "teacher" or "scholar."   *122*

Bar/bat mitzvah means "son/daughter of the commandment" and refers to a Jewish boy or girl reaching the age of a religious adult. A boy becomes a bar mitzvah at age 13, and a girl attains the status at age 12. Bar/bat mitzvah is also the name of the ceremony often held to celebrate this event.   *123*

Torah, meaning Law, refers to the first five books of the Hebrew Bible. However, the word can also be used to denote *all* Jewish religious texts and *all* Jewish law.   *123*

Tanakh refers to three sets of religious texts— "the Law" (Torah), "the Prophets," and "the Writings" that constitute the Hebrew Bible.   *126*

Midrash interprets the Torah with an emphasis on everyday life.   *126*

Talmud, also called the "oral Torah," is a historical collection of rabbinical writings and commentaries on the Torah.   *126*

Mishnah is a compendium of opinions and teachings on the Talmud.   *127*

Gentiles are non-Jews.   *130*

Mitzvot are the commandments of God found in the Torah.   *133*

Diaspora refers to Jews being exiled from Israel to live around the world.   *134*

Hasidim are members of a mystical and pietistic group in Judaism.   *136*

Haskalah is the Hebrew word for the Jewish Enlightenment.   *136*

Find it on  the THINKSPOT
www.thethinkspot.com

- Central Synagogue: The Sacred Place that opens this chapter talks about the Central Synagogue, located in the heart of midtown Manhattan. To explore the deep faith tradition that exists at the Central Synagogue and among its congregation, go to the ThinkSpot to access the web site, which includes music samples, sermons, and access to services in real time. Visiting the site will put the sacred place in context and make you understand the deep and rich tradition that lives within its walls. (www.centralsynagogue.org)

- Walking the Torah: Sifrei Torah: To a historian and student of religion, there is no greater sight than seeing ordinary people live their faith. In this video, members of the Midway Jewish Center march the Sifrei Torah from Bethpage—a temple that is now closed—to its new home in Midway. The pride that the congregants have for their temple and the Torah is apparent as they march down typical suburban American streets to place the Torah in its new home. The number of men, women, and children who come out to participate in this event is moving and a testament to the congregation's spirit of community. (http://www.youtube.com/watch?v=la-eYV0mPVM)

- Torah Café: Religion comes to the Internet! Want to get your religious messages online? Torah Café can help. Visit this site to get videos on a number of topics related to Judaism and living the faith today. Mixing both the modern and traditional, Torah Café is the place for Jews living in our fast-paced, 21st century world. (www.torahcafe.com)

- Dizzie Gillespie's goddaughter blows her own horn in this fascinating interview broadcast on NPR. Turn up your speakers! (http://www.npr.org/templates/story/story.php?storyId=113311070)

Questions for Study and Review

1. What constitutes proof of God in Judaism?

For Jews, the existence of the universe constitutes proof of God. The Torah states that God created everything, and that nothing existed before Him. Thus, God must exist, because only He could be capable of creating such a vast and magnificent universe.

2. Why are Jews called "the chosen people"?

Jews are "the chosen people" because they are the descendants of Abraham, who entered into a sacred agreement with God. Abraham chose God by following His commands willingly. Because of this devotion, God chose Abraham to be the father of the Jewish people.

3. Why must Jews follow so many commandments?

Since Jews are God's chosen people, they must lead a life more religiously rigorous than non-Jews. Although they originally pertained only to the priests who served in the Temple, the commandments became important to all Jews after the destruction of the Temple in 70 CE.

<<< Devout Jews pray at the Western Wall, the last remaining portion of the Temple in Jerusalem. How important is location to the act of prayer?

HOW DO HUMANS INTERACT WITH THE SACRED?
HOW DOES THE SACRED BECOME COMMUNITY?

Call it the Western Wall. Call it the Wailing Wall. Either way, these stones have witnessed some of the best and worst of human history. From the building of the Temple of Jerusalem to its destruction, from the quiet peace of an old woman at prayer to the violence of fighting between young Muslim and Jewish boys, this ancient wall stands as a silent testament to history. Why would people flock there? Why would they lean toward the wall in prayer, or leave a note asking God for help? For Jews across the world, these walls symbolize their history and people's desire to pray in the place where their forebears stood. When a Jew says, "Next year in Jerusalem!" this is what she means.

We explored the foundations of Judaism in our previous chapter. In this chapter, we'll delve more fully into the significance of Jewish prayer: what it means and what Jews hope to accomplish through it. We will also examine the larger Jewish community and how religion and culture intersect in the modern world.

JUDAISM: Israel in the Diaspora

CHAPTER 10

The Eruv

On any given Saturday in Orthodox Jewish communities across the world, you might see people strolling—out for some fresh air, off to the synagogue, or visiting friends. They're walking, not driving. They're also not gardening, shopping, or going to work. This is the Sabbath, or **Shabbat** in Hebrew, the day of rest. Those strolling stay within the **eruv**, a ritually defined area where they can move freely even when observing the Sabbath. You can find one example in Montgomery County, MD, not far from Washington, D.C. One woman put it this way: "What the eruv does is help the Jewish community feel more like a community. There's not much feeling of isolation. I do most of my entertaining on the Sabbath. If the eruv was down, people couldn't come" (Rathner).

The concept of the eruv comes from the Talmud and creates borders for walking and carrying things on the Sabbath (Seltzer, 592). It's a great illustration of how the relationship between the laws of the Torah, the interpretation in the Talmud, and the real life of Jewish communities interact. To create the eruv, Jewish community leaders designate its borders either symbolically—for example in the homes and businesses of community members—or physically, by stringing lines between utility poles to close off the area in a ritual way. Traditionally, the eruv included parcels of property aggregated into a single unit, so that Jews could come and go freely with their children within a *chatzer*, that is, a walled courtyard. You'll also hear the term *eruv chatzerot*, or a collective of courtyards.

The rabbis of the Talmud set forth specific rules to construct an eruv in accordance with the laws of the Sabbath. Community members regularly inspect the eruv to ensure that there are no breaks or make repairs in time for the Sabbath. Often, a group of people or a construction crew holds responsibility for this task and notifies the community if the eruv is operative or not. You can even find eruv notices on the Web, updating the status for specific locales.

In contemporary society, though, an eruv can create problems. For example, the local synagogue's plan to create an eruv created an uproar in Westhampton Beach, NY. People who did not like the idea—including both Jews and non-Jews—said that even a symbolic border could undermine their constitutional rights to freedom of religion. An advertisement in the local newspaper asked, "Is

∧
∧ **This student is enjoying the** eruv on his
∧ university campus.

Westhampton Beach an Orthodox Jewish Community? No it's a secular, open Village with a proud history of welcoming all faiths. The erection of an eruv will proclaim us as an Orthodox Jewish community for all time. Don't let it happen" (Berger). In this case, the eruv's border crossed both neighbors' land and consciousness. Although not physically affected by it, the eruv forced citizens of the village to consider how one group's religious freedom (to create an eruv) might affect other people's perceptions and feelings, even if the eruv never affected their lives directly.

▶ HOW DO HUMANS INTERACT WITH THE SACRED?

The idea of an eruv helps illustrate the ways in which God, people, and community interact with one another in Judaism. The scholars and scribes who first considered the eruv surely did not imagine one in Maryland or Long Island. Rather, they perceived Israel as existing only in its historic home, and so the rabbis conceptualized the eruv based on architectural styles, building patterns, and settlements that they knew. As we learned in Chapter 9, though, in 70 CE the Roman army demolished the Temple and forced the Jews to leave Jerusalem. As a result, they lost the ability to offer ritual sacrifice in the Temple and had to find new ways to interact with the sacred.

Without a temple or society, Judaism changed dramatically. The importance of some groups declined while others grew. People directly related to the Temple—especially the priests, scribes, and Sadducees—

gradually lost significance. The Pharisees, on the other hand, gained momentum after 70 CE. As you remember, they had argued that all Jews, not just priests, ought to follow Torah purity laws. They looked to Hosea 6:6 for proof: "I [God] desire goodness, not sacrifice; Obedience to God rather than burnt-offerings."

Over the next few centuries, the Pharisee tradition developed into the Rabbinic Judaism we know today, which stresses the active pursuit of holiness and ethics. As a result, Judaism focused on interactions with God that relied on the Torah, the Talmud, and the continual interpretation of Jewish law. We'll take our cue from this tradition and look more closely at prayer and following commandments as forms of human contact with God. Additionally, we'll study the mystical system called the Kabbalah, as it offers an alternative path for Jewish interaction with the divine.

Prayer

Prayer—the language of communication with God—beats at the heart of Judaism. In fact, the Jewish prayer tradition has become so ubiquitous that many people in American society use the term "prayer" to refer to *any* communication with God, even if it's not really a form of prayer. Jews pray both privately and as a community in the synagogue. The Torah exhorts them to pray three times per day, so as to remember the importance of God in the morning, at midday, and in the evening.

Many prayers begin with these words: "Blessed are You, Lord, our God, King of the Universe." The prayer upon waking from sleep, for example, also says that "I give thanks to You, Source of life and existence, that you have once again placed my soul within me, great is your faith (in me)" (Robinson 20). Look closely, and you will see that this prayer includes statements that God is good, that God is the Creator, and that God and human beings share a common image. These three concepts, embedded in a prayer for the start of day, also remind Jews of their special heritage of ethical monotheism. In other words, Jewish prayer not only seeks to communicate with God, but also to educate the faithful. Therefore, prayer helps Jews respond to God's goodness by developing their own.

By tradition, there are three categories of Jewish prayer: those that praise God, those that ask for requests of God, and those that give thanks to God. Among the most important prayers in Judaism are the Shema, the Amidah, and the Kaddish. Each of these illustrates important themes in the Jews' search for interaction with God, so we'll investigate them in more depth.

THE SHEMA

Observant Jews read the **Shema** (also known as the *Sh'ma Yisroel* or just the *Sh'ma*), twice a day—once when

> **Shabbat** is the Hebrew word for the Sabbath, the day of rest.
> **Eruv** is a contained space within which Jews observe the Sabbath; plural: *eruvin*.
> **Shema** is a prayer that reminds Jews to remember God and the commandments at all times.
> **Amidah** is a Jewish prayer made up of 19 sections and includes praise, request, and thanksgiving.

lying down to sleep and again when they awake. Here is its first part, taken directly from the Torah:

> Hear, O Israel! The LORD is our God, the LORD alone. You shall love the LORD your God with all your heart and with all your soul and with all your might. Take to heart these instructions with which I charge you this day. Impress them upon your children. Recite them when you stay at home and when you are away, when you lie down and when you get up. Bind them as a sign on your hand and let them serve as a symbol on your forehead; inscribe them on the doorposts of your house and on your gates. (Deuteronomy 6:4–9).

Try to set the beginning of this prayer in your memory, because it offers a succinct definition of Judaism: "The LORD is our God, the LORD alone." After that crucial description of God, the Shema develops a number of extremely important themes. It reminds Jews that they should both fill their hearts with love for God, and also teach their children. It explains the importance of the commandments, which ought to be followed every day in all situations, as illustrated in the line "Recite them when you stay at home and when you are away, when you lie down and when you get up." Even a Jew's body should carry God's commandments ("Bind them as a sign on your hand and let them serve as a symbol on your forehead"), words that explain the *tefillin* described in Chapter 9. And finally, even a Jew's home should carry the sign that God's commandments would be followed, written "on the doorposts of your house and on your gates." The Shema holds such meaning that Jews often say these words in their last breaths (Blech 295; Robinson 34–35).

THE AMIDAH

To recite the **Amidah**, a fundamental part of every prayer service, the faithful stand up and put their feet close together. (In fact, "amidah" means "the standing.") Before beginning to speak, you must take three steps back, then forward, symbolizing entry before the presence of a king. Once finished, you step backward, symbolically returning to the everyday world.

The Amidah includes 19 sections covering the three types of prayers mentioned previously: praise, request, and thanksgiving (Blech 296; Robinson 34–35). Although it is traditionally called "the 18" for its component parts, it actually has 19 sections. More than just trivia, this illustrates how Judaism has changed its prayers to fit different circumstances, the last section appearing after the destruction of the Temple by the Romans. Then, in the 19th century, Reform Jews (including the founders of the Central Synagogue in New York, mentioned in Chapter 9) added Sarah, Rebecca, Rachel, and Leah to the list of Biblical patriarchs in the first section to show respect for the Biblical women.

<<< **How might** prayer link generations?

<<< The words of the Shema are written on a tiny slip of paper that fits into a mezuzah as it hangs on a doorpost. What function might it play in the everyday life of a Jewish family?

The Kaddish

The **Kaddish**, meaning "sanctification," has many forms. It asks for the whole world to become holy and that God's will be done. Often used to link different parts of a synagogue service, the Kaddish expresses Judaism's ultimate hope:

> Glorified and sanctified be God's great name throughout the world. He has created according to His will. May he establish His kingdom in your lifetime and during your days, and within the life of the entire house of Israel, speedily and soon; and say Amen (Seltzer 305–306).

Most famous is the Mourner's Kaddish, words designed to give a deep sense of solace to those whose family member has died. It emphasizes the belief that God created all things and asks for peace in the world; interestingly, the prayer never mentions death itself. Tradition teaches that the Kaddish should be said for 30 days for your closest family, but for 11 months after a parent's death. At the end of a synagogue service, the family of a recently deceased person stands and leads the whole congregation in prayer. The Kaddish ends with words that offer peace and unity with Jews everywhere: "May the One who causes peace to reign in Heaven let peace descend on us and on all Israel" (Robinson 32).

Following the Commandments: The Example of Food

As we learned in Chapter 9, the Torah offers hundreds of commandments that concern all aspects of life. Many of these, as we've noted, include laws regarding the proper keeping of the Sabbath. Let's zoom in on just one kind of commandment—food—to give us a closer picture of the relationship between the commandments and the community.

Religion + EDUCATION

The Importance of Education in Judaism

The Amidah provides a key to many facets of Jewish interaction with God, including the role of education: "[T]hese words, which I command thee this day, shall be upon thy heart," God says in the prayer taken from the Torah, "and thou shalt teach them diligently unto thy children." Although important to the scribes and priests of the Temple, education developed much more broadly in the post-Temple period and has exploded in the last two centuries.

Jewish philosophers (including the great Moses Maimonides and Moses Mendelssohn) considered education a way to develop rational understanding of the Torah among men, so that a Jew could act ethically. The structure of the Talmud itself prompts learning and critical thinking, since it offers multiple interpretations of a single Torah passage all on one page. You might even remember a line from the musical *Fiddler on the Roof*, produced in high schools around the United States every year. In it, the Mamas ask "Who must raise the family and run the home, so Papa's free to read the holy books?"

Since the early 19th century, a period of educational reform across Europe, Judaism has developed a three-branch system of schooling. First, synagogues provide training in Hebrew and the Torah to children and teenagers, who also attend Jewish or secular primary and secondary schools. Followers of the Haskalah opened education (long a male preserve) to girls and added secular subjects. Second, religious institutions like the synagogue (often called by their Yiddish name, *shul*, like "school" in German, and often a male bastion) continue to emphasize the Torah and Talmud.

In the 20th century, American Judaism has focused on the third area, the development of higher education. The Hillel movement (named after the first-century CE Jewish thinker) celebrates Jewish heritage and faith. The group finds inspiration in Hillel's emphasis on peaceful education of Jews and non-Jews, "loving peace and pursuing peace, loving your fellow creatures and drawing them to the Torah" (Seltzer 217–218). Hillel has spread across campuses in the United States. Yeshiva University and Brandeis University offer full college degrees, while specialized theological schools focus on religious education and research. The Hebrew Union College, for example, follows Reform Judaism, while the Jewish Theological Seminary of America observes the Conservative tradition. (We will learn more about those denominational differences later in this chapter.)

This focus on education has paid off for Judaism—by some counts, over 20 percent of all Nobel Prize winners have had Jewish roots, although Jews make up only a tiny fraction of the world population.

<<< Young boys line up for school in Vilnius, Lithuania, in 1929. Before World War II, Central Europe had more Jewish schools than anywhere else in the world.

Deuteronomy 14:1–21

"You are the children of the LORD your God. You shall not gash yourselves or shave the front of your heads because of the dead. For you are a people consecrated to the LORD your God: the LORD your God chose you from among all other peoples on earth to be His treasured people."

"You shall not eat anything abhorrent. These are the animals that you may eat: the ox, the sheep, and the goat; the deer, the gazelle, the roebuck, the wild goat, the ibex, the antelope, the mountain sheep, and any animal that has true hoofs which are cleft in two and brings up the cud—such you may eat. But the following which do bring up the cud or have true hoofs which are cleft through, you may not eat: the camel, the hare, and the daman—for although they bring up the cud, they have no true hoofs—they are unclean to you; also the swine—for although it has true hoofs, it does not bring up the cud—is unclean for you. You shall not eat of their flesh or touch their carcasses."

"These you may eat of all that live in water: you may eat anything that has fins and scales. But you may not eat anything that has no fins and scales: it is unclean for you."

"You may eat any clean bird. The following you may not eat: the eagle, the vulture, and the black vulture; the kite, the falcon, and the buzzard of any variety; every variety of rave; the ostrich, the nighthawk, the sea gull, and the hawk of any variety; the little owl, the great owl, and the white owl; the pelican, the bustard, and the cormorant; the stork, and any variety of heron, the hoopoe, and the bat."

"All winged swarming things are unclean for you: they may not be eaten. You may eat only clean winged creatures."

"You shall not eat anything that has died a natural death; give it to the stranger in your community to eat, or you may sell it to a foreigner. For you are a people consecrated to the LORD your God. You shall not boil a kid in its mother's milk."

the THINK SPOT
www.thethinkspot.com

By following commandments related to food and its preparation, Jews transform eating into a sacred act and recall the animal sacrifices of the Temple. In the last chapter, we learned that following certain dietary laws can help you stay ritually clean. More to the point is that following commandments also offers communion with God. Known as **kashrut**, the commandments come mainly from two sources in the Torah—the books of Leviticus and Deuteronomy. The partial list on this page, taken from the Torah book of Deuteronomy, will show you both how general and how specific the kashrut laws can be.

As you can imagine, some of these rules tend to be easier to keep than others. In contemporary American society, how many people shop for stork, heron, hoopoe, or bat? Yet other rules, like not eating pork, can be a bit more difficult. To make them fit into their contemporary societies, rabbis from the Talmudic period until today have studied these rules and described appropriate ways to follow them. For example, Jews now interpret the directive not to "boil a kid in its mother's milk" as a commandment against mixing milk and meat. In some Jewish traditions, families even keep two completely different kitchens—one for preparing milk-based foods and another for cooking meat. That way, they continually remind themselves of God's mandates for ritually pure food. The issue becomes even more complex in the supermarket. Jews who "keep **kosher**" follow this custom and must eat only food products that have received a rabbinic certification. These products carry the **hekhsher** to identify them as ritually pure (Robinson 251–252).

At this point, you may be asking, Why? In fact, there is no single answer to the question. Over centuries, Jews have

Kaddish is a Jewish prayer used to express the hope that the world will become holy and God's will be done.

Kashrut is a set of Jewish dietary laws.

Kosher refers to the appropriate kind of food to be consumed according to Jewish dietary laws.

Hekhsher is a kosher certification symbol.

Jewish Dietary Laws

Kosher (permitted)	Trayf (forbidden)
Ritually slaughtered beef, sheep, goats, and deer with no flaws or diseases	Pork, camel, rabbit, rodents, reptiles, and any animal that died of natural causes
Chicken, turkey, quail, geese	Eagle, hawk, vulture
Salmon, tuna, carp, herring, cod	Crab, lobster, octopus, clam, swordfish, sturgeon
Meat eaten separately from dairy	Meat with dairy
Wine or grape juice made under Jewish supervision	Any other wine and grape juice
Soft cheese and kosher hard cheese	Most hard cheese

>>> You can easily find a hekhsher on products in your supermarket. Would non-Jews ever look for kosher foods? Why or why not?

Sources: Based on Robinson 251–252; Judaism 101, "Kashrut: Jewish Dietary Laws," http://www.jewfaq.org/kashrut.htm; ReligionFacts, "Keeping Kosher: Jewish Dietary Laws," http://www.religionfacts.com/judaism/practices/kosher.htm.

wondered about kosher, too, trying to figure out the rationale for eating one food or another, preparing it one way or another. One general answer (as we've seen) links prohibited behavior to things that relate somehow to death (Neusner 118). Seeking to lessen cruel treatment of animals and maintain food hygiene also make sense for many—but not all—kosher rules. As we'll discuss later in this chapter, some Jewish traditions have dropped the kosher diet as being a remnant of the past, when we did not strictly control the quality of our food. Others, however, keep kosher for the same reason—because it links them to Jewish tradition. In the end, it may be that many Jews keep kosher to remind themselves of their relationship with God every day, even if they don't understand the specific reasons for doing so (Blech 235–254; Robinson 243–254).

Mystical Judaism and the Kabbalah

While Jewish prayer and law convey their ideas through rational language, the mystical tradition seeks a direct, nonrational link to the divine. Though mysticism has roots deep into Jewish past, it's best known through the **Kabbalah** (meaning "the received" or "tradition"), a form that developed in medieval France and Spain and spread across the Jewish world. As the name implies, Kabbalah Judaism perceives itself as a secret tradition, a form of wisdom that only a few understand in its entirety.

The Kabbalah attempts to answer questions about issues most rabbis believe to be outside the realm of human understanding. These include the mysteries of creation, the hidden meaning of words, and the exact relationship of God and humanity, as described in the *Zohar*, a set of medieval books at the center of the Kabbalah. The Kabbalists agree with the rabbis that the mind cannot grasp God, but the Kabbalah teaches us that the Torah holds mysterious meaning in the letters of the Hebrew alphabet, the arrangement of words, and the commandments that come from God. Once experienced, these letters and numbers and words open us up to a closer relationship with God. Let's look at three important parts of Kabbalistic thought—God (*Ein Sof* and *Sefirot*), the human soul, and the relationship between God and human beings (*tikkun*).

Here's a warning: This material may seem impossible to understand, which is fine. The Kabbalah should not be comprehended but rather experienced; to plumb its depths you'll need years of education, contemplation, and mystical practice. Traditionally, Kabbalah study begins after age 40, when a person has already learned the traditions of rabbinic Judaism.

Like other mystical systems, Kabbalistic Judaism focuses on the interaction between divine and human realms. The *Zohar* teaches that "stirring up holiness below results in stirring up divine grace above" (Seltzer 444). To explain this,

The Sefirot

Keter (Crown)
Binah (Understanding)
Hokmah (Wisdom)
Gevurah (Might)
Hesed (Lovingkindness)
Tiferet (Beauty)
Hod (Splendor)
Netzakh (Victory)
Yesod (Foundation)
Malkhut (Sovereignty)

∧
∧ The Sefirot **is essential to**
∧ Kabbalistic tradition.

Source: Based on Robinson, George. *Essential Judaism: A Complete Guide to Beliefs, Customs, and Rituals.* (London: Pocket Books, 2000), 376.

Kabbalists create a sort of mystical picture of God as the Ultimate One (*Ein Sof*) revealed to us through specific attributes (**sefirot**). God's breathing in and out provided space for the cosmos to come into existence, and the sefirot act as filters for us to experience God's greatness and revelation. Schematically, God's sefirot unite as a symbolic primordial man called the "Adam Kadmon."

Some Kabbalah scholars illustrate the sefirot as concentric circles, a person, or a complex plant. We will use the "Tree of Life," which arranges the 10 attributes in a way that suggests both a tree and a highly abstracted body. The top circle represents the Ein Sof in heaven, the ultimate One beyond understanding. Moving downward through the "Supreme Crown" and toward the earth, we see seven more circles symbolizing aspects of God that we can perceive: understanding, wisdom, judgment or might, greatness or love, splendor, victory or endurance, and foundation. In the middle, the circle corresponding to beauty links them all together. All the energy from Ein Sof flows through the sefirot to the bottom circle, the "Kingdom of the Shekhinah," which is sometimes shown as a symbol of Israel.

Like water moving from the ocean through rivers and back to the sea, the grace of God travels downward through the Tree of Life and ultimately unifies again at the bottom (Seltzer 432).

The sefirot have multiple meanings. In some interpretations, the top circles signify the cosmos, and the bottom ones correspond to the days of creation. The *Zohar* teaches us that left side of the figure represents femininity, and the right stands for male aspects of God. (Paradoxical to Western tradition, power and justice are feminine traits, while unity, harmony, and love are masculine.) The top of the diagram may also embody the head, arms, and chest of Adam Kadmon, while the bottom symbolizes legs and genitals. The tenth circle (in the middle) harmonizes the top, bottom, left, right, heaven, and earth (Robinson 376–379; Seltzer 428–434).

Human souls move from God (at the top) to Earth (at the bottom) to purify themselves and to repair (**tikkun**) the world. Being in the "image of God," the soul has attributes of the sefirot. When Adam sinned in Eden, however, he cut off the bottom of the Tree of Life from the top. Jews can repair this break and restore harmony to themselves and the cosmos by correctly uttering prayers, following commandments, and developing one's spiritual self. The world will end when all souls have performed the tikkun, and some Kabbalists believe that humans may be reincarnated until such time as the repair is finished (Seltzer 442).

The Kabbalah has become much better known in the past few years through publicity surrounding celebrities. Madonna has done the most in this regard, using Kabbalah symbols as part of her stage design, talking about the Kabbalah, and getting involved in a secular version known as the "Kabbalah Center." Some Jews welcome the publicity for the Kabbalah, but many others strongly disagree with people outside Judaism teaching the Kabbalah or using it to turn a profit.

▶ HOW DOES THE SACRED BECOME COMMUNITY?

Think back to different sections of Chapters 9 and 10—the synagogue, the bar/bat mitzvah celebration, the commandments, the chosen people, ethical monotheism, and the eruv. Put them together and you'll begin to see a picture of Judaism as a social system. Like other religions we have studied, Judaism rarely differentiates between ideas that we might call "religion," "society," and "culture." Living a Jewish life combines all of those concepts into one experience.

Take the eruv, for example, where it's permissible to walk around even on the Sabbath. This brings people together to live in a specified neighborhood area. By following the Halakhah, in other words, Jews respect God's will and also create community.

Jews usually meet in prayer at a synagogue. The act of praying there is a social experience; you need to have other Jews around you to feel closer to God and to each other. In fact, the Talmud designates that synagogue prayer must be done by a **minyan**—a group of 10 or more adults. (Different groups disagree if women should be counted in the minyan.) Further emphasizing their social aspects, many Jewish prayers use "we" instead of "I," which promotes a greater sense of community and solidarity (Blech 27–78).

Calendar and Life Cycle Rituals

Jews gather together for a number of important holidays, many of them clustered in early fall. The "Days of Awe" begin in September with Rosh Hashanah, the Jewish New Year, and end with the Day of Atonement called Yom Kippur. (Referring to the words of Genesis that "the evening and the morning" made up the first days, Jews observe holidays as they do the Sabbath, by starting at sundown the night before the actual day.) Rosh Hashanah has two goals—to celebrate a new liturgical year and also to begin reflecting on things you might want to change in your life. The two-day celebration involves services in the synagogue, which are often so overcrowded that congregants need to get tickets beforehand. Back at home, families meet for a meal and top it off by eating honey-dipped apples to represent the hope of a sweet new year.

At the other end of the "Days of Awe," Jews abstain from all food, take off work, and attend services for Yom Kippur. They gather in such crowds for this solemn occasion that buildings literally overflow. The Central Synagogue that we learned about in Chapter 9 has found a novel solution—it rents out a huge hotel ballroom for services, the only way it can accommodate the thousands of congregants who come together on this day.

The fall also welcomes Sukkot, the harvest festival best known for its huts (called sukkot). Jews sometimes build a little hut to live in during the festival, reminding them of the years when God protected them in the wilderness before they made it to the promised land.

In midwinter, Jews celebrate Hanukkah (which you might also see spelled "Chanukah"). Although not historically an important holiday, it has gained popularity since the 19th century, especially in largely

---

Kabbalah refers to a group of books that provide mystical insight into Judaism.

Sefirot are 10 attributes through which God is revealed; singular: *sefirah*.

Tikkun means "repair" in Hebrew, either of one's soul or the whole world.

Minyan is made up of 10 adult Jews, which is the minimum number of people required for congregational prayer.

Seder is a traditional Jewish meal eaten at Passover.

Christian societies, because it lands very near Christmas. Hanukkah recalls a miracle that occurred between 165–163 BCE, when a group of Jews called the Maccabees wrested the Temple from Syrian control as part of a long war. They hoped to celebrate for eight days after rebuilding the altar, but only had enough oil to light lamps for one day. The first, then second, and finally all eight days passed but the oil never ran out—God had kept the lamps lit.

In remembrance of this, Jews light an eight-branched menorah (candelabra) during Hanukkah and sometimes give gifts to each other in memory of God's gift to the Maccabees. This celebration has taken on even more significance as Christmas has become commercialized in Europe and the United States. Likewise, the story of devout Jews fighting for their religious independence has resonated in Israel since its independence in 1948.

In the spring, Jews celebrate the beginning of new life through Passover, which marks their forebears' exodus from Egypt. During the weeklong festival, families and friends gather to read the story of Jewish exodus and to relive the exultation of freedom and subsequent 40 years wandering in the desert. Coming together for generations, the faithful follow the words of the Torah:

> This day shall be to you one of remembrance: you shall celebrate it as a festival to the LORD throughout the ages; you shall celebrate it as an institution for all time. Seven days you shall eat unleavened bread; on the very first day you shall remove leaven from your houses, for whoever eats leavened bread from the first day to the seventh, day that person shall be cut off from Israel.

> You shall celebrate a sacred occasion on the first day, and sacred occasion on the seventh day; no work at all shall be done on them only what every person is to eat, that alone may be prepared for you. You shall observe the [Feast of] Unleavened Bread, for on this very day I brought your ranks out of the land of Egypt; you shall observe this day throughout the ages as an institution for all time. (Exodus 12:14–17)

Like Rosh Hashanah and Yom Kippur in the fall, Passover helps define exactly what it means to be a Jew. By reading, remembering, and eating together, each generation can contemplate the cycles of suffering and redemption that mark Jewish history. Every portion of the Passover meal holds great significance, and families follow traditions year after year. You can get a feeling for the Passover dinner, called the **Seder**, in the chart on the next page.

<<< Although she isn't Jewish, Madonna wears a red string on her wrist that links her to the Kabbalah movement, even when singing in concert. **Do you think Jewish leaders should be upset at her interest in the Kabbalah?**

The Seder

Order of the Seder	Symbolic Foods	Symbolic Actions	Symbolic Words
1 Kadesh	Wine, sitting next to a hard-boiled egg, roasted bone, and the other foods of the ritual.	An opening prayer said over wine.	An opening prayer said over wine.
2 Urkhatz		Washing of Hands	
3 Karpas	Leafy Greens	Dipped in salty water to remind us of tears.	
4 Yakhatz	Matzo	Broken in half and hidden for later.	
5 Maggid			A family member reads the "Haggadah," the story of Exodus. Children sing and read too.
6 Rakhtsah		Washing of Hands	
7 Motzi Matzo	Matzo	Eating Matzo	
8 Maror	Bitter herbs and Kharoset (a chutney-like dish of chopped apples, nuts, cinnamon, wine, and sometimes honey).	Herbs are dipped in kharoset and eaten.	
9 Korekh	Bitter herbs, kharoset, and matzo.	The three are eaten together.	
10 Shukham Orekh	Traditional dishes (different for Ashkenazi and Sephardic traditions)	Dinner	
11 Tsafun	The half-piece of matzo eaten		
12 Barekh			A prayer of thanks after the meal.
13 Hallel			Psalms for the day
14 Nirtzah			The end of the celebration: "Next year in Jerusalem!"

∧ These are the fourteen elements of the Passover seder. What might be the significance of
∧ serving bitter herbs alongside sweet fruit?

At the end of the Passover season comes Shavuot, renamed Pentecost by Hellenized Jews because it comes 50 days after Passover. It marks both the spring wheat harvest (when the Jews received food from God) and the reception of the Torah (when the Jews received wisdom and teaching from God).

RITUALS OF THE LIFE CYCLE

As the year has a certain rhythm to it, as we've just seen, so does a Jewish life. From birth to death, the Jewish life cycle emphasizes an individual's role in the community.

Family and friends come together to celebrate the birth of a Jewish child after eight days. Naming the child welcomes the baby boy or girl into the family and community. With boys, however, one further step brings him into the covenant between God and Israel. This is done with circumcision, when a Jewish ritual surgeon (called a mohel) removes the foreskin of the boy's penis.

As they reach adolescence, both boys and girls regularly celebrate their bar mitzvah and bat mitzvah, as described in Chapter 9. The ritual of adulthood exists in many cultures, but seldom does such a ritual seem more important than the bar/bat mitzvah. The young person now holds the title of "son of the law" or "daughter of the law." From that point onward, the new adult counts in the minyan and thus becomes an active member of his or her congregation. Yet there is more to it; as we've seen, Judaism has long taught that the chosen people have to follow more laws, not fewer, than the rest of humanity. To become a child of the law marks a youth as both crucial to the Jewish community and also subject to the commandments.

∧
∧ A Jewish *katubah* (marriage contract) from
∧ Venice, Italy in 1524. Judaism gave specific legal rights to women long before other religious traditions. Why might this have happened?

∧
∧ A platter of apples and honey on Rosh
∧ Hashanah represents the beginning of a sweet new year.

Typically, marriage occurs next in the cycle of Jewish life. By long tradition, Judaism has perceived itself as matrilineal—children are Jewish because their mothers are Jewish. This gives marriage social power, as it continues the existence of Judaism itself. That's why intermarriage between a Jew and gentile has become one of the most important problems in contemporary Judaism. (This hit home a few years back, when a Jewish friend of mine married a Roman Catholic woman. I asked him how they would bring up their children. He replied, "As Christians. That's what their mom is!") With a quick Google search, you'll find many Web sites that lament intermarriage, track the birth rate of Jewish families, and offer advice to parents of marriage-age children. Web sites such as J-Date also offer to link potential Jewish mates with each other.

Given its crucial role in the history of Judaism, it's no surprise that the wedding itself has developed important characteristics. The first part of the ceremony focuses on signing the katubah, the marriage contract. Next, the couples receive seven blessings that begin with the creation of the world and end by anticipating the restoration of Israel. In other words, the process of marriage replicates both the history of humanity and the hope for its future. In that way, the wedding links the new couple to each other and to the community.

You may already know the last and most famous part of the Jewish wedding—the stomping on a wine glass by the groom. Ask a Jew and you'll get many possible explanations for this. It might recall the destruction of the Temple, be a way to ward off evil, or symbolize a girl's upcoming loss of virginity (Robinson 164–169).

As naming and marriage celebrate new life, the Jewish mourning tradition marks the end of a life. Rituals of death and mourning occur in several stages. By long tradition, Jews bury their dead quickly, nearly always within three days after death. During this time, people may stay with the body and read the Psalms aloud near it. On the third day, family and friends gather for a short burial and begin a weeklong mourning period. If you're Jewish or a friend of a Jewish family, you too may "sit shiva" during the week, enjoying each other's company, contemplating the loss of a loved one, and remembering his or her life. After that, Jewish tradition tells the family to return to their everyday activities. As we learned earlier in this chapter, the family continues to mark their mourning by leading the synagogue congregation in the mourner's Kaddish.

Denominations in American Judaism

Back in Chapter 9, we learned about the founders of the Central Synagogue in New York. They had begun to assimilate into American culture and considered themselves "progressive" Jews. Coming from Bohemia, the founders had experienced integrationist Judaism where it began. They may even have attended Sabbath prayers at the New-Old Synagogue in Prague. Once in America, they became part of the movement called Reform Judaism. Henry Fernbach, the architect of the Central Synagogue, had two themes in mind—first, he hoped to remind Jews of their "Moorish" history in Spain, Northern Africa, and the Middle East. Simultaneously, though, he hoped to build a synagogue that fit into a majority Christian community. So, the reading table (bema) was moved from the center to the front wall, and the pews and pipe organ resembled Christian churches. One stained glass window even shows the Ten Commandments in their Christian form—numbered from left to right in Roman numerals, rather than right-to-left in Hebrew.

In fact, Reform Judaism argues that the faith has continually "reformed" throughout its history. They offer the change from Temple to Rabbinic Judaism as proof positive. For that reason, they say, Judaism should also adapt to the realities of modern life, with its accompanying urbanization and multireligious atmosphere. Reform Judaism therefore perceives "Israel" to be a religious community rather than a distinct "people" and seeks to integrate Jews fully into American society and culture. Reform Judaism has de-emphasized the yearning for a Messiah and exults the importance of the synagogue, sometimes even calling it a "temple." Reform Jews rarely keep kosher and use English in much of their prayer, instead of Hebrew (Neusner 151–154).

Unlike the long tradition of segregationist Judaism, the modern Jewish Orthodox movement has also supported assimilation into society, while arguing for greater adherence to tradition and the religious separation of Judaism than Reform would accept. Orthodox Jews tend still to keep kosher, wear at least some distinctive clothing, and feel bound by the Torah commandments. They are more likely, for example, to create an eruv (Neusner 154–157).

Orthodox Judaism has many separate traditions, ranging from the "ultra orthodox" in Israel to the large Hasidic communities in America. Because they maintain distinctive forms of dress, concentrate in particular neighborhoods, and often cluster in a few related professions, modern Hasidim has become the face of traditional Judaism for much of U.S. and European society. From the outside, it seems a somber form of religion with its dark clothing for men and long skirts and covered hair for women. Yet Hasidism teaches a mystical faith that focuses on the joy of existence and the possible link between God and humanity (Blech 324). It's a case of the cover looking very different from the contents of the book!

Conservatives Judaism developed in the United States after the Reform and modern Orthodox movements developed. Though American, Conservative Judaism closely resembles similar movements in Western Europe and Canada. Conservatives feel uncomfortable with the dramatic changes of the Reform movement, yet they do not embrace Orthodoxy completely. Conservatives believe that integration into society should require much less radical changes in tradition than what Reform Jews practice. Instead, they have relied on the promise of careful scholarship and thoughtful debate to decide when to keep and when to discard tradition (Neusner 157–162).

Judaism in the Modern World

Think back to the beginning of Chapter 9, when we first began to consider the idea of ethical monotheism. There's something truly social about this idea: Judaism's commitment to a single God also includes a promise to act ethically to ward other people. This creates the basis for the Jewish idea of **tikkun olam**, repairing the world. In the Kabbalah, tikkun takes on mystical connotations. For most Jews, though, the idea refers to the need to act ethically in every part of your life—family, home, job, and politics. In this way, bit by bit, Jews may help heal the world, putting it back together when people don't act ethically.

From the late 18th century to today, we human beings have transformed our world at an alarming pace. Industrialization, colonization, secularization, nationalism, scientific innovation—together they drive the relentless changed called modernization. For religions steeped in tradition with identities linked to the past, the modern world can be a treacherous place. European and American Jews, like other religious people, confront their new world in different ways. One of the most important, however, relates to Jewish identity and assimilation. Should Jews emphasize their separate Jewish heritage or their shared European identity?

In Europe, the debate was often referred to as the "Jewish question." Were Jews different from other Europeans? If so, did this difference mean that they should live under unequal laws and suffer persecution?

<<< Hasidic boys in New York City.
How would specific religious clothing affect your life?

Reconstructionist Judaism

No longer content with Orthodoxy, the founder of Reconstructionist Judaism, Rabbi Mordecai Kaplan, became a teacher while serving as rabbi at a New York synagogue he had founded. Kaplan said that Judaism meant more than just "religion" or "nationality"; Jewish history and culture surpassed the historic land of Israel. Judaism held fast to traditions, but could also change to fit new situations as necessary. Kaplan also believed that the commandments, although not binding, should be upheld unless there was good reason otherwise. He went on to declare that the sacred Jewish texts were the creation of people, not of God. A completely American movement, Reconstructionism offers yet another perspective on the relationship between Judaism and the modern world (Robinson 61–62).

the **THINK**SPOT
www.thethinkspot.com

Tikkun Olam, meaning "repairing the world," refers to the need for Jews to act ethically in every part of their lives—family, home, job, and politics.

Pogroms were anti-Semitic riots that occurred in early 20th-century Russia.

In the early modern period, European governments increasingly marginalized Jews. In 1492, the Spanish expelled them despite centuries of peaceful coexistence and rich cultural interactions between Jews and Christians. The Republic of Venice created the first official ghetto—a sequestered area in which Jews were forced to live—in 1516. Although the word "ghetto" originally referred to a nearby iron foundry, over time it acquired a negative connotation. Similarly, in the late 18th century, Empress Catherine II established the Pale of Settlement, restricting where Jews could live within the Russian Empire. At the turn of the 20th century, Jews had to endure a number of murderous riots called **pogroms**, brought on by economic and political hardships that were blamed on them.

As Jews began to integrate into European society, however, anti-Semites redefined their bigotry from religion to race. Instead of focusing on the separateness of Judaism, 20th century anti-Semites turned to theories of racial biology to argue that Jews could never integrate into European society because they were racially distinct. From that point, it was a small intellectual step to scapegoat Jews as the source of all evil in society and to call for their eradication.

ZIONISM

In the late 19th century, Zionism arose as a movement to create an independent political nation called Israel. It was strongly influenced by both the suffering experienced under European anti-Semitism and the philosophy of nationalism, which argues that a people with shared values and backgrounds should live in an independent state. In a time when people

Progressive politicians believed in equality under the law, whereas conservative ones retained the concept of Jews being different from everyone else.

In the 19th century, some countries actively sought to integrate Jews into their legal and social structures. The experience of one Jew—Alfred Dreyfus—crystallized the issue. A French army officer and a Jew from the French-German border region, Dreyfus became a scapegoat for a spying scandal involving the French army and the German government. Using fabricated evidence and stoking anti-Jewish feelings, prosecutors in the 1890s twice found Dreyfus guilty. Only later, when outraged intellectuals and his family helped bring the real events to light, was Dreyfus taken out of solitary confinement and eventually allowed to serve again in the military with his name cleared. The Dreyfus Affair thus brought up many questions about Jewish identity, patriotism, and French bigotry.

ANTI-SEMITISM

To study the significance of the Jewish sacred community, it is crucial to understand the role of anti-Semitism. This term generally describes anti-Jewish ideas and actions that have existed for centuries, especially in Europe where a long history of mistrust between Christians and Jews manifested itself in several key periods of religious anti-Semitism.

In the Middle Ages, for example, Christians were forbidden to lend money and charge interest. As non-Christians, however, Jews were permitted to become moneylenders, which often led to bad feeling between debtor Christians and creditor Jews. In addition, Christians sometimes blamed Jews for the death of Christ and persecuted them for "blood libel," the notion that Jews murdered children to use their blood for Passover meals.

∧
∧ Anti-Semitism sometimes takes the form of desecrating Jewish graves. What can the perpetrators of such actions hope to achieve?

<<< A medieval Christian manuscript illustration of "Heretics and Jews refusing to listen to the Word of God." What forces tend to strengthen or weaken anti-Semitism?

were turning away from a religious identity ("I am Catholic," "I am Jewish") to a national identity ("I am German," "I am French"), Zionists viewed Jews as a "nation" or a "people" in a political sense, lacking an independent nation of their own.

Not all Jews accepted this concept. Some objected to the movement because they believed in the integration of Jews into the larger society. They argued against the Zionist claim that Jews would never be safe from hatred until there was an independent Israel. Other Jews disliked Zionism's secular interpretation of Judaism. To Zionists, for example, King David might be better remembered for his political leadership than as the author of the Psalms.

Although Zionism began as an intellectual movement, it gained practical importance as it helped Jews resettle around Jerusalem. In doing so, they reclaimed land that they called their homeland. This created problems with Palestinian Muslims and Christians who also called Jerusalem their ancestral home. However, as the 20th century wore on, the Zionist belief that Jews needed a place safe from persecution seemed prophetic.

THE HOLOCAUST, JEWISH RESPONSE, AND THE FOUNDING OF ISRAEL

No relic of bygone barbarism, the Holocaust (also called the Shoah) happened within your grandparents' lifetime. During World War II (1939–1945), Germany's Nazi regime murdered millions of Jews and other people deemed to be threats to an ethnically "pure" German race. This Nazi "Final Solution" was intended to eliminate all Jews, homosexuals, and Gypsies.

At first, German soldiers gunned down Jews. Later, the Nazi regime used camps such as Auschwitz, Dachau, and Buchenwald to kill millions more. This was more than the murder of Jews for their beliefs or ethnicity. It was genocide—an attempt to annihilate all Jews

V
V What does this timeline of modern Israel suggest about the ability of Israel and its
V neighbors to coexist in the Middle East?

Timeline of Modern Israel

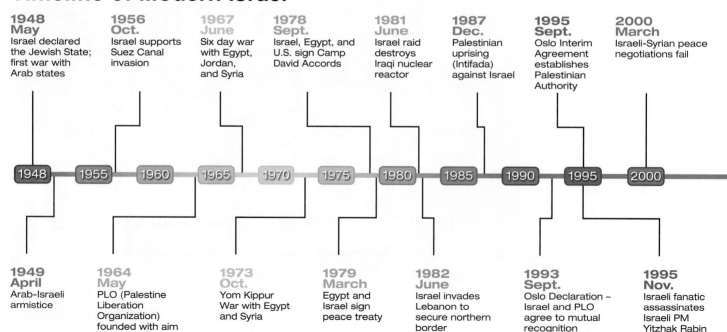

1948 May	1956 Oct.	1967 June	1978 Sept.	1981 June	1987 Dec.	1995 Sept.	2000 March
Israel declared the Jewish State; first war with Arab states	Israel supports Suez Canal invasion	Six day war with Egypt, Jordan, and Syria	Israel, Egypt, and U.S. sign Camp David Accords	Israel raid destroys Iraqi nuclear reactor	Palestinian uprising (Intifada) against Israel	Oslo Interim Agreement establishes Palestinian Authority	Israeli-Syrian peace negotiations fail

1948 — 1955 — 1960 — 1965 — 1970 — 1975 — 1980 — 1985 — 1990 — 1995 — 2000

1949 April	1964 May	1973 Oct.	1979 March	1982 June	1993 Sept.	1995 Nov.
Arab-Israeli armistice	PLO (Palestine Liberation Organization) founded with aim of destroying Israel	Yom Kippur War with Egypt and Syria	Egypt and Israel sign peace treaty	Israel invades Lebanon to secure northern border	Oslo Declaration – Israel and PLO agree to mutual recognition	Israeli fanatic assassinates Israeli PM Yitzhak Rabin

At the beginning of the war, German soldiers rounded up Jews, forced them to dig mass graves for themselves, and then shot them. This picture was taken just outside Ivangorod, USSR. Why would the Nazis want to kill Jewish women and children, and why would they change their methods from shooting to gassing? >>>

and Jewish culture—using the most modern methods available. Put plainly, this was industrial-scale murder.

With the defeat of Germany in 1945, many Holocaust survivors found themselves in territory occupied by the victorious Allies. Having experienced the horrors of the Holocaust, many Jews renewed their support for Zionism. What they wanted was a homeland of their own, which they finally achieved in the formation of the state of Israel in 1948.

But what of God? How could the Creator, the Divine One who interacts with and is worshipped by the Jews, allow such atrocities to occur? Jewish responses to this question arise out of agonized attempts to reconcile horrific experience with the traditional concerns of Judaism. A few might argue that the Holocaust took place to punish Jews for the sin of forgetting the 613 commandments. Some others have said that Jewish people have been forced to suffer for all of the world's sins. More mystical Jews sometimes describe the Shoah as a terrible event that transcends human understanding.

Some Jews, however, have said that the Holocaust proved that God could not exist. How could a good, ethical god let such an event take place?

One of the most widespread interpretations of these horrific events might be called "Judaism of Holocaust and Redemption." This idea "joins the Holocaust to the creation of the state of Israel. It links the secular and the theological, the Israeli and the diaspora communities of Judaism" (Neusner 171). This interpretation brings Judaism back to its traditions of expulsion and return to the homeland. Worse than Egypt or Babylon, the Holocaust has proven the need for Jews to maintain their identity and to defend it militarily in Israel. To this way of thinking, it's possible to be Jewish without ever entering a synagogue or keeping kosher. Rather, Jewish identity confers the responsibility to remember the past and to shield future generations from reliving the horrors of the 20th century.

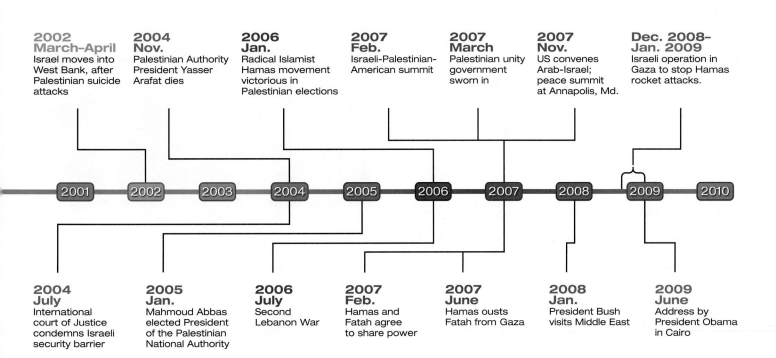

2002 March–April
Israel moves into West Bank, after Palestinian suicide attacks

2004 Nov.
Palestinian Authority President Yasser Arafat dies

2006 Jan.
Radical Islamist Hamas movement victorious in Palestinian elections

2007 Feb.
Israeli-Palestinian-American summit

2007 March
Palestinian unity government sworn in

2007 Nov.
US convenes Arab-Israel; peace summit at Annapolis, Md.

Dec. 2008–Jan. 2009
Israeli operation in Gaza to stop Hamas rocket attacks.

2001   2002   2003   2004   2005   2006   2007   2008   2009   2010

2004 July
International court of Justice condemns Israeli security barrier

2005 Jan.
Mahmoud Abbas elected President of the Palestinian National Authority

2006 July
Second Lebanon War

2007 Feb.
Hamas and Fatah agree to share power

2007 June
Hamas ousts Fatah from Gaza

2008 Jan.
President Bush visits Middle East

2009 June
Address by President Obama in Cairo

Holocaust Denial

On June 10th, 2009, an 89-year-old white supremacist named James W. von Brunn shot and killed an African American security guard at the Holocaust Museum in Washington, D.C. In his car after the shooting, police found this note: "You want my weapons—this is how you'll get them. The Holocaust is a lie. Obama was created by Jews. Obama does what his Jew owners tell him to do" (Drost; see also Rutten).

Beginning with Nazis in war crimes trials and continuing to the present day, anti-Semites have somehow claimed—against all evidence—that Allied governments fabricated the Holocaust to help Jews. The growth of the Internet has helped these extremists spread their ideas, and von Brunn had posted his screeds on Web sites devoted to the matter. Although generally linked to far-right politics in America, the idea gained an unusual adherent in the past few years: The Iranian president Mahmoud Ahmadinejad has repeatedly questioned the Holocaust in public speeches and even sponsored a conference of Holocaust deniers in Tehran in 2005.

In part to honor the dead, in part to shame those who deny the Shoah, President Barack Obama had spoken at the Buchenwald concentration camp just a week before the deadly attack in Washington, D.C. "To this day," he said, "there are those who insist that the Holocaust never happened, a denial of fact and truth that is baseless and ignorant and hateful. This place is the ultimate rebuke of those thoughts—a reminder of our duty to confront those who tell lies about our history. These sites have not lost their horror with the passage of time." In later remarks, Obama added that the Iranian president "should make his own visit" to see proof of the atrocities (Squires; see also Paterson).

>>> A chart of prisoner markings used in German concentration camps. The horizontal categories list markings for the following types of prisoners: political, professional criminals, emigrants, Jehovah's Witnesses, homosexuals, Germans shy of work, and other nationalities shy of work. The vertical categories begin with the basic colors, and then show those for repeat offenders, prisoners in punishment commands, Jews, Jews who have violated racial laws by having sexual relations with Aryans, and Aryans who violated racial laws by having sexual relations with Jews. The remaining symbols give examples of marking patterns. Why would the last category have a special marking according to the Nazi way of thinking?

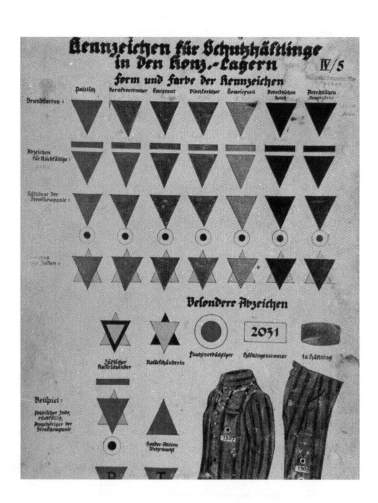

Conclusion

The next time you read the news, listen to the radio, or watch a movie, think about all the references to God. They are everywhere, from our politics to our schools, from our television shows to the Internet. When we argue about "religion," for example, it is often another way of discussing ethics—the way in which people should live and treat others. Underneath all the rhetoric lie assumptions about God, prayer, and a personal or communal relationship with the divine.

In the United States, these ideas come directly from Judaism. This religion, more than any other, has affected the way American society has grown and developed. Need proof? Take a coin out of your pocket and check out the monotheistic prayer stamped on it: "In God We Trust." The words could have come from Abraham in the Torah, from a rabbi in the synagogue, or from the president of the United States.

By placing the words of the Shema in their houses, Jews are reminded of God's constant presence.

v
v
v

Although Jews are considered "chosen", the story of Isaac's sacrifice illustrates the fact that Abraham also had freedom of choice. Because of this, Jews are considered to have both been chosen by God and to have chosen God.

v
v
v

IS THERE A GOD?
Judaism believes in a single God who has a direct relationship with humanity. According to Jewish scripture, God created everything and thus has power over all creation.

HOW DOES THE SACRED BECOME COMMUNITY?
Like other traditions, Judaism has highly social elements. Following the Halakhah, praying and celebrating holidays together, getting married to another Jew, and becoming a bar mitzvah or bat mitzvah all provide ways to create community within Judaism.

?

WHAT DOES IT MEAN TO BE HUMAN?
According to the first book of the Torah, God created humanity in God's image. This means that people share free will and innate goodness with God. Human beings, however, have chosen to use their free will to do good (like God) but also to do evil. The father of Judaism, Abraham, chose to follow God and was rewarded by having his progeny become the "chosen people."

HOW DO HUMANS INTERACT WITH THE SACRED?
In the millennium before the Common Era, Jewish interaction with God focused on Temple sacrifice and ethical conduct based on commandments from the Torah. After the Romans destroyed the temple in 70 CE, Judaism developed its present Rabbinic tradition, which emphasizes prayer, following the Torah, concentrating on education, and acting ethically. Mysticism, such as Kabbalah tradition, uses a less rational approach to interact with God than Rabbinic Judaism and seeks an intense communion with God.

<<<
For Jews, prayer brings all Jews— past, present, and future—together.

What is it about communal prayer that can bind people together in this way?

>>>
The Torah is the most sacred of the writings of Judaism. How important is a written law to a religious community?

Summary

HOW DO HUMANS INTERACT WITH THE SACRED?   p. 142

- Prayer, whether private or communal, is at the heart of Judaism. Prayer allows Jews to communicate with God as well as remember their shared heritage and beliefs. Important prayers include the Shema, the Amidah, and the Kaddish.
- Followers of Judaism keep commandments such as special dietary laws, which regulate what foods are kosher and what are trayf. These laws link Jews to tradition and remind them daily of their relationship with God.

HOW DOES THE SACRED BECOME COMMUNITY?   p. 147

- Jews observe holidays such as Rash Hashanah, Yom Kippur, and Sukkot. These holidays usually involve ritualized eating, and a coming together of family. By keeping these traditions alive through generations, Jews retain a link to the past.
- As they reach puberty, Jewish boys and girls celebrate their bat and bar mitzvahs to mark a coming of age. From that day on, they are expected to take on a full adult role in the religious community and are subject to the commandments.
- Unfortunately, Anti-Semitism has existed for centuries, affecting Jewish people around the world. This has led to a Zionist movement, as some Jews seek refuge in their ancient land.

Key Terms

Shabbat is the Hebrew word for the Sabbath, the day of rest.   *143*

Eruv is a contained space within which Jews observe the Sabbath; plural: *eruvin*.   *143*

Shema is a prayer that reminds Jews to remember God and the commandments at all times.   *143*

Amidah is a Jewish prayer made up of 19 sections and includes praise, request, and thanksgiving.   *143*

Kaddish is a Jewish prayer used to express the hope that the world will become holy and God's will be done.   *145*

Kashrut is a set of Jewish dietary laws.   *145*

Kosher refers to the appropriate kind of food to be consumed according to Jewish dietary laws.   *145*

Hekhsher is a kosher certification symbol.   *145*

Kabbalah refers to a group of books that provide mystical insight into Judaism.   *146*

Sefirot are 10 attributes through which God is revealed; singular: *sefirah*.   *146*

Tikkun means "repair" in Hebrew, either of one's soul or the whole world.   *146*

Minyan is made up of 10 adult Jews, which is the minimum number of people required for congregational prayer.   *147*

Seder is a traditional Jewish meal eaten at Passover.   *147*

Tikkun olam, meaning "repairing the world," refers to the need for Jews to act ethically in every part of their lives—family, home, job, and politics.   *151*

Pogroms were anti-Semitic riots that occurred in early 20th-century Russia.   *151*

Find it on

the THINKSPOT
www.thethinkspot.com

- West Hampton Beach/Eruv: The construction of the eruv in the community of West Hampton Beach sparked a great debate. Go to the ThinkSpot to visit two sites—one that publishes a letter in support of the eruv, and one that has devoted an entire site against—that detail the discussion that raged regarding the denoting of a one-square mile area, or one third of the town proper, to proclaim the area an Orthodox Jewish community. After you've read both sides of the argument, what do you think? (http://www.adl.org/ADL_Opinions/Religious_ Freedom/Newsday_Westhampton_Eruv.htm)(http://alliance separationofchurchandstateforgreaterwesthampton.org/)

- Madonna practices it. So did Britney Spears, for a time. It's Kabbalah, a "mystical" interpretation of the Torah. Practitioners can be identified by the thin, red thread that they wear around

their wrists. If you want to learn more, go to the ThinkSpot to read about this ancient religious tradition that has grown in popularity in recent years. (http://www.kabbalah5.com/ INDEX.htm)

- A defining moment in time for the Jews of the world is the Holocaust, a genocide that occurred during the 1930s and 1940s. The Holocaust History Project is devoted to "never forgetting" the tragedy. This is a free archive of documents, photographs, recordings, and essays related to the Holocaust, including refutation of Holocaust denial. Visit the ThinkSpot www.thethinkspot.com to visit this moving and profound site devoted to the memory of those lost during this horrific and unimaginable event. (www.holocaust-history.org)

Questions for Study and Review

1. What is an eruv, and how is it used in Jewish tradition?

In traditional Judaism, the eruv surrounds a Jewish neighborhood. Sometimes, it is physically closed off, for example, by stringing cables between telephone poles. Sometimes, the borders are symbolic, designated by homes, businesses, or streets. On the Sabbath and on other designated worship days or holidays, Orthodox Jews may continue to walk and carry things in the eruv, even when prohibited from doing so outside of its borders.

2. What is Passover?

Passover recalls the Jews' enslavement by the Egyptians and their eventual flight to the desert and Israel.

3. What is Jewish mysticism?

Jewish mysticism seeks a nonrational link to the divine. One of the most well-known mystical traditions is Kabbalah, which strives to answer the questions of existence in unique ways, relying on secret wisdom handed down from generation to generation. In recent years, this mystical tradition has been the center of some controversy because of its introduction into popular culture.

For Further Study

BOOKS:

Armstrong, Karen. *A History of God: The 4,000-Year Quest of Judaism, Christianity and Islam.* New York: Ballantine Books, 1994.

Blech, Benjamin. *The Complete Idiot's Guide to Understanding Judaism.* New York: Alpha, 2003.

Berlin, Adele and Marc Zvi Brettler, eds., *The Jewish Study Bible,* New York: Oxford, 2004.

Cohn-Sherbok, Dan. *Fifty Key Jewish Thinkers.* New York: Routledge, 2007.

Heschel, Abraham Joshua. *The Sabbath.* New York: Farrar Straus Giroux, 2005.

Neusner, Jacob. *Judaism: The Basics.* New York: Routledge, 2006.

Robinson, George. *Essential Judaism: A Complete Guide to Beliefs, Customs, and Rituals.* New York: Pocket Books, 2000.

Seltzer, Robert M. *Jewish People, Jewish Thought: The Jewish Experience in History.* New York: Macmillan Publishing Co., Inc., 1980.

Tanakh: The Holy Scriptures, Philadelphia: The Jewish Publication Society, 1988.

WEB SITES:

Hebrew-English Bible. http://www.mechon-mamre.org/p/pt/pt0.htm

Jewish Virtual Library. http://www.jewishvirtuallibrary.org

Judaism 101. http://www.jewfaq.org/index.htm

MavenSearch: Jewish Web Directory. http://www.mavensearch.com/

<<< Santa Maria in Trastevere is one of Rome's ancient churches. This building reveals the influence of many forms of Christianity. The huge mosaics in the dome have a Byzantine style, but the pews and other art reflect later Roman Catholic additions. The icon on the altar, recently added, comes from the Russian Orthodox tradition.

IS THERE A GOD?
WHAT DOES IT MEAN TO BE HUMAN?

The next

time you are out for a drive or a walk, start looking at churches. Count how many you see. I think there are at least four within a couple blocks of my house. There must be nearly two dozen within a five-minute drive from my office. Some soar into the Philadelphia skyline, but many more proclaim themselves from storefronts.

Why are there so many different churches in the United States? Are they all the same? Are they all Christian? Do they all worship the same God or different ones? Chapters 11 and 12 will help you figure out the origins of Christianity, how it grew, and how it spread across the globe.

We will also consider how Christianity has developed very differently from other religions we have studied. While Hinduism layers ideas on top of one another (remember the sand art?), Christianity seems to prefer precise definitions. Yet, if Christians aim to clarify the relationship of God and humanity, why are there so many different opinions among Christians today?

You'll notice a few ways that Chapters 11 and 12 differ from other parts of *Think World Religions*. Most American students feel more familiar with Christianity than any other religion, and the United States has a dizzying number of Christian denominations. Because of those facts, we'll study the differences among Christian groups in more detail than other traditions we learn about in this book. After all, you too may drive past Roman Catholic, Primitive Baptist, Apostolic Holiness, Albanian Orthodox, or Ethiopian Coptic churches as you hurry to classes. Here's your chance to begin learning about that rich tapestry of Christian faith.

CHRISTIANITY:
The God-Man Messiah

St. Stephen's of Walbrook

THINGS JUST FEEL RIGHT IN ST. STEPHEN'S OF WALBROOK IN LONDON, ENGLAND. It's tucked inside the bustling City of London, the financial center of Great Britain. As you walk through the doors, the blaring of urban life slips away. You step past a mosaic of St. Stephen as you enter, reminding you of Christianity's first martyr. Listen for bells from the tower on your left. Even their ethereal sounds won't prepare you for the soft light that floods in from the dome and the windows. It illuminates flowers and vines cast in plaster. Look up, look around: the room's geometric proportions are perfect. The dome soars above your head. You can see and hear from any part of the room, a testament to the church's 17th-century designer, the famous English architect Christopher Wren. The columns and dome give it an ancient Roman feeling; dark wood carvings add the English touch. Other elements look more northern European, like the carved baptismal font, the pipe organ, and the high pulpit for preaching the word of God. In 1953, the priest here, Chad Vallah, decided to take those words to people considering suicide. He began The Samaritans. An easy-to-remember phone number linked you to a Good Samaritan. Now The Samaritans have such phone numbers all over the world.

Wren gave the pulpit more prominence than the altar, a testament to his Protestantism. Yet now, a rough rock altar stands directly under the dome, quite different from its elegant surroundings. Made for the church by Henry Moore in 1972, the altar feels modern and ancient at the same time. It reminds you of the sacrifice of Abraham and the stone altars of Roman gods, which once stood near this very spot. Though an altar used to be at the east end of the church, the new one feels right here, at the center St. Stephen's.

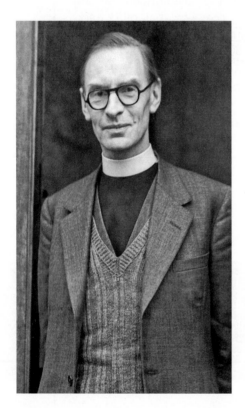

*Portrait of **E.C. Varah**, rector of St. Stephen's and founder of the Samaritans, a group that helps people in despair and considering suicide.*

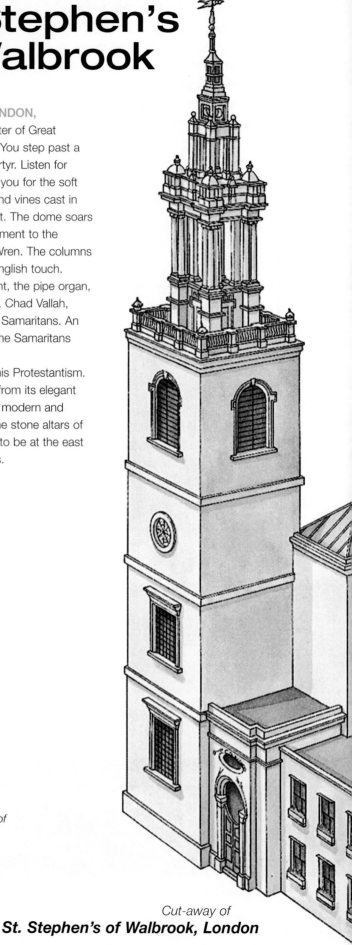

Cut-away of
St. Stephen's of Walbrook, London

Painting showing **St. Stephen's Walbrook** *in the 18th century*

In this picture, all eyes are trained on the preacher in the corner pulpit. Nowadays, the stone altar in the middle of the church provides the focus of worship. What might that mean in the context of Christian theology? What other changes do you see in the church's interior? How might they affect the way people interact with God and each other?

Modern Altar

The Messiah: Jesus Christ

Is there a God in Christianity? The answer is "Absolutely yes!" Christianity grows out of the Judaic belief in a single creator god. Christians accept ethical monotheism from Judaism but then add elements of Greek philosophy and other local traditions. They have created a religion on the foundation of others, actually building Christian altars atop ancient Roman ones. Why? Around the time of Jesus' birth (traditionally 1 CE, but now thought to be a little earlier) the Roman Empire controlled what is now modern-day Israel. Roman government and previous rule by the Greek conqueror Alexander the Great had introduced Greek and Roman influences into the region. This linked Israel to the rest of the "civilized" (read: Roman) world, but it also shackled it under non-Jewish rulers (Spickard and Cragg 24–27).

As we have learned in Chapters 9 and 10, these were turbulent years for Judaism. Pharisees, Sadducees, and other groups debated the roles of priests, lay believers, and Mosaic Law. Hellenized Jews, educated in Greek philosophy, began to integrate Jewish theology with Greek ideas about God and the cosmos. They discussed whether God would send a messiah to free Israel from Roman rule, and they wondered if their lives would end when they died or whether some other world existed after death.

During this turbulent time, a very young woman named Mary bore a son and named him Jesus. According to Christian tradition, Mary never had sexual relations with anyone before giving birth to her son. Tradition says that Mary's mother, Anna, and her father, Joachim (who was a priest at the Jewish temple), had dedicated Mary to the Temple service as a child. When she became old enough, she left to live independently, under the care of Joseph of Nazareth, an older man (perhaps a widower) who was supposed to take care of her. That's when she brought Jesus into the world.

We know little about Jesus's childhood, except that he learned carpentry under Joseph's tutelage in Nazareth. As an adult, his cousin John the Baptist, a holy man preaching the coming of a messiah, baptized Jesus. Afterward, Jesus spent 40 days and nights in solitude to confront temptations and reaffirm his obedience to God's will.

Jesus taught for three years, traveling through the region around Jerusalem. During this time, he chose 12 disciples who would later help form the core of the Christian church. As he traveled, Jesus taught that people should care for one another, welcome the downtrodden, feed the poor, and care not for money but cultivate selfless love. He preached in synagogues and performed miracles. He lived and ate with people

---

A SACRED ACTION ▶▶▶

Liturgy and Eucharist

As the priest steps away from the altar at the Church of the Holy Spirit in Minsk, Belarus, a line forms in the crowded room—hundreds of people stand in the church. He has just finished chanting a prayer that has quieted the rustle: "I believe, O Lord, and I confess that Thou art truly the Christ, the Son of the Living God, who came into the world to save sinners, of whom I am the first. I believe also that this is truly Thine own most pure Body, and that this is truly Thine own most precious Blood. Therefore I pray Thee: Have mercy upon me and forgive me my transgressions, committed in word and deed, whether consciously or unconsciously."

People move amiably out of the way of those who want to receive communion. Mothers prop their children on a hip and take them to the front of the line that meanders back toward the entrance of the building. Moving forward toward the priest, each person first kisses a painted icon and then folds her hands over her chest. The priest, meanwhile, faces the line holding a large silver chalice with a deep cup and an oversized base. He grasps a spoon with a longish handle, which he dips into the mixture of wine and small cubes of bread inside the chalice.

Coming toward the priest, a woman leans slightly forward and two altar boys hold a cloth under her chin to catch any drops. The priest spoons a small amount of bread and wine from the large chalice into her mouth. He calls her by name, adding that the wine and bread are "for the remission of sins and life eternal." She kisses the chalice, the altar boys remove the napkin, and the woman turns away to make room. Another person steps up to the chalice and repeats the ritual—leaning forward toward the chalice, receiving a spoon of bread and wine, and kissing the chalice. This happens as many times as there are people in line.

As the woman returns to her place, friends whisper congratulations to her for receiving the Eucharist, since they believe that she has communed with God in a direct way—by accepting God's "own pure body" and "precious blood."

<<< People stand for prayers and communion in the Church of the Holy Spirit in Minsk, Belarus.

who Jewish society considered ritually impure, such as lepers, prostitutes, and thieves. He interacted with women, respecting them as equal to men before God, an attitude that was uncommon for the times (McGrath 84–106).

Jesus' life and teaching confounded people in his society, including some of the men closest to him. In some ways, he seemed completely normal—he understood the political and social rules of Roman-occupied Israel. He was a Jew, not some other ethnic or religious tradition. He claimed that he would fulfill Jewish law, not break it.

Yet in other ways, Jesus seemed completely unlike the men and women of his day. Even when he spoke plainly, it seemed something mysterious was happening. For example, he might command his disciples to throw their fishing nets into the sea after a long day with no catch. Of course, when they did it one more time, their boats nearly sank with the fish. Jesus also introduced new ideas about God and Israel through parables. What may seem common sense to us now sounded revolutionary then:

> Jesus replied, "A man was going down from Jerusalem to Jericho, and fell into the hands of robbers, who stripped him, beat him, and went away, leaving him half dead. Now by chance a priest was going down that road; and when he saw him, he passed by on the other side. So likewise a Levite, when he came to the place and saw him, passed by on the other side. But a Samaritan while traveling came near him; and when he saw him, he was moved with pity. He went to him and bandaged his wounds, having poured oil and wine on them. Then he put him on his own animal, brought him to an inn, and took care of him. The next day he took out two denarii, gave them to the innkeeper, and said, 'Take care of him; and when I come back, I will repay you whatever more you spend.' Which of these three, do you think, was a neighbor to the man who fell into the hands of the robbers?" He said, "The one who showed him mercy." Jesus said to him, "Go and do likewise." (Luke 10: 30–37)

You'll remember from Chapter 9 that Jewish society gave great respect to the priests and Levites as the men who could offer sacrifices and serve in the Temple. Jesus said that a Samaritan—an outcast in Israelite society—might act in a more neighborly way than did Jewish elites. This did not enamor Jesus to the priests and Levites. So, while the message might seem reasonable to us ("help the needy") Jesus' audience understood its radical subtext ("the elite of society may not be better than the outcast").

In some cases, Jesus' followers found it difficult to understand exactly what he meant. Was Jesus really the messiah? If so, was he a leader, a judge, a prophet, or a warrior? Imagine if you heard the following parable—in whose role would you place yourself?

> The kingdom of heaven may be compared to a king who gave a wedding banquet for his son. He sent his slaves to call those who had been invited to the wedding banquet, but they would not come. Again he sent other slaves, saying, "Tell those who have been invited: Look, I have prepared my dinner, my oxen and my fat calves have been slaughtered, and everything is ready; come to the wedding banquet." But they made light of it and went away, one to his farm, another to his business, while the rest seized his slaves, mistreated them, and killed them. The king was enraged. He sent his troops, destroyed those murderers, and burned their city. Then he said to his slaves, "The wedding is ready, but those invited were not worthy. Go therefore into the main streets, and invite everyone you find to the wedding banquet." Those slaves went out into the streets and gathered all whom they found, both good and bad; so the wedding hall was filled with guests. But when the king came in to see

the guests, he noticed a man there who was not wearing a wedding robe, and he said to him, "Friend, how did you get in here without a wedding robe?" And he was speechless. Then the king said to the attendants, "Bind him hand and foot, and throw him into the outer darkness, where there will be weeping and gnashing of teeth." For many are called, but few are chosen. (Matthew 22: 1–14)

The Jewish public responded in various ways to Jesus. Some, including many leaders of the Temple, the Pharisees, and the Sadducees, questioned his teachings as being insufficiently Jewish and perhaps felt threatened by him. Others, especially groups of poor Jews and people looking for a messiah, took solace in his teachings and

∧ **The Monastery of St. Catherine,** deep in the Sinai desert, has preserved this very early depiction of Jesus. What influence do you think this image has had on our ideas about him?

Eucharist is the Christian ritual based on the Passover seder held by Jesus and his disciples.

hoped he would lead Israel toward a new period of independence. In those years, Israel had both a Jewish tetrarch (Herod) and a Roman governor (Pontius Pilate). Herod controlled issues relating to Jewish events or local customs, while Pilate maintained order and ensured Israel's acquiescence to Roman taxes and laws.

On the Jewish feast of Passover around the year 33 CE, Jesus shared a "last supper" with his disciples. During this meal he told his disciples that it would be his last Passover meal, instructing them to eat

bread and drink wine as "his body and his blood" in remembrance of him. This would later become the ritual of **Eucharist**, or communion. One of Jesus' disciples, Judas Iscariot, took a bribe to tell where Jesus was staying, so that a group of Jewish and Roman men could arrest him. When Jesus was unwilling to defend himself, Pilate might have freed him, but a raucous mob called for his death. Calling it an internal Jewish issue, Pilate allowed Jesus to be crucified along with common criminals.

Flogged, beaten, and humiliated, Christian sacred writings explain that Jesus hung on the cross for three hours before he died, constantly watched by a group that included soldiers, his mother Mary, and a young disciple named John. On the Friday before sundown that began the Passover Sabbath, Pilate allowed Jesus' body to be entombed and

∧
∧ Consider how each artist portrays Jesus on the cross. The picture above shows a Roman
∧ Catholic version of the crucifixion. The one on the top right is an Orthodox mural icon on a church wall. The bottom left is by Russian-Jewish painter Marc Chagall, and includes elements of Jewish life at the beginning of the 20th century.

sealed. Three days later, three women named Mary (Jesus' mother, Mary Magdalene, and Mary, the mother of John) went to anoint the corpse, only to find the tomb empty. Christ had risen from the dead, breaking the power of death over humanity. Christians mark this as Easter or Pascha, shorthand words for the resurrection of Jesus. For 40 days after that, Jesus appeared to his disciples and many others, teaching them that the messiah was not to be a political, but rather a spiritual savior for both Jews and non-Jews alike.

After his last period of miraculous teaching, Christian sacred writings explain that Jesus rose into heaven, a day commemorated as the Ascension. Unclear as to what to do next, his disciples continued to meet in semi-secret until the Jewish holiday of Pentecost. Then, as they gathered together, tradition says that the spirit of God infused each of them with the power to speak different languages to teach Jesus' message across the Roman Empire and beyond. From this point, people began to call them "apostles" rather than "disciples." Christians sometimes commemorate this as the birthday of their religion, when the apostles began a ministry outside their own circle of friends and relatives.

After Pentecost, Jesus' disciples began to re-interpret Jewish law and scripture in light of their new circumstances. They traveled across the Roman Empire as teachers. Most people saw them as just another sect

---

>>> **After having a mystical experience** on the road to Damascus, **Paul became a very devout Christian.** How might this conversion story affect later Christians?

Old Testament refers to the Jewish Tanakh.

New Testament is made up of 26 books related to Jesus' life, teachings, and the teachings of his disciples.

of Jews who sometimes met at the Temple and regularly attended services at synagogues outside Jerusalem. The movement expanded dramatically when a Hellenistic Jew named Paul (previously named Saul) stopped persecuting Christians and instead joined them. Paul and others like him made Christianity more understandable to a non-Jewish audience (McManners 23–26).

WRITING ABOUT THE CHRISTIAN GOD

As the apostles spread out around the Roman Empire, people began referring to them as "Christians," based on the idea that Jesus was the "Christ"—another word for "messiah." Christianity expanded and interacted with many non-Jewish people. Similar to Hellenistic Jews, who integrated philosophy with Judaism, Christians began to use Greek philosophy and Jewish ideas to explain Jesus' teachings to those outside his core of followers.

Not only did they augment Jewish ideas about God, but Christians often interpreted Biblical prophesies to show that Christ was the Messiah. In this way, Christianity differentiated itself from Judaism. Christians began to write about two "testaments" of God to humanity: the Jewish law (**Old Testament**) and the Christian Gospel (**New Testament**).

The New Testament slowly took shape in the form of letters (Epistles) and sacred history (Acts of the Apostles). Christians also circulated different versions of the "Good News," accounts of Jesus' life, teaching, and miracles. In English, we update the archaic term

---

THINK World Religions

Paul's Mystical Experience

Here is how the Acts of the Apostles relates Paul's experience:

"While I was on my way and approaching Damascus, about noon, a great light from heaven suddenly shone about me. I fell to the ground and heard a voice saying to me, 'Saul, Saul, why are you persecuting me?' I answered, 'Who are you, Lord?' Then he said to me, 'I am Jesus of Nazareth whom you are persecuting.' Now those who were with me saw the light but did not hear the voice of the one who was speaking to me. I asked, 'What am I to do, Lord?' The Lord said to me, 'Get up and go to Damascus; there you will be told everything that has been assigned to you to do.' Since I could not see because of the brightness of that light, those who were with me took my hand and led me to Damascus."

"A certain Ananias, who was a devout man according to the law and well spoken of by all the Jews living there, came to me; and standing beside me, he said, 'Brother Saul, regain your sight!' In that very hour I regained my sight and saw him. Then he said, 'The God of our ancestors has chosen you to know his will, to see the Righteous One and to hear his own voice; for you will be his witness to all the world of what you have seen and heard. And now why do you delay? Get up, be baptized, and have your sins washed away, calling on his name.'"

"After I had returned to Jerusalem and while I was praying in the temple, I fell into a trance and saw Jesus saying to me, 'Hurry and get out of Jerusalem quickly, because they will not accept your testimony about me.' And I said, 'Lord, they themselves know that in every synagogue I imprisoned and beat those who believed in you. And while the blood of your witness Stephen was shed, I myself was standing by, approving and keeping the coats of those who killed him.' Then he said to me, 'Go, for I will send you far away to the Gentiles.'" (Acts 22:6–21)

the THINK SPOT
www.thethinkspot.com

<<< Here are two pages from the oldest known manuscript of the New Testament, the Greek Codex Sinaiticus. How might different translations of the Bible affect the way people interpret it?

"godspel" to become "gospel." The last book of the New Testament is also its most controversial. The Revelation of St. John (or the Book of Revelation) describes a mystical dream about the end of the world experienced by an early Christian named John on the island of Patmos.

In some cases, as in the letters of St. Paul or Revelation, scholars of Christianity generally agree on who wrote books of the New Testament. In other cases, especially regarding the Gospels, you can find dozens of opinions regarding who wrote the texts, when, and in what order. Each gospel gives a different perspective of Jesus as seen by that author.

Books of the New Testament

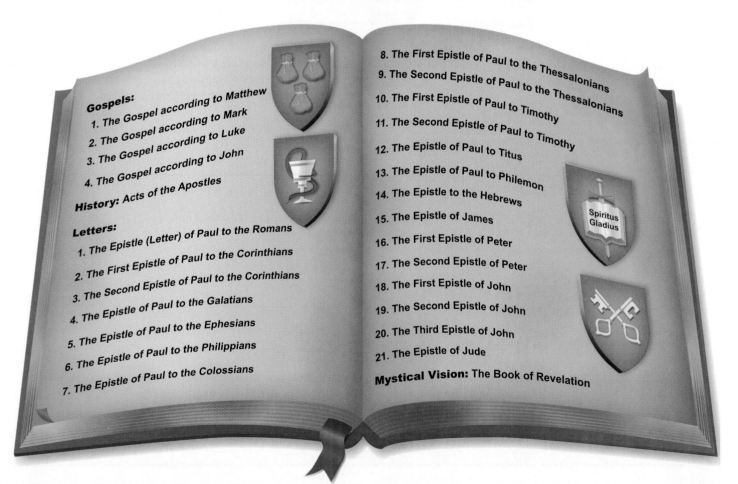

Gospels:
1. The Gospel according to Matthew
2. The Gospel according to Mark
3. The Gospel according to Luke
4. The Gospel according to John

History: Acts of the Apostles

Letters:
1. The Epistle (Letter) of Paul to the Romans
2. The First Epistle of Paul to the Corinthians
3. The Second Epistle of Paul to the Corinthians
4. The Epistle of Paul to the Galatians
5. The Epistle of Paul to the Ephesians
6. The Epistle of Paul to the Philippians
7. The Epistle of Paul to the Colossians
8. The First Epistle of Paul to the Thessalonians
9. The Second Epistle of Paul to the Thessalonians
10. The First Epistle of Paul to Timothy
11. The Second Epistle of Paul to Timothy
12. The Epistle of Paul to Titus
13. The Epistle of Paul to Philemon
14. The Epistle to the Hebrews
15. The Epistle of James
16. The First Epistle of Peter
17. The Second Epistle of Peter
18. The First Epistle of John
19. The Second Epistle of John
20. The Third Epistle of John
21. The Epistle of Jude

Mystical Vision: The Book of Revelation

Spiritus Gladius

Varieties of Early Christianity

Given its lack of cohesive structure and fear of persecution, you can see how difficult it would have been to build an organized "church" in the first few centuries of the Christian movement. Instead, try to imagine many different Christian traditions sprouting up in various parts of the Roman empire, sometimes interacting with one another, other times isolating themselves. Depending on philosophical, political, or personal situations, Christians might appear to be Jewish, Greek, a mixture of the two, or something quite different from either. Students from some Christian traditions feel comfortable with this idea, but others find it difficult to accept. When I was a graduate student, a younger colleague dropped out of a course called "Varieties of Early Christianity" because she couldn't accept that they didn't all see eye to eye with each other and with her own Christian tradition.

Here's an example: The **Gnostics** had their own beliefs regarding God based on secret knowledge called "gnosis." They wrote their own gospels and interpretations of Jewish ideas, emphasizing a struggle between good and evil on Earth (Gnosticism). The Gnostics viewed the world as an imperfect version of reality, to be overcome only through mystical, secret gnosis. Other early Christian leaders vehemently disagreed with the Gnostic position and wrote blistering anti-Gnostic tirades.

We have only begun to learn about Gnosticism from its own works, based on documents found at Nag Hammadi in Egypt in 1945. Their ideas about gender, the body, Mary, Jesus, and the disciples give us new interpretations on some very old themes (McManners 26–28).

∧
∧ The Nag Hammadi texts, written around
∧ 400 CE, help us learn about Gnosticism.
How might they also change our views of
modern Christianity?

the **THINK** SPOT
www.thethinkspot.com

Although the gospels provide historical and biographical information, they also interpret Jesus' message to different audiences. Three of them (Matthew, Luke, and Mark) relate closely to one another. The authors of these three surely knew of each other's texts and perhaps used a common source to produce them. The Gospel of John came much later and had a different intended audience. Instead of Jews, John's writing was aimed at Greek-speaking people who might have understood philosophy better than they did Jewish law (Sanders 71).

The Acts of the Apostles follows the Gospels. This long book shows how Christians traveled across the Roman empire while suffering internal disagreements and external persecution. The next 20 books are all letters from Christianity's early leaders, defining doctrine and practice as well as encouraging Christians, especially when facing hostility. The final book, the Revelation, uses symbolism and figurative language to detail the vision John of Patmos had of the end of the world. It encourages the belief that present suffering will some day be overcome in a New Jerusalem (McGrath 55–74).

Seeking God in the Early Christian Church

If you were a Christian in the year 200 CE, you might have a difficult time figuring out how to explain Jesus to your Jewish or Roman friends. After all, you wouldn't have one accepted book called the "New Testament." Instead, you might read different versions of the Gospel, including a couple not even mentioned in the list on the previous page. You might read Greek, Latin, or Hebrew, but would most likely be illiterate. You'd hear friends and preachers talking about the Word of God and the Holy Spirit. What do those terms actually mean?

Gnostics were a Christian sect that taught that the physical world was flawed. Gnostics believed that salvation could be found in hidden knowledge.

Apostolic succession refers to the Christian act of being blessed by an Apostle who was blessed by Christ.

To find some answers, we need to learn a little more about early Christian communities. Of course, the first Christians didn't originally call themselves by that name—they were mostly Jews who believed Jesus was the Messiah. For that reason, they still attended synagogue, celebrated Jewish holidays, and probably made sacrifices at the Temple in Jerusalem. Yet, little by little, the followers of Jesus began to pull away from Judaism: They welcomed gentiles into their communities, struggled with understanding the role of Jewish law to their lives, and started to alter Jewish practices and words. Some time after the Roman destruction of the Jewish Temple in 70 CE, Christians began to call some of their leaders "priests," a term previously used only for men who made sacrifices in the Temple. (Paul had described Christ as a "high priest," in his Epistle to the Hebrews 9:11). The term "priest" came directly from Jewish usage, but Christians gave it new meaning. Instead of a class of men who made sacrifices in the Temple of Jerusalem, Christian priests received their blessing from men who had walked and lived with Jesus or from those who had themselves received such a blessing. Priests who rose to leadership positions took the name "bishop," or sometimes "high priest" (McManners 33–35).

This process—laying hands in a transfer of blessings from the apostles on down—defines **apostolic succession**. Jewish priests descended from one of the 12 tribes of Judah, but Christians created a spiritual family tree

>>> In this picture, Emperor Constantine bows down to an icon of Saints Peter and Paul, held by Saint Sylvester. What messages was the artist trying to convey? Who seems more or less powerful in this depiction?

Picture Desk, Inc./Kobal Collection

through this process of laying of hands. We can read about it in the Acts of the Apostles:

> And the twelve called together the whole community of the disciples and said, "It is not right that we should neglect the word of God in order to wait at tables. Therefore, friends, select from among yourselves seven men of good standing, full of the Spirit and of wisdom, whom we may appoint to this task, while we, for our part, will devote ourselves to prayer and to serving the word." What they said pleased the whole community, and they chose Stephen, a man full of faith and the Holy Spirit, together with Philip, Prochorus, Nicanor, Timon, Parmenas, and Nicolaus, a proselyte of Antioch. They had these men stand before the apostles, who prayed and laid their hands on them. The word of God continued to spread; the number of the disciples increased greatly in Jerusalem, and a great many of the priests became obedient to the faith. (Acts 6:1–7)

For approximately 300 years, Christianity remained an underground religion, lacking official recognition by the Roman government. When Christians opposed rituals in honor of the Roman gods or disagreed with local political leaders, they sometimes suffered persecution from the state. Before his conversion to Christianity, Paul had been personally responsible for persecuting followers of Jesus. Roman officials tended to do this most vehemently when Christians refused to acknowledge Roman state gods or if they violated Roman cultural and social norms.

In 313 CE, the Roman world got turned upside down. The new emperor, Constantine, turned his back on centuries of Roman religious heritage, which included both

<<< This ancient manuscript recounts the killing of 40 Christians by Roman soldiers, just a few years before Constantine made Christianity the state religion.

sacrifices to the Roman gods and also periodic persecution of Christians. (The worst had occurred under Emperor Diocletian, shortly before Constantine, who used Christians as bait for wild animals in Colosseum games in Rome.) Influenced by his mother Helen, who had converted to Christianity, Constantine promulgated the Edict of Milan (313 CE), offering freedom of religion across the empire.

Tradition says that Constantine had a vision before an important battle with a rival for the imperial throne. In his dream, Constantine saw a Christian cross and the words "In this sign conquer" written in the sky. The next morning, he directed that crosses be painted on all his soldiers' shields. Constantine's army, though severely outmanned, defeated his rival. This posed an interesting paradox for Christianity. Although its core ideas were thoroughly nonviolent and apolitical, suddenly a warrior emperor found meaning in Christianity's message and symbols.

In the years after the Edict of Milan, Constantine dismantled the Roman state polytheism and raised Christianity to the status of state religion. By 325 CE, Constantine had become increasingly interested in Christianity on a personal level. Educated in Greek philosophy, he looked for a consistent definition of God in Christianity but found a range of opinions. As emperor, Constantine had the power to convene bishops from across the empire, asking them to come up with an exact definition of Jesus' relationship to God and the Holy Spirit, another term that had grown in use during the previous centuries.

From 325 CE onward, Christian leaders met in different cities around the Roman empire in what became known as the **ecumenical councils**. This process combined political, theological, spiritual, and personal elements. Bishops from one region would band together for one or another reason. Leaders from big cities sometimes carried more influence than ones from rural areas. Better orators could sway the crowds inside and outside the meetings. Still, the councils' decisions met with surprisingly broad support as the will of God, even if the process was a little messy and sometimes downright divisive (Spickard and Cragg 57–61). They debated, fought, prayed, and cajoled. In the end, they believed that God had directed them toward the truth, no matter how difficult it might have been.

Christianity and Popular Culture: The DaVinci Code

Dan Brown described the ecumenical councils in his runaway hit from 2003, *The Da Vinci Code*. In it, he claims that Christians did not believe Christ was God until told to do so by the First Ecumenical Council. In the movie version with Tom Hanks, the first council gets a short scene where lots of old men in beards scream at each other in a large room. The book has a little more detail, but still gets the basic idea wrong. By the time the First Ecumenical Council met, most Christians already identified Christ with God. The Council then defined the *relationship* among God, Christ, and the Holy Spirit.

the THINKSPOT
www.thethinkspot.com

DEFINING GOD: THE ECUMENICAL COUNCILS

The First Ecumenical Council took up a question not so different than this book has. What did "Jesus Christ" and "God" really mean? By this point, 325 CE, Christians generally agreed that Jesus was God, not just a

Ecumenical councils were gatherings of Christian bishops organized to define the basic elements of Christianity.

prophet or teacher. But how did that relate to the Jewish God of Israel? Or to the Holy Spirit, mentioned in Christian writings but never explained? To answer these questions, the councils used four overlapping sources:

- Judaism's long tradition of ethical monotheism
- Writings by the early Christians about Christ (these would become known as the New Testament)
- Greek philosophical ideas about perfection
- Highly precise philosophical language (Spickard and Cragg 19–24, 57–61)

Much of the discussion centered on the idea of Jesus' "nature," in other words, his exact existence. For Jews, this was never a problem, since they perceived God as completely different from human beings. After all, that's what made God *God*. The problem for the Christians was that people had lived with and spoken to Jesus, had met his mother and his friends.

Early Christian leaders turned in part to Greek philosophy to answer the problem. Specifically, they used Plato's (and his followers') ideas about perfection. Plato taught that philosophers should try and grasp "eternal and unchangeable" perfection (Plato, *Republic*). Hellenistic Jews and Christians used this idea to describe God as the one eternal and unchangeable thing in the universe, who created everything else. Up to this point, Jews and Christians could agree, because both defined God the same way: as an unchangeable being who created the world and its inhabitants.

The philosophical problem arose when they tried to add Christ to this picture—how could he be unalterable (God) if he was also a changeable human (Jesus)? Views differed. The Christian theologian Arius taught that Christ *couldn't* be both god and human, since being *created* by God (as human) would preclude his *being* God, too. Arius reasoned, with good Greek logic, that Christ had to have been of a different "substance" than God and that Christ must have been created at some point after God. So, as a created being, Christ could not be "co-eternal" or equal with God.

Opposed to Arius, Bishop Athanasius of Alexandria taught that Jesus and God shared the same substance and therefore Jesus had always existed along with God. In other words, Jesus came to earth in the form of Christ but did not lose his divine substance. He was "consubstantial" and "co-eternal" with God.

Picture Desk, Inc./Kobal Collection

∧
∧
∧   Compare this sculpture of Emperor Theodosius and the Second Council of Nicaea to the picture of Emperor Constantine on the previous page. Did the painter and the sculptor have the same opinion of emperor–Church relations? Why or why not?

(I realize this is a tough philosophical slog. Try to stay with me, because it is important in understanding Christianity.) Depending on which book and translation they read, the Bible seemed to agree with both points. To make things philosophically more complicated, no one had yet decided precisely which writings should be in the "canon," the list that every Christian would agree as being the most important.

The Council of Nicaea, after rancorous debate, agreed with Athanasius. It concluded that Jesus was both "perfect God" and "perfect Man." In other words, he was the God-Man, two *natures* fused into one *person*. This sealed the break with Judaism, which knew God as independent of humans, without form or a body.

The Problem with the Holy Trinity

If you agreed with the "two nature, one person" definition, that still left another problem. Christians said they were monotheistic, yet openly talked about God the Father, God the Son, and God the Holy Spirit. Wasn't that polytheism? The ecumenical councils said "no." To explain themselves, the fathers wrote a kind of constitution for Christianity called a **creed** (or "symbol of faith") that outlined the things Christians should believe. In terms of the Trinity, the ecumenical fathers wanted to make three main points:

1. Christians retain the Jewish concept of a creator God who can pass judgment on humanity.
2. Christians also emphasize an intimate relationship between God and humanity through Jesus.
3. Christians believe that human relations with God have evolved. In the Old Testament, human beings recognized God (Father) mostly as a creator and a judge. In the New Testament, humans also learned to recognize God's mercy (Son) and compassion (Holy Spirit).

If you're Christian you may already have heard the Nicene Creed, written during councils held in 325 CE and 381 CE. Although it would later become a point of contention, most Christians accept it as the basis for Christian perceptions about God (Harvey and Hunter 432–433). As you read it, notice how precisely the Fathers of the Church picked their terms.

> We believe in one God, the Father almighty, maker of heaven and earth, and of all things visible and invisible: and in one Lord Jesus Christ, the only-begotten Son of God, begotten of the Father before all ages, Light of Light; true God of true God; begotten, not made, of one essence with the Father, through whom all things were made; who for us men and for our salvation came down from the heavens, and was made flesh of the Holy Spirit and the Virgin Mary, and became man, and was crucified for us under Pontius Pilate, and suffered and was buried and rose again the third day according to the scriptures, and ascended into heaven, and sits on the right hand of the Father; and comes again with glory to judge the living and the dead, of whose kingdom there shall be no end.
>
> And in the Holy Spirit, the Lord and Giver of Life, who proceeds from the Father, who with the Father and the Son together is worshiped together and glorified together, who spoke by the prophets:
>
> In one Holy, Catholic, and Apostolic Church:
>
> We acknowledge one baptism for the remission of sins. I look for the resurrection of the dead, and the life of the world to come. (Spickard and Cragg 58)

HOMO-OUSIOS VS. HOMO-I-OUSIOS

Much of the debate on the Holy Trinity swirled around one little Greek letter: the iota. Were Jesus and the Holy Spirit "the same essence" as God (*homo-ousios*) or "a similar essence" as God (*homo-i-ousios*)? The councils decided on the first term—homoousios. To make things more difficult, though, the Council added that the one *ousia* (essence) had three *hypostases* (persons).

Your initial response to this may be, "Huh?" Don't worry if these concepts need some more work to understand. In fact, we have to use foreign words because English doesn't have appropriate terms to translate the Greek concepts. Frankly, most modern Christians don't ever think about "essence" versus "person." Yet it did bother early Christian leaders (McManners 191–200). The issue also came up when Christian theologians debated Jews or Muslims, both of whom argued that the Holy Trinity smacked of polytheism.

OTHER DEFINITIONS OF GOD, CHRIST, AND THE TRINITY IN CHRISTIANITY

As you can imagine, centuries of controversy led to many different opinions on the Trinity. Although "Trinitarian Christianity" has become the norm across the world, many important groups have questioned

<<< **Why do the three people in this Ethiopian picture of the** Holy Trinity **look** exactly alike?

THINK World Religions

Don't Understand the Holy Trinity? Try These Techniques!

D o *homoousios* and *homoiousios* look the same to you, and you wouldn't know *hypostases* if they hit you on the head? Think instead about God's roles. Christians often describe God the Father as the creator and judge. God the Son links divinity to humanity. God the Holy Spirit helps people feel strong or at peace, earning the title the "Comforter." In other words, people experience different parts (persons) of God, but that doesn't keep the other parts from existing.

Here's another method. Remember the creation story in Genesis, when "God said 'Let there be light. And there was light.'"

1. God the Father = voice
2. God the Son = words
3. God the Holy Spirit = breath

All together, they are the single Creator God.

Here's another one: The Holy Trinity is to human beings as the sun is to Earth. The sun is simultaneously gas, light, and heat. Without all three, there could be no life on Earth.

One more: The Holy Trinity might not make sense as addition (1 + 1 + 1 = 3 gods) but rather as multiplication (1 × 1 × 1 = 1 God).

the **THINK**SPOT
www.thethinkspot.com

Creeds, or symbols of faith, served as a kind of constitution for the Christian ecumenical fathers.

Five Patriarchates were five cities (Rome, Constantinople, Antioch, Alexandria, Jerusalem) around which large groups of Christian churches grew.

the meaning of the trinity in their faith. Some of these include the Unitarians, Jehovah's Witnesses, some Assemblies of God, and the Church of Jesus Christ of Latter-day Saints (usually called Mormons). Their views range widely on the issue and continue to develop.

Unitarians, for example, developed from Protestants who questioned the rationality of a Trinitarian concept. Present-day Unitarian-Universalism, though, no longer considers itself strictly a Christian church, but rather an inclusive religion based on personal experience and rationality.

The Latter-day Saints believe that the Book of Mormon, revealed to Joseph Smith in the early 1800s, clears up problems left over from earlier Christian history. The Mormon tradition teaches that both God the Father and Son have physical bodies, but the Holy Spirit does not. Calling the three "Godhead" rather than "Trinity," Mormons tend to emphasize the separateness of each "person" much more than most Christian churches.

In yet another view, the Jehovah's Witnesses teach that God created Jesus (who is therefore *not* God but rather the "Word," or God's "Messenger"). Likewise, Jehovah's Witnesses explain the Holy Spirit as God's force on Earth but not a separate entity.

▶ WHAT DOES IT MEAN TO BE HUMAN?

Christianity takes its foundational ideas about humanity from Judaism. These include the Genesis story about the first human beings, and the Abraham story, which introduces the idea of ethical monotheism and a chosen people. Judaism interprets these stories as describing humans as basically good but flawed. Christians aren't so sure.

Christian Confessions

As it grew and spread across the ancient world, Christians slowly developed differing opinions about humans and our relationship to God. Let's take a look at the main "confessions" of Christianity, so we can identify different ways that they define humanity. (We'll return to these groups in Chapter 12.)

Five Patriarchates (4th to 11th centuries CE): For the first thousand years of Christian history, the church developed around five large cities: Rome, Constantinople, Antioch, Alexandria, and Jerusalem. As fathers, or "patriarchs" of a region, the bishop in each of these cities guided all Christians in that area. These Patriarchs and other bishops met to discuss important issues in the Ecumenical Councils. As bishops in the major Roman cities, the Pope (Patriarch of Rome) and the Patriarch of Constantinople held the most power. If there were administrative

>>> **What do you think this medieval manuscript is telling us about human beings?**

Organizational Chart of Christian Denominations

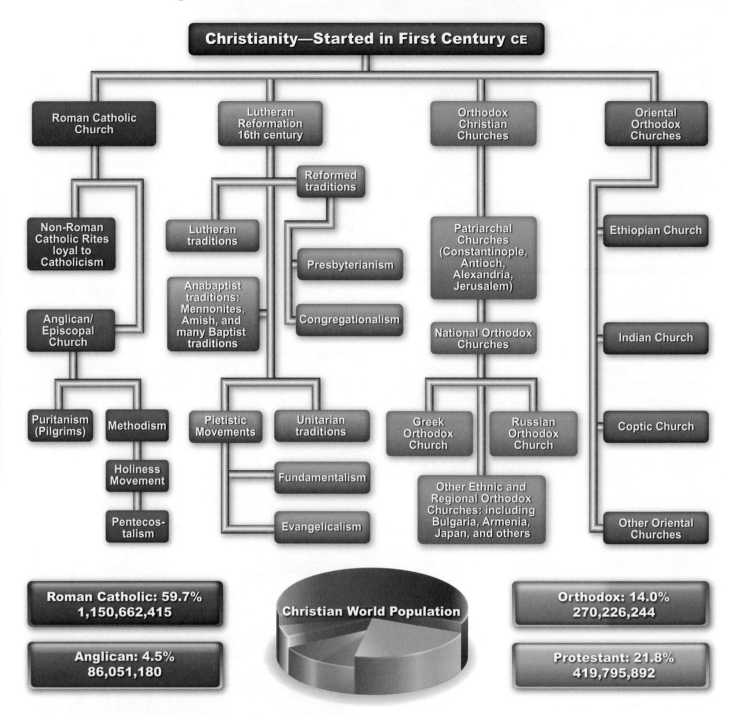

Christianity—Started in First Century CE

- Roman Catholic Church
  - Non-Roman Catholic Rites loyal to Catholicism
  - Anglican/Episcopal Church
    - Puritanism (Pilgrims)
    - Methodism
      - Holiness Movement
        - Pentecostalism
- Lutheran Reformation 16th century
  - Reformed traditions
  - Lutheran traditions
  - Presbyterianism
  - Anabaptist traditions: Mennonites, Amish, and many Baptist traditions
  - Congregationalism
    - Pietistic Movements
    - Unitarian traditions
    - Fundamentalism
    - Evangelicalism
- Orthodox Christian Churches
  - Patriarchal Churches (Constantinople, Antioch, Alexandria, Jerusalem)
  - National Orthodox Churches
    - Greek Orthodox Church
    - Russian Orthodox Church
    - Other Ethnic and Regional Orthodox Churches: including Bulgaria, Armenia, Japan, and others
- Oriental Orthodox Churches
  - Ethiopian Church
  - Indian Church
  - Coptic Church
  - Other Oriental Churches

Christian World Population

- Roman Catholic: 59.7% — 1,150,662,415
- Anglican: 4.5% — 86,051,180
- Orthodox: 14.0% — 270,226,244
- Protestant: 21.8% — 419,795,892

Source: Based on World Christian Database, "2010 Population of Christians in the Four Largest Traditions," Accessed April 11, 2010, http://www.worldchristiandatabase.org.

disagreements between bishops, however, the Pope was supposed to arbitrate and make a final decision.

The Non-council Churches (from the 5th century CE onward): As we just learned, some Christians did not agree with the majority definition of Christ's nature and person. This led to a theological split from the rest of the Five Patriarchs. Based nearly completely in the Middle East and North Africa, this tradition calls itself the Oriental Orthodox Church." You'll sometimes hear the term "non-Chalcedonian," as these churches did not agree with the decisions of the Council of Chalcedon in 451 (Spickard and Cragg 126–145). The term "Oriental" as used here does not relate to

"Orientalism," a pejorative term coined by the scholar Edward Said to describe Western European paternalism of Asian societies. In this case, the churches use the term to show their differentiation from (yet spiritual proximity to) the Eastern Orthodox Church. You're likely to hear them called by their national names: Assyrian, Coptic, and Ethiopian, for example. (Spickard and Cragg 126–145).

The Eastern Orthodox Churches (1054 CE—present): When he became Emperor, Constantine moved the capital city from Rome to Byzantium, which received the new name "Constantinople." Over the next 700 years, the Byzantine Empire struggled with the rise of Islam and trade with eastern Europe. The Roman Empire had its hands full with the barbarian invasions from the north. Slowly, the Eastern and Western traditions diverged along linguistic, cultural, and theological lines. In the year 1054 CE, the Christian Church broke into two parts, roughly aligned by East and West. The four Eastern Orthodox Churches (Constantinople, Antioch, Alexandria, and Jerusalem) spread north and east into Europe while simultaneously interacting with Islam in the Middle East. These churches agreed on doctrine, but developed their own practices and traditions (Spickard and Cragg 102–125).

The Roman Catholic Church (1054 CE—present): This was the other half of the 1054 **Great Schism**. Geographically remote from the other patriarchs and dealing with "barbarian" rather than Muslim threats, Rome relied more heavily on Latin than Greek and considered itself the leader of all Christians. Its influence grew in central and western Europe, South America, and parts of Asia. During the Crusades, however, the Roman Catholic Church also spread into traditionally Orthodox lands, crusading against Islam but often angering and even attacking the Christians who

lived there (Spickard and Cragg 146–170). For much of the next five centuries, the Roman Catholic Church dominated religious and scholarly life in Western Europe. The Pope gained increasing political power, which often put him in direct conflict with other leaders (such as the Holy Roman Emperor—the West's version of the Byzantine Emperor).

The Protestant Churches (mid-1600s—present): The great architectural and scholarly marvels of the medieval period gave way to the 14th century Black Death, when about one-third of Western Europe perished. Western European elites also began to change their intellectual focus from scholasticism (using Aristotelian philosophy to understand God) to Humanism, which emphasized our place as being just "a little lower than the angels."

What's in a Name? Describing Christian Tradition

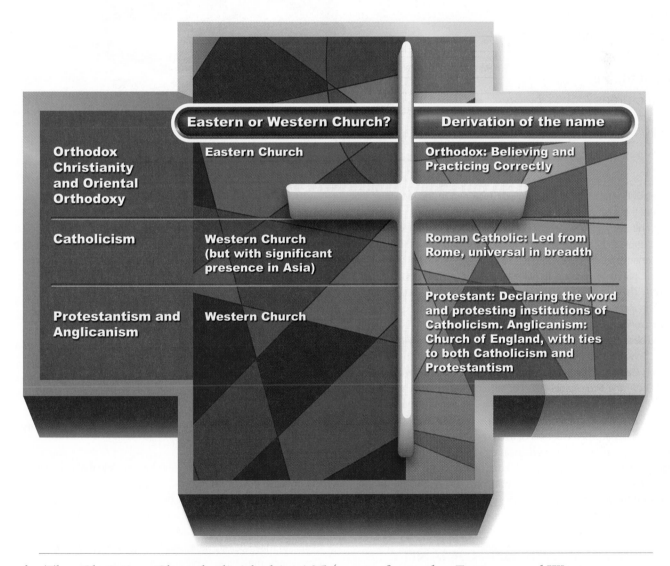

	Eastern or Western Church?	Derivation of the name
Orthodox Christianity and Oriental Orthodoxy	**Eastern Church**	**Orthodox: Believing and Practicing Correctly**
Catholicism	**Western Church (but with significant presence in Asia)**	**Roman Catholic: Led from Rome, universal in breadth**
Protestantism and Anglicanism	**Western Church**	**Protestant: Declaring the word and protesting institutions of Catholicism. Anglicanism: Church of England, with ties to both Catholicism and Protestantism**

∧
∧ The Christian Church divided in 1054 CE to form the Eastern and Western
∧ branches, which then split again. What effect do you think this had on the spread of Christianity?

>>> After the Great Schism in 1054 CE, many Christians started to travel on different paths. This map shows the distribution of religions in the 17th century. Can you identify these forms of Christianity in your city or town? Why do you think that different traditions have settled in specific areas?

MAJOR RELIGIOUS DIVISIONS

Roman Catholic	Anglican
Lutheran	Orthodox
Calvinist	Moslem

The Roman Catholic Church also actively took part in the growth of this movement that later would be called Renaissance Humanism.

By the early 1500s, though, the spread of printing and literacy offered people the chance to read the Bible for themselves. Reformers, strengthened by their personal interpretations of scripture, pushed the Catholic Church to give up its wealth, political power, and hierarchal structure. They wanted a more egalitarian church that relied on local languages instead of Latin and emphasized personal piety over institutional or clerical power.

The clash between the Roman Catholic Church and the reformers got progressively hotter throughout the 1500s. Martin Luther led a movement protesting Catholic Church and which became known as Protestantism. By 1648 CE, the Protestants had broken completely from the Roman Catholic Church, which itself experienced a revival and reformation.

Although Martin Luther, English King Henry VIII, and John Calvin come to mind first when we think of this period called the Reformation, many Christian leaders protested against the Roman Catholic Church. As variations of opinion grew, so did the number of different Protestant denominations. Some sources say that there are more than 30,000 different Protestant denominations, but far fewer have large followings (Spickard and Cragg 200–258).

ORTHODOX VIEWS ON HUMANITY

Eastern Orthodoxy and the Oriental Orthodox churches emphasize **theosis** (or "divinization"). These Christians believe that human beings were once naturally good because we are made in the "image and like-ness" of God. After Adam and Eve, however, we use our free will to sin,

and so give up our likeness. Jesus came to Earth to reunite the image and likeness once and for all, showing how we too could embody these traits. Orthodox Christians see Christ as the perfect icon of God, which they should try to emulate. Orthodox Christians hope to regain this like-ness of God just as Jesus did as the God-Man. The Orthodox empha-size the parable of the tax collector and the Pharisee:

> Two men went up to the temple to pray, one a Pharisee and the other a tax-collector. The Pharisee, standing by himself, was pray-ing thus, "God, I thank you that I am not like other people: thieves, rogues, adulterers, or even like this tax-collector. I fast twice a week; I give a tenth of all my income." But the tax-collector, standing far off, would not even look up to heaven, but was beating his breast and saying, "God, be merciful to me, a sinner!" I tell you, this man went down to his home justified rather than the other; for all who exalt themselves will be humbled, but all who humble themselves will be exalted. (Luke 18:10–14)

We should, according to the Orthodox, emulate that publican rather than the Pharisee if we seek theosis.

From the Orthodox point of view, so long as we're alive, our path toward theosis never ends, so we're never really sure if we have achieved that state or not. A person who may seem to be a good Christian may secretly hate people. A person not following the rules of Christianity may have a pure heart. Perhaps, say the Orthodox, that second person is actually further toward theosis than the first Christian. The only people we know to be deified are the saints. Because they lived exemplary lives, Orthodox Christians ask saints for help in the human path toward theosis.

Good Nature but Evil Deeds?

If people are made in the "image and likeness" of God, as Genesis says, then why do they kill, steal, or lie? How can God, the definition of goodness, allow evil to exist? Polytheistic religions don't have to worry about this issue, since they distinguish different moral attributes in various deities. If you rely on a single creator, though, you're left with a problem that goes like this: If God is perfect, and if God has created everything, then has God also created evil?

Traditionally, Christianity defines evil as a form of illness or as separation from God. Angels and humans, like God, have free will. Evil first occurred when the angel Satan decided he was just as important as God. This pride led to his separation from God. Then, taking the form of a snake, Satan convinced Adam and Eve to distance themselves from God by eating the fruit.

When we draw closer to God, we do good deeds. When we distance ourselves from God, we perform wicked acts. Following this logic, we are "good" or "healthy" when we acknowledge that God controls the world and not us. However, when we try to create or destroy things by our own power, we distance ourselves from God, do evil things, and suffer spiritual sickness. Satan, of course, would like us to keep doing bad things, because, well, misery loves company (Ward 18–26, 36–45).

Christians tend to agree on three things about humanity:

1. We're created by God in the divine "image" and "likeness," so we're special.
2. Led by Adam and Eve, we tend to do bad things, often called "sins."
3. Jesus helped bring humans back to God (although how this works is up for debate).

ROMAN CATHOLIC VIEWS ON HUMANITY

Roman Catholicism emphasizes the *interaction* between God and humanity. Though God has ultimate power, humans, too, play a role in the relationship. After the fall, Adam passed on a bit of his "original sin" to all subsequent humans, but that is washed away through baptism. As Christians, we strive to recreate that sinless state through our relationships with God and other human beings.

In general, the Catholic Church teaches that we can have a hand in transforming ourselves from a sinful to an eternal life. The Church offers sacraments to bring us closer to God. If we faithfully receive them and treat fellow human beings with love, then we draw closer to God. You can see this especially in the Letter of James,

> **Theosis**, meaning divinization, is an important concept in Eastern Orthodoxy and the Oriental Orthodox churches. By living a Christian life within the Church, individuals can become more like Jesus and regain the image and likeness of God.

where he reminds his disciples they need to have faith in God, but also to do good works:

> What good is it, my brothers and sisters, if you say you have faith but do not have works? Can faith save you? If a brother or sister is naked and lacks daily food, and one of you says to them, "Go in peace; keep warm and eat your fill," and yet you do not supply their bodily needs, what is the good of that? So

∧
∧ Look at the incredible detail in this painting of heaven and hell by Hieronymus Bosch (c.1510). Where did he get those ideas? Contrast it to the 1948 German film updating the Genesis story called *Der Apfel ist Ab* (Released in English as *Original Sin*).

Creationism argues that God created human beings as we now exist, as described in the Book of Genesis.

Darwinism claims that all life has evolved from other forms, becoming ever more complex.

faith by itself, if it has no works, is dead. But someone will say, "You have faith and I have works." Show me your faith without works, and I by my works will show you my faith. You believe that God is one; you do well. Even the demons believe—and shudder. (James 2:14–19)

Like Orthodox Christians, Catholics never know their status in terms of salvation; the process continues throughout life. They too appeal to saints for help on their Christian path. Unlike the Orthodox idea of Jesus as an icon, though, Roman Catholics tend to think of Jesus as taking on punishment that we rightly deserved through sin. In this way, he "justifies" our cause before God.

PROTESTANT VIEWS ON HUMANITY

In opposition to Roman Catholicism, Protestantism emphasizes grace. As human beings, we are so distant from God that nothing we can do will help us. Rather, only a divine gift—"grace"—can reunite us with God. Jesus brought that grace to earth when he suffered and rose from the dead. As Abraham was willing to sacrifice Isaac for God, God sacrificed Jesus for us. In doing so, he "justified us by faith," which Protestants have historically contrasted to their view of Catholicism as "justification by works."

Protestant traditions place a lot of importance on Paul's words regarding faith:

We ourselves are Jews by birth and not Gentile sinners; yet we know that a person is reckoned as righteous [justified] not by the works of the law but through faith in Jesus Christ. And we have come to believe in Christ Jesus, so that we might be justified by faith in Christ, and not by doing the works of the law, because no one will be justified by the works of the law. (Galatians 2:15–16)

Some Protestants claim that grace actually makes free will irrelevant; God knows everything and gives the gift of salvation to us no matter how wantonly we act. The Protestant view sometimes emphasizes human weakness that leads to sin but other times focuses not so much on human frailty as on God's love. For example, in 1739 CE the

minister Jonathan Edwards preached on this topic. It has become one of the most famous sermons in American history, however, you'll find it difficult to meet any contemporary Protestant with such a dark view of human nature.

The God that holds you over the pit of hell, much as one holds a spider, or some loathsome insect, over the fire, abhors you, and is dreadfully provoked; his wrath towards you burns like fire. . .you are ten thousand times so abominable in his eyes as the most hateful venomous serpent is in ours. . . . . [But] now you have an extraordinary opportunity, a day wherein Christ has flung the door of mercy wide open, and stands in the door calling and crying with a loud voice to poor sinners; a day wherein many are flocking to him, and pressing into the kingdom of God. . . . How awful is it to be left behind at such a day! (Edwards)

For nearly 500 years, debate has continued between proponents of human free will (which Orthodox and Catholics accept) and divine predestination (as taught by some Protestants).

What Happens When Human Beings Die? Christian Ideas of Heaven and Hell

As you can guess from the descriptions in the last few paragraphs, death plays a greater part in Christian thought than it does in Judaism. Jews can imagine many possibilities of what happens after death. Christians, on the other hand, often try to define precisely what will occur.

Christianity generally teaches that Satan, not God, created hell as a place far from God. As a result, people may end up in hell if they die separated from God. Some traditions imagine hell in physical terms, where fires burn and people scream. The great example of this comes from Dante's *Inferno*, which describes each painful characteristic of the place. In other traditions, though, hell has a more spiritual quality, the ultimate place of disconnection from God. A few Christian traditions even teach that there is no hell because Jesus made it possible for all human beings to come back to God.

All these ideas—God, the Trinity, the Church, theosis, works, grace, heaven, and hell—build a foundation for us to understand how Christians interact with God and how they have created so many different groups over the past 2,000 years. We'll dig deeper into these ideas in Chapter 12.

Christianity + LITERATURE

Dostoevsky, On Hell

Fyodor Dostoevsky wrote a fascinating Christian vision of Hell in his great novel *The Brothers Karamazov*. In this passage, hell only exists because of our inability or refusal to give and receive love and love. It's difficult language but worth the work.

Fathers and Teachers, I ask myself: "What is hell?" And I answer thus: "The suffering of being no longer able to love. . . ." People

speak of the material flames of hell. I do not explore this mystery, and I fear it, but I think that if there were material flames, truly people would be glad to have them, for, as I fancy, in material torment they might forget, at least for a moment, their far more spiritual torment. And yet it is impossible to take this spiritual torment from them, for this torment is not external but is within them." (Dostoevsky, 1880)

Christianity and Evolution

In contemporary America, it seems like Christians constantly battle scientists about human evolution. More specifically, some Protestants argue for **creationism** as opposed to **Darwinism**. You can see this on the back of people's cars, where folks affix a fish symbol on their trunk. This harkens back to ancient Rome, where Christians often used the fish to symbolize Christ. To tease "creationist" Christians, other people stick decals on their cars that resemble a fish with little feet, as if it had evolved toward a higher form of life. Inside the fish they write "Darwin." In response, creationists add a bigger fish with the word "Jesus" eating the "Darwin" fish. How many other issues would produce car-trunk warfare?

In fact, though, Christians do not agree on evolution. The root of the disagreement comes from differing opinions about the Genesis story of creation. Those "Christians" described in the news are almost always Evangelical Protestants, often called "born again" or "fundamentalist" Christians who believe in a literal meaning of the Bible: God created everything in six 24-hour days, ending with the formation of human beings. This would seem to disprove evolutionary theory, which claims that human beings developed slowly over time. Andrew McIntosh, an Evangelical Protestant, professor, and scientist, puts it this way: "Many believers have tried to harmonize the early chapters of Genesis and evolutionary philosophy. But any attempt to move away from the literal interpretation of these grand opening statements undermines the authority of Scripture" (McIntosh).

On the other hand, Orthodox, Roman Catholic, and many Protestant churches have no problem letting science untangle the prehistory of humanity. They tend to interpret Genesis as both metaphorically true (with God as ultimate creator) and beautifully poetic, instead of concretely scientific. Even early Christian theologians may have considered some sort of evolution. St. Augustine, for example, wrote that "There have always been creatures . . . but these creatures have not always been the same, but succeeded one another" (Augustine). In 2008, the Roman Catholic Church sponsored an academic conference marking the 150th anniversary of Darwin's *The Origin of Species*. There, Archbishop Gianfranco Ravasi said that evolutionary theory "is not incompatible with the teachings of the Catholic Church or the Bible's message" (Ravasi, 2008). Earlier, Pope Benedict XVI also weighed in on the conflict, saying that the clash between evolution and science was absurd (Benedict XVI, 1996).

∧∧∧ **Does the second symbol actually** discount or support evolution? **Why?**

Summary

IS THERE A GOD?   p. 162

- Definitely, yes. Christians consider themselves monotheistic, although most Christians say that three separate entities make up God: the Father, the Son, and the Holy Spirit.

WHAT DOES IT MEAN TO BE HUMAN?   p. 171

- Christians view humans as created by God in his image and likeness. Like Adam and Eve, however, we often perform bad deeds. Christianity offers the path back to God.

- Orthodox teachings stress that our sins come as a result of free will; however we can still achieve theosis by cultivating a pure heart and living as a good Christian within the Church.
- Roman Catholicism teaches that, because of the actions of Adam and Eve, we are all born with original sin that gets washed away through baptism. Continuing to sin, we can bring ourselves closer to God by receiving sacraments and doing good deeds.
- Protestants emphasize grace as the only way to reconnect with God. Through Jesus' sacrifice, God offered us the gift of salvation. Some Protestant groups teach divine predestination—the idea that some of us are destined for heaven—and reject the idea of free will.

Key Terms

Eucharist is the Christian ritual based on the Passover seder held by Jesus and his disciples.   *164*

Old Testament refers to the Jewish Tanakh.   *165*

New Testament is made up of 26 books related to Jesus' life, teachings, and the teachings of his disciples.   *165*

Gnostics were a Christian sect that taught that the physical world was flawed. Gnostics believed that salvation could be found in hidden knowledge.   *167*

Apostolic succession refers to the Christian act of being blessed by an Apostle who was blessed by Christ.   *167*

Ecumenical councils were gatherings of Christian bishops organized to define the basic elements of Christianity.   *168*

Creeds, or symbols of faith, served as a kind of constitution for the Christian ecumenical fathers.   *170*

Five Patriarchates were five cities (Rome, Constantinople, Antioch, Alexandria, Jerusalem) around which large groups of Christian churches grew.   *171*

Great Schism marked Christianity's branching into two different streams roughly delineated by east and west. The Western branch developed into Roman Catholicism and Protestantism, while the Eastern branch became the Eastern Orthodox Church.   *173*

Theosis, meaning divinization, is an important concept in Eastern Orthodoxy and the Oriental Orthodox churches. By living a Christian life within the Church, individuals can become more like Jesus and regain the image and likeness of God.   *174*

Creationism argues that God created human beings as we now exist, as described in the Book of Genesis.   *177*

Darwinism claims that all life has evolved from other forms, becoming ever more complex.   *177*

Find it on

http://www.youtube.com/watch?v=ijtSNnxOru8

Pentecost Sunday is an incredibly important event in the Christian church. If you'd like to see the ceremony that accompanies the celebration of the founding of the Church, visit the ThinkSpot to see how Pentecost Sunday is commemorated at a typical Christian Church. The Parish of Hamilton is an Anglican Church whose ceremony is representative of the ceremonies that take place at other Christian churches on this important Sunday.

http://gwydir.demon.co.uk/jo/gospels/index.htm

Many of the individual readings in the gospels tell the same story. How are they same? How are they different? If you're interested in seeing how different gospels interpret the same message, go to the ThinkSpot to see how they each place their individual stamp on the teachings of Jesus, the miracles of Jesus, and the Resurrection, to name a few.

http://www.catacombe.roma.it/

It may be hard for you to imagine a world in which you could not practice your faith tradition openly and freely. Or maybe you come from—or know someone who does—a place where religious persecution is a part of everyday life. The sad news is that religious persecution has been around for thousands of years, as evidenced the by Catacombs in Rome, where early Christians met to avoid punishment, torture, and possibly death for practicing their faith. Visit the ThinkSpot to see photographs of the Catacombs and to read about each individual underground place of worship.

Questions for Study and Review

1. **What role did the ecumenical councils play in the history of Christianity?**

   The ecumenical councils determined the definition of Christianity and its creeds. This included defining God, Jesus, the Holy Trinity, and combining elements of ethical monotheism from Judaism, early writings of the Christian Church, and Greek philosophy as it applied to perfection and language. Furthermore, the ecumenical councils were believed to speak with the voice of God.

2. **Why was the concept of a Holy Trinity difficult to define?**

   The Holy Trinity was difficult to define because conceptually, the idea of God the Father, God the Son, and God the Holy Spirit appeared to go against the idea of monotheism. To reconcile this, the ecumenical councils determined that God was "one essence" in which there were "three realities," the Father, the Son, and the Holy Spirit.

3. **Compare and contrast Jewish and Christian perspectives on whether human beings are good or bad.**

   Judaism says that human beings are basically good because they are made in the image and likeness of God. Christianity says that God created everything except evil, which is committed by an individual's own free will. When human beings use their power to control, create, and destroy things, they distance themselves from God.

4. **What role does theosis play in Christianity?**

   Christians believe that people are naturally good, but human beings give up their likeness to God by sinning. In Eastern Orthodox Christian tradition, human beings reunite with God through theosis, thereby recreating their image and likeness of God.

5. **Discuss the views that different forms of Christianity have toward evolution.**

   The scientific view of evolution, or Darwinism, maintains that all life evolved from one original source. Some branches of Christianity, however, interpret evolution in terms of the Genesis story in its strictest, most literal sense, arguing that the theory of evolution is not correct. On the other hand, other branches of Christianity interpret the Genesis story more poetically and see God as the creator of evolution.

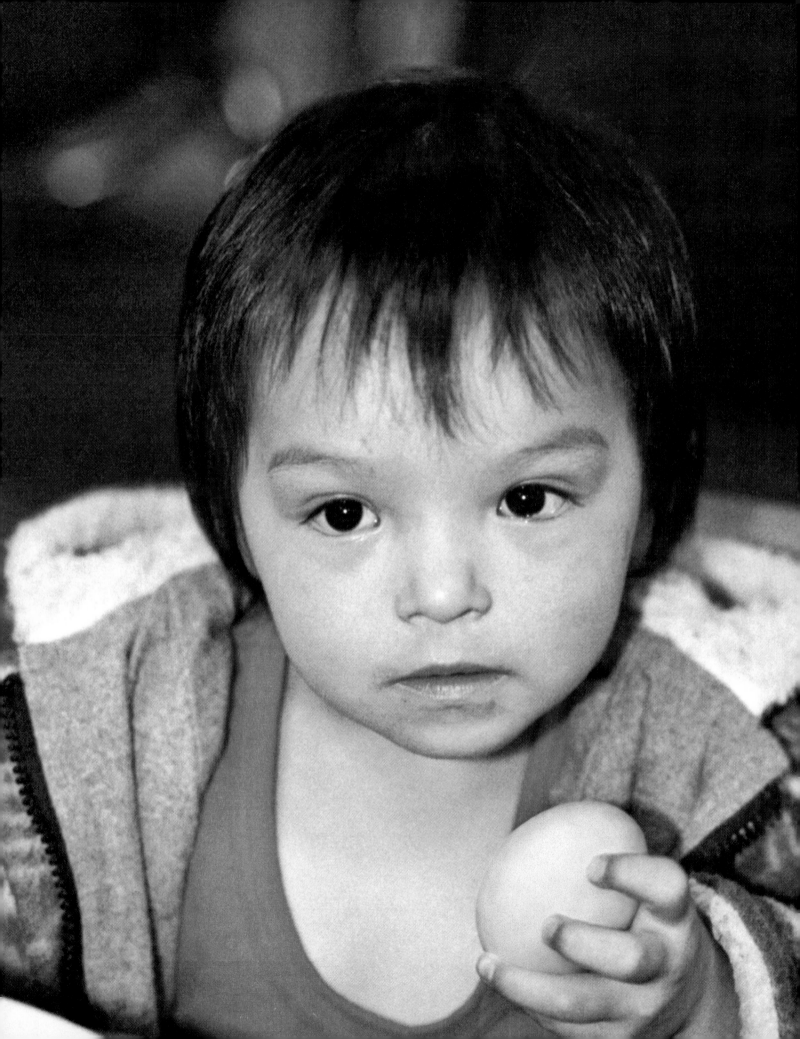

<<< A little girl dyes Easter eggs at a soup kitchen in Minneapolis. Why do you think eggs became part of nearly all Christian Easter celebrations?

This little

girl looks beautiful, hopeful, but a little reticent. Her face cannot hide her hunger. Soon, we hope, she'll be allowed to break open that Easter egg and eat a good breakfast. You can see this scene repeated from Los Angeles to Lagos, as Christians mix spiritual nourishment with "feeding ministries" for the poor and homeless. These simple kitchens help Christians follow Jesus' command to feed the hungry while also following his example of sharing a meal with both friends and strangers.

When the Romans demolished the Temple in 70 CE, both Jews and Christians had to respond. This dramatic event forced Christianity to define itself in new ways, just as rabbinic Judaism did in the post-Temple period. We don't know all the details, but ancient sources teach us that Christians gradually moved away from Jewish traditions and created their own. Christians focused on prayer, oral teaching, writing to one another, taking care of the downtrodden, and meeting in groups for a sacred meal. These practices created the foundation for Christian practices in the present day.

Based on their opinions about God and humanity, churches vary widely in the ways they interact with the sacred world. In these pages, we'll explore both common themes and dramatic differences among different Christian traditions. As in Chapter 11, we'll generally move from East to West in our discussions, following the roads that Christianity took as it moved from Jerusalem, Rome, and Constantinople to the rest of the world.

Chapter 12 will investigate how Christians identify themselves, relate to their sacred world, and strive for salvation. Whether discussing the bread and wine of Eucharist or the social renewal of liberation theology, Christians return again and again to this simple idea—feeding the body will also nourish the soul.

CHRISTIANITY:
Communion and Community

Mother Teresa of Calcutta

In August 1910, a tiny baby came into the world in Skopje, a town in present-day Macedonia. Her family was Albanian, and they called her Agnes Gonxha Bojaxhiu. By the time she was 21 years old, she had become a Roman Catholic nun and was teaching in the slums of Calcutta. As she worked with the poor, her fame grew. She started a new Catholic group called the Missionaries of Charity in 1950, all the while struggling with her own faith in God, wondering why people suffered, why God did not seem closer to her, and even if God existed. And yet she continued her aid to the poorest of the poor, finding new support for her mission to help and introduce them to the Roman Catholic concept of God.

We know her as Mother Teresa of Calcutta. When she accepted the Nobel Prize for Peace in 1979, Mother Teresa said these words:

> The poor are very wonderful people. One evening we went out and we picked up four people from the street. And one of them was in a most terrible condition— and I told the Sisters: You take care of the other three, I take of this one that looked worse. So I did for her all that my love can do. I put her in bed, and there was such a beautiful smile on her face. She took hold of my hand, as she said one word only: Thank you—and she died.
>
> I could not help but examine my conscience before her, and I asked what would

∧ **Do you think that poor people** ∧ **can offer wisdom** different from their wealthy neighbors?

I say if I was in her place. And my answer was very simple. I would have tried to draw a little attention to myself, I would have said I am hungry, that I am dying, I am cold, I am in pain, or something, but she gave me much more—she gave me her grateful love. And she died with a smile on her face. As that man whom we picked up from the drain, half eaten with worms, and we brought him to the home. I have lived like an animal in the street, but I am going to die like an angel, loved and cared for. And it was so wonderful to see the greatness of that man who could speak like that, who could die like that without blaming anybody, without cursing anybody, without comparing anything. Like an angel—this is the greatness of our people. And that is why we believe what Jesus had said: I was hungry—I was naked—I was homeless—I was unwanted, unloved, uncared for—and you did it to me. (Mother Teresa, 1979)

Mother Teresa died in 1997, and since then many Roman Catholics have called on the church to recognize her as a saint. Scholars and Christians study her letters, which show a person usually at peace with service but always searching for God. Her official name is now Blessed Mother of Teresa. Watch the news, because she may soon be St. Teresa of Calcutta.

▶ HOW DO HUMANS INTERACT WITH THE SACRED?

What's in a Name?
Churches, Denominations, and Communities

Years ago, I was traveling on a tour with my college singing group. We stayed with families in the towns where we sang. I remember that one host in Georgia had a final question for me as we parted: "Are you Christian?" This scene comes back to me whenever I hear a song called "Walking in Memphis," which describes a musician in that city. At the end of a long night of "singing with all my might," the singer's accompanist (named Muriel) asks him, "Are you a Christian, child?" and he responds: "Ma'am, I am tonight!"

What did my host and Muriel mean? Did they wonder if we were Catholic, or perhaps Lutheran? Probably not. Although the term "Christian" describes anyone who follows the teachings of Jesus Christ, some people use the word as shorthand for "Evangelical Protestant Christian." More likely than not, these people were asking if we were "born again" Christians, rather than any other kind.

Depending on time and place, Christians have viewed each other with a mixture of respect and distaste. Would a Baptist say that a Roman Catholic was part of the church, or vice versa? That depends on the person, the period and the way each one would define the church; there is no single answer. So what's in a name? As we learned in Chapter 11, Christianity has developed along four major streams—Anglicanism, Orthodoxy, Protestantism, and Roman Catholicism. Some scholars call these "megablocs," but we'll use the term "traditions" or "churches." Here's a short introduction to the groups we'll discuss in this chapter:

Oriental Orthodoxy, Orthodox Christianity, and Roman Catholicism consider themselves independent "churches." Within each one, we can find regional, local, and ritual variation. These groups magnified their differences for centuries, but have recently begun to explore similarities. Present scholars, in fact, believe that theological distinctions may have grown as a result of differences in language rather than belief. Although a Greek Orthodox might find a Finnish Orthodox service hard to understand, they agree on most points of theology and practice. Similarly, a Lebanese Maronite Catholic and a Canadian Roman Catholic would recognize each others' theology, if not rituals.

Anglicanism straddles Catholicism and Protestantism. Based on reforms of English King Henry VIII but later associated with Protestant ideas, the Anglican tradition has fostered a number of variations in belief and practice. In the 19th century, for example, some Anglicans began to preach openly against social problems. They created Methodist, Wesleyan, and Holiness communities that emphasized a direct relationship with God and a desire to help the needy. These groups found fame by battling slavery in Great Britain and the United States.

Contemporary Anglicanism (often called Episcopalianism outside of England) extends across the world, growing more quickly in Africa than anywhere else. Those who prefer a traditional Catholic-style ritual call themselves High Church, whereas less formal worshipers are Low Church. The Anglican tradition presently struggles with a division between cultural liberals and conservatives, especially in matters of sexuality and gender. In a fascinating reversal of traditional power structures, conservative American Episcopalians have begun to ally themselves with their brothers and sisters in African churches. A generation ago, few people would have imagined this alliance, which may loosen both groups' ties to the home Church of England.

Five Solas distinguish Protestantism from Roman Catholicism and Orthodox Christianity. Created by early Lutherans, they include a belief in salvation through faith, an eschewing of religious texts beyond the Bible, and an emphasis on the grace of God.

When Luther began to preach against corruption in the Roman Catholic Church in the early 1500s, he sparked a wave of change that would become known as the Reformation. Its believers were called Protestants. Rather than distinct "churches," we often call Protestant groups "denominations." The Lutherans (also called Evangelicals in Europe) spread across central and northern Europe, growing especially strong in the Germanic and Nordic countries. They defined themselves by the **Five Solas** (see the next page) that distinguished Protestant from Catholic Christianity.

Another group would ultimately call itself "Reformed" Christianity instead of "Lutheran." Based on the teachings of John Calvin (in Switzerland) and John Knox (in Scotland), Reformed denominations emphasize the power of God to be merciful and the powerlessness of

THINK World Religions

Justin Martyr Describes Christian Interaction with the Sacred

Approximately 120 years after Jesus' life, a Christian named Justin described how his community interacted with God. A few years later, he was executed for his Christian beliefs, and since then has been known as Justin Martyr. Here's what he wrote:

> And the wealthy among us help the needy; and we always keep together; and for all things wherewith we are supplied, we bless the Maker of all through His Son Jesus Christ, and through the Holy Ghost. And on the day called Sunday, all who live in cities or in the country gather together to one place, and the memoirs of the apostles or the writings of the prophets are read, as long as time permits; then, when the reader has ceased, the president verbally instructs, and exhorts to the imitation of these good things. Then we all rise together and pray, and, as we before said, when our prayer is ended, bread and wine and water are brought, and the president in like manner offers prayers and thanksgivings, according to his ability, and the people assent, saying Amen; and there is a distribution to each, and a participation of that over which thanks have been given, and to those who are absent a portion is sent by the deacons. And they who are well to do, and willing, give what each thinks fit; and what is collected is deposited with the president, who succors the orphans and widows and those who, through sickness or any other cause, are in want, and those who are in bonds and the strangers sojourning among us, and in a word takes care of all who are in need. But Sunday is the day on which we all hold our common assembly, because it is the first day on which God, having wrought a change in the darkness and matter, made the world; and Jesus Christ our Savior on the same day rose from the dead. For He was crucified on the day before that of Saturn (Saturday); and on the day after that of Saturn, which is the day of the Sun, having appeared to His apostles and disciples, He taught them these things, which we have submitted to you also for your consideration. (First Apology of Justin, Chapter 67)

In this passage, Justin Martyr describes a number of practices that we'll study in this chapter. They include reading, preaching, and teaching the Bible; celebrating the Eucharist; helping people in financial need; and meeting on Sunday rather than the Jewish sabbath of Saturday. Over the past 2,000 years, though, Christians have developed many different ways to do these things. More often than not, different practices and ideas split the Christian Church into separate, ever-more numerous groups.

the THINKSPOT
www.thethinkspot.com

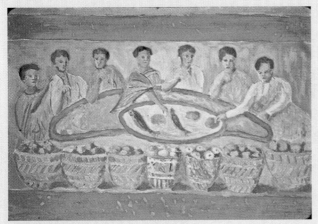

Copyright The British Museum

<<< You can still see ancient Christian art in the catacombs outside Rome, Italy. Why do you think that early Christians had to use bread and fish as symbols for Christ in their art?

human beings to do anything by their own will. (Jonathan Edwards, whose sermon we read last chapter, followed Reformed Protestantism.) They have also developed structures to ensure equality and fairness in Christian communities, giving more power to committees of lay members and less to ordained ministers. Some of the most well-known Reformed groups include Congregationalists and Presbyterians.

Anabaptists, including Mennonites and the Amish, took the Five Solas to a logical conclusion, calling for adults to make a rational decision to become Christian, arguing for the separation of church and state, teaching adherence to the Bible (rather than tradition), and emphasizing the importance of a society based on Christian morals. Originally a highly political—even revolutionary—group, they are now best known as "plain people" in the United States. They try not to use modern conveniences and rely on one another for religious, economic, and social strength.

At the turn of the 20th century, a number of Protestant groups grew rapidly, especially in the United States. Like the Anabaptists, they

The "Five Solas" (or "Five Onlys")
How Protestants Disagree with Orthodox and Catholic Christians

By scripture and tradition— We can come to know God through the Bible but also via holy traditions and other writings.

Orthodox and Catholic Perceptions

With a little help from our friends— We can interact with God directly, but we can also ask the holiest humans (saints) and the Virgin Mary to intercede on our behalf.

By faith and works— We gain salvation through faith, sacraments, and good works. In Orthodoxy, that is a process of deification: becoming more like the image and likeness of God.

By Christ, through the Church— We gain salvation (or deification) through our life in the Church, which is often called "the bride of Christ."

Only by the scripture— We don't need any sacred writings other than the Bible. Every other ritual, tradition, or idea is made by humans, not by God.

Only to God— We don't need to have any intermediaries, like priests or saints, between us and God. We can have a direct relationship with God, so we pray only to Him.

Only by faith— We cannot gain salvation by anything we do. Only faith brings salvation.

Protestant Perceptions

Only by grace— Because we cannot do anything to be saved, we must rely on grace, another word for a gift from God.

Only by Christ— We can't be saved through anyone other than Jesus Christ, so there is no need for saints, popes, or priests.

said that the Bible was never wrong. This made them skeptical of modern science and secular education. These denominations placed great importance on emotionally powerful preaching. Because of their "Bible-based" views, they became known as Evangelicals. Sometimes they stayed within their home denominations, but other times broke away to form new ones.

Evangelicals often call themselves "born again Christians" because they believe that a person must make a conscious choice to accept Jesus Christ as a personal savior. Once that is done, there is no more need to worry; you have accepted the gift of heaven from God and can rest assured of your eternal life there. Here are the major Evangelical movements:

- *Baptists* believe in the power of adult baptism in water as a form of Christian rebirth. They share the theological roots with the Anabaptist tradition.

- *The Christian Missionary Alliance* focuses on the "great commission," in which Christ sent out people to teach all nations.

- *Pentecostal* and *Holiness* churches accentuate the direct working of the Holy Spirit within individuals—we'll talk more about them later in this chapter.

- *Fundamentalists* question any ideas that they believe do not come literally from in the Bible. Their movement has become synonymous with a political and social conservatism that disbelieves modern scientific views of evolution, as we saw in Chapter 11.

Other denominations have sprouted up, sometimes based on truly new and unique ideas or practices. A number of these groups have developed a global presence:

- *Jehovah's Witnesses* began in Pennsylvania but have since spread to other regions of the world. They introduced new ideas about the apocalypse, teaching that the world would ultimately be inherited by 144,000 "spiritual sons of God" who would rule with Christ. Jehovah's Witnesses discount all traditional symbols and holidays of Christianity, including the cross and Christmas, and deny the existence of an eternal soul.

- *The Church of Jesus Christ of Latter-day Saints* (also known as Mormonism) developed from the revelations of Joseph Smith in rural New York during the mid-1800s. He disseminated a new gospel—the Book of Mormon—as a basis for a new kind of church. Based in Salt Lake City, Utah, the Mormons have become one of the most visible missionary groups of the 20th and 21st centuries.

- *The Church of Christ, Scientist* seeks to heal the sick through the belief that human beings exist in a spiritual (not material) world. Christian Scientists try to heal physical ailments through spiritual growth and health rather than traditional medicine.

- *Seventh-day Adventists* prepare for the imminent second coming of Christ to Earth and are most famous for keeping Saturday, not Sunday, as the Sabbath.

- *The Unification Church* arose from the teachings of Rev. Sun Myung Moon in Korea. Often derided as "Moonies," followers of the Unification Church hope to unify all Christians under the leadership of Rev. Moon, the Messiah returned to Earth.

The list is dizzying in its size. Christians often disagree with each other even over basic terms. For example, the word "church" can have many meanings. On the one hand, you might consider "the Church" to mean something like "all Christians." On the other, the Church may refer to a single denomination (the Episcopal Church), a region (the Albanian Church), or a single building (my church down the street). Orthodoxy and Catholicism describe the Church as the "bride of Christ." This idea (odd if you're not used to it) states that Christ and the Church produce children—human beings—as a sort of family. In this opinion, the Church defines itself through apostolic succession and the Nicene Creed.

Some Protestant traditions take a different view, saying that the Church is "the community of the saints" who believe in Christ. Luther, for example, famously defined the Church as "the holy believers and lambs who hear the voice of their Shepherd." This tends to downplay structure and to emphasize individual relationships with God (Smalcald, Articles III: 12).

The Eucharist: An Ancient Christian Form of Communion with God

As we read in the passage by Justin Martyr, early Christians met to eat a ritual meal with each other. In another place, he explained, "the food which is blessed . . . is the flesh and blood of that Jesus who was made flesh" (First Apology, 66:1–20). This was the Eucharist, a term based on the Greek word for "thanksgiving." As the Eastern and Western halves of Christianity grew apart, their views on the Eucharist slowly diverged. By studying how this happened, we can learn how different Christians interact with the sacred. As you read, try to keep in mind the words "mystery," "sacrament," and "symbol," because these terms will illustrate different views of this ancient practice.

COMMUNING WITH GOD THROUGH THE ORTHODOX EUCHARIST

The Eastern and Oriental Orthodox churches emphasize the mysterious nature of the Eucharist. In fact, they say "holy mystery" rather than a "sacrament." Using "mystery" highlights both the exclusive nature of the Eucharist (only baptized Orthodox Christians may receive communion) and also its nonrational basis—something happens in the Eucharist that we humans will never understand.

Like Justin Martyr, Orthodox Christianity teaches that people take the "flesh and the blood of Jesus" into their bodies through the Eucharist. All other forms of sacred interaction pale in comparison to the Eucharistic liturgy. (By the way, this explains why Orthodoxy places so much importance on priests and bishops, because only they can perform the liturgy and bless other men to do the same. Why? It's because only priests and bishops have received the apostolic succession.)

Remember the description of communion at the beginning of Chapter 11? The priest and people in the Church of the Holy Spirit in Minsk said they believed that the bread and wine *actually became* the body and blood of Christ. No Orthodox Christian knows how it happens, except to say that it happens mysteriously during the liturgy.

For the Orthodox, communion has become closely related to the idea of resurrection. As people take communion, the choir repeats the same words over and over again: "Receive ye the Body of Christ; taste ye the fountain of immortality" (Antiochian Library). Communion is both intensely personal—just you and God—but also communal. You can see this in their practice: Orthodox Christians hear their name said by the priest as they approach the cup, yet they share the same spoon (McManners 161).

Continuum of Opinions by Present-day Christian Denominations

Human nature:

Humans are inherently evil.	Humans are inclined to evil.	Humans pass on sin from Adam.	Humans tend to sin, but have some good.	Humans are inherently perfect.
	Protestantism	Catholicism	Orthodoxy	

Salvation:

Salvation is a gift of God and humans can do nothing to gain it.		Salvation comes from God but humans also play a role, especially in taking sacraments.		Salvation equals theosis—the unification of God and man through love, sacraments, and moral life.
Protestantism		Catholicism		Orthodoxy

State or process in the quest for salvation:

State of being—a believer is assured salvation			Process—a believer is never sure if he or she is saved
Evangelical Protestants; Fundamentalist Protestants	Mainline Protestantism	Anglicanism	Orthodoxy Catholicism

Rational or mystical theology?

Rational Theology			Mystical Theology	
Some Reformed Protestantism	Independent Evangelical and Fundamentalist Protestantism	Mainline Protestantism	Catholicism	Orthodoxy

Attitude toward change:

Open to Change			Honors tradition	
Independent Evangelical Protestantism	Mainline Protestantism		Catholicism	Orthodoxy

Attitude toward saints:

Define "saints" as all Christians who have been saved by personal acceptance of Christ.		Venerate saints as intercessors with God
Independent Evangelical Protestantism	Mainline Protestantism	
		Orthodoxy and Catholicism

Importance of spontaneity and emotion:

Spontaneous and Emotional		Structured and Liturgical	
Independent Evangelical Protestantism	Low-Church Anglicanism and Mainline Protestantism	Catholicism and High-Church Anglicanism	Orthodoxy

Because it's a mystery that goes beyond any rational explanation, Orthodox argue that even a baby can receive it, obtaining the Eucharist's benefits at any age. Once we get older, though, no one is spiritually clean enough to be united with God. That's why people prepare themselves for communion through prayer and fasting. As a result, some Orthodox Christians receive communion frequently, while others only do so on rare occasions. The power of God's presence is so great during Eucharist, that you can receive strength and blessing just by being present in the church, even if you have not taken communion.

COMMUNING WITH GOD THROUGH THE ROMAN CATHOLIC MASS

The Orthodox and Roman Catholic Churches agree on most elements of the Eucharist and the role of clergy. Catholics usually call the Eucharist "Mass," though you'll also hear "communion" and "Eucharist." While the Eastern Orthodox prefer "mystery," Catholic Christians emphasize "sacrament," a term that comes from the Latin word for a solemn oath. Unlike a mystery, a person can understand and explain an oath. Only a person old enough to understand should take one. Likewise, The Catholic Church has developed more philosophically precise descriptions of the Eucharist than the more mystically inclined Orthodox (McGrath 363–365). The Roman Catholic Church agrees with the Orthodox Churches that the bread and wine actually become the body and blood of Christ. But Catholics also focus on the big question: "How?" The answer comes in the term **transubstantiation**. It's a difficult concept, but generally means this: The outward *form* of the Eucharist remains as bread and wine, but the bread and wine's *substance*—what they're really made of—has changed into the body and blood. That why Christians aren't cannibals—a claim made by some Romans when they persecuted early Christians (Spickard and Cragg 75).

For centuries, the Catholic Church typically offered both wine and bread only to the clergy, while lay Catholics took communion only in one form—the wafer. Now, however, all Catholics can receive both the blood (wine) and body (wafer). That pure white sliver of unleavened bread helps Catholics experience the Eucharist as a sacrifice cleansing us of sin, a divine version of sacrifices in the Jewish Temple. Just before taking communion, for example, people hear these words from the priest: "Behold the Lamb of God, behold Him who takes away the sins of the world" (Latin Mass). Like other sacraments and a charitable life, Roman Catholicism calls on its members to attend mass and receive communion regularly as an aid toward salvation.

ATTENDING THE LORD'S SUPPER AT A PROTESTANT CHURCH

Protestant groups use differing terms, including mass, Eucharist, communion, and the Lord's Supper. Many Protestants don't agree with the concept of transubstantiation, preferring the more general idea of the "real

Transubstantiation occurs when the Eucharist transforms into the body and blood of Christ.

presence" of Christ. That way you don't have to accept either the "mystery" of Orthodoxy or the "magic"—as some Protestants disparagingly call it—of changing bread and wine into body and blood. Some Protestants go even further, arguing that that the bread and wine are just symbols. In other words, they claim that it's irrational to imagine bread and wine being "mysteriously" or "sacramentally" transformed. It's just bread and wine, and people eat them "in remembrance" of Christ, as in the Last Supper:

> Then [Jesus] took a cup, and after giving thanks he said, "Take this and divide it among yourselves; for I tell you that from now on I will not drink of the fruit of the vine until the kingdom of God comes." Then he took a loaf of bread, and when he had given thanks, he broke it and gave it to them, saying, "This is my body, which is given for you. Do this in remembrance of me." (Luke 7:17–19)

You can see from this passage that the Protestant tradition stresses the "remembrance" idea, while the Orthodox and Catholic Churches accentuate the words "this is my body" and "this is my blood." Orthodox and Catholic churches would not disagree with the Eucharist as a symbol, but would strongly disagree with calling it *only* a symbol (Ward 166–167).

As Protestant traditions vary, so do the ways in which they celebrate the Eucharist. You can learn a lot by watching closely. In the most traditional Anglican and Episcopal communities, you'll experience Mass with all of the

>>> **A Priest** consecrates the bread in a Roman Catholic mass.

Christian Rites of Passage

Baptism

Mystery in Orthodoxy, *Sacrament* in Catholicism and Anglicanism, *Sacrament* in Protestantism

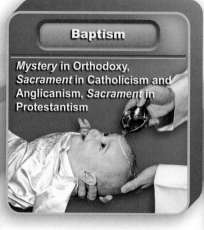

Burial

Mystery in Orthodoxy, *Ceremony* in Catholicism and Anglicanism, *Sacrament* in Protestantism

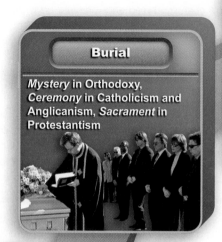

Confirmation

Mystery in Orthodoxy, *Sacrament* in Catholicism and Anglicanism, *Ceremony* or *Sacrament* in Protestantism

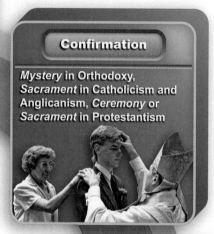

Ordination

Mystery in Orthodoxy, *Ceremony* in Catholicism and Anglicanism, *Sacrament* in Protestantism

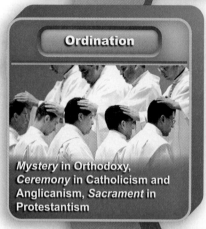

Mysteries, Sacraments, or Ceremonies?

These rites of passage have more meaning in some traditions than others.

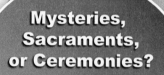

Marriage

Mystery in Orthodoxy, *Sacrament* in Catholicism and Anglicanism, *Sacrament* in Protestantism

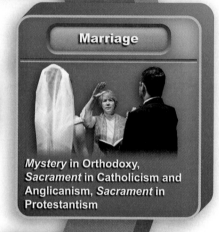

Anointing the sick

Mystery in Orthodoxy, *Ceremony* in Catholicism and Anglicanism, *Sacrament* in Protestantism

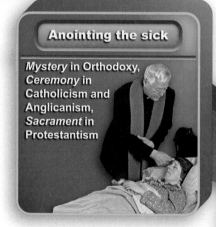

Individual Confession and Absolution

Mystery in Orthodoxy, *Sacrament* in Catholicism, but not always done in Anglicanism, and almost never in Protestantism

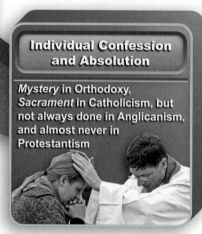

Eucharist

Mystery in Orthodoxy, *Sacrament* in Catholicism and Anglicanism, *Ceremony* or *Sacrament* in Protestantism

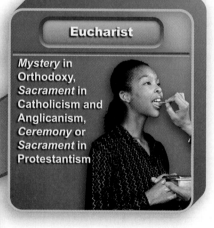

∧∧∧ While Christianity holds some practices nearly universal, not all denominations agree on their importance. Here are several rites of passage that are sometimes considered oaths (sacraments), sometimes considered rituals (ceremonies), and sometimes considered events beyond comprehension (mysteries).

∧ This picture, by the famed artist Lucas Cranach the Younger, is called "The Holy Communion of
the Protestants and Ride to Hell of the Catholics." Why did communion become such an
intense area for debate?

bells, chants, incense, and movements popular 150 years ago in England or Rome. In a Finnish Lutheran church, on the other hand, the service consists mostly of communal singing and Bible reading. You don't need a priest to prepare communion. People file up the front of the church to take bread from a minister and drink wine from many tiny chalices, a small version of the one used in the service. In this way, the Finnish church stresses the equality of all Christians (by having identical chalices) while also honoring individuality (by keeping them separate). In many American Protestant congregations, ministers hand out small glasses to people as they sit in the pews. This further highlights the equality of all people while also allowing families to sit together and commune without the ruckus of lining up at the altar. How might that compare to the way people receive communion in the Orthodox and Catholic traditions?

Prayer: Personal and Communal Interaction with the Sacred

Christians have inherited many Jewish ideas about prayer. Yet, as you can imagine, Christians also differ widely in their views. The Lord's Prayer, which appears twice in the New Testament, forms the foundation for all others. Varying a little by language, every Christian church uses it somewhere in their prayer life. Here it is the context of the Gospel according to Matthew. Jesus tells his disciples that:

> When you are praying, do not heap up empty phrases as the Gentiles do; for they think that they will be heard because of their many words. Do not be like them, for your Father knows what you need before you ask him. Pray then in this way:

> Our Father in heaven, hallowed be your name. Your kingdom come. Your will be done, on earth as it is in heaven. Give us this day our daily bread. And forgive us our debts, as we also have forgiven our debtors. And do not bring us to the time of trial, but rescue us from the evil one.

> For if you forgive others their trespasses, your heavenly Father will also forgive you; but if you do not forgive others, neither will your Father forgive your trespasses. (Matthew 6:7–15)

PRAYER IN THE ORTHODOX TRADITIONS

Walk into an Orthodox church and you're likely to see many pictures, candles, and banners. You'll smell incense and hear chanting or singing. People will move their bodies in specific ways, often standing

What's in a Name? Christian Priests and Preachers

	Orthodoxy	Catholicism	Anglicanism	Protestantism
Deacon	Ordained by a priest, the deacon serves the parish, especially during Eucharist. Though possibly either sex in the ancient church only males today.	Ordained by a priest, the deacon helps the priest in the parish, especially during Eucharist. Always a man.	Helps the priest in the parish, especially during Eucharist. A man or woman.	Helps the ministers in the parish. A man or a woman.
Priest	Ordained by a bishop, the priest may celebrate communion. Always a man. May be celibate or married, but only before ordination	Ordained by a bishop, the priest may celebrate communion. Always a man. Must be celibate in the Roman tradition.	Ordained by a bishop, the priest may celebrate communion. May be a man or woman, celibate or married.	Never used: Protestants believe in the "priesthood of the people"
Minister	Rarely used	Rarely used	Sometimes used to describe a priest	Often used to describe an ordained leader who is not a priest. Only men in some denominations; men and women in others
Preacher	Rarely used	Rarely used	Rarely used	Especially popular in the Evangelical and Fundamentalist traditions. Usually only a man.
Bishop	A priest who has been ordained to lead a large geographic area or city. All bishops have equal votes on matters of theology.	A priest who has been ordained to lead a large geographic area or city. All bishops can vote on matters of theology but final decision is made by the Pope	A priest who has been ordained to lead a large geographic area or city. All bishops have equal votes on matters of theology, however authority is largely regionalized.	Sometimes used to denote a respected leader of the denomination or community
Patriarch	The bishop of a national church	Rarely used	Rarely used	Rarely used
Pope	The bishop of Rome, but not the leader of the Orthodox Church	The bishop of Rome, also called the "Vicar of Christ" and leader of the Roman Catholic Church	Rarely used in the low-church tradition; sometimes used in the high-church liturgy	Never used

for hours, tracing a cross on their bodies with their hands, kneeling, or kissing sacred objects. Orthodox believers hope that a Christian from a thousand years ago could walk into their church and feel at home, because the liturgies have changed very slowly. For them, all of the words, smells, sounds, and pictures integrate in prayer. In their prayers, Orthodox Christians emphasize deification, or becoming more like God. Written prayers (said in church services or by yourself) often include deep theological and historical meaning, meant to educate the person reading or hearing it. Prayers also help people become more and more like Jesus by letting them become peaceful rather than anxious, and full of love rather than anger. Finally, Orthodox prayers help people understand what is really important and what is not; remember that the Lord's Prayer asks for daily bread but also that God's will be done on Earth and heaven.

>>> Consider the role of candles and light in the prayer life of this Greek Orthodox priest.

Orthodox churches generally use prayers that have been handed down for centuries. New prayers often take years to write, to make sure they are done just right. Orthodox believers also often feel comfortable praying with both their minds and bodies—for them, human ideas and actions cannot be separated.

Orthodox churches have developed a very rich tradition of prayer through the saints—people who lived such holy lives that we feel sure they're in heaven. We might hope to emulate a saint or ask one to be an intercessor for human beings with God. Mary ranks above all the saints and angels because she alone was chosen to bear God in His human incarnation. For that reason, you'll often heard her called "Theotokos," or "God-bearer."

CATHOLIC PRAYER

The Roman Catholic Church defines prayer as the "vital and personal relationship" of a human being with his or her church. Orthodox and Catholic Churches mostly agree on the basic form and importance of prayer. In fact, the Catholic Catechism defines prayer in ways that may also remind you of our discussion of Jewish prayers from Chapter 10:

- Prayers are not gifts to God, but gifts from God—they help us to become humble
- Prayers mark a covenant between humans and God—they are a commitment by both God and people
- Prayers are a form of communion—they link us to God. (Catechism of the Roman Catholic Church)

Catholics often like to use prayers written for special occasions or needs, praying to God through other holy people, especially saints and the Virgin Mary. Although they have thousands of different ones, Catholics regularly rely on the prayer "Hail Mary" as a way to find peace, ask God for help, and remind themselves to try to emulate Mary's life. It says:

> Hail Mary, full of grace, the Lord is with thee. Blessed art thou amongst women, and blessed is the fruit of thy womb, Jesus. Holy Mary, Mother of God, pray for us sinners, now and at the hour of our death. Amen.

This short text symbolizes some important aspects of Catholic prayer. First, it takes its first words directly from the Bible. It then adds lines to help explain Mary's importance in Catholicism. According to Roman Catholic doctrine, other than Jesus, only Mary was born without original sin (thus making her mother Anna's pregnancy an "immaculate conception"). Given her special status, the Virgin mediates between us and her son, God. The phrase "Hail Mary" reminds us that our work is never done—we need help from God through Mary until the moment we die.

PRAYER IN THE PROTESTANT TRADITIONS

As they shifted focus away from the sacraments, Protestants redoubled their emphasis on prayer as the best way to interact with the Word of God (John 1:1). Protestants tend to emphasize prayers devoted to a particular place and moment in time. A Presbyterian minister may, for example, write a "call to worship" that begins each worship service. In it, he or she can talk about issues that are important to that congregation on that day.

Protestants have also developed spontaneous prayer to a very high degree. This reflects their heritage of *declaring* (which you'll remember is part of the meaning of "Protestant"). Baptist, Evangelical, and Fundamentalist groups especially emphasize this form of prayer.

Whereas Orthodox and Catholic Christians might take comfort in praying the same words as their forebears and co-religionists, Protestants exult in declaring an immediate and intimate relationship with God. Spontaneous prayer also downplays communal interactions while magnifying the personal link of believers to God. Here's a hint: Study the ways in which people use the name "Jesus Christ"; Orthodox and Catholics tend to use "Christ," but Evangelicals prefer the more intimate "Jesus."

Music and Prayer

Many Christians set their prayers to music, just as a psalm instructed Jews thousands of years ago: "Praise [God] with trumpet sound; praise him with lute and harp! Praise him with tambourine and dance; praise him with strings and pipe! Praise him with clanging cymbals; praise him with loud clashing cymbals!" (Psalm 150). Some Christian traditions only use singing in their prayers, while others prefer organs and other instruments accompanying the human voice. The oldest Christian hymn may be the "Phos Hilaron," named for its first lines in Greek:

> O gracious Light,
>
> pure brightness of the ever-living Father in heaven,
>
> O Jesus Christ, holy and blessed!
>
> Now as we come to the setting of the sun,
>
> and our eyes behold the vesper light,
>
> we sing your praises, O God: Father, Son, and Holy Spirit.
>
> You are worthy at all times to be praised by happy voices,
>
> O Son of God, O Giver of life,
>
> and to be glorified through all the worlds. (Sacred Texts)

The Christian tradition has inspired much of the greatest European music ever written. Some scholars argue that the greatest of all composers was Johann Sebastian Bach, who wrote music for both the Roman Catholic and Lutheran churches. His skill and huge output—about 1,120 pieces—earned him the nickname "The Fifth Evangelist." His most famous piece may be "Jesu, Joy of Man's Desiring," but he also wrote masses, cantatas, and hundreds of hymns.

the **THINK**SPOT
www.thethinkspot.com

Picture Desk, Inc./Kobal Collection

∧
∧ An autographed page from J.S. Bach's
∧ Missa Solemnis. Why do you think Bach was able to write for both Catholics and Protestants?

Spontaneous prayer and television complement each other because both have an immediate impact—not something pre-considered. Spend a few minutes watching Evangelical TV shows, which have really developed the idea of "praying over" a problem or a person (Spickard and Cragg 420–421; McManners 590–594).

Contemplation and Quiet as Forms of Interaction with the Sacred

We've studied contemplation in a number of previous chapters—Hinduism and Buddhism meditation, for example. Christians rarely meditate in the same sense; for them, contemplation offers a path to leave daily problems behind. As you've probably guessed, various Christian groups employ different contemplative practices. In general, the older

>>> Televangelist Robert Tilton preaches to viewers at home. Think of two or three reasons that he would be showing his telephone number on the screen.

(214) 620-6200

Andrei Rublev, "Old Testament Trinity (Three Angels). Icon. Tempera on panel. 1410–1420. Sovfoto/Eastfoto.

∧
∧ This icon depicts the story of the three
∧ angels visiting Abraham near the Oak of
Mamre. Why would Andrei Rublev, the greatest
Russian iconographer of all time, choose to
depict the Holy Trinity this way? Why did he
leave a place open at the table?

traditions (such as Orthodoxy and Catholicism) emphasize contemplation to a higher degree than their Protestant counterparts do.

Here are three examples, which are snapshots of a long tradition of Christian contemplation. Christians sometimes borrow from one another, so you may see each of these practices in more than one church. (It is now commonplace, for example, to find Orthodox-style icons in Roman Catholic churches. Look back to the first pages of Chapter 11 and note that a Russian Orthodox icon of Christ hangs on the altar of the Catholic church of Santa Maria in Trastevere.)

∧
∧ This Greek mosaic icon shows Jesus as God
∧ and also as a young child playing in his
mother's arms.

Icons symbolize sacred persons in the Orthodox Christian Church. They act as windows to the spiritual realm and aid believers in worship.

CONTEMPLATION WITH ORTHODOX ICONS

Orthodoxy focuses intently on the contemplation of **icons**. When you're in an Orthodox church, icons are all around you. In the home of an Orthodox person, you'll likely see them too.

Take a look at the icons on this page. Do they look a little unnatural, the bodies a little too long, the eyes a bit too big? That's on purpose—icons represent a person who has achieved deification. Iconographers choose to portray their subjects in a slightly abstract way. Instead of painting a saint

THINK World Religions

Spiritual Double-Clicking

In the past few years, it's gotten much easier to introduce the idea of icons to college students than when I began teaching. You already know the word "icon" as it refers to the little picture on your computer screen. Stop and think about the attributes of that computer icon:

• It symbolizes something else—often a program—in a graphically stylized way
• It acts as a portal or window for that program
• You don't just look at the icon, you interact with it by pointing and clicking
• That interaction takes you to another place—the program or file symbolized by the icon.

For over a thousand years, Orthodox Christians have used sacred icons in much the way I just described the ones on your desktop. For them, icons act as windows and doorways to the heavenly realm. Orthodox followers gaze at icons, touch them, kiss them, light candles in front of them, and carry them when traveling. They celebrate holidays in their honor and try to save them from burning buildings. They explain that no one prays to the icon as a god—that would be idol worship. Rather, Orthodox Christians view their interaction with icons as a way to help them believe, act, and think like the holy women and men portrayed on the icons. By spiritually double-clicking, as I like to call it, these Christians hope to transform— to deify—themselves.

the THINK SPOT
www.thethinkspot.com

∧
∧ What does the ornate design of this Mexican
∧ monstrance tell us about the adoration of
the gifts?

or depicting a holiday with naturalistic perspective or perfect body proportions, iconographers show people as we imagine them in a world without cares, work, or change. In other words, the icons represent people as they might look in heaven rather than on Earth. In that way, too, icons help us connect with God because they remind us of our ultimate goal: transforming our image to be like that of God. Orthodox believers contemplate God through the icons. The quiet act of seeing helps icons become windows to another world (Spickard and Cragg 107–108; 121–122).

ROMAN CATHOLIC ADORATION OF THE GIFTS

In a Roman Catholic church you're likely to see a contemplative practice called the **adoration of the gifts**. The priest will place a small

>>> This engraving from the late 1800s depicts a Quaker meeting house. Why do you think the men are seated on one side and the women on the other?

portion of transubstantiated bread (the Body of Christ) in a vessel called a monstrance, which offers protection and a clear view. People come to sit, usually for an hour, in front of the monstrance. They take this time to consider God's closeness to them in the stillness of a quiet church. Often, one person follows another all through the night, sometimes for 40 hours at a stretch. In rare cases, the adoration of the gifts can last for years in an unbroken line of quiet contemplation. In the pews, the Catholics feel closer to God by looking at the monstrance and remember the line from the Psalm 46:10: "Be still and know that I am God" (Papal Instruction).

UNPROGRAMMED QUAKER WORSHIP—A PROTESTANT FORM OF CONTEMPLATION

Though more rare than in Orthodoxy or Catholicism, you can find some contemplative practices in Protestant churches, too. One of the most important is the Unprogrammed Quaker Worship developed by the Society of Friends, also known as Quakers.

Instead of the sacred liturgy or worship service, Quakers often meet and sit in silence. Anyone may speak, but the main idea is to come together in quiet contemplation. This has been called "expectant waiting," because the silence eventually opens you up to interaction with God. For some people, it seems difficult—just sitting in a plain room, not *doing* anything. But, after a while, the silence begins to help people contemplate God (Avery, "Unprogrammed Quaker Worship"). This attracts many people to Quakerism, as they seek relief from their busy lives. In fact, Quakerism has expanded from its traditional strongholds in England and the East Coast of the United States. On the U.S. West Coast, for example, some people integrate ideas from Zen Buddhism with Quaker principles and practices. How do you think other Quakers might respond?

Philadelphia: Quäkerkirche.

Finding a Direct Link to God: The Charismatic Movement

Contemplation seeks a quiet way to interact with God. The Charismatic Movement, on the other hand, celebrates a direct link to the sacred world through movement, song, and exciting sermons and prayers. Charismatic Christians hope to feel the Holy Spirit working within them, just as the Apostles did on Pentecost.

> When the day of Pentecost had come, they were all together in one place. And suddenly from heaven there came a sound like the rush of a violent wind, and it filled the entire house where they were sitting. Divided tongues, as of fire, appeared among them, and a tongue rested on each of them. All of them were filled with the Holy Spirit and began to speak in other languages, as the Spirit gave them ability. (Acts 2:1–4).

Charismatic Christians often refer to the scene described above as a "baptism in the Holy Spirit." A charismatic Christian may feel as though God has actually entered his or her body. As with other mystical experiences, it's not

rational or explainable—it just happens. But once it does, you may have the power to do wonderful things. Some people "speak in tongues," as they are moved to pray in an unknown language. Others may "lay hands" on sick people to heal them. A few may even receive a gift of prophecy—speaking the truth about the world and God's instructions for us. Some denominations, such as the Pentecostal Churches and Assemblies of God, strongly encourage charismatic worship. Others, both Protestants and Catholics, include charismatic activity as part of a bigger tradition. In fact, the Charismatic Movement may be the most powerful development in Christianity across the world in the past 50 years (McManners 584–590).

<<< From her outstretched hands to her "Christ" T-shirt, we know that this woman is a Charismatic Christian.

Adoration of the gifts is a Roman Catholic practice that involves contemplation of the Body and Blood of Christ, sometimes displayed in a monstrance.

▶ HOW DOES THE SACRED BECOME COMMUNITY?

Christianity has long grappled with the relationship between the individual believer and the community. In its first centuries, Christian men and women sought refuge in the desert of Syria and Egypt. In some cases, they hoped to live alone in a life of quiet contemplation and fasting. In others, they sought out like-minded people to create monasteries devoted to God. Yet they were a minority; like today, most Christians lived in their local communities, constantly interacting with many different kinds of people. It's good to remember this range of human experiences as we explore how Christians have developed sacred communities of many different forms.

Monasticism

In general, Christian monks and nuns seek simplicity and contemplation in their lives. They desire to follow an ancient tradition in which a man or woman leaves the old life, seeking total devotion to God. Monks and nuns may live far from society or completely within it, depending on their tradition. The number of monks and nuns has risen and fallen many times in the past 2,000 years, and today seems to be dying out in some places even as it revives in others. Here are some examples from across the Christian spectrum.

Orthodoxy has a long and deep relationship with monasticism. Orthodox believers revere the early "desert fathers" and "desert mothers" who lived in physical poverty and spiritual wealth. They ate little, wore shabby

(or even no) clothing, and spent their day in rigorous prayer. They developed two basic kinds of monasticism that would continue in Orthodoxy: the hermitage and the communal monastery. A hermit lives alone or with a couple other people, subsisting simply and spending most of his or her time in prayer. A monastic person prays for himself or herself, but also to ask God for the salvation of the entire world. In addition to this spiritual work, communal monasteries also produce scholarship, build libraries, paint icons, and teach children. Monks work together, constructing impressive complexes of buildings and welcoming pilgrim visitors.

In present-day Orthodoxy, bishops usually come from communal male monasteries. Although not allowed to be priests or bishops, Orthodox women find the monastic life to be a good way to serve God because convents offer more opportunities for female leadership than parishes, where men often take leadership roles.

<<< Although founded in 362 CE, by 2002 only a few monks still lived at the Syrian Orthodox monastery of Mar Mata, near the ancient city of Nineveh, Iraq. Why might the number of monks in Iraq be so low?

Catholicism and Anglicanism add another rite to monasticism: holy orders. After years of helping the poor, for example, Mother Teresa created her own order, the Missionaries of Charity, to aid the very poorest people of Indian society. If you want to become a monk or nun, you can then pick a group that focuses on one kind of service, such as education of children, aid to the poor, baking of communion wafers, or contemplative prayer. The religious orders form the backbone of Roman Catholic organization and administration, and they include famous groups such as the Benedictines, Cluniacs, Trappists, and Jesuits.

Protestantism has no formal monastic tradition, and early Protestants often attacked it, saying that people should live inside the community, not set apart from it. Nevertheless, a few Protestant groups have come close to monasticism in spirit, if not in name. Take the Shakers, for example. Although never a large group, the Shakers once had communities across America, full of men and women who lived with one another in celibate lives devoted to work and service. They influenced furniture design and religious music through their conviction that life was full of "simple gifts" from God. Their most famous hymns explains it well: "'Tis a gift to be simple, 'tis a gift to be free. 'Tis a gift to come down where we're supposed to be" (McManners 110–120; Spickard and Cragg 88–94; McGrath 255–256; "Shaker Music").

Calendars, Rituals, and Community Celebrations

Like many of the traditions we study in *THINK World Religions*, Christianity builds its sense of community through shared holidays

The Christian Calendar

Christian Year

Holiday Name	Advent	Christmas/ Nativity of Christ	Epiphany	Baptism/ Theophany	Presenta- tion/ Candlemas	Lent	Palm Sunday and Holy Week	Memorial of Christ's Death	Easter/ Pascha
Commemo- rates what event	Prepara- tion for Christmas	Birth of Jesus	Visit of Wise Men to Christ	Baptism of Christ by John the Baptist	Presenta- tion of Jesus to the Jewish Temple	Prepara- tion for Easter/ Pascha	Seven days before Easter/ Pascha, including Jesus' entry to Jeru- salem and crucifixion	Christ's death as noted in the Bible	Resurrec- tion of Christ from the dead
Orthodox Celebrate it	Yes	Yes	No (celebrated during Christmas)	Yes	Yes	Yes	Yes	No	Yes
Catholics Celebrate it	Yes	Yes	Yes	Yes	Yes	Yes	Yes	No	Yes
Anglicans Celebrate it	Yes	Yes	Yes	Some	Some	Yes	Yes	No	Yes
Protestants Celebrate it	Some	Yes, except Jehova's Witness	Rarely	Rarely	Some	Most	Most	Only Jehova's Witness	Yes, except Jehova's Witness

and rites of passage. We discussed the rites of passage in Chapter 11. Most Christians follow a calendar of holidays that mainly revolve around events in the life of Jesus Christ. Orthodox and Catholics often celebrate more holidays, while Protestant denominations range from many celebrations (Anglicanism) to nearly none at all (Jehovah's Witnesses).

Western Christians (Catholics and Protestants) tend to celebrate Christmas with more gusto than any other Christian holiday. And why not? On that day, Christians commemorate the moment when God and humanity united in the incarnation of Christ. Eastern Christians often focus on Pascha (Easter) because it marks the resurrection of Christ from the dead and the final between God and Humanity. The word Pascha comes from "Passover," in commemoration of the Jewish holiday, and for the Orthodox it always lands after the Jewish celebration. Orthodox often say that the Jewish Passover marks the movement from Egypt to Israel, and the Christian Passover marks the transition from death to life. (In fact, they use leavened instead of unleavened bread for the Eucharist as a reminder of this "New Passover.")

Communal Worship and Identity

At the beginning of Chapter 11, we read about the Eucharist in the Belorussian Orthodox Church. A few pages back in this chapter, we added Mother Teresa's description of Christian life and Justin Martyr's portrayal of ancient Christian practices. These scenes remind us how

Christian Year

Transfiguration	Ascension	Other days devoted to Jesus' life and works	Pentecost/Trinity	Nativity of Mary	Annunciation	Mary's Assumption/Dormition	Immaculate Conception	Other Days to Commemorate Mary	Days to Commemorate Saints
Christ appearing to disciples as God	Christ going back to heaven	Varies	Holy Spirit coming to the apostles	Jesus' mother's birth	Gabriel telling Mary she will bear Jesus; Mary accepting	Mary's death (or transfer of her body to heaven)	Joachim and Anna's conception of Mary without Original Sin	Events in Mary's life or her protection of people on earth	Remembering the suffering, works, death, and help people on Earth
Yes	Yes	Yes	Yes	Yes	Yes	Yes	No	Yes	Yes
Yes	Yes	Yes	Yes	Yes	Yes	Yes	Yes	Yes	Yes
Some	Yes	Some	Yes	Some	Some	Some	Some	Some	Some
Some	Some	Usually not	Some	Usually not	Usually not	Usually not	No	No	No

important community can be for Christians. But how does it develop? What are its boundaries? How does the sacred become community for Christian groups?

In Orthodoxy and Catholicism, believers who reside near one another typically unite into a parish tied to a village, town, or city neighborhood. This helps create spiritual, social, educational, and even economic ties with your neighbors. It is usually anchored by the service of a priest who is involved in life of the community. Living in a Catholic neighborhood can often affect your identity, even if you're not Catholic. I remember that my first apartment as a professor was advertised as "St. Theresa's Parish" in the local newspaper. If I had wanted to live a little further out, I would have gone to "Holy Name Parish." It didn't matter if I was Catholic or not; the local identity was strong enough to affect how everyone perceived our hometown.

RITUAL AND COMMUNITY IN ORTHODOX AND CATHOLIC TRADITIONS

In Orthodoxy, community develops via liturgical rituals, especially the Eucharist. By retaining the same prayers and movements from centuries ago, Orthodox Christians think of their community as stretching all the way back to Christ. This comes from apostolic succession, but also from the way that Orthodox churches try *not* to change, which offers a sense of community with one another and also with those in the past and future. In fact, disagreements in the Orthodox tradition have sometimes occurred because people resisted change. These include the Old Believers in Russia and the Old Calendrists in Greece.

Roman Catholics emphasize the Mass as a place to interact with God and to create community. Three Catholic councils produced important guidelines. The Council of Trent (starting in 1545) strengthened traditional Catholic practices and ideas in the face of rebellion by Luther and other Protestants. While Luther had argued that rituals should take place in the people's own language and that you need not be a priest to conduct the Lord's Supper, the Council claimed that prayer should be in Latin and celebrated by a priest. Retaining Latin reinforced Catholicism as a worldwide community and helped to keep non-Catholic ideas from creeping into the Mass.

Three hundred years later, the first Vatican Council (1869–70) offered a cohesive definition of the word "Church" and solidified the Pope's position as infallible when speaking as the Vicar of Christ. The Second Vatican Council (1962–65, also called Vatican II), dramatically changed the course of Roman Catholicism. It embraced Mass in the local language, integrated monks and nuns into society, and changed many "rules" of the faith to "guidelines." This served to open up Catholicism, but also made traditionalists feel like their faith had become too "modern." Today, the Mass tends to be less formal than it was before Vatican II and the rules less strict than a generation ago, but it remains central to Catholic life.

>>> Does this picture of the Lakewood Church in Texas look very "churchy" to you? Why or why not?

<<< In America, religion and sports often work together to create the feeling of community. Here is a "plain" Mennonite girl from Ohio playing softball. How might her clothing and her swing both affect the girl's place in a community?

BLESSINGS OF CONGREGATION IN ANGLICAN AND PROTESTANT CHURCHES

As we learned a few pages ago, Anglicans often think of themselves in terms of a "high church" or "low church." The first one retains many rituals from Roman Catholicism, while the second resembles Protestant churches. In one Anglican church, for example, you might see a monstrance or hear a mass in Latin. In another, however, you might not even see candles—just a plain Bible and a cross on a table. The distinctions between high and low church do not, by the way, always follow social or theological lines. High Church Anglicans can be theologically liberal, while those from the Low Church often argue a more conservative line. The worldwide Anglican communion seeks to embrace both high and low, conservative and liberal.

As a general rule, non-Anglican Protestantism views rituals with some healthy skepticism. Instead of elaborate rituals, Protestants tend to rely on the reading of the Bible, singing hymns, and hearing the sermon. They welcome many different forms of group worship. Nowadays, this often includes singing, electric musical instruments, and pop-style music or dance. In embracing "praise bands" and other crossovers from secular society, Protestant communities seek to bring popular culture into the church. As the Orthodox find solace in tradition, Protestants often seek excitement and relevance in change.

Protestantism, especially in the United States, has largely avoided geographically distinct parishes. Instead, people choose a church to attend. Scholars sometimes call this phenomenon "shopping for a church" to see what fits you the best, regardless of exact denomination or neighborhood.

Some Evangelical churches have grown to a huge size. When more than 2,000 people attend prayer services weekly at one place, we often use the term "mega-church." Typically, they look less like traditional church and more like a theater, complete with food concessions, lighting, sound systems, and even special effects. To help people feel like they are part of a community, mega-churches regularly host dozens, even hundreds, of "affinity ministries"—for athletes, mothers, caregivers, or college-aged kids.

This desire, to welcome many different people and to give them a place to feel at home, has sometimes fractured denominations. Many Protestants disagree about women and openly homosexuals serving as ministers, priests, and bishops. Liberals points out that Jesus embraced many marginalized people, so it seems only appropriate to welcome anyone who seeks a Christian community. Conservatives counter that ministry has been a male form of service since apostolic times. They also note that Christianity has long accepted homosexuals as members of the community without welcoming their "alternative lifestyle," which seems to threaten the status quo.

The Spread of Christianity

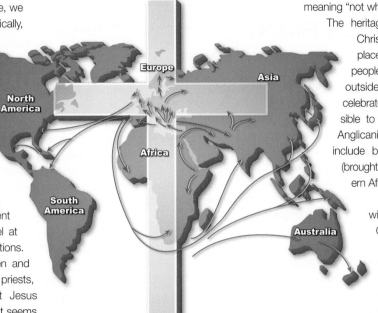

∧∧∧ From the 1500s to the 1800s, Christianity spread rapidly from Europe and Asia to the rest of the world. Why might such a religion appeal to both dominators and the oppressed?

viewed local traditions and religions as "pagan" or "uncivilized." These tended to be code words meaning "not white" or "not European."

The heritage of imperialism has made Christian life complex in many places. In Africa, for example, some people see Christianity as a tool of outside domination, while others celebrate it as a local tradition. Is it possible to be both? Can South African Anglicanism, for example, somehow include both the Anglican Christianity (brought from England) and also southern African spiritual traditions?

Although sometimes siding with invaders and imperialists, Christianity has also offered people a path of resistance against oppression. The African American tradition, for example, includes both Protestant and non-Christian elements. As it grew among slave communities in the American South, Christianity offered solace and strength to slaves. Here are three dramatic case studies to show how Christianity and politics interacted in the 20th century.

Christians in the World

Whether parish or mega-church, Christian groups often reach out to their communities and beyond, even to foreign lands. They call this "mission" or "missionary work." As we have seen in Mother Teresa's Nobel Lecture, a mission has three parts:

1. Working to alleviate suffering or poverty
2. Introducing Christian ideas to other people through service
3. Strengthening your own religious commitment through service

Different missionaries emphasize one or the other of these. A nondenominational soup kitchen in Moscow might never mention its religious affiliation, but a Mormon food bank may offer both physical and spiritual aid. If you think back to Mother Teresa, it's clear that her work with the poor helped both her and them.

From the 16th to 20th centuries, Christian missionaries traveled with European armies and merchants as they colonized the Americas, Asia, and Africa. In some cases, missionaries tried to integrate their beliefs into the local society. The Catholic priest Matteo Ricci (1552–1610), spoke and lived as a Chinese person, and introduced Christianity in a way that related to Confucianism, Daoism, and Buddhism.

Catholics and Protestants dominated missionary activity in the "new worlds" of North America, South America, Asia, and Africa. Often, Christian missionaries accompanied military and economic domination. The example of Matteo Ricci was the exception, not the rule; missionaries often

ORTHODOX CHRISTIANITY IN THE USSR

During the period of communist rule in the USSR (1917–1991), the Soviet government often persecuted Christians, especially the Russian Orthodox in the 1920s and '30s and Catholic or Protestant groups after World War II. Intent on getting rid of all religion, which they saw as an impediment to scientific progress, the Soviets government killed thousands of priests and closed churches, turning them into garages, theaters, or even labor camps. One of the most notorious was Solovki—a historic Russian Orthodox monastery that became the first Soviet prison camp.

As a result of these persecutions, Christianity became a medium of dissent against communism, but often underground or at the edges of society. When the USSR collapsed after eight decades of communism, Christian communities again sprouted across Russia—including Russian Orthodox, Protestant, and local denominations (CIA Country Studies).

LIBERATION THEOLOGY IN CENTRAL AND SOUTH AMERICA

While not attacked as viciously as the Russian Orthodox in the former USSR, some Roman Catholic priests have also suffered for their beliefs. As liberation theology spreads across much of Latin America, governments (and even popes) have tried to stop it. Why? Because liberation theology asks the Catholic Church to focus nearly all of its energy on aiding the poor and oppressed, even if that means political revolution. It also calls for constant self-criticism by the Catholic Church: Where have we helped the rich and powerful instead of the poor and oppressed? (McGrath 42; Spickard and Cragg 428–432).

Religion + POLITICS IN THE USA

THE RELIGIOUS RIGHT

Long before Barack Obama and Rev. Jeremiah Wright, Christians have struggled with defining the relationship between faith and politics. Think back on the emperors whose pictures we studied in Chapter 11.

Yet America is a special case, because we insist on the separation of church and state. So, why do they so often mix? During the past 20 years, this debate has centered on the Evangelical tradition. For much of the 20th century, Evangelical Christians completely stayed away from the political process. However, the rise of new groups and the wide reach of televangelism changed everything. From the 1980s to today, the "religious right" has influenced every presidential election in the United States. Is that now changing? Consider this recent article from the *New York Times*:

> The hundred-foot white cross atop the Immanuel Baptist Church in downtown Wichita, Kan., casts a shadow over a neighborhood of payday lenders, pawnbrokers and pornographic video stores. To its parishioners, this has long been the front line of the culture war. Immanuel has stood for Southern Baptist traditionalism for more than half a century. Until recently, its pastor, Terry Fox, was . . . the public face of the conservative Christian political movement in a place where that made him a very big deal.
>
> With flushed red cheeks and a pudgy, dimpled chin, Fox roared down from Immanuel's pulpit about the wickedness of abortion, evolution and homosexuality. He mobilized hundreds of Kansas pastors to push through a state constitutional ban on same-sex marriage, helping to unseat a handful of legislators in the process. His Sunday-morning services reached tens

of thousands of listeners on regional cable television, and on Sunday nights he was a host of a talk-radio program, "Answering the Call."

> For years, Fox flaunted his allegiance to the Republican Party, urging fellow pastors to make the same "confession" and calling them "sissies" if they didn't. "We are the religious right," he liked to say. "One, we are religious. Two, we are right."
>
> And Fox's confrontational style packed ever more like-minded believers into the pews. He more than doubled Immanuel's official membership to more than 6,000 and planted the giant cross on its roof.
>
> So when Fox announced to his flock one Sunday in August last year that it was his final appearance in the pulpit, the news startled evangelical activists from Atlanta to Grand Rapids. Fox told the congregation that he was quitting so he could work full time on "cultural issues." Within days, The Wichita Eagle reported that Fox left under pressure. The board of deacons had told him that his activism was getting in the way of the Gospel. "It just wasn't pertinent," Associate Pastor Gayle Tenbrook later told me.
>
> These days, Fox has taken his fire and brimstone in search of a new pulpit. He rented space at the Johnny Western Theater at the Wild West World amusement park until it folded. Now he preaches at a Best Western hotel. "I don't mind telling you that I paid a price for the political stands I took," Fox said. "The pendulum in the Christian world has swung back to the moderate point of view. The real battle now is among evangelicals."

(David D. Kirkpatrick, "The Evangelical Crackup," *The New York Times*, October 28, 2007.)

CIVIL RIGHTS AND AFRICAN AMERICAN PROTESTANTISM

Finally, the American Civil Rights Movement illustrates how Christianity sometimes supports social change through nonviolent protest, prayer, and preaching. Although it is a political speech, Rev. Martin Luther King, Jr.'s, famous "I Have a Dream" has the cadence of a great sermon:

> With this faith we will be able to transform the jangling discords of our nation into a beautiful symphony of brotherhood. With this faith we will be able to work together, to pray together, to struggle together, to go to jail together, to stand up for freedom together, knowing that we will be free one day. (King, "I Have a Dream")

African Americans in the 1950s and '60s relied on King and other Christian leaders to support their cause for equal rights. For these children and grandchildren of slaves, Ezekiel and Moses were not distant Jewish patriarchs, but rather prophets of freedom and deliverance. Singing "Ezekiel Saw the

Wheel" reminded civil rights activists that progress happened because of divine intervention: "The big wheel moved on faith, the little one by the grace of God" (Burleigh).

Conclusion

Now that you've finished this chapter, go stroll through your neighborhood. You'll have a better idea about the great diversity of Christianity in the world. Although it began with a tiny movement in a corner of the Roman Empire, the Christian faith has spread further across the globe than any other religious tradition. Its strength may come, ironically, from the many different answers to Christianity's big questions: Is Christ both God and human? Are human beings good or bad? Do Christians find salvation through beliefs or actions? Is there one church or many? Should Christianity be separate or part of society?

As it changes, one thing is sure: Christianity today looks much different than it has at any other time. Christianity has been used both to oppress and to deliver from oppression. At the beginning of a new century, Christianity sometimes retains its historic face—candles still flicker in front of icons St. Petersburg, Russia. Other times, though, Christians show a new face to the world, looking heavenward, hands to the sky in charismatic worship in Accra, Ghana.

>>> Rev. Martin Luther King, Jr.
speaks to the March on Washington in support of civil rights.

The Trinity is one of the key concepts in Christianity. **How might the shape of this church in Tromsoe, Norway be symbolic?**

v v v

Here is a depiction of Satan tempting Christ from the 12th century CE. **Why is Jesus portrayed as a humanlike figure, while the devil has claws, horns, and a tail? >>>**

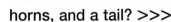

IS THERE A GOD?

Christians believe in a single god, usually described as the Trinity (the Father, the Son, and the Holy Spirit). God is the creator and ultimate judge, but possesses compassion and mercy. Unlike Judaism, Christianity believes in the physicality of God through the Son—Jesus Christ.

HOW DOES THE SACRED BECOME COMMUNITY?

Most Christians celebrate several important holidays each year, often corresponding to events in the life of Christ. Christmas commemorates his advent to Earth, Good Friday marks his death on the cross, and Easter celebrates his rebirth. The Orthodox and Roman Catholic Churches strive to retain traditional practices and rituals in order to universalize Christianity across time and space. Protestants and Anglicans, however, tend to modernize and expand Christian traditions in order to appeal to a wider audience.

WHAT DOES IT MEAN TO BE HUMAN?

Christians believe that human beings were created in the likeness of God, but have strayed away. Satan, the antithesis of God, was once an angel, but pulled away and fell into evil. When we distance ourselves from God, we end up committing evil as well.

HOW DO HUMANS INTERACT WITH THE SACRED?

There are variations between regions and churches. Eastern and Oriental Orthodoxy emphasize the mysterious nature of the Eucharist, and use traditional prayers that have been passed down for centuries. Roman Catholics consider the Eucharist a sacrament in which the bread and wine are transubstantiated, and consider prayers to be a communal covenant between human beings and God. Protestantism argues that the Eucharist is a symbol of remembrance, not the actual blood and body of Christ. Some Protestant denominations focus on spontaneous and personal prayer.

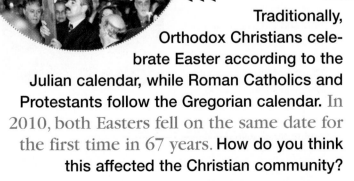

<<< **Traditionally, Orthodox Christians celebrate Easter according to the Julian calendar, while Roman Catholics and Protestants follow the Gregorian calendar.** In 2010, both Easters fell on the same date for the first time in 67 years. **How do you think this affected the Christian community?**

>>> Da Vinci's famous mural "The Last Supper" adorns the wall of Santa Maria delle Grazie in Milan. **How do different Christian traditions memorialize this final meal?**

Leonardo da Vinci (1452–1519), "The Last Supper." 1495-97/98. Mural (oil and tempera on plaster), 15′ 1 1/8″ × 28′ 10 1/2″. Refectory, Monastery of Santa Maria delle Grazie, Milan, Italy. IndexRicerca Iconografica. Photo: Ghigo Roli

REVIEW

Summary

HOW DO HUMANS INTERACT WITH THE SACRED?   p. 182

- There is a wide range of beliefs in Christianity, and thus, many different denominations. The three major divisions are Orthodox Christianity, Roman Catholicism, and Protestantism. Each interacts differently with the sacred through rituals that can be considered mysteries, sacraments, or ceremonies.
- All forms of Christianity stress the importance of prayer. Prayer brings humans closer to God and sometimes allows them to communicate directly with Him. While denominations such as the Society of Friends cultivate prayer through quiet reflection and meditation, others like the Pentecostal and Holiness Churches seek divine interaction through movement and song.

HOW DOES THE SACRED BECOME COMMUNITY?   p. 195

- Orthodox Christians take pains to preserve centuries-old traditions; in this way, they are connected to a community of believers that stretches all the way back to Christ himself. The Roman Catholic Church also preserves tradition but emphasizes the importance of Mass as a way of interacting with God and strengthening the community of followers.
- Protestants (and some Anglicans) seek to bring popular culture to the church, incorporating modern music and other secular crossovers. Some churches can have thousands of members, and push to appeal to a wide audience.
- Christian missionary work serves to strengthen the religious commitment of followers as well as help those in need and spread the word of Christ. Historically, this has provided imperialists with the justification necessary to dominate other cultures; however it has also provided the oppressed a means of achieving social change.

Key Terms

Five Solas distinguish Protestantism from Roman Catholicism and Orthodox Christianity. Created by early Lutherans, they include a belief in salvation through faith, an eschewing of religious texts beyond the Bible, and an emphasis on the grace of God.   *183*

Transubstantiation occurs when the Eucharist transforms into the body and blood of Christ.   *187*

Icons symbolize sacred persons in the Orthodox Christian Church. They act as windows to the spiritual realm and aid believers in worship.   *193*

Adoration of the gifts is a Roman Catholic practice that involves contemplation of the Body and Blood of Christ, sometimes displayed in a monstrance.   *194*

Find it on

- http://vodpod.com/watch/989322-mother-teresa-advice-from-a-saint-calcutta-is-everywhere
"Calcutta is everywhere." So says Mother Teresa on this short video, which you can access on the ThinkSpot. In her own words, Mother Teresa talks about her life's work of helping the poor and instilling in them a belief that they are worthy of God's—and their neighbor's—love. She speaks of the "poverty of the heart" which she finds a much greater need to fulfill than "material hunger."

- http://www.chapellenotredamedelamedaillemiraculeuse.com/
The significance of the Blessed Virgin, Mary, cannot be overemphasized when talking about Catholicism. It is through Jesus'

mother that Christians learned of the "immaculate conception," in which Mary was conceived without original sin in order to make her worthy and holy enough to bear the Son of God. Go to the ThinkSpot to learn more about the Church of the Miraculous Medal in Paris, which is devoted to Mary and in which you can learn about the significance of the "miraculous medal," a religious icon that is important to those with a devotion to Mary.

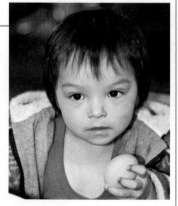

Questions for Study and Review

1. What is the Eucharist, and how is it viewed by different branches of Christianity?

The Eucharist is a communion of wine and bread that recalls the Last Supper. Eastern and Oriental Orthodox churches refer to it as a mystery, and emphasize its mystical nature. They believe that during communion, the bread and wine become the body and blood of Jesus Christ, and he is, in a sense, resurrected. Roman Catholics refer to the Eucharist as a sacrament, and believe in transubstantiation—although the bread is still bread, and the wine is still wine, its inner substance has changed. Protestants tend towards the idea that the substances used in the Eucharist are symbols of Christ, not actually his flesh and blood. They believe that Christ is present during the communion, but not because of transubstantiation.

2. What is the Charismatic Movement?

Charismatic Christians worship through movement and song, and sometimes experience a direct link to the spiritual through bodily possession. In these cases, followers feel as though the Holy Spirit literally enters their body, a mystical experience that may cause them to speak in tongues or receive healing powers.

3. How does monasticism play a role in Christianity?

Traditionally, Orthodox monks and nuns lived in poverty, eating little and spending much of their day in prayer. They developed two forms of monasticism: hermitage and communal. The Catholic and Anglican Churches expanded on the tradition by creating holy orders, groups that focused on one type of service, such as education, or aid to the poor. Protestantism has no recognized monastic tradition, but groups such as the Shakers have created communities dedicated to service to God.

For Further Study

BOOKS:

Harvey, Susan Ashbrook and David G. Hunter. *The Oxford Handbook of Early Christian Studies*. New York: Oxford University Press, 2008.

Kim, Sebastian and Kirsteen Kim. *Christianity as a World Religion*. New York: Continuum, 2008.

McGrath, Alister E. *An Introduction to Christianity*. Cambridge, MA: Blackwell Publishers, Inc., 1997.

McManners, John, Ed. *The Oxford Illustrated History of Christianity*. New York: Oxford University Press, 1990.

Spickard, Paul R. and Kevin M. Cragg. *A Global History of Christians*. Grand Rapids, MI: Baker Academic, 1994.

Ward, Keith. *Christianity: A Beginner's Guide*. Oxford, UK: Oneworld, 2008.

WEB SITES

A Comparative Chart of Christian Beliefs.
http://www.saintaquinas.com/christian_comparison.html

Flowchart of Christianity.
http://philtar.ucsm.ac.uk/encyclopedia/christ/index.html

The Internet Sacred Text Archive: Christianity.
http://www.sacred-texts.com/chr/index.htm

Religion Facts: Christianity.
http://www.religionfacts.com/christianity/index.htm

<<< Sitting on the floor in their mosque in Oman, these three Muslim men study a beautifully illustrated version of the Qur'an, Islam's most sacred text. What can we guess about Islam just by looking at this picture? Why do they wear special hats? Why do the books have as much color as text? What do their body postures reveal to us about their religious traditions?

"Your God

is the one God: there is no god except Him, the Lord of Mercy, the Giver of Mercy" (Haleem, trans., Sura 2: 163). If you remember no other words about Islam, it should be these. God's unity, God's uniqueness, God's mercy and judgment: these themes fortify Islam. As you read this chapter, also remember two more words: *islam* and *imam*. The first one doesn't just refer to the name of the religion; it means "submission" and has the same root as the Arabic word for "peace." The second word means "faith." Together, they refer to Islam's three crucial teachings:

1. Realize that there is only one God who creates everything.
2. Accept that Muhammad was God's last and greatest prophet.
3. Live with complete submission and faith in God.

That wasn't so hard, was it? Yet, like all the traditions we have studied in *THINK World Religions*, Islam has taken this simple structure and developed rich practices to help human beings follow the three steps outlined here. In Chapters 13 and 14, we'll investigate how Muslims' views of God, people, and community have developed and spread across much of the world. In addition, we'll focus on the ways that Muslims agree and disagree with the other "peoples of the Book": Christians and Jews.

Living together has proven to be a challenge for much of Jewish-Christian-Islamic history. I think back to Chapter 2, when we considered how much harder it was to get along with people similar to us than with people who had very different backgrounds. It seems like followers of the three great monotheistic religions should get along pretty well because they share many beliefs and practices. In fact, often they *do* get along—the end of the Ramadan fast brings out a good many non-Muslims to my university's dining hall, and no Christian or Jew seems to mind when the Muslim Students Association has Friday prayers in a college lounge. But say the following words to different people, and you'll probably get some heated responses: crusade, jihad, Taliban, Zion, Jerusalem. It's clear that similarity breeds interaction, but sometimes it highlights tensions as well.

ISLAM:
Submission and Faith

CHAPTER 13

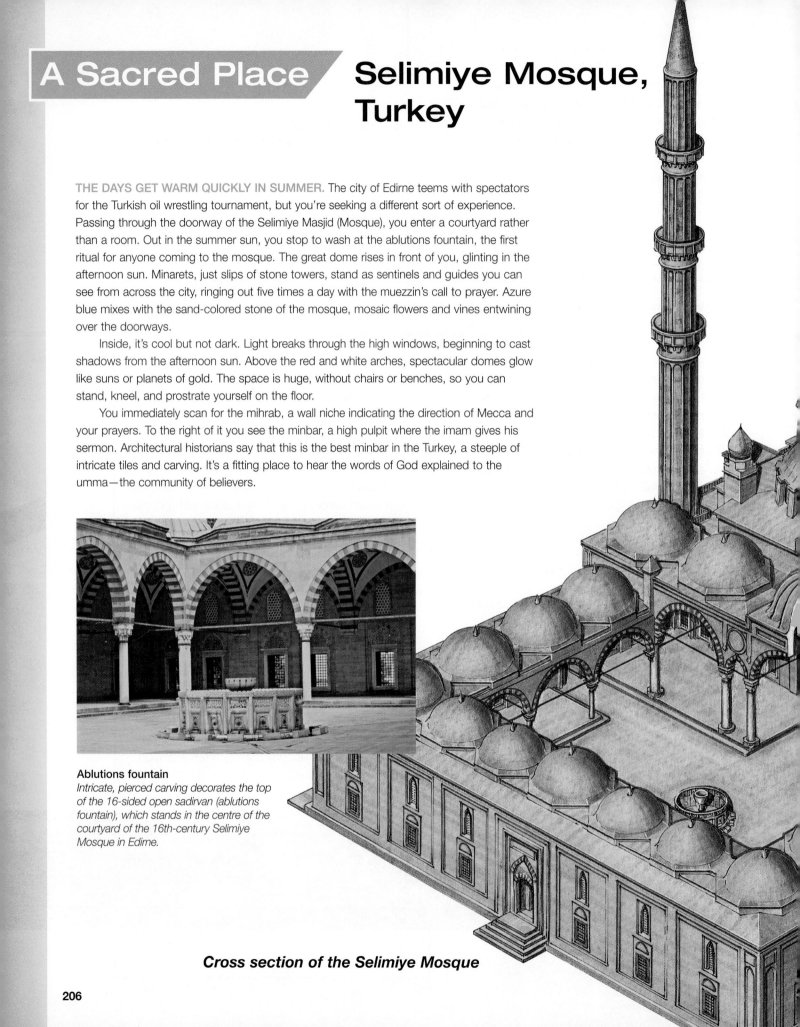

A Sacred Place Selimiye Mosque, Turkey

THE DAYS GET WARM QUICKLY IN SUMMER. The city of Edirne teems with spectators for the Turkish oil wrestling tournament, but you're seeking a different sort of experience. Passing through the doorway of the Selimiye Masjid (Mosque), you enter a courtyard rather than a room. Out in the summer sun, you stop to wash at the ablutions fountain, the first ritual for anyone coming to the mosque. The great dome rises in front of you, glinting in the afternoon sun. Minarets, just slips of stone towers, stand as sentinels and guides you can see from across the city, ringing out five times a day with the muezzin's call to prayer. Azure blue mixes with the sand-colored stone of the mosque, mosaic flowers and vines entwining over the doorways.

Inside, it's cool but not dark. Light breaks through the high windows, beginning to cast shadows from the afternoon sun. Above the red and white arches, spectacular domes glow like suns or planets of gold. The space is huge, without chairs or benches, so you can stand, kneel, and prostrate yourself on the floor.

You immediately scan for the mihrab, a wall niche indicating the direction of Mecca and your prayers. To the right of it you see the minbar, a high pulpit where the imam gives his sermon. Architectural historians say that this is the best minbar in the Turkey, a steeple of intricate tiles and carving. It's a fitting place to hear the words of God explained to the umma—the community of believers.

Ablutions fountain
Intricate, pierced carving decorates the top of the 16-sided open sadirvan (ablutions fountain), which stands in the centre of the courtyard of the 16th-century Selimiye Mosque in Edirne.

Cross section of the Selimiye Mosque

Interior of the Mosque with Dome
Daylight comes through windows on the dome and along the walls to show a colorful decorative ceiling with red and white arches supported by tall large columns in a room of the Selimiye Mosque.

Sultan's Loge
Turkey, Edirne, Selimiye Mosque, Sultan's Loge, arch with shuttered window, surrounded by blue tiles and inscription in Arabic script.

Window
Asia, Turkey, Edirne, window in the 16th-century Selimiye Mosque, white script on dark blue and green tiling in arch above with metal latticing protecting window pane.

minbar
Many experts claim that the Selimiye Mosque's minbar, with its conical tiled cap, is the finest in Turkey. Its lacelike panels are exquisitely carved.

There is one god in Islam: God. Muslims worship the "capital-g" God of Abraham, Moses, Mary, and Jesus. They share sacred stories of creation and redemption with Jews and Christians. Yet Muslims see Islam as both the first and the final version of monotheism: the primordial religion of all people, but also the fulfillment of Judaism and Christianity's promise. According to Islam, each of the holy people in the past, from Abraham to Jesus, paved the way for the final messenger from God, Muhammad. But even he cannot come close to the glory of God the Creator.

First, let's turn to the Qur'an (Koran) as the source for understanding God. Then we'll study Muhammad's life as an example of perfect submission and faith in God.

The "Glorious Qur'an"

Turn back to the beginning of this chapter and compare the opening photograph with the ones on this page. The former one shows three Omani men studying the Qur'an, while below is a 17th-century copy of the sacred text. What can we learn from them? The men wear simple white robes and beautifully embroidered hats. One is pointing to the mid-dle of a page. Take a closer look—the words of the Qur'an fit into the middle circle. In the picture below, the text also takes up only a portion of the page. The rest of the sheets have multi-colored designs and embellishments that resemble the men's hats. Is it possible that the graphic designs on the hats and the page both point us toward the holiness of the text? Could both act as illuminations for the words, reminding the students of the Qur'an's importance? Can you guess why there are no pictures of Muhammad or God on these pages?

Muslims turn to their holy book—the Qur'an—as the primary source to learn about God. For them, the Hebrew Tanakh and the Christian New Testament act as prefaces to the Qur'an, which answers questions posed by Jews and Christians. Likewise, the Qur'an corrects mistakes found in those earlier texts. In fact, Muslims tend to think of the Qur'an in ways that might remind you of Christians' views of Jesus (Ayoub 41). For example, Muslims generally believe that the Qur'an has always existed, that it is the Word of God that was ultimately written down on Earth. For that reason, it's a perfect book, complete and unchangeable. (In fact, it's not strictly correct even to quote the Qur'an in any language other than Arabic,

A SACRED ACTION ▶▶▶

Sandys Travailes

Similar to us, 17th-century Europe loved a good travel story, especially if it described foreign lands and unknown religious traditions. The reading public wanted confirmation that Christian European culture was better than any other, but also wondered what life was like in far-away places. In 1658, a book was published that promised all that and more—*Sandys Travailes*.

In the past few chapters, we have encountered many different ways to describe sacred actions, including charts, newspaper accounts, and ethnographic descriptions. In this passage, consider what George Sandys intended to tell his readers about Islam. Did he want Christian Englishmen to find Muslims to be similar or different from themselves? Why? Does the description sound like things you've heard on the radio or read online about Islam? How do you imagine people reacted to reading these words?

Read through this passage, but don't be surprised if the language sounds out of date or the ideas seem a little odd. Come back to it as you learn more about Islam in Chapters 13 and 14. Where do you think George Sandys accurately described Muslim practices, and where did he make mistakes?

> The Alcoran [Qur'an], which containeth the sum of their Religoin, is written in *Arabicke* rhime, without due proportion of numbers: and must neither be written nor read by them in any

other language. . . . They never touch it within-washed hands: and a capital crime it is, in the reading thereof to mistake a letter or displace the accent. They kiss it, imbrace it, and swear by it: calling it, The book of Glory, and director into Paradise.

> To speak a little of much; they teach that God is onely to be worshipped, onely one, and the Creator of all: righteous, pitofull; in wisdome and power incomprehensible. . . . Idolatry they hold to be the most accursed of crimes, and therefore they interdict all images and counterfeits whatsoever; reputing the Christians Idolaters, for that they have them in their Churches and houses: imagining also that we worship three Gods, as not apprehending the mystery of the Trinity. . . .

> Congregated they are as aforesaid by all chanting of the Priest [muezzin] from the tops of steeples: at which times lightly though they be in the fields, they will spread their upper garments on the earth, and fall to their devotions. Moreover, I have seen

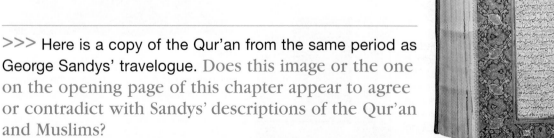

>>> Here is a copy of the Qur'an from the same period as George Sandys' travelogue. Does this image or the one on the opening page of this chapter appear to agree or contradict with Sandys' descriptions of the Qur'an and Muslims?

since translations never exactly reflect their original texts.) Many Muslims would even argue that the words, the sounds, and the letters of the Qur'an are sacred, actually fragments of God. And so how you treat the Qur'an equals how you treat God; if you get the Qur'an dirty or do something disrespectful with it, you're blaspheming God.

When you pick up a Qur'an, you'll immediately notice that it does not read like a story. Unlike the Jewish and Christian Bibles, it offers no sense of narrative. Its **suras** (chapters) each exist as a unit on their own, teaching us something about God and humanity. For that reason, "chapter" doesn't completely reflect the word, but neither does "essay." We'll just use the term "sura" throughout these chapters (El "Sura"). Although it has suras, the Qur'an has no

>>> The Qur'an includes a lot of material about Jews and Christians as "People of the Book." Why do you think Jesus' donkey and Muhammad's camel seem so happy in this picture?

From: Al-Biruni, "Chronicle of Ancient Nations" ORMS.161.f.10v. Courtesy of Edinburgh University Library.

Sandys Travailes:
CONTAINING
A HISTORY
OF THE
Original and present state of the *Turkish* EMPIRE: Their *Laws*, *Government*, *Policy*, *Military Force*, *Courts* of *Justice* and *Commerce*.

The MAHOMETAN *Religion* and *Ceremonies*.
A Description of CONSTANTINOPLE.
The *Grand Seignior* SERAGLIO, *and his manner of living*.
ALSO,
Of GREECE, with the RELIGION and Customes of the GRÆCIANS.

Of EGYPT; the *Antiquity*, *Hieroglyphicks*, *Rites*, *Customes*, *Discipline*, and *Religion* of the *Egyptians*:
A VOYAGE on the River *Nilus*, and of the Crocodile:
Of *Armenia*, *Grand Cairo*, *Rhodes*, the *Pyramides*, *Colossus*, *Mummies*, &c.
The former flourishing and present state of *ALEXANDRIA*.

A Description of the HOLY-LAND; of the *Iews* and several Sects of CHRISTIANS living there; of *Ierusalem*, *Sepulchre* of *Christ*, *Temple* of *Solomon*; and what else either of Antiquity, or worth Observation.

Lastly, *Italy* described, and the Islands adjoyning; As *Cyprus*, *Crete*, *Malta*, *Sicilia*, the *Æolian* Islands; Of *Rome*, *Venice*, *Naples*, *Syracusa*, *Messena*, *Ætna*, *Scylla* and *Charybdis*, and other places of note.

Illustrated with Fifty Graven Maps and Figures.

THE SIXTH EDITION.

LONDON,
Printed by R. and W. Leybourn, and are to be sold by JOHN SWEETING at the Angel in Popes-head-Alley, M.DC.LVIII.

them con-joyntly pray in the corner of the streets, before the opening of their shops in the morning. Friday is their Sabbath, and yet they spend but a part thereof in their devotion, and the rest in recreations: but for that time they observe it so rigorously that a *Turke* here lately had his ears nailed to his shop-board for opening it too timely. Before they pray, they wash all the organs of their senses; their legs to their knees, and their arms to their elbows: their privities after their purging of nature; and sometime all over from top to toe: for which there are houses of office with conducts belonging to every principall Mosque. Where water is wanting they doe it with dust. At the dore of the Mosque they put off their shoes; and entring, fit crosse-legged upon rows of mats one behind another, the poor and the rich promiscuously. The Priest in a pulpit before them; not otherwise distinguished in habit, but by the folding up of their Turbant. When they pray they turn their faces towards *Mecca*: first standing upright; without any motions of their bodies, holding the palmes of their hands upward; sometimes they stop their eyes and ears, and oft pull their heir on the sides of their faces: then thrice they bow, as in their salutations; and as often prostrating themselves on the earth, do kiss it. . . . The priest doth sometimes read unto them some part of the Alcoran [Qur'an] (holding it, in reverence to the book, as high as his chin) sometime some of their fabulous Legends, intermixing expositions, and instructions: which they hearken unto with heedy attention and such steddy posture of body as if they were intranced. Their Service is mixed with songs and responses: and when all is done they stroke down their faces and beards with lookes of devout gravity. (Sandys 42–43)

<<< Why do you think the title of this book would be so long—178 words?

chronological beginning, middle, or ending. In fact, it's organized by length of sura, going from long to short. The exception to this rule is the very first one, called the Fatiha, which introduces the subject of God and his relationship to humanity:

In the name of God, the Lord of Mercy, the Giver of Mercy!

Praise belongs to God, Lord of the Worlds,

the Lord of Mercy, the Giver of Mercy,

Master of the Day of Judgment.

It is you we worship; it is You we ask for help.

Guide us to the straight path:

The path of those You have blessed, those who incur no anger and who have not gone astray. (1: 1–7)

Selected Suras

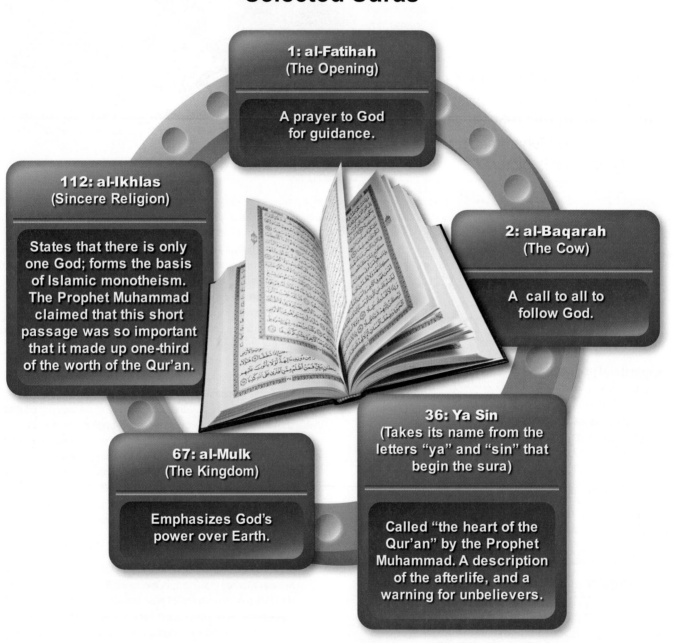

1: al-Fatihah (The Opening)

A prayer to God for guidance.

112: al-Ikhlas (Sincere Religion)

States that there is only one God; forms the basis of Islamic monotheism. The Prophet Muhammad claimed that this short passage was so important that it made up one-third of the worth of the Qur'an.

2: al-Baqarah (The Cow)

A call to all to follow God.

67: al-Mulk (The Kingdom)

Emphasizes God's power over Earth.

36: Ya Sin (Takes its name from the letters "ya" and "sin" that begin the sura)

Called "the heart of the Qur'an" by the Prophet Muhammad. A description of the afterlife, and a warning for unbelievers.

Sources: Based on The Qur'an: The Scripture of Islam, "Important Surahs of the Qur'an," Retrieved March 4th, 2010, http://www.bible.ca/islam/library/Gilchrist/Vol1/4a.html; Islamic Academy, "Jewels of Quran," Retrieved March 4th, 2010, http://www.islamicacademy.org/html/Articles/English/Jewels_of_Quran.htm; Syed Abdul, "Commentary on the Holy Qur-an," Retrieved March 4th, 2010, http://www.arabicbible.com/christian/maududi_tafsir.txt; A.R. Kidwai, Muslem Access, "English Translations of the Holy Gur-an," Retrieved March 4th, 2010, http://www.muslimaccess.com/quraan/translations/index.asp.

Λ
Λ   Here are a few important suras from the Qur'an. What comparisons can you draw between
Λ   these and other religions texts?

<<< Sura 46 in the Qur'an is entitled "Curving Sand-Hills." **How do you think the geography and climate of the Arabian Peninsula might relate to its people and their religious traditions?**

In Chapter 14, we'll return to the practice of reciting the Qur'an. For now, just remember that the text has a specific organization and function, quite different from other religions' sacred texts.

The Qur'an also includes things that no one can comprehend. Some words don't seem to make sense, while others confuse us more than enlighten us. Muslims accept this; the Qur'an accurately portrays God, so why expect that human beings would fully understand it? For example, the Sura entitled "The Curved Sand-Hills" begins with the letters "Ha-Mim." One translation explains that the "letters are one of the miracles of the Qur'an, and none but Allah knows their meanings" (Saudi 46: 1). Another word, "jinn," appears at the end of the Qur'an. Muslims theologians and scholars, storytellers and poets have debated its meaning from the earliest days of Islam. Jinn seem to be beings, created by God but different from angels or humans. Some scholars claim that the word refers to Bedouins—non-Arab nomadic traders—but most traditions see them as spirits, separate from us, but still part of God's creation. The English word "genie" derives from this term.

God and the Kaaba

So, who is the Islamic God, and how might He be different from the God of Israel or Christianity? The idea of Allah—God—existed in many

Muslims learn the Fatiha by heart at a young age, as they say it over a dozen times a day in their prayers. In the next 113 suras, the Qur'an describes the attributes of God, the way that humans should live, and the fate that awaits good and bad people. The 114th sura brings the Qur'an full circle, reminding us that God is the "controller of people" who offers refuge from the devil, the "slinking whisperer—who whispers into the hearts of people" (114: 1–3).

You may also notice that suras often begin with the words "Say" or "Recite." That's a clue to the way Muslims think about the book. Though written down, the Qur'an may be most beautiful and meaningful when it's recited aloud. Sura 16 explains that God has revealed the Qur'an "in parts, so that you can recite it to people at intervals; We have sent it down little by little" (17: 106).

THINK World Religions

"Allah" or "God"?

When we discuss Islam, should we use the word "God" or "Allah"? People disagree on this issue. Some scholars worry that using "Allah" incorrectly differentiates the Islamic God from that of the Jews and Christians (and in fact Arabic Christians use "Allah" in their liturgy). Yet English-language translations of the Qur'an (sometimes written "Koran") use both "Allah" and "God." In Chapters 13 and 14, we'll generally use the term "God," unless it's a quotation from another source. After all, the highly respected *Encyclopedia of Islam* puts it this way: "God: see Allah" (*Encyclopedia of Islam*, 116, column 2).

>>> The Kaaba, **Islam's holiest shrine, is a cube-shaped structure that includes a black stone used by Abraham to build the first Kaaba. What message does this picture convey about the Kaaba's importance to Islam?**

Arabian communities well before Islam developed in the seventh century. Jews and Christians mingled and traded with polytheistic Arabs, exchanging religious beliefs. Among the Arabs, Allah seemed to hold a preeminent place among the gods as the creator. You could see this especially in the Arab city of Mecca, with its cube-shaped shrine called the **Kaaba**. Among many statues or symbols of the gods (perhaps as many as 360 different ones), Meccan Arabs especially revered the Black Stone, which they linked to Allah. People would come to the Kaaba as pilgrims, beginning a sacred action that Muhammad and later generations of Muslims would continue.

As Islam developed, Muslims purified the Kaaba by getting rid of all remnants of polytheistic religion. The black stone of the Kaaba remained, put back into place by the young Muhammad when the Kaaba was redesigned. For Muhammad and all later Muslims, God did not *actually* reside in the Kaaba, even though they called it the House of God. Rather, the Kaaba marks the most sacred spot on earth, the geographical focus of all Muslim prayers. In a world that constantly experiences the effects of the supreme God, the Kaaba feels it most of all.

Comprehending God in Islam

Muslims explain that no person can totally understand God, any more than an infant might fully appreciate her mother and father. Still, they believe that human beings yearn to recognize God, just as a child needs to know her mother is close by. To do this, Muslims explain that we should consider God's three interlocking traits: God is one and unique; God is the creator; God is all-powerful.

GOD IS ONE AND UNIQUE

According to Islam, people naturally experience God's unique oneness, but they also tend to stray from His path. Maybe people just think too much, rather than simply having faith and submission. Muslims say that you're bound to get confused when you discuss multiple persons, or different faces of God. In your desire to know God, you've let human imagination take the place of God's uniqueness and unity. Specifically, Muslims disagree with the Christian idea of God having two natures (Father and Son) and three persons (Father, Son, Holy Spirit).

∧
∧   Here is an image of the Shahada, the words
∧   Muslims speak to declare their submission
and faith to God: "There is no other God but God, and Muhammad is the Messenger of God." Why do you think that calligraphy, rather than pictures, is preferred to describe God?

Muhammad revered Jesus but said that he wasn't God. "Praise belongs to God, who has no child nor partner in His rule. He is not so weak as to need a protector. Proclaim His limitless greatness!" (17: 111).

If that weren't clear enough, the Qur'an directly speaks to Christians about Isa (Jesus) and Mary (Marium): ". . . the Messiah, Jesus, son of Mary, was nothing more than a messenger of God, His word, directed to Mary, a spirit from Him. So believe in God and His messengers and do not speak of a 'Trinity'" (4: 171). In case people didn't understand even this statement, Muhammad direly warned Christians, saying "Those people who say that God is the third of three are defying [the truth]: There is only One God. If they persist in what they are saying, a painful punishment will afflict those of them who persist" (5:73).

With these words, Muhammad directed Muslims to witness God's unity. They must bring everyone back to humanity's original understanding of God's uniqueness and unity.

> Say, "He is God the One,
>
> God the eternal.
>
> He begot no one nor was He begotten.
>
> No one is comparable to Him" (112).

GOD IS THE CREATOR

If God's completely one and unique, it follows logically that he also created everything; after all, there is no one else out there to do the job. Muslims agree completely with Jews and Christians on this point. God exists outside of time and space, and he created the universe and all its inhabitants. Unlike Brahman in the Hindu tradition, God existed before creation and apart from it. A Hindu may say that we are all part of Brahman's unity but simply don't realize it. A Muslim, on the other hand, cannot actually hope to *become* part of God but rather to submit faithfully to divine will.

God's role as the creator also gives him ultimate power to judge people for their actions and beliefs. As the one who created humanity from a "clinging form" or "bit of coagulated blood," (96: 1–5) God is also "the most decisive of judges" (95: 8). For Muslims, only acknowledging God's creative power can keep them safe from eternal suffering. Here are some the Qur'an's most poetic yet terrifying lines:

> When the sky is torn apart, when the stars are scattered, when the seas burst forth, when the graves turn inside out: each soul will know what it has done and what it has left undone. Mankind, what has lured you away from God, your generous Lord, who created you, shaped you, proportioned you, in whatever form He chose? Yet you still take the Judgment to be a lie! (82: 1–9)

GOD KNOWS EVERYTHING, AND HE IS MERCIFUL

If God were to be completely just, how many of us would pass the test? Who has actually submitted faithfully to God every minute of his or her life? Realizing this, Muslims take solace in God's omniscience and His mercy. After all, people really can try to do the right thing, to live according to God's laws, but still have problems. In those cases, they can find peace knowing that God can offer a softer side of judgment than we read about in the last Qur'an quotation. Other sections therefore teach people not to despair. The Qur'an reminds us that "God is fully aware of everything you do. Whatever is in the heavens and in the earth belongs to God and, whether you reveal or conceal your thoughts, God will call you to account for them. He will forgive

Judaism and Christianity in the Qur'an

Since its early years, Islam has had a complex relationship with Christians and Jews. On the one hand, all three were monotheistic "people of the book." Yet Christians and Jews did not accept Muhammad as the messenger of God. How do you interpret the following passages from the Qur'an?

> The [Muslim] believers, the Jews, the Christians, and the Sabians—all those who believe in God and the Last Day and do good- will have their rewards with their Lord. No fear for them, nor will they grieve. (2:62)

> They also say, "No one will enter Paradise unless he is a Jew or a Christian." This is their own wishful thinking. [Prophet], say, "Produce your evidence, if you are telling the truth." (2:111)

> The Jews say, "The Christians have no ground whatsoever to stand on," and the Christians say, "The Jews have no ground whatsoever to stand on," though they both read the Scripture, and those who have no knowledge say the same; God will judge between them on the Day of Resurrection concerning their differences. (2:113)

> The Jews and the Christians will never be pleased with you unless you follow their ways. Say, "God's guidance is the only true guidance." If you were to follow their desires after the knowledge that has come to you, you would find no one to protect you from God or help you. (2:120)

> Abraham was neither a Jew nor a Christian. He was upright and devoted to God, never an idolater. (3:67)

For the wrongdoings done by the Jews, We forbade them certain good things that had been permitted to them before: for having frequently debarred others from God's path for taking usury when they had been forbidden to do so; and for wrongfully devouring other people's property. For those of them that reject the truth we have prepared an agonizing torment. (4: 160–61)

> The Jews and the Christians say, "We are the children of God and His beloved ones." Say, "Then why does He punish you for your sins? You are merely human beings, part of His creation: He forgives whoever He will and punishes whoever He will. Control of the heavens and earth and all that is between them belongs to Him: all journeys lead to Him." (5:18)

> You who believe, do not take the Jews and Christians as allies: they are allies only to each other. Anyone who takes them as an ally becomes one of them—God does not guide such wrongdoers. (5:51)

> For the [Muslim] believers, the Jews, the Sabians, and the Christians- those who believe in God and the Last Day and do good deeds- there is no fear: they will not grieve. (5:69)

> The Jews said, "Ezra is the son of God," and the Christians said, "The Messiah is the son of God": they said this with their own mouths, repeating what earlier disbelievers had said. May God confound them! How far astray they have been led! (9:30)

> We forbade the Jews what We told you about. We did not wrong them; they wronged themselves. (16:118)

> Say [Prophet], "You who follow the Jewish faith, if you truly claim that out of all people you alone are friends of God, then you should be hoping for death." (62:6)

whoever He will and punish whoever He will: He has power over all things" (2: 283–84). And even if God decides whom to punish, human beings can still "turn to God and ask His forgiveness . . . God is most forgiving, most merciful?" (5: 74).

DOES GOD HAVE HUMAN TRAITS?

Similar to the Jewish and Christian Bibles, the Qur'an often describes God in ways that make him seem human. For Christians, this isn't a problem, because Christ unites humanity with divinity. For Muslims (like Jews), though, words like God's "hand" or "voice" can bring up an important debate: Should we believe that God actually has hands and a tongue and a throat? Does he, as some Muslims believe, have long, black, curly hair?

Muslim scholars have debated this question for hundreds of years. In their discussions we can see traces of Greek philosophy as it interacted with

Muslim thought, just as it did with Jewish and Christian ideas. Many faithful Muslims would not think twice about using words like "hands" or "face" to described God. Muslim theologians, however, argued over the relationship of God's "essence" and his "attributes," just as Christians had a few centuries before. In addition, by surveying Muslim attitudes toward God's attributes, we can also get a feeling for the theological differences of Islam. Here are the three general points-of-view (*EI*, Vol. I, 406):

1. Some ancient scholars argued that we should not try to apply human intellect or philosophy to the "plain truth" of the Qur'an. For them, God has human features like hair and eyes. We may not see

>>> Muslims disagree on how to interpret God's "hands" as described in the Qur'an. Why then do you think that the handprint became an important symbol for Muhammad? (Bain 149–152)

Attributes of God in Islam

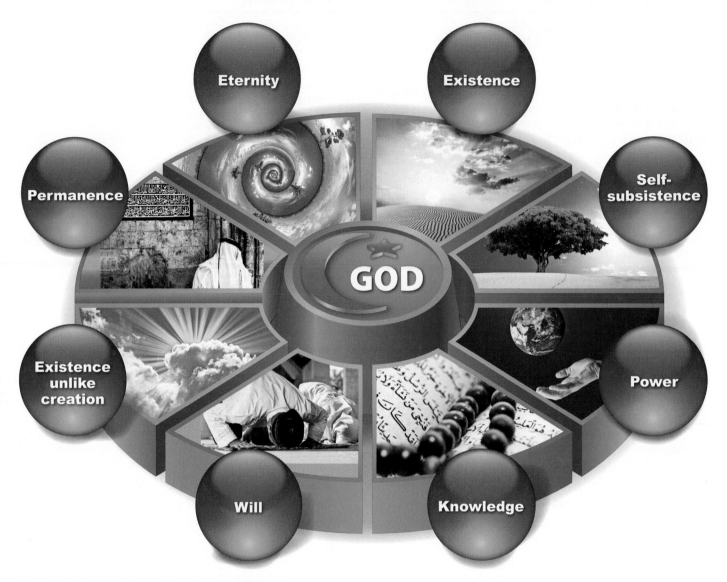

Source: Based on *EI* Volume I, page 406, column 1.

∧
∧ Muslims perceive God as omniscient and omnipotent, existing beyond the realm of human
∧ understanding. How does the Islamic sense of God compare to that of other religions?

them on Earth, but perhaps when we get to Paradise, God will show them to us. They might translate Sutra 48: 10 in the following way—*"Those who pledge loyalty to you [Prophet] are actually pledging loyalty to God Himself—God's hand is placed on theirs—and anyone who breaks his pledge does so to his own detriment: God will give a great reward to the one who fulfils his pledge to Him."*

2. Other Muslim theologians take a middle position, saying that God has real hands, eyes, and a throne. As human beings, though, we cannot guess what those words mean to God. So, although we use the word, God's "hands" are completely beyond our comprehension. Though the following translation uses quotation marks to highlight the metaphorical nature of "hands," Muslim believers could also interpret it as a middle-of-the-road translation from the Arabic: *"Those who swear allegiance to you*

(O Messenger), swear allegiance to God only. God's 'Hand' is over their hands. Whoever then breaks his oath, breaks his oath only to his own harm; and whoever fulfills what he has covenanted with God, He will grant him a tremendous reward" (Ali Ünal, *The Qur'an with Annotated Interpretation in Modern English* Clifton, NJ: Tughra, 2006).

3. A third group of scholars claims that God gave us the ability to use intellect to interpret the Qur'an. In this case, words like "hand" or "hair" have poetic and metaphorical meaning, but they don't refer to real body parts. To get past this problem, these scholars might approve of the following translation of Sura 48: 10: *"Those who swear allegiance to you indeed swear allegiance to God; and God's protection is over them. Then whosoever breaks the promise breaks it to his own loss; but whosoever fulfills the promise made to God will receive a great reward from Him."*

Islam's view of humanity can be summed up in a single name: Muhammad. Neither a god nor an angel, Muhammad nevertheless linked God with humanity through the text. Crucially, the Qur'an explains that Muhammad never erred in his decisions—he always made the right choice. For that reason, his life can teach us how we might also live in perfect Islam (submission) and imam (faith).

Muhammad had three separate but related roles: as messenger of God, military leader, and head of state. This makes him different from Jesus, Buddha, or Confucius, none of whom held political power. For Muslims, Muhammad's three vocations illustrate how the world should work; Muslims should not separate religion from politics, economics, or even war. All human decision should flow directly from Islamic teaching.

Muhammad's Biography

Paradoxically, we know both a lot and very little about Muhammad's world. Around 600 CE, the Arabian Peninsula teemed with travelers crossing its difficult terrain. Bedouin and Arab caravans carried goods from the Red Sea and the Arabian Sea to the great cities of Jerusalem, Antioch, and Alexandria. The harsh conditions meant that many people lived a nomadic life of caravan trade. Life revolved around extended families, clans, and tribes.

Far from barren, the Arabian desert sprouted religious groups of all kinds. As caravans and traders crisscrossed the region, they brought their religious and philosophical traditions with them. Jews had settled for centuries throughout the region. Christians, especially monks and nuns, found refuge in the desert. (Even today, the Monastery of St. Catherine in the Sinai Desert traces its roots to the centuries before Muhammad was born.) The Zoroastrians taught a form of monotheism, while Manicheans followed Mani, who claimed to be the last prophet in a line starting with Adam (Brown 33–43). Muhammad was born into this culture in which religious ideas shifted and changed like the dunes.

Like many great religious figures throughout history, we know little about Muhammad's early life. He was born around 570 CE to a family with prestige in the Arab city of Mecca. Tradition tells us that his father died before Muhammad was born, and his mother died when the young boy was only nine years old.

History obscures the early years of his life, but legends say that Christians realized Muhammad's future greatness when they met him.

∧∧∧ Here is Muhammad's name with sacred text written inside it. What might the artist be telling us in this composition?

His family fell into poverty, but still Muhammad made a name for himself as a capable and extremely honest person. A woman of means named Khadijah first offered Muhammad work as her agent selling goods. Impressed with him, Khadijah (who was older than Muhammad) then offered to marry him. With her wealth and his honesty and intelligence, the couple thrived. They had five or six children together, and Khadijah supported Muhammad in his growing spirituality.

When he was 35, God gave the people of Mecca a glimpse of Muhammad's future greatness. The local leaders decided to rebuild the

<<< According to Muslim tradition, Muhammad's special qualities could be seen even before he became the messenger of God. Why would his setting the Black Stone be seen as prophetic of his later feats?

Kaaba. The destruction of the shrine went well enough, but reconstruction faltered when the builders could not decide who should place the sacred black stone in place. To stop the fight over this honor, an elder recommended that the next man to arrive would have the honor, whoever he was. Of course, it was Muhammad. Not only did he move the black stone by himself, but he also rebuilt the Kaaba spiritually as well, making it a shrine for Allah alone (Brown 53–54).

We can thank Khadijah, Muhammad's wife, for helping him understand his true calling. When he was around 40, Muhammad went into the mountains outside Mecca. We don't know what exactly he did there, but he apparently used the month as a time to meditate and reflect on his life. While there, according to Muslim tradition, the angel Gabriel came to him and explained that he would receive messages from God, which he then needed to teach far and wide.

> Read! In the name of your Lord who created:
>
> He created man from a clinging form.
>
> Read! Your Lord is the Most Bountiful One
>
> who taught by [means of] the pen,
>
> who taught man what he did not know.
>
> But man exceeds all bounds
>
> when he thinks he is self-sufficient:
>
> [Prophet], all will return to your Lord. (96: 1–8)

Returning home, Muhammad recounted this terrifying event to his wife, who then enlisted the aid of a Christian friend. They assured Muhammad that he was not being tempted by a devil, but being contacted by an angel of God.

The messages continued to come from God to Muhammad for three years. During this time, Muhammad taught quietly, bringing together a small group of friends and family who realized he had received a new revelation from Allah, the God of Creation. They began the process of discarding their previous polytheistic ways and submitting completely to a single God. At the same time, Muhammad and his followers began to question the wealth and complacency of society in Mecca: Could you submit with faith to God if you focused so much on money and comfort?

As you can imagine, more people questioned Muhammad's message than accepted it. Some people wanted to simply silence the Prophet, but others sought to kill him, especially when he kept attacking their traditional gods and preaching the complete power of Allah. In addition to his family, though, early Islam did attract a mixture of people, including slaves. These companions suffered with him as Muhammad's own tribe, and neighbors refused to trade or interact with the Muslims.

Finally, people began to realize Muhammad's gifts. The people of Yathrib, a city not far from Mecca, asked Muhammad to help resolve a war they had been fighting. Broken down but unbowed, in 622 CE Muhammad took his small band of followers—perhaps a few hundred people—and trekked from Mecca to Yathrib (later renamed Medina al Nabi—the City of the

Prophet—usually shortened to "Medina."). Muslims call this period the Hijra, or "great emigration." Muhammad's success as a political leader brought more interest in his message, and Medina offered a safe refuge for six years. Muhammad responded by developing a successful political system based on Islam, creating a monotheistic theocracy. In those same years, Muslim tradition relates that God sent Muhammad on a mystical night journey to Jerusalem, where he met and prayed with Abraham, Moses, and Jesus. From there, he traveled back to Medina, able to describe the caravans and events he had experienced that night. He became convinced that Jews were people of the book, but ought to be expelled from Medina if they did not conform to Islamic practice.

In Medina, Khadijah died, leaving Muhammad bereft. He married again numerous times, some wives having been widowed during wars with the Meccans. No other wife, however, rises to the prominence of Khadijah in Islamic tradition.

Opponents continued to attack the Muslims, as Meccans sought to undercut the religious and political progress Muhammad was experiencing in Mecca. From 625 to 628 CE, the Muslims and the Meccans fought a series of battles. Although grossly outnumbered, Muhammad's followers won the first and last of these, outlasting his enemies at the Battle of the Trench in April, 627. A peace treaty—not always maintained—secured the right of Muslims to travel across Arabia in peace. Muhammad's reputation as political and military leader grew each year, bolstered by his incorruptibility and honesty. For Arabs watching the conflict between Mecca and Medina, it must have seemed that Muhammad did have God on his side: "When God's help comes and He opens up your way [Prophet], when you see people embracing God's faith in crowds, celebrate the praise of your Lord and ask His forgiveness: He is always ready to accept repentance (110: 1–3).

Muhammad's Names

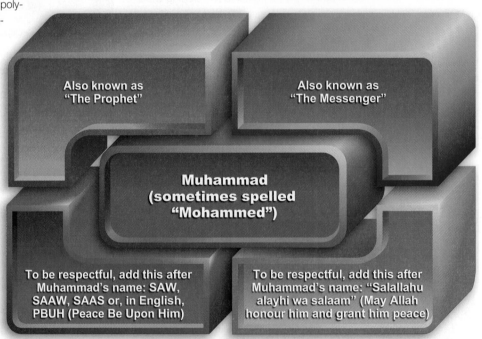

Also known as "The Prophet"

Also known as "The Messenger"

Muhammad (sometimes spelled "Mohammed")

To be respectful, add this after Muhammad's name: SAW, SAAW, SAAS or, in English, PBUH (Peace Be Upon Him)

To be respectful, add this after Muhammad's name: "Salallahu alayhi wa salaam" (May Allah honour him and grant him peace)

∧
∧ When reading an Islamic text, you'll often see Muhammad referred
∧ to as "The Prophet (PBUH)." What do Muhammad's different descriptions tell us about him?

The Life of Muhammad (570 CE–632 CE)

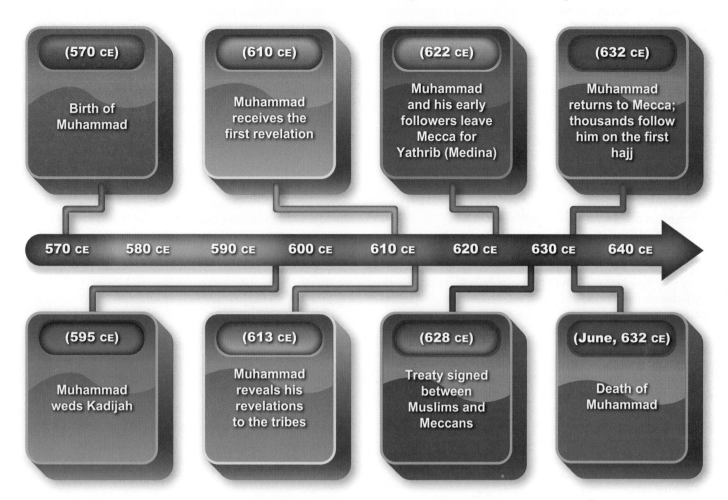

| (570 CE) | (610 CE) | (622 CE) | (632 CE) |
| Birth of Muhammad | Muhammad receives the first revelation | Muhammad and his early followers leave Mecca for Yathrib (Medina) | Muhammad returns to Mecca; thousands follow him on the first hajj |

570 CE   580 CE   590 CE   600 CE   610 CE   620 CE   630 CE   640 CE

| (595 CE) | (613 CE) | (628 CE) | (June, 632 CE) |
| Muhammad weds Kadijah | Muhammad reveals his revelations to the tribes | Treaty signed between Muslims and Meccans | Death of Muhammad |

Source: Based on PBS.org, "Muhammad: Legacy Of A Prophet," Accessed March 4, 2010, http://www.pbs.org/muhammad/timeline_html.shtml.

∧
∧ Because scholars disagree on exact dates, the order of events in Muhammad's life can often be
∧ confusing. Use this brief timeline to help you remember important events in early Islam.

In 630 CE, Muhammad left Medina and went home to Mecca, gaining supporters as he traveled. He entered the city to pray at the Kaaba and build his own mosque; by that point, the city had come to its senses and opened its arms to him. Although Mecca was his, Muhammad continued to live in Medina. He directed or led expeditions against other tribes, winning over converts to Islam. He oversaw the integration of Jews and Christians into his lands. He did not force them to accept Islam, but did expect payment of extra taxes if they refused to follow God's prophet.

Muhammad went one last time to Mecca in 632 CE. Tens of thousands joined him on the journey. This was the first hajj, the triumphant return of Muhammad to his ancestral city. From the Qur'an and tradition, Muslims learn that Ibrahim (Abraham) and his son Ismail (Ishmael) were the first true monotheists. They laid the first stones of the Kaaba. In returning to Mecca, Muhammad highlighted the return of his people to ancient monotheism. The Qur'an makes this clear: "Abraham was neither a Jew nor a Christian. He was upright and devoted to God, never an idolater" (3: 67).

Muhammad died in Medina on June 8, 632, held in the arms of his favorite wife, Aisha. It had been six years since he had been forced to leave Mecca for Medina. In that brief time, he had risen from persecuted prophet to leader of the great nation of Islam. Accordingly, Muslims restart the calendar from the date of Muhammad's emigration. By that calendar, the Prophet died in the Islamic Year (AH) 11.

Islam After Muhammad's Death

When Muhammad died, he left no instructions regarding a successor. His role as spiritual, political, and military leader, not to mention his stature as the Prophet with a direct link to God, made it very difficult to follow in his footsteps. The history of those first years, though, can help us to understand how Islam considers the human condition.

After the Prophet himself, Muslims pay high respect to his family, the first people to accept Islam, and then the companions who directly knew or saw the Prophet. The Prophet's first wife holds a special honor, as we already discussed. Muslims also respect his third wife, who taught us many things about virtue and honor. The men who first learned from Muhammad, then suffered and fought next to him, also receive high praise as his "companions." Finally, Muslims hold a special place for the men and women who heard Muhammad preach and whom he touched spiritually. These people, often also called "companions," helped spread the Prophet's message quickly across the Middle East and beyond.

What can we learn from this structure of respect? First, a principle of proximity affects the importance of the person. Muslims believe that the people closest to Muhammad felt the power of God more completely. Their witness, actions, and suffering command the most respect. Their memories and sayings about Muhammad have strongly influenced later Muslim perceptions of the Prophet. Though they did not always agree, and in fact fought bitterly, the early Companions still had the daunting task of cultivating both the religion and the political regime that Muhammad had started.

The growing circles of Muslim adherents provide an example for more general Islamic views of humanity. By definition—remember, it means "submission"—Islam focuses on the individual. No one can force another person to become Muslim, even if your family and culture are Islamic. From the beginning of their education, Muslim boys and girls learn that they must define themselves as Muslims by publicly proclaiming their belief in God and acceptance of Muhammad as God's Prophet on Earth.

Yet family and culture do matter to Islam. Like the wives, children, and extended family of the Prophet, Islam teaches that a person's close family, extended kin, and clan make up circles of familiarity that ripple outward from the individual. As we'll discuss more in Chapter 14, close family members may act more intimately with one another than people outside that small circle. One can be more open and less modest with parents and kin than extended family. Although your decision to be a Muslim may ultimately be personal, it's difficult to divorce yourself from your network of kinship and history.

The early companions of the Prophet, like other families, sometimes disagreed on the path Islam should take after his death. The first successor to Muhammad—his *caliph*—seemed like an easy choice. He was Abu Bakr, Muhammad's friend, fellow member of Muhammad's tribe (the Quraysh), and father of Aisha, Muhammad's third wife. However, Abu Bakr was not a member of the Hashim, Muhammad's clan. The closest Hashimite to the Prophet was Ali Ibn Abi Talib—Muhammad's nephew and son-in-law. Although very close to Muhammad, at his death Ali was only about 30 years old, much younger than Abu Bakr, which meant that Ali received less respect than the older man.

Muhammad's close circle supported Abu Bakr's rise to the position of caliph. Not just a religious successor to the Prophet, the caliph had to extend the political and military influence of Islam while also defending the faith against nonbelievers. By picking Abu Bakr, Islam began to develop its post-Prophet structure that (as we've seen) relied on piety, proximity, and kinship. These principles were not set in stone; some early Muslims argued that Ali made a better choice because of his blood ties to Muhammad, while others

preferred a larger circle of possible leaders, including men from his tribe and other early adherents.

Including Abu Bakr, four successors to Muhammad received the title of "rightly guided caliph." Each of them held power for a short time, and every one had to struggle with internal fighting among Muslims. As you can see in the chart on the opposite page, it took a while for Islam to work out forms of succession. Some Muslims emphasized the importance of close kinship, while others focused on the Muslim community's acceptance of a leader. That trend, however, turned into traditional dynasties as a son inherited his father's caliphate. These differences outline the variations in opinion related to community, kinship, and heredity in Islam's view of humanity.

In general terms, one group followed Uthman Ibn Affan (654–66 CE), who was killed by his Christian slave. This faction grew eventually into the *Sunni* branch of Islam, which spread incredibly quickly across Arabia, Africa, and into Europe (especially Spain). The other group argued for caliphs picked from among Prophet's kinsmen through the familial line of Ali Talib. They developed into the *Shia* branch of Islam, which found its home mostly in Persia (now Iran).

Women in Islam

By now (especially if you're a woman), you've probably noticed that all the leaders of Islam have been men. Muslims generally also use a masculine pronoun for God, although they believe that Allah transcends any gender distinction. What does this say about women in Islam?

In the Qur'an and throughout Islamic history, men and women developed complementary yet distinct roles and lines of authority. Although the Muslim community as a whole has naturally included women, men almost always take the leadership positions. Men could take multiple wives, but only if they could provide for all of them equally. Men could marry non-Muslims, but women had to convert their fiancés to Islam before getting married. Women could not take multiple husbands, and Qur'an taught that good wives were "devoted to God, true believers, devout, who turn to Him in repentance and worship Him, given to fasting, whether previously married or virgins" (66: 5).

Clearly, the structure and tradition of Islam places men in a position of authority. They are to take care of the women in their family and have far more avenues of expression and power than women. That being said, Muhammad introduced a level of civility and equity between men and women. He condemned the murder of baby girls by burying them in the sand, a practice often seen in pre-Islamic Arab societies. No longer could a man take as

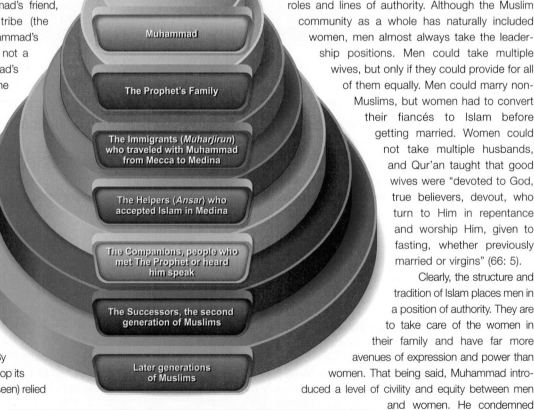

Muhammad

The Prophet's Family

The Immigrants (*Muharjirun*) who traveled with Muhammad from Mecca to Medina

The Helpers (*Ansar*) who accepted Islam in Medina

The Companions, people who met The Prophet or heard him speak

The Successors, the second generation of Muslims

Later generations of Muslims

> Islam most respects those who were closest to the Prophet. Their testimony has more influence on Islamic tradition than those who came afterward.

Caliphs and Sultans: The Successors to Muhammad

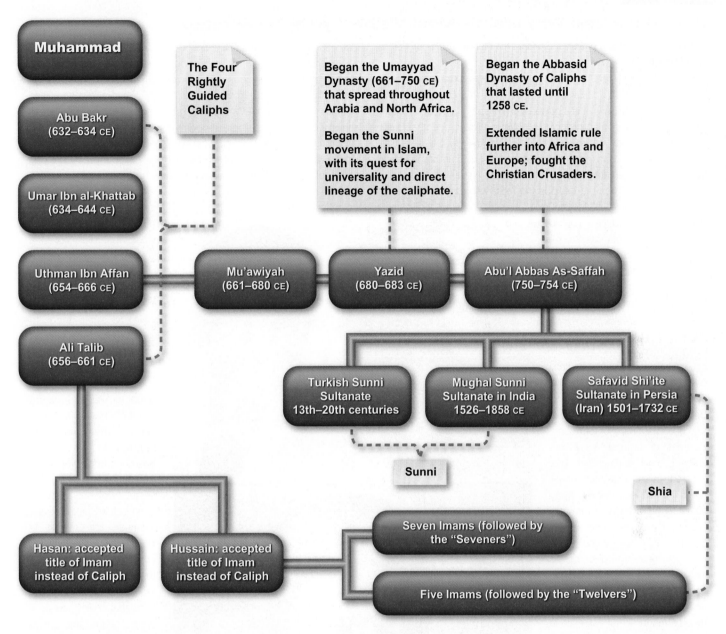

Muhammad

Abu Bakr (632–634 CE)

The Four Rightly Guided Caliphs

Began the Umayyad Dynasty (661–750 CE) that spread throughout Arabia and North Africa.

Began the Sunni movement in Islam, with its quest for universality and direct lineage of the caliphate.

Began the Abbasid Dynasty of Caliphs that lasted until 1258 CE.

Extended Islamic rule further into Africa and Europe; fought the Christian Crusaders.

Umar Ibn al-Khattab (634–644 CE)

Uthman Ibn Affan (654–666 CE)

Mu'awiyah (661–680 CE)

Yazid (680–683 CE)

Abu'l Abbas As-Saffah (750–754 CE)

Ali Talib (656–661 CE)

Turkish Sunni Sultanate 13th–20th centuries

Mughal Sunni Sultanate in India 1526–1858 CE

Safavid Shi'ite Sultanate in Persia (Iran) 1501–1732 CE

Sunni

Shia

Hasan: accepted title of Imam instead of Caliph

Hussain: accepted title of Imam instead of Caliph

Seven Imams (followed by the "Seveners")

Five Imams (followed by the "Twelvers")

Source: Based on Encyclopædia Britannica Online, Accessed March 8, 2010, http://search.eb.com/eb/article-9018680.

⋀⋀⋀ This chart details the development of the two modern branches of Islam. How do you think the origins of each branch affect how current-day Muslims view their groups?

many wives—and their riches—as he wanted. The "bride price" had to stay under a wife's control, to make sure she had income if her husband died (4: 2–13). Divorce became more mutual and less tilted toward male power: "When you divorce women and they have reached their set time, then either keep or release them in a fair manner. Do not hold on to them with intent to harm them and commit aggression: anyone who does this wrongs himself" (2: 231).

Muhammad himself found financial and spiritual support from his 13 wives, especially Khadijah (his first wife), and Aisha (who nursed him before his death). Remember that Muhammad first worked for Khadijah and that she—as a widow—offered herself in marriage to the future Prophet. After Muhammad's death, Aisha actively supported some caliphs over others,

distancing herself from Ali and personally fighting in battle. Both give examples of how Islam offers a more subtle approach to gender roles than we often assume.

The question of gender relations has become one of the most important topics in contemporary Muslim society. We will study this in greater detail in Chapter 14, but you should consider it whenever you think about the definition of humanity in Islam. Pick up any introduction to this tradition and you're sure to find at least one chapter devoted specifically to women. Some Muslim communities have active feminist communities, while others strongly oppose gender equality based on Islamic traditions. Yet even these distinctions don't explain the situation completely.

Behind the Veil: Why Islam's Most Visible Symbol Is Spreading

Embraced or banned, a prayer or a prison, the Muslim veil is spreading: Who wears it - and why?

(Caryle Murphy, "The Christian Science Monitor," December 12, 2009)

It liberates. It represses. It is a prayer. It is a prison. It protects. It obliterates. Rarely in human history has a piece of cloth been assigned so many roles. Been embroiled in so much controversy. Been so misjudged, misunderstood, and manipulated. This bit, or in some cases bolt, of fabric is the Islamic veil.

For non-Muslims, it is perhaps the most visible, and often most controversial, symbol of Islam. From Texas to Paris, it has gained new prominence and been at the center of workplace misunderstandings, court rulings, and, in Europe, parliamentary debates about whether it should be banned. The veil's higher profile stems from several factors, including greater awareness and curiosity about Islam since 9/11, U.S. military interventions in Muslim countries like Iraq and Afghanistan, and the rising visibility of Muslim immigrant communities in the United States and Europe. It has also become a magnet for trouble in times of distress, as Illinois resident Amal Abusumayah discovered when a woman upset about the Fort Hood, Texas, killing spree tugged Ms. Abusumayah's head scarf in a grocery store.

But the veil—in its many manifestations—also gives rise to disagreement among Muslims. And their contemporary debate about it, while not yet widespread, raises fundamental questions relating to free will, women's status in society, and even how to interpret Islam's holy book, the Koran.

In its broadest sense, the "Islamic veil" refers to a large variety of coverings. The most widely worn is the head scarf. Covering hair and neck, it can be black and simple, or colorful and sweeping, as in Cairo, where scarves are tightly wound around women's heads and then cascade luxuriously to their waists. The head scarf is often referred to as **hijab** or hejab, an Arabic word meaning a covering or a screen. *Mujahabat* means "women who are covered." There is sweeping consensus among Islamic religious scholars around the world that Muslim women are required to, or at least should, cover their hair. So the head scarf, or some type of head covering, is widely viewed as mandatory in Islam. Other coverings worn by Muslim women also fall within the category of "veil." Depending on the country, these outfits can be regarded as either optional or compulsory. Often they are said to be required on either religious or cultural grounds—categories that overlap in most Muslim countries. Iran's traditional covering, for example, is the chador, an ample black cloth that fits over the head and reaches to the ground. Women often hold part of it over their face in mixed company. The more modern Iranian cover is a head scarf accompanied by a longish, coat-type garment. Women in Saudi Arabia wear an oblong black scarf flipped twice over their heads, along with the abaya, a loose black robe. Many add the niqab, a square piece of cloth that covers the mouth and nose, or sometimes hides the entire face with only a slit for the eyes. The most restrictive covering by far is the burqa of Afghanistan, a long billowy smock that totally covers a woman from head to toe, including her face. She sees the world only through a small square of cloth webbing.

Non-Muslims tend to regard veiling as a sign of women's repression. That is true in highly patriarchal societies like Iran and Saudi Arabia, where women have second-class status and are required to cover both head and body when outside the home. But most Muslim women, including most in the United States, voluntarily opt to wear the head scarf out of religious commitment. They believe they are following God's wish, and reject suggestions that their head covering means they have less autonomy at home or on the job. "It's something that you love to do because it makes you feel that you are closer to Allah, that you're doing the right thing," says Reem Ossama, an Egyptian mother of three who covers her head when she leaves her home. "Allah ordered us to wear the scarf . . . to protect our dignity, to protect women, [so we would] not be looked at just as a beautiful body, a beautiful face, [so others would] look at our minds and our personalities." In addition to religious reasons, many Muslim women have adopted the head scarf to show pride in their faith, particularly in times like these when Islam is under attack from non-Muslims. It's a way for women to say, "I'm proud to be a Muslim and I want to be respected."

The Sira, Sunna, and Hadith

Because the Qur'an does not include many details of Muhammad's life, Muslims have relied on the *Sira*, the name for Muhammad's biography. By studying, interpreting, and applying the Sira, Muslims have created the *Sunna*, a compilation of traditions that teach us how to live. As Rabbinic Judaism relies on both the Torah and the Talmud, Islam uses both Qur'an and Sunna. Unlike much of Christian theology, it concentrates on correct actions instead of exact beliefs. According to legend, Muhammad himself defined a Muslim as anyone who follows its food rituals and faces Mecca while performing its prayers. Everything else, he implied, is secondary (Ayoub 110).

Muslims believe that over the centuries most humans have forgotten that only God controls the universe. They raise false idols and glorify themselves, rather than God. People assume that *they* have control over their surroundings and future. To counter this human tendency, Muhammad offered three ways to "return to your Lord" (96: 8):

1) His life (called "the actions")
2) Things he allowed (called "the consent")
3) His teachings (called "the sayings")

Muslim scholars created a branch of scholarship called **Hadith** to discover a chain of attribution (called an *isnad*) that led back to Muhammad himself. A strong isnad gives a tradition more power than one with a weak isnad.

The Qur'an and the Sunna thus provide the two main sources for **sharia**, Islamic law. In a way, they highlight Islam's understanding that all humans have two natures, spiritual and physical. We might think of the Qur'an as emphasizing the spiritual nature of humanity, while the Sunna focuses on the physical one. Muslim scholars also employ two other methods, called *Qiya* and *Ijma*, to develop sharia. Qiya refers to the search for God's will through rational analogy, using a system of precedent and history in coming to a decision. Ijma seeks consensus among legal scholars on interpretations. Defined as "the unanimous doctrine and opinion of the recognized authorities at any given time," Ijma gives Islam an organized way to interact with the changing world without giving up its core beliefs (El "Ijma" and Brown 158–159). Two main compilations (called "al Buhham" and "Muslim") codified sharia in the ninth century. Muslims in various regions follow four different schools of jurisprudence, each of which has produced its own interpretations, explanations, and directives. These tend to regulate Muslim behavior in worship and in social transactions according to five categories (Ayoub 123):

1. Obligatory (also called *halal*)
2. Recommended
3. Permitted
4. Disliked
5. Forbidden (also called *haraam*)

Finally, an individual sharia scholar (called a **mufti**) can hand down a precise ruling (called a **fatwa**) based on his own interpretation of sharia. Some Muslims are concerned that sharia cannot keep up with contemporary life and its issues, because its main structure has been fixed for more than 1,000 years. Others, however, argue that God's plan for humanity does not change; instead, human beings ought to follow sharia rather than try to change it.

Hijab is the head scarf worn by many observant Muslim women.

Hadith, a branch of Islamic scholarship, searches for a chain of attribution that leads back to Muhammad.

Sharia is Islamic law.

Mufti is a scholar of Islamic law.

Fatwa is a ruling handed down from an Islamic scholar based on his interpretation of Islamic law.

Religion + SECULAR LITERATURE

The fatwa of Salman Rushdie

Many non-Muslims first heard the term "fatwa" in 1989, when Iranian religious leader Ayatollah Khomeini called for the death of Salman Rushdie for insulting Islam in his novel *The Satanic Verses*. As a result of this extraordinary fatwa, Rushdie went into hiding for 10 years. The Iranian government dropped its support of the ruling in 1998, but Rushdie still worries about being attacked. Recently, he announced plans to write a book describing his ordeal. *(Associated Press)*

>>> Both Salman Rushdie (left) and Ruhollah Khomeini (right) were raised as Muslims, but their views on religion differ immensely.

The Organization of Islam

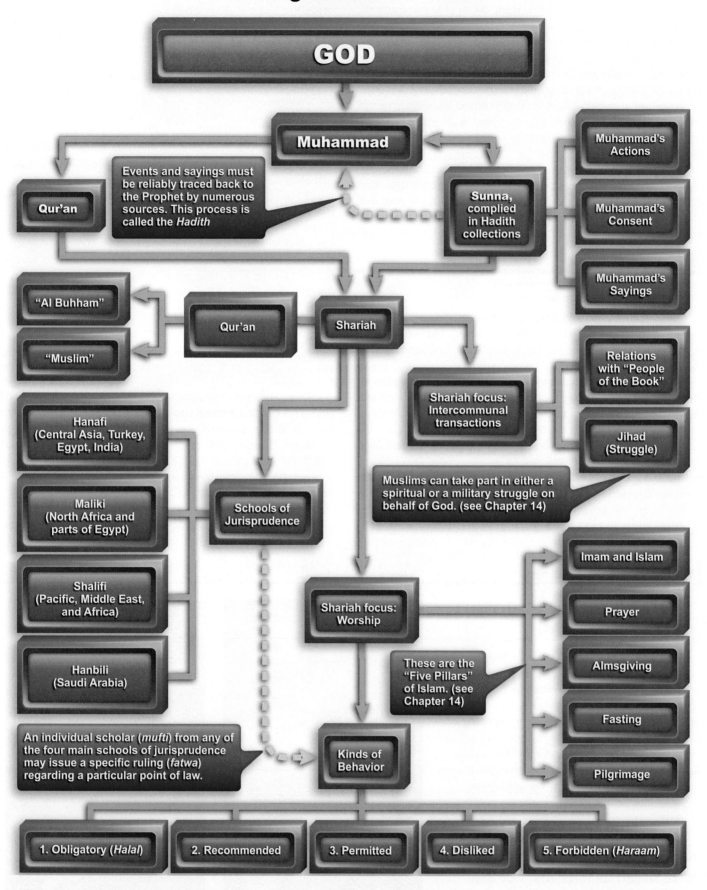

^ Follow the arrows on this chart to see how Islam traces God's will from Muhammad to
^ today.

> ∨
> ∨ Here are a few religious duties that all Muslims are expected to
> ∨ perform, as outlined in Islamic legal texts.

Religious Duties of Muslims

Pray a set number of times per day, in a set manner

Contribute to the yearly *zakat*, or donation to the less fortunate

Abstain from food, drink, and sexual intercourse from dawn until dusk during the month of Ramadan

Complete the Hajj to Mecca

Make war, or *jihad*, against polytheists

Complete proper funeral rituals, such as bathing the dead and speaking the required prayers

Source: Based on Brown 163–164.

What Happens After Humans Die?

Like Christianity, Islam developed a much more specific conception of heaven and hell than had existed Judaism. Also like Christianity, Muslims wrestled with the question of who might get to heaven, and who decides. On the one hand, if God is almighty, then we have little recourse through our own actions: Either we go to paradise or we do not. On the other hand, God has given us the ability to choose submission and faith to Him. This implies a form of free will that would seem to take away some of His power. The middle line, developed by Muslim theologians, explains that human beings constantly decide if and how they will submit themselves to God. On the other hand, God gets to decide whether he wants to act with righteous judgment or mercy on each one of us (Brown 174–176). The Qur'an explains it this way:

"Hurl every obstinate disbeliever into Hell,

everyone who hindered good, was aggressive, caused others to doubt, and set up other gods alongside God.

Hurl him into severe punishment!"—and his [evil] companion will say, "Lord, I did not make him transgress; he had already gone far astray himself."

God will say, "Do not argue in My presence. I sent you a warning and My word cannot be changed: I am not unjust to any creature."

We shall say to Hell on that day, "Are you full?" and it will reply, "Are there no more?"

But Paradise will be brought close to the righteous and will no longer be distant:

"This is what you were promised—this is for everyone who turned often to God and kept Him in mind,

who held the Most Gracious in awe, though He is unseen,

who comes before Him with a heart turned to Him in devotion—

so enter it in peace. This is the Day of everlasting Life." (50: 16–20; 24–34)

REVIEW

Summary

IS THERE A GOD?   p. 208

- There is one god: God (often called Allah). This is the same God as in Christianity and Judaism, however Muslims emphasize submission and faith toward Him more than the other two do.
- God is unknowable and unique. He is the omnipotent creator who exists outside of time and space.
- God is an omniscient judge, however He also shows mercy.
- The Qur'an holds the words of God, and it is thus perfect and unchangeable.

WHAT DOES IT MEAN TO BE HUMAN?   p. 215

- Muhammad is regarded as the quintessential Muslim, and by following his example, other Muslims can live devout lives.
- Islam is a deeply personal, as well as communal, matter. No one can force another to be a Muslim, as each must proclaim their own faith in God. However, the community of believers is also important, and good Muslims need not separate their religious lives from their social or political ones.

Key Terms

Suras are chapters of the Qur'an.   *209*

Kaaba, Islam's holiest shrine, is located in Mecca, Saudi Arabia.   *212*

Hijab is the head scarf worn by many observant Muslim women   *220*

Hadith, a branch of Islamic scholarship, searches for a chain of attribution that leads back to Muhammad.   *221*

Sharia is Islamic law.   *221*

Mufti is a scholar of Islamic law.   *221*

Fatwa is a ruling handed down from an Islamic scholar based on his interpretation of Islamic law.   *221*

Find it on

- http://www.islamfortoday.com/women.htm

The role of women in Islam is a topic that is often discussed. How do women see themselves in Islam? Visit the ThinkSpot to learn more about Muslim women and their role in today's Islamic society.

- http://www.islamicity.com/mosque/quran/

I don't know about you, but I find other sacred texts fascinating. It's interesting to see how religious texts from other faiths send similar messages to a particular faith's followers. If you are as interested in the "word" of Islam, go to the ThinkSpot to read different passages from the Qur'an and to learn more about Islam.

- http://www.youtube.com/watch?v=5P6NOl3-f-A

What does traditional Muslim worship look like? Visit the ThinkSpot to get an idea of how Islam is put into practice.

Questions for Study and Review

1. **Who are "people of the book," and what is their relationship to Muslims?**

   Jews and Christians are considered people of the book (aka, the Qur'an) because they worship the same monotheistic God as Muslims do. However, Islam does not consider Jesus the Messiah, or Abraham the father of Judaism. Instead, Muslims say, these men were great prophets who paved the way for the final messenger of God: Muhammad.

2. **Who was Muhammad, and how does he relate to the sacred?**

   Muhammad is considered God's prophet, and the final messenger of Islam. During his life, Muhammad acted as a religious, political, and military leader, uniting the Arabian Peninsula under Islam. Although Muhammad is revered in Islamic tradition, he is not considered a division of God—he was the perfect Muslim, but still simply a man.

3. **What role do women play in Islam?**

   Although leadership in Islam has traditionally stemmed from male authority, Muslim women enjoyed certain rights under Islam (such as the ability to divorce) that they had not been previously allowed. Muhammad's wives, especially Kadijah and Aisha, hold an important status in Islam, as they supported the Prophet and helped spread his teachings.

4. **Explain Islamic views on death and the afterlife.**

   Unlike Judaism, Islam has developed a specific idea of the afterlife. Muslims believe that human beings choose whether to submit to God, and in return, He decides whether to be merciful. When those who are faithful die, they enter Paradise. When those who have turned away from God die, they are cast into Hell.

<<< This Indonesian woman clasps her hands in a prayer for peace. What blend of cultures can you see in this photo? What does this tell us about the Muslim community?

HOW DO HUMANS INTERACT WITH THE SACRED?
HOW DOES THE SACRED BECOME COMMUNITY?

Imagine

the whole of Islam—every woman, child, and man who accepts God and Muhammad as his prophet. All together, they're called the *umma*, the community of all Muslims. It includes followers of Islam from Mecca to Manhattan to Malaysia.

On March 9, 2003, the woman in this photo gathered with a half-million other Indonesian Muslims in a field on the island of Java. Hands together, head covered with a beautiful green-embroidered cloth, she asked God to bring peace to the Middle East. The birthplace of Islam, the Middle East suffered from war in Iraq, hopelessness in the Palestinian region, and popular unrest in Saudi Arabia and Egypt. She asked for peace as the United States and Iran quarreled and Lebanon struggled to find harmony among its religious groups. The Indonesian woman hoped that God would hear her voice with a chorus of other faithfuls, renewing their submission to him and asking that he show mercy on the umma. She prayed the words of the *Bismillah*, taken from the Qur'an: "In the name of God, the Merciful Benefactor." And she surely remembered Muhammad's promise that communal prayer is 25 times more effective than praying alone (Waines 197). If that was the case, how might God receive the prayer of 500,000?

Prayer is one of Islam's five pillars. Along with witness, giving alms, fasting, and pilgrimage to Mecca, the five pillars focus on action rather than belief. Although they have developed different theological traditions, Muslims more often diverge on practice than on theology. Who should lead the Islamic community? How should you pray? How do you interpret sharia? This makes Islam different from Christianity, which has struggled to find precise definitions for its relationship to God. Look at this verse from the Qur'an, which describes good Muslims as people who *act* like good Muslims but also keep God in their hearts:

For men and women who are devoted to God-believing men and women, obedient men and women, truthful men and women, steadfast men and women, humble men and women, charitable men and women, fasting men and women, chaste men and women, men and women who remember God often—God has prepared forgiveness and a rich reward. (33: 35)

ISLAM:
The Pillars and the Umma

CHAPTER 14

Mecca

The highlight of a Muslim's religious life is the **hajj**, a once-in-a-lifetime pilgrimage to Mecca. Once there, Muslims reenact rituals performed by millions of other faithful, going back to Muhammad and, before him, Abraham. Here is a description of a hajj by Robert R. Bianchi, an American lawyer who has worked and taught in the United States and Egypt.

I spent the bulk of my time with Muhammad, the Egyptian tour leader, who was a university student in Chicago, and Sultan, a towering African American postal worker from Oakland. Most days, we were joined by Ashraf, an Egyptian engineer from Milwaukee, and Hussain, a Pakistani who ran a tourist shop in New Orleans. There were also a couple of married men who enjoyed our company whenever their wives had to share sleeping quarters with the other women. We jokingly called them the "brothers from Ohio," but they were really brothers-in-law—Middle Western farm boys married to sisters from a family of Syrian immigrants.

. . . The focal point of the [Prophet's Mosque in Medina] is a small area toward the front where the Prophet's pulpit and tomb are located. A narrow passage between the pulpit and tomb is known as Rauda al-Nabawiya—the Prophet's Garden—because tradition says he was accustomed to praying there. No matter how many additions the Saudis construct to expand the space for prayer, everyone still wants to be as close as possible to this tiny corner.

Security guards in the mosque allow pilgrims to pray briefly in the Rauda and then to pass quickly by the Prophet's tomb. Pilgrims can greet the Prophet as they would any dear friend, but they are not permitted to pray in front of his tomb because it would seem they were worshiping another human instead of God, especially because their backs are facing the *Ka'ba*. The steady crush of emotion-filled visitors and their recurrent clashes with whip-wielding guards makes this a flash point under any circumstances . . .

When we visited the Prophet's tomb, Sultan and I were astonished by the power of Muhammad's emotions. We had already made several trips to the mosque at different hours of the day and night, so we assumed this visit would be like the others—crowded but relaxed and convivial. Then, as we squeezed into the line passing in front of the tomb, we realized Muhammad was weeping uncontrollably.

Overcome by the surge of feeling he experienced in the Prophet's "presence," he froze, closed his eyes, and prayed in whispers, holding his open hands near his temples. Soon, others stood at his side, each in a similar posture. The flow of visitors slowed to a trickle and then stopped completely, putting unbearable pressure on the already weary crowd behind us.

∧∧∧ **Why would Muslims change into white** as they **start their pilgrimage?**

. . . After weeks of failure, Sultan finally pushed close enough to kiss the Black Stone, but just a few feet behind him the "brothers" from Ohio lost all their cash to thieves who slashed their clothes and money belts. Back in the hotel, Sultan—fearless and elated—boasted of his feat, giving heart to the hapless brothers, listening intently as they peeked out from their bunk beds, dazed and shaken but unharmed. (Bianchi 16–20)

▶ HOW DO HUMANS INTERACT WITH THE SACRED?

Each of the five pillars of Islam helps Muslims interact with God. We'll discuss three of them—bearing witness, prayer, and fasting—in this part of Chapter 14. We'll focus on the last two, pilgrimage (hajj) and almsgiving, in the second part of this chapter, because they also link Muslims to one another in the Islamic umma. Although we will generally use the English terms, you may also see the five pillars described in Arabic. Here are both forms, but I have taken off the diacritical marks used in scholarly works.

Arabic word	English Equivalent
Shahada (or shahadah)	Witness or profession of faith
Salat (or salah)	Prayer
Sawm (also called siyam)	Fasting
Zakat	Almsgiving or "religious tax"
Hajj	Pilgrimage

Shahada: Witnessing and Professing Faith in God

The first pillar of Islam supports all the others, for it requires Muslims to profess their faith in a single God and His final prophet, Muhammad. It acts both as a creed—a definition of faith—and also as a kind of initiation into Islam. As soon as a baby is born, parents whisper the Shahada, the first words the infant will hear: "There is no God but God and Muhammad is the Prophet of God." The child may grow up in an Islamic household with Muslim parents and siblings. Yet she will not be a Muslim until she says, with conviction and faith, these words herself. Direct, simple, and eloquent, the Shahada echoes passages throughout the Qur'an, as in Sura 3:62: "This is the truth of the matter: there is no god but God; God is the Exalted, the Decider."

The Shahada sums up Islam and summons believers to prayer. If you've ever been in an Islamic country, you've surely heard the words called out by the **muezzin** (or sometimes a recording) from the minarets of the town.

Yet this familiar call also introduces us to the largest disagreement among Muslims. If you listen to the muezzin ringing out from the top of a Sunni mosque like the Selimiye Masjid in Turkey, you'll hear exactly one version of the words. But if you were to walk the streets of Karbala, Iraq, the words will be a little different. There, the Shiite muezzin of Karbala will add, "I bear witness that Ali is the vice regent of God."

How could this be so controversial? To figure out the meaning behind that line, we need to learn more about the differences between

> **Hajj** is a sacred pilgrimage to Mecca and the fourth pillar of Islam.
> **Muezzin** is an official who calls Muslims to prayer.
> **Sunni Islam** includes about 80 percent of Muslims in the world, and emphasized scholarly and communal decision-making after the death of Muhammad.
> **Shia Islam** emphasizes the lineage of Muhammad and places great spiritual importance on the imams. Followers are referred to as Shiites.

Sunni and **Shia Islam**. As we do, you'll see how these variations affect different ways that Muslims witness and profess their belief in God.

THE SUNNI SHAHADA: EXPANDING THE UMMA

The roots of the Sunni-Shia split go back to the first generation of caliphs (successors) to Muhammad. As you'll remember from Chapter 13, Muhammad left no explicit instructions regarding who should lead the movement of Islam after he died. The social dynamics among these men, all Muhammad's friends, created the precursor to the divisions we see today. The group that became Sunni Islam emphasized communal decision-making by the *ulama*, scholars of the Qur'an, hadith, and sharia. A famous hadith explains that Muhammad preferred consensus among his people, saying, "Truly my umma will never agree together on an error" (El "Umma").

Sunni Muslims have both enjoyed the benefits and felt the responsibility of being the majority. The branch includes about 80 percent of all Muslims

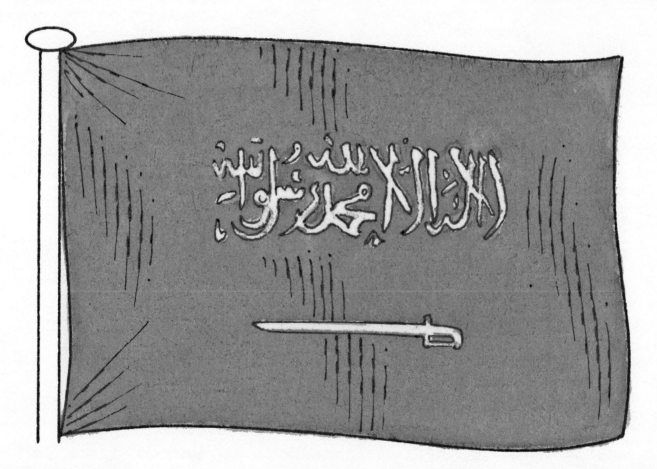

∧∧ The flag of Saudi Arabia, home of Mecca and Medina, includes the Shahada. Why would the kings of Saudi Arabia pick that to be on their flag? What does it say about the relationship of Islam and politics there?

There are slight differences in the Sunni and Shiite prayer calls. **How do you think this affects the Islamic umma?**

Adhan, the Call to Prayer

In Arabic	Translation	Sunni	Shiite	Number of Recitations
Allahu Akbar	God is great	✓	✓	four
Ash-hadu alla ilaha illallah	I bear witness that there is no lord except God	✓	✓	two
Ash-hadu anna Muhammadan rasulullah	I bear witness that Muhammad is the Messenger of God	✓	✓	two
Ash-hadu anna Aliya wali-ul-lah	I bear witness that Ali is the vice regent of God		✓	two
Hayya 'alas-salat	Make haste towards prayer	✓	✓	two
Hayya 'alal-falah	Make haste towards welfare	✓	✓	two
Assalatu khayru min an-naum	Prayer is better than sleep	✓		two
Hayya- al Khair al amal	Make haste towards the best thing		✓	two
Allah u Akbar	God is great	✓	✓	two
La ilaha illallah	There is no lord except God	✓	✓	two

Source: Based on Brown 10–11.

>>> An interior photo of the Hagia Sophia. It was first a church, then a mosque, and now a museum. Why would Muslim rulers in Istanbul leave a mosaic showing Jesus and Mary, but also install verses from the Qur'an?

worldwide, an incredibly diverse group. Sunni Muslims follow many local traditions regarding clothing, language, and interpretations of the sharia. When you think of this global umma, remember that the Qur'an explains, "All people were originally one single community, but later they differed" (10: 19). Islam's goal is to reunite them again in submission to God.

The political history of Sunni Islam relates directly to the dynasties that began shortly after the Prophet's death and continued into the 20th century. Yazir, the son of Mu'awiyah, left the caliphate to his son in a tradition that became the Umayyad Dynasty, lasting for 89 years. The Umayyad Empire grew with incredible speed, spreading across the Arabian Peninsula, North Africa, and edging toward Europe. It took Jerusalem from the Byzantine Empire and built the Dome of the Rock mosque, one of the most important in the world, on the spot where the Jewish Temple once stood.

In its success, the Umayyad leaders began to develop a form of Islam based on the twin authorities of the Qur'an and the sunna as revealed through the hadith. Jews and Christians were permitted to retain the structure of their communities and worship openly. These "people of the book" simply had to pay a special tax to the caliph. If they converted to Islam, that tax disappeared (Ayoub 81–86).

As the years following Muhammad's death wore on, piety and religious authority waned as the Umayyads focused increasingly on political, economic, and military leadership. Political power stayed with the caliphs, but they did not retain the spiritual authority of the first few. As time went on, Muslims began to identify the Umayyad leaders with laxity in Muslim discipline and impious focus on political or military power. Islam seemed ready for a revival.

∧∧∧ The Muslim Dome of the Rock stands in the right foreground of this picture, with the Christian Church of the Holy Sepulchre to the left. What point might the Umayyad caliphs have been trying to make when they built the Dome of the Rock?

In 750 CE, a renewal movement, led in part by Shiites (followers of Shia Islam), ousted the Umayyad caliphs from power and installed the new Abbasid Dynasty. The Shiites lost influence, however, after instigating an insurrection that led to bloody reprisals. Instead, Abbasid rulers paradoxically supported Sunni scholarship while also introducing a measure of worldly enjoyment to the court. (Charlemagne's Europe of the same time, to the contrary, had a much more austere culture.) The umma continued to grow as the Abbasids expanded Islam even further into Africa and Europe, but that led to decentralization and competition among dynastic parties. Like the Umayyad caliphs before them, the Abbasid rulers proved to be incredibly successful, as they too had the goal of establishing Islam all over the world. But also like their predecessors, the Abbasid caliphs could not simultaneously lead a political empire and maintain spiritual authority. Again and again, pious Muslims called for renewal to strengthen the empire's witness to God and to revive the piety of the umma (Ayoub 86–90).

In 1258 CE, ruthlessly efficient Mongol armies swept through Asia. On their tiny, tireless ponies, the Mongols had already broken Chinese, Russian, and other powers as they sped westward. They took Baghdad, the Abbasid capital, and the already shaky dynasty fell. Ironically, though, this setback eventually helped the umma spread, as lines of communication and travel expanded eastward. The Mongols had less interest in religion than tribute, so Christians in Moscow or Muslims in Baghdad could continue to live so long as they appropriately bowed down to Mongol leadership and paid heavy taxes.

The Mongols proved to be less adept at long-term rule than they were at taking over vast territories. Over the course of a couple hundred years, the Mongol groups integrated into local elites and gave way to three regional and highly successful Muslim empires: the Ottoman Empire (based in Turkey), the Safavid Empire (in Persia), and the Mughal Empire (in India). In turn, each of these developed its own traditions, always broadening the lens of Islam on the world.

The Ottomans pushed their way into Europe, conquering the Byzantine Empire and taking its capital, Constantinople in 1453 CE. The victors remade the Cathedral of Hagia Sophia into a mosque, covering its mosaics of saints with a fresh coat of plaster. In this way, the Ottomans transformed the spiritual center of Orthodox Christianity into a symbol of Islamic success.

In the 16th century, the legendary Ottoman ruler Suleiman the Magnificent led an army more deadly than any in Europe. No wonder George Sandys so breathlessly recounted life among the Ottoman Muslims to his English audience. Suleiman, the successor to Constantine, hung huge round calligraphic signs in the cathedral, reminding everyone that God was great and Muhammad, not Jesus, was the final prophet who gave us the Word of God.

The Spread of Islam

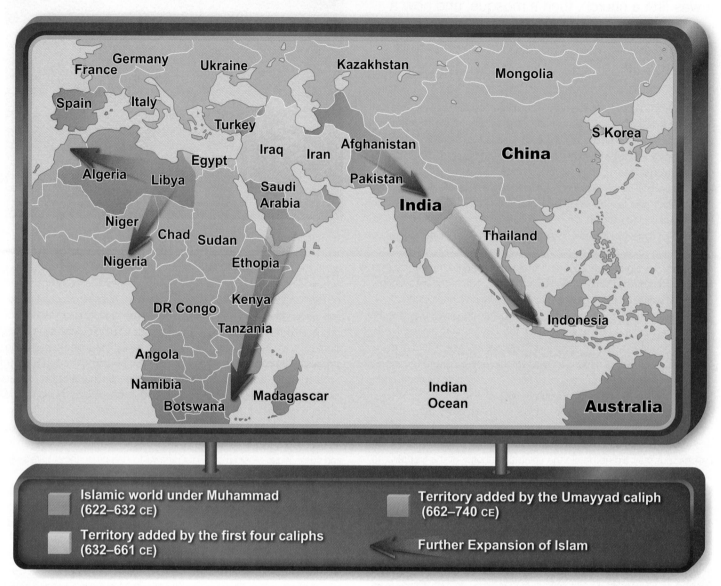

Source: Based on "The Spread of Islam," http://wps.ablongman.com/wps/media/objects/262/268312/art/figures/KISH_07_156.gif.

> ∧
> ∧ Islam spread rapidly in the century following Muhammad's death. How does this
> ∧ expansion compare to the spread of Christianity, as discussed in the previous chapters?

The Ottoman Empire renamed Constantinople as "Istanbul" and incorporated elements of Byzantine and European culture. If the Hagia Sophia were to be the empire's main mosque, then smaller masjids (like the one opening Chapter 13) could sometimes take on architectural features of Christian churches. Sitting at the edge of Europe and Asia, the Ottoman Empire looked both southeast toward Mecca and northwest into Europe. Its ships and scholars crossed the Adriatic and Mediterranean seas, interacting with Venetians and Greeks, and fighting the Holy Roman Emperors in Eastern Europe for religious, political, and economic control of the region. Cities like Budapest developed a cosmopolitan feel that had aspects of both European Christian and Ottoman Muslim culture. The Crimean and Black Seas also became melting pots for Christians and Muslims as the Muscovite Russians sought to wrest control in the name of Orthodox Christianity and reclaim the mantle of Byzantium.

The Ottoman Empire struggled with other peoples of the book. The Mughals, however, spread Islam through the Indian subcontinent and across the islands of the Pacific Ocean. Led by Emperor Akbar ("the Great"), the Mughal Empire expanded its witness of God and the Prophet into Hindu and Buddhist lands. Naturally, in areas where Hinduism or Buddhism predominated, Muslims conversion did not happen as readily as it did when it spread to a region where no single religion dominated. It was more difficult to meld local traditions with Islam in India because Hinduism seemed to celebrate everything that Islam forbade: multiple gods, avatars, sculptures, and the belief that gods and people shared the divine essence of creation (Brahman) rather than being made by a creator god.

The spread of Islam throughout India often created tension, especially as the ruling dynasty was Muslim, not Hindu. Yet Islamic leaders

∧∧∧ **Muslim empires** often developed highly sophisticated centers of learning, maintaining ancient knowledge otherwise lost to the rest of Asia and Europe. **Pictured here are Ottoman Muslim astronomers at an observatory founded in 1557.** Why might Muslim scientists be particularly interested in astronomy?

chapter. Look back at that photo and you'll be able to realize just how large the Sunni Islamic umma really is.

The Shia Shahada: Purity and Fidelity

Tradition says that all the close companions of Muhammad agreed on Abu Bakr as the first caliph, even though some people thought that Ali, the Prophet's nephew, made a better choice. Tensions remained between the two groups for decades, as Muslims had to figure out whether family, clan, tribe, or other relationship to Muhammad ought to matter the most when picking his successor. In a small group that had no ambitions of growth, this would not have been so important. But early Islam was growing rapidly through military, social, religious, and economic ties with other regions. Should Muslim leadership always reside with Muhammad's family, to ensure pure leadership, even as Islam spread further from Mecca?

The first four "rightly guided" caliphs sought to strengthen Islam's political power while also keeping a firm hand on religious leadership. They felt pressure from the family of Ali, but also tried to rein in other new interpretations of Islam. Similar to the development of Rabbinic Judaism

∧∧ What Muslim and Hindu influences do you see in this picture of the **Mughal king, Akbar?**

like Akbar frequently found common ground with the wise yogis of Hinduism and even sought out their advice. As it interacted with local traditions and cultures, Islam in Asia developed a different focus than in Arabia. Though sometimes borne by arms, Islam more often spread through cultural and economic contacts. From 1300–1500 CE, it grew quickly along South Asia and South East Asia. Muslim traders introduced Islam in port cities throughout the Pacific, sometimes by marrying local women and converting them. Though often overshadowed by their Arab brothers and sisters in the news, Asians now account for about one-third of all Muslims worldwide (Ayoub 106–08). Finally, as it moved eastward, Islam took on an increasingly Asian feel. You can see this in the head-covering worn by the woman in the beginning of this

Message to the Blackman in America by Elijah Muhammad

Islam's spread around the world did not stop in ancient times. Its message of faith and submission to God resonates today with people struggling to find meaning in the modern world. For thousands of African Americans over the last century, Islam has offered a way to stand up to injustice and to seek strength from within. First led by Wallace D. Fard (Wallace Fard Muhammad), the Nation of Islam mixed traditional Islam with Black Nationalist ideas. It grew under the leadership of Elijah Muhammad and then Malcolm X, who broke away from the movement when he re-aligned himself with Sunni Islam. Elijah Muhammad's son, Warithuddin Muhammad, also found solace in orthodox Islam. Louis Farrakhan, however, led much of the Nation back to Elijah Muhammad's teachings. The movement now has two main parts, divided on their relationship to traditional Islamic teaching and organization (El "Muslimun").

Here are a few verses from Chapter 8 of Elijah Muhammad's classic text. As you read it, consider how the author connects Biblical language, Islamic teaching, anti-White sentiment, and a call for Black self-help. You may want to return to *Message to the Blackman in America* in Chapter 16, when we study New Religious Movements.

Chapter 8: The Coming of God and the Gathering Together of His People

⁵ Allah came to us from the Holy City Mecca, Arabia, in 1930. He used the name Wallace D. Fard, often signing it W. D. Fard, in the third year (1933). He signed his name W. F. Muhammad which stands for Wallace Fard Muhammad. He came alone. He began teaching us the knowledge of ourselves, of God and the devil, of the measurement of the earth, of other planets, and of the civilization of some of the planets other than earth.

⁶ He measured and weighed the earth and its water; the history of the moon, the history of the two nations, black and white that dominate the earth. He gave the exact birth of the white race, the name of their God who made them and how; and the end of their time, the judgment how it will begin and end.

⁷ He taught us the truth of how we were made "slaves" and how we are kept in slavery by the "slave master's" children. He declared the doom of America for her evils to us was past due. And that she is number one to be destroyed. Her judgment could not take place until we hear the truth.

⁸ He declared that we were without the knowledge of self or anyone else. How we had been made blind, deaf and dumb by this white race of people and how we must return to our people, our God and His religion of peace (Islam), the religion of the prophets. We must give up the slave names of our slave masters and accept the name of Allah (God) or one of His divine attributes. He also taught us to give up all evil doings and practices and do righteousness or be destroyed from the face of the earth.

⁹ He taught us that the slave-masters had taught us to eat the wrong food and that this wrong food is the cause of our sickness and short span of life. He declared that he would heal us and set us in heaven at once, if we would submit to Him. Otherwise He would chastise us with a severe chastisement until we did submit. And that He was able to force the whole world into submission to his will. He said that he loved us (the so-called Negroes), his lost and found, so well that he would eat rattlesnakes to free us if necessary for he has power over all things.

¹⁰ I asked him, "Who are you, and what is your real name?" He said, "I am the one that the world has been expecting for the past 2000 years." I said to him again, "What is your name?" He said, "My name is Mahdi; I am God, I came to guide you into the right path that you may be successful and see the hereafter." He described the destruction of world with bombs, poison gas, and finally with fire that would consume and destroy everything the present world.

¹¹ Nothing of the present world of white mankind would be left. Those escaping the destruction would not be allowed to carry anything out with them.

. . . .

¹⁵ This includes the history of the world and a knowledge of God and the devil. He condemned the teachings of God not being a man as a lie from the devils for the past 6,000 years; he said that Christianity was a religion organized and backed by the devils for the purpose of making slaves of black mankind.

¹⁶ I also bear witness that it certainly has enslaved my people here in America, 100 per cent. He chose me to bear the message of life (Islam) to my people here. Islam is our salvation. It removes fear, grief, and sorrow from any believer and it brings to us peace of mind of contentment.

¹⁷ The greatest hindrance to the truth of our people is the [sic] of Christianity. He will not accept it, nor is he content to let others alone who are trying to accept the truth. He is the man who stands in the way of the salvation of his people, and as soon as the people awaken to the knowledge of this man in their way to God, freedom, justice and equality and stop following him, the sooner they will be in heaven while they live.

The Internet Archive, "Message to the Blackman in America," Accessed April 9, 2010, http://www.archive.org/details/MessageToTheBlackmanInAmerica.

the **THINK**SPOT
www.thethinkspot.com

∧
∧ This 17th-century fresco depicts Shiite
∧ women mourning the death of their
men, who fell in combat with the Sunni majority.

and the Christian church of the ecumenical councils, it wasn't clear at the time exactly which group would dominate Islam in the years to come. (Scholars would say that no single strain of Islamic belief and practice had become normative.) Instead, different groups vied for power through a mixture of political, religious, and even military actions. Arab and Bedouin tribes had long resorted to violence to defend their authority and honor, and this fighting also affected Islam.

Ali, the Prophet's nephew, served as caliph for just five years, picked by the umma after the pious Uthman had been murdered by his Christian slave. Uthman's supporters argued that Ali had not effectively brought the slave to justice, intimating that Ali might have been behind the killing himself. Aisha, Muhammad's beloved wife, backed this group against Ali, and open warfare broke out. Aisha even took to the battlefield, but Ali's troops captured her and sent her safely away. Ali sought compromise, which angered his most ardent supporters as giving in to the enemy, and who then turned against him, too. Called the Kharijites, they murdered Ali for accepting arbitration with Uthman's supporters. Rather than compromise, the Kharijites interpreted Ali's actions as losing religious purity and not standing up for the truth.

Ironically, this left the caliphate to the successor of Uthman (named Mu'awiyah), rather than to Ali's sons Hasan and Hussein. They accepted the title **imam**. The Kharijites suffered complete defeat, but their ideal of purity lived on even after their movement died. Ali's son Hussein agreed to wait until Mu'awiyah had died before pressing to succeed him as caliph. It was not to be. Mu'awiyah's army attacked Hussein and his supporters in Karbala, now part of Iraq. They showed no mercy to the son of Ali, brutally killing him, his family, and his troops. This cemented Mu'awiyah's control as caliph, but at a great cost: Hussein's martyrdom marked the symbolic birthday of Shia Islam, as Ali's supporters looked to the Prophet's familial lineage for leadership, and endeavored to keep Islam pure.

Having lost political power, the growing party of Ali—the Shiites—looked to their imams for spiritual leadership. After all, they were the true heirs to the Prophet, because they came from the same family

Imam is a Muslim leader and successor of Muhammad (following the line of Ali).

as Muhammad, Ali, and Hussein. Some Shiites claim that seven men rightly held the title "imam." They're called "Seveners" for this reason. Most Shiites, however, recognize twelve imams, and thus receive the name "Twelvers." The last imam, according to Twelver tradition, never died. Instead, he disappeared—hid himself—from the world and is living on until he is ready to reappear to the faithful. The Ismaili tradition, related to the Twelvers, had a highly militaristic view of Islam, and they developed a huge empire through North Africa and into Sicily (Brown 134–136).

Over the next centuries, Shia and Sunni Islam developed along roughly parallel paths, each with its own hadith and sharia traditions. Except in Persia, where the Safavid Empire embraced the Shiite tradition, most political leaders preferred the Sunni system. The majority of Shiites, therefore, had to figure out how to exist with neither a caliph nor a visible imam (although they believed that one lived somewhere). Often, in fact, the Shiites had to hide their true beliefs, so that they might live to witness a dominant Shia Islam at some later date.

The Shiites developed ways of thinking about the world and God that seemed strange to Sunni Muslims. For example, Shiites added a line to the Shahada to remind all Muslims that that Ali and Hussein had died in defense of the truth. Shiite judgments from the sharia tended to be stricter than Sunni ones. Hussein took on nearly messianic qualities in Shiite theology, which taught that his suffering helped to assuage the guilt of all human beings, and faith in him could bring salvation to a believer. As a result, Shiite Muslims travel far and long to commemorate Hussein's death in Karbala.

∧ Every year, Shiite Muslim men come to
∧ Karbala to remember the death of
Hussein, son of Ali and family member of Muhammad. This photo was taken in 2006. What effect would this intense form of worship have on people?

Ayatollah is a top-ranking scholar of Muslim law in Shia Islam.

Salat, or prayer, provides Muslims a direct way of interacting with God. It is the second pillar of Islam.

Today, Shiites often perceive the world in more apocalyptic terms than their Sunni counterparts do, recounting Shiite stories about the affliction of their leaders and persecution by the Sunni majority. For Shiites, professing the truth of Islam has held far more risks than for Sunni Muslims, and the stakes are also higher. When will the Twelfth Imam choose to return to our sight, leading all people back to the true witness of God through his prophet's family and their successors?

Shiite Muslims tended to develop their traditions based on their minority status. The Twelver tradition taught that all secular power (even held by Shiites) could never be legitimate, because only the Imam could rule in Muhammad's place. The Safavid Empire, though, gave Shia the opportunity to develop as a majority. Although not as long-lived as the Ottoman or Mughal Empires, the Safavid Empire did develop Shiite Islam to new heights. Most importantly for our study, it gave political backing to the Shiite movement. Under Safavid rule, *mullahs* (the Shiite equivalent to the ulama) worked out the problem of the hidden Imam: if he were not present, who should lead the state? Although Shiites disagreed on this important point, some mullahs began to claim that they could hold power as representatives of the Imam until he showed himself on Earth. They took the name *mudjtahid*, independent scholars of Muslim law. Ultimately, the highest-ranking of the mudjtahid received the name **Ayatollah**, the "Miraculous Sign of God" (Waines 193–95; E.I. "Ayatullah" and "Mudjtahid").

The split between Sunni and Shiite Muslims illustrates the paradox of unity and diversity in Islam. The Qur'an often states that all people will eventually unite in Islam. Yet, in other places, it seems to acknowledge disagreements. A famous hadith explains that Muhammad foresaw 73 different sects of Islam, though only one

would be correct. This varied heritage sometimes leads Muslims to emphasize the unity of all monotheistic Peoples of the Book. Other times, however, Muslims focus on pan-Islamic unity. In many cases, though, Muslim equally condemn rival Islamic groups, while also denouncing non-Muslims.

Interacting with the Divine Through Prayer: The Second Pillar of Islam

Like its Jewish and Christian neighbors, Islam has long emphasized prayer as the most direct way to interact with God. If the first pillar celebrates Muslims' submission to God, then the second—prayer—gives every Muslim a language to speak to Him.

Muslim prayer emphasizes form and structure, more like Jewish, Catholic, and Orthodox Christian prayer than the freestyle approach in Evangelical Christianity. The Qur'an tells Muslims to stop everything— work, school, or cooking—five times each day. They follow a traditional set of steps in **salat** (prayer) that integrate words of the Qu'ran, gestures, bows, and prostrations. As you examine the chart on the opposite page, consider how prayer can help a devout Muslim to reinforce his or her faith and submission to God.

Interacting with God through Food and Fasting: The Third Pillar of Islam

In addition to prayer, Islam uses food as a form of interaction with the sacred. Eating or touching pork results in ritual uncleanliness. The Qur'an and hadith prohibit other substances, too, especially alcohol. Unlike Judaism or Christianity, which elevate wine to ritual importance in some situations, Islam offers no such exception to the general prohibition of alcoholic beverages. (This does not extend to all intoxicating

V
V **In China,** Muslim men stop everything for prayer, while a young girl prays with other
V women on a city street. How would stopping five times a day to pray affect the way you interact
with the world?

Steps of Salat

1 **Face the Kabaah**
Wherever you are located, you must face the direction of the holy shrine in Mecca.

2 **State your intention**
State your intent to observe the specific prayer you're about to perform.

3 **Raise your hands to the side of your head and say "Allahu Akbar"**
This statement acknowledges that God is great. Repeat this phrase every time you change position throughout the salat.

4 **Lower your hands and recite the first sura of the Qur'an**

5 **Bow at the waist**
Repeat "Allahu Akbar" (God is great), and keep your gaze on the floor.

6 **Return to standing**
Say "Sami' Allahu liman hamidah" (God hears those who praise him).

7 **Kneel prostrate on the floor**
Touch your forehead to the floor and say "Subhaana Rabbiyal Allaa" (Glory to my Lord, the Highest).

8 **Rise to a sitting position, then return to prostration.**
Touch your forehead to the floor and again say the phrase "Subhaana Rabbiyal Allaa" (Glory to my Lord, the Highest). This completes the first *Rukkah* (unit) of the salat, which is then repeated.

9 **Sit back and recite the Shahadah**
After you have finished repeating the correct number of *Rukkahs*, sit back on your knees and recite the First Pillar of Islam.

10 **Turn your face to the right and to the left, repeating "Assalaamu Alaikum"** (Peace be with you)

Sources: Based on Ayoub 56–58 and Maqsood 61–73. For online descriptions of Islamic prayer, see "How to Perform *Salah*," the Islamic Association of Raleigh, http://islam1.org/how_to_pray/salah.htm, retrieved March 11, 2010, and "Islam Unraveled," "The Submitters Contact Prayers," http://www.islamunraveled.org/islam-basics/religious-duties/contact-prayer.php#howtoperform, retrieved March 11, 2010.

∧
∧ While variations exist among regions, the general Islamic salat, or prayer,
∧ includes these ten basic steps. How does the combination of words and actions mirror the overall philosophy of Islam?

Islam and Ritual Purity

By this point in your study of *THINK World Religions*, you've probably noticed that many religious traditions differentiate between ritually clean and unclean states. We first saw this in Hinduism, but it appears other places, too, including Judaism and Christianity. Islam has developed a keen sense of the ritually pure and impure. For Muslims, impurity tends to relate to death, blood, and to things that come out of the human body. These include semen, menstrual blood, urine, and excrement. Coming into contact with a dead body or any of those substances makes you ritually unclean. In that state, you should not take part in daily prayers, meet for Friday congregational services at the mosque, or take part in any ritual interactions with God. Muslims will often use their right hand for clean actions (such as handling prayer beads) while reserving the left hand for unclean actions (such as cleaning up after using the toilet).

Ritual purity and health often go together. Washing with water often takes care of both physical and ritual dirt, and mosques generally have a ritual washing place outside their doors. They are following this command from the Qur'an:

O believers, when you stand up for the service of prayer wash your faces and hands up to elbows, and also wipe your heads, and wash your feet up to the ankles. If you are in a state of seminal pollution, then bathe and purify yourself well. But in case you are ill or are travelling, or you have satisfied the call of nature, or have slept with a woman, and you cannot find water, then take wholesome dust and pass it over your face and your hands, for God does not wish to impose any hardship on you. He wishes to purify you, and grace you with His favors in full so that you may be grateful. (5: 6)

A well-known hadith of Muhammad continues the instruction on ritual purification, often called "ablution." The Encyclopedia of Islam, an excellent source for scholarly descriptions of Islam, describes the two versions of ablution. The first is *wudu*, a more minor ritual. More intense uncleanness leads a person to perform *ghusl*.

[O]nce the proper amount of fluid is procured, the believer inclines his heart to the purpose; recites the [bismillah]; washes his hands three times up to the wrists, making sure to reach the spaces between his fingers; takes water in his right hand and brings it up to his mouth, where he gargles it and then spits it out, each three times (if possible, cleaning the teeth with a toothpick is performed at this point); he takes water with his right hand again, snuffs it up his nose and blows it out into his left hand, also three times; washes his face from forehead to chin and from ear to ear, and runs his moistened fingers through his beard, all three times; washes his right arm up to the elbow three times, then his left arm up to the elbow three times; wipes his whole head once (according to al-Shafii and some others, thrice), including the outside and inside of the ears; and washes his right foot, then his left, each three times up to the ankles, making sure to reach the spaces in between the toes.

Ghusl begins, after the niyya, with a washing of the private parts with the left hand, followed by a washing of that hand thrice; wudu is then performed, excluding the feet; next, water is poured over the head three times, thoroughly wetting the hair; the whole head and body are then washed, starting with the right side and making sure water reaches every part of the body; finally the feet are washed. (E.I. "Ablution")

As you can imagine, Muslims around the world interpret ritual cleanness and impurity in different ways, based on varying traditions. George Sandys noticed that in his description of Islam, printed over three centuries ago. Shiites tend to wash their feet a little less intently than Sunnis during wudu because of differing interpretations of Qur'anic texts. More generally, a Muslim in Saudi Arabia will tend to view ritual purity quite differently than his counterpart in northern China or Detroit, Michigan. An Indian student of mine says her parents remind her only to give and receive money with the "clean" right hand.

Why do you think that ritual cleanness and impurity exists in so many religious traditions? Why might these ideas intensify or die away?

<<< Here men wash their feet at the Sultan Mosque. Why would Muslims wash their feet before beginning prayer? Why do feet and shoes seem to play a part in so many religious traditions?

Meat must be killed in a ritually pure way before observant Muslims can eat it. In a practice very similar to following Jewish kosher laws, a Muslim butcher kills the animal swiftly with a sharp knife-cut to the throat. He must then drain the blood of the animal before butchering it into edible pieces. In big cities in America and Europe, you can easily find these *halal* butchers or *halal* restaurants, especially near a mosque. Some Muslim scholars recommend that Muslims buy kosher meat if no halal butcher is nearby.

In addition to abstaining from particular foods at all times, Muslims reserve one month a year—Ramadan—as a time of abstinence from daybreak to sunset. Anyone without age or health problems should fast during Ramadan, not even drinking water during the day. Because Islam follows a lunar calendar, Ramadan changes each year in relation to the secular calendar. Sometimes, Ramadan falls during the winter, when the days are short. Other times, though, it coincides with the longest days of the year, making fasting much more difficult. Yet Muslims try to view this as a gift from God rather than as a hardship to be endured. They seek solace in the words of the Qur'an as it instituted the Ramadan fast:

> You who believe, fasting is prescribed for you, as it was prescribed for those before you, so that you may be mindful of God. Fast for a specific number of days, but if one of you is ill, or on a journey, on other days later. For those who can fast only with extreme difficulty, there is a way to compensate—feed a needy person. But if anyone does good of his own accord, it is better for him, and fasting is better for you, if only you knew. It was in the month of Ramadan that the Quran was revealed as guidance for mankind, clear messages giving guidance and distinguishing between right and wrong. So any one of you who is present that month should fast, and anyone who is ill or on a journey should make up for the lost days by fasting on other days later. God wants ease for you, not hardship. He wants you to complete the prescribed period and to glorify Him for having guided you, so that you may be thankful. (2: 183–185)

The ritual of Ramadan both complies with the Qur'an and reenacts Muhammad's experience of spending a month in the mountains, during which he began to receive the Qur'an from God. During parts of

∧
∧ This McDonald's offers Islam-approved
∧ chicken nuggets. **Where do you think this picture was taken?**

substances: Muslims often smoke tobacco, and millions of people in Africa chew chat, a leaf with some mild mind-altering effects.) Like observant Jews, Muslims must simply accept some of these prohibitions as divinely inspired, even if they do not understand them. Perhaps pork should not be eaten because it used to be difficult to keep it from going bad. Perhaps alcohol loosened the tongue and lowered inhibitions between men and women.

>>> Muslims celebrate the holiday of Eid-al-Fitr at the end of Ramadan. **This Malaysian family prays before breaking the fast.**

Sufism is a mystical branch of Islam that emphasizes the constant remembrance of God.

Ramadan, people may cut themselves off from society, even living inside the mosque so that they can completely focus on God. On the night in the month of Ramadan that Muslims believe God first spoke to Muhammad, many believers will pack the local mosque, listening to the Qur'an recited aloud by people who have memorized the entire text. In the morning, Muslims often break their fast with a handful of dates, just as the Prophet did.

Here is a contemporary Muslim author describing Ramadan for an English-speaking audience. He describes the month as one of work, but also joy:

> Ramadan is seen as the most significant of months, a time of spiritual and physical discipline, and a time for making extra effort to spread love, peace, and reconciliation.
>
> Muslim fasting involves deliberately cultivating a peaceful and prayerful attitude of mind, and undergoing the physical discipline of giving up all food, liquid, smoking and sexual intercourse during the hours of first light of dawn to sunset for the entire month. Nobody starves to death,

for all these things are allowed after sunset, until the first light of the next day's dawn when a black thread can be distinguished from a white one. It is not just a question of going without food; that is only one aspect of it, and indeed, it is not the most important aspect. Allah pointed out that if a person could not give up evil ways, violence, greed, lust, anger and malicious thoughts, he had no need of their giving up food and drink. It would be meaningless. (Maqsood 77–78)

Sufism: Mystical Interaction with the Sacred

Take another look at the quotation from the Qur'an at the beginning of this chapter, in which God promises forgiveness and reward to "men and women who remember God often" (33: 35). What might that mean? How can anyone "remember God" when we are creation and God is the creator? For Muslims, the mystical path of **Sufism** offers a path toward remembrance.

Sufis take their name from the Arabic word for wool, because early mystical Muslims sometimes wore harsh wool clothing to remind them always to remember God. The Sufi tradition crosses into Shia and Sunni, Arab and non-Arab, as it "disperses in the land" and looks for "God's bounty" (Surah 63:20).

You may see hints of mystical Christianity in Sufism, for the two grew up side by side on the Arabian Peninsula. Both, for example, seek a life completely in tune with an ultimate reality. Both hope that our very breathing can ultimately praise God and link us to him. Mystical Islam, like that of Judaism and Christianity, also uses neo-Platonic

>>> Sufi Muslims perform many kinds of dikhr. The most famous may be the "whirling dervishes," seen here in Damascus, Syria. Other forms of dikhr can help put Sufis into a trance-like state. How might dancing have that effect on Sufis like the Tanoura of Egypt?

Religion + POETRY

The Poet Rumi

Rumi, born Maulana Jalaluddin Rumi al-Balkhi, is the most famous Sufi poet in history. His lines about love—human and divine—have immortalized his poetry. Here are a few:

> It is greater than a hundred resurrections,
> for the resurrection is a limit, whereas love is unlimited.

> Love has got five hundred wings, each of them reaching from the Divine Throne to the lowest earth.

—and—

> Open the veil and close our door—
> You are and I, and empty the house. (Schimmel 134, 320)

>>> Why might mystics like Rumi, the great Sufi poet, prefer poetry to other kinds of interaction with the sacred?

Source: G. Dagli Orti, "Mevlana Celaleddin Rumi". The Art Archive/Picture Desk, Inc./Kobal Collection

Steps on the Path Toward Sufi Islam

Struggle (*mujahada*) – The struggle of the soul on its spiritual quest

Ascetism (*zuhd*) – Renouncing pleasures to pursue the spiritual path single-mindedly

Silence (*samt*) – The silent acceptance of God's will

Trust (*tawakkul*) – Ceaseless contentment with what God has provided

Servanthood (*ubudiya*) – Complete subjection to God

Desire (*irada*) – The replacement of personal desires with the singular desire for God

Remembrance (*dikhr*) – Continual awareness of God

Friendship (*wilaya*) – Sainthood; protection by God and the ability to perform miracles

Mystic Knowledge (*ma'rifa*) – Knowledge that comes directly from God

Love (*mahabba*) – A love of God that overwhelms all else

Yearning (*shawq*) – Passionate longing to be near God

Source: Based on Brown 196–197.

∧
∧ The path toward Sufism can be a long but joyful one. Which of these steps seems the hardest
∧ to accomplish? Why might someone join a Sufi tariq?

philosophical sources in explaining how God's perfection comes to exist on earth (Brown).

Let's go back to the idea of "remembering God," which appears regularly in the Qur'an. Mystical Islam explains that people will never be able to remember God completely until we get rid of our own personal desires, our own individuality. After all, aren't all of our worries and cares ultimately related to our own selfish needs? When you procrasti- nate studying for a test, and I dawdle instead of grading them, aren't we both being selfish? How can we constantly remember God when we can't even concentrate on our academic jobs? Sufis answer this question by explaining that ultimately we must seek a direct relationship with God, in which our individuality melts away as we experience our creator. Sufis can't explain *how* this happens, because human words cannot explain God. But they can explain *why* it happens: Ultimately, creation (the human race) needs to reunite with the creator (God). Put another way, a Sufi might say that unity with God is the ultimate submission to Him.

Sufi practices and ideas tend to describe the world in complementary pairs that resolve to a single truth, just like our relationship with God). This gives Sufi Islam a lot of room to maneuver. Although all Muslims should stay sober by not drinking, Sufis seek divine intoxication that breaks down borders between people and between us and God. While Muslims emphasize that even the Prophet was ultimately just a man, the Sufis explain that all human beings can ultimately become one with God. And while Muslims must follow God through sharia laws, Sufis celebrate God through mystical poetry (E.I. "Tasawwuf").

Say that you'd like to become a Sufi mystic. How do you do it? Over the centuries, Sufis have developed a system. Because it involves a lot that can't be rationally explained, you won't be able to sit down and read about it in a book. Instead, you'll go on a personal journey. Your guide will be a *shaykh*, a master who has been trained by an earlier generation of Sufi masters. First, you should repent for your sins. You'll then completely submit yourself to the shaykh's teaching. This will begin the process of getting rid of your ego, while simultaneously opening you up to the mystical understanding that the shaykh can give to you.

Ultimately, you'll learn specific Sufi practices, called **dikhr**, the remembrance of God. Although they teach different techniques to remember God, Sufis unite in the desire to say the name of God—Allah—with every breath. By bringing God into us, we experience the oneness that human beings all desire, like finally coming home after a long journey away from your loved ones. How you celebrate may differ, but the feeling of unity will be the same. So it is with dikhr; the celebrations may differ, but the goal of constantly interacting with God remains the same. You may learn to remember God through breathing exercises, dance, or even jumping in the air. The twirling dikhr of the "whirling dervishes" have come to symbolize Sufi practices, but they are just the most well-known.

THINK World Religions

The Intoxication of Qalandar

In Pakistan, Sufis often disagree with the stricter sharia-based interpretations of Islam. Like the Taliban in Afghanistan, Pakistani Islamists also seek to establish a purely Muslim government and society. Islamists often denounce Sufism as being too mystical and disinterested in following sharia laws. Sufis refuse to leave their path, though, and continue to remember God in their own ways. Here's a description of the celebrations that commemorate the 1274 death of Lal Shahbaz Qalandar, the Sufi mystical poet of the Qalandar brotherhood. As you read, look for the cry "Mast Qalandar," which translates to "intoxication of Qalandar." What do you think it means?

The campsites began appearing about five miles from the shrine. Our car eventually mired in a human bog, so we parked and continued on foot. The alleys leading to the shrine reminded me of a carnival fun house—an overwhelming frenzy of lights, music and aromas. I walked beside a man blowing a snake charmer's flute. Stores lined the alley, with merchants squatting behind piles of pistachios, almonds and rosewater-doused candies. Fluorescent lights glowed like light sabers, directing lost souls to Allah.

Groups of up to 40 people heading for the shrine's golden dome carried long banners imprinted with Koranic verses. We followed one group into a tent packed with dancers and drummers next to the shrine. A tall man with curly, greasy shoulder-length hair was beating on a keg-size drum hanging from a leather strap around his neck. The intensity in his eyes, illuminated by a single bulb that dangled above our heads, reminded me of the jungle cats that stalked their nighttime prey on the nature shows I used to watch on TV.

A man in white linen lunged flamboyantly into a clearing at the center of the crowd, tied an orange sash around his waist and began to dance. Soon he was gyrating and his limbs were trembling, but with such control that at one point it seemed that he was moving only his earlobes. Clouds of hashish smoke rolled through the tent, and the drumming injected the space with a thick, engrossing energy.

I stopped taking notes, closed my eyes and began nodding my head. As the drummer built toward a feverish peak, I drifted unconsciously closer to him. Before long, I found myself standing in the middle of the circle, dancing beside the man with the exuberant earlobes. If only for a few minutes, it didn't matter whether I was a Christian, Muslim, Hindu or atheist. I had entered another realm. I couldn't deny the ecstasy of Qalandar. And in that moment, I understood why pilgrims braved great distances and the heat and the crowds just to come to the shrine. While spun into a trance, I even forgot about the danger, the phone calls, the reports of my disappearance and the police escort.

"Mast Qalandar!" someone called out. The voice came from right behind me, but it sounded distant. Anything but the drumbeat and the effervescence surging through my body seemed remote. From the corner of my eye, I noticed photographer Aaron Huey highstepping his way into the circle. He passed his camera to Kristin. In moments, his head was swirling as he whipped his long hair around in circles.

"Mast Qalandar!"

(Schmidle, 2008).

the **THINK**SPOT
www.thethinkspot.com

Don't worry, because you won't be alone on your journey. You will be part of a brotherhood called a *tariq*, an order of Sufis with its own unique practices. Generally, brotherhoods develop in specific geographic areas, using the local language and attracting people from that culture. Brotherhoods exist in most traditionally Islamic lands; Persia, Arabia, India, Pakistan, and North Africa all have active brotherhoods that trace their lineage through shaykhs all the way back to Muhammad himself. (However, the brotherhoods don't all get along, and many have developed a kind of spiritual rivalry.) You'll also seek the company of the great Sufi masters who have achieved saint-like stature in Islam. Having experienced oneness with God, these people can help you too, if you seek out the celebrations that occur at their tombs or the poetry they've left behind.

▶ HOW DOES THE SACRED BECOME COMMUNITY?

Giving to the Poor: The Fourth Pillar of Islam

The Qur'an teaches Muslims two important things about giving to the poor. First, your wealth belongs ultimately to God, not to you. Second, by giving away your wealth, you incur more riches in heaven. Here are God's words in Sura 2:

> You who believe, give charitably from the good things you have acquired and that We have produced for you from the earth. Do not give away the bad things that you yourself would only accept with your eyes closed: remember that God is self-sufficient, worthy of all praise. Satan threatens you with the prospect of poverty and commands you to do foul deeds; God promises you His forgiveness and His abundance: God is limitless and all knowing, and He gives wisdom to whoever He will. Whoever is given wisdom has truly been given much good, but only those with insight bear this in mind. Whatever you may give, or vow to give, God knows it well, and those who do wrong will have no one to help them. If

The Eight Groups that Receive Zakat

Debtors

The impoverished

The poor

Travelers stranded without money

Military volunteers

The zakat collecting agents

Slaves who wish to purchase their freedom

Converts to Islam

Source: Based on E.I. "Zakat"

∧
∧   **Eight different groups** traditionally receive zakat, although the categories are sometimes
∧   combined or reinterpreted by Muslims scholars to fit modern times. How is zakat similar to the
Buddhist practice of alms-giving?

The Steps of the Hajj

1 Ihram – A state of holiness
Pilgrims dress in special clothing: Women cover all but their faces, hands and feet, and men wear white sheets of cloth. They are not permitted to wear jewelry (except for wedding rings), or use perfume or scented toiletries. Women are expected to leave their faces uncovered in tribute to the atmosphere of purity—all lustful feeling must be cast aside. Pilgrims may not shed animal's blood or uproot any plants. This symbolizes unity with nature.

2 Tawaf – Circling the Kaaba
Upon arrival to Mecca (no matter what time of night or day), the first act a pilgrim must take is to circle the Kaaba seven times counterclockwise. If possible, the first three circuits are run. Afterwards, pilgrims perform two cycles of prayer.

3 Sa'i – Walking Between the Two Hills
Pilgrims run or walk briskly between the two hills Safa and Marwah. This is done in memory of Hajarah, the mother of Ismail (Isaac), and her frantic journey while on the lookout for caravans bringing water.

4 Mina – The Valley
On the eight day of the Hajj, pilgrims travel on foot to the valley of Mina (approximately six miles away). There, they camp in tents and await *wuquf*.

5 Wuquf – The stand before God
On the ninth day of the Hajj, before noon, all pilgrims must arrive at Arafat. Between noon and dusk is a period of prayer and meditation on God. If pilgrims do not arrive in time for wuquf, their Hajj is considered invalid.

6 Stoning the Jamrahs
Pilgrims toss small pebbles at three pillars, or *jamrahs*, that represent Satan. While "stoning the devil," the pilgrims reaffirm their vows to drive out the evil in themselves.

7 Eid al-Adha – The Festival of Sacrifice
Those who can afford it purchase a sheep or a goat and sacrifice it for the feast. This represents Ibrahim's dedication to God and his willingness to sacrifice his own son. No meat is wasted during the celebration, and pilgrims often take what remains with them when they leave.

8 The final tawaf
After returning from Arafat, pilgrims must circle the Kaaba once more. This completes the hajj.

Source: Based on Maqsood 84–96.

∧ Although many Muslims perform other rituals such as shaving their heads or kissing
∧ the black stone of the Kabbah, these eight steps form the backbone of the hajj. How might
these individual actions relate to the other four Pillars of Islam?

you give charity openly, it is good, but if you keep it secret and give to the needy in private, that is better for you, and it will atone for some of your bad deeds: God is well aware of all that you do. (2:267–71)

As Islam developed, it created a set of rules to help Muslims give appropriate amounts of their wealth to the poor. It's a little confusing, because Muslims often interchange the terms they use for charity, **zaka** and **sadaqa**. (The plural of zaka is *zakat*, and you'll hear both versions of the word.) Let's use zakat when referring more specifically to mandatory giving of money, and sadaqa as a more general term for charity.

You're more likely to learn about zakat than sadaqa in a class on Islam. Like the other four pillars, all Muslims must follow the rules of zakat to the extent that they're able. Hadith rules have reinterpreted zakat in the light of changing circumstances. If not, everyone would still be expected to pay zakat in camels! To give zakat is to help the Islamic umma: This money must be given to Muslims, not to non-Muslims or other charities. In fact, hadith practice describes eight groups that should receive zakat. As you study the graphic on the next page, notice how this system helps build up the umma.

Almsgiving—sadaqa—comes from the heart, a completely individual action to help others. In the best cases, no one even knows who has given money to a charitable cause, a beggar on the street, or a pilgrim needing financial help. The Qur'an and the hadith praise people who give money this way, since they go beyond the basic five pillars.

Although sadaqa ought to be given freely, Muslim traditions do describe specific benefits from it. Many Muslims will give alms to help purify themselves after doing something inappropriate. It's especially powerful if you give sadaqa immediately after you have sinned. It can even make up for zakat that you've forgotten or sinfully chosen not to give. You should consider giving sadaqa when you're leaving on a journey or going into harm's way. And though you can give anytime, sadaqa when you're young and healthy produces more merit than when you're infirm and near death (E.I. "Sadaqa").

Sadaqa also helps shield you from evil. You can almost see a hint of karma in this concept, for the gifts you give now can help keep you safe from harm in the future. Some people even give sadaqa early in the morning (the same time the Buddhist monks receive alms!), to keep you safe all day long.

Ultimately, zakat and sadaqa help everyone involved. The giver gets the merit and good feeling that comes along with his or her gift. The umma receives the funding necessary to continue its work. And the receiver of sadaqa, whoever that might be, benefits from what is given. An old Muslim saying describes the transformative power of sadaqa in the voice of the person receiving aid. "I was little and you made me much, I was small and you made me great, I was your enemy and you made me your friend, I was perishable and you made me permanent, I was guarded and you made me your guard" (E.I. "Sadaqa").

>>> Like the earth around the sun, Muslims on the hajj circle the sacred Kaaba shrine in a ritual called the Tawaf.

Zaka(t), is the mandatory giving of money, and the fourth pillar of Islam. **Sadaqa** is the Muslim word for charity.

The Hajj: The Fifth Pillar of Islam

Consider how the Kaaba creates a worldwide Muslim umma: Since the time of the Prophet, Muslims everywhere have turned toward Mecca five times a day to pray. At any given moment in the last minute, someone somewhere has turned in that direction and bowed down. No single place in the world has that kind of power for other religions—not Jerusalem, the Bodhi Tree, or Rome. It's as if the Kaaba is a sacred magnet, pulling each Muslim into alignment. Even if there were no hajj, the Kaaba would still have an incredible power to link Muslims together in a huge sacred community that goes backward and forward in time.

Imagine the hajj. If you spent your entire life turning toward Mecca and the Kaaba, how would you feel when you finally arrived? You wouldn't have to turn toward Mecca for prayers—you'd be there. It would seem like Earth had turned on its axis. Instead of the North and South Pole, you'd feel the Muslim world spinning around you, facing the spot where you stand. If you were a Sufi, you may have symbolically created this feeling during the dikhr, spinning around your shaykh like the moon around Earth. In Mecca, you'd realize that you were also spinning like the umma around the Kaaba.

Muhammad made the first Muslim pilgrimage to Mecca after he had won the city back for God and stripped the Kaaba of its 360 heathen Arab idols. Muslims believe that, even before Muhammad, Ibrahim (Abraham to Jews and Christians) stood at that very place, ready to sacrifice his son to God. Ibrahim set the corner stone of the Kaaba and showed himself to be the first Muslim—a man wholly subservient to God.

Because of this, Muhammad instructed all Muslims to join him on a trek to Mecca. Although you can go more often if you have the

Jihad, or "struggle," is often called the sixth pillar of Islam. Various Islamic traditions interpret jihad differently: an inner effort to seek faith and submission to God, the overall attempt to expand Islam throughout the world, or physical defense of Islam when it is under attack.

money, the vast crush of people each year means that Saudi authorities try to convince people to make the journey only once. Reread A Place in the World at the beginning of this chapter, and you'll get a feeling for the flood of emotions that people have on the hajj. It's both exhausting and exulting, sacred and scary. At times, there are so many people that hundreds of hajjis can be trampled to death. The press of people is so great that pickpockets—surely not good Muslims—often prey on the pilgrims.

The hajj has a set number of activities, each to be done at a particular time and way. The rituals have been handed down for generations, each based on texts from the Qur'an and the hadith. By following these same steps, hajjis help remind Muslims everywhere that the umma is alive and well, made up of people from across the world, rich and poor, old and young. The chart on the previous page describes the precise actions of the hajj. As you read through it, think about how these actions simultaneously foster individual religious commitment and cultivate the sacred Islamic community.

Jihad in a Modern World?

Jihad. To non-Muslim Americans, the word conjures up mental images of Osama bin Laden calling for the death of Americans around the world. Could a religion really tell young people to become suicide bombers, killing themselves and others in a reign of terror?

The idea of jihad runs deep in Islamic history. Some people call it the Sixth Pillar because it defends the Muslim umma from outside attack. Other Muslims interpret jihad as a mostly internal spiritual struggle, not a military or violent one. In that case, the jihadi (the struggler) tries to vanquish the power of the devil and his or her own sinful actions. There is no one else to blame, no person, culture, or nation that you can say led you astray.

Jihad's multiple shades of meaning illustrate how Islam perceives itself and its neighbors. Islam sees itself as the universal religion, the original faith of all human beings that has been corrupted over the millennia in thousands of ways. Unlike Hinduism or Judaism, Islam actively seeks converts. All people, Muslims believe, must ultimately submit to God. For that reason, Muslims must struggle to develop Islam in themselves and also strive to convert others, sometimes even using force. This lends multiple interpretations to the struggle for Islam:

- Jihad describes the struggle of all Muslims to live according to the precepts of Islam. Complete submission and faith to God don't come easily: we struggle to live according to the five pillars. This might be called the "inner jihad," though many Muslims also call it the "greater jihad."
- Jihad also describes the struggle to expand Islam to all parts of the world. Sunni jurists say that Muslims can never enact it against one another, since jihad should bring people to Islam. Likewise, Sunni Islam has long taught that Jews and Christians should not be forced to accept Islam but rather made to pay extra taxes for their errors. Shiites disagree with this view, saying that even Sunni Muslims are proper targets of jihad, because they have strayed from the path of true Islam. It's a

paradox we've discussed earlier in this chapter. On the one hand, the Qur'an states that no one can be forced to be a Muslim. On the other hand, the Qur'an also commands Muslims to follow Muhammad's example by cultivating Islam in new lands.
- Finally, jihad can be used defensively, coming to the aid of Islam when under attack. Muslims often explain the Crusades this way, because the caliphs had to defend themselves against the invading Christians. (You can see why "crusade" has negative connotations for Muslims.)

The main legal schools have many different interpretations of these three forms of jihad, especially in relation to the forcible expansion of Islam to non-Islamic cultures. Present-day Muslim scholars tend to fall along a spectrum of ideas. The most pacifist have concluded that the days of armed struggle are over and that jihad must be undertaken only through education and living as a good example to other people. According to this view, anyone who accepts Islam under threat of violence can't be called a real Muslim, because it was not a voluntary act.

Scholars in the middle of the spectrum would argue that the jihad will continue until all people submit to God. However, that does not mean that Muslim leaders should recklessly attack other nations in the name of God. The widespread influence of Christianity also counsels against an active jihad, since Christians might be in error but they're still monotheists. Judaism also presents a problem here, since Jews too are a people of the book. Many Muslims, though, see the state of Israel as an interloper in the Middle East, no better than the Crusaders who tried to wrest Jerusalem from Muslim hands. From this point of view, Israel has attacked Islam through its creation of a Jewish state on historically Muslim lands. Aiding Palestinian Muslims may then count as a defensive jihad.

At the other end of the spectrum, some Muslim scholars say that the struggle for Islam must happen everywhere, but especially in Muslim lands now contaminated by infidel non-Muslims. Following this line of reasoning, the European and American presence in Iraq or Afghanistan, the state of Israel, and even secular government in Turkey may all be targets of Muslim jihad. Looking at the situation from this vantage, the struggle between truth (Islam) and falsehood (all other religions) must be fought both spiritually and militarily. According to these scholars, Muslims must be willing to suffer any kind of pain or death in the jihad to cleanse Muslim lands and to expand Islam.

Conclusion

Some of the words from the beginning of Chapter 13 may now sound a little more familiar to you: Allah, caliph, jihad, Shiite, Sunni, Sufi, and umma. What were once foreign (and maybe a little scary) words may now sound more like new acquaintances. You've undoubtedly learned how Islam recognizes and interacts with other monotheistic traditions, especially Judaism and Christianity. The five pillars offer support for Muslims to believe and for us to learn about Islam. As I asked at the beginning of our study on Islam, "That wasn't so hard, was it?"

Maybe not. But for students in the United States and Europe, Islam has political overtones that we rarely hear from Buddhism or Daoism. You can read about the competing visions of Islam at the end of this chapter. In one fatwa, Osama bin Laden calls for armed struggle against the "Crusaders." In the other, the Islamic scholar Tahir-ul-Qadri writes that Islam must forsake terrorism because the "Muslim Umma, as well as humanity, is heading towards catastrophe." This is an argument that cannot be resolved in two chapters of a book. But maybe, just maybe, our deeper understanding of Islam will translate into better relationships around the world.

Here, Ali removes pagan idols from the Kaaba. Even before the rise of Islam, polytheistic Arabs worshipped Allah as the god of creation. **How might these early beliefs have influenced the Islamic movement?**

vvv

Some women see the veil as oppressing, while others argue that it displays their pride as Muslims and shows their devotion to God. **How might this controversy affect the unity of the Islamic umma?**

vvv

IS THERE A GOD?

Muslims worship one God, the creator and ruler of all. God is omnipotent and un-knowable, and although Muhammad was the messenger of God, he was still just a man. Many passages of the Qur'an reflect this, as they are confusing to us, but ultimately make sense from a divine viewpoint. References to God's "hands" and "eyes" are interpreted by some to mean that God has human-like features, but other scholars argue that these terms are simply metaphorical in nature. Although we may never understand God completely, Muslims believe that we yearn to be near Him and receive His grace. Since no one is perfect, human beings must rely on God's mercy and forgiveness when He judges us.

HOW DOES THE SACRED BECOME COMMUNITY?

The fourth and fifth pillars of Islam—giving to the less fortunate and completing the pilgrimage to Mecca—function to unite the Muslim umma. By donating money to those in need, Muslims purify themselves and strengthen their commitment to the community. Through charity, both the receivers and the givers of sadaqa benefit. Likewise, the hajj plays a crucial part in Muslim life, as it increases personal and communal religious ties.

WHAT DOES IT MEAN TO BE HUMAN?

Muhammad is seen as the perfect Muslim; therefore by studying his life, we can learn to follow his example. Like Muhammad, Muslims seek to incorporate Islam into their political and social lives. The global community of Muslims is called the *umma*, and although it is a personal decision to become Muslim, the family and community play important roles in spiritual life. Controversy has risen up in recent years over the Islamic tradition of male authority. Debates continue on the practice of female veiling, as some see it as a form of oppression, and others as a means of liberation and pride.

HOW DO HUMANS INTERACT WITH THE SACRED?

The five pillars of Islam hold a prominent place in the life of Muslims. Professing his or her faith through the Shahada brings a Muslim closer to God and the community of believers. Prayer, the second pillar, offers a way for Muslims to communicate with God directly and ask for grace. By fasting during Ramadan, they commemorate the transfer of the Qur'an from God to humans, and through observing a halal diet, they acknowledge God's will over men.

<<< Launched internationally in 2003, Mecca Cola advertises itself as the Muslim alternative to American soft drinks, **and emphasizes that 20 percent of the proceeds goes to charity. How would purchasing this drink strengthen Muslims' bonds with the community?**

>>> Many Muslims consider following the rules of halal a means of accepting God's will even if humans cannot understand it. **How is this similar to Jewish views on kosher laws?**

Summary

HOW DO HUMANS INTERACT WITH THE SACRED?   p. 228

- The first pillar of Islam requires Muslims to profess their faith in God and Muhammad. The Sunni and Shia traditions disagree as to exact Islamic beliefs, however.
- The second pillar of Islam is salat, or prayer. Muslim prayer emphasizes form and structure as a way to communicate directly with God.
- Muslims also interact with God through keeping a halal diet and fasting during the month of Ramadan.
- Sufi Muslims seek a more mystical interpretation of the sacred, and place great importance on the constant remembrance of God.

HOW DOES THE SACRED BECOME COMMUNITY?   p. 243

- The fourth pillar of Islam is zakat, or giving to the poor. By giving away wealth on Earth, Muslims incur riches in heaven.
- All Muslims must participate in the hajj at least once in their lifetimes. The pilgrimage strengthens the umma by fostering a feeling of community between believers.

Key Terms

Hajj is a sacred pilgrimage to Mecca and the fourth pillar of Islam.   228

Muezzin is an official who calls Muslims to prayer.   229

Sunni Islam includes about 80 percent of Muslims in the world, and emphasized scholarly and communal decision-making after the death of Muhammad.   229

Shia Islam emphasizes the lineage of Muhammad and places great spiritual importance on the imams. Followers are referred to as Shiites.   229

Imam is a Muslim leader and successor of Muhammad (following the line of Ali).   235

Salat, or prayer, provides Muslims a direct way of interacting with God. It is the second pillar of Islam.   236

Ayatollah is a top-ranking scholar of Muslim law in Shia Islam.   236

Sufism is a mystical branch of Islam that emphasizes the constant remembrance of God.   240

Dikhr ("remembrance of God") are Sufi practices that teach constant interaction with

God. They include breathing exercises, dancing, and twirling.   242

Zaka(t) is the mandatory giving of money, and the fourth pillar of Islam.   245

Sadaqa is the Muslim word for charity.   245

Jihad, or "struggle," is often called the sixth pillar of Islam. Various Islamic traditions interpret jihad differently: an inner effort to seek faith and submission to God, the overall attempt to expand Islam throughout the world, or physical defense of Islam when it is under attack.   246

Find it on

http://www.metacafe.com/watch/2358242/hajj_pilgrimage_to_the_holy_land_mecca_in_arabic/

Describing the pilgrimage to Mecca really doesn't do the event justice. It is something that needs to be seen to be believed, so great in scope is this annual journey to the Muslim holy land. Visit the ThinkSpot to see a recent pilgrimage and read a history and commentary on Hajj.

- http://www.3dmekanlar.com/en/al-madinah-prophets-mosque.html

Visit the ThinkSpot to take a virtual tour of an Islamic mosque. Let the Sacred Place come to life as you visit the Prophet's Mosque in Saudi Arabia.

Questions for Study and Review

1. What are the Five Pillars of Islam, and what purpose do they serve?

The Shahada, the first pillar of Islam, requires Muslims to acknowledge their faith in God and His prophet, Muhammad. The second pillar, prayer, celebrates Muslims' submission to God and allows them a language in which to communicate with the divine. The third pillar involves ritual fasting and keeping a pure diet. Foods such as pork and beverages such as alcohol are forbidden in Islam, and animals must be slaughtered in a certain way. The month of Ramadan is observed by fasting from sunrise to sunset, in remembrance of Muhammad's time spent in the mountains outside of Mecca. The fourth pillar of Islam dictates charity to the poor, and the fifth pillar requires all Muslims to complete the hajj at least once in their lifetime.

2. What is Sufism, and how does it differ from other forms of Islam?

Sufis emphasize the mystical side of Islam and seek to become closer to God through every action. Sufism explains that individualism is a form of selfishness, and that we must give up our individuality in order to reunite completely with God. Dikhr, the remembrance of God, can be achieved through divine intoxication. To accomplish this, Sufis practice breathing exercises, dancing, and twirling.

3. What is jihad, and how does it relate to modern Islam?

Jihad can refer to an external struggle, such as defending the Muslim community from outside attack, or the internal struggle of Muslims to submit to God and adhere to the tenets of Islam. Modern scholars disagree on the exact meaning, however many believe that jihad refers to Muslims' duty to encourage the spread of Islam.

For Further Study

BOOKS:

Ayoub, Mahmoud. *Islam: Faith and History*. Oxford: Oneworld, 2004.

Bianchi, Robert R. *Guests of God: Pilgrimage and Politics in the Islamic World*. New York: Oxford University Press, 2004.

Brown, Daniel W. *New Introduction to Islam*. Malden, MA: Wiley-Blackwell, 2009.

Endress, Gerhard. *Islam: An Historical Introduction*. NY: Columbia University Press, 2003.

Grieve, Paul. *Brief guide to Islam: history, faith and politics: the complete introduction*. New York : Carroll and Graf Publishers, 2006.

Madelung, Wilferd and Farhad Daftary, eds. *Encyclopaedia Islamica*. http://www.brillonline.nl/ Publication: Leiden: Brill 2007–.

Maqsood, Ruqaiyyah Waris. *Teach Yourself Islam*. New York: McGraw-Hill, 1996.

Waines, David. *An Introduction to Islam*. NY: Cambridge University Press, 2004.

WEB SITES:

Tahir-ul-Qadri, Muhammad. *Fatwa on Suicide Bombings and Terrorism*. London: Minhaj-ul-Qur'an International, 2010. Available at http://www.minhaj.org/images-db2/fatwa-eng.pdf.

The Holy Quran from all Tafseer Schools. http://www.altafsir.com.

Online Qur'an Project. http://www.al-quran.info

Schmidle, Nicholas. "Mas Qalandar!" *Smithsonian magazine*, December 2008. http://www.smithsonianmag.com/people-places/Faith-and-Ecstasy.html

Q

IS THERE A GOD?

WHAT DOES IT MEAN TO BE HUMAN?

HOW DO HUMANS INTERACT WITH
THE SACRED?

HOW DOES THE SACRED BECOME
COMMUNITY?

When I

was 11 years old, my college-age brother gave me a book called *Seven Arrows*, an "adventure of the People, the Plains People" (Storm 1). When I think about it, it was a funny gift for a preteen. What was my brother thinking? Did he expect that I'd like the pictures? Did he remember that the Boy Scouts, which I had just joined, held many Native American ideas? Looking back, I suspect that he wanted to head me into a new way of experiencing the world—including things like the medicine wheel and the vision quest—while I was still a kid.

Back then, in 1974, many Americans had become interested in Native American history and culture. *Bury My Heart at Wounded Knee* introduced us to the darker side of American history, where the American Indians weren't always bad and the cavalry didn't always ride to the rescue, as we had seen on Saturday-morning TV. Ironically, the more we learned and respected the indigenous people of America, the more confused we became about their names: Indians? American Indians? First Nations? First Peoples? Aboriginal Americans? As it turns out, each of those names works well sometimes but there are so many

Native American groups that no one word encompasses them all.

In Chapter 15, we'll study Native Americans as an introduction to indigenous religions across the world. Given the huge number of local religions on Earth, we can't study them all. However, although they're different from one another, many local traditions do share some traits: reverence for the land, seeking sacred power in nature, and retaining oral traditions. Now that you've gotten used to using the Four Questions approach to studying religion, you'll be able to branch out on your own and study indigenous traditions from around the world.

To tell the truth, I never made it all the way through *Seven Arrows*. But more than 35 years later, I still keep it in a special place on my bookshelf, where I take it out to read and gaze at the pictures. In fact, here's a riddle based on the stories in *Seven Arrows*: What animal is like a mouse, an eagle, a buffalo, and a bear?

251

RELIGIONS OF PLACE:
A Sacred World Around Us

CHAPTER 15

A Sacred Place / The Tipi

THE TIPI SEEMS TO GROW FROM THE EARTH, YOUNG TREES BENDING TOWARD ONE ANOTHER AND COVERED WITH ANIMAL SKINS. Walk up to it and you'll see it's pretty small. Pictures of people, horses, buffalo, and other tipis cover the outside. A shield made of skins and paint marks the entrance. Flip back the flap and your senses will begin to tingle; your pupils dilate in the dimness and sting a bit from the lingering smoke. A shaft of light from the smoke vent drifts downward, illuminating motes in the warm air. The aroma of leather blends with tobacco and wood. The char from a fire, now put out, smells a little like the smoke from a long-stemmed pipe.

These are all sacred elements to Plains Indian life: the smoke, the buffalo hides, the wood, and the light. The tobacco pipe links person to person to the earth, passed around a circle inside the tipi. A pipe could be a sacred lie detector—if you accept the pipe, you have not told a lie. The shield hanging outside illustrates a name given the tipi's owner, one he received after a vision quest, that solitary spiritual journey taken by Native Americans.

Each of these things seems completely organic, taken from the land. For Native Americans, the land is a sacred place, stretching for a thousand miles across the prairie. When you step toward the tall poles holding up the tipi, you're coming toward the sacred center of the world. Move your tipi and the center of the universe moves with you, always radiating out from that lodge pole. The tipi, the leather, the wood, the tobacco, the clay, the stones, and you are a continuum of living creation
(Epes and Cousins, 36–38).

A Native American Tipi

A Native American Shield

Detail of a tipi painting showing horses,
people, and buffalo surrounding the image of a tipi.

A Plains Indian Peace Pipe

Sacred Mystery is a life force shared by all things in the world.

Now that we've studied five major religious traditions, you're ready for any ambiguous answers to this question. Given how many indigenous cultures exist across the world, you can already guess the answer for this chapter: one god, many gods, no gods, and everything is a god. These statements make sense for the variety of indigenous sacred traditions.

We can be a little more specific than that. Indigenous cultures across the world tend to perceive gods as being linked to the land. In many cases, the concept of a god or spirit works in a specific locale. Look at Black Elk's dream in the feature below. Notice that the things he describes in his dream also exist in his waking world: horses, eagles, buffalo, elk, clouds, thunder, and lightning. For Black Elk, as well as many other indigenous people,

creation exists on a continuum that includes Earth, water, rocks, animals, people, and spirits. Instead of a creator god, Black Elk would likely talk about a **Sacred Mystery** (or a Great Mystery) called Wakan Tanka, a "mysterious life power permeating all natural forms and forces and all phases of man's conscious life" (Fletcher 106). All the things we just listed from Black Elk's dream would have been a realization of the Sacred Mystery. Each goose or mouse has a bit of the Sacred Mystery, but precisely how all of it works together is, well, a great mystery.

Let's think of this another way. For the monotheistic religions, you might imagine a deep canyon between God and humanity, brought on by Adam and Eve's decisions to disobey God. Only God can step across the gorge; human beings must rely on God to help them cross the valley. For indigenous religions, though, you might imagine a vast prairie instead of a canyon. You can travel across that wide, flat land only if you get help from

A SACRED ACTION ▶▶▶

Black Elk's Vision

In 1931, an American scholar named John G. Neihardt met the Lakota Indian Black Elk, hoping to interview him for an ethnographic study of the Plains Indians. To begin, Neihardt described his own ideas, his scholarship, and even his dreams. Black Elk sat quietly, watching the ethnographer instead of being watched. And then Black Elk began to talk. Over the next years, he would tell his own story to Neihardt, which was full of visions, rituals, and bloody fights alongside the great warrior Crazy Horse. As he listened, Neihardt realized that Black Elk's "medicine" (his power and link to the divine) was to tell stories—to heal wounds through words. In the following passage, Black Elk describes a sacred dream he had as a young man. As you read it, consider how people, nature, spirits, and animals relate to one another in the dream. That will help as you learn more about indigenous traditions, as it offers a picture to the link between the sacred and everyday life. How might Black Elk's vision compare or contrast to other mystical experiences?

As I lay in the tipi I could see through the tipi the same two men whom I saw before and they were coming from the clouds. Then I recognized them as the same men I had seen before in my first vision. They came and stood off a ways from me and stopped, saying: "Hurry up, your grandfather is calling you." When they started back I got up and started to follow them. Just as I got out of the tipi I could see the two men going back into the clouds and there was a small cloud coming down toward me at the same time, which stood before me. I got on top of the cloud and was raised up, following the two men, and when I looked back, I saw my father and mother looking at me. When I looked back I felt sorry that I was leaving them.

I followed those men on up into the clouds and they showed me a vision of a bay horse

∧
∧ **Here is Black Elk,**
∧ the Lakota Sioux Indian whose visions will help us understand the sacred world of Native Americans.

standing there in the middle of the clouds. One of the men said: "Behold him, the horse who has four legs, you shall see." I stood there and looked at the horse and it began to speak. It said: "Behold me; my life history you shall see. Furthermore, behold them, those where the sun goes down, their lives' history you shall see." I looked over there and saw twelve black horses toward the west, where the sun goes down. All the horses had on their necks necklaces of buffalo hoofs. [I saw above the twelve head of horses birds. I was very scared of those twelve head of horses because I could see the light[ning] and thunder around them. Then they showed me twelve white horses with necklaces of elks' teeth and said: "Behold them, those who are where the giant lives [the north]." Then I saw some white geese flying around over the horses. Then I turned around toward the east, where the sun shines continually. The men said: "Behold them, those where the sun shines continually." I saw twelve head of horses, all sorrels [and these sorrels had horns and there were some eagles flying above the sorrels]. Then I turned to the place where you always face, the south, and saw twelve head of buckskin horses. They said: "Behold him, those where you always face." These horses had horns. At the beginning of the vision they were all horses, only two (sets) had necklaces (the blacks and the whites) and two had horns (the sorrels and the buckskins).] When I had seen it all, the bay horse said to me: "Your grandfathers are having a council, these shall take you; so take courage." Then these horses went into formation of twelve abreast in four lines-blacks, whites, sorrels, buckskins. As they stood, the bay horse looked to the west and neighed. I looked over there and saw great clouds of horses in all colors and they all neighed back to this horse and it sounded like thunder. Then the horse neighed toward the north and the horses came through there and neighed back again. These horses were in all colors also. Then the bay looked

everything on it—the stones for paths, the plants for food, animals to show you water, and the sun and moon to guide you on your way. As you travel, you begin to realize that the land, its inhabitants, and you are all connected to one another. Where on that prairie is the line between the creator and the creation? Can we ever fully grasp the relationship between creation and creator? The answer depends on which indigenous tradition you're studying. Black Elk and many other Native Americans might say that we'll never know for sure, for it is part of the Sacred Mystery; that is, it may vary depending on the terrain, the plants, the animals, and you.

<<< What elements of this photograph of the cloud dance help us understand the sacred ideas of Black Elk and other Native Americans?

toward the east and he neighed and some more horses neighed back. The bay looked southward and neighed and the horses neighed back to him from there. The bay horse said to me: "Behold them, your horses come dancing." I looked around and saw millions of horses circling around me—a sky full of horses.

Then the bay horse said: "Make haste." The horse began to go beside me and the forty-eight horses followed us. I looked around and all the horses that were running changed into buffalo, elk, and all kinds of animals and fowls and they all went back to the four quarters. I followed the bay horse and it took me to a place on a cloud under a rainbow gate and there were sitting my six grandfathers, sitting inside of a rainbow door, and the horses stopped behind me. I saw on either side of me a man whom I recognized as those of the first vision. The horses took their original positions in the four quarters.

One of the grandfathers said to me: "Do not fear, come right in" (through the rainbow door). So I went in and stood before them. The horses in the four quarters of the earth all neighed to cheer me as I entered the rainbow door. The grandfather representing where the sun goes down said: "Your grandfathers all over the world and the earth are having a council and there you were called, so here you are. Behold then, those where the sun goes down; from thence they shall come, you shall see. From them you shall know the willpower of myself, for they shall take you to the center of the earth, and the nations of all kinds shall tremble. Behold where the sun continually shines, for they shall take you there." (DeMallie)

>>> How well do you think this contemporary yarn painting captures a Native American mystical vision?

Glooskap the Divinity

The Algonquin Indians lived a thousand miles east of the Plains tribes. Yet this story includes a trickster god in some ways similar to ones you might learn about among the Sioux or others. This tale describes two characters: Glooskap (a good spirit) and Malsumsis (an evil spirit). Is it always clear here which of the brothers is good and which is evil? Do both have a little bit of the Trickster in them? Why do you think that the Trickster might occur in many indigenous American sacred traditions? Finally what role does the beaver play in this story?

Now the great lord Glooskap, who was worshiped in after-days by all the Wabanaki, or children of light, was a twin with a brother. As he was good, this brother, whose name was Malsumsis, or Wolf the younger, was bad. Before they were born, the babes consulted to consider how they had best enter the world. And Glooskap said, "I will be born as others are." But the evil Malsumsis thought himself too great to be brought forth in such a manner, and declared that he would burst through his mother's side. And as they planned it so it came to pass. Glooskap as first came quietly to light, while Malsumsis kept his word, killing his mother.

The two grew up together, and one day the younger, who knew that both had charmed lives, asked the elder what would kill him, Glooskap. Now each had his own secret as to this . . . and Glooskap, to test his brother, told him that the only way in which he himself could be slain was by the stroke of an owl's feather, though this was not true. And Malsumsis said, "I can only die by a blow from a fern-root."

Then the false man led his brother another day far into the forest to hunt, and, while he again slept, smote him on the head with a pine-root. But Glooskap arose unharmed, drove Malsumsis away into the woods, sat down by the brook-side, and thinking over all that had happened, said, "Nothing but a flowering rush can kill me." But the Beaver, who was hidden among the reeds, heard this, and hastening to Malsumsis told him the secret of his brother's life. For this Malsumsis promised to bestow on Beaver whatever he should ask; but when the latter wished for wings like a pigeon, the warrior laughed, and scornfully said, "Get thee hence; thou with a tail like a file, what need hast thou of wings?"

Then the Beaver was angry, and went forth to the camp of Glooskap, to whom he told what he had done. Therefore Glooskap arose in sorrow and in anger, took a fern-root, sought Malsumsis in the deep, dark forest, and smote him so that he fell down dead. And Glooskap sang a song over him and lamented (Leland 15–17).

the THINK SPOT
www.thethinkspot.com

<<< Here Glooskap is shown holding an eagle. According to legend, the bird's flapping caused terrible storms until Glooskap caught it and bound its wings.

Plains Indians (and other Native Americans) often describe the Sacred Mystery in two ways. The first one focuses on a complementary pair: the Mystery Above and the Mystery Below, for example, earth and sky, fire and water, left and right, up and down: All these can help us understand the cosmic linkage of the Mystery Above and the Mystery Below. As an example of this, we might think of Black Elk traveling from our world to the Mystery Above when he had his dream.

Other Native American traditions describe the dyad as twins who create the world together, as in the story of Glooskap at the top of this page.

Often, one of the pair has some mischief or even some evil in him. He's called the Trickster—always teaching us about the world by turning it upside-down or taking things that he shouldn't. In the American Southwest, you're likely to see images of the Trickster as a dancing coyote on T-shirts, tote bags,

∧∧∧ In the American Southwest, the Trickster may be called Kokopelli, who plays a flute or smokes a pipe. This picture appears on an ancient rock painting in New Mexico. Do you know of a Trickster in your own religious background?

and tattoos. For Native Americans, though, the Trickster is not so much a cute marketing gimmick as a reminder of the changing nature of things; when you think you understand the world, the Trickster is sure to play a joke to remind you otherwise.

The Medicine Wheel

Black Elk's vision also illustrates the "medicine wheel," another way that some Native Americans describe the relationship between the Mystery Above and the Mystery Below. From the longhouse lodges built by Lenape Indians to the Medicine Wheel on the Great Plains, Native Americans have often used space as a way to talk about their sacred world. Think about Jewish, Christian, and Muslim ideas about God. Those traditions tend to employ terms related to *time*, reminding us that God

<<< This photograph gives you a bird's-eye view of the Medicine Wheel on Medicine Mountain, Wyoming. Although it can be small, or huge like this one, the medicine wheel links Native Americans to their sense of the sacred. Have we seen other, similar traditions before in *THINK World Religions*?

existed even before time began, even before Adam and Eve. Native Americans, on the other hand, traditionally describe the sacred world in terms of *space*, especially the four directions—north, south, east, and west. The Plains Indians often describe the world in these terms:

> Each one of these . . . stones within the Medicine Wheel represents one of the many things of the Universe. One of them represents you, and another represents me. Others hold within them our mothers, fathers, sisters brothers, and our friends. Still others symbolize hawks, buffalo, elks, and wolves. There are also stones which represent religions, governments, philosophies, and even entire nations. All things are contained within the Medicine Wheel, and all things are equal within it. The Medicine Wheel is the Total Universe (Storm 5).

In his highly influential book *God Is Red*, the Native American writer Vine Deloria, Jr., introduced the idea of sacred geography to the non-Indian public. His words highlight the Indian ideal of human linkage to the land, on this idea of sacred space, writing, "The vast majority of Indian tribal religions, therefore, have a sacred center at a particular place, be it a river, a mountain, a plateau, valley, or other natural feature. This center enables the people to look out along the four dimensions and locate their lands, to relate all historical events within the confines of this particular land, and to accept responsibility for it" (Deloria 66). Another Native American sums up the relationship of land and spirit with just a few words: "To us when your land is gone, you are walking towards a slow spiritual death. We have come to the point that death is better than living without your spirituality" (Brown 23).

A Native American Medicine Wheel

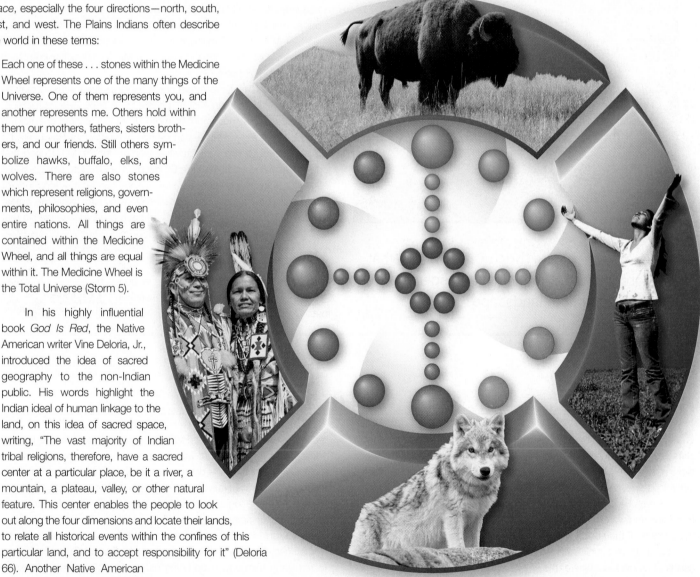

Source: Based on Storm 5.

∧ Each stone in a medicine wheel represents a facet of life.
∧ To live in harmony with the universe, we must first find our own place within the wheel.

Sacred Land and Sacred Power Across the Globe

Although Native Americans teach that the Sacred Mystery exists within and around us, its power is magnified in some places. The great Medicine Wheel on Medicine Mountain is one such place, but there are others: "buttes, canyons, river crossings, and old roads" that hold special meaning (Deloria xv). Other indigenous cultures have found their own places of sacred power. Just below the Arctic Circle, indigenous people created stone labyrinths on the shore of Great Solovetsky Island in Russia. Thousands of miles to the south, Nigerians describe Benin City as the "cradle of the world," where the High God's son created the first dry land in a world of water (Olupona 190).

∧
∧ Mt. Shasta, in northern California. What
∧ might make this mountain an especially
sacred place in the landscape?

In the United States, many non-Indians have begun to explore the concepts of sacred space and powerful forces in nature. As interest has grown, so have disputes and problems between Native Americans who want to preserve their sacred places and other people who desire to learn (or even profit) from popular interest in events such as sweat lodge ceremonies, which exist in nearly every indigenous American culture. Mount Shasta, for example, has been singled out as a "power vortex," one of seven areas of intense energy fields across the globe. This might not bother Native Americans, except that they too consider Mount Shasta a sacred place. Instead of coming to Mount Shasta with respect and silence (as some Buddhist monks have), Native Americans claim that New Age seekers clamber about the mountain in groups, making noise and desecrating holy ground. "No Christian church or Moslem [sic] mosque would be asked to endure the kinds of violations that the sacred locations on Mt. Shasta suffer from New Age activities" (Olupona 77).

Sometimes, things really get out of hand. Sedona, Arizona may be even better known than Mount Shasta as a New Age destination. (We'll discuss this movement in more detail in the next chapter.) In October 2009, a self-help expert named James Arthur Ray offered a five-day retreat to find your "spiritual warrior" for $9,000. During that time, he crowded approximately 60 people at a time into a huge sweat lodge, for them to experience a Native American purification ritual for themselves. Two healthy people, however, died in the lodge that week, possibly because the sweat lodge had been covered with plastic that kept steam from escaping, or because burning sandalwood had created a toxic gas inside the lodge. A Native American sweat-lodge leader was not surprised at the sad result, saying, "It's important to know who is responsible for your spiritual and physical safety in that lodge" (Dougherty A-13).

the THINKSPOT
www.thethinkspot.com

▶ WHAT DOES IT MEAN TO BE HUMAN?

When Black Elk described his vision, he told John Neihardt a lot about Native American beliefs on humanity. In his dream, Black Elk's grandfathers represented the cardinal directions. Yet they were not disembodied voices or even angels—they were his family, showing him the way to live. Even as he conversed with his grandfathers, Black could also talk to horses and watch them dance. He could see geese that represented the corners of the earth, just as his grandfathers did.

What do you think it all means? For Black Elk in 1931, and thousands of readers elsewhere, the story of his vision reinforced the Native American idea that human beings exist together—not separate from—the rest of creation. Although they are very different from rocks, horses, and spirits, human beings share a direct link with place—the land, the mountains, the water, and the sky of a particular region. (Native American sensitivity to such connections mirror similar ideas and experiences in many other indigenous cultures worldwide.)

Imagine your grandfathers, even if you don't know them. You exist because they did. Your life depends on their having lived, and you may

feel more affectionate toward your grandfather than your dad. He gave you life, and you return that with respect, love, communication, and even a gift once in a while. He doesn't need much, but still, it's the right thing to do, isn't it? The Native American view of human beings and nature follows the same logic, but broadens the focus to include it to the land, animals, and spirits. According to Native American opinion (or Confucianism, for that matter), human harmony comes from reciprocity. Sometimes, American Indians call this the **giveaway** (Storm 5). For nature to remain in harmony, each being must take only what is necessary to survive, but also give away what he or she does not need. The plants take carbon monoxide and give away oxygen. The sheep take the oxygen but give the carbon monoxide. The wolf takes a sheep but leaves remains for the bugs. Bugs eat dead carcasses and give nutrients to the soil.

We human beings differ from animals through our inability to give away. We're often takers, not providers. "Each individual," writes one Iroquois author, "both genders, each clan, each community has its place in Creation, just as each other-than-human species does. Each has a

things and are linked to everything on the land where you're born (Hirschfelder & Molin 191–92).

For Native Americans, the path from childhood to adulthood—from innocence to responsibility—often includes rituals that culminate in receiving a new name. The rites of passage for young adults paint a vivid picture of Native American views about humanity and help us understand the human potential for growth. Girls become women at first menstruation, often accompanied by an intense period of ritual purification. Sometimes marked by a massage to transform a girl into a woman, the puberty rite also begins a girl's path away from selfishness toward reciprocal life with the world. Newly able to bear children, many Native American tribes feel intense power from the girl as she changes into a woman, and people sometimes seek her out for healing.

Historically, the passage from boyhood to manhood could be more intense and more severe than for young women. For a young boy, the process of developing reciprocity might happen on his first hunt. Killing an animal, the boy needed to learn the reciprocal arrangement that gave meat to his family but demanded respect in return. This didn't always happen, of course, because human beings often take a long time to develop giveback. People who want to revive Native American sacred ways must not forget Head-Smashed-In Buffalo Jump, the spot in Alberta, Canada, where the Blackfoot Indians hunted by herding hundreds of animals over a cliff. Although the ritual was executed with

∧∧∧ This painting is called "Celestial Germinators" by Hopi-Choctaw artist Dan V. Lomahaftewa. How might it illustrate Native American ideas about humanity?

part in the 'Original Instructions. . . .' But human beings often fail in their designs—fall short of their ideals. Cycles of revenge, self-indulgence, and violence ensue" (Olupona 142).

As a result of humanity's inability to give back as much as we receive from the world, we must take steps toward a better relationship with our world. That would include the past and future, people and animals, rocks and plants. We must try to emulate the best aspects of animals who intrinsically understand giveback. Each one of us can develop some of the strengths and weaknesses that animals display. Native American names often reflect individual traits, including animals, colors, or other natural phenomena. As we saw on the medicine wheel, each point on the compass reflects a color, an animal, and a personality trait. Yet just as the compass has limitless gradations, so too do human names. In fact, in some tribes children don't receive a name until they show their personality. In a number of Native American groups, every person even has a secret name known to the family but never used in public. Some groups give children names to remind them of their grandparents, while still others add one related to the season the child was born. You can see how this works out, right? Your name as a Native American might include a mixture of family members, weather conditions, animals, and seasons. This makes sense because you exist on a continuum with all of those

∧∧∧ Hopi teenager Smiling Sun prepares for his ceremony into manhood. How do such puberty rituals bring together the entire community?

Plains Indian Concept of the Four Souls

Niya: The life-breath

Niya fills all physical forms with life. During ceremonies, a person's Niya can leave the body and return to the spirit world to interact with other spiritual beings.

Sicun: The spirit power

Sicun resides in beings regardless of life or death. When an animal is killed, for example, its Niya is taken away, but its Sicun still remains.

Nagila: Cosmic energy

Nagila is the source of all things, and the essence of life. Because all living things share this spiritual energy, they are all related to one another.

Nagi: The ghost

Nagi mirrors a person's physical form and personality. A young person with great knowledge of the world may have the Nagi of a person who lived previously. When a man or woman goes on a vision quest, his or her Nagi speaks with the Nagi of animals and other spiritual guardians.

Source: Based on Epes and Cousins 89–90.

∧
∧ All things in the world are related through possession of these four souls. How might you view the world differently if you perceived every rock, plant, and animal as a relative?

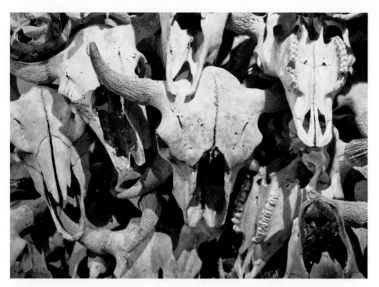

<<< These bison skulls are kept at the Head-Smashed-In Buffalo Jump in Alberta, Canada. The site derives its name from the story of an unfortunate young man who stood beneath the cliff to watch the bison stampede.

intense preparation and concern for the buffalos' spirits, the results were often brutal to witness:

> A dreadful scene of confusion and slaughter then begins, the oldest and strongest animals crush and toss the weaker; the shouts and screams of the excited Indians rise above the roaring of the bulls, the bellowing of the cows, and the piteous moaning of the calves. The dying struggles of so many huge and powerful animals crowded together, create a revolting and terrible scene. (Brink 147)

▶ HOW DO HUMANS INTERACT WITH THE SACRED? HOW DOES THE SACRED BECOME COMMUNITY?

Surprised you, right? Suddenly, after 14 chapters, I've combined the last two questions. To tell the truth, I tried to write them separately, but they kept getting mixed up with one another. Then I understood why: In Native American spiritual traditions, you simply cannot separate sacred interaction from community. Even when they're feeling lonely or solitary, Native Americans believe that they're not alone. The world around them is their community, alive with the Great Mystery. You may find this idea in other indigenous religions too.

Native Americans, like other indigenous peoples, interact with their sacred world every day. Sleeping, eating, breathing, walking, hunting, even attacking and killing each other in wars—each of these can reinforce the sacred and reciprocal relationship with the world around them. To explore this relationship, Native Americans developed hundreds of rituals. For Black Elk's Lakota, these included the begging dance, the kettle dance, the sweat lodge, and the Wakan feast. We can break down Native American interaction with the sacred into three areas: words, steps, and rituals.

Sacred Words

Words carry meaning, but not just as symbols. Like Native Americans' names, their words both reflect and change the world. You can see it all through this chapter, as different Native Americans tell stories about their

∧ An Apache girl undergoes her puberty ritual
∧ ceremony in Arizona. What rites of passage do
you have in your culture or faith tradition?

∧ Storytelling in a Native American longhouse.
∧ How do these stories affect people's
spiritual lives?

sacred world. That's on purpose; words carry power to describe and to create at the same time. From an American Indian point of view, you'll never be the same after reading the stories on these pages. I change just by typing them into my computer.

Like the world around us, words appear in different forms as Native American links to the sacred. Written words probably have the least power because they only change a little (depending on who is reading them). But when we sing, chant, and tell stories, the words are constantly changing and growing with the situation. The general term for this might be "teachings," but even that doesn't celebrate the transformative and creative power that words give to the world. One Native American says, "An oral story is not an object of art or any other kind of object. It is an action, it is something I do. It's an action that's now, and that speaks of ancient things" (Epes and Cousins 54).

Of course, a story needs an audience. You could speak to the wind and the four directions, but words carry the most meaning when they're part of a community interaction, as people listen and respond. "When I was a little girl, every so often in the evening my family would invite some old man into our home. We would make cherry pudding for him and have him tell stories to us kids. As long as we said, 'Eh,' which is 'yes,' he kept on telling the story. When nobody said 'Eh' that was the end of the story. He'd quit and go home. Then he'd come back and do it again another time" (Epes and Cousins 54).

From Words to Steps: The Vision Quest

Native American spirituality has traditionally taught that people learn to overcome senseless violence and selfishness by finding a kindred spirit. To do this, both boys and girls could undertake a **vision quest** (as I read about in *Seven Arrows*). This was a form of spiritual growth, a way to recognize the interaction of all creation (Irwin 236). During the vision quest, a person would leave his family for some extended period, eating little and walking alone across the land, often toward some place in the sacred geography. He could stay in a sacred cave, follow a river, or sleep alone among the stones, animals, and spirits of his land. Back home, the community continually talked about the youth, asked animals and the Great Mystery to watch over him, and kept him in their minds as they fell asleep at night. As he traveled, the youth sought a vision, perhaps like Black Elk's dream that we've just read. In this search, the person hoped to experience a direct link to the land and its inhabitants, that could then help him to become a truly reciprocal human, one who has learned to give back as well as to take. The vision might appear during that first quest, or during another quest later in life, or perhaps not at all. In any case, the land taught something valuable to the young person, who might receive a new name based on what happened during the quest.

In some cases, especially in Plains Indian tribes, a boy's vision quest could culminate in an intense ritual linked to the sun dance. After ritual purification through a sweat

∧ Looking toward the sun and tethered with
∧ leather to a pole, this Creek Indian undergoes
∧ the ritual piercing that will introduce him to manhood. How do you think Native Americans interpreted the elements of this ritual?

∧ Blackfoot Indians use this bison skull as part
∧ of their sun dance. What can you learn
∧ about the sacred world by studying this painted skull?

lodge ceremony, elders prepared the young man to endure pain as a way to give back to the world. During the sun dance, a tribal leader would cut the youth's chest or back and insert a wooden peg with a leather rope connected to it, threading the wood behind the muscle. The leather piece connected to a pole standing high above the ground. Leaning backward to tighten the connection, dancing in a circle and hearing his tribal elders drumming, chanting, and singing, the young man pulled until the leather and wood ripped out of his chest.

I remember reading about this a kid, probably around the same time my brother gave me *Seven Arrows*. Then and now, looking at the picture, I'm not sure I could have gone through with it. What I did not understand, I suppose, was the strength that the man in the photo would have received from everything *not* shown there—the wood from the earth, leather from animals, the sun, and his tribe's support through ritual preparations, music, and songs.

^ ^ ^ Harrington Luna is a Pima Medicine Man.
Here he says a morning prayer for the winter solstice.

Steps Become Ritual: The Sun Dance

Of all Native American celebrations, the sun dance may be the most famous. Occurring in the springtime as a way to heal, connect, and be reborn, American Indians from many tribes still celebrate this multi-day ritual. (See the graphic on the next page to get a better sense of each step of this sacred practice.)

Participants in the sun dance sought out a medicine man for spiritual and physical aid. Sometimes called a holy man or a shaman (a term we'll encounter again in Chapter 16), this member of the tribe held special power to contact and interact with the sacred world.

Vision Quest is a form of spiritual growth derived from journeying alone to seek a vision linking the self with the land and its inhabitants.

Scholars hold different opinions about the term "shaman," but such a person almost always exists in the indigenous traditions of the world. For Native American tribes, this holy man helps heal people and connect them to the rest of creation through the words and actions that make up rituals. It would be hard to imagine the sun dance lasting for hundreds of years if not for the wise men who remember its steps, its songs, and its power. We'll learn more about shamans in Chapter 16.

American Indian Spirituality Meets Christian Spirituality: Is God Red or White?

White settlers regularly brought Christianity with them as they journeyed westward into American Indian country. Many Catholic missionaries carried the gospel of Jesus into Native American lands, sometimes successfully integrating the two worlds. In the past 30 years, though, many American Indians have resisted Christianity and returned to a more "Indian" way of looking at the world. The bible of this movement may be *God Is Red*. In it, the Native American author dissects Christianity as he sees it, constantly illustrating his interpretation of religion: Christianity has become a tool of power, dominance, and ecological suicide. Native American spirituality, to the contrary, embraces giving back, equality, and oneness with Earth.

Some Native Americans, though, feel a kinship between Christianity and American Indian culture. Look at the historic photo on this page, taken at Pueblo de Cochiti, New Mexico, in 1888. You can see immediately how Native Americans integrated their traditional ways with Christianity.

As in other religious systems that we have studied, Indian and Christian traditions sometimes mixed syncretically. For example, Native Americans have often used substances in their quest to broaden their comprehension of nature and humanity. These include tobacco and peyote, a small cactus, that grows in present-day Texas and Mexico. Peyote provides a more intense and hallucinogenic experience than tobacco. Some Indians then transformed the Christian sacrament of communion (using wine) into a Native American equivalent—eating peyote.

In the following passage, the Winnebago Indian John Rave describes his first peyote use, probably around 1893. He found wisdom and power in peyote, enough

<<< Pictured is a photograph from 1888 of a Pueblo Indian sun dance. **How are Christian ideas blended with Native American spirituality?**

The Sun Dance

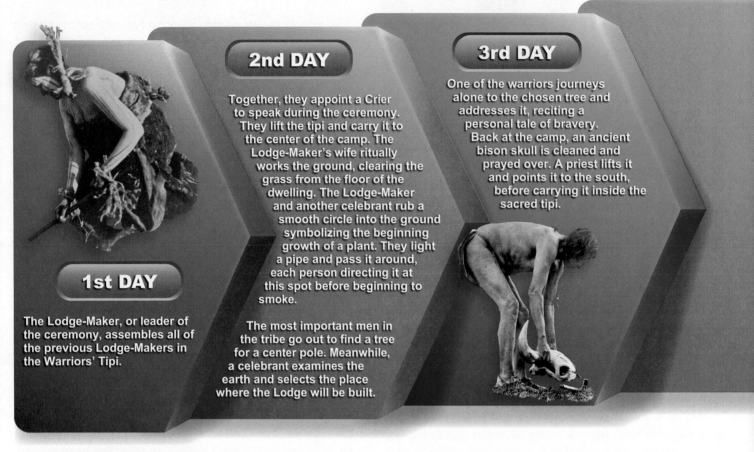

1st DAY

The Lodge-Maker, or leader of the ceremony, assembles all of the previous Lodge-Makers in the Warriors' Tipi.

2nd DAY

Together, they appoint a Crier to speak during the ceremony. They lift the tipi and carry it to the center of the camp. The Lodge-Maker's wife ritually works the ground, clearing the grass from the floor of the dwelling. The Lodge-Maker and another celebrant rub a smooth circle into the ground symbolizing the beginning growth of a plant. They light a pipe and pass it around, each person directing it at this spot before beginning to smoke.

The most important men in the tribe go out to find a tree for a center pole. Meanwhile, a celebrant examines the earth and selects the place where the Lodge will be built.

3rd DAY

One of the warriors journeys alone to the chosen tree and addresses it, reciting a personal tale of bravery. Back at the camp, an ancient bison skull is cleaned and prayed over. A priest lifts it and points it to the south, before carrying it inside the sacred tipi.

Source: Based on Jamake Highwater, *Ritual of the Wind: North American Indian Ceremonies, Music and Dances*, (New York: The Viking Press, 1977: 64–71.

∧
∧ This is a description of the Sun Dance, as performed by the Plains Indians. The dance is
∧ a ritual of renewal and an expression of hope that the coming seasons will provide good
hunting, gathering, and planting.

to create the John Rave Cross Fire Ritual that integrated Rave's Christian education with Native American concepts and actions. In the following passage, pay special attention to the language—how does he mix Indian and Christian ideas?

The following night we were to eat peyote again. I thought to myself, "Last night it almost harmed me." "Well, let us do it again," they said. "All right, I'll do it." So there we ate seven peyote apiece.

Suddenly I saw a big snake. I was very much frightened. Then another one came crawling over me. "My God! Where are these coming from?" There at my back there seemed to be something. So I looked around and I saw a snake about to swallow me entirely. It had legs and arms and a long tail. The end of this tail was like a spear. "O, my God! I am surely going to die now," I thought. Then I looked again in another direction and I saw a man with horns and long claws and with a spear in his hand. He jumped for me and I threw myself on the ground. He missed me. Then I looked back and this time he started back, but it seemed to me that he was directing his spear at me. Again I threw myself on the ground and he missed me. There seemed to be no possible escape for me. Then suddenly

it occurred to me, "Perhaps it is this peyote that is doing this thing to me?" "Help me, O medicine, help me! It is you who are doing this and you are holy! It is not these frightful visions that are causing this. I should have known that you were doing it. Help me!" Then my suffering stopped. "As long as the earth shall last, that long will I make use of you, O medicine!"

This had lasted a night and a day. For a whole night I had not slept at all. Then we breakfasted. Then I said, when we were through, "Let us eat peyote again to-night." That evening I ate eight peyote.

. . .

In the middle of the night I saw God. To God living up above, our Father, I prayed. "Have mercy upon me! Give me knowledge that I may not say and do evil things. To you, O God, I am trying to pray. Do thou, O Son of God, help me, too. This religion, let me know. Help me, O medicine, grandfather, help me! Let me know this religion!" Thus I spoke and sat very quiet. And then I beheld the morning star and it was good to look upon. The light was good to look upon. I had been frightened during the night but now I was happy. Now as the light appeared, it seemed to me that nothing would be invisible to me. I seemed to see

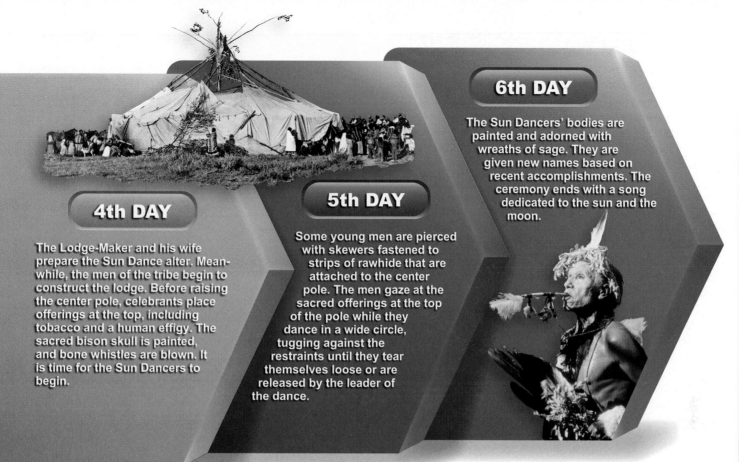

4th DAY

The Lodge-Maker and his wife prepare the Sun Dance alter. Meanwhile, the men of the tribe begin to construct the lodge. Before raising the center pole, celebrants place offerings at the top, including tobacco and a human effigy. The sacred bison skull is painted, and bone whistles are blown. It is time for the Sun Dancers to begin.

5th DAY

Some young men are pierced with skewers fastened to strips of rawhide that are attached to the center pole. The men gaze at the sacred offerings at the top of the pole while they dance in a wide circle, tugging against the restraints until they tear themselves loose or are released by the leader of the dance.

6th DAY

The Sun Dancers' bodies are painted and adorned with wreaths of sage. They are given new names based on recent accomplishments. The ceremony ends with a song dedicated to the sun and the moon.

everything clearly . . . It is a cure for all evil. Before, I had thought that I knew something but I really knew nothing. It is only now that I have real knowledge. In my former life I was like one blind and deaf. My heart ached when I thought of what I had been doing. Never again will I do it. This medicine alone is holy and has made me good and has rid me of all evil. The one whom they call God has given me this. That I know positively. Let them all come here; men and women; let them bring with them all that they desire; let them bring with them their diseases. If they come here they will get well. This is all true; it is all true. Bring whatever desires you possess along with you and then come and eat or drink this medicine. This is life, the only life. Then you will learn something about yourself, so come. Even if you are not told anything about yourself, nevertheless you will learn something of yourself. Come with your disease, for this medicine will cure it. Whatever you have, come and eat this medicine and you will have true knowledge once and for all. Learn of this medicine yourself through actual experience.

If you just hear about it you are not likely to try it. If you desire real knowledge about it try it yourself, for then you will learn of things that you had never known before. In no other way will you ever be happy. I know that all sorts of excuses will run through your mind for not partaking of it, but if you wish to learn of something good, try this (Radin 342–343).

>>> A candle and a peyote cactus are held together in this man's hands. What does this image tell us about the blending of religions and cultures?

Breaking the Sacred Bonds of the Land: Native Americans and the U.S. Government

By now, you've gotten a general sense of Native American spirituality and how it interacts with the land and with outside influences like Christianity. Unfortunately, Native Americans and the U.S. government had very different plans for the vast lands of the American West. One simplified version of the story says that primitive Indians could not assimilate to European-style American society, so they were forced to move into reservations in the name of progress. On the reservations, the American Indians remained illiterate, drank too much, and slid into poverty.

The other account of the story goes something like this: Honorable Native Americans lived peacefully on their sacred lands until the White Man arrived, bringing smallpox, alcohol, guns, and violence. The U.S. government supported white settlers in their struggle

against noble Indians. Through force, treachery, and lies, the government knowingly committed genocide and herded Native Americans into reservations where they could not harm white people.

In this case, both stories hold some truth. Tensions did arise between white Americans and Native Americans. Settlers wanted to farm, settle, and build townships in America, developing capitalism and private ownership of the land. American Indians saw themselves as members of a great family, living in reciprocity with the land and everything on it. Looking back, it seemed inevitable that the two cultures would clash.

Three events illustrate the spiritual losses related to the fight between the U.S. government and Native Americans. In trying to subdue the Indians and get them to settle down as ranchers or farmers, the U.S. Army cavalry waged a low-intensity war with the American Indians for years. In 1876, a group of Lakota Sioux (including Black Elk and Crazy Horse) demolished the forces of General George Custer at the Battle of Little Big Horn. From then on, the U.S. government redoubled its efforts to control the American Indians.

The Dawes Act of 1887 began forcing Native Americans to give up their idea of collective harmony with the land, and instead bullied them into buying private parcels. The Indian School in Carlisle, Pennsylvania, began to re-educate American Indian children to act like "civilized" whites.

In the midst of this, a spiritual revival began among the Plains Indians. A Paiute medicine man named Wovoka had a vision in which he saw a revival of Indian life that wove together many ideas we've discussed.

> When you get home you must make a dance to continue five days. Dance four successive nights, and the last night keep up the dance until the morning of the fifth day, when all must bathe in the river and then disperse to their homes. You must all do in the same way. Do not tell the white people about this . . . Jesus is now upon the earth. He appears like a cloud. The dead are still alive again. I do not know when they will be here; maybe this fall or in the spring. When the time comes there will be no more sickness and everyone will be young again. Do not refuse to work for the whites and do not make any trouble with them until you leave them. When the earth shakes [at the coming of the new world] do not be afraid. It will not hurt you (Mooney 781).

News of this vision spread quickly through American Indian groups, and the "ghost dance" (as American newspapers called it) triggered a renewal in American Indian spirituality, with a Christian twist. People swore that they saw Wovoka survive a shotgun blast, and they believed that their "ghost dance" shirts might shield them from gunfire—a kind of spiritual bulletproof vest.

Most settlers did not seem bothered by this revival, but some newspaper reporters began to claim that the ghost dance was a charade to hide plans for an uprising. In response, U.S. President James Harrison called out the troops, Sitting Bull was killed in a botched arrest attempt, and other Lakota began a trip off reservation to the Standing Rock Agency reservation, where he had been killed. On their way, the cavalry intercepted the American Indians and forced them to stop at Wounded Knee Creek. In confusion over the peaceful or violent intentions of each group, someone shot off a rifle, which erupted into a massacre. The cavalry killed about 300 Lakota men, women, and children on December 29, 1890. The ghost dance renewal died, and with it the last organized resistance to the American government (Mooney 843–886 and The Wounded Knee Museum online, http://www.woundedkneemuseum.org/ main_menu.html).

Frederic Remington, "Ogallala Sioux performing the Ghost Dance at the Pine Ridge Indian Agency, South Dakota, 1890"/The Granger Collection, New York

∧
∧ **This painting by Frederic Remington from the late 1800s shows** the South Dakotan Sioux Indians **performing their version of the** ghost dance.

Thinking About Indigenous World Religions

We have learned about the American Plains Indians, but don't forget that indigenous cultures survive around the globe, either in large groups or small patches. As their cultures succumb to the pressure of modern life, we risk losing nearly all knowledge of them, because they tend to pass down knowledge orally rather than written books. When the stories do get written down, as in my old friend *Seven Arrows*, they're sometimes hard to understand. Even so, we can try to apply what we've learned from Native American traditions to other indigenous cultures around the world. Shawn Wilson, a Native American who works in Australia, puts it this way:

> It is necessary to provide you with a background of myself as the storyteller, and why I am interested in the fields of Indigenous Spirituality, education and psychology. I am an Opaskwayak Cree from Manitoba, Canada. My mother is of Scottish ancestry and my father is Opaskwayak Cree. My Cree cultural heritage has been more influential in my life because I was raised on an Indian reserve that is part of Opaskwayak Cree Nation traditional lands. My upbringing and culture as a Cree person have been very important in the formation of my values, ideals and outlook on life. The importance of respect, equality and personal growth has been stressed to me since I was born. . . .

> Travelling and meeting new people from different cultures have always held a fascination for me. My upbringing has taught me to view differences between cultures as something to be treasured; though in meeting Indigenous people in Canada, United States, South-east Asia, Norway, New Zealand and Australia, I have noticed that we all share very similar beliefs and spirituality. I have often wondered how Indigenous peoples from opposite sides of the earth

Casinos and Native American Life

In the past few years, casinos have started popping up on Indian Reservations all over the United States. If you're in Connecticut, you may not have known much about the Pequot Indians until the Foxwoods Casino became a major tourist destination. It's far removed from the bingo halls and cigarette shops that used to welcome Americans to Native American lands. Other tribes across the country have imitated Foxwoods' success.

It's a funny turnaround—for years, reservations acted like huge jails without walls for many Native Americans. The U.S. government prohibited many sacred traditions, and American economic success rarely found its way to "the rez." In fact, some scholars have called government actions a form of "spiritual genocide" that subsided only with the American Indian Religious Freedom Act in 1978 (Talbot 7).

These casinos illustrate some of the paradoxes of Native American life in the 21st century. How can Indian land be sacred *and* poverty-stricken *and* lit up like Las Vegas, all at the same time? It comes down to the particular relationship that Indians have with the U.S. government. As sovereign nations, Native American tribes have some legal rights that the states do not enjoy. This includes the power to open casinos even in places where gambling is illegal in neighboring towns or cities.

As a result, non-Indian gamblers might only know of the Cherokee, Pequot, or Seminole Indians through the glitzy Indian-themed decorations at the casinos. Still, billions of dollars have flowed into tribal bank accounts. They underwrite education, housing, and even powwows and religious ceremonies. Some Native Americans worry that the casinos will ruin indigenous religious life, luring Indians with materialism and wealth. One Indian scholar puts it this way: "If we lose the ability to exercise our rights as Native people, to exercise our traditional and spiritual practices to protect those sites that are sacred and that are essential to the ability to exercise those practices, we will have lost everything, and the ability to operate a successful casino won't mean anything. The white man will have won. We will have become just like everybody else, and there will be no need to wage the struggle any more. I don't think it's going to come to that; I think that we will succeed, that we will continue" (Echo-Hawk 167).

Poverty and promise. Do you think there is irony in calling this casino "Mystic Lake?"

---

could have values that are so alike. Consequently, my interest in this topic has grown, as I contend that Indigenous people share a unique way of thinking (Used by permission of Shawn Wilson ©. ucahs.nsw.gov.au.)

We can't possible consider all the world's sacred traditions in *THINK World Religions*, but you may want to branch out and do some of your own research. Check out the ThinkSpot.com to find more resources and study many of the traditions listed on the map on the following page. The possibilities are nearly endless. You can start by asking the Four Questions we have studied throughout this book. Then branch out and consider some other topics. Here are a few ideas to start you off:

- How do indigenous traditions interact with others—do they mix together or try to stay separate?

- Does the tradition have a person who acts similar to a shaman?

- Do indigenous politics and religion interact? How and why?

- Do men or women tend to dominate sacred traditions? How?

- Does the religion seem to change rapidly or slowly?

- How have imperialism and modern life affected indigenous sacred life?

As you study, don't forget to use the skills you've developed here. Analyze visual data such as pictures, photographs, and videos. Look for biases in arguments. Consider different forms of asceticism. Try to learn how an indigenous group lives authentically on its sacred lands. As you dig deeper, I'm sure you'll begin to see ideas that relate to things you've read about in *THINK World Religions*. Do the similarities come from contact between indigenous and outside groups, or do they seem universal? Why?

Good luck!

Indigenous Cultures

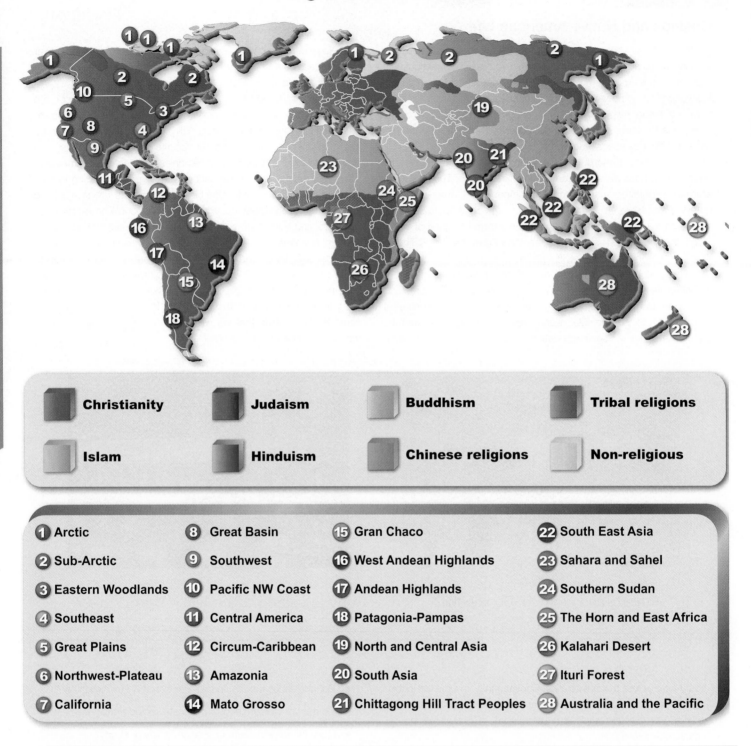

Christianity **Judaism** **Buddhism** **Tribal religions**

Islam **Hinduism** **Chinese religions** **Non-religious**

1 Arctic	8 Great Basin	15 Gran Chaco	22 South East Asia
2 Sub-Arctic	9 Southwest	16 West Andean Highlands	23 Sahara and Sahel
3 Eastern Woodlands	10 Pacific NW Coast	17 Andean Highlands	24 Southern Sudan
4 Southeast	11 Central America	18 Patagonia-Pampas	25 The Horn and East Africa
5 Great Plains	12 Circum-Caribbean	19 North and Central Asia	26 Kalahari Desert
6 Northwest-Plateau	13 Amazonia	20 South Asia	27 Ituri Forest
7 California	14 Mato Grosso	21 Chittagong Hill Tract Peoples	28 Australia and the Pacific

∧
∧ This map shows the distribution of current belief systems, as well as the location of
∧ modern indigenous peoples. Pay close attention to how the two overlap. How does this mix affect
the spirituality of different cultures?

Conclusion

And so, what is the answer to the riddle from *Seven Arrows*? Here it is again: What animal is like a mouse, an eagle, a buffalo, and a bear? By now, you know the American Indian answer: We are that animal when we human beings are wise. We can see things up close and innocently, like a mouse. We can see for miles like an eagle. We can achieve the spiritual introspection of the bear and, we hope, the wisdom of the buffalo.

Even today, people journey to the medicine wheel in Sedona, Arizona for spiritual healing and learning. **Why do you think Native American spirituality might appeal to people from other cultures?**

Some Native American groups celebrate a girl's passage into puberty with a four-day reenactment of the creation myth. The girls are sprinkled with a pollen mixture that remains on their bodies throughout the ceremony. **Can you think of similar rituals in other religions?**

IS THERE A GOD?

The answer varies. Different Native American groups recognize individual gods such as the Trickster (known in the Southwest as Kokopelli), or the Creator. In general, however, all share a spiritual belief in the interconnectivity of humans to the land around them. Many Native Americans believe in the Sacred Mystery that is shared by all things plant, animal, and mineral, and thus perceive all of creation as related. Although the sacred is everywhere, power can be magnified in certain locations.

HOW DOES THE SACRED BECOME COMMUNITY?

Native Americans perceive the world around them as their community, and the sacred is involved in every aspect. Holy men, sometimes known as medicine men or shamans, help people connect to the rest of creation through the words and actions of rituals. Due to the interaction of cultures over the past couple centuries, many Native Americans have incorporated aspects of Christianity into their spiritual life. An example is the use of peyote during communion, instead of the traditional wine.

WHAT DOES IT MEAN TO BE HUMAN?

No man is an island—all human beings exist together with the rest of creation. In the Native American tradition, all things in the world are related through the possession of four souls, and harmony comes from reciprocity. The notion of "giveaway," or giving back to nature, is sometimes reflected in Native American naming rituals. The passing from childhood to adulthood marks the beginning of developing giveback, and often young adults take new names to represent their new identities.

HOW DO HUMANS INTERACT WITH THE SACRED?

It is hard to separate the sacred from the community in Native American traditions because the community is a part of the sacred; thus Native Americans are constantly interacting with the sacred as they interact with the world. However, there are also specific rituals, such as sun dances and vision quests, which help people communicate directly with the spiritual realm. The telling of stories also holds a place of importance, since words forever alter our experiences and perceptions of the world.

The Church of Saint Francis of Assisi in Ranchos de Taos, New Mexico was built in 1730. **Does this look like a traditional Christian church to you? Why might it have been built to reflect the architecture of the Pueblo Indians?**

This totem pole is one of many from Saxman Totem Park in southeastern Alaska. **What is symbolic about the human figure being encompassed by the bird?**

Summary

IS THERE A GOD?   p. 254

• Yes, no, and maybe. Indigenous cultures around the world tend to perceive spirituality as linked to the land. Some believe in specific gods, such as the Trickster, while others simply accept the idea of the Sacred Mystery, a life force shared by all of creation.

WHAT DOES IT MEAN TO BE HUMAN?   p. 258

• There is no spiritual separation between human beings and nature; humans share a deep relationship with everything in the world.

• Some Native Americans believe in four souls that are shared by all of creation.

• Giveaway plays an important role in Native American cultures, as all beings are expected to give back to the world in return for what they have taken.

HOW DO HUMANS INTERACT WITH THE SACRED? HOW DOES THE SACRED BECOME COMMUNITY?   p. 261

• The community itself is sacred, as it is a part of the sacred world.

• Some cultures use medicine men, or shamans, to incorporate rituals into their lives. Practices such as the Sun Dance and sweat lodge ceremonies strengthen people's ties to the spiritual.

Key Terms

Sacred Mystery is a life force shared by all things in the world.   *254*

Giveaway is the Native American idea of the reciprocity of the universe.   *258*

Vision quest is a form of spiritual growth derived from journeying alone to seek a vision linking the self with the land and its inhabitants.   *262*

Find it on

www.tipis.org

Go to the ThinkSpot to learn more about the structure we call the "tee-pee" but that is actually spelled "tipi." See historic and modern drawings of this structure, thought to represent a "life of freedom on the Plains." Maybe you'll be inclined to try tipi dwelling out at some point after reading about different tipi competitions that are held around the country, or maybe you'll join a discussion group about the practicality and building of this type of Native American shelter.

• http://www.nebraskahistory.org/sites/neihardt/memorial_room.htm

If you'd like to learn more about John G. Niehardt and his experiences documenting the American West experience, visit the ThinkSpot. Nebraska's poet laureate recorded the oral traditions of many indigenous Americans, allowing modern-day Americans to experience the "tragedies and triumphs of the frontier experience.

• http://1onewolf.com/lakota/music4.htm

Learn more about the Lakota culture and tribe by visiting the ThinkSpot. Your exposure to different songs and dances of this group will give you insight into their traditions.

Questions for Study and Review

1. How are medicine wheels important in Native American tradition?

Medicine wheels symbolize creation; the individual stones represent aspects of creation such as family members, animals, or even concepts such as government or religion. Medicine wheels are one of the ways in which Native Americans celebrate the relationship between physical space (the land) and incorporeal spirituality (the sacred).

2. What are the four souls present in every being?

Nagila is the source of all things, and the essence of life. Niya is the life-breath of beings, and leaves the body eventually to return to the spirit world. Sicun, the spirit power, resides in all things regardless of life or death. Nagi is the essence of a person's physical form and personality, and can communicate with spiritual guardians.

3. What is a sun dance, and how does it relate to Native American spirituality?

Often performed in the spring, sun dances celebrate rebirth and reconnection to the earth. In some traditions, the dance includes a ritual that marks a boy's transformation into a man. Sun dances are led by holy men, sometimes called shamans, who maintain knowledge of the words and actions of the ritual.

For Further Study

BOOKS:

Brown, Joseph Epes, and Emily Cousins. *Teaching Spirits—Understanding Native American Religious Traditions.* New York: Oxford University Press, 2001: 23. Oxford Scholarship Online. Oxford University Press. Retrieved 18 March 2010.

Deloria, Vine Jr. *God Is Red: A Native View of Religion.* Golden, CO: Fulcrum Publishing, 2003.

DeMallie, Raymond J. Ed., *The Sixth Grandfather: Black Elk's teachings given to John G. Neihardt, 1881–1973.* Lincoln: Bison Books, University of Nebraska Press, 1985.

Storm, Hyemeyohsts. *Seven Arrows.* New York: Harper & Row Publishers, 1972

WEB SITES:

Brink, Jack W. *Imagining Head-Smashed-In: Aboriginal Buffalo Hunting on the Northern Plains.* Edmonton, Alberta: AU Press, Athabasca University, 2008. Available at http://www.aupress.ca/books/120137/ebook/99Z_Brink_2008-Imagining_Head_Smashed_In.pdf. *Retrieved 31 March 2010.*

Wilson, Shawn. Recognising the Importance of Spirituality in Indigenous Learning." Australia Corrections Education Association, 1999: 1. Available at www.acea.org.au/Content/1999%20papers/Shaun%20Wilson%20-%20paper.pdf. *Retrieved 17 March 2010.*

Wounded Knee Museum Online, http://www.woundedkneemuseum.org/main_menu.html. *Retrieved 31 March 2010.*

State of the World's Indigenous Peoples. http://www.un.org/esa/socdev/unpfii/en/sowip.html.

<<< Many New Religious Movements seek wisdom from places long held sacred by indigenous cultures. **The elements of water, earth, fire, and air all seem to merge dramatically in** Sedona, AZ.

IS THERE A GOD?

WHAT DOES IT MEAN TO BE HUMAN?

HOW DO HUMANS INTERACT WITH THE SACRED?

HOW DOES THE SACRED BECOME COMMUNITY?

There

have always been seekers: Hindu ascetics, living in the forest and learning the most esoteric practices; Christian monks perched atop a pedestal in the desert; a Jewish king writing sacred poetry; a Pakistani youth twirling in ecstatic circles, seeking unity with God. People have long searched for the spark of meaning, the path toward enlightenment, or the taste of eternity. Often they mixed traditions and practices in a stew of sacred activity, one adding spice to another. Christianity began as Judaism, but accommodated the ancient holly, ivy, and Yule log to celebrate its good news in England.

Nowadays, though, things change rapidly. In the contemporary world, the search has expanded further than our grandparents' traditions. We sometimes feel the need for new kinds of wisdom, since old ways have left us disenchanted (Lewis 40–53). After all, we can wake up in San Francisco and go to sleep in Adelaide, all the while texting our brother in Brazil. In a world like that, it's no surprise that we've begun to look across the globe to find new paths and unearth ancient traditions in an attempt to construct our sacred lives.

In the years that spawned two world wars, jet planes, and computers, people across the globe have often felt unmoored from their communities. They have sought new ways to explain the cosmos, themselves, and their world. As a result, many new sacred movements have grown and spread. Scholars have tried to understand this great diversity, to find the underlying forces behind the creation of New Religious Movements (NRMs). That's extremely difficult to do—NRMs develop rapidly and sometimes secretly. They mix old ideas and new concepts more readily than any tradition we have studied so far in *THINK World Religions*. You can see this in the Sacred Place and the Sacred Action features that follow on the next three pages. As you read through Chapter 16, remember that NRMs cross every possible border—land, history, tradition, and even the cosmos. We can organize this multitude into two general types—the "new paths" forged from well-established religions and "ancient wisdom" that people seek to explain the modern world. As you can imagine, these often mix and overlap with one another, as you'll see in Chapter 16. Our study will concentrate on two very different NRMS: the Unification Church and Wicca—especially as it interacts with the New Age Movement. Though Wicca and New Age are not synonymous, I think you'll find enough correspondences to study them together.

NEW RELIGIONS:
A Quest for the Sacred

CHAPTER 16

A Sacred Place / Stonehenge

THEY'RE TRAPPED MOST OF THE TIME, THE STONES ARE. Huge, lurking bluestones stand alone or as dolmens, Pi-shaped monuments with a huge rock sitting on top of two others. A large circle of chain-link fence runs around the site, as if someone wants to keep the stones from running away. Don't laugh—for hundreds of years, people described Stonehenge as "The Giants' Dance." According to legend, the great magician Merlin transferred them from Ireland, where ancient giants had brought them from Africa! In truth, ancient people pulled, pushed, rolled, or floated them over 250 miles from Wales, all to build this sacred circle. One scholar estimates that it took *2.1 million* hours to build the two largest sections of the monument (Ray 232).

Around the stones, scores of people lay buried in the earthen barrows that rise slightly above the flat farmland of Salisbury, England. Some were local people; some were sick pilgrims who led their cows from as far away as Scotland, only to die a disfigured death. And others, perhaps, were kings.

Leave the rainy Sussex plain and come back for the summer solstice, when you can get through the fence and close to the stones. Druids will arrive too, in their robes and hoods. They play the long horn and drum, invoking the spirits of generations past and asking them to watch over the world for another summer. For these people, some wearing antlers on their heads, Stonehenge symbolizes light and dark, life and death. Its stones are male and female, huge legs and genitals (Hatto 103; Ray 260–69). Druids look to Stonehenge to find ancient meanings, seeking to recreate a lost religion from the centuries before Christianity.

When the Druids leave, the party begins. Girls with backpacks and boys with crazy hats made of ivy descend on the site. Celtic drumming and Scottish pipes turn to African drums and dance circles, lit by fires around the megaliths. Jugglers, hula-hoop dancers, saxophone players, and penny whistlers join together on the plain to wait for the sun to rise. In a modern take on ancient rituals, the dancers greet the sun as it traces a path perfectly across Stonehenge's axis. In this ancient place, they have found a quicksilver community.

The party at Stonehenge.

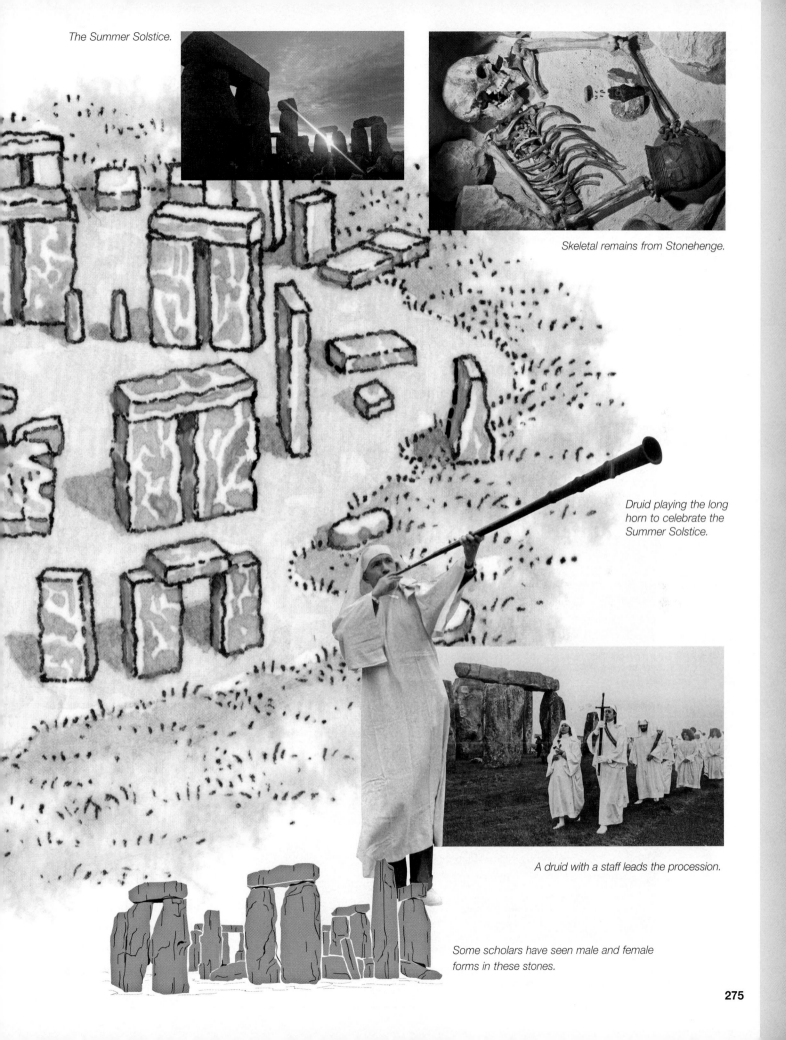

The Summer Solstice.

Skeletal remains from Stonehenge.

Druid playing the long horn to celebrate the Summer Solstice.

A druid with a staff leads the procession.

Some scholars have seen male and female forms in these stones.

The Blessing Ceremony

A huge crowd, yes, but otherwise the scene couldn't be more different from Stonehenge at the solstice. Ten thousand people sit peacefully, dressed in similar suits and dresses. They have come to get married or to renew their vows in a **Unification Church** Blessing Ceremony. Standing above them in an elegant cream-colored robe, the Rev. Sun Myung Moon reaches out his hand in blessing. To them, he is the True Father, successor to Christ, and the new messiah. He has begun the **True Family**, which these couples hope to expand across the world.

They do not need to know one another—Rev. Moon has joined them, and together they'll follow the Divine Principle as revealed by Christ to Rev. Moon. "In the Unification Church, following the Principle, God and

Marriage:
The Blessing Ceremony

1 **The Chastening Ceremony:**
Husband and wife chasten each other three times. This represents the acceptance that all humans err, but also that all humans forgive. God looks kindly on all who seek forgiveness for their faults.

2 **The Holy Wine Ceremony:**
Holy wine is given to the woman, who bows and drinks half of it. She then gives it to the man who also bows and drinks the remainder. This marks the transition from false parenthood (started by Adam and Eve, the first dysfunctional family) to True Parenthood, free from original sin.

3 **The Holy Blessing:**
This is the official marriage ceremony. Couples are sprinkled with holy water, recite vows, and exchange rings.

4 **The Separation Period:**
For 40 days following the ceremony, couples maintain sexual abstinence. This reflects Jesus' 40 days of fasting in the desert.

5 **The Three-Day Ceremony:**
To signify the transition to True Husband and True Wife, the couple consummates their marriage through a ritual of rebirth. The woman acts as both mother and wife, "rebirthing" and receiving the man as a husband. The man does the same, "rebirthing" his wife and also receiving her as wife.

then Father [Rev. Moon] are supposed to select your spouse. Your fathers and mothers who live in the fallen world do not know the Principle. They do not know. They do not follow any rules. Do you understand? But Reverend Moon of the Unification Church knows the standard that can establish the order centering on this Principle, and the covenant which must be followed to fulfill the law of heaven" (Blessing and Ideal Family, Chapter 4, Part 1).

The marriage process has five steps: the Chastening Ceremony, the Holy Wine Ceremony, the Holy Blessing, the Separation Period, and the Three-Day Ceremony. By following these steps, a young couple learns to communicate with each other and to commune with God. Eventually, they hope, they will begin their own True Families.

<<< The five steps of marriage are sacred to Unificationists. **Can you spot influences from other religions?**

Defining the New Religious Movements

Before we jump into our familiar Four Questions, let's take a minute to consider the very idea of "New Religious Movements." Back in Chapter 1, we studied the controversy over defining the word "religion." Over the years, dozens of scholars have tried their hands at it, but no one classification seems to cover humanity's great variety of sacred experiences. It's the same with New Religious Movements— we disagree on what the term means, though it does seem to describe phenomena of our modern life.

Think about it: How do we know when something stops being "new"? What if an idea (like karma) exists for thousands of years in one culture but suddenly arrives in a different one? Is it new or old? The same problem exists with the words "religious" and "movement," which mean different things to various people. For example, in this chapter we'll study the **New Age Movement**. Many people who ascribe to New Age ideas emphasize health and wellness, not religion. Yet the New Age generally falls under the umbrella of NRMs. What if you leave the Catholic Church to follow the Unification Church? Have you simply changed denominations or become a member of an NRM? Finally, if a group has close ties to more mainstream religions, does that mean it can't be a "new movement" (Chryssides 11–18)? You can see the problems.

Another approach is to think about each religion in its own context. Perhaps a New Religious Movement strays from the norms of dominant culture. One infamous example happened in 1994, when an Evangelical Christian preacher in North Carolina published a booklet entitled *Barney: The Purple Messiah*. That's right; the preacher claimed that the purple TV dinosaur had begun taking the place of Jesus in little kids' hearts. By singling out Barney as a fake messiah, the preacher was trying to redefine Barney from being a cuddly TV creature to being a false messiah in a New Religious Movement designed to supplant Christianity (Gallagher 210–11).

NRMs seek to blaze a new path that originates from an established religion. The Unification Church illustrates this idea, since it adds Korean folk ideas and the Supreme Ultimate to established Christian theology.

Unification Church is a modern interpretation of Christianity and East Asian traditions that stresses marriage within the church as a way of rebuilding God's kingdom on Earth.

True Family is composed of male and female members of the Unification Church united in sacred matrimony, free from original sin. These families produce True Sons and Daughters.

New Age Movement describes the overarching belief in developing one's spiritual, physical, and psychological self outside traditional boundaries, often with the ultimate goal of transforming the world.

But wait—if they're *old* Korean traditions, can they really be *new* paths? It makes your head spin. Other groups, like the Druids who gather at Stonehenge, seek to rediscover remnants of pre-Christian traditions in their indigenous cultures. A big problem: no one really knows what the Druids actually believed or how they acted, so modern Druids have to extrapolate from ancient sources or recreate Druidism based on their own imagination.

Finally, scholars point out that NRMs often form around highly charismatic leaders, such as the Rev. Sun Myung Moon (Unification Church) or L. Ron Hubbard (Scientology). But what happens when the original leader dies? Does the movement fade away? Or does it simply stop being "new?" Other groups, like Wicca or the New Age, however, bristle at the very idea of a single leader.

By this point in *THINK World Religions*, you know that a world of possibilities awaits you outside the covers of this book and beyond the walls of your classroom. The chart on the next page will help you identify NRMs that you might like to investigate in greater depth than we can do in this chapter. Even this long list, though, cannot include all the different groups and offshoots. It's also possible that you'll consider some of these groups to be quite mainstream. That will depend on many factors, including where you live and how diverse your community is. As you read about the Unification Church, Wicca, and the New Age in the rest of the chapter, consider how they might illustrate aspects of other NRMs too.

▶ IS THERE A GOD?

A New Path for Christianity: The Unification Movement

We encountered the Unification Movement in the Sacred Action section earlier in this chapter. Founded by the Rev. Sun Myung Moon, it has spread across the world from its beginnings in Korea. To put the church in context, let's take a quick look at that country's history in the last 100 years. At the turn of the century, Korea had its own emperor. Though not a strong country militarily, Korea celebrated its language, culture, and very rich religious traditions. In 1910, however, Japan annexed Korea after threatening to invade, taking firm control by the 1930s. Unlike Japan, which was largely Buddhist and Shinto, Korea had an extremely complex religious scene that included Roman Catholicism and Protestantism in addition to Daoist, Confucian, and local shamanic traditions. In fact, many Koreans saw Christianity as a force for independence and salvation in the face of Japan's imperial power.

On Easter Sunday 1935, a 16-year-old Sun Myung Moon prayed on a remote Korean hillside. There, he had a vision of Jesus, who instructed the young boy to lead a new kind of Christianity and unite nations in peace. For the next ten years, Moon continued to receive revelations, even as World War II raged across Asia. In 1945, as the war ended, Moon began to teach publicly about the need for a universal family of love. Korean Communists persecuted him in the North, torturing him in prison for three years at Hungnam, one of its notorious prison camps. In 1950, the camp fell to the South Koreans and Moon escaped (Clarke 343). In the South, he lived like an early Christian monk—penniless in a hut made from mud, stones and cardboard. There, he began to write down his *Divine Principle*, the guiding force for his new church. Mainline Christian denominations condemned him, but Moon's message of Divine Unification spoke loudly to some people in the divided Korean nation. His indigenous interpretation of the Bible incorporated both Confucian ideas of the family and shamanic perceptions, including the idea of spirits with sexual desires. Perhaps because it unified Christian and East Asian thought, the Unification Church grew quickly in Korea. It expanded into other parts of the world too, especially Japan, Great Britain, and the United States (Partridge 71). Often called "Moonies,"

New Religious Groups and Alternative Spiritualities

New Paths

Roots in Christianity

- The New Apostolic Church (1906)
- The Nazareth Baptist Church (Shembe) (1911)
- Oneness Pentecostalism (1913)
- Iglesia ni Cristo (1914)
- Kimbanguism (1921)
- The Zion Christian Church (1924)
- The Church of the Lord (Aladura) (1925)
- Rastafarianism (1930)
- The Worldwide Church of God (1933)
- The Celestial Church of Christ (Aladura) (1947)
- The Brotherhood of the Cross and Star (1950s)
- The Family Federation for World Peace and Unification (Unification Church) (1954)
- The Way International (1955)
- The Peoples Temple (1955)
- The Branch Davidians (1959)
- The Jesus Movement (1960s)
- The Family (Children of God) (1968)
- The Holy Order of MANS (1968)
- The Jesus Fellowship (Jesus Army) (1969)
- The World of Faith Movement (1974)
- Creation Spirituality (1977)
- The International Churches of Christ (1979)
- The Embassy of Heaven Church (1987)

Roots in Judaism

- ALEPH: Alliance for Jewish Renewal (1962)
- Humanistic Judaism (1965)
- The Havurot Movement (1973)
- Gush Emunim (1974)
- Meshihistim (1994)

Roots in Islam

- The Sufi Movement (International Sufi Movement) (1923)
- The Nation of Islam (1931)
- Subud (1932)
- The Sufi Order of the West (Sufi Order International) (1960s)
- United Nuwaubian Nation of Moors (1965)
- The Bawa Muhaiyaddeen Fellowship (1971)

Roots in Zoroastrianism

- Mazdaznan (1902)
- Iim-e Khshnoom (1907)

Lost Wisdom

Roots in Indigenous and Pagan Traditions

- Heathenism (20th century)
- The Native American Church (1918)
- Umbanda (1920s)
- Wicca (1954)
- The Church of All Worlds (1968)
- The Covenant of the Goddess (1975)
- The Fellowship of Isis (1976)
- Eco-Paganism: Protest Movement Spiritualities (1990s)

Roots in Western Esoteric and New Age Traditions

- Ordo Templi Orientis (OTO)
- The Anthroposophical Movement (1912)
- The Society of the Inner Light (1922)
- Gurdjieff and Ouspensky Groups (1922)
- The Arcane School (1923)
- The Emissaries of Divine Light (1932)
- The 'I AM' Religious Activity (1934)
- The School of Economic Science (1937)
- The Church Universal and Triumphant (Summit Lighthouse) (1958)
- The Findhorn Foundation (1962)
- Satanism (1966)
- The Movement of Spiritual Inner Awareness (1971)
- The Servants of the Light (1972)
- The Share International Foundation (1972)
- The Universal Christian Gnostic Church (1972)
- The Order of the Solar Temple (1973)
- A Course in Miracles (1976)
- Damanhur (1977)
- Fiat Lux (1980)
- The Impersonal Enlightenment Foundation (1988)
- The Temple of the Vampire (1989)
- Jamuheen and the Breatharians (1990s)
- The Celestine Prophecy (1994)
- The Company of Heaven (2001)

Roots in Modern Western Cultures

- Transpersonal Psychologies (1901)
- URANTIA (1935)
- Psychedelic Spirituality (1938)
- Silva Mind Control (1944)
- The Church of Scientology (1954)
- The Aetherius Society (1954)
- The Unarius Academy of Science (1954)
- The Synanon Church (1958)
- The Human Potential Movement (1962)
- Neuro-Linguistic Programming (1970s)
- Emin (1973)
- The Raëlian Religion (1974)
- Heaven's Gate (1975)
- Landmark Forum (est) (1985)
- Thee Church ov MOO (1990s)
- Chen Tao (God's Salvation Church) (1993)
- Doofs and Raves in Australia (1997)

Source: Based on Partridge 7–9

New Paths

Roots in Indian Religions

- The Meher Baba Movement (1923)
- The Self-Realization Fellowship (1925)
- The Self-Revelation Church of Absolute Monism (1927)
- The Brahma Kumaris (1936)
- Hao Hao (1939)
- The Church of the Shaiva Siddhanta (1949)
- The Satya Sai Baba Society (1950)
- The Muttappan Teyyam (1950s)
- Ananda Marga (1955)
- Transcendental Meditation (1957)
- ISKCON: The International Society for Krishna Consciousness (Hare Krishna Movement) (1965)
- Eckankar (1965)
- The Osho Movement (1966)
- The Friends of the Western Buddhist Order (1967)
- Krishnamurti and the Krishnamurti Foundation (1968)
- Auroville (1968)
- The 3HO Foundation (Healthy, Happy, Holy Organization) (1969)
- Mother Meera (1970s)
- Sahaja Yoga (1970)
- Elan Vital (1971)
- Adidam (1972)
- The Santi Asoke Movement (1973)
- Lifeware (1975)
- The New Kadampa Tradition (NKT) (1976)
- The Dhammakaya Foundation (1977)
- The Mata Amritanandamayi Mission (1981)
- Shambhala International (1992)

Roots in the Religions of East Asia

- Reiki (1914)
- Perfect Liberty Kyôdan (1924)
- Reiyûkai (1924)
- Cao Dai (1926)
- Gedatsukai (1929)
- Seichô no Ie (1930)
- Sôka Gakkai (1930)
- Yiguandao (Tian Dao) (1930s)
- Sekai Kyûseikyô (1935)
- Shinnyoen (1936)
- Risshô Kôseikai (1938)
- Kôdô Kyôdan (1939)
- The Cult of Mao and the Red Guards (1940s)
- Tenshô Kôtai Jingûkyô (1946)
- Bentenshû (1948)
- Ananaikyô (1949)
- Byakkô Shinkôkai (1955)
- Mahikari (1959)
- GLA (God Light Association) (1969)
- Daesunjinrihoe (1969)
- Agonshû (1978)
- Aum Shinrikyô (1986)
- Suma Ching Hai (1990)
- Falun Gong (Falun Dafa) (1992)

the movement goes by the names "Unification Church" and "Family Federation for World Peace and Unification." Other acceptable names include "Unification Movement" and "Unificationism."

If you read the *Divine Principle*, you'll see some East Asian ideas that you've learned in earlier chapters of this textbook. For example, the book teaches that God has two parts, Spirit and Energy, which may remind you of qi from Chapters 7 and 8.

> God, the Creator, is infinite, invisible Spirit and does not appear fully in any finite or visible form. . . . God is the Absolute; the eternal I AM. In other words, God is perpetual, self-generating energy. Therefore, He is the First Cause and the Source of all energy.
>
> This Source Energy is polarized into masculine and feminine within God. The give and take between them forms the foundation for His eternal existence. Source Energy operates throughout the creation and is the cause of its existence and maintenance. God's Energy appears through the medium of give and take, and causes all things to exist in give-and-take relationships (*Divine Principle* Chapter 1, Section 1).

As you can see, God's "source energy" has a dual quality. Looked at in some ways, it seems to exist in two parts (masculine and feminine). Yet seen another way, God is One. You can also hear the echo of yin and yang in these lines:

> Derived from God's harmonized polarity, all things are created in pairs so that they might form relationships. . . . Through give and take with their complements, they are again to unite. Through this union they form a receptive base and produce new life. These three stages are called origin (God), division (subject and object), and union (new life)" (*Divine Principle* Chapter 1, Section 2, Part D).

Because it comes from God, all creation follows this same dualistic path and shares its attributes with God. Some of them include:

- True Love
- Beauty
- Truth
- Goodness, Justice and Freedom
- Eternity
- Creativity
- Order and Harmony
- Absolute Values

Taken together, all of God's qualities illustrate the Perfect Father, who then created his Perfect Family (Quinn 9–12). But here's the problem—God is perfect, but creation is not. How could this have happened? To understand, we must turn to the Unification Movement's view of humanity. We'll do that in a few pages.

Wicca and the New Age: Ancient Magick for a Modern Era

The Unification Church offers a highly structured religion with a strong central leader. Nothing could be further from the experience of Wicca. You could also sense that lack of top-down organization

New Religious Movements + Violence = Cults?

Though we use the neutral term "New Religious Movement," many people prefer the word "cult," with all of its negative connotations. Instead of alternative sacred choices, they emphasize the idea that NRMs sometimes "brainwash" people into submission and giving up their money. One popular definition claims that cults have six characteristics. In this analysis, a cult includes

1. Authoritarian leadership
2. Total control over life
3. Aggressive outreach to other people
4. A system of indoctrination ("brainwashing")
5. A short history
6. An attraction to disaffected middle-class people
   (Gallagher 213)

From this point of view, a single person usually creates a cult, then lures disenchanted youths from middle class families into his alternative community. Once the followers feel at home and loved, the cult begins to control their lives, brainwashing them into agreeing with the leader's ideas, no matter how kooky. Cult leaders take their money and force them to entice their friends or neighbors into the trap.

In some dramatic and terrible cases, religious groups have turned to violence and suicide. Even if you don't know the details, the names will sound familiar: Jonestown, Solar Temple, Waco, Aum Shinrikyo, Heaven's Gate. In each of these cases, a New Religious Movement has become entangled with violence, murder, or large-scale suicide. Each time a tragedy occurs, public leaders and politicians seek legal, social, and cultural ways to rein in the effect created by New Religious Movements. While some scholars of religion agree with anti-cult laws and activities, most others argue that New Religious Movements rarely employ violence, and that anti-cult laws tend to create a "moral panic" more destructive than cults themselves (Richardson and Introvigne 213).

in the description of Stonehenge at the summer solstice, where sacred actions and youthful hijinx exist side by side.

In the 20th century, the United Kingdom experienced an explosion of interest in New Religious Movements. Many people, including the Druids we met at the solstice celebration, turned away from the Church of England in search of a spiritual path unconnected to the political and social status quo. In 1951, Gerald Brosseau Gardner published a book called *Witchcraft Today*. In it, Gardner explained that **Wiccans** (an ancient word for witches) had existed secretly for thousands of years in England, Scotland, Wales, and Ireland. They kept secret, he said, to avoid persecution from Christians and the government until 1951, when Parliament repealed the Witchcraft Act of 1735. During the 1950s and 60s, Gardner continued to publicize "The Old Religion," also called "Wisecraft" or "The Craft" in addition to "Wicca." While some people believe that Gardner had really learned his magick from witches, others have argued that he actually created the modern Wiccan movement through his publications.

And so, either Wicca represents the most ancient religion, or very new one. In the past 50 years, the "Old Religion" has spread across Europe and America. No one knows how many Wiccans actually take part in witchcraft rituals, in part because they swear to "keep a secret, and never reveal, the secrets of the Art, except it be to a proper person, properly prepared within a Circle" (Farrar and Farrar). Gerald Gardner and his followers, who first published information about Wicca, claimed that they had been initiated into "The Craft," but many scholars believe that he spliced together bits and pieces of information from folklore, literature, art, and his own imagination to create the books.

Wiccans seek personal enlightenment and harmony with the world by reviving the wisdom vanished from modern society. Part of a larger movement called **Neo-Paganism**, Wiccan beliefs and practices

<<< A New Religious Movement, or a cult?
Here, Rev. and Mrs. Moon bless a group of Unificationist newlyweds.

<<< This watercolor illustration of a goddess comes from the late 19th century. The writing along the edges explains how to develop an astral connection with an entity based on the letters of its name. This practice is heavily influenced by Kabbalistic teachings.

often overlap with groups like the Druids at Stonehenge or the New Age practitioners that we'll meet later. In general, the Neo-Pagans want to breathe life into our dying planet by returning to pre-Christian, non-monotheistic traditions. From their point of view, all of our social, economic, political, and environmental problems have grown out of monotheism, which makes humans dominate nature while paradoxically feeling impotent before our Maker. What's the answer? Look to the witches, wise women, medicine men, shamans, and other people who have kept the "old ways" in the face of constant persecution. However, since much of the magick has been lost, it might be necessary to establish new traditions too, based on concepts taught in ages past.

So, is there a god in Wicca? Because there is no one thing we can define as "Wicca," you're likely to hear many different answers to this question. Nowadays, Wiccans search for gods all over. If pressed, many Wiccans will discuss a great creator who resembles the Native American "Sacred Mystery" much more than the Jewish God. Yet Wiccans do sometimes invoke "Adonai," the Hebrew word for Lord, in their rituals. They might also venerate Gaia, a Greek goddess of the earth, or Perkuna, the Lithuanian god of thunder—both pre-Christian deities related to nature. Wiccans may focus on gods

<<< The Health and Harmony Music Festival in Santa Rosa, California, includes a Goddess Altar. How many different traditions can you find represented among the statues? What do you think the altar-builders are trying to say?

from their region of the world, nearby places, or halfway across the globe. Followers generally say that The Creator includes both male and female energy (Partridge 296). Some even consider The Creator, nature, males, females, and gods the same thing. Others focus internally, seeking the god or goddess inside of themselves. Though they look to the earth and stars for knowledge and magic, these Wiccans view god as Shakespeare saw fate: "It's not in the stars, dear Brutus, but in ourselves" (*Julius Caesar* I: ii).

Many contemporary Wiccans do emphasize female goddesses as an antidote to male focus in Judaism, Christianity, and Islam. The Wiccan witch Starhawk (Miriam Simos) published a guide to feminist witchcraft in 1979 entitled *The Spiral Dance: A Rebirth of the Ancient Religion of the Great Goddess*. It has become a standard reference work and spiritual guide for feminist Wiccans. Starhawk explains that the Goddess often takes on three appearances: the "virgin," "mother," and "crone." Each form celebrates a stage in a woman's life, and all are equally beautiful, important, and sacred (Partridge 297). Feminist Wiccans often link their traditions to broader movements in American society, sometimes called "women's spirituality" or "the Goddess Movement." From the Wiccan point of view, these terms intertwine with each other. They say: Seek the Goddess instead of God. Develop your Women's Spirituality rather than your Men's Religion. This will lead you on the path to the Old Religion (Hanegraff 86).

THE NEW AGE: BREAKING DOWN BOUNDARIES

At this point, you may be wondering if you see Wiccans everywhere. After all, you can walk into a shopping mall and buy crystals, oils, or candles that seem like they might be used by a witch. This familiarity highlights the relationship between Paganism and Wicca and a broader search for health and authenticity outside of traditional Western boundaries. Generally known as the New Age Movement, it seems to

thrive in regions of America and Europe that welcome counter-cultural lifestyles. Rather than an organized religion, or even a philosophy, the term "New Age" describes people who hope for a better future through development of their own spiritual, physical, and psychological conditions. As I write this chapter, I've struggled to decide where to put the Four Questions when it comes to the New Age. Every time we discuss a deity, it seems like we're also considering humans. When I think we're turning to interactions with the sacred, we seem also to be defining deities. So, in the next couple of pages, consider how the New Age tries to break down even these broad categories of comparison.

Like Neo-Paganism and Wicca, the New Age refuses to submit to a single philosophy, authority, or deity. You'll find no New Age Pope or New Age Dalai Lama. At some point, however, New Age ideas intersect with all nearly all of the movements we've studied in *THINK World Religions*. New Age ideas derive from Wiccan and Pagan concepts, the Goddess Movement and Women's Spirituality, Buddhism and Christianity. Though sometimes the New Age seems to be mostly a women's movement, men too have tried to regain their "past warrior" through retreats, drum circles, and writing.

Instead of a single deity, some New Age philosophy relies on the idea of **correspondence**, where one thing relates to another. Candles, crystals, incense, humans, and the stars correspond to one another. If we can find the correct harmony between them, we'll also produce harmony in ourselves. Take a look at the chart on the opposite page, taken from Starhawk's book. It shows us a Wiccan view of correspondences that many followers of the New Age also embrace. Elements of the chart on this page should look familiar to you from other chapters of *THINK World Religions*. You'll see the names of Hindu goddesses, Judeo-Christian-Muslim angels, and Wiccan rituals. Parts of the Native American medicine wheel coincide with the Hebrew YHWH. In this way, aspects of the New Age combine elements of many traditions. You might even say this equalizes all the world's religions, as it offers the correspondence between them. In other ways, though, a correspondence table brings up new questions. If, for example, YHWH is the God, how does He relate to Isis?

>>> The New Zealand All Blacks rugby team performs a ritual Maori dance called the *haka* before a match. What message does the dance send to the dancers and to their opponents? Do you consider the dance to be a religious action? Why or why not?

Elements from the Table of Correspondences

Element	Air	Earth	Fire	Water	Spirit
Direction	East	North	South	West	Center and circumference
Angel	Michael	Gabriel	Ariel	Raphael	(none)
Sense	Smell	Touch	Sight	Taste	Hearing
Jewel	Topaz	Rock crystal	Fire opal	Aquamarine	(none)
Tree	Aspen	Oak	Almond, in flower	Willow	Flowering almond
Animal	Birds	Bison, cow	Fire-breathing dragons, lions, snakes	Dolphins, porpoises, fish, sea mammals	Sphinx
Goddesses	Aradia, Cardea, Nuit, Urania	Ceres, Gaia, Persemone, Prithivi	Brigit, Hestia, Pele, Vesta	Aphrodite, Isis, Mari, Tiamat, Yemaya	Isis, The Secret Name of the Goddess, Shekinah
Gods	Enlil, Khephera, Mercury, Thoth	Adonis, Dionysius, Pan, Tammuz	Agni, Hephaetus, Horus, Prometheus, Vulcan	Dylan, Neptune, Osiris, Poseidon	Akasha, Iao, JHVH

∧ Followers of Wicca and the New Age Movement seek healing through natural harmony.
∧ Do you see elements of other religious traditions that we've studied in this table? How would you interpret their inclusion in it?

UFOlogy

So far, we've studied how NRMS look for deities in established religions (Unificationism) or through the revival of lost wisdom (Wicca and the New Age Movement). Other seekers, however, have looked to outer space to find their deity. When I was young, a book called *Chariots of the Gods* hit the best-seller lists. Its author, Erich von Däniken, claimed to have sold a total of 60 million copies of his books about UFOs. In addition to *Chariots of the Gods*, they include *Gods from Outer Space*, *Signs of the Gods*, *According to the Evidence*, *The Gods were Astronauts*, and *History is Wrong*. He explained that supernatural beings came to Earth in ancient times, seeded humanity with special wisdom, and then returned home. As our memories dimmed, we re-imagined the aliens as gods, and thus religion formed.

Another UFOlogist named Claude Vorilhon says that alien scientists actually wrote the Bible. Unfortunately, though, successive generations of humans have changed the text, added their own interpretations, and altered the original meaning. In 1973, the aliens returned and chose Vorilhon as their messenger. He took the name Raël, meaning "messenger" in Hebrew, and began teaching his ministry to the world.

Here is a passage from *The Book Which Tells the Truth*, recently republished as *Intelligent Design: Message from the Designers*. As you read it, consider how Raël has combined ancient wisdom, new paths, and a new story in his religious text.

> The following day I was at the meeting place again as arranged with a notebook, a pen, and the Bible. The flying machine reappeared on time, and I found myself face to face once more with the little man who invited me to enter the machine and sit in the same comfortable chair.
>
> I had spoken to nobody about all this, not even to those closest to me, and he was happy to learn that I had been discreet. He suggested I take notes, and then he started to speak:

∧
∧
∧ Erich van Daniken claimed that the mammoth drawings in Nazca, Peru portrayed aliens, not people.

> "A very long time ago on our distant planet, we had reached a level of technical and scientific knowledge, comparable to that which you will soon reach. Our scientists had started to create primitive, embryonic forms of life, namely living cells in test tubes. Everyone was thrilled by this. . . ."
>
> [The "little man" explains that his beings had developed intergalactic travel and so went to study Earth. Their activities on Earth have been partially written down in the Bible.]
>
> "Now I would like you to refer to the Bible where you will find traces of the truth about your past. . . . So let us start with the first chapter of the Book of Genesis: 'In the beginning Elohim created the heaven and the earth (Genesis 1:1).'"
>
> "*Elohim*, translated without justification in some Bibles by the word *God*, means in Hebrew 'those who came from the sky,' and furthermore the word is plural. It means that the scientists from our world searched for a planet that was suitable to carry out their projects. They 'created,' or in reality discovered the Earth, and realized it contained all the necessary elements for the creation of artificial life, even if its atmosphere was not quite the same as our own" (Raël 10–11).

<<< Pictured is the Raëlian Headquarters in Maricourt, Canada. Recently, the Raëlians have claimed to clone a human by using supernatural information.

▶ WHAT DOES IT MEAN TO BE HUMAN?

Unificationism

As you'll remember from earlier in the chapter, Rev. Sun Myung Moon began having visions of Jesus when he was just sixteen years old, and the visions continued throughout his life. During these revelations, Sun Myung Moon learned the true interpretation of the Bible, which had long been lost to humanity. It turns out that original sin—brought about by eating the forbidden fruit—is actually a metaphor for illicit sex. Here's how it happened: God created Lucifer before Adam and Eve, so he was more mature than them but also jealous. Adam and Eve lived as brother and sister in Paradise, not yet developed enough to see each other as mates. Lucifer, however, saw the blossoming sexuality in the beautiful Eve. He tempted Eve into having sex with him, and in doing so deviated from God's plan for complementary and creative love. As a result of her fornication, Eve felt guilt but also realized that Adam was to be her partner. She then seduced Adam before they had the opportunity to marry and constitute God's family.

> Through God's blessing, Adam could have fulfilled goodness together with Eve. However, by uniting with her prematurely, he fulfilled evil. . . . If Adam and Eve had reached maturity, God would have blessed them in marriage. Had they been united by the love of God, they would have produced children free of inherited sin. But because Adam and Eve joined with Satan through the act of unprincipled love, their descendants were the children of the fall, and the world came under Satanic rule (*Divine Principle* Chapter 2, 6–7).

By not allowing the Holy Spirit into their life through a "divine marriage in Perfection," Adam and Eve missed the chance to create a Holy Trinity with God. It should have worked this way:

Adam + Eve + Divine Marriage = Holy Trinity

but instead it turned out like this:

Satan + Eve + Adam = Damnation

Jesus, the second Adam, came to Earth to set things right. He planned to establish the Messianic Kingdom of Israel by marrying and having perfect children. Yet people were not ready to follow him. Sadly, Jesus "was unable to bring his kingdom and subjugate Satan completely. Sin and evil still run rampant in the world" (*Divine Principle* 3, 8). Instead of creating a divine kingdom based on love, Jesus realized he would have to face crucifixion and lead his followers toward redemption by suffering.

After he rose from the dead, Jesus created the Christian Church as a comfort to his followers who still suffered under Satan's rule. Though they could not yet create the perfect family, Christians could become spiritual children of God through the interaction of Jesus (Male) and the Holy Spirit (Female). This created a new equation: Christ + Holy Spirit = Spiritual Rebirth.

On that fateful Easter Day in 1935, Jesus spoke directly to Sun Myung Moon. He was to become a new messiah, a third Adam (or the "Lord of the Second Advent"). The Unification Movement believes that Rev. Moon and his wife Hak Ja Han have created the True Family, finally realizing Adam and Eve's original potential for a Holy Trinity with God.

God and Humanity in Unification Teaching

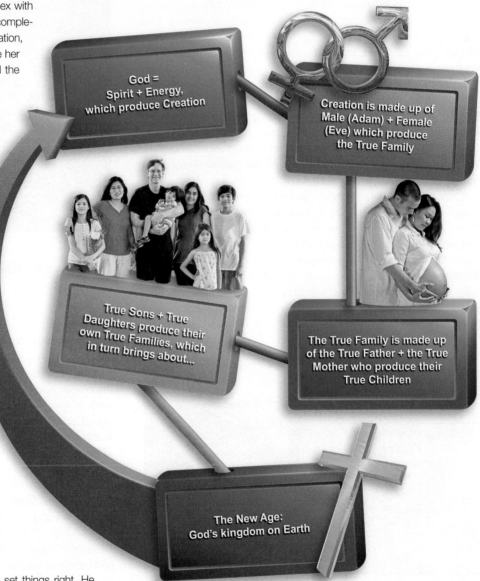

God = Spirit + Energy, which produce Creation

Creation is made up of Male (Adam) + Female (Eve) which produce the True Family

True Sons + True Daughters produce their own True Families, which in turn brings about...

The True Family is made up of the True Father + the True Mother who produce their True Children

The New Age: God's kingdom on Earth

∧
∧ By creating a global community of
∧ believers, **Unification members hope to banish Satan and** create a new spiritual paradise on Earth.

Wicca and the New Age

In studying the gods of Wicca, we have already learned a lot about its views on humanity. Many Wiccans follow the example of indigenous cultures and place humans on a continuum that includes rocks, animals, spirits, and the cosmos. Unlike many other New Religious Movements, however, Wicca has never had a single charismatic leader. Just the opposite, in fact—Wiccans tend to reject *any* leader who might infringe on individual or communal values or beliefs. Starhawk writes that "each of us embodies the divine. Our ultimate spiritual authority is within, and we need no other person to interpret the sacred for us. We foster the questioning attitude, and we honor intellectual, spiritual, and creative freedom" (Starhawk 6).

In their search for ancient wisdom, Wiccans have often turned to anthropology, sociology, and religious studies for clues about both ancient and indigenous ideas. In doing this, Wiccans resemble the religious studies scholars we read about in Chapter 1 who seemed nearly obsessed with discovering the source of human religion. Unlike scholars looking for the origins of religion, however, Wiccans search for the authentic human—one who has not been affected by monotheism, capitalism, industrialism, or patriarchy.

Of course, Wiccans know that they are not actually indigenous Maori or Sioux Indians. Even so, they hope to find elements of truth in those traditions and apply them to new situations, to create a "reclaiming tradition" that will help heal the world and themselves. Wiccans, Neo-Pagans, and others often explain their movement as a way to reclaim the human body from Western culture. They say that monotheism hates the body, and that Western medicine especially belittles the female body. To counteract these forces of disharmony, Wicca celebrates the human body as sacred. Wiccans believe that we should search for sacred interactions using our own bodies. When they celebrate the virgin, mother, and crone, Wiccans highlight the relationship between a woman's changing body and her sense of spirituality by linking, beauty, childbearing, and magic. For example, a witch might use her own menstrual blood in a ritual to sanctify a new magical tool.

∧
∧ **A pagan dance.** What elements of Wicca
∧ did the artist include in this painting?

Unlike many Wiccans, New Age followers often define their interests as health-related rather than religious. I know a highly skilled, very well-trained massage therapist who has an incredible knowledge of the human body and how it reacts to stress. You might consider her work completely physical. Yet her treatment room is full of crystals, animal sculptures, and what would be considered "New Age" music. In this way, she illustrates the New Age's search for alternative paths to health.

Western medicine tends to emphasize causal relationships: Fix the cause, and you'll get healthy. In contrast, the New Age looks to indigenous and Asian traditions: Fix the mind and spirit, and the body will heal. Instead of using only Western medicine, many medical professionals hope to find holistic remedies that include mind, body, and spirit. My massage therapist friend illustrates this trend—in her quest to heal the body, she may also consider interactions with the sacred world.

<<< Some study Wicca through rituals, while others turn to texts such as Gardner's famous *Book of Shadows* or studies on witchcraft.

Unificationism

As we've seen, in Unificationism marriage provides the best way to interact with God. Once you have accepted Rev. Moon's teaching, you can join the Unification Movement, get married and begin a new family. The old ways of marriage developed through sinful lust that led to damnation. The new kind of marriage, though, purifies the sacrament through the leadership of Sun Myung Moon. Before Jesus called on Rev. Moon to accept the Second Lordship, human sexuality produced only more sinful humans. But now, the True Family can evolve without sin, a building block of a new age.

Recently, the Unification Church has begun its transition from the charismatic leadership of its founder, Rev. Sun Myung Moon, to his children. On Easter Sunday of 2010, In Jin Moon, the new president of the Church, commemorated the holiday with a sermon in Las Vegas, Nevada. As you read this passage, think back to Chapters 10 and 11 where we discussed Christianity. How does In Jin Moon's sermon about the second coming of Christ also describe how Unificationists interact with God? Do members of the Unification Church interact with God in the same way as older Christian groups? Would the Rev. In Jin Moon's message sound odd to other Christians? Why or why not?

> But because of the failure of John the Baptist and the failure of the Israelites to truly unite with Jesus Christ and understand why he was given as a gift to this world, Jesus had to go the way of the cross. For the millions and millions of Christians all around the world, the day of resurrection is the citadel of Christian faith. Christians understand this day as a day when Jesus conquers death, and therefore, in Jesus Christ we can have eternal life.
>
> But brothers and sisters, if we understand that the crucifixion was not the goal of Jesus' mission, and that crucifixion was the way that Jesus had to go because he had no foundation to stand on as the Son of God, then we realize that when the Bible says that there has to be a Second Coming, we understand that the mission of Jesus Christ was left unfulfilled, and therefore, somebody who can stand in that position as the perfected Adam, as the True Parent, having found and raised up a perfected Eve, that Jesus' mission has yet to be fulfilled (Moon, 2010).

Wicca and the New Age

As we've seen, the Unification Church adds a new dimension to marriage, a widely accepted Christian rite. Wiccans, to the contrary, search for multiple sources of sacred interactions instead of relying on just one tradition. Wiccan manuals are full of examples and instructions for rituals, which often happen inside a ritual sacred circle. Some examples include Casting the Circle, Closing the Circle, Charge of the God, Charge of the Goddess, Yule Ritual, Candlemas Ritual, Summer Solstice Ritual, Tool Consecration, Drawing Down the Moon, and the Magick Ordeal.

By performing these rituals, Wiccans believe that their actions spark the correspondence between nature and the sacred world. Take the initiation ritual as an example. While developing a witch's magical powers, the rite also introduces the new witch into the circle of Wiccan practitioners. You may or may not be able to observe the effects of the ritual. That's part of its mystery. Even so, Wiccans agree with Native Americans that

∧
∧ How do you think that the ritual dance of a
∧ Mongolian shaman might help him connect
to the sacred world around him?

focusing on actions (like rituals or dancing) can create a harmony between humans, the earth, and the cosmos.

Like Wiccans, many New Agers look to indigenous shamanic traditions to create harmony among humans, spirits, and nature. One field anthropologist, Michael Harner, has taken this "reclaiming" one step further, and started a non-profit organization. After studying shamans all over the world, Harner realized that some ideas and practices crossed all national, cultural, and language barriers. Since they appeared everywhere, he reasoned, these must be universal characteristics of humanity that modern people have forgotten. To reclaim your authentic self, it's now possible to take courses that teach you the universal principals of "core shamanism." Harner defines this as

the universal or near-universal principles and practices of shamanism not bound to any specific cultural group or perspective, as originated, researched, and developed by Michael Harner. Since the West overwhelmingly lost its shamanic knowledge centuries ago due to religious oppression, the Foundation's programs in core shamanism are particularly intended for Westerners to reacquire access to their rightful spiritual heritage through quality workshops and training courses. Training in core shamanism includes teaching students to alter their consciousness through classic shamanic non-drug techniques such as repetitive drumming so that they can

discover their own hidden spiritual resources, transform their lives, and learn how to help others. Core shamanism does not focus on ceremonies, such as those of Native Americans, which are part of the work of medicine men and women, persons who do both shamanism and ceremonial work.

(The Foundation for Shamanic Studies, 2010)

In the end, followers of the New Age believe that their path may help save the world. Paradoxically, this fresh beginning comes from the revival of ancient and indigenous traditions. As they transform themselves in a new context, they will also transform the world around them. As one scholar puts it, "Personal enlightenment in enough numbers will bring about collective enlightenment, that is, a new age" (Partridge 312).

▶ HOW DOES THE SACRED BECOME COMMUNITY?

Unificationism

As we've seen, the Unification Wedding Blessing starts a couple on the road to creating a new kingdom on Earth, led by Rev. Moon and populated by the Church. In a very physical sense, Unificationism

hopes to literally create a sacred community by recommending its followers to have large families. The True Father and True Mother (Rev. and Mrs. Moon) had 15 children, and you'll often hear sayings like "12 before 40!" or "15 before 40!" as a guide to the number of children a couple should have before the wife hits the age of 40. Following a yin-yang model, the parents and children will embody the "high and low," "left and right," and "above and below." As Rev. Sun Myung Moon writes, "Thus, in order to complete the realization of the ideal, both the horizontal and vertical axes of the sphere must be established. When a man and a woman experience this realized two-fold realm, they can finally say that they are living in the ideal" (*Blessing and Ideal Family*, Part 1). A three-year period of public service after marriage can also help to bring couples together and to create a community. In this period, the young couple dedicates their time and effort to expanding the Unification Movement.

Rev. Moon has fought back against claims of tax evasion and that his church brainwashes its members, forcing them into mass marriages and giving up their incomes. By the 1990s, the movement had become much more accepted in the Korean (and to lesser extent) American mainstream. The Unification Movement uses its great wealth to influence public opinion through its News World Communications, which owns *The Washington Times*, Universal Press International, *Insight Magazine*, and a half-dozen other media outlets. The church has begun to develop huge tracts of land in Paraguay in addition to its real estate in the United States and South Korea. Through these activities, Unificationists hope to guide the world toward a divine order on Earth.

Wicca and the New Age

In her introduction to Wicca, Skyhawk describes the link between ritual, magic, and community. "Our rituals are participatory and ecstatic, celebrating the cycles of the seasons and our lives, and raising energy for personal, collective, and earth healing. . . . We know that everyone can do life-changing, world-renewing work of

<<< Over 20,000 couples are blessed in a mass wedding in Seoul, South Korea.

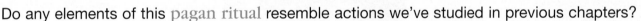

∧
∧ Do any elements of this pagan ritual resemble actions we've studied in previous chapters?
∧

magic, the art of changing consciousness at will. We strive to teach and practice in ways that foster personal and collective empowerment, to model shared power, and to open leadership roles to all" (Skyhawk 6).

The Wiccan experience can be intensely communal, as some members meet regularly as a coven. For many Wiccans, however, witchcraft can be a lonely affair. Some may be afraid to talk openly about it at work, or don't have other members of The Craft in their towns. And so, although they focus on nature, many Wiccans also embrace the power of the Internet. Though this may seem paradoxical, one Wiccan explains that "Once we enter Cyberspace, we are no longer in the physical plane; we literally stand in a place between the worlds, one with heightened potential to be as sacred as any circle cast upon the ground" (Cowan 1).

Community and Celebrity in the New Age

Some New Religious Movements create a community through the charismatic message and life of their founders. We've read about Sun Myung Moon, who teaches that he is the Messiah returned to Earth. In many other cases, however, celebrities are the public face of New Religious Movements. Perhaps rock musicians and movie actors feel deeply disconnected from their world and turn to NMRs for enlightenment. Perhaps

∧ Timothy Leary pioneered the link
∧ between celebrity and religion. How did
∧ his clothing and body position help to convey his message?

Religious Pluralism

Wicca shows up pretty regularly in the news. The idea of witchcraft scares some people and fascinates others. Books, movies, TV shows—stories about witches seem to be everywhere these days. This article appeared in the *New York Times* on Halloween, 2009. Pay attention to the ways in which Neo-Paganism and Wicca have moved into the mainstream of movies, academia, and even politics. Why do you think that Americans accept these practices more than they have in the past?

If personal tradition holds, just before sundown Saturday, Michael York will stand before a colonial-style wooden cabinet in his Bayside town house here and light a candle. As night falls, it will illuminate the surrounding objects: tarot cards, Tibetan silver bowls, a bell and statues or icons of deities like the Greek earth-mother, Gaia, and the Lithuanian thunder god, Perkunas.

While facing the altar, if past practice holds, Mr. York will invoke the names of the ancestors and loved ones who have died. He will often write down their names, too, and keep that piece of paper in the cabinet. One can mourn on any day, as Mr. York put it recently, but on this occasion, "the veil between the worlds is understood to be thinnest."

The day that most Americans know as Halloween, a commercial bonanza and secular holiday with only the faintest remnants of its pantheistic origins, Mr. York celebrates as Samhain, the autumnal new year for Pagans. And for Mr. York, Paganism is indeed a proper noun, connoting a specific religion that he has observed for decades.

Shortly after Samhain ends, Mr. York plans to travel to Montreal for the annual meeting of the American Academy of Religion, an umbrella group for scholars from the United States and Canada. There, as a chairman of the Pagan Studies Group, he will help oversee three panel discussions, and present his own academic paper, "Idolatry, Ecology and the Sacred as Tangible."

In both guises, as an individual practitioner and a credentialed expert, Mr. York embodies the increasing mainstream acceptance of Pagan religion. From academia to the military, in the person of chaplains and professors, through successful litigation and online networking, Paganism has done much in the last generation to overcome its perception as either Satanism or silliness.

"Academically, it's much more open and accepted and respected," said Mr. York, 70, who retired five years ago from the faculty of Bath Spa University in England. "And on a more personal level, we don't proselytize or anything like that, but most of my friends know that I'm Pagan and most of them are not, and we can discuss it. They understand that there is a Pagan spirituality, and the misconceptions about it have diminished."

Because the federal census does not ask about religious affiliation, and because ridicule or discrimination tended to keep Pagans closeted in the past, statistics on the number of adherents in the United States are imprecise and probably too low. Still, the recent growth is evident in surveys done in 1990 and 2001 by the City University of New York.

Over the course of those 11 years, the survey went from tabulating 8,000 Wiccans nationally—that branch of Paganism was the only one to turn up—to 134,000 Wiccans, 33,000 Druids and 140,000 Pagans. (Others identify as Heathens.) The sociologist Helen A. Berger, who is doing research on Pagan demography, said she believed that a more accurate current number would fall between 500,000 and one million.

Certainly, there is nothing new about Paganism per se. From Halloween to May Day to Yuletide, said Prof. Diana L. Eck of the Harvard Divinity School, "there's a way in which all of us, especially in the Christian tradition, follow a religious calendar that is pegged to ancient Pagan festivals."

But in the grand scheme of the Western world, polytheism was seen as being superseded by monotheism and faith itself by science, leaving Paganism as some kind of atavistic orphan of history. The fact that its practitioners lacked any formal denominational structure added to the religion's relative invisibility, except as the object of fears or the butt of jokes.

In several ways, though, Paganism was waiting for modernity to catch up with it. The emphasis on the worship of nature in virtually all variations of Pagan faith, and the embrace of a female divinity in many, situated the religion to mesh with the environmental and feminist movements that swept through the United States in the 1970s.

In the 1970s, Wiccan groups began seeking and obtaining tax-exempt status from federal and state authorities, said the Rev. Selena Fox, the founder and spiritual leader of an early, influential Wicca church, Circle Sanctuary in Barneveld, Wis. By the decade's end, Wicca was included in the handbook for military chaplains and had been written about in such popular books as "Drawing Down the Moon," (Penguin, 2006), by Margot Adler.

^^^ **A magical seal with a central pentacle.** You can now find similar ones on American military gravestones.

Since then, Wiccans have served as chaplains in prisons and hospices, as well as in the armed forces. Just this week, Ms. Fox supplied the invocation for the daily session of the Wisconsin State Assembly. And, of course, the popular culture of the Harry Potter books, the television series "Buffy the Vampire Slayer" and the current zombie vogue have defanged Pagan religion for a mass teenage audience.

Nothing did more to secure Paganism's place in the religious mainstream, though, than a highly serious, indeed somber, court battle. Brought by Americans United for Separation of Church and State on behalf of Circle Sanctuary and several widows, the decade-long litigation sought permission from the federal Department of Veterans Affairs to have the gravestones of deceased Wiccan soldiers marked with the symbol of the pentacle.

Since winning that right as part of an out-of-court settlement two years ago, Wicca followers have marked more than a dozen military graves with the five-pointed star.

"This got us the most widespread support and had the most wide-ranging import," Ms. Fox said. "Our symbol was literally being carved in stone and taking its place alongside the symbols of other religions. Our religion was at last getting equal treatment. It was one of those crossroads moments." (Freedman 13)

∧
∧ The Circle expands: the psychedelic
∧ movement, rock 'n roll, nudity, dance, and
Stonehenge in the 1960s.

Psychedelic Spirituality teaches that people can find enlightenment through hallucinogenic drugs. The movement borrows elements from East Asian religious philosophy as well as Wicca and Judaism.

some religious leaders enjoy the company of influential individuals. For whatever reason, New Religious Movements often thrive on the financial and vocal support of famous people.

We can trace this back to the 1960s and Timothy Leary, who founded the **Psychedelic Spirituality** movement, which gained steam through the support of Aldous Huxley, the famous author of *Brave New World*. The psychedelic movement taught that people could find enlightenment, even Nirvana, by taking hallucinogenic drugs. While peyote played a key role, acid-seekers preferred LSD as a spiritual short-cut to enlightenment. Some even considered LSD to be the reincarnated version of soma, the legendary drug of the Hindu Vedas (Partridge 377–78).

In 1968, Leary published *High Priest*, his sacred text for the psychedelic movement. He claimed that "the authentic priests, the real prophets of this great movement are the rock-and-roll musicians. Acid-rock is the hymns, odes, chants of the turned-on love generation. . . . We turn our work and our planet over to the young and their prophets: The Beatles, The Byrds, The Rolling Stones, Country Joe and the Fish, Charlie Lloyd, The Monkees,. . .The Grateful Dead, The Animals,. . .The Doors, The Quicksilver Messenger Service and many other ecstatic combinations" (Leary iv-v).

High Priest includes elements of East Asian philosophy, Buddhism, Wicca, Judaism, and science. Instead of chapters, the book has "trips," each of which starts with a quotation from the *Yijing* (*I Ching*). Look at these two pages from a first edition of the book, including notes made by readers over the years. Does the layout of the pages look familiar? They follow the same general structure as the Talmud, with different sections of text commenting on each other across the page. Check out the bottom right portion of the page, where you'll find the Leary's famous message: "And to TUNE IN you must DROP OUT" (Leary 3). This became the mantra of the Psychedelic Movement, repeated millions of times by rock and roll stars and their fans.

A few years ago, the actress Shirley MacLaine became an unofficial spokeswoman for the New Age movement. A believer in reincarnation, she has described her quest to discover her earlier lives on television shows, newspaper articles, and magazine features. A recent article says that "Ms. MacLaine has palpitated every corner of her soul in an effort to know herself, and she makes no apology for the affectionate self-regard her investigations have yielded. 'Who can say it's crazy if it's my experience?' she asks

---

TRIP 1

In the beginning God created the heavens and the earth.

The earth was without form and void, and darkness was on the face of the deep.

∞

Nicholas in *The Magus* by John Fowles:

For a while I let my mind wander into a bottomless madness.

Supposing all my life that last year had been the very opposite of what Conchis so often said—so often, to trick me once again—about life in general.

That is, the very opposite of hazard.

∞

And God said let there be light; and there was light. And God saw that the light was good; and God separated the light from the darkness.

∞

In the beginning was the TURN ON. The flash, the illumination. The electric trip. The sudden bolt of energy that starts the new system.

The TURN ON was God.

All things were made from the TURN ON and without Him was not any thing made.

In this TURN ON was life; and the life was the light of men.

It has always been the same.

It was the flash that exploded the galaxies, from which all energy flows. It was the spark that ignites in the mysterious welding of amino-acid strands that creates the humming vine of organic life. It is the brilliant neurological glare that illuminates the shadows of man's mind. The God-intoxicated revelation. The Divine union. The vision of harmony, samadhi, satori, ecstasy which we now call psychedelic.

What happens when you turn on? Where do you go when you take the trip? You go within. Consciousness changes. Your nerve endings, neural cameras, cellular memory banks, protein structures become broadcasting instruments for the timeless humming message of God located inside your body.

The external world doesn't change, but your experience of it becomes drastically altered.

You close your eyes and the thirteen billion cell brain computer flashes multiple kaleidoscopic messages. Symbolic thought merges with sensory explosions; symbolic thoughts fuse with somatic-tissue events; ideas combine with memories—personal, cellular, evolutionary, embryonic—thoughts collapse into molecular patterns.

You open your eyes and you see your tidy television-studio world of labeled stage-props fusing with sensory, somatic, cellular, molecular flashes.

2

Your nervous system is prepared to register and coordinate up to one thousand million units of flashing information each second.

A psychedelic trip lasts from five to twelve hours. Each trip takes off from a stage-set structured by the physical surroundings and the cast of characters present. Each person in the session is a universe of two billion years of protein, protean memories, and sensations. A heady mix.

How to describe this multiple, jumbled, rapidly changing process? What do you do after you TURN ON?

The Light shineth in the darkness and the darkness comprehendeth it not.

You TUNE IN.

TUNE IN means to bear witness to the Light, that all men might believe.

The TURN ON bolt shatters structure. Reveals the frozen nature of the artificial stage-set men call reality. Certitude collapses. There is nothing but the energy which lighteneth every man that cometh into the world. $E = MC^2$.

We discover we are not television actors born onto the American stage-set of a commercially sponsored program twenty centuries old. We are two-billion-year-old carriers of the Light, born not just of blood nor of the will of the flesh, nor of the will of man, but of the Light that flashed in the Pre-cambrian mud, the Light made flesh.

TUNE IN means that you sit in the debris of your shattered illusions, and discover that there is nothing, you are nothing except the bearer of the wire-coil of life, that your body is the temple of the Light and you begin once again to build a structure to preserve and glorify the Light. You bear witness crying, the Sun that comes after me is preferred before me, and your days are spent preparing the earth for the Son to come. That is TUNING IN.

And to TUNE IN you must DROP OUT.

DROP OUT means detach yourself tenderly, aesthetically, harmoniously from the fake-prop studio of the empire game and do nothing but guard and glorify the Light.

My first trip came in the middle of the journey of this life (when I was thirty-five years old) and

January 1959 ∞ 3

Nicholas in *The Magus:*

I stared at myself. They were trying to drive me mad, to brainwash me in some astounding way. But I clung to reality.

∞

And God saw that it was good.

∞

From *The Magus:*

I cannot believe Maurice is evil. You will understand.

∞

And God made the beasts of the earth according to their kinds and the cattle

according to their kinds, and everything that creeps upon the ground according to its kind. And God saw that it was good.

∞

∧
∧ Leary's *High Priest* encourages its readers to "tune in" by "dropping out."
∧

rhetorically. 'It's a very self-centered time of life, which you could say is selfish but you have the right, I think.'" (Hampson, 2008)

Other singers and actresses have offered their public support to New Religious Movements. Look at Gwyneth Paltrow's web site, goop.com, where she blogs about alternative healing, spirituality, and women's health. Scientology, which characterizes itself both as a religion and a self-help movement, celebrates its link to famous people at the Church of Scientology Celebrity Centre International in Hollywood. Gossip columns and television shows regularly showcase people like Tom Cruise and John Travolta as famous Scientologists. Behind-the-scenes celebrities in the Church of Scientology apparently include Nancy Cartwright, the voice of Bart Simpson (Betts).

Sometimes, this association between New Religious Movements and celebrity comes in for some affectionate teasing. The movie *This Is Spinal Tap* has become a cult classic (no pun intended), portraying aging rockers looking for fulfillment in loud music, drugs, and New Religious Movements. Jane Chadwick plays the girlfriend of David St. Hubbins (Michael McKean). She tries to bring success to the band through New Age techniques, but her efforts only get Spinal Tap second-billing to a puppet show at an amusement park.

The best reference to New Religious Movements, though, comes in Spinal Tap's song "Stonehenge," loosely based on a show put on by the band Black Sabbath. The lyrics parody both Druid ceremonies and rock bands that use Wiccan and Pagan themes in their music.

In ancient times
Hundreds of years before the dawn of history
Lived a strange race of people: the Druids.

No one knows who they were or what they were doing
But their legacy remains

Hewn into the living rock
Of Stonehenge.

Stonehenge! Where the demons dwell
Where the banshees live and they do live well.
Stonehenge! Where a man's a man
And the children dance to the Pipes of Pan.
Hey!

Stonehenge! 'Tis a magic place
Where the moon doth rise with a dragon's face.
Stonehenge! Where the virgins lie
And the prayers of devils fill the midnight sky.

And you my love, won't you take my hand?
We'll go back in time to that mystic land
Where the dew drops cry and the cats meow
I will take you there, I will show you how.
Oh!

(Spinal Tap, *This Is Spinal Tap*, Polydor/Umgd, 1984)

Conclusion: Thinking About New Religious Movements

Though we've only studied a small fraction of the New Religious Movements, I think that you've begun to see some patterns. The next step will be to use your knowledge of the Four Questions and the examples of Unificationism and Wicca/New Age to study other NRMs. You can use the chart near the beginning of this chapter to find other traditions to study, or see if your own spiritual path is listed. Remember that all those on the list aren't necessarily totally new religions or denominations. Instead, the chart points you toward trends in religion occurring over the last century. If that seems like a long time to call something a "New Religious Movement," remember that Hinduism is already around 5,000 years old. From that point of view, the twentieth century is but a blink of the divine eye.

<<< Why would Spinal Tap want to have its promo picture taken in front of an ancient castle? Could it relate to any New Religious Movements?

Pilgrims hug an Energy Tree in Sedona, Arizona to receive a physical and mental boost. **How is this perception of the spiritual similar to Native American beliefs?**

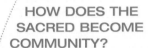

Men and women gather for an adult finger-painting workshop as part of spiritual therapy. **How might art help people connect with their inner feelings and beliefs?**

IS THERE A GOD?

Yes and no; some new religions seek lost wisdom, while others create new religious paths. UFOlogy, for example, argues that what were perceived as gods in the past were actually alien beings bringing enlightenment. Unificationism, on the other hand, follows the Christian tradition of monotheism. Wiccans often differ in their beliefs. Some accept a great creator, while others invoke a pantheon of ancient gods. Many new religious movements share the belief that the spiritual originates from within, rather than from an outside god or gods.

HOW DOES THE SACRED BECOME COMMUNITY?

In general, New Religious Movements don't separate the community from the sacred. Unificationists strive to produce a True Family of believers, bearing as many children as possible in order to bring about a divine order on Earth. On the other hand, Wiccans view the entire world as naturally divine. By interacting with the world around us, they argue, we gain ancient knowledge that leads to personal enlightenment.

WHAT DOES IT MEAN TO BE HUMAN?

According to Unificationists, human beings developed original sin after Eve seduced Adam into having sex out of wedlock. To become True Children, followers must go through a spiritual rebirth in the form of a highly ritualized Unification wedding. Wicca and Neo-Paganism, on the other hand, celebrate individuality and freedom in spiritual matters. Wiccans hope to discover the authentic human being, one who has not been corrupted by modern influences such as capitalism, industrialism, and patriarchy.

HOW DO HUMANS INTERACT WITH THE SACRED?

Marriage is the most important way a person can interact with God in Unificationism, since only through marriage can a sacred True Family form. Many Wiccans and Neo-Pagans interact with the sacred through rituals to create a harmony between humans and the divine.

Although many religions we've studied so far can be practiced individually, there seems to be an inclination to form a community of believers. **Why might this be?**

Druids celebrate the spring equinox at Stonehenge. **Why might these followers perceive power in this ancient structure?**

REVIEW

Summary

IS THERE A GOD?   p. 277

• Unificationists believe in one god—the capital "g" God of Judaism, Christianity, and Islam. However, the Unification Movement also incorporates East Asian spiritual traditions, describing God as a form of self-generating energy. This Source Energy is made up of two parts: the masculine and the feminine. Because of this, Unitarians argue, all things have a dual quality.

• Wicca has traditionally eschewed a single definition of God or gods, preferring to look at the world around it for divine inspiration. Belief in a deity (or deities) spans the religious spectrum. Some Wiccans invoke the Jewish God, while others focus on internal development or the spirituality of nature.

WHAT DOES IT MEAN TO BE HUMAN?   p. 285

• The Unification Movement teaches that humans inherited original sin from Adam and Eve, who forsook a divine unity with God in favor of sexual temptation by the devil. In order to bring about a new holy kingdom on Earth, followers must marry and produce True Sons and Daughters of the Church.

• Wiccans and Neo-Pagans focus on reclaiming the human body. Western culture, they argue, has corrupted our idea of ourselves, causing us to lose sight of the innate spirituality of humanity. Both Wiccans and Neo-Pagans celebrate the body, believing it to be an essential link to the divine.

HOW DO HUMANS INTERACT WITH THE SACRED?   p. 287

• Marriage is the ultimate bond between humans and God in Unificationism. Through the Blessing Ceremony, followers are initiated into the True Family, and begin spreading the Divine Principle.

• Wiccans believe that actions, such as rituals and ceremonies, can produce harmony between humans and the universe. Shamanic practices grow out of this tradition, and seek to bring together humans, spirits, and nature.

HOW DOES THE SACRED BECOME COMMUNITY?   p. 288

• The Unification Church teaches that its followers should strive to create a new, holy community on Earth. Worshipers are encouraged to establish a large family rooted in the teachings of the Church, and spread the word of Unificationism.

• Wiccan practices can be both private and communal. Some Wiccans meet together in a coven, while others embrace the power of the Internet in order to connect to other practitioners around the world.

Key Terms

Unification Church is a modern interpretation of Christianity and Confucianism that stresses marriage within the church as a way of rebuilding God's kingdom on Earth. *276*

True Family is composed of male and female members of the Unification Church united in sacred matrimony, free from original sin. These families produce True Sons and Daughters. *276*

New Age Movement describes the overarching belief in developing one's spiritual, physical, and psychological self outside traditional boundaries. *277*

Wiccans are modern believers and practitioners of witchcraft *280*

Neo-Paganism is a wide-ranging movement that seeks to return to pre-Christian, polytheistic religious practices. *280*

Correspondence refers to the elemental quality of nature, and the relationships between natural objects. *282*

Psychedelic Spirituality teaches that people can find enlightenment through hallucinogenic drugs. The movement borrows elements from East Asian religious philosophy, as well as Wicca and Judaism. *291*

Find it on the THINKSPOT

www.thethinkspot.com

http://www.metacafe.com/watch/3568023/10_000_
marriages_big_white_wedding_for_unification_church/

What does it look like when 10,000 couples get married? Visit
the ThinkSpot to watch a video, with a rather tongue-
in-cheek commentary, of a Unification Church marriage
ceremony.

• www.wicca.com
Do the Celts have a connection
to Wicca? Find out by visiting
the ThinkSpot. See Kardia's blog
on "Nature's Ancient Wisdom"
where she tackles the universal
questions of religion and how
they relate to Wicca and other
ancient traditions.

Questions for Study and Review

1. **Describe the steps of the Unification Blessing Ceremony.**
   Husband and wife begin by chastening each other three times, representing human error, but also the power of forgiveness. Next, the
   couple drinks holy wine, indicating the transition from false parenthood to True Parenthood. Couples are sprinkled with holy water and
   exchange rings. After the official wedding, couples are expected to
   follow a 40-day period of sexual abstinence, recalling Jesus' 40 days
   of fasting in the desert. Finally, couples reenact a birthing ritual, marking their ultimate transition to True Wife and True Husband.

2. **What is UFOlogy, and how does it compare to other New
   Religious Movements?**
   While some NRMs look to ancient traditions and others expand upon
   established religious ideas, UFOlogy focuses on the extraterrestrial.

   Popularized by Swiss author Erich von Däniken, UFOlogy teaches that
   celestial beings came to Earth long ago, bringing wisdom to humanity.
   In the centuries after their departure, humans slowly began to worship
   them as gods, and religion was founded.

3. **What is correspondence, and what is its importance in New
   Age spirituality?**
   Correspondence refers to the relationship between objects. Often, correspondence incorporates gods and goddesses from multiple religions,
   as well as objects in nature. Knowledge of the relationship between
   things can be used in mental and physical healing and harmonization
   with the universe.

For Further Study

BOOKS:

Clark, Peter. *New Religions in Global Perspective*. New York: Routledge,
2006.

Cowan, Douglas E. *Cyberhenge: Modern Pagans on the Internet*. New
York: Routledge, 2005.

Davy, Barbara Jane, Ed. *Paganism: Critical Concepts in Religious
Studies*. New York: Routledge, 2009.

Hanegraff, Wouter J. *New Age Religion and Western Culture:
Esotericism in the Mirror of Secular Thought*. New York: E. J. Brill,
1996.

Lewis, James R. and Jesper Aagaard Petersen, Eds. *Controversial New
Religions*. New York: Oxford University Press, 2005

Lewis, James R., ed. *New Religious Movements*. New York: Oxford
University Press, 2004.

Lewis, James R. *The Oxford Handbook of New Religious Movements*.
NY: Oxford University Press, 2004.

Lynch, Gordon. *The New Spirituality*. New York: Palgrave MacMillan,
2007

Partridge, Christopher, Ed., *New Religions: A Guide*. New York: Oxford
University Press, 2004.

Partridge, Christopher, Ed. *UFO Religions*. New York: Routledge, 2003.

Starhawk. *The Spiral Dance: A Rebirth of the Ancient Religion of the
Goddess: 20th Anniversary Edition*. New York: HarperOne, 1999.

WEB SITES:

The Divine Principle in Simple Language.
http://www.divineprinciple.com/1_dp/dp_menu.html

Kim, Young Oon. *Divine Principle and Its Application*. Internet edition at
http://www.tparents.org/Library/Unification/Books/DP69/0-Toc.htm

Wicca and Neo-Paganism. http://www.sacred-texts.com/pag/index.htm

Teampall Na Callaighe: The Website of Janet Farrar and Gavin Bone.
http://www.callaighe.com/bos/firstdegree.php

Using the  the THINKSPOT

www.thethinkspot.com

The THINKSpot is an open-access Web site for *THINK World Religions* that gives students the freedom to study however and wherever they want. Whether they are studying online or on the go with a mobile phone, music player, or printout, this Web site provides all the resources students will need. The chapter summaries, flash cards, audio summaries, and chapter quizzes in the THINKSpot reinforce and build upon what is learned with the exercises, news, and Web sites. This well-rounded body of examples and exercises goes beyond the text, assisting students in developing their own critical skills through comparison, contrast, and analysis.

Whether online or on the go, students can access the same great study tools:

CHAPTER SUMMARY

In addition to reviewing each chapter's central themes and key terms, the section called "Find It on the THINKSpot" contains nearly fifty links to video clips, news stories, and Internet URLs that are called out in the body of the chapters, in some of the exercises, and at the end of the chapters. The "Questions for Study and Review" section contains suggestions that guide students through the main ideas in every chapter. "THINK World Religion" sections encourage students to continue their learning by answering questions and exploring additional Web resources.

FLASH CARDS

The flash card tool makes it easy for students to learn at their own pace. Customized flash card decks can be read online, exported to a mobile phone, or printed out.

AUDIO SUMMARY

Audio summaries of each chapter are available for streaming online or for purchase through the iTunes store.

CHAPTER QUIZ

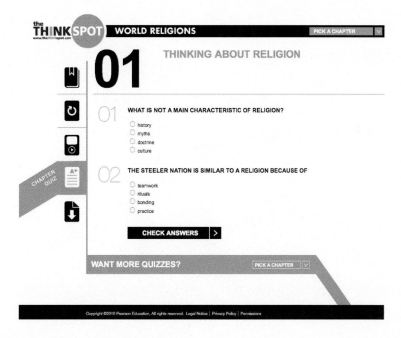

The chapter quizzes feature short-answer questions that ask students to apply the principles covered in the text.

DOWNLOAD FILES

All of the chapter summary material, audio, and flash cards are downloadable in one place.

GLOSSARY

Acupuncture uses tiny needles to remove blockages of qi in the body. (110)

Adoration of the gifts is a Roman Catholic practice that involves contemplation of the Body and Blood of Christ, sometimes displayed in a monstrance. (194)

Alchemy is the ancient practice of transforming one matter into another. In Eastern Asia, practitioners focused on the transformation of the human body. (106)

Amidah is a Jewish prayer made up of 19 sections and includes praise, request, and thanksgiving. (143)

Anatman literally means "not self." In contrast to the Hindu concept of atman, Buddhists do not believe that there is an essential self that moves from one body to another as we are reincarnated. (56)

Anjali is a gesture of greeting one makes by putting the palms together at the chest. (74)

Apostolic succession refers to the Christian act of being blessed by an Apostle who was blessed by Christ. (167)

Arhat is a person who has achieved enlightenment, a "worthy one." In the Theravada Buddhist tradition, to become an arhat is the goal of humanity. (63)

Atman is the true self; Hindus work to achieve understanding of atman. (33)

Ayatollah is a top-ranking scholar of Muslim law in Shia Islam. (236)

Bar/bat mitzvah means "son/daughter of the commandment" and refers to a Jewish boy or girl reaching the age of a religious adult. A boy becomes a bar mitzvah at age 13, and a girl attains the status at age 12. Bar/bat mitzvah is also the name of the ceremony often held to celebrate this event. (123)

Bhakti is a form of devotion by Hindu individuals and groups toward a specific god. (43)

Bodhisattva is a person who has achieved enlightenment but chooses to stay on Earth to help others reach enlightenment rather than entering nirvana. Becoming a bodhisattva is the goal of Mahayana Buddhists. (63)

Brahma is often considered to be the creator of the world in Hinduism. (29)

Brahman is the original source of all things and the composition of the cosmos in Hinduism. (29)

Brahmins are the priestly caste in the Hindu caste system. (32)

Caste system divides people into separate social groups that have varying rights, responsibilities, professions, and status. (26)

Correspondence refers to the elemental quality of nature, and the relationships between natural objects. (282)

Creationism argues that God created human beings as we now exist, as described in the Book of Genesis. (177)

Creeds, or symbols of faith, served as a kind of constitution for the Christian ecumenical fathers. (170)

Dao can mean the path, or The Way; it encompasses the nature of everything. (86)

Darwinism claims that all life has evolved from other forms, becoming ever more complex. (177)

De is virtue attained by acting in harmony with the Dao. (92)

Devas are gods who live in the highest realms of existence in Buddhism. (61)

Dharma can mean religion, universal law, application of universal law to Indian society, regulation of life through universal law, social responsibilities and duties, and the virtuous path of life. In Buddhism, it refers to the teachings of the Buddha and the natural law that the universe follows. (26; 60)

Diaspora refers to Jews being exiled from Israel to live around the world. (134)

Dikhr ("remembrance of God") are Sufi practices that teach constant interaction with God. They include breathing exercises, dancing, and twirling. (242)

Divination tells the future by showing people their place in the cosmos. (89)

Doctrines explain how to understand the world and how to behave based on a specific religion. (13)

Duhkha is the Sanskrit word for suffering, which Buddhism states is the primary condition of life. (60)

Ecumenical councils were gatherings of Christian bishops organized to define the basic elements of Christianity. (168)

Eruv is a contained space within which Jews observe the Sabbath; plural: *eruvin*. (142)

Ethical monotheism is a foundational principle of Judaism that encapsulates three main ideas: 1) the need to recognize only one God; 2) the need to act appropriately toward God; and 3) the need to act appropriately toward other people. (122)

Eucharist is the Christian ritual based on the Passover seder held by Jesus and his disciples. (164)

Falun Gong combines a system of exercise and movement with a spiritual emphasis on self-improvement. (107)

Fatwa is a ruling handed down from an Islamic scholar based on his interpretation of Islamic law. (221)

Feng shui focuses on the flow of qi in a specific place (often a room or building). (108)

Five Patriarchates were five cities (Rome, Constantinople, Antioch, Alexandria, Jerusalem) around which large groups of Christian churches grew. (171)

Five Solas distinguish Protestantism from Roman Catholicism and Orthodox Christianity. Created by early Lutherans, they include a belief in salvation through faith, an eschewing of religious texts beyond the Bible, and an emphasis on the grace of God. (183)

Four Noble Truths are the essence of Buddhist dharma; they state that life is suffering; suffering is caused by desire; it is possible to end suffering; and there is a path to follow to end suffering. (60)

Gentiles are non-Jews. (130)

Giveaway is the Native American idea of the reciprocity of the universe. (258)

Gnostics were a Christian sect that taught that the physical world was flawed. Gnostics believed that salvation could be found in hidden knowledge. (167)

Great Schism marked Christianity's branching into two different streams, roughly delineated by east and west. The Western branch developed into Roman Catholicism and Protestantism, while the Eastern branch became the Eastern Orthodox Church. (173)

Hadith, a branch of Islamic scholarship, searches for a chain of attribution that leads back to Muhammad. (221)

Hajj is a sacred pilgrimage to Mecca and the fourth pillar of Islam. (228)

Harijan means people of God, a term used by Gandhi for the outcastes of the Hindu caste system. (48)

Hasidim are members of a mystical and pietistic group in Judaism. (136)

Haskalah is the Hebrew word for the Jewish enlightenment. (136)

Hekhsher is a kosher certification symbol. (145)

Hijab is the head scarf worn by many observant Muslim women. (220)

Icons symbolize sacred persons in the Orthodox Christian Church. They act as windows to the spiritual realm and aid believers in worship. (193)

Imam is a Muslim leader and successor of Muhammad (following the line of Ali). (235)

Jati refers to a subcaste of the Hindu caste system. (33)

Jihad, or "struggle," is often called the sixth pillar of Islam. Various Islamic traditions interpret jihad differently: an inner effort to seek faith and submission to God, the overall attempt to expand Islam throughout the world, or physical defense of Islam when it is under attack. (246)

Kaaba, Islam's holiest shrine, is located in Mecca, Saudi Arabia. (212)

Kabbalah refers to a group of books that provide mystical insight into Judaism. (147)

Kaddish is a Jewish prayer used to express the hope that the world will become holy and God's will be done. (143)

Kaivalya is the experience of ultimate timelessness or detachment in Hinduism. (43)

Kandhas (see Skandhas)

Karma (in Hinduism) is the effect of a person's actions; good actions result in good karma, and bad actions result in bad karma. In Buddhism, karma has both an immediate and a later effect; it ultimately determines one's status in the next life. (34; 61)

Kashrut is a set of Jewish dietary laws. (145)

Kosher refers to the appropriate kind of food to be consumed according to Jewish dietary laws. (145)

Ksatriyas are the warrior or governmental caste in the Hindu caste system. (32)

Lama is someone who has achieved a certain level of spirituality in Buddhism and has the authority to teach others. (72)

Legalism assumes that all human beings act selfishly and need government and its laws to create a working society—in direct contradiction to both Confucianism and Daoism. (98)

Li denotes rituals and rites in Confucianism. (94)

Life cycle rituals are performed at the important stages of a person's life, such as birth, marriage, and death. (45)

Mahayana means "the great vehicle," and is a branch of Buddhism that developed after Theravada. (63)

Man of humanity nurtures others to help them become superior persons in Confucianism. (96)

Mandalas are geometric designs symbolic of the universe. They act as spiritual maps, leading one to a world beyond suffering. (54)

Mantra is a sacred verbal formula repeated in prayer and meditation. (72)

Maya is the illusory, transient world that distracts Hindus from the universal truth that Brahman is in all things. (33)

Midrash interprets the Torah with an emphasis on everyday life. (126)

Minyan is made up of 10 adult Jews, which is the minimum number of people required for congregational prayer. (147)

Mishnah is a compendium of opinions and teachings on the Talmud. (127)

Mitzvot are the commandments of God found in the Torah. (133)

Moksha is the experience of oneness with the entirety of creation in Hinduism. (33)

Muezzin is an official who calls Muslims to prayer. (229)

Mufti is a scholar of Islamic law. (221)

Murtis are statues of Hindu deities in which the god is present. (40)

Myths explain important ideas about the world through narrative stories. (12)

Neo-Paganism is a wide-ranging movement that seeks to return to pre-Christian, polytheistic religious practices. (280)

New Age Movement describes the overarching belief in developing one's spiritual, physical, and psychological self outside traditional boundaries. (277)

New Testament is made up of 26 books related to Jesus' life, teachings, and the teachings of his disciples. (165)

Nirvana is enlightenment, the ultimate goal of Buddhism. After a Buddhist becomes enlightened, he or she reaches a state of existence in which suffering ends and the cycle of rebirth and reincarnation is broken. (61)

Old Testament refers to the Jewish Tanakh. (165)

Om is the sound of the universe and the sound emanating from all Brahman. (43)

Pandit studies and teaches Hindu law. (45)

Path of knowledge is a means by which one can arrive at an understanding of all things in Hindu belief. (43)

Petty person is the lowest position on the moral hierarchy of Confucianism. A petty person often seeks to make profit. (96)

Pogroms were anti-Semitic riots that occurred in early 20th-century Russia. (151)

Prostration is an act of bowing down to the ground. (72)

Psychedelic Spirituality teaches that people can find enlightenment through hallucinogenic drugs. The movement borrows elements from East Asian religious philosophy, as well as Wicca and Judaism. (291)

Puja is the ritual by which Hindus connect with their gods and goddesses; the puja can be held by a priest in a temple or by Hindu followers themselves in their homes. (26)

Puranas often teach morality lessons or other parables relating to correct living in Hinduism. (28)

Qi is matter or energy that comes from the Dao. Qi is the totality of things and is in perpetual motion. (86)

Rabbi is a Jewish religious leader. The term literally means "teacher" or "scholar." (122)

Reincarnation is the concept in which a soul moves from one being to another after death. (34)

Rituals are repeated actions that have meaning. (13)

Sacred Mystery is a life force shared by all things in the world. (254)

Sadaqa is the Arabic word for charity and is related to zaka(t) as a pillar of Islam. (245)

Sage leads many people to self-cultivation and higher moral positions, and spreads harmony among multitudes of people. It is the highest level that a human being can attain in the Confucian moral hierarchy. (96)

Salat, or prayer, provides Muslims a direct way of interacting with God. It is the second pillar of Islam. (236)

Samana is a wandering religious beggar. (57)

Samsara is the wheel of time, or cycle of rebirth and re-death. In Buddhism, it represents our bondage to time and our inability to escape change. (34; 61)

Sanatana dharma refers to Hindu religion and life; it translates roughly as "eternal law" or "eternal virtue." (26)

Sangha is the monastic order created by the Buddha. Although the Buddha created the order for men only, he later created a separate order of nuns. (59)

Sati was a Hindu funeral practice in which a widowed woman would, voluntarily or by force, be burned on a pyre with the body of her husband. (47)

Seder is a traditional Jewish meal eaten at Passover. (147)

Sefirot are 10 attributes through which God is revealed; singular: *sefirah*. (147)

Shabbat is the Hebrew word for the Sabbath, the day of rest. (143)

Sharia is Islamic law. (221)

Shema is a prayer that reminds Jews to remember God and the commandments at all times. (143)

Shen are spirits of ancestors in traditional China. (91)

Shia Islam emphasizes the lineage of Muhammad and places great spiritual importance on the imams. (229)

Shiva is the Hindu god of transformation and destruction that ultimately leads to new creation. (29)

Shu complements zhou, and represents the Confucian concept of empathy or reciprocity. (94)

Skandhas are five elements that combine to form an individual. (62)

Smrti refers in Sanskrit to sacred Hindu traditions, both orally transmitted and written down. (28)

Sruti means "scripture" in Sanskrit and refers to the Vedas as well as the other sacred texts of Hinduism. (28)

Sudras are laborers and servants in the Hindu caste system. (32)

Sufism is a mystical branch of Islam that emphasizes the constant remembrance of God. (240)

Sunni Islam includes about 80 percent of Muslims in the world, and emphasized scholarly and communal decision-making after the death of Muhammad. (229)

Superior person rises above a petty person and seeks, through self-cultivation, The Way, rather than personal profit; this term is used in Confucianism. (96)

Suras are chapters of the Qur'an. (209)

Talmud, also called the "oral Torah," is a historical collection of rabbinical writings and commentaries on the Torah. (126)

Tanakh refers to three sets of religious texts: "the Law" (Torah), "the Prophets," and "the Writings" that constitute the Hebrew Bible. (126)

Tantra is a set of instructions said to be given by the Buddha to a group of his students. These teachings are widely used in Tibetan Buddhism. (71)

Theosis, meaning divinization, is an important concept in Eastern Orthodoxy and the Oriental Orthodox churches. By living a Christian life within the Church, individuals can become more like Jesus and regain the image and likeness of God. (174)

Theravada means "teaching of the elders" and refers to the oldest Buddhist tradition. (63)

Thread ceremony, also called the second birth, is a coming-of-age ceremony in which a boy's hair is shaved except for a topknot and he is initiated into Hindu education. (45)

Three Jewels of Buddhism are Buddha, dharma, and sangha. (70)

Tikkun means "repair" in Hebrew, either of one's soul or the whole world. (147)

Tikkun olam, meaning "repairing the world," refers to the need for Jews to act ethically in every part of their lives—family, home, job, and politics. (150)

Torah, meaning Law, refers to the first five books of the Hebrew Bible. However, the word can also be used to denote *all* Jewish religious texts and *all* Jewish law. (123)

Transubstantiation occurs when the Eucharist transforms into the body and blood of Christ. (187)

Trigrams are symbols of three lines each that show how yin and yang interact in the world. (88)

Tripitaka are the sacred texts of Theravada Buddhism. (63)

True Family is composed of male and female members of the Unification Church united in sacred matrimony, free from original sin. These families produce True Sons and Daughters. (276)

Truthfulness seeks the truth or tries to find a way to live authentically or genuinely. (17)

Truthiness refers to a satirical idea describing verifiable falsehoods repeated so often that they seem to be true. (17)

Unification Church is a modern interpretation of Christianity and Confucianism that stresses marriage within the church as a way of rebuilding God's kingdom on Earth. (276)

Untouchables, also called outcastes, dalits, or the scheduled castes, represent a group below the four traditional castes in Hinduism. (32)

Vaisyas are the caste of farmers, merchants, businesspeople, and professionals in the Hindu caste system. (32)

Varna means "color" and refers to caste in Indian society. (47)

Vedas are the most sacred texts in Hinduism. (28)

Vishnu is the Hindu protector of the world. (29)

Vision quest is a form of spiritual growth derived from journeying alone to seek a vision linking the self with the land and its inhabitants. (262)

Wiccans are modern believers and practitioners of witchcraft. (280)

Wu wei is a Daoist concept that describes "action without effort" in Chinese. By practicing wu wei, we reflect nature rather than act against it. (98)

Yajna is the sacrifice that Hindus use to connect to deities. (41)

Yang, together with yin, makes up qi. Yang is active energy and cannot exist without yin. (88)

Yin is passive energy and makes up a part of qi. Yin cannot exist without yang. (88)

Yoga generally refers to any religious practice, but it is often used in connection with the development of physical and spiritual discipline toward the goal of kaivalya. (43)

Zaka(t) is the mandatory giving of money, and the fourth pillar of Islam. (245)

Zhong is loyalty, an important part of self-development according to Confucius. (94)

REFERENCES

AcademicInfo: "Religion Gateway," http://www.academicinfo.net/Religion.html.

Adele Berlin and Marc Zvi Brettler, eds., *The Jewish Study Bible* (New York: Oxford, 2004).

Ahmed Ali (trans.), *Al-Qur'an: A Contemporary Translation* (Princeton, NJ: Princeton University Press, 2001).

Alexandra Bain, "The Late Ottoman 'En'am-i Serif': Sacred text and images in an Islamic prayer book" (unpublished dissertation, University of Victoria, 1999).

Ali Ünal, *The Qur'an with Annotated Interpretation in Modern English* (Clifton, NJ: Tughra, 2006).

Alice C. Fletcher, "Wakondagi," *American Anthropologist*, 1912. 14(1): 106–108.

Andrew Buncombe, "Burma's angry monks 'excommunicate' junta by refusing donations," *The Independent* (London) September 20, 2007, World Section: 34.

Annemarie Schimmel, *Mystical Dimensions of Islam* (Chapel Hill: University of North Carolina Press, 1978).

Antiochian Orthodox Christian Archdiocese of North America, "Sacred Music Library," Accessed September 27, 2009, http://www.antiochian.org/music/library/813.

Anuj Chopra, "Burma's Buddhist Monks take to the Streets," *Christian Science Monitor*, September 20, 2007, World Section: 6

Arlene Hirschfelder and Paulette Molin, eds., *The Encyclopedia of Native American Religions* (New York: Facts on File, 1992).

Arthur T. Hatto, "Stonehenge and Midsummer: A New Interpretation," *Man*, 1953. 53: 101–106.

Ashutosh Varshney, "Contested Meanings: India's National Identity, Hindu Nationalism, and the Politics of Anxiety," *Daedalus*, 1993. 122(3): 227–261. http://www.jstor.org/stable/20027190 (accessed July 1, 2009).

Axel Michaels, *Hinduism: Past and Present*, trans. Barbara Harshav (Princeton, NJ: Princeton University Press, 2004).

Beliefnet, "Belief-o-Matic," http://www.beliefnet.com/Entertainment/Quizzes/BeliefO-Matic.aspx.

Benjamin C. Ray, "Stonehenge: A New Theory," *History of Religions*, 1987. 26(3): 225–278.

Bharatiya Temple, Inc., *Pran Pratishtha Mahotsava-2009*. http://pranpratishtha.ettitudemedia.com (accessed October 2, 2009).

Brill Online, "Encyclopaedia Islamica," http://www.brillonline.nl/.

Buddha Dharma Education Association, Inc., *Buddhanet: Buddhist Education and Information Network*, http://www.buddhanet.net.

Buddhist Temples.com, *Buddhist Temples: Paths to Salvation*, http://www.buddhist-temples.com.

Cameron Stewart, "Tibet's Looming Eruption," *The Australian*, November 13, 2008, All-Round Country Edition: 11.

Cardinal James R. Knox, "Inaestimabile Donum: Instruction Concerning Worship of the Eucharistic Mystery." http://www.ewtn.com/ library/PAPALDOC/JP2INAES.HTM (accessed March 31, 2010).

Carl Olson, *The Different Paths of Buddhism: A Narrative-Historical Introduction* (New Brunswick: Rutgers University Press, 2005).

Caryl Murphy, "Behind the Veil: Why Islam's Most Visible Symbol Is Spreading; Embraced or Banned, a Prayer or a Prison, the Muslim Veil is Spreading: Who Wears It—and Why?" *The Christian Science Monitor*, December 12, 2009.

Charles G. Leland, *The Algonquin Legends of New England* (Cambridge, MA: The Riverside Press: 1884). Available online at *Sacred-texts.com*, http://www.sacred-texts.com/nam/ne/al/al00.htm.

Christopher Partridge, ed., *New Religions: A Guide*, (New York: Oxford University Press, 2004).

Craig A. Forney, *The Holy Trinity of American Sports: Civil Religion in Football, Baseball, and Basketball* (Macon, GA: Mercer University Press, 2007).

Dalai Lama, *The World of Tibetan Buddhism: An Overview of Its Philosophy and Practice* (Somerville, MA: Wisdom Publications, 1995).

Damien Keown, *Buddhism: A Very Short Introduction* (Oxford, UK: Oxford University Press, 1996).

Dan McDougall, "Indian Cult Kills Children for Goddess: 'Holy Men' Blamed for Inciting Dozens of Deaths," *Observer* (UK), Foreign Pages: 39.

Daniel W. Brown, *New Introduction to Islam* (Malden, MA: Wiley-Blackwell, 2009).

David O'Reilly, "Rare Ceremony Consecrating New Hindu Temple in Bucks," *Philadelphia Inquirer*, May 24, 2009, Section B, 1.

David Ownby, *Falun Gong and the Future of China* (New York: Oxford University Press, 2008).

David Waines, *An Introduction to Islam*. New York: Cambridge University Press, 2004.

Douglas E. Cowan, *Cyberhenge: Modern Pagans on the Internet* (New York: Routledge, 2005).

Eugene V. Gallagher, "Compared to What? 'Cults' and 'New Religious Movements,'" *History of Religions*, 2008. 47(2/3): 205–220.

Frederick E. Hoxie, *Encyclopedia of Native American Indians* (Bellmawr, NJ: Houghton Mifflin Harcourt, 1996).

Friedrich Nietzsche, *The Gay Science*, in *The Complete Works of Friedrich Nietzsche*, trans. Oscar Levy (New York: The Macmillan Company, 1924), 168.

Gene R. Thursby, *Religious Worlds*, http://www.religiousworlds.com.

George Sandys, *Sandys travailes: containing a history of the original and present state of the Turkish Empire, their laws, government, policy military force, courts of justice and commerce : the Mahometan religion and ceremonies : a description of Constantinople : the grand seignors seraglio and his manner of living : also, of Greece, with the religion and customes of the Graecians : of Egypt, the antiquity, hieroglyphicks rites, customs, discipline and religion of the Egyptians : a voyage on the river Nilus, and of the crocodile : of Arminia, Grand Cairo, Rhodes, the pyramides, colossus, mummies, &c. : the former flourishing and present state of Alexandria : a description of the Holy-land : of the Jews and several sects of Christians living there : of Jerusalem, sepulchre of Christ, temple of Solomon and what else either of antiquity or worth observation : lately, Italy described, and the Islands adjoyning, as Cyprus, Crete Malta, Sicilia, the Aeolian Islands, of Rome, Venice, Naples, Syracusa, Messena, Aetna, Scylla and Charybdis and other places of note : illustrated with fifty graven maps and figures* (London : Printed by R. and W. Leybourn, 1600).

Gerald B. Gardner, *Witchcraft Today*. (New York: Citadel, 2004).

Graham Harvey, *Indigenous Religions: A Companion* (New York: Continuum International Publishing Group, 2000).

Graham Harvey, *Readings in Indigenous Religions* (New York: Continuum International Publishing Group, 2002).

Hemant Kanitkar and Owen Cole, *Teach Yourself Hinduism* (London: McGraw-Hill, 2003).

Hyemeyohsts Storm, *Seven Arrows*. (New York: Harper & Row Publishers, 1972).

"In Depth: Dalai Lama in exile now for 50 years," (transcript), *NBC Nightly News*, March 10, 2009, Accessed March 30, 2010.

Internet Sacred Text Archive, Hinduism, http://www.sacred-texts.com/hin/index.htm.

Internet Sacred Text Archive, "Phos Hilaron," Accessed September 27, 2009, http://www.sacred-texts.com/chr/bcp.txt.

Jack Maguire, *Essential Buddhism: A Complete Guide to Beliefs and Practices*. (New York: Pocket Books, 2001).

Jack W. Brink, *Imagining Head-Smashed-In: Aboriginal Buffalo Hunting on the Northern Plains* (Edmonton, Alberta: AU Press, Athabasca University, 2008). Available online at http://www.aupress.ca/books/120137/ebook/99Z_Brink_2008-Imagining_Head_Smashed_In.pdf.

Jacob K. Olupona, ed., *Beyond Primitivism: Indigenous Religious Traditions and Modernity* (New York: Routledge, 2004).

Jamake Highwater, *Rituals of the Wind: North American Indian Ceremonies, Music, and Dances* (New York: The Viking Press, 1977).

James Mooney, "The Ghost-Dance Religion and the Sioux Outbreak of 1890," in *Fourteenth Annual Report of the Bureau of Ethnology, Part 2*. Reprinted as *The Ghost-Dance Religion and Wounded Knee* (Dover Publications, Inc., 1973: 781).

James R. Lewis, ed., *New Religious Movements* (New York: Oxford University Press, 2004).

James T. Richardson and Massimo Introvigne, "'Brainwashing' Theories in European Parliamentary and Administrative Reports on 'Cults' and 'Sects,'" *Journal for the Scientific Study of Religion*, 2001. 40(2):143–168.

Janet Farrar and Gavin Bone, "First Degree Initiation," Accessed March 31, 2010, http://www.callaighe.com/bos/firstdegree.php.

Janet Lubman Rathner, "A Neighborhood Built Around Religious Ritual; Border Helps Potomac Jews Observe Sabbath," *Washington Post*, October 4, 2008: G1.

Jeaneane Fowler, *Hinduism: Beliefs and Practices*. Eastbourne (UK: Sussex Academic Press, 1997).

Jeff Zeleny and Adam Nagourney, "An Angry Obama Renounces Ties to His Ex-Pastor," *New York Times*, April 30, 2008, A, 1.

Jeffry F. Meyer, "Salvation in the Garden: Daoism and Ecology" in *Daoism and Ecology: Ways within a Cosmic Landscape*, N. J. Girardot, et al. (Cambridge, MA: Harvard University Press, 2001), 228.

Jeremy Laurence, "Science Proves Acupuncture is Sound Medicine," *The Independent* (London), March 14, 2009: News 8.

John B. Hare, *Internet Sacred Text Archive*, http://www.sacred-texts.com.

John Dougherty, "Sweat Lodge Deaths Bring Soul-Searching to Area Deep in Seekers," *New York Times*, October 12, 2009: Section A, 13.

John Quinn, *Divine Principle in Plain Language: The Basic Theology of Sun Myung Moon*, (Principled Publications, 2006).

Joseph Berger, "Orthodox Jews' Request Divides a Resort Village," *New York Times*, June 22, 2008: Section LI, 1.

Joseph Epes Brown and Emily Cousins, *Teaching Spirits—Understanding Native American Religious Traditions* (New York: Oxford University Press, 2001) 23.

Joseph L. Price, ed., *From Season to Season: Sports as American Religion* (Macon, GA: Mercer University Press, 2001).

Justin Martyr, *The First Apology of Justin,* Accessed March 31, 2010, http://www.earlychristianwritings.com/text/justinmartyr-firstapology.html.

Karen Armstrong, *Buddha* (New York: Viking Adult, 2001).

Kim Knott, *Hinduism: A Very Short Introduction* (New York: Oxford University Press, 2000).

Kingdom of Saudi Arabia, Ministry of Islamic Affairs, Endowments, Da'wah and Guidance, "Al Islam," Accessed March 31, 2010, http://quran.al-islam.com/.

Klaus K. Klostermaier, *A Survey of Hinduism* (Albany, NY: State University of New York Press, 2008).

Klaus K. Klostermaier, *Hinduism: A Beginner's Guide* (Oxford, UK: Oneworld, 2008).

Lee Irwin, "Dreams, Theory, and Culture: The Plains Vision Quest Paradigm," *American Indian Quarterly,* 1994. 18(2): 229-245.

Leslie V. Grinsell, "The Legendary History and Folklore of Stonehenge," *Folklore,* 1976. 87 (1): 5-20.

Li Hongzhi, *Zhuan Falun,* Accessed March 31, 2010, http://falundafa.org/eng/books.html.

Liturgica.com, "Spiritual Growth: Daily Prayers—Morning Prayers," Accessed March 31, 2010, http://www.liturgica.com/html/growO2.jsp.

Madeline Anita Slovenz, "The Year Is a Wild Animal: Lion Dancing in Chinatown," *The Drama Review: TDR,* 1987. 31(3): 74-75.

Mahmoud Ayoub, *Islam: Faith and History* (Oxford: Oneworld, 2004).

Mao Zedong, *Quotations from Chairman Mao Tse-Tung* (San Francisco, CA: China Books & Periodicals, Inc.).

Marianne Betts, "Host of Celebrities in Scientology's Fold," *Herald Sun* (Australia), January 10, 2009: Section 1, 24.

Mark MacKinnon, "Is This the Last Great Dalai Lama?" *The Globe and Mail,* March 7, 2009, Section A: 1.

Martin Forward, *Religion: A Beginner's Guide* (Oxford, UK: Oneworld Publications, 2001).

Mechon Mamre, "A Hebrew-English Bible According to the Masoretic Text and JPS Edition," Accessed March 31, 2010, http://www.mechon-mamre.org/p/pt/pt0.htm.

Medieval Sourcebook, "Mass of the Roman Rite: Latin/English," Accessed September 27, 2009, http://www.fordham.edu/halsall/basis/latinmass2.html.

Meir Shahar, *The Shaolin Monastery: History, Religion, and the Chinese Martial Arts* (Honolulu: University of Hawaii Press, 2008).

Michael Cooper, "McCain Criticizes Clergyman's Remarks," *New York Times,* April 28, 2008, A, 21.

Michael Drost, "Museum Slaying Suspect Charged; Police Weigh Hate Crimes, Rights Offenses," *The Washington Times,* June 12, 2009: Section A, 1.

Michael Martin, "Buddhist Chaplain Prepares for Deployment," *National Public Radio,* September 11, 2009, Accessed November 29, 2009, http://www.npr.org/templates/story/story.php?storyId=112743568&ft=1&f=1010.

Muhammad A. S. Abdel Haleem, *The Qur'an: A New Translation* (New York: Oxford University Press, 2005).

Muhammad A. S., Abdel Haleem (trans.), *The Qur'an: A New Translation* (New York: Oxford University Press, 2005).

Muhammad Tahir-ul-Qadri, *Fatwa on Suicide Bombings and Terrorism* (London: Minhaj-ul-Qur'an International 2010). Available online at http://www.minhaj.org/images-db2/fatwa-eng.pdf.

Nicholas Schmidle, "Mas Qalandar!" *Smithsonian Magazine,* December 2008, http://www.smithsonianmag.com/people-places/Faith-and-Ecstasy.html.

Nick Squires, "Denying Holocaust is Hateful, says Obama," *The Daily Telegraph,* June 6, 2009: International, 22.

Paul Grieve, *Brief Guide to Islam: History, Faith and Politics: The Complete Introduction* (New York : Carroll and Graf Publishers, 2006).

PBS NewsHour Online, "Bin Laden's Fatwah," Accessed March 31, 2010, http://www.pbs.org/newshour/terrorism/international/fatwa_1996.html.

Public Broadcasting Service, "Muhammad: Legacy of a Prophet," Accessed March 31, 2010, http://www.pbs.org/muhammad.

Quaker Information Center, "Your First Visit to an Unprogrammed Friends Meeting," Accessed September 30, 2009, http://www.quakerinfo.org/quakerism/worship.html.

Raë, *Intelligent Design: Message from the Designers* (Nova Distribution, 2005).

Rainer Maria Rilke, *Letters to a Young Poet.* Translated by Joan M. Burnham (Novato, CO: New World Library, 2000), 35.

Rapola Rahula, *What the Buddha Taught: Revised and Expanded Edition with Texts from Suttas and Dhammapada* (New York: Grove Press, 1974).

Raymond J. DeMallie, ed., *The Sixth Grandfather: Black Elk's teachings given to John G. Neihardt, 1881-1973* (Lincoln: Bison Books, University of Nebraska Press, 1985).

ReligionFacts, *Welcome to ReligionFacts,* http://www.religionfacts.com.

Robert L. Winzeler, *Anthropology and Religion* (New York: AltaMira Press, 2008).

Robert R. Bianchi, *Guests of God: Pilgrimage and Politics in the Islamic World* (New York: Oxford University Press, 2004).

Rudolf Otto and John W. Harvey (trans.), *The Idea of the Holy: An Inquiry into the Non Rational Factor in the Idea of the Divine 1926* (Whitefish, MT: Kessinger Publishing, LLC, 2004), 7.

Ruqaiyyah Waris Maqsood, *Teach Yourself Islam* (New York: McGraw-Hill, 1996).

"Rushdie to Write Book About Decade in Hiding," Associated Press, February 23, 2010.

Sacred Texts: Buddhism. http://www.sacred-texts.com/bud/index.htm

Samuel G. Freedman, "Paganism, Slowly Triumphs Over Stereotypes," *New York Times,* October 31, 2009: Section A, 13.

Shawn Wilson, *Recognising the Importance of Spirituality in Indigenous Learning* (Australia Corrections Education Association, 1999). Available online at www.acea.org.au/Content/1999%20papers/Shaun%20Wilson%20-%20paper.pdf.

Smithsonian Institution, *Chinese American Teens on Ancestor Worship Today,* Accessed December 9, 2009, www.asia.si.edu/exhibitions/online/teen/default.htm.

Starhawk, *The Spiral Dance: A Rebirth of the Ancient Religion of the Goddess: 20th Anniversary Edition* (New York: HarperOne, 1999).

Sun Myung Moon, "Blessing and Ideal Family: Part 1," Accessed March 31, 2010, http://www.tparents.org/moon-books/bif1/BIF1-1-101.htm.

Sun Myung Moon, "The Process of Blessing," Accessed March 31, 2010, http://www.tparents.org/Moon-Books/bif/BIF-4-1.htm.

T. Dean Thomlinson, "Monologic and Dialogic Communication," Accessed November 11, 2009, https://umdrive.memphis.edu/ggholson/public/Dialogue.html.

Tanakh: The Holy Scriptures (Philadelphia: The Jewish Publication Society, 1988).

The Pulse, "Is Acupuncture just a Sham?" June 17, 2009: 18.

The Writing Center, University of North Carolina at Chapel Hill, *Religious Studies,* www.unc.edu/depts/wcweb/handouts/religious_studies.html.

Thomas H. Kean et al., *The 9/11 Commission Report* (Washington, DC: The National Commission on Terrorist Attacks Upon the United States, 2004), 55-62.

Tim Rutten, "Hatred and the Far Right," *Los Angeles Times,* June 13, 2009: Part A, 29.

Tonio Andrade, "Introduction," *Emory Endeavors in World History,* http://history.emory.edu/endeavors/volume1/Introduction.pdf.

Tonio Andrade, "Introduction: Why Truthiness?" Accessed November 11, 2009, http://www.emoryprof.googlepages.com/Introduction.pdf.

Tony Paterson, "A Powerful rebuke to Israel's Enemies; Obama Pays His Respects at the Former Buchenwald Concentration Camp," *The Independent* (London), June 6, 2009: World, 30.

Tparents.org, "Unification News for July 2000," Accessed March 31, 2010, http://www.tparents.org/UNews/unws0007/ Sato-Ocean.htm.

Unification. org, "Introduction to the Blessing Ceremony," Accessed March 21, 2010, http://www.unification.org/intro_blessing.html.

United States Conference of Catholic Bishops, "Catechism of the Catholic Church, Part Four—Christian Prayer," Accessed March 31, 2010, *United States Conference of Catholic Bishops.* http://www.usccb.org/catechism/text/partfour.shtml.

Vine Deloria, Jr., *God Is Red: A Native View of Religion* (Golden, CO: Fulcrum Publishing, 2003).

Walter H. Capps, *Religious Studies: The Making of a Discipline* (Minneapolis, MN: Fortress Press, 1995).

William Cromie, "Meditation Changes Temperatures," *Harvard University Gazette,* April 18, 2002, Science & Research Section.

William J. Baker, *Playing with God: Religion and Modern Sport* (Cambridge, MA: Harvard University Press, 2007).

William James, *The Varieties of Religious Experience: A Study in Human Nature* (London: Longman, Green, and Co., 1905), 28.

Wounded Knee Museum Online, Accessed March 31, 2010, http://www.woundedkneemuseum.org/main_menu.html.

Wouter J. Hanegraff, *New Age Religion and Western Culture: Esotericism in the Mirrore of Secular Thought* (New York: E. J. Brill, 1996).

Young Oon Kim, "Divine Principle and Its Application," Accessed March 21, 2010, http://www.tparents.org/Library/Unification/Books/DP69/0-Toc.htm.

PHOTO CREDITS

CHAPTER 10 PAGE 140: Mira.com/David Paterson; **142:** Mark Peterson/Redux Pictures; **143:** Geoff Manasse/Getty Images, Inc.—Photodisc./Royalty Free; **144: (top)** Moskol, Sally/PhotoLibrary.com; **(bottom)** Yivo Institute for Jewish Research; **147:** Ted S. Warren/AP Wide World Photos; **148:** Michael Newman/PhotoEdit Inc.; **149: (top)** Eileen Tweedy/Picture Desk, Inc./Kobal Collection; **(bottom)** Joel S. Fishman/Photo Researchers, Inc.; **150:** © Nathan Benn/Corbis; **151:** © ALEXANDER DEMIANCHUK/Reuters/Corbis; **152:** Dagli Orti/Picture Desk, Inc./Kobal Collection; **153:** © United States Holocaust Memorial Museum, courtesy of Instytut Pamieci Narodowej; **154:** KZ Gedenkstaette Dachau/Library of Congress; **155 (clockwise from top left):** Moskol, Sally/Photolibrary.com; Geoff Manasse/Getty Images, Inc.—Photodisc./Royalty Free; Andy Crawford/Dorling Kindersley © Jewish Museum, London; Michael Kappeler/AFP/Getty Images, Inc.; **156 (clockwise from top left):** Michael Newman/PhotoEdit Inc.; Mark Peterson/Redux Pictures; Mira.com/David Paterson.

CHAPTER 11 PAGE 158: James McConnachie © Rough Guides; **160: (left)** Getty Images, Inc.—Hulton Archive Photos; **(right)** © Dorling Kindersley; **161 (from top):** Private Collection/The Bridgeman Art Library; Hulton Archive/Getty Images; Stephen Oliver © Dorling Kindersley, Courtesy of Henry Moore Foundation; **162:** Greenberg, Jeff/Omni-Photo Communications, Inc.; **163:** Hachette Photos; **164: (top left)** Villa Tasca, Palermo, Sicily, Italy/The Bridgeman Art Library; **(top right)** © ANCIENT ART & ARCHITECTURE/DanitaDelimont.com; **(bottom right)** Art Institute of Chicago, IL, USA/The Bridgeman Art Library; **165:** Duomo, Siena, Italy/The Bridgeman Art Library; **166:** British Library; **167:** Institute for Antiquity and Christianity, Claremont, California; **168: (top)** Picture Desk, Inc./Kobal Collection; **(bottom)** Biblioteca Nazionale, Turin, Italy/The Bridgeman Art Library; **169:** Picture Desk, Inc./Kobal Collection; **170:** ANCIENT ART & ARCHITECTURE/DanitaDelimont.com; **171:** Picture Desk, Inc./Kobal Collection; **174:** Karen Minot; **175: (left)** Hieronymus Bosch, "Creation of Eve in the Garden of Eden"; "Garden of Earthly Delights"; "Hell" (interior of the "Garden of Earthly Delights" triptych). c. 1510-15. Oil on wood, 7' 2 5/8" × 6' 4 3/4" (each wing). The figures in the foreground of the central panel are approximately 10-14 inches tall. © Museo Nacional del Prado, Madrid, Spain. All rights reserved; **(right)** Getty Images, Inc.—Hulton Archive Photos; **177: (left)** Corbis RF; **(right)** © Gary Braasch/Bettmann/CORBIS All Rights Reserved; **178: (top)** ANCIENT ART & ARCHITECTURE/DanitaDelimont.com **(bottom)** Picture Desk, Inc./Kobal Collection; **179:** James McConnachie © Rough Guides.

CHAPTER 12 PAGE 180: Skjold Photographs; **182:** Kapoor Baldev/Sygma/Corbis; **183:** Copyright The British Museum; **184: (top)** PhotoEdit Inc.; **(bottom)** Getty Images, Inc.; **187:** PhotoEdit Inc.; **188 (clockwise from top left):** PhotoEdit Inc.; Stock Boston; Catholic News Service; The Image Works; PhotoEdit Inc.; Dimitar Dilkoff/AFP/Getty Images; Silver Burdett Ginn; Chicago Tribune; **189:** Bildarchiv Preussischer Kulturbesitz/Art Resource, NY; **190 (from top):** Peter Arnold, Inc; Getty Images, Inc.—Photodisc/Royalty Free; © Jim Bourg/Reuters/CORBIS All Rights Reserved; Photo Researchers, Inc.; **191: (top)** Getty Images, Inc.—Image Bank; **(bottom)** Peter Arnold, Inc.; **192: (top)** Picture Desk, Inc./Kobal Collection; **(bottom)** Stock Boston; **193: (left)** Andrej Rublev, "Old Testament Trinity (Three Angels). Icon. Tempera on panel. 1410-1420. Sovfoto/Eastfoto; **(right)** Stock Connection; **194: (top)** Robert Fried/robertfriedphotography.com; **(bottom)** Library of Congress, Washington D.C., USA/The Bridgeman Art Library; **195: (top)** PhotoEdit Inc.; **(bottom)** Peter Arnold, Inc. **196–197:** Bruce Rolff/Shutterstock; **198: (top)** PhotoEdit Inc.; **(bottom)** AP Wide World Photos; **199: (top)** Kheng Guan Toh/Shutterstock; **(bottom)** Peter Arnold, Inc.; **200:** CORBIS—NY; **201 (clockwise from top left):** © imagebroker/Alamy; The Art Archive/Church of Saint Martin Zillis/Gianni Dagli Orti; Leonardo da Vinci (1452-1519), "The Last Supper". 1495-97/98. Mural (oil and tempera on plaster), 15' 1 1/8" × 28' 10 1/2". Refectory, Monastery of Santa Maria delle Grazie, Milan, Italy. IndexRicerca Iconografica. Photo: Ghigo Roli; © Andrew Holt/Alamy; **202 (from top):** Peter Arnold, Inc.; Peter Arnold, Inc.; Skjold Photographs.

CHAPTER 13 PAGE 204: Robin Laurance/Photo Researchers, Inc.; **206: (left)** Linda Whitwam © Dorling Kindersley; **(right)** Maltings Partnership © Dorling Kindersley; **207 (clockwise from top left):** Adam Woolfitt/Robert Harding World Imagery; Linda Whitwam © Dorling Kindersley; Linda Whitwam © Dorling Kindersley; Linda Whitwam © Dorling Kindersley; **208:** The Art Archive/Museum of Islamic Art Cairo/Dagli Orti; **209: (top)** From: Al-Biruni, "Chronicle of Ancient Nations" ORMS.161.f.10v. Courtesy of Edinburgh University Library; **(bottom)** Roy Robson; **210:** © Ramzi Hachicho/Shutterstock; **211: (top)** Navajas, Carlos/Getty Images, Inc.—Image Bank; **(bottom)** Nabeel Turner/Getty Images,

Inc. Stone Allstock; **213:** Hayes, Dannielle/Omni-Photo Communications, Inc.; **214 (clockwise from top left):** Mikhail Levit/Shutterstock; Amid/Shutterstock; Galyna Andrushko/Shutterstock; Eastimages/ Shutterstock; olly/Shutterstock; Sinan Isakovic/Shutterstock; Distinctive Images/ Shutterstock; Veronika Vasilyuk/Shutterstock; **215: (top)** Peter Sanders/Peter Sanders Photography; **(bottom)** Edinburgh University Library; **220 (clockwise from top left):** Thierry Nauger/Photo Researchers, Inc.; ADAM BUCHANAN/DanitaDelimont.com; © Bryan Peterson/CORBIS All Rights Reserved; **221: (left)** Joe Kohen/Contributor/WireImage/Getty Images; **(right)** Gabriel Duval/Staff/AFP/Getty Images; **223:** Alex Mares-Manton/Asia Images/Getty Images; **224 (clockwise from top left):** olly/Shutterstock; ADAM BUCHANAN/DanitaDelimont.com; Robin Laurance/Photo Researchers, Inc.

CHAPTER 14 PAGE 226: EPA/Empics; **228: (top)** AP Wide World Photos; **(bottom)** M.Freeman/Getty Images, Inc.—PhotoDisc; **229:** John Woodcock © Dorling Kindersley; **230:** RIA Novosti/Alamy Images; **231: (top)** Robert Frerck/Getty Images, Inc.—Stone Allstock; **(bottom)** Annie Griffiths Belt/National Geographic Image Collection; **233: (left)** University Library, Istanbul, Turkey/The Bridgeman Art Library; **(right)** Prince of Wales Museum, Bombay, India/The Bridgeman Art Library; **235: (top)** Art Resource, NY; **(bottom)** Hadi Mizban/AP Wide World Photos; **236: (left)** Susan Van Etten/PhotoEdit Inc.; **(right)** David Grossman/Photo Researchers, Inc.; **237 (from top):** Getty Images, Inc./Zubin Shroff; Andy Crawford © Dorling Kindersley; Getty Images, Inc./Image Source; Getty Images, Inc./David Silverman; Louise Batalla Duran/Alamy Images; **238:** © Dorling Kindersley; **239: (top)** Ed Kashi/IPN/Aurora Photos, Inc.; **(bottom)** Michael Newman/PhotoEdit Inc.; **240 (top)** Mary K. Love/Creative Eye/MIRA.com **(bottom)** G. Dagli Orti, "Mevlana Celaleddin Rumi." The Art Archive/Picture Desk, Inc./Kobal Collection; **244 (from top):** Mohammad Hamza Mian/Alamy Images; (c) Reuters/CORBIS; © Art Directors & TRIP/Alamy; © Tengku Mohd Yusof/Alamy; Alamy/Trip/Art Directors & TRIP; AP Wide World Photos; © Art Directors & TRIP/Alamy; Alamy/Athar Akram/ArkReligion.com/Art Directors & TRIP; **245:** Alamy/Athar Akram/ArkReligion.com/Art Directors & TRIP; **247 (clockwise from top left):** Art Resource/Bildarchiv Preussischer Kulturbesitz; Paul Prescott/Alamy Images; michaeljung/Shutterstock; C.Garroni Parisi/Das Fotoarchiv/Peter Arnold, Inc.; **248 (clockwise from top left):** David Grossman/Photo Researchers, Inc.; Alamy/Athar Akram/ArkReligion.com/Art Directors & TRIP; EPA/Empics.

CHAPTER 15 PAGE 250: Andy Holligan © Dorling Kindersley **252:** Jason Lewis © Dorling Kindersley, **253 (from top):** Lynton Gardiner © Dorling Kindersley, Courtesy of The American Museum of Natural History; Viesti Associates, Inc.; EMG Education Management Group; **254:** Courtesy of The Smithsonian Institution, National Anthropological Archive. Joseph Epes Brown (neg.3303c); **255: (top)** Ira Block/National Geographic Image Collection; **(bottom)** Suzi Moore/Woodfin Camp & Associates, Inc.; **256: (top)** © Dorling Kindersley; **(bottom)** Jack Parsons/Omni-Photo Communications, Inc.; **257: (top)** Jim Wark/Peter Arnold, Inc.; **(bottom, clockwise from left):** St. Nick/Shutterstock; Tom Antos/Shutterstock; Shutterstock/© Denis Pepin; Sergei Bachlakov/Shutterstock; **258:** Corbis RF; **259 (top):** Dan V. Lomahaftewa, "Celestial Germinators," 1992, 48" × 36", acrylic on canvas; **(bottom)** Sara Wiles; **260:** © John Mitchell/Alamy; **261: (top)** © WALTER BIBIKOW/DanitaDelimont.com; **(bottom left)** Paul Chesley/Stone/Getty Images; **(bottom right)** The Ndakinna Wilderness Project/Ndakinna Wilderness Project; **262: (top)** Edward S. Curtis/CORBIS—NY; **(bottom)** Lynton Gardiner © Dorling Kindersley, Courtesy of The American Museum of Natural History; **263: (top)** Arne hodalic/CORBIS—NY; **(bottom)** The Granger Collection; **264: (left)** Buyenlarge/ Contributer/Hulton Archive/Getty Images; **(right)** Buyenlarge/Contributer/Hulton Archive/Getty Images; **265: (top left)** Buyenlarge/Contributor/Hulton Archive/Getty Images; **(top right)** Michael Ochs Archives/Stringer/Getty Images; **(bottom)** Maria Stenzel/National Geographic Image Collection; **266:** Frederic Remington, "Ogallala Sioux performing the Ghost Dance at the Pine Ridge Indian Agency, South Dakota, 1890"/The Granger Collection, New York; **267: (left)** Jim Noelker/Image Works **(right)** Jeff Greenberg/PhotoEdit Inc.; **271:** offiwent.com/Alamy Images; **269 (clockwise from top left):** © MARKA/Alamy; Paul Chesley/National Geographic/Getty Images; Nigel Hicks © Dorling Kindersley, Courtesy of Saxman Totem Park; Mira.com; **270 (clockwise from top left):** Dan V. Lomahaftewa, "Celestial Germinators," 1992, 480" × 360", acrylic on canvas; Edward S. Curtis/CORBIS—NY; Andy Holligan © Dorling Kindersley; Sergei Bachlakov/Shutterstock.

INDEX